Thinking
THE·FAITH

"Douglas John Hall combines contemporary contextual and liberationist emphases with Luther's theology of the cross better than anyone else I know. His writing is consistently vigorous and interesting."

GEORGE LINDBECK

"Douglas John Hall here initiates a radical redoing of theology as it grows out of our North American context and is not simply an imitation of theology done in other countries. The task has long needed doing, and Dr. Hall is the first to treat it with the seriousness and creativity it deserves. His book will be the benchmark for future North American theology. This is a seminal volume."

ROBERT MCAFEE BROWN

"Douglas John Hall is Karl Barth's type of theologian, with the Scriptures in the one hand and a daily newspaper in the other. He has a deep perception of the Christian tradition—moving Christologically—and razored insights into the problems of our culture."

JAMES A. NESTINGEN

ALSO BY DOUGLAS JOHN HALL

God and Human Suffering:
An Exercise in the Theology of the Cross (1986)

Professing the Faith:
Christian Theology in a North American Context (1993)

God and the Nations
(with Rosemary Radford Ruether, 1995)

Confessing the Faith:
Christian Theology in a North American Context (1996)

Thinking
THE·FAITH

Christian Theology in a
North American Context

DOUGLAS JOHN HALL

FORTRESS PRESS
Minneapolis

THINKING THE FAITH
Christian Theology in a North American Context

First Fortress Press edition 1991
First paperback edition 1991

Scripture quotations from the Revised Standard Version of the Bible are copyrighted 1946, 1952, and 1971 by the Division of Christian Education of the National Council of Churches.

Cover design: Judy Swanson

Library of Congress Cataloging-in-Publication Data

Hall, Douglas John, 1928–
    Thinking the faith: Christian theology in a North American
context / Douglas John Hall.
        p.   cm.
    Bibliography: p.
    Includes index.
    ISBN 0-8006-2545-5
    1. Theology, Doctrinal—North America. 2. Christianity and
culture. I. Title.
    BT30.N7H35 1988
    230'.097—dc19   91-8536
                                                                 CIP

The paper used in this publication meets the minimum requirements of American National Standard for Information Sciences—Permanence of Paper for Printed Library Materials, ANSI Z39.48-1984. ∞™

Manufactured in the U.S.A.   AF 1-2545

01   00   99   98   97   4   5   6   7   8   9   10   11   12   13

Jesus says in his society there is a new way for [people] to live:

> you show wisdom, by trusting people;
> you handle leadership, by serving;
> you handle offenders, by forgiving;
> you handle money, by sharing;
> you handle enemies, by loving;
> and you handle violence, by suffering.

In fact you have a new attitude toward everything, toward everybody. Toward nature, toward the state in which you happen to live, toward women, toward slaves, toward all and every single thing. Because this is a Jesus society and you repent, not by feeling bad, but by *thinking different.**

---

*Rudy Wiebe, *The Blue Mountains of China* (Toronto: McClelland and Stewart, 1970), pp. 215-216.

CONTENTS

PART II: THE DISCIPLINE

PREFACE

As the Christian movement nears the end of its second millennium, it faces a crisis that could not have been anticipated at the close of the first thousand years—or, indeed, by most of our own great-grandparents. In North America, which in some respects is the last stronghold of Western Christendom, the continuing material viability of the churches, aided by periodic "revivals," shields the average churchgoer from direct exposure to what Albert van den Heuvel called "the humiliation of the church." But those of us who are close enough to the internal life of the churches, yet sufficiently free of ecclesiastical promotionalism to be a little honest, know that the worldwide currents which have been altering the face of once-proud Christendom are subtly at work on this continent as well. We also know that Christian hope lies in the direction, not of ignoring or minimizing these influences, but of facing them forthrightly and seeking the positive meaning that they may contain for serious faith.

Since the most conspicuous dimensions of the waning of Christendom have to do with material decline (the decline in church membership and active attendance of Sunday services, the decline in financial and physical prosperity, the decline of influence in high places), such analyses as there are usually belabor the obvious: something drastic is happening to the churches! Yet another such analysis has recently made its appearance in my country, and, ecclesiastical imagination being almost as limited as secular imagination, it has quickly achieved the status of a "media event"—largely on account of its excited reception by the churches.[1] To anyone possessing even a minimal acquaintance with trends in religion over the past two centuries, the study in question is about as newsworthy

---

1. Reginald W. Bibby, *Fragmented Gods: The Poverty and Potential of Religion in Canada* (Toronto: Irwin, 1987).

as the fact that population concentrations are now found in cities and towns rather than in the country. But it is symptomatic of the churches' incapacity to confront the deeper malaise that they are ready to devote such unwarranted attention to superficial accounts of the situation. No doubt, certain statistical and other aspects of that deeper malaise *are* made visible through the activities of pollsters and popular sociologists; but the crisis behind the crises cannot be submitted to computer programming.

For that rudimentary crisis is *a crisis of thinking*.

Throughout most of its long history, Christianity has not required of its adherents that they should *think* the faith. The historical accident of its political and cultural establishment 15 centuries ago—an eventuality which today can be considered providential only in the most Kierkegaardian sense!—ensured that a thinking faith would be purely optional for members of the church. Indeed, it ensured that the vast majority would not "opt" for anything where religious belief was concerned, but would be ushered into Christendom automatically, baptism following birth as a matter of course. Under such sociological circumstances, to think the faith required an exceptional degree of curiosity and determination—not to mention leisure and, perhaps, an inclination to doubt authority!

More than that, with Feuerbach, Marx, Freud, and Nietzsche looking over our shoulders as we discuss such matters, we should have to admit that for countless millions the Christian religion has not only been an unthought affair but an aid to thought's repression, a tranquilizing agent assisting one to pass through this "vale of tears" with a minimum of original reflection upon the whole wondrous and perilous journey.

But that misuse of the Christian faith has come to an effective end. While a remarkable feature of religion in North America is still its capacity to perform, for many, this palliative service, "the end of the Constantinian era" is in sight also among us. This is particularly true of the churches representing the remnants of classical Protestantism. Perhaps that is because Protestantism, even in its North American mode, was never able to suppress thought altogether. While, apart from Wycliffe, they did not openly question the Constantinian model of the church, the Reformers envisaged a disciple community in which *all* members, not only the clergy and theological professionals, wrestled with the meaning of what they believed. "The true genius of Protestantism is to make extraordinary spiritual demands on very ordinary people."[2] This has never been truer than it has become in our own time and place.

---

2. Ronald Goetz, "Protestant Houses of God: A Contradiction in Terms?" *The Christian Century*, March 20–27, 1985, p. 299.

The new, post-Christian situation has naturally resulted in a winnowing process. That process has been at work in Europe for more than a century; it has been manifesting itself among us in the "New World" since the end of World War II in particular. Wherever it becomes evident that Christian discipleship now entails new depth of thought—indeed, that it will plunge one into profundities that a people pursuing "happiness" instinctively avoids!—there is an exodus from the churches. Some of those who leave the thinking churches make their way to other "sanctuaries" where incipient thought is assuaged at once with ready-made answers, or lulled by old, familiar tunes. Thus religion continues to play, among us, its habitual role.

But thought-less faith, which has always been a contradiction in terms, is today a stage on the road to the extinction, not only of Christianity itself, but of whatever the architects of our civilization meant by "Humanity." Only a thinking faith can survive. Only a thinking faith can help *the world* survive!

There are immense barriers to the creation of a truly thought-full Christian community in the North American context. The long-established function of religion as an effective sanctuary from thought is only one such barrier, though perhaps the most formidable. Even in ecclesial communities where thought has been permitted its place, perhaps even welcomed on occasion, one quality that is indispensable to plenitude of thought has seldom been conspicuous on this continent: originality. It will be pointed out by the erudite that originality, at least where questions of "ultimate concern" (Tillich) are at issue, is rarely—if ever—come by. What thought of God, of human destiny, of the path to redemption is ever truly new?

Perhaps. But it can be new *to me, to us*. Indeed, if the quality of newness and discovery is lacking from the thought that belongs to Christian faith, then, in a real sense, everything is lacking. For the "word of the cross," however venerable, only achieves its rightful hearing as it becomes altogether new and unheard-of—that is, as it engages my and our existence quite concretely and as "good *news*."

For the most part, North American Christianity has been deficient in this quality. At the personal and experiential level we have often accentuated the dimension of discovery; but our faith, however heartwarming it may sometimes have been, has been lacking in *intellectual* depth—in theology!—and it has seldom been carried into the arena of corporate life. Where thought is concerned, we have been content, as a rule, to borrow our ideas from the original struggles of other provinces of the

13

ecumenical church—a habit which is still visible today, for instance, in our consumer orientation towards Latin American liberation theology.

What would it mean to "think the faith" quite consciously in the North American context?

That is the confronting question and challenge that I have assumed in this book. It is not an easy task. It would be difficult even without the aforementioned cultural and ecclesiastical barriers to originality of thought. For there are, besides these, inherent obstacles in any theological exercise that wishes to meet the internal requirements of thought in the Christian mode. On the one hand, such thought is responsible to a tradition. It is not spun out of one's untrammeled entelechy. It is *the faith* which is to be thought—not merely one's own faith, but something given, pondered over by centuries of the faithful, shared by a worldwide community of faith. If such a work as this is intended as an introduction to theology for students and serious Christians of whatever background (and it is), then it has the responsibility of inculcating the tradition, including its terminology, its development or evolution, its sources and resources, the alternatives it offers, the many-faceted dialogue in which it is presently engaged, and other aspects.

On the other hand, the faith can be *thought*—that is, such reflection can become in the strict sense *theology*—only if, in the process of remembering all that precedes and excludes "us," we are simultaneously brought into a more articulate awareness of ourselves, our own identity, our "situation in life" *(Sitz im Leben)*: Who am I? Who are we? What do we bring to this struggle to understand? Why do we feel it to be necessary to do this? What is at stake for us? What are we afraid of? What do we hope for? This alone is a an arduous task. Perhaps it is impossible. Certainly it is never finished. Nevertheless, it is absolutely indispensable to Christian theology. Without this, one ends with mere doctrine.

Whether the present work succeeds in keeping these two fields of reflection in dialogue with each other will have to be determined by the community for which the work is intended: the community of Christ's disciples on the North American continent, circa the final decade of what was supposed to have been "the Christian century."

ACKNOWLEDGMENTS

I am grateful to McGill University for a small research grant which has helped with some aspects of this work; to my colleagues and students in McGill University's Faculty of Religious Studies, who have encouraged me in many and various ways, not least by granting me the freedom to pursue this study over the past eight years; and, above all, to Rhoda Palfrey Hall, my wife, who rightly spurns the title "research assistant" (though that is what the academic world would call her). While I have *written* the book, it is in reality the work of two authors and should bear the names of both; one of them, however, is more modest than the other.

INTRODUCTION

If I myself were an American . . . and a Christian theologian, then I would try to elaborate a theology of freedom—a theology of freedom from . . . any inferiority complex against good old Europe. . . . You do not need to have such an inferiority complex. . . . You may also have freedom from a superiority complex over against Asia and Africa. . . . Freedom for which you would stand would be the freedom for—I like to say a single word—humanity.[1]

1. The Summons to Contextualization

In August of 1975, about 200 Christian thinkers from South and North America met in Detroit to consider the future of theology in the Americas "by taking as their starting point their respective historical experiences."[2] In particular, the North Americans, whose numbers greatly surpassed those from the other America, wanted to learn from Latin American theologians of liberation what meaning their enterprise might have for the theological community in the United States and Canada. The burden of the message they received from their South and Central American colleagues is implied in the opening paragraphs of the report that was issued, later, by a "Follow-Up Conference":

1. Karl Barth, "Introduction to Theology: Questions to and Discussion with Dr. Karl Barth," April 25, 1962, Rockefeller Memorial Chapel, The University of Chicago; recorded in *Criterion,* vol. 2, no. 1 (Winter 1963), p. 24.

2. Gregory Baum, "The Christian Left at Detroit," in *Theology in the Americas,* ed. Sergio Torres and John Eagleson (Maryknoll, N.Y.: Orbis, 1976), p. 399.

INTRODUCTION

The future of North American theology concerns many people today, especially those who are preoccupied with the concepts of pluralism and the contextualization of theology. We hear about Latin American, African, and Asian theologies. What we call Western theology has been largely, if not exclusively, a European theology.

This seems for many Christians the right time to develop more authentic North American theologies. Otherwise Christianity in the United States will lack the prophetic voice required of it by the ecumenical demands of today and the future.

The context would include many different aspects and issues, one of which, by itself, is far-reaching: the U.S. dominates a large part of the world in economic and technological power. There must be a critical Christian word addressed to the great human issues that arise just from that fact.

The American dream has been increasingly challenged in recent years. For many North Americans, U.S. history expressed in religious symbols is a covenant of freedom and democracy; for some people at home and many in the Third World, it is an enterprise of oppression, domination, and imperialism.

North American theology has to be concerned with the deeper questions of how to speak of Christ in the midst of the ongoing moral crisis of the U.S. It is necessary to recover the tradition of idealism and struggle against oppression in our own history, both secular and religious, and work towards shaping a theology for the future.[3]

While the present work was not inspired by the above statement or the deliberations out of which it emerged (I was not personally involved in the Detroit conference), the statement nevertheless expresses rather pointedly some of the main concerns that have persuaded me of the need to articulate a Christian theology quite consciously out of the North American context. I have quoted at considerable length from the conclusions arrived at by the Follow-Up Conference because they indicate that this need, and the experiences that have brought it to light, do not pertain to any one person or group but are shared widely among sensitive North American Christians today. There is a growing awareness that too much of our theology has been secondhand. It has been gleaned from the spiritual struggles of other peoples and "applied" to our United States and Canadian societies with little concern for genuine interpretation or dialogue with the particularities of our milieu. Indeed, the most consistent aspect of such "application" has probably been oversimplification—the sloganization and watering-down of the complexities of more nuanced deliberations.

3. Ibid., p. 433.

INTRODUCTION

The historical moment in which we find ourselves, if we are citizens of the United States or Canada, calls for *original* thinking of a caliber that, heretofore, only a few individuals among us have attempted or attained. It will not do for Christians in our part of the "First World" today to mouth simplistic or revamped versions of the theological confessions hammered out on the anvils of European *or Latin American* experience. We must learn to do theology for ourselves.

Doing theology, as distinct from imbibing the results of the theological exertions of others, involves entering at depth into the historical experiences of one's own people. As the Detroit statement intimates, this prerequisite of all authentic theology entails for *us*—a people at the nerve center of the affluent nations of the Northern hemisphere—the acquisition of a critical self-awareness which may well produce in us acute forms of mental discomfort. To do theology anywhere in the First World today means to suffer. Precisely in those parts of the world where humanity still regularly congratulates itself on its high achievements, Christians are required to suffer—to permit—dark thoughts to enter their consciousness. They are called to this cruciform vocation, not out of any fascination with the negative, but because the rhetorical positive lauded by the image makers of the First World is sustained at an inestimable cost to millions of God's beloved creatures, human and extrahuman, and threatens the future of the planet itself. In the midst of societies that are "First," someone has to remind the human species that the first may well be last.

Within such contexts, serious theological thinking cannot be engaged in apart from deliberate and frequently renewed acts of courage. No one *wants* to suffer—nor should one want to. But spiritual and cerebral—as well as, on occasion, physical—suffering belongs to the life of "the people of the cross." If it surprises us that we should be asked, as Christian thinkers, to take up a mode of reflection which may be painful, even *excruciating*, this only indicates how far we have come from the Newer Testament's description of the church, which has more to say about the suffering of the *sōma Christou* than about any other single ecclesiological subject.

The dimension of suffering in theology which belongs to all First World settings today is especially poignant in the two northern nations of the North American continent, because our whole project as peoples has been to eliminate every form of suffering. Yet it is necessary for all who respond today to the summons to contextualization in theology to come to terms with the fact that, for all our fabled success, not to mention our still more mythic innocence, we North Americans are a highly problematic people. If the Christians among us—at least the Christians!—

19

cannot fight our way through the cloying layers of official light to the heart of our real darkness, then we shall have failed to rise to the challenge implicit in this historical moment.

It is a truly monumental challenge, and one with far-reaching consequences. For one must doubt that there can be any lasting hope for Western civilization if we, the people of a continent privileged to explore at length the expansive visions of occidental modernity, fall short of the stamina and imagination needed to engage the strange despair that has come upon us, uninvited and largely unacknowledged, in these latter decades.

The call for an indigenization of Christian theological reflection, expressed at Detroit and elsewhere, is therefore not to be construed as yet another exhortation from the heart of academe urging the churches to become more mature and intellectually serious. Neither is it the product of a New World boast, in the face of a long and somewhat humiliating reliance upon European academic theology, that we are finally disengaging ourselves theologically, as we have already done in other respects, from the parental cultures.

As for academic excellence in theology, it is something always to be striven for. But the most brilliant theological ratiocination does not necessarily contribute to the spiritual authenticity that is required of North American Christians today; in fact, it may even impede that authenticity, especially when pursued as an end. What the moment demands of us is not that we produce theologians capable of competing in the intellectual Olympics of the world church, but that we raise up a community of thinking Christians who are able to bear prophetic witness to the truth of God as it manifests itself in the life of the world—not some theoretical world, and not somebody else's world, but our world, our problematic First World.

The distinction between theory/practice and *praxis* is useful here (as it was at Detroit).[4] The summons to contextualization is not a challenge to produce impressive theoretical statements of the faith but to engage in faithful Christian praxis. Kierkegaard had some such distinction in mind when he wrote,

> The moment I take Christianity as a doctrine and so indulge my cleverness or profundity or my eloquence or my imaginative powers in depicting it, people are very pleased; I am looked upon as a serious Christian. The moment I begin to express existentially what I say, and consequently to

---

4. Ibid., p. 435.

bring Christianity into reality, it is just as though I had exploded existence—
the scandal is there at once.[5]

Those who are prone to think that a term like *praxis* easily translates into
"practice" and thus supports a straightforward activism over against all
who ponder should remember, however, that Søren Kierkegaard was first
of all a ponderer! The point of praxis is not to substitute act for thought,
deed for word, but to ensure that thinking is rooted in existence—and
committed to its transformation. To say that the summons to contextualization is a call to faithful Christian praxis is *not*, therefore, to say, "Let
us leave off all this wearisome business of theology and get on with *doing
the truth!*" It means, rather, to pledge oneself to the overcoming of the
(after all, artificial) gap between thought and act, and so to become more
serious *about both*. To attempt a disciplined and faithful Christian praxis
as North Americans today means, concretely expressed, to enter into our
historical destiny *as North Americans*, to suffer the critical dimensions
of our new consciousness of that identity and destiny and, so far as
possible, to alter the direction of our society in ways consistent with the
gospel that we are brought to hear in and through this discriminating
encounter with our context.

Such an attempt is far from being a bid for independence vis-à-vis
the European theological community and the traditions that it represents.
No theological province of the *oikumēnē* can be independent of the others.
Every theological community, however, must work out its witness in
dialogue with the particularities of its own sociohistorical situation. Otherwise, it will in any case have nothing to contribute to the ecumenical
discussion. It is in this sense that the venerable Barth, addressing the
largest audience of his career, in Chicago in 1962, employed the term
"freedom." Not independence from "old Europe," but freedom in relation
to that parental civilization and church—this is what is required of us.

Precisely such freedom is presupposed by the method and spirit of
contextualization. Contextualization, as I shall hope to demonstrate in
what follows, is the sine qua non of all genuine theological thought, and
always has been. The wonder is that North America has been able for so
long to evade the call to contextuality in theology. We take refuge in our
novelty, but we are, after all, no longer a *very* new "New World." The
first musical concert in the European mode was given in my city of
Montreal (then the Indian settlement of Hochelaga) in 1535—when Luther

---

5. Søren Kierkegaard, *Journals*, ed. and trans. Alexander Dru (London: Oxford University Press,
1938), entry #988, p. 343.

was at the height of his career. Along with others who will read these words, my own Caucasian ancestors arrived on these shores in the early 1600s—and some of my people, being Mohawk, were already "here to meet the boat." Surely, half a millennium is long enough to achieve a measure of real freedom. One of the historical mysteries that we shall have to explore in these pages (for it has high theological significance) is why a culture almost 500 years old still cherishes the notion of its newness; and why, in particular, the church within that culture has been content to order its ideas from abroad, playing in the ecumenical dialogue of Christendom the role of administrator, publicist, diplomat, and financier, but rarely that of thinker.

2. The Point of View

In previous writings, particularly in *Lighten Our Darkness,*[6] I attempted to intuit the *kind* of theological emphasis appropriate to North America, especially to the remnants of classical Protestantism on this continent. As the subtitle of the above-named work indicates ("Towards an Indigenous Theology of the Cross"), the more I have been compelled by events and by my vocation to enter consciously and in a spirit of critical responsibility into the life of this civilization, the more convinced I have become of the appropriateness for our situation of some variation on that theological approach which Martin Luther named *theologia crucis,* "theology of the cross."

That I have felt the necessity of searching the past for a way into the future—for roots—will no doubt already reveal something about the character of my basic theological approach. I do not believe that Christian theology can be spun out of our own personal or collective entelechy, with no reference to what has gone before us. Christianity is a historical faith, and we are the inheritors of a tradition. This, as I shall try to show in the opening chapter, is inherent in the contextualizing process. Every new generation of the *koinōnia* is required—not by external authority but by the inherent claims of the gospel as such—to live in an ongoing dialogue with that tradition, and to preserve what is true, beautiful, and good within it. This responsibility comes to us, not only as a vocational duty, but as a privilege. It is also, plainly, a necessity without which we cannot

---

6. Douglas John Hall, *Lighten Our Darkness* (Philadelphia: Westminster, 1976); I attempted to speak specifically to the Canadian situation out of this same tradition in a small work entitled *The Canada Crisis* (Toronto: Anglican Book Centre, 1980).

pursue our "modest science" (Barth). Christian belief and thought *needs* the past. Our need for what Martin Marty insightfully called "a usable past" is today very close to the surface of our New World consciousness. The future we confront is uncertain, and the present moment is an enigma. We turn to the past for help, for perspective—not, it should be hoped, for refuge!

But the past, for Christians, is no more unitary a thing than is the present. There are in fact *many* traditions within the Christian past, and every existential (as distinct from merely curious or "scholarly") resort to the past is an attempt to locate the lineage of *that* tradition which can be, for our present, a source of wisdom and courage.

It is my view (and as such it will color everything that is said in the course of this study) that the tradition North American Christians today are most in need of contemplating and assimilating is that thin, neglected, and frequently *rejected* one to which Luther gave the nomenclature (he did not invent it) *theologia crucis*.

Obviously, the process of reflection through which, over the years, I have been led to this conclusion is not readily explained. It is still less accessible to verification or even, perhaps, justification. That it is bound up with personal experience, including psychological as well as conceptive dimensions of my own character, and contains therefore a highly subjective component I should be the last to deny. I doubt that theology can ever avoid that component, or that it should. There are, however, besides various personal and other *causes* for this orientation, certain *reasons* why, as a North American Christian living at the end of the modern era, I am moved to explore the potentiality of that particular tradition for yielding something like "gospel."[7] These reasons are inseparable from the raison d'être of the present work as a whole, and they

---

7. I owe the distinction between reason and cause to Alaisdair MacIntyre. It is a useful distinction, particularly in a society which rather too automatically psychologizes every decision or belief. MacIntyre insists that arguments from psychology do not bring out the fallacies they are supposed to show; in particular, they do not dispose of religious belief, because "the distinction in question is that between the *causes* of a particular belief's being held and the *reasons* for its being held. If I say that 9 x 9 equals 81, my reasons for this belief will be a matter of my reliance on my memory of the multiplication table, and my belief in its validity as a method of calculation. But the causes of my belief may go back to such factors as the impressive voice in which the infant teacher uttered this truth and my own suggestibility as a child. To give a psychological explanation to the holding of a belief is to say what kind of past events in an individual's history or what kind of personality structure tend to lead on to the holding of a particular kind of belief; to explain why a particular individual holds the belief that he does hold is to identify him as being an example of this kind of history or temperament producing this kind of belief. It is to speak entirely of causes, and not at all of reasons. On the other hand, to discuss the validity of an argument for belief or its truth is to say what sort of logical connections must hold between different types of statements, or what evidence it is appropriate to offer for or against a particular kind of belief. It is to speak entirely of reasons, and not at all of causes" (*Difficulties in Christian Belief* [London: SCM, 1959] pp. 97-98).

must therefore be introduced gradually. Whatever justification there is for the studied contemplation of this minority tradition will depend upon the integrity and persuasiveness of the whole work which is its consequence.

The lineage of the *theologia crucis* passes through some of the medieval mystics by whom Luther himself was deeply influenced, and finds its way eventually to Paul—with, I think, a considerable impetus along the way from the christological deliberations of the school of Antioch and certain aspects of the many-sided Augustine of Hippo. Its *deepest* roots, however, are found in the prophetic tradition of ancient Israel. It is therefore not accidental that the rediscovery of this minority Christian tradition must mean both the rediscovery of the Older Testament as theologically normative, and of the living community of Israel—a people who, as one may well say, have *lived* the theology of the cross, and have had to do so partly because Christians, who always had a good deal to say about *Jesus'* cross, themselves lived in accordance with a very different conception of the calling of the people of God![8]

This is not the place to enter into a full-scale description of the tradition under discussion,[9] but some preliminary response should nonetheless be given to the question that is no doubt begged by the preceding comments: What *is* the *theologia crucis?*

Contrary to the way in which the term is frequently heard in the English-speaking world, the "theology of the cross" is not a synonym for the doctrine of the atonement. It designates rather a whole theological and faith posture. "*Theologia crucis,*" as Jürgen Moltmann has aptly

---

8. Dietrich Bonhoeffer, in this as in so many other matters, set the tone for many of us in his Advent letter of 1943: "My thoughts and feelings seem to be getting more and more like the Old Testament, and no wonder, I have been reading it much more than the New for the last few months. It is only when one knows the ineffability of the Name of God that one can utter the name of Jesus Christ. It is only when one loves life and the world so much that without them everything would be gone, that one can believe in the resurrection and a new world. It is only when one submits to the law that one can speak of grace, and only when one sees the anger and wrath of God hanging like grim realities over the head of one's enemies that one can know something of what it means to love and forgive them. I don't think it is Christian to want to get to the New Testament too soon and too directly. . . . We live on the next to last word, and believe on the last, don't we?" (*Letters and Papers from Prison,* ed. Eberhard Bethge, trans. Reginald H. Fuller [London: SCM, 1953], p. 79).

9. Among the many works which can assist in the comprehension of the spirit of this tradition, the following may be named at this juncture as having special significance: Walther von Loewenich, *Luther's Theology of the Cross*, trans. Herbert J. A. Bouman (Minneapolis: Augsburg, 1976); Jürgen Moltmann, *The Crucified God: The Cross of Christ as the Foundation and Criticism of Christian Theology*, trans. R. W. Wilson and John Bowden (London: SCM, 1973); Eberhard Jüngel, *God as the Mystery of the World: On the Foundation of the Theology of the Crucified One in the Dispute between Theism and Atheism*, trans. Darrell L. Guder (Grand Rapids: Eerdmans, 1983).

said, "is not a single chapter in theology, but the key-signature for all Christian theology."[10] Indeed, one hesitates to use the terminology at all. It would be preferable in so many ways simply to speak about the gospel and the theology which attempts to address itself to the most rudimentary meaning of the Christian gospel! Certainly "theology *of the* cross" should be distinguished sharply from that tendency of the North American ecclesiastical community in the past several decades to be swayed by one "theology *of*" after another. We are not dealing here with another in the series. We are attempting to recover and restate, in terms adequate to our own epoch, a tradition which has been present from the outset of the Christian movement, though present, unfortunately, as a *minority* tradition, and one which for the most part could only with the greatest difficulty sustain itself against the dominant theology of Christendom—what Luther called *theologia gloriae*. As Moltmann, again, has put it, "There is a good deal of support in tradition for the theology of the cross, but it was never much loved."[11]

At the heart of the theology of the cross is—of course—the cross of the Christ. Such a statement, however, says both everything and nothing—and it can do so rather piously. Let us therefore try to express the core of this theological tradition in a way that may be at the same time less explicitly dogmatic and more faithful to what the tradition intends: the theology of the cross, at base, is about *God's abiding commitment to the world*. Borrowing again from Barth's moving "final words" in Chicago—and they are the words of one who knew a good deal about this same tradition—the theology of the cross has to do with the "freedom for humanity" that is the core of the gospel of "Jesus Christ and him crucified" (1 Cor. 2:2).[12] Over against and in opposition to every "religious"

---

10. *The Crucified God*, p. 72.

11. Ibid., p. 3. I wonder, however, whether Prof. Moltmann does not underestimate the scope of the tradition since, in the sentences immediately following this, he affirms that the tradition "begins with Paul, to whom its foundation is rightly attributed, and then leaps forward to Luther, in whom it is given explicit expression, and is present today in the persecuted churches of the poor and the oppressed. It returns to life in a distinctive way in Zinzendorf. It left its mark on the better side of early dialectical theology and on the Luther renaissance of the 1920s" (ibid.).

12. I am of course aware of the ambiguity of the term *world*. James Gustafson rightly criticizes "much . . . recent theology" for its lack of clarity in the employment of this term, and he is particularly critical of the implication (which he finds, for instance, in the work of Jürgen Moltmann) that the term *world* too often suggests that "the whole of this universe was created solely for the sake of man" (*Ethics from a Theocentric Perspective* [Chicago: University of Chicago Press, 1981], pp. 44-45).

While Karl Barth's phrase, "freedom for humanity," as well as my own formulations in the text above, can seem to court such an equation, I have no wish to single out the *human* species as the sole object of redemption through the cross. *Kosmos* (as in John 3:16) incorporates the whole creation—and its ineffable connectedness. It is necessary, however, for Christian theology to con-temptation to abandon creation and to seek security and hope in a supra-mundane denouement to the riddles of existence, the representatives of this tradition insist that it is the world that the biblical God loves and wills to redeem. The transcendent and transforming *agapē* of the "high and holy One of Israel" is as firmly fixed upon "fallen" creation as the cross of the Christ is planted in "the place of the skull."

It is this world-orientation of the *theologia crucis* which requires of us that we locate its deepest roots in the prophets of Israel. (In this connection, incidentally, it should not be forgotten that the man who gave the name to this minority tradition, Luther, was as much a student of the Psalms and the prophets as he was of Romans and 1 Corinthians.)[13] In particular, what binds the *theologia crucis* to the faith of Israel is its indelible continuity with what Abraham J. Heschel considered the essence of prophetic faith, *divine pathos:*

> Prophecy consists in the inspired communication of divine attitudes to the prophetic consciousness. . . . The divine pathos is the ground tone of all these attitudes. . . . It is echoed in almost every prophetic statement.
>
> To the prophet . . . God does not reveal himself in an abstract abso-luteness, but in a personal and intimate relation to the world. He does not simply command and expect obedience; He is also moved and affected by what happens in the world, and reacts accordingly. Events and human actions arouse in Him joy and sorrow, pleasure or wrath. He is not con-ceived as judging the world in detachment. He reacts in an intimate and subjective manner, and thus determines the value of events. . . .
>
> God's pathos was not thought of as a sort of fever of the mind which, disregarding the standards of justice, culminates in irrational and irre-sponsible action. There is justice in all His ways, the Bible insists again and again.
>
> There is no dichotomy of pathos and ethos, of motive and norm. . . . It is because God is the source of justice that His pathos is ethical; and it is because God is absolutely personal—devoid of anything impersonal—that this ethos is full of pathos.
>
> Pathos, then, is not an attitude taken arbitrarily. Its inner law is the moral law; ethos is inherent in pathos. *God is concerned about the world and*

---

centrate upon the human, for it is the human species which, for this tradition, constitutes the disruptive and destructive aspect of ("fallen") creation. A phrase like "freedom for humanity" should not be heard, then, as denoting an exclusive interest in the human, but as implying a concern for the whole created order, which is victimized by human *un*freedom.

13. He was, in fact, lecturing on the Psalms at the time when he coined the term *theologia crucis*. See Roland H. Bainton, *Here I Stand: A Life of Martin Luther* (New York: Mentor Books, New American Library, 1950), p. 51.

shares its fate. Indeed, this is the essence of God's moral nature: His willingness to be intimately involved in the history of man.[14]

The passion of Jesus *(passio Christi)* is inseparable from the pathos of the God of Israel; indeed, when the cross of Christ *is* separated from the pathos of Yahweh it is grossly distorted, becoming on the one hand the soteriological basis for the heaven-bent world rejection of much avowed Christian orthodoxy, and on the other the model for that peculiar form of personalistic sentimentalism which characterizes bourgeois neo-Protestantism. The abiding commitment to creation that marks classical Hebraic thought as well as much contemporary Jewish theology and faith[15] is the matrix for our contemplation of the meaning of the cross. We can recover the full significance of Jesus' suffering and death only if we regard it against the backdrop of that ancient tradition, and in company with our brothers and sisters of Israel who still live and think that prophetic faith-tradition.[16]

It is not accidental, therefore, that when, a few days before his death by hanging, Dietrich Bonhoeffer penned some important words about the gospel of the cross, he began his reflections with the sentence, "Now for some further thoughts *about the Old Testament.*" He continued,

Unlike the other oriental religions, the faith of the Old Testament isn't a religion of redemption. It's true that Christianity has always been regarded as a religion of redemption. But isn't this a cardinal error, which separates Christ from the Old Testament and interprets him on the lines of the myths about redemption? To the objection that a crucial importance is given in the Old Testament to redemption (from Egypt, and later from Babylon—cf. Deutero-Isaiah) it may be answered that the redemptions referred to here are *historical*, i.e. on *this* side of death, whereas everywhere else the myths about redemption are concerned to overcome the barrier of death. Israel is delivered out of Egypt so that it may live before God as God's

---

14. Abraham Heschel, *The Prophets* (New York: The Jewish Publication Society of America, 1962), pp. 223-224; emphasis added.

15. See, e.g., Emil L. Fackenheim, *To Mend the World: Foundations of Future Jewish Thought* (New York: Schocken Books, 1982).

16. The brief dialogue between Hans Küng and the Jewish theologian Pinchas Lapide is excellent documentation of this claim. "For eighteen hundred years," says Lapide, "the Church has done three things to Jesus: it has de-judaized him, it has hellenized him, and it has very effectively put us off him." Yet Jesus belongs within the story of Israel and Israel's God: ". . . for the Jewish people what better embodiment could you find than this poor rabbi of Nazareth? Eli, Eli lama sabachthani is not merely a psalm of David and a word of Jesus from the cross, but—I would almost say—the leitmotiv of those who had to go to Auschwitz and Majdanek" (*Brother or Lord? A Jew and a Christian Talk Together*, trans. Edward Quinn [Glasgow: William Collins Sons, 1977], pp. 17, 20).

people on earth. The redemption myths try unhistorically to find an eternity after death. Sheol and Hades are no metaphysical constructions, but images which imply that the "past," while it still exists, has only a shadowy existence in the present.

The decisive factor is said to be that in Christianity the hope of resurrection is proclaimed, and that that means the emergence of a genuine religion of redemption, the main emphasis now being on the far side of the boundary drawn by death. But it seems to me that this is just where the mistake and the danger lie. Redemption now means redemption from cares, distress, fears, and longings, from sin and death, in a better world beyond the grave. But is this really the essential character of the proclamation of Christ in the gospels and by Paul? I should say it is not. The difference between the Christian hope of resurrection and the mythological hope is that the former sends a man back to his life on earth in a wholly new way which is even more sharply defined than it is in the Old Testament. The Christian, unlike the devotees of the redemption myths, has no last line of escape available from earthly tasks and difficulties into the eternal, but, like Christ himself ("My God, my God, why hast thou forsaken me?"), he must drink the earthly cup to the dregs, and only in his doing so is the crucified and risen Lord with him, and he crucified and risen with Christ. *This world must not be prematurely written off; in this the Old and New Testaments are at one.* Redemption myths arise from human boundary-experiences, but Christ takes hold of a man at the centre of his life.[17]

Commitment to the world, which is the foundational theo-anthropological rationale of the cross of Christ and of which that cross is (for Christians) the supreme statement, prevents those who follow in the spirit of this tradition from espousing religious "solutions" in which the ills of the world have already been met and resolved. In contrast to the theological triumphalism (*theologia gloriae*) which has accompanied the ecclesiastical imperialism of dominant forms of Christendom throughout the ages, the theology of the cross takes as its point of departure the brokenness of the human spirit and the human community. It places its hope in God's transformative solidarity with fallen creation, with the world *in* its brokenness. It wants to serve, not as a ready-made ideological panacea for every form of human and worldly suffering, but as the salvific base from which the courage may be found willingly to participate in the suffering of the earth and its creatures. Thus the community that is moved

---

17. The quotation is from one of Bonhoeffer's last letters to Eberhard Bethge and is found in the larger edition of *Letters and Papers from Prison* (London: SCM, 1971), pp. 336f. Italics added.

Note: While I shall avoid exclusive language in my own text, I shall not alter quotations, even when (as in the present instance) I deplore the sexist connotations implicit or explicit within them.

by the gospel of the cross inevitably finds itself drawn towards earth's suffering ones, for they are in particular those in whom the divine pathos and compassion become especially transparent.[18] By contrast, the "theology of glory" instinctively draws away from the sufferer, except where it can play the role of benefactor and miracle worker, because every unresolved negation calls in question its ideology of triumph. Invariably, therefore, Christian triumphalism ends in world-denial, either in the form of blatant otherworldliness or as the ecclesial embodiment of theoretical systems which repress or suppress knowledge of the real world. The theology of the cross does not *celebrate* the world's status quo, and it certainly eschews the brand of "realism" which is simply fatalism in disguise; but it is marked by a determination to be entirely honest about the evil and negation that is "there" in existence, and to work out its strategies of hope only in dialogue with the suffering that is consequent upon that evil and negation. As Luther put it succinctly in his Heidelberg Disputation, thesis 21: "A theology of glory calls evil good and good evil. A theology of the cross calls the thing what it actually is."[19] Karl Rahner could be considered a faithful exegete of the meaning of Luther's aphorism when he writes that

> the real and total and comprehensive task of a Christian as a Christian is to be a human being, a human being of course whose depths are divine. . . . And to this extent the Christian life is the acceptance of human existence as such as opposed to a final protest against it. But this means that Christianity *sees reality as it is. Christianity does not oblige [the Christian] to see the reality of his historical experience of life in an optimistic light. On the contrary, it obliges him to see this existence as dark and bitter and hard, and as an unfathomable risk.*[20]

Precisely here lies the point of inescapable convergence between the *theologia crucis* tradition and theological contextuality. *Theology done in the spirit of this tradition is bound to be a contextual theology.* For it would be the height of contradiction to insist that what is revealed in the suffering, death, and resurrection of Jesus Christ is God's abiding commitment to this world, and then to enucleate a theology which in effect ignored the specific realities of the here and now. If it is taken seriously

---

18. I know of no more moving documentation of this claim than is provided by Jean Vanier in his *Eruption to Hope* (Toronto: Griffin House, 1971).

19. *Luther's Works,* vol. 31 (Philadelphia: Fortress, 1957), pp. 40-41.

20. Karl Rahner, *Foundations of Christian Faith*, trans. Wm. V. Dych (New York: Seabury, 1987), p. 403.

that the whole movement of the God of the Bible, culminating for Christians in the incarnation and humiliation of the Word, is a painful but determined journey towards creation ("he set his face steadfastly to go to Jerusalem," Luke 9:51, KJV), then the faith which emanates from such a gospel *must* be a matter of praxis, i.e., of an ever more intensive *concretization* of the divine solidarity with creaturely being. It is possible that there are other types of theological emphases which provide a basis and rationale for Christian involvement in this world; but the *theologia crucis* not only *offers* the believing community such a basis and rationale, it positively drives the church out into the world—just as, according to the (highly instructive) legend of *Quo Vadis*, St. Peter, bent upon escaping from dangerous Rome, was impelled by his vision of the crucified and risen Christ on the Appian Way to return to the *civitas terrena*, there to share the suffering of his Lord.

There are thus more reasons than one for exploring this not-much-loved tradition. Not only is it appropriate within a First World context because of its capacity to unmask triumphalism and provide an alternative statement of the meaning of the Christian message; it is, besides, the most insistent *material* basis for a *formal* or methodological principle that is centrally informed by the desire to engage the context.

What the most compelling *contemporary* statements of the theology of the cross have demonstrated[21] is that the people of the cross are drawn, not only towards *individual* sufferers, but towards suffering *peoples* and indeed towards all creatures, human and extrahuman, which are being deprived of the fullness of life for which God intends what God has made. The *pastoral* impulse has always been part of this theological tradition (as witness Luther's many *Letters of Spiritual Counsel*).[22] What has not always been part of it, unfortunately, is the recognition that this same pastoral impulse implies a *political* dimension and in fact is itself impoverished until that concern for the *polis* is made good. It has taken contemporary social experience and theory (including Marxist social analysis)[23] to help Christians standing within this minority tradition to discern its sociopolitical implications. Too often, the theology of the cross has articulated itself in the type of pastoral and personal orientation which is

---

21. I am thinking here of the work of many of the most influential theological thinkers of our century, including Karl Barth, Emil Brunner, Reinhold Niebuhr, Paul Tillich, Dietrich Bonhoeffer, Jürgen Moltmann, Dorothee Sölle, C. S. Song, Kosuke Koyama, and many others.

22. Martin Luther, *Letters of Spiritual Council,* ed. and trans. Theodore G. Tappert, Library of Christian Classics 18 (Philadelphia: Westminster, 1955).

23. In this connection see Nicholas Lash, *A Matter of Hope: A Theologian's Reflections on the Thought of Karl Marx* (Notre Dame, Ind.: University of Notre Dame Press, 1982).

frankly privatistic: the sufferings of the Christ are presented as a model (*imitatio Christi*) and a source of meaning for our personal trials. When this is accompanied by a certain (perhaps Nordic?) fatalism about worldly life in general, as it frequently has been and is, it is productive of the kind of *social* quietism and resignation which ends in an otherworldliness that can be just as detrimental to the *shalom* of the earth as any other form of world denial. Such mottos associated with this theological posture as "through cross to crown," or "life is a cross that must be borne," are often in fact pietistic betrayals of the very essence of this tradition. For that essence is its intense and eloquent articulation of the divine compassion, the pathos of God, God's unaccountable and entirely gracious but nonetheless (for faith) *definitive* commitment to creation—in short, God's ḥesed/agapē.

Individuals are certainly recipients of this "spontaneous and unmotivated love" (Nygren), but we are not dealing here with religious individualism. Even the most (reputedly) otherworldly of the Gospels offers as its *rudimentary* explanation of the passion of the Christ an unqualified and radical statement of the divine love *for the world* (*kosmos*, John 3:16). The recognition of this *cosmic* thrust of the gospel of the cross has demanded of all serious modern exponents of the *theologia crucis* that they develop, in a manner seldom if ever explored in the past, its potential as a basis for *political* theology. This has of course been facilitated greatly by the disestablishment of the Christian religion. Under the conditions of the Constantinian arrangement, Christianity may have been at liberty to set forth exceptional faith-postures for individuals, but to offer a political gospel so thoroughly at odds with empire was virtually unthinkable. Even a mind as prolific and critical as Luther's could not undertake, in such a context, the full exploration of this tradition for its larger, public meaning.

With the disestablishment of the Christian religion, however, such an exploration begins to be seen as being of its essence. Thus it can be observed already with Kierkegaard that the theology of the cross becomes a tool and perspective of social analysis; for, despite his own brand of individualism, "SK" realized full well that the Christian community could no longer rely upon "Christendom" for its understanding of and relation to the world. In our own period, this potential of the *theologia crucis* for yielding a political theology and ethic has been probed by many, from Karl Barth to some of the contemporary feminist and liberation theologians. The tradition is of course more explicit in some than in others. Theologians for whom the Reformation has had a particular authority and meaning (e.g., Kitamori, Moltmann, Sölle, Koyama, Song) have developed their own thought, often, in conscious response to the theology of the cross. Yet traces of this tradition are in some measure present wherever the life and destiny of this world are believed to be a matter of "ultimate concern" (Tillich) for Christian faith.[24]

In such contemporary expressions of the theology of the cross, it is clear that we do not have to do only with *understanding* the world and that which negates the life of the world. The comprehension of reality, though in itself entailing an act of unusual intellectual courage, could never satisfy a theology whose object, i.e., whose living subject, is a God intensely committed to creation, for whom the fate of the earth is a matter of parentlike yearning. Such a theology is bound always to move from theology to ethic, indicative to imperative, gospel to command (*Torah*), comprehension to transformation. From the discernment of the suffering of the world and the most rigorous and disciplined study of its causes, the community influenced by this tradition is compelled by its involvement in its discipline (by its *discipleship!*) to enter into a working solidarity with those most vulnerable to the effects of this suffering, and to attempt to turn the suffering body politic towards life rather than death. Today the very *mission* of the church must, in my view, be expressed in just such terms. As I have phrased it elsewhere, Christian mission today means "the stewardship of life in the kingdom of death."[25] Without ceasing to be a personal and pastoral theology—in fact, enhancing the personal dimension by setting persons where they actually live, within their social contexts—the theology of the cross becomes today, of necessity, a political theology. That is, it is the life of the *polis* that grips it, and the *polis* from now on is the whole earth and all creatures, the "global village."[26]

---

24. Thus it is not surprising to discover strong intimations of the *theologia crucis* tradition in Catholic liberationists like Gutierrez, Segundo, and others, as well as in critical First World theologians who write out of a Roman Catholic identity, such as Johannes Metz and Rosemary Ruether. Moreover, the best *artistic* representations of this theological tradition are almost always Roman Catholic (e.g., Shusaku Endo's novel *Silence*, trans. William Johnston [Tokyo: Sophia University, 1969]; Graham Greene's *The Power and the Glory* [Harmondsworth: Penguin, 1962], and Georges Bernanos's *Diary of a Country Priest*, trans. Pamela Morris [New York: MacMillan, 1937]).

25. See my book, *The Stewardship of Life in the Kingdom of Death*, rev. ed. (Grand Rapids, Mich.: Wm. B. Eerdmans, 1988).

26. Here and there, there are encouraging signs that Christians are making new and necessarily painful attempts to achieve a global perspective and orientation that is distinct from Christian expansionism on the one hand and liberal ecumenism on the other. In New York City, due mainly to the efforts of Edward Huenemann, Paul Lehmann, and others, an "Association for Global Theology" has been formed, incorporating theological-ethical concerns from all three "worlds." A moving testimony to the need for global vision is presented in the inaugural address of Choan-Seng Song, professor at the Pacific School of Religion. The address, given on October 14, 1985, is entitled, "Ecumenical Horizons of Theology in a Global Context."

Such a theology is a theology *of the cross* because it fastens upon that which negates and threatens the life of creation and upon God's intention, through incarnational solidarity with the world's suffering, to turn history towards life rather than death. If it concentrates upon suffering, it is not because this tradition manifests a morbid interest in pain, but because there *is* pain, because disintegrative pain[27] is not part of what *should* be, and because there can be no healing that does not begin with the sober recognition of the reality of that which needs to be healed. It goes for societies—even for "Worlds"—as for individuals: "Only the sick have need of a physician." If so many of the changes constantly clamored after in our First World are cosmetic, it is surely due to the paucity of truthful reflection upon and confession of our real condition. Ill persons frequently die when only the symptoms of their diseases are treated. It is not unthinkable that a civilization could be in the throes of "the sickness unto death" (Kierkegaard) while experiencing periodic economic recoveries! If on the other hand the suffering of societies, as of persons, is explored with sufficient depth and commitment, life *can* become the outcome even of the terminally ill. It is that hope which gives the people of the cross the courage to probe to the very heart of our darkness.

3. The Theology of the Cross and the North American Experience

But why should such a theological tradition be meaningful within the North American context in particular? Far from appearing an appropriate tradition for the church in our part of the First World to investigate, it would seem entirely foreign to the spirit of our historical experience. It is hardly commensurate with the regnant conventions and values of New World optimism to think in terms of brokenness, suffering, and failure— not to mention the violence which the symbol of the cross inevitably conjures up.

Precisely! It is so incongruous with the dominant themes and pursuits of our success-orientated society to think in these terms that as a people we do not know what to make of brokenness, suffering, death, and failure

---

27. In my *God and Human Suffering: An Exercise in the Theology of the Cross* (Minneapolis: Augsburg, 1986) I have made what I regard as an important distinction between suffering which is integrative and suffering which merely negates. Suffering which is ultimately integrative belongs to our creaturely status, and we should not pursue theories of theodicy or redemption which mistake salvation for a pain-free existence.

when we actually experience them. Much less can we deal with violence, though our cities are full of it and our foreign policies aid and abet it throughout the planet.

In her moving novel *Obasan*, Joy Kogawa depicts, through the eyes of a child who was one of the victims, the pathetic story of Canadians of Japanese origin during and immediately after World War II. Not only were these citizens of Canada, most of them living in British Columbia, herded into camps in the interior (as happened also in the United States) but their properties were confiscated and, after the war, they were again uprooted—"exiled from their exile," as Kogawa puts it—and either deported or relocated in other parts of the country, where many of them had to engage in what was virtually slave labor. As with other minorities in our midst, the traditions still alive among the North American Japanese (some of them Christian traditions) enabled them to endure the unspeakable hardship and humiliation of this shameful episode in Canadian history. The Christian pastor who lives among them and is one of them, in Kogawa's documentary novel, gives words to the tradition by which significant numbers of them were sustained (and it is a profound instance precisely of the *theologia crucis*)[28] when he says

> that there is brokenness . . . . That this world is brokenness. But within brokenness is the unbreakable name. How the whole earth groans till Love returns.[29]

What the novel tells us of the dominant, Anglophone,[30] and (in its Western-Canadian context) largely Protestant culture of our society, however, is that it is almost entirely bereft of self-knowledge in the face of such suffering. Not only are the average Canadians who appear in this account awkwardly ill at ease in the presence of another race, but they seem incapable either of compassion or guilt. Reading this history, written from the perspective of another cultural tradition, one wonders at the apparently impenetrable complacency of one's own kind, and one darkly suspects that certain forms of "Christianity" have had something to do with its

---

28. It is perhaps not accidental that this is so. If one thinks of a theologian like Kitamori, with his "theology of the pain of God," one suspects that Japanese Christianity has a certain predisposition towards this theological tradition—perhaps in part because of the Buddhist influence. "The dominant theological influence upon Kitamori," however, "has been Lutheran" (see Carl Michalson, *Japanese Contributions to Christian Theology* [Philadelphia: Westminster, 1960], pp. 73 ff.).

29. Joy Kogawa, *Obasan* (Harmondsworth: Penguin, 1981), p. 240.

30. In order to distinguish between the two founding peoples of Canada, those whose mother tongue is French are called "Francophone" while those whose first language is English (whether or not they are Anglo-Saxon in origin) are designated "Anglophone."

formation. The same suspicions are raised by present-day media reporting of hostage-taking and other violent acts in which American citizens are involved. Seldom if ever is the question asked: *Why* do these desperate peoples of other races and political spheres hate us so?[31]

That we resist the knowledge of our oppression of other peoples is of course a dimension of the same repressive mind-set which enables us to resist the knowledge of our own subtle oppression. We too are a broken people, covertly broken. Every news broadcast documents our strange, unheralded night.[32] Our art, literature, and popular music are amanuenses of a pain that would have been inconceivable to the founders of our Experiment. Those who measure history by the decade, and call that being "contextual," will point out that (for example) Paul Simon's "American Tune" has been superseded by Reaganomics and Yuppies and yet another "return to religion."[33] Serious persons are required to take a longer and deeper view of historical realities. Periodic ups and downs—largely significant to the affluent only—are not what contextual theological thinking is all about. The context to which Christian theology in North America has to relate is itself one of a cultural malaise that has been a long time in the making. It is characteristic of that malaise that it robs human beings

---

31. Another Canadian author, the late Margaret Laurence, has characterized very precisely the kind of "Christianity" that I have in mind in her novel *The Diviners,* where she depicts a stained-glass window in a local Protestant church showing Jesus on Golgotha looking like "a slightly effeminate traveling salesman . . . expiring with absolutely no inconvenience on what might in other circumstances have been a cross" (New Canadian Library 3 [Toronto: McClelland & Stewart, 1971], p. 41).

32. In her insightful work *Lives of Girls and Women* (Toronto: McGraw-Hill Ryerson, 1974), p. 26, Alice Monroe comments on the familiar North American family pastime, "listening to the news": "Though my parents always listened to the news and were discouraged or relieved by what they heard (mostly discouraged, for this was early in the war), I had the feeling that, to them as to me, everything that happened in the world was out of our control, unreal yet calamitous."

33. It is perhaps helpful to distinguish contextuality in theology from what may be called *situationalism.* Within any given sociohistorical context there will be a great variety of different situations. For example, one will expect to find significant differences between the conditions of the poor and the rich, male and female, the young and the elderly. Obviously, it will be mandatory for practical theology to be sensitive to these differences. Again, due to the rapidity of social change, situations are not likely to remain static. For example, the category "Yuppie," meaning young urban professional, only recently discovered by social analysts, is already being displaced by another grouping: advertising agencies now address their claims, not to Yuppiedom, but to a new social stratum which is, apparently, much more susceptible to advertisements because of an advanced consumerism, ready cash, and a notorious lack of commitment to home and permanent values. This stratum has been dubbed "the Skoties"—"spoiled kids of the eighties"—by some social analysts (see the Toronto *Globe and Mail*, September 24, 1986, p. B8). Christian ethics and pastoral theology must certainly be cognizant of such changes. "Systematic" theology, however, while not *ignoring* such specifics, must attempt to discern the greater movements of history of which these may be variations on more extensive and sustained themes. The context, in my interpretation, refers to these more sweeping movements.

of the wit and will to acknowledge it; and that characteristic is nowhere more pathetically present than in the two northern nations of this continent.

We are a people wondrously afraid of the dark. It is not surprising that we should be so, however pathetic and even tragic it is. For our whole foundational *mythos* assured us that the darkness was being gradually but surely banished, that now it would grow always lighter, and that we ourselves were the vanguard of the new age of light. Without operative spiritual and intellectual traditions for honest and open confrontation of that darkness, we can only languish in perplexity—or seek refuge in the private "good life." As Robert Bellah and his associates have recently written in the concluding chapter of their study of current American mores, *Habits of the Heart: Individualism and Commitment in American Life,*

> There is a widespread feeling that the promise of the modern era is slipping away from us. A movement of enlightenment and liberation that was to have freed us from superstition and tyranny has led in the twentieth century to a world in which ideological fanaticism and political oppression have reached extremes unknown in previous history. Science, which was to have unlocked the bounties of nature, has given us the power to destroy all life on earth. Progress, modernity's master idea, seems less compelling when it appears that it may be progress into the abyss. And the globe today is divided between a liberal world so incoherent that it seems to be losing the significance of its own ideals, an oppressive and archaic communist statism, and a poor, and often tyrannical Third World reaching for the very first rungs of modernity. In the liberal world, the state, which was supposed to be a neutral night-watchman that would maintain order while individuals pursued their various interests, has become so overgrown and militarized that it threatens to become a universal policeman.[34]

There is no greater public task for theology in North America today than to help to provide a people indoctrinated in the modern mythology of light with a frame of reference for the honest exploration of its actual darkness. The point of such a theology is not to wallow in despair, and not to judge the past, but to facilitate a process of self-knowledge, self-criticism, and truth-seeking that is necessary if, as a people, we are going to overcome the "impasse of modernity"[35] and find our way into the future. "The job of thought in our time is to bring into light the darkness

---

34. Robert N. Bellah et al., *Habits of the Heart* (Berkeley, Calif.: University of California Press, 1985), p. 277.
35. Ibid.

as darkness.''[36] The knowledge of our darkness is not the end, but it is the necessary means to the end that—at least as Christians—we are obliged to desire for ourselves and for the privileged culture to which we belong. For, as Joseph Sittler wisely wrote more than three decades ago, "Darkness *realized* is creative of a receptive theater for the drama of God's salvatory action in Christ; there is a *dynamics* of damnation, a process of perdition, that may be used by the Spirit in such a way as to constitute of it a positive preparation for the Gospel.''[37] The fate of the North American peoples as they struggle with a cultural malaise that their operative myths and beliefs prevent them from facing is a matter of enormous consequence to other peoples of the planet, and for two reasons: first, because our malaise is only an acute and advanced form of the sickness of most modern societies—a sickness that Third World societies are also courting, unawares, as they reach "for the very first rungs of modernity"; second, because the failure to cope creatively with this grave disorder on the part of a society as powerful as that of the United States in particular could result in global disaster.

The malaise of modernity is the legacy of a Promethean optimism which did not take into account the limits of human power and the ubiquity and subtlety of evil. This optimism was first conceived by the humanistic thinkers of the Renaissance. It was honed to ideological perfection by the Enlightenment, mobilized for action by 19th-century industrialism, and brought to full flower in the 20th century's technological society. But, as frequently happens in history as in nature, in its maturation this brave hope has shown its false, naive, and ominous underside. The irony of what modernity dreamed of as humanity's mastery of nature and "the overcoming of chance"[38] is now visible for all who can bear the sight: in the moment of conquering nature, humanity, being part of nature, must itself be conquered, hoisted by its own petard. While that conquering could as well mean the mutilation of the human *spirit* as the destruction of the body, the great symbol of the irony of our situation is of course "the Bomb." Thirty years ago, Reinhold Niebuhr, with his special sensitivity to the ironic, phrased it thus:

> We had imagined that the very technics that finally produced atomic destruction would make us the masters of history. But they merely produce

---

36. George P. Grant, "The Computer Does Not Impose on Us the Ways It Should Be Used," in *Beyond Industrial Growth,* ed. Abraham Rotstein (Toronto: University of Toronto Press, 1976), p. 130.

37. Joseph Sittler, "A Theology for Earth," *The Christian Scholar* 37/1 (March 1954): 369-370.

38. Grant, "The Computer," p. 130.

an increased amount of power over nature that has a dubious role in the affairs of men. . . . Thus we have come into the tragic position of developing a form of destruction which, if used by our enemies against us, would mean our physical annihilation; and if used by us against our enemies, would mean our moral annihilation. What shall we do?[39]

We have managed, thus far, to avoid the doomsday of nuclear confrontation, and we nervously congratulate one another on this achievement; but almost half a century after Hiroshima we are still totally lacking in any international guidelines for the limitation of nuclear power.[40] The future of the earth revolves around the physical and moral questions implicit in this situation. For theology—in particular one which intends to be contextual—the situation holds its own special problematic. Later we shall discuss that problematic more extensively. Here we go only so far as to recognize that one of the two great empires whose activities and predispositions are determinative for earth's future *is* the context in which we are doing theology. Whether the other empire has resources for self-knowledge, self-criticism, and truth-seeking is held in doubt by many. *Its* commitment to the religion of progress is *perhaps* even more ironclad and single-minded than ours. But the question which must concern us is whether there are resources for critical self-awareness and restraint within the traditions, values, and institutions of *this* continent. Is it possible that in the United States and Canada there could come to be a sufficiently profound awareness of the limits and dangers of mastery that this awareness would be reflected in the international policies, the approach of our governments and institutions to Third World peoples, and the military budgets of our nations? Is it too much to hope that there could occur in the heart of North America a *metanoia*—a revolution of spirit and hope—deep enough to turn it from the blind pursuit of oblivion towards the sincere and intelligent quest for world peace? Not merely of "happiness" but of peace—the *shalom* of earth?

This is not a rhetorical question, nor is it a question belonging to

---

39. D. B. Robertson, ed., *Love and Justice: Selections from the Shorter Writings of Reinhold Niebuhr* (Cleveland and New York: World, 1967), p. 235.

40. Half a century of "peace" (during which there have been some 130 "limited" wars!) is a very brief span in the life of the species; besides, as C. F. von Weizsäcker has recently remarked, it requires only one mishap to usher in the conflagration: "In the final analysis, necessary world peace can by no means be guaranteed technologically, but only politically. Technology, which, in addition, is caught in the constant stream of development, cannot provide a permanent guarantee against technical failure, the escalation of regional conflicts, and human madness. And *one* failure a century is enough for the catastrophe" (*Die Zeit drängt* [Munich and Vienna: Carl Hanser Verlag, 1986], p. 41; my trans.).

some other discipline and not in a book of theology. The theological tradition to which I am trying to be faithful is one that refuses "to abandon the world prematurely." It is precisely "the fate of the earth" (J. Schell) that we are all being asked to consider and decide upon today. Whoever does not live with this question and put it on the agenda of his or her "science" in a prominent place has fallen victim to the alienation and fragmentation of knowledge that is itself part of the general malaise. There is no place in theology—the theology of the cross—for escape into specialization, especially not theological specialization. A theology which looks to God's solidarity with the broken creation and aims to participate in God's healing of that creation *must* involve itself in the specifics of its society's problematique, including its economics, its foreign policies, its long- and short-range goals. The logic of this "must" is the same as that which moved Jesus to tell his disciples, their repeated protests notwithstanding, that "The Son of man *must* suffer many things and be delivered up. . ." (Luke 9:22, par.). That logic, being the consequence of a divine *agapē* rooted in world-orientation, is not easily understood by a self-preoccupied human rationality. It is "beyond reason," as love always is. But there is perhaps some remnant of a deeper-than-rational wisdom in us which knows that there can be no healing that does not come to be from within the broken body, even though the healing agent must be introduced into the body from beyond its own resources.

4. A Capacity for Disillusionment

What is there within the broken body-politic of our North American society which, if it could be reached and entered into by the community of belief, might prove a point of contact for some measure of healing? I am convinced that the conclusions of the Detroit conference are right in this: theology must work with what is there in the society for whose life it has responsibility. The revolution that the gospel creates must be an indigenous one—as Dom Helder Camara has said so pointedly in his exhortation to First World Christians who rush into the Third World hoping to discover "where the action is":

> Instead of planning to go to the Third World to try to arouse violence there, stay at home in order to help your rich countries to discover that they too are in need of a cultural revolution which will produce a new hierarchy of values, a new world vision, a global strategy of development, the revolution of mankind.[41]

---

41. Dom Helder Camara, *Church and Colonialism*, trans. William McSweeney (Denville, N.J.: Dimension Books, 1969), p. 111.

I am, however, not convinced that either the Detroit consultation or the more recent sociohistorical study to which reference has been made (*Habits of the Heart*) are as perceptive as they might be concerning that within North American experience which could, if adequately explored, prove a point of entry for such a revolution of values.

The formulators of the Detroit follow-up statement locate this resource in "the tradition of idealism and struggle against oppression in our own history, both secular and religious." I agree that North American history does contain a remarkable tradition of idealism and struggle against oppression. As I have put it elsewhere, the first European settlers on this continent were, for the most part, the Third World of their times: poor and marginalized people, pushed out of the Old World by the political, technological, and religious upheavals of their epochs, and by economic forces over which they had no control. They appeared on these shores, not as Hobbesian lords and masters of the universe, armed with utopian visions and inflexible "New World" ideologies, but as the victims of ideologies and worldviews, who turned to this frontier as their only hope, their last resort. Their dreams were mostly modest dreams: they sought a place in these forests where they could raise their children, earn their bread by the sweat of their brow, and worship God in their own manner. If and wherever the memory of this modest vision can be appropriated by us, it can indeed provide a background of historical experience enabling us as peoples both to rethink our own later, swollen expectations and to link ourselves more sympathetically with the victims of those expectations.[42] The effort—through education, through drama and story, through history and the social sciences—to recover these humbler beginnings and apply their lessons critically to the present situation should never be abandoned.

But both the Detroit statement and, in certain of its conclusions, the Bellah analysis are too sanguine, it seems to me, concerning the prospects

---

42. Recently I heard one of the great literary figures of my country, Hugh MacLennan, say that after years of reflection he had finally discerned the one thing that all of our citizens, representing a veritable patchwork quilt of races and tribes and nations, have in common: "We are all offspring of ethnic losers!" Such an image is not without promise today in the very practical business of nation building and global responsibility. It could have untold influence for good in the areas of international trade and immigration policies, for example, if the older, established peoples of both northern nations of this continent achieved a renewed and imaginative consciousness of their roots as homeless, economically deprived, and politically and religiously oppressed peoples. Thus the indignation of many Canadians, in connection with the recent illegal entry of 150 Tamil and 176 Sikh refugees might well be reconsidered if these same Canadians recalled the desperate voyages of their own Irish, Scottish, English, and French forebears to these shores. Especially if they did so under the impact of the Native North American's contemporary question: What *legal* right did *you* have to all this?

of recovering this foundational vision. The team of sociologists which produced *Habits of the Heart*, while by no means underestimating the "impasse of modernity," found that "there are still operating among us, with whatever difficulties, traditions that tell us about the nature of the world, about the nature of society, and about who we are as a people. Primarily biblical and republican, these traditions are . . . important for many Americans and significant to some degree for almost all." It is, they conclude, worth considering

> whether the biblical and republican traditions that the small town once embodied can be reappropriated in ways that respond to our present need. Indeed, we would argue that if we are ever to enter that new world that so far has been powerless to be born, it will be through reversing modernity's tendency to obliterate all previous culture.[43]

Laudable as this conclusion is, both for its honest analysis of the demise of the modern vision and its refusal to capitulate to hopelessness, it shares with the Detroit prescription a rather conspicuous nostalgia for the same brand of idealism and human potentiality that is the very stuff out of which the modern vision was constructed. I frankly doubt that we shall be able to pass from the modern to the postmodern era in the evolutionary manner that such statements assume. I suspect that we must experience a far more profound exposure to the *demise* of modernity than we have yet experienced, as a people, before we can acquire sufficient humility to learn another way of being in the world. The modest vision cherished by our earliest forebears can certainly function as a source of wisdom for us *if we can grasp it unadorned.* But how shall we find our way back to that vision, even to the understanding of it, to say nothing of recapitulating it in our lives today? That humbler vision was all too soon corrupted by its incorporation into the grand schemes of 18th-century social philosophers, and the cheaper, sloganized packaging of those schemes by the entrepreneurs and developers of the age of colonization. All too soon, what began unpretentiously as a second chance was turned into a success story—at least rhetorically, and to a considerable extent materially as well. Even the modest beginnings were made to contribute their special effects to the well-worn tale, the "American Dream": "from rags to riches," "the land of unlimited opportunities," "they said it couldn't be done," and so on. How is it possible—especially in a television era which has reduced the Horatio Alger mythology to even cheaper forms of New World

---

43. *Habits of the Heart,* pp. 282f.

bravado—to reach back behind the American Dream (or its paler Canadian version) to the more authentic, human hope represented by the remnants of unembellished testimony to our pioneer ancestry?

In short, I find too much cultural-religious triumphalism still in the Detroit statement and in aspects of the later study. Rather, there is too little of that more subtle "wisdom of the cross." What is present in our historical experience as a people to be turned to account by those who desire to "speak of Christ in the midst of the ongoing moral crisis" (Detroit) is not, surely, our much-publicized potential for idealism and derring-do, but whatever could bring us a greater realism and a greater *fundamental humility* as a people. The revolution called for in North America is not a repeat a fortiori of 1776, lifting us to yet greater heights of power and glory. It is rather a revolution of spirit that would bring us into compassionate proximity with those who suffer now from our power and glory!

For this reason, I am led to think along quite different lines when I search (as today all persons of good will must do) for some foothold in our social history for the Christian witness to that quite *other* glory that belongs to the tradition of Jerusalem. Professor Bellah and his associates come closer to *that* perspective, I think, when they write that

> we will need to see the story of our life on this earth not as an unbroken success but as a history of suffering as well as joy. We will need to remember the millions of suffering people in the world today and the millions whose suffering in the past made our present affluence possible. . . . We have been called a people of plenty . . . . Yet the truth of our condition is our poverty. We are finally defenseless on this earth. Our material belongings have not brought us happiness. Our military defenses will not avert nuclear destruction. Nor is there any increase in productivity or any new weapons system that will change the truth of our condition.[44]

These words, too, are the musings of North Americans. Fortunately, there is today a significant minority of such persons—persons who have begun to enter *profoundly* into the demise of modernity; and in *that* direction, it seems to me, lies our hope.[45] Such a resource of hope has seldom been tapped by popular culture in our milieu—including popular

---

44. Ibid., pp. 295-296.
45. I am not thinking here only of the few truly learned analyses of our contemporary condition, like that of the Bellah team, but also of popular accounts through which millions of North Americans are touched by questions that probe very deeply the received myths and values of our culture. Films like *Platoon* and *The Decline of the American Empire* are only two such instances of the type of critical self-awareness that is becoming increasingly conspicuous on this continent.

religion, whose very popularity depends upon its supplying the cultic foundations for the optimism demanded by the culture. In the tradition of that theology that is still "not much loved," and on this continent all but unheard-of as well, a tradition which finds that "life only begins when the whole framework is shaken,"[46] what appears to me most encouraging theologically in the North American context today is the shaking of the foundations which has been occurring since the end of our post–World War II euphoria. Our revolution/*metanoia* could begin as more of us find the confidence to acknowledge and meditate upon the meaning of that experience.[47]

The framework that is being shaken is the framework not only of the American Dream but of the dream of modern Western technocracy, a dream which in various guises and degrees has spread over the entire globe. What is of particular significance in the current incipient sense of the failure of this dream among North Americans lies in the fact that we have dreamed it longer, with greater devotion, and under physical conditions more favorable than any other people on earth. Not only have we possessed the space, time, and natural resources requisite to such an expansive vision, but we have given our hearts to it—hearts largely unencumbered by the skepticism and cynicism of older civilizations. If ever a human worldview has been afforded a chance to prove itself, the modern Weltanschauung is it! The shaking of such a worldview in such a place is therefore immensely instructive. As I have sometimes put it, employing a metaphor which is certainly limited but perhaps useful, there have been automobiles in my family (a family of "ordinary people," most of them laborers or farmers) for four generations. We ought by now to *know* that automobiles do not bring "happiness," however convenient they may be for certain limited purposes. Such knowledge is not—and in a real sense cannot *be*—possessed by the majority of the peoples of the planet earth, most of whom are dreaming some version of the same dream we have dreamed. In Russia and the countries of the Second World, where one waits for several *years* to get the car one ordered, this most immediate personal symbol of modern technology is almost worshiped. Even in

---

46. Alfred Delp, S. J., *The Prison Meditations of Father Delp* (New York: Macmillan, 1969), p. 40.

47. Reinhold Niebuhr's 1940 address, "Optimism, Pessimism, and Religious Faith," republished in Robert McAfee Brown's collection, *The Essential Reinhold Niebuhr: Selected Essays and Addresses* (New Haven: Yale University Press, 1986), pp. 3ff., gives notice of this new public awareness of the "superficial religion" of modernity when he writes: "Though there is a horde of moderns who still live by and in this kind of uncritical naturalism and optimism, it could not long claim the credulity of the more critical spirits."

newly affluent and technologized nations of Western Europe it is frequently treated as a childish and dangerous outlet for individual "freedom" in the midst of crowded conditions and restrictive conventions.[48] In the Third World, the automobile is revered as an unreachable divinity, yet an enticing symbol of what might be—if only! There are, in short, abundant resources of potential wisdom in a society like our own, which has been granted the time, the space, and all the accoutrements that are needed (and they are legion) for the dreaming of this particular dream.

Yet, experience alone, contrary to the old adage, is not necessarily the best teacher. To meditate profoundly upon the experiences of up to four centuries of devotion to the modern vision, a people requires intellectual and spiritual resources that are not automatically provided along with the experience itself, and may even be denied by it. As George Grant wrote at the end of his learned discourse "In Defence of North America,"

> We live . . . in the most realized technological society which has yet been; one which is, moreover, the chief imperial centre from which technique is spread around the world. It might seem then that because we are destined so to be, we might also be the people best able to comprehend what it is to be so. Because we are first and most fully there, the need might seem to press upon us to try to know where we are in this new found land which is so obviously "terra incognita." Yet the very substance of our existing which has made us the leaders in technique, stands as a barrier to any thinking which might be able to comprehend technique from beyond its own dynamism.[49]

There is, however, a dimension within North American historical experience to which the Christian community may turn for an entrée in its attempt at contextualization. It is the incipient *disillusionment* of a people which has given itself long and wholeheartedly to the modern illusion. In this hesitant but no longer dismissable skepticism and disbelief, perhaps a point of contact can be found for a gospel that dares to pronounce that real hope can begin where illusions end, and real life where death is tasted.

---

48. Witness the vain attempts of West German authorities to introduce speed limits on the autobahns. Though it is estimated that one half of Germany's trees are dying, on account of industrial pollution, including the acid rain produced by automobiles, the limitless speed permitted on superhighways appears to be an immutable symbol of personal autonomy amidst a highly regulated society. One is reminded of Ortega's statement: "The new man wants his motor-car, and enjoys it, but he believes that it is the spontaneous fruit of an Edenic tree. In the depths of his soul he is unaware of the artificial, almost incredible character of civilization. . ." (Jose Ortega y Gasset, *The Revolt of the Masses* [New York: W. W. Norton, 1957], p. 82).

49. George Grant, *Technology and Empire* (Toronto: Anansi, 1969), p. 40.

But in order to achieve this encounter with ancient wisdom and grace, and thus contribute to the revolution of values and vision that global society requires of our continent, it is first necessary to provide the conditions within which our embryonic discontent and sense of alienation can be brought into the open and become the subject of more extensive and honest inquiry. It is, I believe, our very *capacity for disillusionment* that creates our growing potentiality for wisdom, hope, and life. But so long as disenchantment with our foundational and rhetorical worldview is prevented from direct expression, and must instead work itself out in defensive and aggressive political and economic behavior, it is no advantage at all but only an increasing threat to ourselves and to the world at large. We stand at the edge of a metaphorical Red Sea, where an open acknowledgment of our "impasse" (Bellah) could become the catalyst for the courage we need to seek passage into a better future; where living through the *impossibility* could open to us a new *possibility*. Yet there can be no admission of the impossible, no recognition of our subtle suffering under the yoke of a dream-become-illusion—we *must* repress it—unless a frame of reference were given, on whose basis we could feel the permission forthrightly to face our limits, and honestly confess the pain that we must now hide. Without such a point of vantage, exposure to our real condition—our "poverty" (Bellah)—would only prove debilitating.

The question for Christian theology implicit in this situation is whether Christian faith can contribute to the provision of such a frame of reference. What is there in the tradition of Jerusalem that could assist in inducing a climate of trust and wisdom enabling North Americans to examine and confess the decline of their experiment, to explore the deeper meaning of that decline, and to begin again with better, chastened hopes?

5. A Systematic Theology?

That, in one form and another, is the question which has preoccupied me in previous writings. What I hope to do in the present work is to appear, so to speak, as a bearer of that question *before the whole tradition*. In this necessarily modest enterprise, I should like to regard myself as a child and contemporary representative of this New World pilgrimage, returning at a point of crisis to the cultic roots of the vision that has inspired our corporate sojourn, and asking of that tradition what it may still hold for such a critical context as ours. Did we misunderstand? Was there perhaps even a *rudimentary* misconception in our appropriation of this tradition? Are dimensions missing? Perspectives lacking? What might the tradition have to say to us at this juncture of our sojourn—at the edge of this Red Sea—that it could not convey to us at the height of our success among the fleshpots? Is it possible that in this ancient tradition of Jerusalem, so familiar as to have become distasteful and boring to many, there are new and untried and "strange" (Barth) teachings which, if they were contemplated under such conditions, might prove avenues of grace towards alternatives other than those that have created among us "future shock"?

Is it implied that I am thinking, then, of a "systematic theology"? Yet another?

No . . . and (qualifiedly) yes. No, if systematic theology means, as clearly it does for many, a statement of faith whose primary aim is the internal coherence of doctrine, its articulation in propositional or cognitive terms, and its a priori sufficiency for every situation. Against such entrenched presuppositions concerning the nature of dogmatic or systematic theology, I am in agreement with my former teacher, Robert McAfee Brown, who in his introduction to the aforementioned Detroit conference report remarks, "For a while at least, the writing of theology needs to be done in loose-leaf notebooks. New pages will continue to be needed, and some older pages will need to be replaced."[50]

Systems of theology in the sense developed from the High Middle Ages onwards must be questioned on four counts at least: First, they almost inevitably suggest a greater wisdom than their subject matter warrants. Who dares to reduce God and the things of God to a system? A term like "systematic theology," said Karl Barth, is as paradoxical as "wooden iron."[51] Second, they too easily imply a permanence of theological truth and thus betray the livingness of God and of creation. Again Barth: "There can be no completed work. All human achievements are no more than prolegomena; and this is especially the case in the field of theology."[52] Third, they seldom do justice to the fragmentation (brokenness) of existence, for even if their content makes room for this, their form—the system as such—contains an implicit denial of it. A theology in which everything is present and accounted for is hardly consistent with a world in which so many things (including God) seem absent and incomprehensible. Working within the parameters of the theology of the cross, one must take one's stand with the crucified Christ in the midst of

50. *Theology in the Americas,* p. xi.
51. Karl Barth, *Dogmatics in Outline* (New York: Harper & Row, 1959), p. 5.
52. Karl Barth, *The Epistle to the Romans,* Preface to the Second Edition (London: Oxford University Press, 1933), p. 2.

this world's alienation and disjointedness. It would be a conspicuous contradiction of this mode of doing theology if it then became one's object to produce a fully coherent system of doctrine.

To these perennial reasons for questioning the enterprise usually labeled (in our part of the world) systematic theology, a fourth should be added out of faithfulness to our concern for contextuality. It is perhaps implied in Professor Brown's half-whimsical suggestion about "loose-leaf notebook" theology. There is something altogether too predictable about systematic theologies undertaken in First World contexts today. Without intending to do so (so little of what we in fact perpetrate is intended), they nevertheless imply a noticeable measure of control, certitude, well-being, magnaminity, and personal security characteristic of the affluent. To the victims of our society, our theologies must on the whole appear as self-satisfied as our economics and our technology. Anyone who does theology within the "have" nations today needs to be aware of the contribution that his or her scholarship may be making to the spirit of "oppression, domination, and imperialism" (Detroit) projected by our affluent societies. We must do our theology in such societies as a theological community that knows that its work is being observed by both oppressors and oppressed, and may be used for ends quite contrary to its stated purposes. Therefore we cannot give ourselves to systems which preclude the grace of recanting, or at least of revising, what proves productive of questionable consequences.

Yet, on the other hand, I believe that the project of systematic theology cannot be abandoned altogether. For whatever ill use has been and can still be made of it, the principle which brought this "modest science" into being in the first place and sustained it over the centuries still pertains, namely, that the biblical God is One, and that God's ways with the world, however mysterious, seem to have a rationale that now and then can be glimpsed by faith. Unless we are ready to say with Tertullian that we believe because it is absurd (*Credo quia absurdum est*), then we are bound to affirm with Augustine and Anselm that, believing, we are driven to attempt fullness of comprehension (*Credo ut intelligam; Fides quaerens intellectum*). As in our individual lives, so in the life of the church there are times when it seems possible to comprehend much and other times when avowed understanding can only appear unwarranted and pompous. Our time is no doubt closer to the latter experience. Yet to capitulate to incomprehension, or perhaps to court it and make a fetish of fragmentation in thought and word, is no real alternative for those who feel responsibility "to see life steadily and whole" (Matthew Arnold). It is possible to discern in the North American context a certain disturbing connection between the failure of professional theology to think comprehensively and contextually, and the spirit of anti-intellectualism present within the churches.

At the same time, the paucity of serious but accessible systematic theological work on the part of professionals in our context is one of the reasons why North American Christians who do "seek understanding" so consistently turn to European and other articulations of the faith. The popularity of a work like Hans Küng's *On Being a Christian*[53] indicates a hunger for theological statements capable of being digested by ordinary Christians, which serve the function of "getting it all together." There is in fact in North America today what may well be an unprecedented desire, on the part of a significant minority of thinking persons who remain in or around the so-called mainline churches, to "find a *reason* for the hope that is in them." They are no longer kept in congregations or pushed into ecclesiastical offices—or even ministry!—by social forces extraneous to the faith. If they remain, it is because they sense in the tradition of Jerusalem something profound, and profoundly needed by them. They will not be content with homilies and sermonettes, nor are those to whom I have reference here satisfied by the hysterical outpourings of the electronic church. They need to enter into the tradition at some depth, and with the real questions of their existence consciously and openly present. They need to discover whether the Christian message is comprehensive enough, even if it is not always altogether comprehensible, to encompass and respond to the totality of their quest for meaning.

This leads to an observation which may help us to achieve a compromise between the no and the yes to systematic theology expressed in the foregoing. In the past, theologians have been used to writing, chiefly, for other theologians—mature scholars, students of the discipline, professionals in ministry. The extent to which theological "science"[54] has been shaped by this fact alone can hardly be overestimated. Nor can the equally decisive and related factor that professional theology has normally been conducted within universities and similar settings, and has thus been unusually conscious of an academic audience.

This situation has been changing, however, within the past decades— and markedly so. We have come to a time when we must be conscious,

---

53. Hans Küng, *On Being a Christian,* trans. Edward Quinn (Glasgow: Collins, 1978).

54. The very notion that theology is a science, albeit a "modest" one (Barth), discourages lay education in the faith. It would be preferable for this reason, as well as others, to think of theology as an art—that is, a work of the imagination, which is surely what it is. Great art is certainly not every human being's calling or potential, but most of us are capable of artistic expression at some level, being creatures of imagination.

on all sides, of *non* professionals whose lives are affected by what theologians do or do not say.[55] On one side, as we noted earlier, there are the oppressed within and beyond our own society, whose situation may be helped or hindered by the witness of the theological community in the First World. On the other side, there are persons within and on the edges of the middle-class Christian denominations that most theologians themselves represent, who look for guidance to those whose education and occupation have given them the occasion to be more deeply exposed to "the mysteries of God." The needs of these two listening groups may be very different. The one has reason to fear "systematic" accounts of Christianity, especially when they are proffered by representatives of the dominant culture of imperial societies. The other group hungers for a comprehensiveness that is more filling than the tidbits of dogma and morality that it has too often been offered. But both segments of theology's listening audience today are comprised of persons whose primary identity is the world and not the academy; both need help for living, not just for making a living; both ask for understanding of an existential nature, not just for purposes of intellectual satisfaction or ordered rationality. Moreover, even among the professionals and academicians with whom (one hopes) theology will continue to have discourse, the problematic of the times has meant that a purely "professional" approach to Christian theology could no longer have much meaning. The students we teach, the colleagues with whom we associate—even many of the (formerly suspicious) academics of our universities—are in the main as keen as are nonprofessionals to know whether anything good can still come out of Nazareth.

---

55. Both Edward Farley and James Gustafson have made this same point. Gustafson delineates three groups which constitute theologians' "expected audience": professional colleagues in universities, other theologians, and ministers and laity. He notes that the first two groups appear to be uppermost in the minds of professional theologians, with the consequence that the third group is deprived of guidance. "The gulf between the specialized and sometimes arcane interests of the academician and those who engage in the activities about which academics want to think properly exists in large measure as a result of the necessary specialization of vocabulary and symbol, but also because of the lack of interest in a wider readership." "Ordinary" Christians "do have theological quandaries, and face them not only when they have to preach but when they experience the limits of human satisfactions, the issue of the basis for personal integrity, the need for some meaningful objects of confidence and for orientations towards their activities. For such persons the substantive theological questions arise first in the course of human experience and professional responsibilities. In many instances the questions that preoccupy the philosophers of theology are real but inchoate" (*Ethics from a Theocentric Perspective*, vol. 1, p. 67).

"Education in the truest and most serious sense," writes Edward Farley, "needs to be introduced into the church. It may be surmised that as long as the church educator is conceived as a specialist in program administration and in developmental psychology, this will not occur. Further, if a Christian *paideia* is introduced into church education, it too will involve the recovery of theological understanding. The reason is simply that *theologia*, a dialectical reflection which presides over faith's self-conscious and critical responses to the world, is the heart and soul of any Christian *paideia*" (*Theologia: The Fragmentation and Unity of Theological Education* [Philadelphia: Fortress, 1983], p. 196).

INTRODUCTION

This means that new demands are being made of theological discourse, and in the process a new role for systematic theological thought is emerging. While there have always been theologians who were conscious of the nonprofessional church and world, this consciousness has become, and must become more *deliberately*, normative. Without detracting from intellectual "excellence" (which in any case should never be confused with mere obscurity),[56] those who perform the church's more disciplined reflection on its belief must become increasingly conscious of the call for integrity coming from church and world. In that call for integrity there is an implicit demand for the ordering of our ideas and beliefs, for tracing relationships among the various teachings of the tradition, for perceiving the ethical and other consequences of dogma, and for many other things that add up to the need for theological integration. In other words, the impetus for the integration and reconstruction of theological thought comes to us now, not from the merely scholastic prerequisites of a discipline wishing to defend its membership in the guild of the intellectuals, and not only from the quest for cohesion inherent in the faith itself, but also and more insistently from the very human needs that are present within our historical context. We are being pressed into disciplined reflection, not because such reflection simply belongs to our discipline and is expected of professionals and "academics," but because a world torn by disintegrative irrational as well as narrowly rationalistic forces requires reintegration of thought and life from all who care about its "fate."[57]

---

56. It is impossible to estimate the extent to which Christian theology has suffered from the academic disease of obscurantism. Perhaps in direct proportion to its divorce from modern scientific and philosophic thought, theology seems often to have managed to eke out a place for itself in the academy only by becoming increasingly specialized and inaccessible to ordinary intelligence. Theologians who *have* succeeded in communicating with those outside their own discipline have frequently been discounted by their colleagues as popularizers. It is a travesty of the gospel when thinkers as profound as Karl Barth, on account of their capacity to "speak with authority and not as the scribes" are written off by those who dub themselves and one another "scholars." Perhaps this kind of professional snobbery is disappearing, and perhaps its disappearance is related precisely to the new openness to a theology that is capable of addressing the life situation, to which I have referred here. It is indicative of this new openness that, when John Coleman Bennett was presented with the Union Theological Seminary Medal in January of 1986, President Shriver said: "When obscurity has been stylish, you have written with clarity, honesty, and fervor. You have never feared to face the hard issues of scholarship, public policy, and personal integrity. In you the roles of intellectual and public activist come together in mutuality and complementarity. For you theology and ethics are inextricably intertwined" (unpublished citation).

57. It may be expedient at this juncture to distinguish the concerns of this project from a school (or mood) which seems to have arisen in the United States, and is represented by the Duke team, Stanley Hauerwas and William H. Willimon. In their 1985 explanation of their theological program (*The Christian Century*, January 30, 1985, vol. 101, no. 4, pp. 98ff.), these American churchmen go on record as being strictly opposed to a theology which aims at worldly survival. "For too long

INTRODUCTION

Our position is therefore in important respects comparable to that of theologians who were at work during previous periods of great historical transition and upheaval—the collapse of the Roman Empire (Augustine), the failure of the Platonist vision (Thomas Aquinas), the breakdown of the medieval synthesis (the Protestant reformers), the waning of Enlightenment rationalism (Schleiermacher and the liberals). Out of each of these ages of social upheaval, great systems of theology came to be. In time, the "creative chaos" (Tillich) that gave them birth was replaced by ordered forms of existence; and then the theological systems (Calvin's, for example) were caused to serve the often questionable ends of the guardians of that new order. Ironically, such systems of Christian thought became, under new sociological conditions, indispensable elements in the established order against which still newer manifestations of prophetic faith had in turn to struggle. But it remains that in their origins, the truly luminous theological systems of the West functioned as courageous and life-giving attempts of the human spirit to preserve civilization in times of social disintegration and spiritual chaos.[58]

Christians have presented their faith (most recently in much talk about peace and ecology) as a survival tactic for the modern world: the church primarily has been seen as something of extrinsic, functional value to the culture—helping Caesar keep society in good working order." Such a focus, they define frankly as "incipient atheism."

There is, I think, a sense in which those of us who must live *alongside* the American empire can be grateful for persons living *within* it who have become so "pessimistic" about "American patriotism" and "arrogance" as Hauerwas and Willimon in this manifesto declare themselves to be. As "children of Vietnam," they are rightly sickened by the identification of the Christian mission with the preservation and enhancement of modernity. Rightly, they protest what Sydney Mead called "the Americanization of Christianity." Rightly, as well, they posit over against a "liberal" faith which always seeks to accommodate itself to "the spirit of the age," a church which is faithful to the Scriptures and attempts to discern the "radical" import of its message *for* "the social order." One can only be grateful that such thoughts (which, however, are hardly as "new" as these authors insist!) have taken hold of some younger Christians living at the epicenter of the First World.

But perhaps from the edge of empire one may be permitted to remind these American colleagues that human civilization is not to be equated with modern America, and the preservation of "the world" as the object of the gospel does not immediately translate into the preservation of modern technocratic society! They are quick to dissociate themselves from the program of those (Neuhaus and Novak are named) who want the church to function as "a useful component in keeping constitutional democracy afloat." Agreed! But we must ask them whether it is in any serious sense the church's business to keep *the human project* afloat. Is "the fate of the earth" a matter of Christian ultimate concern? These theologians want a church with its own "intrinsic worth"—one that refuses to let the world "set the agenda." But is the agenda that the church is to set, in their view, one that is conscious of the world's needs, including (certainly) "peace and ecology"? If it is not, then have they not opted for a new kind of ecclesiastical-theological "imperialism" (their term)? If it is, then, in our attempt to construct a responsible theology, we cannot be as independent of "the spirit of the age" as they suggest.

58. This is transparent in the case of Luther. Luther never achieved the systematic output of Calvin, and perhaps he could not have done so, even if he had had the leisure that is needed for it. But the frequently pronounced opinion that Luther was not a systematic theologian is only partly true. It depends upon what connotation is being given to the adjective *systematic*. As Joseph Sittler writes,

51

The question to be asked, then, is not simply whether the subject matter of Christian belief lends itself to systematic statement, but *what prompts the attempt at the ordering of faith's self-understanding, what end it serves, and whom it serves.* The history of dogma contains enough evidence of the possibility that systematic thinking *may* serve the good, particularly in periods of crisis, that one must risk the limits and dangers of all systems, as well as the bad uses to which they may now or later be put, and try once again—in a time of alienation, specialization, and disintegration—to "see life steadily and whole."

Too much, however, should not be claimed for any theological statement, systematic or fragmentary or—as the present one shall very likely be—a mixture of both! To speak of the biblical God—of the God who acts in the life of the world—is always to rush in where angels dare not tread. Only fools will do it without fear and trembling.

6. The Plan of This Theological Statement

Perhaps the most common schema adopted by systematic treatments of Christian doctrine is some version of the following: after attending to preliminary questions of method and the character of theology (the so-called prolegomena), the work moves successively through the five or six major doctrinal areas of traditional belief: the doctrine of God (Theology, in the restrictive sense of the term),[59] the doctrine of creation; the Christian teaching concerning human nature and destiny (anthropology), the doctrine of the Christ (Christology and soteriology), the doctrine of the church (ecclesiology), and the doctrine of "last things" (eschatology). It is my judgment that all of these elements must still be incorporated into any statement of Christian belief that tries to be comprehensive. But

---

"There is, to be sure, a sense of the term *systematic thinker* before which Luther would not qualify— which in fact he would not understand. If, that is, the connotation of system which is proper to propositional logic is made absolute, then Luther was not systematic. But we must decidedly reject any such presumption. There is a system proper to the dissection of the dead; and there is a system proper to the experience and description of the living. There is a system proper to the inorganic; and there is a system proper to an organism. A crystal has a system. But so does a living personality in the grip of a central certainty. If, then, by system one means that there is in a man's thought a central authority, a pervasive style, a way of bringing every theme and judgment and problem under the rays of the central illumination, then it must be said that history shows few men of comparable integration" (*The Doctrine of the Word in the Structure of Lutheran Theology* [Philadelphia: Muhlenberg, 1948], pp. 3-4; cited in *Luther the Expositor,* Companion Volume, *Luther's Works* [St. Louis: Concordia, 1959], pp. 42-43.

59. I shall capitalize the word *Theology* when I intend it to refer to the doctrine of God; otherwise it will connote the discipline as such.

it is not necessary to treat them in that order, or with equal attention to each doctrinal area. One of the limits of conventional schemas of this sort is that they give too little time and space to the development of questions arising out of the context in which the theological work is being done. In our historical moment, for example, it may be necessary apologetically and strategically to spend more time on the Christian doctrine of humanity and history than on the doctrine of God. Another, related concern is that such schematization tends to encourage a very *theoretical* treatment of all doctrinal areas, often devolving into catechetical or straight propositional doctrinalism.[60] This is unfortunate for the whole subject matter, but it is particularly detrimental with respect to the doctrines of the church, the kingdom of God, and eschatology in general. For in these areas especially, theology has to treat our own immediate existence as Christians, and to do so theoretically is to impart to this discussion a quality of artificiality. If praxis and not simply "theory (theology) plus practice (ethics)" is to be our approach, then thought-processes that *we bring* to the study of theology, as well as the existence to which we are called within the Christian community, must be prominent interior aspects of the whole discussion.

On the basis of this and other considerations which I hope to clarify in the process, I have decided upon a schema which divides the material into three distinct classifications, to be published in three separate monographs.

1. The first (the present volume) concerns *Thinking the Faith.* How as Christians do we think about what we believe? If our faith is something to be *understood* and not merely felt or lived, what is the character of this quest for understanding, and how does it relate to other aspects of our life as Christians and as human beings?

Here I shall have to speak to the customary questions of theological method and epistemology, including reason and revelation. But in doing this I wish always to keep in view the fact that we are not raising such questions in the abstract but concretely within a quite specific time and place. Therefore I shall attempt to avoid becoming so preoccupied with the theoretical questions pertaining to this division of the subject as to forget that, as North American Christians living in the last years of the 20th century, we bring to the whole discussion particular problems and possibilities. (A more detailed introduction to the first volume follows in the subsequent subsection.)

---

60. See George A. Lindbeck, *The Nature of Doctrine: Religion and Theology in a Postliberal Age* (Philadelphia: Westminster, 1984), p. 16.

2. The second volume will concentrate upon the three primary doctrinal areas of Christian belief: God, creaturely being, and the Christ. While the first book asks *how* we think as Christians, the second asks *what* we think; that is, what is the *focus* of our thinking, its *meditative core*, so to speak? What in particular do Christians think *about*? What is the fundamental credo that we profess? I shall call this, accordingly, *Professing the Faith*.

This division will of course entail reviewing and interpreting (so far as the scope of the project allows) the primary traditions of Theology, anthropology, and Christology. Again, however, it is not my intention merely to present *the tradition*, but I shall attempt to bring it into dialogue with the secular and religious assumptions dominant in our culture, as I am able to discern them. We are, of course, recipients of a tradition; therefore we are conscious, in this part of the study particularly, that that upon which our faith impels us to concentrate our deliberative energies is not simply part of *our* faith. It lies outside our own subjectivity. Nonetheless, unless our "I" and "we"—with all the specificity and uniqueness that these personal pronouns entail—are brought to the encounter with the scriptural and traditional witness to these central doctrinal areas, we shall not be "doing theology," but only reciting doctrine.

3. The third volume in the series has to create the bridge between theology and ethics—or rather, to demonstrate the fact that such a bridge is implicit throughout this discipline. I shall focus here upon two doctrinal areas particularly, the church and the reign of God—ecclesiology and eschatology. This will mean treating such questions as that of the relation between church and world, the mission of the church, the meaning of ministry, worship, and sacraments, and, above all, the character of Christian hope.

In keeping with the summons to contextualization which is the aim of the entire study, however, I shall again opt for specificity rather than historical breadth or doctrinal inclusivity in this discussion. As North American Christians, persons living at the nerve center of the First World, we bring to the discussion of ecclesiology, for instance, certain presuppositions and experiences that pertain neither in the parental European situation, past or present, nor in other parts of the ecumenical church. For one thing, the church has never been "established" among us—not, at least, in the de jure sense of the term. For another (and this marks us off very distinctly from the European theological scene) we exist in a situation that is conspicuously pluralistic, both sociologically and religiously speaking. Again, we are in a unique way a manifestly "religious" society, even in the post-Constantinian, postmodern era; and the role of religion in our midst (especially of truncated versions of the *Christian religion*) is by no means unambiguously laudatory—not, at any rate, from the perspective of classical forms both of Protestant and Catholic thought. Such conspicuous contextual realities must inform this part of the project in particular. The third volume will be entitled *Confessing the Faith*.

The distinctions between the second and third volumes, as to both their general tone and their purpose within the schema, is implied in the two titles. The full significance of this nomenclature cannot be discussed here; it is, in a real sense, the core of my program in these volumes, and in particular their methodological presuppositions, which are treated extensively in the first volume. Since the terms *profession* and *confession* are frequently used interchangeably, however, it may be expedient to insert at this juncture a brief explanatory note.

Expressed in its most direct form, the calling of the Christian community is to *confess* the faith. That is, the church is summoned, always, to discover and announce for its time and place what it believes to be "gospel." It will not be *gospel* if the church simply recites its accumulated dogma, whether in the form of scripture and exegesis, historic creeds and confessions, liturgies, or systems of theology. It will be *gospel* only if it is *the right word, the right deed*—namely, what is *then and there* appropriate. To say everything is to say nothing. In other words, the *profession* of belief is no substitute for faith's *confession*.

At the same time, however, confession and the desire obediently to confess the faith must not *displace* the ongoing act of faith's *profession*. On the contrary, the *professional* practice and awareness of the faith, its Scriptures, its traditions, its historic struggles, are the sine qua non of appropriate, that is, *faithful* confession. Professional awareness by itself can never *guarantee* faithful confession. But without the professional dimension, confession all too often degenerates into contentless sentiment and indistinct or confused utterance. The church is required continually to contemplate and profess its sources and the bases of its belief if it is to discern the right word and deed for the *hic et nunc*. This is the reason why volume two, which will consist of a disciplined meditation on the three *primary* doctrinal areas of faith's profession (Theology, anthropology, Christology) precedes volume three, which addresses the question, What would it mean to confess, i.e., *to live*, this faith as the church in North America today?

What must be understood, however (and hopefully volume one will establish this point more decisively), is that the process of profession and confession *is* a process, that is, that it is recurrent and reciprocal. It is not a simple movement from stage one (profession) to stage two (confession), but a continuous dialogue. Therefore aspects of the confessional mode must constantly invade professional meditation of the substance of belief, and vice versa.

The second and third volumes will be introduced more explicitly at the appropriate junctures. It remains for the present to explain in greater detail the procedure to be followed in this first volume.

INTRODUCTION TO VOLUME I

Thinking the Faith

Christian faith cannot exist apart from thinking. . . . Thinking faith is Christian faith, and . . . today true Christian faith can be only thinking faith.[1]

The object of the first division of our study is to think about thinking—theological thinking. It will be clear from what has already been said that this does not imply pure ratiocination, speculation, or the kind of thinking that could be separated from either being or doing. Christian *thinking* is a dimension of Christian *being*—a very important dimension. *Doing* and *thinking* are inseparably linked in the being of the believer. *Doing* is an extension of thought, and thought is already deed—one of the points that Jesus intended to make, surely, when in the Sermon on the Mount he contrasted shallow interpretations of sin along the lines of manifestly evil deeds with the more profound knowledge that sinful thought (greed, lust, hatred, etc.) is already an *enactment* of evil.

Thought in this inclusive sense is integral to what Christians *do* and who they *are*. In a real way, it is our *thinking* that determines whether the adjective *Christian* rightly applies to us. This is by no means to diminish the significance of the deed. Deeds are indeed the fruits by which we are known and judged (Matt. 7:16). Thought which does not issue in deed is not Christian thought, no matter how doctrinally "correct" or how pious it may be. (Surely this is what James meant when he said that faith without works is "dead" [2:26]). But deeds—*good* deeds!—are performed by persons who are not, and would not accept the designation "Christian." Christians, after all, have no monopoly on good works! Moreover, there are deeds, performed by Christians as by other persons, which in themselves and as such may be considered good, since they effect beneficial consequences, but which upon careful scrutiny would have to be questioned as to their origin in Christian discipleship; for they proceed from orientations of spirit and mind that are contrary to the law of love—for instance, from an inordinate pride in one's own

---

1. Fritz Buri, *Thinking Faith*, trans. Harold H. Oliver (Philadelphia: Fortress, 1968), pp. 86-87.

goodness. In other words, the identity called "Christian" is inextricably bound up with the ongoing process of reflection which informs the life and work of the believing person and community.

But how shall we describe this thought? What is involved in it? How do we think as Christians? What are the sources and resources of our thought? Is our thought just a type of ordinary human reasoning? Or, on the other hand, is it totally unlike other forms of human rationality? (Some Christians, for instance, seem to believe that the divine Spirit had replaced their regular mental apparatus.) Is our thinking based upon the acceptance of certain precepts or absolutes or religious principles, and do we then reason from these as from laws of science? Or do we think as persons who have submitted to some higher authority—the Bible, the tradition, ecclesiastical authorities—and are obliged simply to accept the dictates of that authority?

Who are we who are thus defined by our thinking, and what is the nature of our thought?

This is the basic question to which we address ourselves in this first division of our study and, in keeping with the terms of the question, I have organized this volume into two main parts. Part I ("The Disciple Community") seeks to answer the first aspect of the summary question posed above: Who are the disciples, that is, who are *we* as persons engaged in this thinking, at this time, in this place? Part II ("The Discipline") responds to the second part of the question: What is the nature of our thought? What is the *discipline* to which as a disciple community we are called? What is . . . theology? It will help to clarify the intention and procedure of this volume if we reflect briefly on the juxtaposition of the two categories, disciple/discipline.

Although I intend them primarily as descriptive, these categories can also serve the structural function of an integrating metaphor binding the two distinctive parts of this first book. I have three reasons for using these particular categories:

1. *Theology as the church's self-reflection:* The first is that Christian theology must concern itself not only with the subject matter of the Christian faith (the discipline) but also with those who struggle with (who think) this subject matter and live in the sphere of its influence (the disciple community). One is of course aware that the term *disciple* is usually applied to the biblical figures grouped around their Master, Jesus, and his memory. But as many discussions of the church in recent theology

have cogently argued (foremost among them, perhaps, Dietrich Bonhoeffer's *The Cost of Discipleship*),[2] restriction of the term to the original
disciple community deprives the contemporary *koinōnia* of an important
insight into itself, namely, that in the same tradition of the Twelve, who
understood themselves to stand in the succession of the twelve tribes of
Israel, the present-day church is part and parcel of the message it announces: "And I believe in the holy catholic church. . . ."

The Newer Testament knows this very well. This is why it presents
itself, not only as an account of the rabbi Jesus, what he said and did,
who he seemed to be; and not only as a statement of what his various
followers thought about him or about the One to whom he testified; but
also as an account of those followers themselves—their origins, their
encounters with representatives of the society in which they lived, their
doubts and their faith, their destinies, their "Acts." This had to be the
case, of course, because the gospel is "good news" only if it is heard
by somebody;[3] and, as Paul knew, the *process* of hearing is itself a profound dimension of what is heard (Rom. 10:14ff.). The community in
which this hearing is taking place, and which engages in the proclamation
without which this hearing cannot take place, and which learns this proclamation as it submits itself to the discipline of a faith which seeks understanding—this community is itself part of its own theological reflection. Despite the early church's essential modesty about itself, it is possible
to perceive in the Synoptic writings intimations of the vast astonishment
that those fisherfolk and tax collectors and servants of the rich must have
felt as they grasped the fact that they had been chosen for this mission.
Their very identity already speaks volumes about the primary thrust of
their message—sheer gift! " 'I thank thee, Father, Lord of heaven and
earth, that thou hast hidden these things from the wise and understanding

---

2. Dietrich Bonhoeffer, *The Cost of Discipleship,* trans R. H. Fuller (London: SCM, 1948). A
very suggestive Roman Catholic treatment of this theme is that of Avery Dulles, *A Church to Believe
In: Discipleship and the Dynamics of Freedom* (New York: Crossroad, 1984). Dulles points out that,
while "the idea of the Church as community of the disciples is not common in Catholic ecclesiology,"
it not only "has a certain biblical basis," but it "suggests a more modest concept of the Church
than some others we have mentioned (perfect society, Body of Christ, People of God, sacrament of
unity . . .). The disciple is by definition one who has not yet arrived, a learner trying to comprehend
strange words and unravel puzzling experience." For this reason, he says, it is a particularly appropriate way of designating the Church today. "The vision of the Church as a community of disciples
. . . is congruent with our everyday experience of Church. At a time when convinced Christians
are a 'cognitive minority' (to use Peter Berger's term) in nearly every country of the world . . . the
believer can identify rather easily with the early Church as a company of witnesses engaged in a
difficult mission" (pp. 7f.).

3. See Paul Tillich, *Systematic Theology*, vol. 1 (Chicago: University of Chicago Press, 1951),
p. 111.

and revealed them to babes; yea, Father, for such was thy gracious will . . .' " (Matt. 11:25-26, par.).

Much too consistently, the theological scribes of evolving Christendom neglected this rudimentary connection between the theological discipline and the community whose discipline it is. This neglect must be attributed in part to the fact that, as a rule, the theological work of the church has been undertaken by a few especially trained individuals, who had the intellectual's habit of objectifying truth. The force of this heritage, which of course has also some beneficial features, is still manifested in most theological circles today. Many Christian scholars feel that it is their calling to devote themselves impersonally to their discipline, to keep their own ideas and struggles of soul out of sight as far as possible, and so to preserve truth unimpeded by biography.[4]

One must say, in defense of earlier schools of theological scholarship, that they could hardly have been expected to regard the church as a whole as a disciple community, whose formation and reformation was part of the story that had to be told; for throughout approximately 1600 years (by far the greater share of its history) the church has consisted of persons who—most of them—were not in the least conscious of wrestling with "the word of the cross" but were pushed into Christendom, generation after generation, by unthinking forces of social custom. Under the conditions of the Constantinian arrangement, the original disciple-community depicted in the Gospels and Epistles assumes a significance that the post-canonical church of the centuries cannot have. The first disciples, elevated to a status of exceptional sanctity, are seen as *participants* in the story, while all Christians who succeed them are only its *recipients*.

This situation has however already been greatly altered by historical providence, and within the next few generations the change will probably become increasingly visible. The church of the immediate future (for the most part already of the present) will be "little flocks"[5] of persons whose only reason for staying will be the occurrence in them of some ongoing *metanoia* of soul and mind. Then (and to a large extent already now) the false division of Christendom into thinking Christians and automatic or acculturated Christians will be (already is) reduced conspicuously; and then it may again be obvious that the *disciplina theologica* belongs to the

---

4. But see James Wm. McClendon, *Biography as Theology* (Nashville: Abingdon, 1974).

5. See "A Theological Interpretation of the Position of Christians in the Modern World," by Karl Rahner, in *Mission and Grace*, vol. 1, trans. Cecily Hastings (London, Melbourne, and New York: Sheed and Ward, 1963), pp. 3ff.

whole people of the cross, and that part of this discipline involves ongoing *self*-reflection.[6]

Self-reflection here does *not* mean a narrow and privatistic type of introspection, but the contemplation of the "self," understood both individually and corporately (*sōma Christou*), as it perceives itself in the larger framework of its world. It was such contemplation, for example, that led the prophet Isaiah in the presence of the Holy to confess,

> "I am a man of unclean lips
> and I dwell in the midst of
> a people of unclean lips."
> (Isa. 6:5)

The discipline to which the disciple community is called requires of it a life-long struggle to know both itself and the "people" in whose midst it dwells.[7] As the resolutions emerging from the Detroit discussions have rightly put it: "To understand the meaning of the Christian faith, the Christian community must come to a correct understanding of its concrete historical situation. Conversion to God implies self-knowledge. This principle also applies to communities; they must come to a correct collective self-understanding."[8]

2. *Theological discipline as the work of a community of persons:* A second reason for the juxtaposition of the terms *disciple* and *discipline* is that the former term helps to offset certain unfortunate connotations of the second, and in this way to restore its hermeneutical usefulness. For reasons which certainly invite lively speculation, it became habitual in the church to identify "discipline" almost exclusively with harsh or at

---

6. Edward Farley concludes his important study *Theologia* (Philadelphia: Fortress, 1983) with a section called "*Theologia* in the Church and in the University," in which he argues that "the recovery of *theologia* as a fundamental feature *of Christian existence itself* would issue in the reform of church and graduate as well as clergy education." The separation of clergy and laity has been, he says, "decisive in the history of the church's conception of education. . . . Modern movements of 'religious' and 'Christian' education have changed all this. Yet a certain ambivalence about education for the laity continues to characterize the churches. Because the clerical paradigm defined theology as an undertaking of clergy education, the education left to the laity could not be 'theological education.' " When theology is understood as a "*habitus* of the understanding, a dialectical of reflection" that belongs to the life of faith as such, this will alter—for the better—the character of education for clergy and professional church workers as well" (pp. 195f.)

7. In this connection, it is impossible for Christians of the Reformed tradition not to recollect Calvin's famous opening sentence in *The Institutes*: "True and substantial wisdom principally consists of two parts, the knowledge of God, and the knowledge of ourselves" (Book 1, Chapter I: "The Connection Between the Knowledge of God and the Knowledge of Ourselves").

8. *Theology in the Americas*, ed. Sergio Torres and John Eagleson (Maryknoll, N.Y.: Orbis, 1976), p. 434.

any rate rigorous methods of "educating" (i.e., indoctrinating, controlling) the person. Frequently, "disciplining" someone meant—and for more conservative ecclesial communities still means—straightforwardly punishing them. In the Calvinist traditions, which have made special use of this concept,[9] "the Discipline" sometimes became the working equivalent of what "the Inquisition" implies within the Roman Catholic past. This is hardly what one would have expected from the etymological meaning of the word, which derives from *discere* (to learn, discern). Obviously, what happened was that the unfortunate measures which were too often employed in the practice of teaching the faith were themselves identified as the process necessary to Christian "discernment." Thus, while the obvious primary meaning of the verb *discere* ("to discipline") is contained in English verbs like "train, educate, teach, instruct, school, lead, guide,"[10] the connotation which has survived as primary is exactly what the *Concise Oxford Dictionary* lists as such: "Bring under control, train to obedience and order, drill . . . chastise."[11] In short, the derivative sense of the verb (derived from bad educational practice!) has succeeded the original meaning and, for the most part, altogether obscured it.

This is what happens when "the discipline," understood as intellectual and moral content, is divorced from those who are its practitioners—from their lives, their personal struggles, their social condition, their racial and sexual identities. For those who regard themselves as experts and "professors" of the theological discipline (are they not also disciples?), the recipients of their tutelage have too often been looked upon as empty vessels into whom the fullness of truth must be poured—as much of it as they could contain! (That this is not merely a practice of our dark past but a habit indulged by Christian "experts" still today can be observed in the average television church service, in many seminary classrooms, and in much "missionary" activity at home and abroad.) A significant corollary of this approach is that the discipline (theology) has emerged in substantially the same manner whether it is practiced in South Africa or Venezuela, Tokyo or Chicago. It could be professed in the same way, and stand for essentially the same content, with variations, in any and every circumstance. Whether offered to black or white, male or female,

9. Cf. F. L. Cross, ed., *The Oxford Dictionary of the Christian Church* (London: Oxford University Press, 1958), p. 406.

10. Listed verbatim from Webster's *Dictionary of Synonyms* (Springfield, Mass.: G. & C. Merriam, 1951), p. 257.

11. *The Concise Oxford Dictionary of Current English*, 5th ed. (Oxford: Clarendon, 1964), p. 347.

bond or free, rich or poor, young or old, it could be the same basic doctrinal product. It was the recipients of the product who had to conform.

A monumental difference is made once one begins seriously to regard the disciple community as itself being part of the discipline. Often, Christian educators have understood this much better than professional theologians. The point is not that the disciple community sets the tone for the whole process of theological reflection, determining both what is to be believed and how. The point is rather that what is "there" to be "handed over" (*tradere*) from one hearer to another—the discipline as such—can only be handed over in any *meaningful* sense of the term if it enters into dialogue with the persons who are ready to receive it. It will be shaped by them, by their experience and their needs, just as it was shaped by the experiences and needs of the original disciple community. It will be appropriated according to their questions, their anxieties, their hopes. And so it will never be the same—never quite the same—from one hearer to another, one epoch to another, one theological province to another.

And *that does not matter!* Those for whom the discipline is an end in itself have always behaved as if what mattered ultimately and utterly were verbal agreement or conformity with some doctrinal norm. This is the disease of religious rationalism, especially the pseudo-intellectualism of those "who combine unusual insecurity with naivete."[12] ("Those are the worst: they have the cruelty of doctrine without the poetic grace of myth.")[13] Such dogmatism can be cured only by a better hearing of the gospel. What matters is not that every Christian should give assent to the same ideas in the same terminology, but that whatever they assent to should emerge from a real struggle within their own souls, and should have the effect of overcoming the alienation of *spirit* which exists between them and "the others." In a word, the discipline is secondary to the disciples. To use Buber's well-known distinction, the discipline is always an "it," no matter how significant an it. The disciple community is comprised of persons whose human integrity should never be compromised for the sake of superficial agreement at the level of religious ideas. Theology was made for human beings, not human beings for theology!

That is why, as I shall attempt to demonstrate in the ensuing chapters, it is such a travesty of the *kerygma* when theologians pursue their discipline without any genuine concern for the context in which they are working. The disciple community, including the theologians themselves, belongs to this context: "I dwell in the midst of a people of unclean lips."

---

12. George Lindbeck, *The Nature of Doctrine,* p. 21.
13. Robertson Davies, *Fifth Business* (Harmondsworth: Penguin Books, 1977), p. 226.

They breathe the air of their social milieu, they reflect the spiritual climate of their environment, they bear in their bodies and souls the marks of their society's crises and longings, they benefit from the particular treasures of its cultural heritage. They cannot divest themselves of these things, this identity. They can become hearers of the good news, recipients of new creaturehood, only as persons whose humanity has been shaped by that past and that present.

> Human temporality in its changing historical context sets the condition for the way we are human; it thus also sets the condition for the way we are or are not religious. Our humanity, our action, our religiousness and thus our theology are essentially intertwined with our historicity.[14]

This means that submitting to the discipline of theological thought *is* in a real sense a matter of being "brought under control," opening oneself to the authority of another Way. It *is* to be "trained in obedience" to this other Way—not *only* in intellectual terms, of course, though also intellectually. Exposure to the theological discipline which belongs to faith means therefore a struggle within the disciple community. This was true of the first disciples of the Christ—of Peter, who thought that Jesus meant friendship when in fact he meant love; of Matthew the tax collector, who had to struggle with his particular anti-Jewish bias; of Paul, the victim, perhaps, of a guilt complex honed to perfection by religious purism.[15] They went about the discipline of faith-reflection in the ways that they did because they were the people they were. It is a mockery of the Christian concept of authority when their profound reflections are turned into absolutes to be swallowed whole by succeeding generations of Christ's disciples. There are very good reasons (as we shall see) for the Reformation's *sola scriptura* principle. But it is one thing to make the testimony of the original disciple communities of Israel and the church *normative* and something else to regard them as being *absolute*. Theology, when it is true to its own best traditions, must always imitate the original disciples, not in their precise narration of the meaning of the faith so much as in

---

14. Langdon Gilkey, *Reaping the Whirlwind: A Christian Interpretation of History* (New York: Seabury, 1976), p. 9.

15. Although John Howard Yoder, following Krister Stendahl, questions the attribution of a "Luther-type experience" to Paul (in Yoder's case, for the good purpose of combatting Christian individualism), it seems to me equally questionable to deny the presence of this theme in Paul's works. Paul is no Luther or Kierkegaard, certainly; but the psalmist also knew about personal guilt and its psychic devastations long before Protestant theology made it a station of the cross! See John Howard Yoder, *The Politics of Jesus: Vicit Agnus Noster* (Grand Rapids, Mich.: Eerdmans, 1972), pp. 219f.

the manner of their quest for that meaning, namely, the way in which they themselves, with all the particularity of their existences, were an integral part of what they are trying to understand—they themselves, caught between the pursuits and assumptions of their world and the untried freedom of a Spirit beckoning them into discipleship.

3. *Discipleship as disciplined thought about the faith*: The third reason why the juxtaposition of disciple and discipline is an instructive metaphor for designating the subject matter of the present volume is the obverse of the second. If "disciple" helps to offset the *doctrinaire* quality of conventional conceptions of the theological discipline, it is also possible that "discipline" can help to redeem some unfortunate connotations of discipleship. Disciple and discipleship have acquired a "heavy" quality. They are terms that suggest a spirituality, piety, obedience, devotion, and earnestness of the sort that often repels *thinking* persons. The language of discipleship lacks not only the quality of play and humor, which must season the life of the mind if it is not to become morose; it lacks ordinary humanness. In particular, it seems to rule out that sense of duplicity and doubt and uncertainty—indeed, of disbelief—that for most of us constitutes being human, and is, besides, a primary factor in the theological imagination. Whenever someone speaks piously about "the disciple community," it can be presupposed that most of those who hear the term are applying it to other people, not to themselves.

Juxtaposing discipleship with the *discipline* to which the disciple community is called could help to rehabilitate the real meaning of discipleship. Discipleship is not merely a "spiritual" (i.e., in the pejorative sense, a rather mindless) commitment to the Christ. It is the decision, taken not once but constantly renewed, to explore in depth the *meaning* of the message in which the Christ is central. Discipleship is submission to the discipline of understanding, without which the discipline of obedience-in-act lacks foundation and rationale. It is the assumption of the posture of one who is willing to "learn" (*discere*). Freed from its associations with moralism and authoritarianism, Christian *discipline* means the quest of the mind and will for a better comprehension of what is believed. It is the attempt of the disciple to align his or her life at every level with what authenticates itself to the human spirit as truth. It is not possible to *command* discipline in this sense. It either happens from within or it does not happen at all. What happens under the name of "discipline" is too frequently mere acquiescence to someone else's prescription for belief and obedience. But Christian theology as discipline is undertaken by the church in obedience *to its Lord*, and therefore in freedom.

The point, however, is that *theology* is a dimension of this Christian discipline. The disciple community is not only concerned to bring its *conduct* into line with the "new law of Christ." It is concerned to let its *thinking* conform to this sphere of obedience. In the past, the discipline undertaken by Christians has concerned primarily the *doing* of what is "right." Today, when Christians are not born as such but must continuously nurture their belief through serious thought, discipline has again to do in a primary sense with thinking. Christian disciples are persons who are seeking to discipline their minds, to wrestle in great earnestness with what their hearts and wills assent to, to comprehend that which has grasped them as their "ultimate concern" (Tillich). When the discipline with which this disciple community is engaged means understanding, assimilating, articulating, and enacting in the world what it believes, then discipleship can be relieved of its reputation for otherworldly solemnity and intellectual laxity, and become a life in which honestly searching human beings can participate without compromising their integrity.

Thinking faith, as Buri insists, is the only kind of faith that can be taken seriously in today's world. This already represents an enormous challenge to us in the North American context; for it has been, almost, a tradition with us to keep thought at a distance where "religion" is concerned, and even to use our religion to help banish thought. As Martin E. Marty reports, one of the observations of the famous Alexis de Tocqueville concerning the "New World" was that

> "the majority draws a formidable circle around thought. Within its limits, one is free: but woe to him who dares to break out of it." Religion, he saw, was a major element in the formation of this circle. He believed there was no country in the world where the Christian religion retained a greater influence over the souls of men than in America.[16]

Tocqueville might still find the Christian religion a force to be reckoned with in North America; but if he were to remain in our midst long enough today he would also come to realize, I think, that here and there probing and provocative thought actually *originates* in some Christian circles and is accompanied by the desire to extend itself into the larger community. It is for the nurture of this nascent thinking-faith wherever it may be found, inside the churches or beyond them, that the present work is undertaken.

---

16. Martin Marty, *Righteous Empire: The Protestant Experience in America* (New York: Harper Torchbooks, 1970), p. 90.

PART I
THE DISCIPLE COMMUNITY

CHAPTER · ONE

The Meaning of Contextuality in Christian Thought

None of us is asked to speak to everybody in all places and in all periods. Communication is a matter of participation. Where there is no participation there is no communication. . . . The really serious problem for us is participation.[1]

1. A Reputation for Timelessness

1.1. *Theologia Eterna*. Christian theology is contextual by definition. The term "contextual theology" is, accordingly, a tautology.

This fundamental assumption of the present study is, however, exactly what has to be demonstrated. For, apart from the work of a few individuals and minorities, what has achieved the reputation of theology in North American church and society is not only noncontextual, it is anticontextual. Most Christians do not regard Christian theology as a mode of engaging their historical, cultural, socioeconomic milieu. On the contrary, where they consider the subject at all, laypersons tend to think of theology as a more or less fixed set of beliefs, contained in embryo in the Bible, codified in various historical creeds, confessions, and faith statements, refined in forbidding volumes of doctrine, and relayed to congregations in simplified form through sermon, catechetical instruction, and (for a few) college classes in religious knowledge.

That the laity has held such a view of the nature of theology is not surprising, however, for, with notable exceptions, the professional practitioners of the discipline have themselves done little to convey another conception of it. The orthodox of the past century actively fostered the idea that their subject matter was above the flux of time and the particularities of place. "Christian theology," wrote the Lord Bishop of Durham

---

1. Paul Tillich, *Theology of Culture* (New York: Oxford University Press, 1959), p. 204.

at the beginning of this century, "as presented in Revelation, practically assumes, as otherwise given, certain *great facts* about man, the world, and God."[2] In a similar vein, the Princeton theologian Archibald Alexander Hodge claimed that

> The Christian religion is that *body of truths*, experiences, actions and institutions which are determined by the revelation supernaturally presented in the Christian Scriptures. Christian theology is the scientific determination, interpretation, and defence of those Scriptures, together with the history of the manner in which the truths it reveals have been understood, and the duties they impose have been performed, by all Christians in all ages.[3]

Liberal Christianity somewhat mitigated this tendency of theological conservatism to elevate (or should one not say reduce?)[4] dogma to the status of timeless "truths" and "facts"; but even theologians influenced by the spirit of liberalism could still regard their discipline as a work of interpreting, arranging, and conveying certain permanently true data. Thus, while the language of John MacKintosh Shaw in the following quotation betrays a typical liberal ethos, its tendency to timelessness is also evident. Noting that the principal subject of Christian theology comprises "a two-sided fact, 'the Jesus of history' on the one side and 'the Christ of experience' on the other," Shaw writes:

> Such being the nature of the Fact of Christ which is the determining organizing [!] principle of the system of Christian truth or doctrine, this revelation of God made in Christ and in Christian history and experience has given rise to *certain great fundamental religious convictions and af-*

---

2. Handley C. G. Moule, *Outlines of Christian Doctrine* (London: Hoddern and Stoughton, 1902), p. 1 (emphasis added).

3. A. A. Hodge, *Outlines of Theology* (London: Thomas Nelson, 1883, New Edition), p. 15.

4. An interesting—and nowadays neglected—statement about the nature of church dogma is presented by the great German historian of Christian thought, Reinhold Seeberg, in *The Fundamental Truths of the Christian Religion* (trans. Rev. George E. Thomson and Clara Wallentin [London: Williams & Norgate, 1908], pp. 115ff.). Dogma, writes Seeberg, "is an historical necessity," for the impulse to "coherence" is present in both Christian faith and human nature. "If we had to begin the history of Christianity now, it would be worthwhile pondering for a moment the thought of a Christianity 'without a dogma.' But much would not be gained by that. On account of the nature of the human mind, 'new dogmas' would immediately arise. The new dogmas would become old dogmas, and other newer dogmas take their place beside them or oppose them. In a word, this way would soon lead into the old track again. Dogmas would just as little be avoided now, if we had to begin afresh, as in the Church of fifteen centuries ago." Yet, however "necessary" dogma may be, insists Seeberg, it is not to be regarded as ultimate truth. "The dogmas are not given by God, they are not revelation. Men have created them" (p. 121). In this sense I find it a *reduction* of dogma when it is considered timeless or eternal, for it eliminates the historical process, i.e., the intellectual element of human thought and speech, from the ongoing search for truth.

firmations, which are before us first in the New Testament and then in the Creeds and Confessions of the Church throughout the centuries. It is the task of Systematic Theology, or the study of the system of Christian truth or doctrine, to take *these properly religious convictions and affirmations, and attempt to give them systematic or orderly intellectual or doctrinal expression and formulation.*[5]

These and countless statements like them convey the impression that theology is the study of an assemblage of basically immutable truths—*theologia eterna.* Unlike representatives of simplistic fundamentalism or popular evangelicalism, serious Christian thinkers seldom display the audacity of believing themselves personally in possession of eternal veracity, though many betray a readiness to make excessive claims along these lines for the authorities they honor. Their personal modesty notwithstanding, professionals seem to have left upon the discipline of theology the mark of the absolute, or of certain pretensions in that direction. John Henry Newman's statement of the matter bears a particularly Catholic stamp, perhaps, but it is not difficult to discover Protestant sentiments to parallel it: "The Gospel faith," declared Newman, "is a definite deposit, a treasure, common to all, one and the same in every age, conceived in set words, and such as admits of being received, preserved, transmitted."[6] Other "truths" might change, be altered or set aside by new discoveries, as Einstein's theories displaced some of Newton's. But the "great facts" and "fundamental religious convictions" of Christian belief, contained for Hodge and many Protestants in the Bible supremely and for Newman and traditional Roman Catholics in the *depositum fidei*,[7] were incontrovertible. No doubt theological truth had to be interpreted, sheathed in more contemporaneous language, and constantly nourished by example in order that it might be "received, preserved and transmitted." No doubt, too, in the process of such Christian apologetics[8] certain differences, nuances, and errors might creep in. But the truth of "revelation" would outlast these accretions of time and human frailty. In any case, the task of the theological servants of the church was to keep the truths of faith

---

5. J. M. Shaw, *Outlines of Christian Doctrine* (Toronto: Ryerson, 1953), p. 15.

6. John Henry Newman, *Parochial and Plain Sermons*, 8 vols. (London, 1937), vol. 2, pp. 356.

7. "Deposit of faith"; see note 24, §30.2 below.

8. Although it can also be used in a very broad sense, the term *apologetics* is not necessarily compatible with the concerns of contextual theology. Conventionally, *apologetics* conveys the notion of a "defence of the Christian faith on intellectual grounds" (*The Concise Oxford Dictionary of the Christian Church*, ed. Elizabeth A. Livingstone [Oxford, London, and New York: Oxford University Press, 1977], p. 29). Contextual theology intends to *engage* the culture, and therefore that which seems reasonable to the representatives of its host society's best thinking; but its object is not necessarily to *defend* or *commend* the faith.

as free as possible from confusion with the passing concerns, fads, and trends of the moment. What should occupy the mind of the church were the "things eternal," not "things temporal" (2 Cor. 4:18).[9]

As for the context, then, one might well conclude that it has been viewed by professionals more consistently as a handicap to the preservation of the truth of faith than as a positive and necessary dimension in the search for theological understanding. The object of these professionals (by which I refer, chiefly, to generations of theological educators rather than to the few original thinkers of the tradition) would seem to have been to get the truth of Christianity *into* the (normally recalcitrant) consciousness of their students and other charges—precisely, to "transmit" it. The notion that the currents of intellect and spirit abroad, at a given time, within a given social milieu would play a decisive role in the actual process of theologizing does not belong prominently to the discipline as it has been bequeathed to us by the dominant strains of our Christian past.[10]

1.2. The Religious Temptation. We should be naive, however, if we left the matter there, as if the theological professionals, like a jealous and protective guild, had managed to keep the substance of the faith (their trade secrets) from mingling with the ever-changing experience and preoccupations of the human community. On the contrary, professional theology at every level has merely been answering a larger human need—obeying, one might even say, the laws of supply and demand. For surely the fact of the matter is that very many people, both Christians and others, wanted and still want religious truth to be fixed, steadfast, and predictable.

This desire is by no means unique to religious conservatism, so-called, though it is naturally more conspicuous in forms of religion which make the conservation of established precepts their priority. In impeccably

---

9. It is significant that charismatic forms of Christian faith and community, manifesting (as one would expect) more interest in the immediacy of the human relation to God, did not feel the same compulsion to honor past articulations of belief as was felt in the church at large. But then charismatic Christianity has had very little influence upon the development of church doctrine and the shaping of the discipline of theology. It was precisely its spiritual immediacy that the guardians of the tradition—perhaps justifiably, but still with some dire results for the discipline of theology—mistrusted. *Revelatio immediata* (immediate or unmediated revelation) was denied, by post-Reformation Protestantism, to all Christians after the closing of the canon. Only the authors of the Scriptures could legitimately claim immediacy of revelatory experience.

10. One result of this, of course (and it is a very prominent one in the North American context), is that the existential concerns of the larger Christian community have achieved a life of their own, outside the theological disciplines, manifesting themselves not only in nonprofessional, charismatic, and other forms of religious life but also, organizationally, in the emergence of many different "churches" and sects which reflect the variety of existential and experiential concern.

"liberal" circles of belief too, however, and even among the secularized masses of modern Western societies, it is quite possible to hear that the church should "stand for something"—meaning that it should hold fast to its habitual truth-claims and modes of behavior. For religion still functions socially for many as a symbol of permanency. People turn to the supramundane for forms of psychic stability denied them by the mundane. It is thus not unusual to find persons whose life-style is decidedly post-Christian resenting it when representatives of churches or synagogues appear as innovators.

This is hardly surprising. Human existence is unbelievably vulnerable. "It is appalling, the burden that man bears, the *experiential* burden."[11] Subject at every turn to the unpredictable and the chaotic, the human psyche reaches out for order, certitude, and stability wherever they can be found—and finds them, regularly, in many places where they cannot, in reality, be found! Clearly, the most ancient and in many ways most rewarding haven in such a quest is explicit religion. In religion, Homo sapiens endeavors to place its destiny beyond the rush and tumble of time. The language of religion—of all religions—is full of this seeking and this finding:

> *Change and decay in all around I see;*
> *O Thou who changest not, abide with me.*

In its essence, the comfort of religion is just this assurance that one's transient life is undergirded by a steadfastness which infinitely transcends the exigencies of time and place.

Let it be said at once that biblical faith understands and has the greatest sympathy for this religious quest. The Christian pastor who delights in humiliating those "worldlings" who look in on the church only at Christmas and Easter may have lost touch with his or her own deep need for security in the midst of life's "demon-ridden journey" (Iris Murdoch). Not only is biblical faith sensitive to the search for a place to stand, it speaks directly to this search. For it declares that God is love. God's faithful love *(ḥesed)* is the permanent factor, the reality from which nothing—not death itself, not *life* itself—can separate us (Rom. 8:38-39). God will not change. Jesus Christ is "the same yesterday, today, and forever" (Heb. 13:8).

Characteristically, however, the human spirit is not satisfied with this security. The security of love, whether human or divine, seems perennially

---

11. Ernest Becker, *The Denial of Death* (New York: The Free Press, 1973), p. 51.

to fall short of the human *demand* for security. From Eden and Babel onwards, the human spirit seems to have desired manifestations of security more explicit than the presence of the loving God in the midst of time. As the temptations both of the garden and the wilderness vividly illustrate, human nature longs for forms of certitude that are denied it—that *must be* denied it, for to have such security is to have ceased living the life *of the creature.* Yet humanity's clamor for a supranatural *securitas* is so insistent that every religious community is beseiged by it. More than any other type of human community—more than the state, more than the workplace or the union, more than the family even—the religious community is under immeasurable pressure from its own membership to surpass every limit and provide assurance of the kind that cannot in fact be provided. Human beings turn to the churches, not only to find in the company of their kind the God who "changest not" but doctrines that do not change, moral precepts that do not change, and even aesthetic forms (Gothic architecture and 19th-century hymns!) which do not change.

Consider then what an affront it is to this propensity to make religion the source of tranquility away from the world's "change and decay" when someone insists (as we shall have to do here) that faith in the *Christian* sense, at least, is the very medium through which one enters into *a more intensive and committed encounter with one's ever-changing world.* Religion has been and is a time-honored and well-proved *sanctuary* from "the context." If we try to make of this sanctuary from history a *forum* for engaging our historical moment, we shall find ourselves opposed by forces infinitely more potent than mere doctrinal conservatism!

Yet, despite sympathy for this all-too-human demand that is made of religion (who in our time could fail to sympathize with human attempts to find sanctuary?), a theology which takes seriously the incarnation and humiliation of the divine Word must insist upon the *forum* character of Christian faith and thought. The Christian gospel is not, and must not be allowed to serve, a flight from the world. On the contrary, it is the catalyst of a deeper and more committed worldliness, in Bonhoeffer's sense. Moreover, "the world" here does not refer to some theoretical construct, logically necessary to the doctrines of creation and incarnation. It means the everyday, complicated, beautiful, ugly, and threatened world of our experience, *when* and *where* we are. It means, in short, our *context.*

Faith is the grace-given courage to engage that world. Theology is a disciplined reflection and commentary upon faith's engagement. Theology therefore is contextual, and that by definition.

2. Defining Contextuality

If we have seen why contextual reflection is threatening to the "religious" mentality, we may have gained *via negativa* a certain perspective from which to consider the meaning of contextuality in Christian theology more positively. Several observations must be made.

2.1. A Dimension of the Whole Task. To claim that Christian theology is by definition contextual is to insist that the *engagement* of the milieu in which theology is done is as such a dimension of the doing of theology. The attempt to comprehend one's culture—to grasp at some depth its aspirations, its priorities, its anxieties; to discern the dominant ideational motifs of its history; to distinguish its real from its rhetorical mores—all this belongs to the theological task as such. For example, if it is true that the recurrent leitmotiv of Canadian imaginative literature has been that of "survival," as Margaret Atwood has claimed in her perceptive study of the subject,[12] then such a theme cannot be ignored by the Canadian theological community if it intends seriously to pursue theology and is not interested merely in church doctrine and conventional morality. Or again, if "narcissism" accurately describes a way of life that has become prevalent in middle-class America,[13] this is as significant a datum for the discipline of theology as it is for social psychology. Again, to speak about "the First World," as we have done in the introduction, is already to speak *theologically*. Such data are not just adjuncts to theology, or preparatory aspects which can be quickly attended to in an introduction. Nor are they matters that the theologian can happily leave to practical theology or ethics. Karl Barth was at least anticipating the concerns of present-day *praxis* theology when, in the foreword of his first volume of *Church Dogmatics*, he wrote: "Ethics so-called I regard as the doctrine of God's command and do not consider it right to treat it otherwise than as an integral part of dogmatics, or to produce a dogmatics which does not include it."[14] The split between theology and ethics is not only a false one, but one which has contributed much to the reputation for timelessness earned by a doctrine-centered theology that did not speak both from and to its historical context.

---

12. Margaret Atwood, *Survival: A Thematic Guide to Canadian Literature* (Toronto: Anansi, 1972).

13. As Christopher Lasch claims in *The Culture of Narcissism: American Life in an Age of Diminishing Expectations* (New York: W. W. Norton, 1978).

14. Karl Barth, *The Doctrine of the Word of God: Prolegomena to Church Dogmatics*, I/1, trans. G. T. Thomson (New York: Charles Scribner's Sons, 1936), p. xiv.

To insist upon the contextual character of Christian "systematic" thought, then, is to claim that at every juncture—in its Christology as in its ethics, in its eschatology as in its pastoralia—Christian intellectual reflection entails serious dialogue with the existing situation of one's world. When this dialogical quality is lacking at the level of the church's doctrinal reflection, no amount of practicality and concreteness at the level of "applied Christianity" will make up for the lack. Indeed, a quite obvious reason why, in North America especially, there has been a perennial rift between theological theory and practical religion, making it necessary for the latter in its various forms to become virtually independent of academic theology, is that what theology we have had is conspicuously deficient in just this dialogical quality. You cannot begin the task of doctrinal speculation on a strictly theoretical plane and expect it to evolve quite naturally into a discussion of the most practical issues besetting church and society.

2.2. A Conscious Element.   The fact is, of course, that in a certain sense all theological thought reflects its context, intentionally or not. We are, after all, creatures of time and space. There is no such thing as non-contextual human thought, including theological thought.

What there is, however (and therefore it is necessary to engage in such a discussion as this), is a form of thought *which does not regard itself as contextual*, and which for complex reasons is treated by whole segments of the populace of this continent as if it were contextually neutral. What there *is*, to be specific, is a very extensive and deeply entrenched but no less contextual tradition in theology—a tradition comparatively unified, variations on well-rehearsed themes; a tradition, namely, which took shape within the historical experience of a specific people, the Europeans. This de facto contextual theology actually does echo the many and diverse movements of evolving European civilization—as one would expect it to do. To follow, for instance, the development of the doctrine of the atonement, is to be introduced to rudiments of the long history of Europe's anxieties and its ways of coping with those anxieties. The concept of humanity as *imago Dei*, so important for Christian anthropology, is indecipherable without some awareness of the various stages of European humanity's self-understanding. As Hendrikus Berkhof has said, "By studying how systematic theologies have poured meaning into Genesis 1:26, one could write a piece of Europe's cultural history."[15]

---

15. H. Berkhof, *Christian Faith: An Introduction to the Study of the Faith*, trans. Sierd Woudstra (Grand Rapids: Eerdmans, 1979), p. 179.

But, for many reasons, some of which have already been broached and others which must await their turn, this European theological contextuality in several typical forms (Augustinian, Thomistic, Calvinistic, pietistic, and others) has been permitted to conduct itself throughout the inhabited earth as if it were *not* a thoroughly contextualized statement of the meaning of Christian faith, but something transcendent of history and therefore entirely universal and portable. It could be transplanted in the soils of all the other continents without undergoing any significant metamorphosis—without undergoing the *kind* of metamorphosis, for example, that Christian belief underwent in its translation from the Near East into the "pagan" cultures of ancient and early Medieval Europe itself. And if the soils of those other continents were not hospitable to this Euro-Christian transplant, then European *soil* could be taken abroad as well! (Here we could conduct a very long excursus on the history of Christian missions.)

We shall return to this observation, for more than one comment has to be made in this connection. For the present, our reference to the Europeanization of the Christian theological tradition is intended only to illustrate something of what is at issue in the theological principle of contextuality. It is to point up, namely, that theology will be (in a certain sense of the term) "contextual," even when it does not intend to be so; even when it is considered quite independent of its context. But the observation also illustrates the fact that the most problematic theology, from the standpoint of a faith which wishes to be in a *purposive and conscious* dialogue with its sociohistorical context, is a theology which hides its de facto contextuality under the guise of universality. Such a theology not only discourages the continuous engagement of the human situation by the representatives of the gospel of Jesus Christ, it carries with it assumptions about the human situation which are either not concretely accurate or (as has frequently happened) are quite patently false. Nor is this inaccuracy and falsehood ever merely harmless. For it functions in the new environs in such a way as to preclude struggle, on the part of the Christian community, with the actualities of those new environs. It functions, that is to say, as *ideology*.[16]

---

16. Since I shall use the term "ideology" with some regularity in this study, I should like to clarify the connotation that it has for me. I have not found a better definition than the one provided by Dorothee Sølle in her book, *Political Theology*, trans. John Shelley (Philadelphia: Fortress, 1971), p. 23. I shall quote the entire context of which her brief definition of ideology is a part: "When we analyze Bultmann's understanding of kerygma, we recover the formal structure typical of and necessary for his thought, which in itself is sufficient to vindicate him. Bultmann makes a fundamental distinction between kerygma and theology, an important fact suppressed by the entire Bultmannian right. Kerygma appears 'as a formidable summary of everything which has to be proclaimed, and now threatens to conceal the real problems facing proclamation under a welter of high-sounding

The lesson being taught us today by the deceptive ideological functioning of religion in so many parts of the world (including our own) is that theological activity must involve a quite *conscious and deliberate* engagement of the context, and must develop a critical awareness of the way the church's witness actually operates in its host society. We cannot assume that this will happen automatically. Unless it is intentionally guarded against, what seems to occur as a matter of course in church doctrine is the perpetuation of religious and other presuppositions which deter and deflect the thrust of the gospel towards a more direct encounter with existing social conditions. In short, the habit of ideological eternalism must be countered today by an explicit demand for historical concreteness and topographical particularity in all theological reflection.

2.3. The Context as Contributor to Theological Discourse. We have said that contextuality in Christian theology means that the social situation in all of its uniqueness informs the reflection of the Christian community, and that it must now do this in a deliberate manner. But to leave the matter there would be to invite the suggestion that the compulsion towards contextualization implicit in the gospel of incarnation and cross would be satisfied if, from its side, the Christian community were to be

---

christological terminology.' It becomes a collection of doctrines that can neither be criticized nor questioned, most of which—and this is deemed progress—are no longer formulated mythologically but ideologically. *By ideology I understand a system of propositional truths independent of the situation, a superstructure no longer relevant to praxis, to the situation, to the real questions of life.* The superstructure has lost precisely what Bultmann learned from dialectical theology, the basic relation to life, and thus it is more resistant to transformation and not even interested in working to improve the underlying situation" (emphasis added.)

Another excellent and, for me, definitive statement is provided by Gustavo Gutierrez: "The term *ideology* has a long and varied history and has been understood in very different ways. But we can basically agree that ideology does not offer adequate and scientific knowledge of reality; rather, it masks it. Ideology does not rise above the empirical, irrational level. Therefore it spontaneously fulfils a function of preservation of the established order. Therefore, also, ideology tends to dogmatize all that has not succeeded in separating itself from it or has fallen under its influence. Political action, science, and faith do not escape this danger" (*A Theology of Liberation: History, Politics and Salvation*, trans. Sister Caridad Inda and John Eagleson [Maryknoll, N.Y.: Orbis, 1973], pp. 234-235).

Theology, like all intellectual activity, walks very close to ideology. "All human knowledge is tainted with an 'ideological' taint," wrote Reinhold Niebuhr. "It pretends to be more true than it is. It is finite knowledge, gained from a particular perspective; but it pretends to be final and ultimate knowledge. Exactly analogous to the cruder pride of power, the pride of intellect is derived on the one hand from ignorance of the finiteness of the human mind and on the other hand from an attempt to obscure the known conditioned character of human knowledge and the taint of self-interest in human truth" (*The Nature and Destiny of Man: A Christian Interpretation* [New York: Charles Scribner's Sons, 1953], pp. 194-195).

Theology is prevented from crossing the invisible line into ideology only by one thing, and that is the very thing we have been discussing here, namely, the necessity, inherent to it, of sustaining an ongoing dialogue with the world, and thus of being continuously judged and corrected by the transcendent Word to which it can only bear secondary witness.

a sensitive and observant spectator of its historical setting, its habitat. And that would be unfortunate.

For the notion of a Christian disciple community seeking in its solitude to comprehend its historical moment does not yet capture the meaning of contextuality in theology. We have already used the word "dialogue" to describe the relation between the theological community and its social context, and we must be clear that this means *dialogue!* This dialogue is not merely a conversation conducted within the precincts of the *koinōnia*. It is not a matter of the disciple community, or some part of it, researching its "world," determining its real condition, and then responding to its own world-analysis from the side of its Christian belief. Such an approach has frequently characterized the various traditions of Christian apologetics, and while it is certainly to be preferred to theological stances which feel no responsibility even to reflect upon the world's condition, it is not yet genuinely contextual in nature. True contextuality means the initiating and nurturing of a *dialogue* with one's culture, a genuine give-and-take, in which the world is permitted to speak for itself, and in which therefore the Christian community opens itself to the *risk* of hearing things that it had not anticipated and to which it cannot *readily* respond. In other words, in a fully contextual approach to its subject, the disciple community sees its sociohistorical habitat, not only as a field to be investigated but as a partner in the investigation—and therefore as contributor to the theological task itself.

What the disciple community has to learn from its context—what it can only learn *from* its context—is something of the spirit of the times (*Zeitgeist*). The dominant mood of an age cannot be discerned only by taking note of current events—a thing which can be done without very much actual contact with the world, particularly in these days of rapid communications. To discover "what time it is" (undoubtedly the most difficult aspect of the whole vocation of theology),[17] the Christian community has to have access to those sources within its host culture which can inform it, not only about what is *occurring* in the world, but about what these (external and internal) occurrences are doing to the human spirit. This knowledge is always in some considerable measure hidden from faith, for the basic and obvious (yet subtle) reason that faith as such *protects the believing community from raw exposure to such knowledge.* Faith itself gives us a sense of meaning that is able to cushion our spirits from the shock of events—events which may well constitute for large

---

17. Cf. §5 below.

numbers of our contemporaries the very stuff out of which despair, cynicism, and nihilism are fashioned. Because it is the vocation of the church to address itself in particular to those who are crushed by life, it is necessary for the disciple community always to achieve a comprehension of reality as it is experienced by such persons. The poor, the unemployed, the handicapped, those whom society ostracizes because they deviate from "the norm," the powerless—such persons are important to the community of belief not only because they are those in and through whom the Christ is concretely present to us, pleading for our care, but also because, without them, we shall almost certainly fail to understand "what time it is."

To speak concretely: It is possible for Christians in the First World today—if they can be delivered from the general state of apathy by which our societies are enthralled—to learn a great deal about the desperate state of famine in parts of the continent of Africa. Quite apart from any contact with those who suffer from these conditions of drought and exploitation, North American churches can (and do) amass large dossiers of information, and, moreover, engage in impressive acts of charity. But all of this can occur without *any* significant growth in understanding our world, or even this one dimension of the total world-problematique. In order to approximate genuine understanding of the context in question, we must open ourselves to those who live at the center of it, its victims. Such growth in understanding can only be attained through participation (see the epigraph of this chapter), that is, through a process of recognizing existentially something of our own responsibility, as First World citizens, for this Third World condition—in other words, through a painful confrontation with the realities of *our own specific context*.

An African Christian has stated this in terms more explicit than any that I might devise:

> People are not finally developed by other people. People must develop themselves. Villagers should be talking together to decide what they want and how to get it. This may mean bringing in outside animators for a limited time, people who can help villagers identify their needs and work out appropriate ways of satisfying them. If necessary, villagers can consult with people in neighbouring areas, or other Third World countries. . . . [But] the biggest job of the church of the North is in the North, because that is where the problem lies. You must put pressure on the transnational companies to change their exploitative practices, and pressure on the government regarding aid and military spending. Eight hundred billion dollars is spent annually on arms. If the North can be humanized, development is possible.[18]

---

18. From "The story behind the story of famine," in *Mandate,* a publication of the United Church of Canada; Toronto, September 1985, pp. 21f.

A theology which knows that it is not time*less* will always need to know what time it is *hic et nunc*. Unless it knows this, the Christian community will not know what form of the Word is appropriate—what is address, gospel, *sermo*. But the Christian community never can know this unless it comes to know—rather intimately—those who are oppressed by the silent but powerful principalities governing the here and now.

2.4. Christian Immersion in the Context. As the above illustration concerning the North/South economic disparity makes very plain, however, the disciple community's understanding of its context requires not only that it invite representatives of the world to enter into the theological dialogue, but also that it should itself be prepared to go out into the world. It is, as Tillich has said, a matter of "participation." Really to *know* one's context means to participate *in* it—not only physically and factually, which in any case is unavoidable, but consciously, deliberately, reflectively. The dialogue with one's world which belongs to Christian faith and theology not only involves an ongoing discussion with those who are able, through their experience or skills, to represent the world; it involves personal immersion in one's world.

To put it in other words, becoming Christian means simultaneously becoming *contemporaneous*. Christian belief may indeed lift one, in some real sense, out of immediate preoccupation with the world. Without this, Christians would lack the *perspective* that is necessary for understanding their "here and now," as well as the prospect of *willing* their participation in it. But it is for the sake of participation that we are lifted out; it is in order to achieve a new status of being "in" the world that we are denied the right to be, simply, "of" it.

We are of course speaking here of a process—an *ongoing* process, and one which cannot be undertaken without pain. When Paul Tillich writes that "the really serious problem for us is participation,"[19] he is not thinking only of an academic or intellectual problem. He is speaking existentially about the suffering that belongs to the community of faith as a whole, and specifically to those within it who are called to the vocation of intensive theological thought. The liturgical paradigm of this pain is baptism, and it is in this sense that the word *immersion* should be heard in the subhead of this section. The disciple community can only become what it is called to be as it is again and again (sacramentally) immersed in the problematic of its context, plunged beneath the threatening waters

---

19. *Theology of Culture.*

of the present and impending future, and caused once more to recover its hope in response to the realities of that concrete situation. Tillich has elsewhere poignantly illustrated what such participation means to the theologian, and why it is "the really serious problem for us." The theologian, he writes in the introduction of the second volume of his *Systematic Theology*,

> must participate in the human predicament, not only actually—as he always does—but also in conscious identification. He must participate in man's finitude, which is also his own, and its anxiety, as though he had never received the revelatory answer of "eternity." He must participate in man's estrangement, which is also his own, and show the anxiety of guilt, as though he had never received the revelatory answer of "forgiveness." The theologian does not rest on the theological answer which he announces. He can give it in a convincing way only if he participates with his whole being in the situation of the question, namely, the human predicament. In the light of this demand, the method of correlation protects the theologian from the arrogant claim of having revelatory answers at his disposal. In formulating the answer, he must struggle for it.[20]

Participation is the sine qua non of communication: "Where there is no participation there is no communication." If Martin Luther had not been compelled to experience at first hand the terrible anxiety that gripped his age—the anxiety of an almost inescapable judgment by an almost implacable God[21]—he would never have discovered the gospel of "justification by grace through faith." As we know from Luther's biography, however, that discovery cost him a great deal of personal anguish—and not just at the outset of his career. The *Anfechtungen* (times of utter abandonment) remained permanent, periodic features of his Christian life.

Perhaps it is the threat of such abandonment that has deterred the church so consistently from exposing itself to the always-new circumstances of the present and, conversely, has attracted it to past expressions

---

20. Paul Tillich, *Systematic Theology*, vol. 2 (Chicago: University of Chicago Press, 1957), p. 15. (Of course, this statement suffers, in the present historical context, from its unfortunate use of exclusive language. It also needs to be revised in such a way as to deliver it from the rather blatant individualism of its conception of "the theologian." Without denying that theology, to be challenging, must usually pass through the filter of an individual life, it needs to be recognized that theology is an undertaking of *the church*. It is for this reason that I most often speak here of "the theological community," awkward as such a phrase may be. Despite these limitations, however, Tillich's essentially humble characterization of "the theologian" is a highly instructive one—and as rare as it is instructive.)

21. What Tillich, in *The Courage to Be* (New Haven and London: Yale University Press, 1952), calls "the anxiety of guilt and condemnation."

of the faith which were tried and true. What the Christian community forfeits by adhering so steadfastly to its own established conventions, however, is precisely *communication*. Without communication there is no *gospel*, for gospel cannot be identified with doctrinal treasures hidden under the bushel of ecclesiastical rites and the in-language of professional churchmanship. Gospel means the Word proclaimed and heard—proclaimed in full awareness of what it has to engage, heard therefore as the living Word *(viva vox Dei)* and as good news.

With important exceptions, the Christian church throughout the ages has not distinguished itself by the appropriateness or good timing of its proclamation. It has been much more adept at *profession* than at *confession*.[22] Frequently—perhaps habitually—it has substituted *didachē* (teaching) for *euangellion* (gospel), *doctrina* for *theologia*. On account of its commitment to entrenched systems of belief, it has often announced reconciliation where judgment was called for, and exhortation to repentance where sheer acceptance and mercy would have been more fitting. It has comforted the comfortable and chastized the miserable, liberated the oppressors and laid upon the oppressed the additional spiritual burdens of duty and divine decree. It has leaped into Asia with "glad tidings" fashioned in the English countryside, and it has offered 16th-century doctrines of salvation for 20th-century sinners. Persuaded of the universal relevance of an evangel made in Europe, missioners both militant and gentle "persuaded" the native peoples of South and North America to adopt Christianity. With overwhelming regularity, the majority of the missioners manifested no concern whatsoever for the contexts of the indigenous peoples, not even bothering, often, to learn the rudiments of their languages. But *evangelism*, as distinct from indoctrination or the sheer imposition of religion, assumes on the part of the evangelist something at least approaching love, and on the part of the evangelized something approximating freedom of choice. "Where there is no participation there is no communication"—and must we not face the fact that a great deal of what the church militant has considered communication with the world has in reality been a very one-sided affair? Something more aptly designated, perhaps, "transmission"? Because of its position of power under the conditions of Constantinianism, the church did not really have to communicate with the world; it could simply announce, declaim, and legislate. It must be asked very seriously by those who reflect upon the Christian past today, and upon the impact of that past on continuing theological-

---

22. See the introduction, pp. 55-56 above.

ethical practice, whether the *gospel* in the strictest sense of the term has ever been more than a minority possibility and reality—the exception to the rule.

2.5. Context, Form, and Content. The distinction between a contextual theology and a theology which either *is*, or is readily employable *by*, ideology can be illustrated by the juxtaposition of two statements which come out of that period of awesome clarification in Western history to which again and again those who seek to comprehend our civilization have had to turn: Germany in the 1930s. At that time, the dean of the Berlin cathedral, Heinrich Grüber, founder of the so-called Grüberbüro (an organization which helped Jews and other threatened persons escape from the Nazis), said very simply: "The *gospel* in our time is that Jesus Christ was a Jew." The full impact of this statement can only be appreciated, however, if it is contrasted with a contemporary pronouncement: Hitler's so-called *Reichsbischof*, Ludwig Müller, sensing a certain questioning of his orthodoxy, coyly declared, "I can accept *all* the creeds."

A theology which does not help the church to discern, out of the great riches of its tradition, the *appropriate* word—"the Word from the Lord"—inevitably functions as an ideational construct within which Christians may find refuge from history, and which therefore lends itself to the support of the status quo, whether intentionally (as was certainly the case with the *Reichsbischof*) or by default. The statement of Grüber illustrates that it is precisely immersion in the context, including especially solidarity with the victims of society, that gives the theological community the prospect of such discernment.

To state this in more traditional terms: contextuality in theology means that the *form* of faith's self-understanding is always determined by the historical configuration in which the community of belief finds itself. It is this world which initiates the questions, the concerns, the frustrations and alternatives, the possibilities and impossibilities by which the *content* of the faith must be shaped and reshaped, and finally confessed. Conscious and thoughtful involvement of the disciple community in its cultural setting is thus the *conditio sine qua non* of its right appropriation of its theological discipline. It cannot be a mere spectator of the world's life, like the man at the window in Elie Wiesel's *The Town beyond the Wall*,[23] who watched as the Jews of his city were rounded up for deportation.

---

23. Elie Wiesel, *The Town beyond the Wall*, translated from *La Ville de la chance* (New York: Avon Books, 1967).

The church can become a theologically alive and obedient disciple community only as it permits its thinking to be receptive to and re-formed by the realities of its world.

The statement that the form of the faith is to be determined by the worldly context of the Christian community perhaps suggests that there exists a given content which is in some sense independent of the forms that it assumes historically. Such a suggestion, taken at face value, could lead back to the very assumption that we have been trying to dislodge in this analysis, namely, that there is some immaculate expression of the faith, preceding every concrete articulation of it, and that it is the church's task to protect and preserve this "pure gospel" in the midst of the historical flux. The declaration that theology is by definition contextual, however, precludes entertaining such a notion. For our argument implies that it is a condition of the theological task as such and from the outset of the church's pilgrimage through time that it occurs under the laws of time and place and is inevitably marked by the particularities thereof. I am in complete agreement with Gordon D. Kaufman when he writes, "Theology is human work: theology is done by men and women for human purposes and . . . serves human purposes and needs. . . ."[24] More than that, theology is always *theologia viatorum post lapsum.*[25] Even of the Scriptures this must be said—and it *has* been said now for more than a century, despite the fact that on this continent in particular most of what is claimed for the Bible by Christians seems impervious to this scholarship. God may be above the *fluxus,* but all of our statements about God are conditioned. They are conditioned not only by our historicity but also by our limited intelligence and our sinful inclination. Even if they were not conditioned by these creaturely factors, they would be conditioned by the God about whom they are made, who, being transcendent Person, does not permit description or definition but only *testimony* (the real meaning of the commandment against graven images).

There is then no eternal "text"—no *theologia in se* (ideal theology as distinct from actual theological work)—which it is our duty as Christians to interpret for our context, no abiding "content" that permits itself to be shaped, reshaped, and perhaps inevitably misshapen in response to the molds that time provides. There are only historical testimonies to a Presence, to events in which this Presence was experienced as being very

---

24. Gordon Kaufman, *Theology for a Nuclear Age* (Philadelphia: Westminster, 1985), p. 19.
25. A theology of pilgrims "after the fall"—a term frequently employed in the writings of post-Reformation Protestant scholastics.

near ("with us"), and to utterances which helped and still help to locate and illuminate the mystery of which this Presence is the center.

On the other hand, the rejection of theological absolutes which could form themselves into an eternally true body of doctrine does not mean that we are forthwith landed into a foundationless relativism. The insistence that any attack upon theological absolutes must imply the abandonment of theology to sheer relativism or capricious historicism is not only a non sequitur; it is usually a spurious argument meant to protect some reputed orthodoxy. Besides flying in the face of what Tillich called, with justification, "the Protestant principle,"[26] such an argument overlooks the fact that the most common situation both in faith and in life generally is neither one which can boast of the possession of absolute certitude nor one which is entirely without intimations of truth, but rather one in which the unknown factor (whether that refers to religious mystery or simply the moving edge of time, the mystery of future) is counterbalanced by certain aids which, while they are by no means flawless, at least serve to insulate and to guide. The "content" side of theology should be understood in this sense. While Christians cannot legitimately indulge in the empty boast of those who claim the possession of absolutes, neither are they wholly abandoned to the spirits and whims of the moment. They have inherited a tradition, a "common heritage" (Robert McAfee Brown). None of this heritage—not the Holy Scriptures themselves—can be assigned the status of the ultimate. To do so would be to usurp the sovereignty of God! On the other hand, neither is it a matter of pure relativity and subjectivism. The tradition is there, and it is there *pro nobis*. It cannot be ignored, set aside, or treated at will; or rather, if this or that faction is ready to treat it in such a manner, other influences within the *koinōnia* will see to it that such treatment is challenged. So long as the truth to which we wish to bear witness is bound up with a presence which, however hidden from human sight (*Deus absconditus*) reveals itself to faith within the flux (*Deus revelatus*), the testimony of those who have acknowledged and revered this presence throughout the centuries has to be taken with great seriousness. This of course applies in a special way to the original revelatory events, which though they do not immediately interpret themselves but depend upon a prophetic or spiritual event for their meaning ("Pentecost," in the Newer Testament's mode of understanding), nevertheless are inseparable from the external occurrences as such, and therefore bind us to the testimony of those nearest those occurrences, the so-called eyewitnesses.

---

26. Paul Tillich, *The Protestant Era*, trans. James Luther Adams (Chicago: The University of Chicago Press, 1948), pp. 161ff.

The Scriptures and their authority in theology must become a matter for closer examination presently. For the moment we may characterize the whole of our common heritage, including these earliest and most normative testimonies, by insisting that in itself and as such *it would drive us to the specifics of our own context.*

To elaborate: We may certainly—and gratefully—admit that within this common heritage there are recurrent themes, such as the consciousness of sin, the experience of forgiveness, the sense of purpose in a world that often seems purposeless, the joy of fellowship, the hope of the faithful for a society in which justice and peace prevail, and others. But these recurrent themes should not (and when considered in any depth cannot) be turned into a hard-and-fast set of ideas, "great facts," a perennial textbook of true doctrine, *vera theologia*. Indeed, any really careful study of the persons and movements throughout the Christian centuries in whom this common heritage was most profoundly articulated (those who in fact were largely responsible for creating it) will show that it is both a rich and a flexible heritage, one which *developed* and was not delivered whole, one which evolved quite obviously in response to emerging situations in church and society. Few if any of the greatest exponents of the Christian faith (those whose names immediately come to mind when we employ the word "tradition") would ever have desired that their thought should be treated by subsequent generations of Christians as if it were perennially valid. Most of them, we may confidently surmise, would have agreed with Tillich's statement in the epigraph of this chapter: "None of us is asked to speak to everybody in all places and in all periods." Irenaeus, Origen, Augustine, Anselm, Luther, Calvin, Kierkegaard, Schleiermacher—the very names of such persons tell us about the quite specific periods of history to which they belong, for they were all firmly rooted in their contexts.

Of course, the great thinkers of the premodern past were not *conscious* of the fact that they were being contextual. We should not expect them to have been conscious of this, for such consciousness belongs to the modern period, the period which discovered history—which discovered, that is, the impact of historical particularity upon the human perception of reality. Luther, the medieval man, did not possess this historical consciousness in our sense. He did not think of himself, therefore, as someone who was doing theology contextually. He simply believed that he was discovering God's "lively Word." Nevertheless, what made his theological work compelling was precisely the fact that, wittingly or unwittingly, he had entered profoundly enough into the problematic of his

87

age to be able (by grace!) to express the faith in a way that could truly address that problematic.

Moreover, in order to speak to their specific contexts, these shapers of the tradition were compelled to modify, and sometimes to reject out-right, the power of the theological conventions that *they* had inherited. Thus Augustine had eventually to let go of many of the Neoplatonic influences by which he had at first been enticed, which were powerfully present in his epoch, and which informed much of the Christian tradition to which he was heir. Aquinas, in turn, had to distance himself from significant aspects of the theology that had been dear to Augustine and the whole of the early Middle Ages. Luther found it necessary to rebel against the conventions of Scholasticism which, he believed, could not contain the word of the cross. Barth could only come to terms with his time and place as he let go (not without difficulty) of the liberal com-monplaces into which he had been indoctrinated by the memorable teach-ers of the 19th century, Wilhelm Herrmann and von Harnack and the others. And the process continues.

In short, if we turn to the most gifted thinkers of the Christian past for our understanding of what is involved in the doing of theology, this common heritage itself drives us towards contexual thinking. What we inherit as our "blessed tradition" is no fixed, ordered, and consistent deposit of doctrine, but an astonishingly expansive and variegated story— a story sufficiently rich and nuanced to function in very different times and places *with amazing consistency*! Only, the consistency is not to be located in what the tellers of this story said so much as it is in the effects that their quite different ways of enunciating the story had upon their hearers. What is most provocative about our common heritage in its highest and most decisive expressions, in other words, is that despite the diverse and sometimes even antithetical character of their articulations of the faith, a long-range review of the history of Christian thought leaves one with the definite impression that these many witnesses have been pointing towards a single Truth. But since it is a *living* Truth, it must be testified to in a great many *differing* ways, and it can never be captured in any of them or in all of them together.

The message that we receive from this Christian past is therefore not, "Repeat what we have said!" but rather, "Do what we have done!" That is, with feet firmly planted in our own *hic et nunc*, we in our turn should look and listen for this "elusive"[27] but self-giving presence, this

---

27. I have in mind Samuel Terrien's moving work, *The Elusive Presence: Toward a New Biblical Theology* (New York: Harper and Row, 1978), and especially the concluding paragraphs: "In biblical

truth which our progenitors glimpsed but which, like the collectors of manna in the wilderness, they could not store up for future consumption. The *form* that eternal truth must assume is dependent upon the specifics of historical time. The Word is forever seeking hearers—now! "*Today* if you will hear my voice . . .!" Hence, theology is an always-unfinished undertaking of the disciple community. There will never be a time when the church can cease *thinking*, and this thinking will have to manifest the trait of originality as long as the Christian movement lasts and even if it accumulates, in the process, 10 times the volume of tradition that it now acknowledges.

2.6. Theology as the Meeting of Stories. We may expand our understanding of the meaning of contextuality in Christian theology through the deployment of this metaphor of story. Story is in fact more than a metaphor in our time; it has become the key concept of a whole methodology. That this has occurred is directly related to our present discussion; for it is precisely because so much of the conventional language of theology too readily suggests a body of timeless information that some Christian thinkers and communicators in our period have turned (or perhaps *re*turned) to the language of narration. It is a useful language, and natural to a faith rooted in the Scriptures of the two testaments. The wonder is that Christian theology could so soon and so thoroughly have devolved into conceptual and preceptive expressions which have little in common with either the historical narratives of the Older Testament and parts of the Newer, or the parabolic approach favored by the rabbi Jesus.[28]

---

faith, human beings discern that presence is a surging which soon vanishes and leaves in its disappearance an absence that has been overcome. It is neither absolute nor eternal but elusive and fragile, even and especially when human beings seek to prolong it in the form of cultus. The collective act of worship seems to be both the indispensable vehicle of presence and its destroyer. Presence dilutes itself into its own illusion whenever it is confused with a spatial or temporal location. When presence is "guaranteed" to human senses or reason, it is no longer real presence. The proprietary sight of the glory destroys the vision. . . .

". . . In biblical faith, presence eludes but does not delude. The hearing of the name, which is obedience to the will and the decision to live now for an eternal future, becomes the proleptic vision of the glory.

"Presence is articulated in the Word, but the Word is heard only by those who recognize the promise and already live by its fulfillment. In this sense, Torah is Logos made flesh" (pp. 476-477).

28. I am not, however, among those who would advocate dispensing with the conceptual approach in favor of narrative. I have no doubt that concept without story ends in forms of propositionalism which have little in common with the tradition of Jerusalem; but I also fear that a theology which attempts to rely primarily on story produces fragmentation both of belief and of the community of belief. Narrative theology is essential if we are to escape from the confines of doctrinalism, for it preserves the sense of livingness and mystery without which both God and the world become "too small" (P. Watson). Yet story needs commentary—as the rabbinic tradition knows very well—if it

What we encounter in the tradition of Jerusalem, especially but not exclusively in the Scriptures themselves, does not resemble a collection of theorums, dogmas, principles, truths, or philosophic arguments so much as it resembles drama, saga, narrative, story. Let us call it "God's Story of the World."[29] Like all stories, it has a beginning (a promising one) and an ending (a happy ending, as J. R. R. Tolkien rightly insists).[30] But the way from the promising beginning to the happy ending—the consummation!—is very complicated, and not simply a foregone conclusion. Presumption is thus constantly ruled out: "Therefore let any one who thinks that he stands take heed lest he fall" (1 Cor. 10:12).

The unpredictability of the course that God's story will follow is largely due to the fact that, in the meantime, another storyteller is at work. Humanity is telling its own story, improvising scenarios, creating roles for itself—for all the other creatures, too, and of course for God! The roles that humanity creates are—in the view of these witnesses to God's story—almost always *not* the roles intended for it. Humanity does not have any real aptitude for the parts that it writes for itself. Yet it seems to be perfectly at liberty to experiment very widely.

There are, of course, certain stock roles, familiar also to Athens and to most other human traditions. Two such standard roles are very common, though they are never quite the same from one moment to another (remember: we are dealing here with a *linear, not a cyclical* view of history). Sometimes humanity tells a very heroic story about itself: Prometheus-like, the human race fancies itself greater than its gods—a feat not terribly difficult, since the roles it creates for its divinities are usually underwritten! The literature of the 19th century is full of that particular story.

---

is to avoid falling into a thousand mythic pieces, each inviting a plethora of interpretations, thus opening the door to something far worse than the denominationalism that plagues doctrinally divided Christendom.

There is no reason why concept and story cannot live together. They do in the Bible. The tradition of Jerusalem (unlike Athens) gives story/history a certain priority. This is because Jerusalem understands and loves the livingness of God and the creation, and celebrates the uniqueness of the particular. But even to do this the biblical faith must also resort to concepts and precepts. The Epistles of Paul must always be secondary to the Gospels; yet the Epistles illuminate the meaning of the Gospels. One would not wish to give the musicologists priority over the Mozart concertos they so laboriously analyze! Yet musicology *can* help us to hear Mozart better. So it is with theological concepts and ethical precepts: they *can* enable us to hear more "hearingly" the Story that Christians are, in turn, to tell.

29. In a helpful chapter in his *Truthfulness and Tragedy: Further Reflections in Christian Ethics* (Notre Dame and London: University of Notre Dame Press, 1978), pp. 71ff., Stanley Hauerwas writes: "It is obvious that whatever else it is the message that appears central to the Christian life is in the form of a story. . . . This does not mean that all theology must itself assume the form of narrative, but rather whatever form theological reflection may take, one of its primary tasks is reminding us of a story." See also Sallie McFague Teselle, *Speaking in Parables: A Study in Metaphor and Theology* (Philadelphia: Fortress, 1975).

30. "On Fairy Stories," in *The Tolkien Reader* (New York: Ballantine Books, 1966), pp. 3ff.

At other times, the race's corporate autobiography is dismal—a genuine pathos: Man as Willy Loman. Low Man.[31] There are, however, many variations on these and other themes, and the combinations are never the same, never quite the same. History does not repeat itself, even though similarities and patterns may certainly be observed. Sin may be as old as Eden, but it appears in ever new guises. The human creature is a consummate storyteller, a veritable Scheherazade! In fact, says a great Jewish storyteller of our time, "God created man because he likes stories."[32]

Theology lives *between* the stories—God's story of the world, and humanity's ever-changing account of itself and all things. *Theology is what happens when the two stories meet.*

It is of course the particular vocation of the disciple community to keep listening especially for *God's* story. That is the only reason for distinguishing it from any other community, any other reflective human posture. But contrary to those who think that this community has direct and unmediated access to the divine account of reality, we must insist (on biblical grounds) that it is literally impossible to hear God's story *alone*. The reason is elementary: God's story is itself always interacting with, responding to the human story! Even God, in the *Hebraic*-Christian understanding of God, must wait to find out what the strange creature who is the articulate center of creation will do, what new tale the creature will circulate about itself, its environment, its Creator.

Not that the biblical God lacks *preconceptions*! Certainly, like any imaginative artist, any good parent, the God of the Scriptures has designs for what God brings into being. But according to Jerusalem God will not *impose* God's *oikonomia* (economy) upon the creation. God will wait, react, respond. God will take up into the divine *boulē* ("plan"—cf., e.g., Acts 2:23) the (usually frustrating) acts, deeds, words, and thoughts of the creature, causing them, despite their potentiality for permanent evil, to serve the Creator's and therefore also the creation's ultimate good.

The Joseph narrative of Genesis could be regarded as paradigmatic for the *whole* story which this tradition wishes to preserve. With decidedly malevolent intent, the brothers sell their younger, favored sibling into

---

31. Perhaps the most instructive exercise for anyone wishing to compare 19th- and 20th-century images of the human is to read, in succession, R. M. Ballantyne's *The Coral Island* (London: J. M. Dent, 1949), and William Golding's *The Lord of the Flies* (Harmondsworth: Penguin Books, in association with Faber & Faber, 1954). Golding's novel, which ends with a serviceman's expression of astonishment that "English schoolboys" could prove such uncivilized beings, is the considered response of a sensitive 20th-century artist to the highly positive conception of humanity and society offered in *The Coral Island*, which was first published in 1825 and was read by every English (and colonial) schoolboy.

32. Elie Wiesel, *The Gates of the Forest* (New York: Avon Books, 1969).

slavery. Nothing prevents their doing this. It is their act, their decision. Yet it is finally—and therefore, says faith, also in some mysterious way originally—God's determination; for it becomes God's means of preserving the people of the covenant. "As for you, you meant evil against me; but God meant it for good, to bring it about that many people should be kept alive. . . ," Joseph tells his brothers at the end of the narrative (Gen. 50:20).

God's story of the world, then, is no fixed drama in which all the parts have been written and from which there can be no deviation,[33] but an ongoing tale, the comprehension of which makes it mandatory for those who try to follow it to sustain an equally active attempt to comprehend the *human* story. Unless they know something of the latter, in all the uniqueness of the here-and-now, the disciples will not understand God's story (which may be part of the reason why the *original* disciples were perplexed by Jesus' teaching and in particular by his determination to go the way of the cross.) For, contrary to certain prosaic interpretations which have their spiritual origins elsewhere than in Jerusalem, God does not have the same "old, old story" to tell, regardless of "the context." God's word to Solomon in all his pomp is not simply a rephrasing of God's word to sick, defeated Saul. The postexilic prophets have a message significantly different both in detail and in tone from those who predicted Israel's captivity. Jesus had something quite different to say to John the beloved disciple from what he had to say to the impulsive and demanding Peter (John 21:20f.). The author of the Apocalypse has conspicuously variant messages from "the Spirit" to the churches addressed in chapters 2 and 3. One could go on.

Similarly, the disciple community must always struggle to discern an appropriate testimony to God's story. A theology which continues addressing itself to 19th-century industrial Prometheanism long after Western humanity has cast itself more characteristically in the role of Willy Loman is not only anachronistic; it isn't theology! A theology which offers tried and true remedies for the human anxiety of guilt and condemnation when the regnant anxiety is the anxiety of meaninglessness and despair[34] is no theology; it is probably ideology. God is not *so* "dead,"

---

33. It was the error of the supralapsarians that they confused the divine determination of the world with philosophic determinism; and this error can be correlated quite precisely with the substitution of conceptual for narrative or dramatic patterns of thought. It is one thing to regard the world from the perspective of an impersonal Fate which programs history in advance; it is something else to think of history as the scene of a (redemptive) drama in which the Redeemer incorporates into the redemptive "plan" the very evils ("the wrath," Ps. 76:10) from which creation must be redeemed.

34. See Paul Tillich, *The Courage to Be*.

surely, as to have pronounced the final word on the subject of the meaning of Christ's crucifixion with the publication of Anselm's *Cur Deus Homo?* or Calvin's *Institutes of the Christian Religion*—despite the continuing dominance of the substitutionary theory of the atonement. So long as the *human* story goes on, the divine story of the world will never be wholly . . . finished.[35]

3. Why Theology Is Contextual

We have said that Christian theology is contextual by definition, and we have described in some measure *what* that means. We must now attempt to say *why* this theology is contextual, that is: what is the rationale of theological contextuality? Three fundamental reasons can be adduced: (1) Theology is a *human* enterprise, (2) theology attempts to speak of the *living* God and of God's relation to a *dynamic* creation, and (3) theology exists for the sake of the church's *confession*. The following three sub-sections will explore these hypotheses.

3.1. A Human Enterprise. No human undertaking ever occurs in a cultural vacuum, a historical no-man's-land. Theological thinking shares this limitation with every other attempt of human beings to understand and describe reality. It cannot possess final truth, it may only encounter truth in time, under the conditions of place.

Unlike many religious and other quests for understanding, however, Christian theology, when it is true to its own best traditions, does not experience this simply as limitation. For while Christian faith includes the *longing* for ultimacy of comprehension ("sight") and the completion of the journey ("sabbath rest"), it contains at the same time the realization that our knowledge is not the wisdom of those who have arrived and who "see" (Heb. 11:1), but of faith. If we think sometimes that we see, it is, as Paul said, "through a glass darkly" (1 Cor. 13:12, KJV).

Nor may the disciple community take its rest in yesterday's visions, brilliant as some of them are. The Way goes on, and along this way the truth of God can be apprehended only as one apprehends "a bird in flight" (Barth).[36] Christian theology is necessarily *theologia viatorum* (theology

---

35. Discussion of this theme, intentionally suggestive of our Lord's last "word from the cross," will be continued later in this chapter under the subhead, "God Lives, Life Goes On," §3.2.

36. "The same holds for Christ as it does for a bird in full flight. No picture will convey that flight, except a moving picture. Likewise in theology: you will understand nothing if you try to lay hold of a position, to apply your mind to an assertion. You must follow the positions, follow the assertions and view the whole, not as if it were a system, but as a history. And the Christians are members of the cast of that history. And their small stories exist only as referring to that great history" (Karl Barth, *The Faith of the Church: A Commentary on the Apostle's Creed according to Calvin's Catechism*, trans. Gabriel Vahanian [New York: Meridian Books, 1958], p. 56).

done while "on the move").[37] Ourselves in motion, we perceive now and then, here and there, the traces of a God who moves. Perhaps like Moses we are permitted to see so much as "the back side of God" (Exod. 33:23). The more we are given such glimpses, the more we yearn for fullness of understanding: that we should know as we are known; that we should see "face to face"—the experience to which the medieval theologians gave the nomenclature, the "beatific vision"; that hearing, which is a wondrous but ephemeral sense, might be replaced by sight, thinking by knowing. Yet this longing for finality and the eternal does not wholly dominate our spirits, making us forever discontented with the present. What we do grasp in faith is . . . enough. Sometimes, it is even too much—more than human thought can rightly absorb. On occasion it is even so overpowering as to raise the human intellect to heights of unaccustomed *ex stasis*. Besides, as C. S. Lewis beautifully expressed it, how could we expect to see God face to face "til *we* have faces."[38]

This being the case, Christian theology must entertain the deepest suspicions of any account of reality which underestimates or defies the dimensions of time and space and offers finality. Of *any* account in which this occurs will a vigilant theology be distrustful, whether such an account emanates from the laboratories of the natural scientists, the studies of political theoreticians, or the souls of visionaries. Theology will find in such accounts the age-old Babel-attempt of proud, frightened *Homo sapiens* to capture and domesticate absolutes which, it supposes, can lift it above the ambiguities and particularies of times and seasons. In the name of the one, untamable Absolute, the disciple community knows that it must warn susceptible humanity against putting its trust in domesticated absolutes of any sort.

But in particular it will be vigilant with respect to religious absolutes. Its special critical attention (which is first of all *self*-critical) is to be on the alert against the thirst for absolutes within the church. For the temptation to finality is always stronger in religious communities than anywhere else. There, the sense of proximity to the ultimate proves to be very heady stuff! As the biography of every great spiritual leader and thinker in the history of the church amply illustrates, the propensity to turn the inspired and timely visions of endowed persons into timeless truth is endemic with Christians. It is our Midas touch! In every case it

---

37. Karl Barth, *The Word of God and the Word of Man*, trans. Douglas Horton (New York: Harper, 1957), p. 99; *Church Dogmatics*, vol. II/1, trans. T. H. L. Parker et al. (New York: Charles Scribner's Sons, 1957), p. 209.
38. C. S. Lewis, *Til We Have Faces* (New York: Time-Life Books, 1956).

can be shown that the gifted ones themselves were cognizant of the *conditioned* character of their insights: *that* knowledge was the cornerstone of their wisdom. Karl Barth, as is well known, went to exceptional lengths to warn his hearers of this reality. "From the very beginning of my theological work," he said on the occasion of his 80th birthday celebrations, "I have been very conscious of its relativity."[39] All the same, his warnings have not prevented the emergence of a Barthianism, many of whose advocates seem ready to believe that Karl Barth spoke not only for Western European Protestantism in a critical hour, but for universal Christianity and forever. All this must surely be accounted for in the psychological terms to which we have already made reference: the comfort of absolutes.[40]

For finite human beings there can be no possession of infinite truth. There can only be attempts, more or less faithful, more or less compelling, to describe the mystery of God and of the world as faith perceives this mystery here and now.

> Truth, divine truth, then is not the conformity of the mind to a divine message uttered ages ago, but the discernment of present evil judged by this message and the discovery of the redemptive movement in history promised by this message. The norm of theological truth, then is not drawn from an analogy with classical philosophy; it is drawn rather from its role in the ongoing process of world-building.[41]

This is the condition under which theology labors, a condition which it shares in one way and another with every other discipline. That this condition can nevertheless be experienced as a *gracious* limitation is due

---

39. Karl Barth, *Fragments Grave and Gay*, ed. Martin Rumscheidt, trans. Eric Mosbacher (London and Glasgow: Collins, 1971), p. 112.

Perhaps the most famous—certainly the most puckish!—of all of Barth's attempts to discourage "Barthianism" is his remark about the laughter of angels, originally quoted in an article by Johannes A. Lombard in *Antwort* (Zollikon-Zürich: Evangelischer Verlag, 1956), p. 895, and quoted by Robert McAfee Brown in his "Introduction" to Georges Casalis's *Portrait of Karl Barth* (Garden City, N.Y.: Doubleday, 1964), p. xiii: "The angels laugh at old Karl. They laugh at him because he tries to grasp the truth about God in a book of Dogmatics. They laugh at the fact that volume follows volume and each is thicker than the previous one. As they laugh, they say to one another, 'Look! Here he comes now with his little pushcart full of volumes of the *Dogmatics*!'

"And they laugh about the men who write so much about Karl Barth instead of writing about the things he is trying to write about. Truly, the angels laugh."

40. See H. A. Williams, "Psychological Objections," in *Objections to Christian Belief* (London: Constable, 1963), pp. 35ff.

41. Gregory Baum, in *Theology in the Americas*, ed. S. Torres and J. Eagleson (Maryknoll, N.Y.: Orbis, 1976), p. 404. The statement is from Baum's review of the Detroit meetings in *The Ecumenist*, September-October 1975.

to the fact that the "object" of the theological inquiry is a living God whose presence is finally more satisfying than intellectual or spiritual certitude. The implications of this statement will become the primary subject matter of the subsequent observation. But first we must concentrate briefly on an aspect of the present observation which is frequently over-looked, namely, what occurs when the human and finite, the time-and-place-bound character of the theological enterprise, is not sufficiently recognized.

As we have already noted in passing, the statement that theology is contextual can be understood in two senses: first, that it is a conscious attempt to engage the historical moment from the side of faith; second, it is unconsciously reflective of a given situation, even when it is offered and/or received as though it were contextually neutral. It is the latter sense that concerns us now.

Theology is contextual, we have said, because it is a human enter-prise, and human beings live in contexts and mirror their contexts in all that they do. It can be observed about the *Institutes of the Christian Religion,* for example, that John Calvin spoke out of the socioeconomic and general cultural milieu of a free city in Western Europe during the turbulent 16th century. Internal evidence from the *Institutes* would verify this, even if we had no other historical data to prove it. Another instance: Anselm's *Cur Deus Homo?* a work, as we have noted above, which is still treated by many Western Christians as if it contained a timeless and irreplaceable definition of the meaning of the atonement, quite clearly reflects the conditions of a feudal society—to the extent that the meaning Anselm himself intended for his statement about Christ's salvific work is virtually hidden from persons who know little or nothing of the cultural and economic conditions under which the work was written.[42] Many sim-ilar examples of the same phenomenon might be cited. The question raised by all of them, however, would be the same: What problems are created for a disciple community—say, the Protestant church in the United States today—when its primary corporate principles, symbols, metaphors, and concepts for the perception of truth are in a large part determined by powerful traditions predating the modern era?

Let us first of all be quite clear that whatever problems we shall

---

42. As Roland Bainton points out, "Anselm's views were based on the feudal view of sin, which rated its magnitude in terms of the rank of the person against whom it was committed. Since God is infinite in his greatness, a sin against him is infinite. Such a sin requires infinite satisfaction, or atonement. . ." (*Christendom: A Short History of Christianity and Its Impact on Western Civilization* [New York: Harper & Row, 1966], vol. 1, p. 197).

identify in response to that question are not to be laid at the doorstep of the makers of these traditions. It is certainly interesting, always, to ask about the extent to which theologians like Calvin and Anselm were able to anticipate the misuse of their ideas; but, short of a detailed historical analysis of the matter, we may assume for our present purposes that such authors were responding as best they could to the problems and possibilities of their own contexts. Let us be clear, further, that the concern for contexualization gives no one the license to treat such authors and the traditions to which they contributed in a cavalier manner. We have still to learn from them, and we may and can learn much from them—*provided* that we first learn that it was not their vocation to have done our theological work for us.

Unfortunately, that lesson has seemed a very hard one for Christians to learn—even Christians who for more than a hundred years now have been equipped by scholarship of every variety to consider all such work historically. The longing for finality being what it is, Calvin, Anselm, and countless other contributors to the theological tradition are made to speak for "the gospel" and "the human situation" universally. Under these conditions they *become* problematic—potentially even demonic— because they then make possible *a flight from our own present moment.* That is, the cumulative impact of their authority not only encourages us to *neglect* the struggle to understand our own situation, but offers us implicit and ready-made cultural analyses which we substitute for original research and reflection about our own actual situation.[43] "Our" theology then becomes the perpetuation, long beyond its time, of a worldview substantially or even radically different from the world of our daily experience. Its questions are different; its fears are different; its hopes are different. Not only are the concrete ethical issues of that premodern *Weltanschauung* vastly altered (think of medical ethics, sexual typologies, the "just war" concept), but there are monumental differences at the deepest levels of the corporate psyche. The example of anxiety-types has already been cited: Anselm undoubtedly spoke to an age whose primary anxiety was that of guilt and the fear of eternal punishment. To this society, the

---

43. For this reason I must express a certain uneasiness about David Tracy's definition of "Systematic Theology" as the theologian's "reinterpretation of her or his tradition for the present situation," and more particularly of his linking this "primarily hermeneutical" work with "fidelity to some classic tradition proper to their church relationship" (David Tracy and John B. Cobb Jr., *Talking about God: Doing Theology in the Context of Modern Pluralism* [New York: Seabury, 1983] pp. 1ff.). While agreeing that theology is always responsible for its handling of the tradition, I find that Tracy's statement places too great an emphasis upon "fidelity"; he seems unaware of the prospect that such fidelity may, under the conditions of historical existence and within religious communities which value stability, function in a repressive manner.

message of his work on the atonement announces the possibility and reality of forgiveness through the sacrifice of the one innocent man. Undoubtedly, guilt and fear are still aspects of contemporary life in North America, for they seem to belong to the human condition; but they are certainly not our primary anxiety. None of the "signs of the times," whether our art, our social sciences, or our popular pastimes, betrays a people consumed by their guilt before God and the prospect of eternal damnation. Everything points to a different anxiety-type and, however it may be terminologically designated, it is certainly closer to what Tillich called "the anxiety of meaninglessness and despair" than to existential guilt before the eternal.[44] We are not so much afraid that we do not measure up to a transcendent canon of human righteousness as that there are no transcendent standards of goodness, beauty, or truth beyond our own lingering desire that such standards might exist.

Now, when the church proclaims an Anselmic type of gospel of substitutionary forgiveness (still the *dominant* atonement theology of popular religion on this continent), it may seem to the postreligious mentality of the secular to be innocently anachronistic; but it is in fact far from innocent. It is contributing very significantly to a process of social repression which is probably the most dangerous dimension of North American life. Repression, as we shall argue more extensively later, is perennial in human nature and human societies, and a degree of repression is necessary to life. One cannot live in constant awareness of all that threatens and negates life. But the repressive instinct must be balanced by a courage to face the realities that are there, and in fact the only authentic social function of religious faith is to contribute what it can to the development of that courage. A religious faith whose primary gift to society is to aid and abet the process of blurring reality always does a disservice to the human project; and if this disservice is practiced within a society whose psychic need to ignore and escape reality is very great, perhaps verging on the pathological, then it is more than mere disservice, it is blasphemy. God is a God of Truth—"I am the Truth," declared Jesus. When the church becomes a "zone of untruth" (Charles Davis), therefore, it blasphemes its Lord. There is an almost palpable connection in our time between the preference of popular Christianity in North America for outmoded and anachronistic forms of the Christian religion and the "psychic numbing"—i.e., the advanced form of sociopsychic repression—that

---

44. In *The Courage to Be*, pp. 46ff.

characterizes our continent's response to the great social problems of the day, particularly nuclearism.[45]

Noncontextuality in theology, then, by which I mean the willed or unwilled neglect of the "circumstances" (Gustafson) in which the disciple community finds itself, is no mere academic peccadillo; it is the mortal sin of the disciple community. For it not only helps to create a sanctuary from the real world, the world *God* loves, but it opens the doors to all kinds of nefarious forces which have their own bleak designs on the world. The recent history of Christianity in the Western hemisphere illustrates this with appalling clarity. It is not possible to walk in a Russian cathedral (the Kremlin cathedrals, for example) without realizing that a religion so singularly devoted to the Holy Eternal would have to be attacked one day by a worldliness in which the dimensions of holiness and eternality might well be suppressed—and suppressed ruthlessly (as occurred under the former seminarian, Joseph Stalin). The perpetuation of pseudo-Lutheran devotion to the theology of justification by grace served—as Dietrich Bonhoeffer so poignantly demonstrated in *The Cost of Discipleship*[46]— not only to raise up a people which neglected the radical *imperative* of the gospel, but created a vacuum in the realm of public life which could then be filled by the most virile of recent tyrannies. When the church permits its theology to transcend time and place—that is, *when it substitutes past time and place for the present*—it is always contributing to evil, and sometimes to spectacular evil. What may seem to be preoccupation with the Eternal thus frequently turns out to be the evasion of the Eternal-in-Time. According to the tradition of Jerusalem, time, if not exactly the only dwelling place of the Eternal, is nevertheless the only place where *we* can meet the Eternal One. "Behold, the tabernacle of God is with humanity" (Rev. 21:3). But with this comment we are already on the way to the second reason why Christian theology must be contextual.

3.2. God Lives, Life Goes On!   It would be a mistake to suppose that the *primary* reason for contextuality in theology is that it is a human enterprise and human wisdom is necessarily finite. True—and deceptively obvious—as this may be, by itself it would constitute a mainly negative rationale for contextuality. The primacy of the *positive* basis for contextuality is evidenced by the fact that we could not even think about finitude

45. See Robert Jay Lifton and Richard Falk, *Indefensible Weapons: The Political and Psychological Case against Nuclearism* (Toronto: Canadian Broadcasting Corporation, 1982), pp. 103f.

46. Dietrich Bonhoeffer, *The Cost of Discipleship* (London: SCM, 1948).

as limitation without recognizing that, given the incarnational core of its subject matter, the limit that Christian theology perforce encounters as a human discipline is actually a *gracious* limit. It is gracious, and can be experienced as such, because the Eternal One of our Judeo-Christian tradition is *self*-limiting: God limits God's own self, for our sake, becoming accessible to us *within* the parameters of our creatureliness. In the language of the Newer Testament, the God who is the focus of our thinking as a disciple community of Jesus Christ is "Emmanuel, God with us" (Matt. 1:23). If, as classical texts of the discipline regularly inform us, the "study of God" (*Theou-logos*) is what theology is all about, then so far as it intends to be the study of the God who is Emmanuel, it has to be as well the study of "us"! For we—finite human creatures— are those *with* whom this God chooses to "tabernacle."

But here we must avoid at all costs the doctrinal habit of embracing formulas without concreteness. Many Christian theologians have made passionate protestations concerning God's identification with the creature, yet they have missed the point of this incarnational thrust of the whole biblical picture of God *as it ought to inform our theological method*. The reason is that they turn the "us" of the Emmanuel formula into an abstraction: humanity, creation, the world, the universe. . . . The Emmanuel formula, however, together with the Hebraic theological-historical consciousness that lies behind it, wants to insist that what is implied here is precisely *not* a generalization but a radical particularization of God's gracious *Mitsein* (being with). God does not seek covenant fellowship with a prototype or an amalgam or a cloned humanity, but with "us"— with this person and that one, Jeremiah, Peter, Mary; with this people and that one, Judah, Corinth, Johannesburg, the German Democratic Republic, America. Turning the "us" of the Emmanuel-formula into an abstraction is like identifying the neighbor of Jesus' love-commandment along such universal lines that (very conveniently) it no longer applies concretely to any human being whom we may happen to live with or to meet, especially not those *conspicuously* particular human beings who are in need, or are perceived by us as enemy.

So soon as one claims to be engaged in describing the God who is "with us," one makes oneself responsible for *contextual* theological reflection. God-with-us means: there can be no God-talk which is not at the same time the most explicit sort of us-talk. While that *may* lead to theological parochialism, the avoidance of such a danger in favor of the kind of universalism which functions the same way in bad theology as abstract neighbor-discourse functions in bad ethics hardly constitutes a viable alternative. About the dangers of contextuality in theology we shall have something to say presently. There is risk in *every* theological posture, for theology always "walks close to blasphemy" (Ursula Niebuhr). But the reduction of theology to abstract universalism in order to avoid seeming overly particularistic is itself, surely, a far greater danger to the gospel of the incarnation and crucifixion of the Word than anything erring on the side of specificity. For such abstraction robs God of God's real involvement in the life of the world. In other words, it violates the first principle of the Judeo-Christian conception of deity, namely, that *God lives*. God's very *being* in the tradition of Jerusalem is a dynamic going-forth and being-with: "I shall be *your* God. . . !"

God lives; and if God's living means God's loving, answering, acting, responding, judging, ruling, suffering, redeeming, and if it means all of this in relation to a creation and to creatures which itself and themselves live and move and change, then the disciple community can and should rejoice when it finds that its reflections *mirror* this ongoingness. The condition written over all theology is that it must not only read while it runs, but must read that which itself is in motion. This can be experienced by belief, however, not as a frustrating and lamentable barrier to understanding, but rather as the first principle of genuine comprehension. The only legitimate cause for great theological anxiety in the disciple community is (or should be) when it finds that its descriptions of God and God's world do not themselves participate in the *movement* that belongs to their subject matter, but are static, repetitious, and predictable, as if they related the tale of a history long since past, a story already brought to an end.

The story with which the disciple community has to do is (as we concluded in the previous section) by no means finished. As the writers of the Newer Testament's Acts and Epistles knew, the gospel is our story too, and the story of generations yet unborn. It is true (and here Christians and Jews do present a different witness)[47] that this story contains at its center what Christian belief regards as its effective *denouement*. Already in the midst of historical confusion and incompleteness, the End (*eschatos*) is introduced—and, as we have already affirmed (with Tolkien), it is "a happy ending." *Faith clings to the hope of the happy ending that it remembers*. "In hope against hope" (Romans 4), the faith of the disciple community enters into deadly combat with the despair of the world, the Weltschmertz which arises within itself as it contemplates the almost

---

47. See Pinchas Lapide, *The Resurrection of Jesus: A Jewish Perspective*, trans. Wilhelm C. Linss (Minneapolis: Augsburg, 1983).

infinite constellations of evil, sin, and death which unveil themselves with the swift passage of days and nights. But faith dares not turn this *confidence* (*con fide*) in God's capacity for effecting the proleptic happy ending into a rationale for religious certitude and dogmatic finality. The message of Easter may indeed be symbolized in that final word of the Christ from his cross: "It is finished." But *what* is finished? Not, surely, the continuing story of the God who loves and the object of that love— this narration which like its prototype the Hebrew Bible is so full of nuance, so variegated in its turnings and details. It would be no accomplishment of the God depicted in these Scriptures to have brought all that to an effective end, so that nothing more could be said but only an endless repetition of the "old, old story." However we may wish to have it otherwise, what shines through the Older Testament's convolutions and meanderings is God's delight in the *living* of God's creatures, in their presence and their unfolding. Surely it is a victory of Marcionism in the church when the Newer Testament is made to suppress that ongoingness in favor of a theoretical finality that permits no novelty, no surprises. Surely the burden of the Newer Testament's witness is not that the song has ended, that the last great chapter has been written, but rather that an obstacle to the *continuation* of the epic tale of creation has been removed! The purpose of the End that is introduced already *in medias res* is that the story might really "go on," that *through* that end-event a beginning might be made in which "all things" could be "made new" (Revelation 21). What is "finished" in and with the cross is not the story as such, but the turning point without which the story could *not* "go on." What is finished is that liberating deed which makes new beginnings possible: a beginning beyond the "impasse" (Bellah) to which human alienation led and leads the world; a beginning through and beyond our real and deserved endings; a beginning at the edge of the Red Sea, with certain death behind and unknown depths ahead. The message of Easter is not that the tale has ended, so that the people of God, minstrellike, could only sing of what once occurred and pronounce upon its eternal import. The message of Easter is that there is this "openness to the future" (Moltmann), this "beginning again" (Wiesel). It is a beginning, certainly, which contains within itself a predisposition towards the kind of *ultimate* ending about which the disciple community can use doxological terms like "fulfillment," "consummation," "kingdom." Yet it is always a beginning that is new, unpredictable, a risk.

There is no cause for presumption (see 1 Cor. 9:24—10:13): the disciple community must be ready for surprises, the greatest of which (if we take seriously Matthew 25 and similar statements about the kingdom) may be precisely the *sort* of fulfillment God intends. Yet the disciples are not paralyzed by anxiety over the future; they may really "go on" (Matt. 6:34). Expectantly, without presumption but also without debilitating caution, we may proceed: past the terrors of our outward and our inward states; past wars and rumors of wars; past the accusations of others and of our own hearts (1 John 3:19); past the fears of youth and the resentments of approaching age—past death itself. Proceed!—this is the permission and the command of the living God. Faith means the courage to accept this invitation and imperative.[48]

If we have had to anticipate the christological section of this study in our attempt to explain the why of theological contextuality, this is entirely by design. It is in fact mandatory, and for two reasons: First, because the method of theology is determined by its subject matter; and that means that the core of the Christian message must be recognized already in our methodological discussions. Second, because precisely this subject matter, in what I must regard as a monumental misconstruction of it, has served the purposes of a religious mentality which desires finality and fears the very openness which the Easter message intends.

It is in particular the *Christian* side of the Judeo-Christian tradition which has so consistently transgressed the livingness of the deity and the ongoingness of the creation; and the doctrinal device by means of which this has been achieved is precisely a Christology in which everything is "finished." Judaic faith has also suffered, sometimes, from the natural human longing for finality. Jesus struggled against just that propensity in some of his Jewish opponents, who clung to the old, manageable, and

---

48. The language employed in the foregoing—and particularly the street metaphor "going on"— is a deliberate anticipation of the attempt which must be made in the christological section of this study to speak to *contemporary* forms of human anxiety and alienation. In distinction from our 19th-century forebears, whose attitude towards life and the future enabled them to lace their rhetoric with terms like "challenge" and "adventure" and to name little towns on the western frontier of this great continent "Onward" and "Success" and the like, late 20th-century Homo sapiens asks whether it is possible to . . . "go on." Samuel Beckett's concluding lines in *The Unnamable* capture the mood of our epoch with characteristic sensitivity:

"You must go on, I can't go on, you must go on, I'll go on, you must say the words, as long as there are any, until they find me, until they say me, strange pain, strange sin, you must go on, perhaps it's done already, perhaps they have said me already, perhaps they have carried me to the threshold of my story, before the door that opens on my story, that would surprise me, if it opens, it will be I, it will be the silence, where I am, I don't know, I'll never know, in the silence you don't know, you must go on, I can't go on, I'll go on" (*Three Novels by Samuel Beckett* [New York: Grove Press, 1955], p. 414). It is this form of human experience with which, in the First World at least, Christian theology today must wrestle. The gospel must be expressed in such a way as to speak to this sense of a psychic impasse, which today is as fully public as it is private.

reputedly conclusive interpretations of the Law over against his "but I say unto you" (Matthew 5). Ultimately, however, the Christians were far more successful than the Jews in containing their "new wine" in "old wineskins" (Matt. 9:17, par.). Ironically, they did this by making the Christ event itself the foundational basis of ultimacy of truth. Judaic faith did not have (what Christianity could *seem* to have) a revelatory core event whose soteriological conclusiveness could lend itself to closed systems of belief. Thus in Judaism still today one can often discern the kind of intensive involvement with life in the world that is not characteristic of *most* forms of Christianty—an involvement of the kind that is granted only to those who do *not* know everything in advance, who must therefore "keep watch," whose curiosity is not dulled by foreknowledge, whose alertness for the battle is not diminished by the certitude of ultimate victory, whose commitment to the present is not reduced by preoccupation with the past and future, or with an eternity which supposedly transcends all time. If Judaic faith has produced an unusual and even singular engagement with its worldly context (the kind of engagement that has been much *too intensive* for so many Western, "Christian" cultures, in fact) it is because Judaic faith possessed no *mythos* through which it could relieve itself of the burden of the *living* God.[49] Christianity—not, I think, in its earliest expressions so much as in its established forms (and of course the entire process about which we are thinking here is inextricably linked with the *establishment* of Christianity)—turned its end-event into precisely that kind of myth, viz., a final pronouncement, a Word to silence all words, a revelation beyond which nothing more remained to be unveiled. The fundamentalistic treatment of *the Bible* as the locus of once-for-all Truth is really therefore no aberration, but only a rather gauche extension of the general "Christian" thirst for finality.

To this, it could be objected that Christianity had also to live with the Paraclete—that Spirit who "blows where it wills" (John 3:8); and that therefore, while its Christology might have led to theological positivism, its pneumatology ought to have constituted a dialectical tension and pull in the other direction. But, as the history of the church's treatment of the Holy Spirit makes abundantly clear, it was exactly this potentiality of the third person of the Trinity to reintroduce life and nuance and movement that was felt in the church as an enormous threat. So that even

---

49. Kafka has captured this Judaic ethos in his "magnificent pronouncement" (Arendt): "It is difficult to speak the truth, for although there is only one truth, it is alive and therefore has a live and changing face" (quoted by Hannah Arendt, *Men in Dark Times* [New York: Harcourt, Brace, Jovanovich, 1955], p. 28).

before Christianity had permitted itself to become the handmaid of empire, thus distancing itself even more decisively from pneumatic religion, it had seen fit—in its handling of the Montanists, for instance—to chain the Spirit to its Christology.

There are of course good reasons why an ungrounded Spiritism had to be checked; still today it must be restrained. But there are also questionable reasons why this has been and is being done in the churches. It is not possible to take with great earnestness the kind of Spirit-theology offered, in embryo, in Paul's Epistle to the Romans or the Acts of the Apostles, for example, and to construct, simultaneously, the *type* of Christology and eschatology which precludes openness to the future, the historical *development* of doctrine, and the capacity for surprise. Had the Spirit been given its (her?) biblical due in the evolving church, it would have been impossible to make of Christian theology the type of ideological undertaking that was required for the production (e.g.) either of late medieval or of 17th-century Protestant forms of scholasticism, for example. As it happened, Western Christendom in particular virtually silenced the Spirit, along with most of the Spirit-inspired movements (e.g., the Anabaptists). The doctrinal instrument by means of which this was achieved was precisely Christology: the Spirit bound hand and foot to the doctrine of the "second person."[50]

This is germane to any discussion of contextuality in theology because, in terms of the Theology (doctrine of God) embraced by Christianity, it is particularly the Holy Spirit who provides the dogmatic basis for the insistence that theological reflection necessarily means engagement with the historical context. The corrective to a theology which has neglected or dismissed the context by means of a rationalized and doctrinaire concentration on the second person of the Trinity is a theology which is goaded into engagement with its worldly reality by a fresh apprehension of the Holy Spirit. For the Spirit will permit us to rest neither in the church nor in doctrinal formulations that know everything ahead of time. The Spirit will drive us, as it drove Jesus, to the wilderness of worldly temptation and the garden of worldly suffering.

Christian theology must be contextual, then, because the *Theos* whom it seeks to understand lives and interacts with a lively creation.

---

50. It is of course necessary on the other side of this issue to laud the decision of the Council of Toledo of 589 C.E., with its introduction of the *Filioque* clause into the Nicene Creed. An undifferentiated Spiritism leads in many directions that Christians cannot and must not go. But it is one thing to insist that the Spirit proceeds from the Father *and the Son,* and something else to say that the Spirit must conform to our Christologies!

Neither of the participants in this drama has yet played out his or her part; nor is it by any means *determined* what the parts are, or what the concrete outcome of their interaction. To be sure, promises have been made, and it behooves faith to trust at least the promises of the initiating Partner in this covenant. But exactly what God's faithfulness may mean for creation's destiny, or even for the next generation—*save that it will be greatly loved!*—who can say? As for the other (articulate) partner in the covenant relationship, evidence from the past suggests that the human creature does indulge in recurring and typical responses, tendencies and patterns. Yet *anthrōpos* in the tradition of Jerusalem is no automaton and (who knows?) may surprise creation with wisdom and courage as yet not realized. Besides, the capacity of the Creator to bring something out of nothing is, as we have noted, a highly prominent feature of this tradition. In short, the working out of the kingdom in the specifics of time and place always remains to be seen.

The point in all of this for the thinking of the disciple community, however, is that this working-out, this ongoing process of God's providential activity within history, is exactly what theological meditation attempts to discern. Without very precise attention to what is "going on" in our here and now, we shall never achieve the transition from doctrine to theology. Christian theology is a studied contemplation of the Eternal *in time*. That is to say, it is incarnational theology, theology of the Spirit, and theology of the cross.[51]

---

51. It will be obvious to the discerning reader that the foregoing statement has much in common with North American process theology. It shares with that theological school a distaste for static conceptions of God and the world, and an insistence that the dynamic nature of reality must be taken seriously in theological as in other kinds of reflection. "Process-theologians are sure that modern man is right in seeing himself as part of a changing, moving, living, active world, in which we have to do not with inert substances but with dynamic processes, not so much with *things* as with events. Hence their conception of divine Reality . . . is not that of an unmoved mover or changeless essence, but rather of a living, active, constantly creative, infinitely related, ceaselessly operative Reality; the universe at its core is movement, dynamism, activity, and not sheer and unrelated abstraction. Whitehead's view, that the cosmos is 'alive,' is basic to the whole enterprise of process-thought; and this carries with it a conviction that the only reasonable explanation of the living cosmos is in fact 'the living God' " (Norman Pittenger, "Process Thought: A Contemporary Trend in Theology," in Ewert H. Cousins, ed., *Process Theology: Basic Writings by Key Thinkers of a Major Movement* [New York and Toronto: Newman Press, 1971], pp. 25-26).

Given this basic agreement with the process school, however, I must confess to certain differences, which will no doubt manifest themselves in the course of this study. Particularly I am bothered by the reminiscence of liberal optimism in the writings of process theologians. They seem to me too certain that "the process" moves in a direction human beings in general (and Americans in particular?) can regard favorably. I, too, want to speak about *love* as the informing principle of the historical process; and as the foregoing statement should confirm, I do not see how anyone taking the Hebraic and Christian Scriptures seriously can avoid thinking that the tradition of Jerusalem posits "a happy ending." But the process school seems to me to place all this too undialectically within the terms

3.3. Theology Is Confessional. The third reason why Christian theology must be contextual is that it is confessional. Put more precisely, what is meant is that Christian theology is an undertaking of the church, and its mandate is to help the disciple community to make its rightful confession in the world. But it can do this only if and insofar as it *knows* that world—and from the inside. For confession, as distinct from the recitation of dogma or the reiteration of already-formulated religious beliefs, implies the kind of intelligent participation in one's culture that is suffiently profound to render the confession of faith arresting. I do not say *credible*, because with classical Protestantism I assume the indefinable leap (Kierkegaard) between reason and belief. However, I do think that the confession of faith, when it is authentic, will always function as a matter of encounter and engagement. At least confession will be heard to address realities within the human situation, and therefore it will not be easily dismissed as simply *in*credible, ridiculous, or unworthy of serious consideration. Confession of the faith occurs when the church is sufficiently identified with the world's doubt and despair and evil that the world, in its turn, is made curious about the church's persistent belief, hope, and message of deliverance from evil.[52]

---

of inevitability, whereas I should like to speak rather of possibility. "The new" is possible; it is not necessary. Transformation of the world is a matter of grace and of hope which may indeed *use* the processes of nature, but which is not as such nature. Along with the possibility of ever-greater realization, in the world, of the divine *agapē*, there is the possibility of continuing and worsening manifestations of alienation. In short, I do not see redemption belonging to "the process" as such, but as that which is continuously offered, continuously *introduced into* the worldly process from beyond its own *inherent* resources. Too much in the process school reminds me of the "religion of Progress." I accept with gratitude the insights of the leading exponents of this school, but I attempt to interpret their insistence upon the dynamic character of reality along the lines of Reformation grace and hope, rather than modern historical optimism.

Perhaps this criticism jibes with that of James Gustafson, who, while he also voices his appreciation for process thought, finds it deficient in what is of "primary moment in a religious view of the world . . . and therefore an assumption in theology," namely, "a sense of dependence on, and respect and gratitude for, what is given" (*Ethics from a Theocentric Perspective* [Chicago: University of Chicago Press, 1981], p. 61). In short, there seems to be a quite different theology of *grace* at work in this school.

52. The extent to which noncontextual or even anticontextual sentiment pervades much academic theology can be perceived in the attempt of established and self-styled "classical" schools of systematic theology to sustain clear distinctions between the "science" of systematics and what they designate "Practical Theology." A typical example: "Systematic Theology is concerned with the study of a definite object. This insight is obscured if theology is presented as a kind of confession. . . . Such an attempt would place theology in the same category as preaching. It would then be a confessional proclamation in a complete and logical form" (Gustav Aulén, *The Faith of the Church*, revised ed., trans. Eric Wahlstrom [Philadelphia: Fortress, 1960], p. 3). The implicit relegation of "preaching" to an inferior status in this statement is itself noteworthy; but more significant for our present purposes is the assumption that Theology, as distinct from the practical art of communicating the evangel, deals with a subject matter ("definite object") quite unrelated to the church's concern to bear witness to its Lord in the place where it finds itself. Surely such an attitude could have

THE DISCIPLE COMMUNITY

With characteristic precision and directness, Luther makes the point to which I am alluding here in the following powerful distinction:

> If I profess with the loudest voice and clearest exposition every portion of the truth of God except precisely that little point at which the world and the devil are at that moment attacking, I am not *confessing* Christ, however boldly I may be *professing* him. Where the battle rages, there the loyalty of the soldier is proved, and to be steady on all the battlefield besides is mere flight and disgrace if he flinches at that point.[53]

The metaphor of the battlefield belongs, of course, to an age in which battles were very different from present or fearfully anticipated warfare. All the same, it casts the role of the theological community in the right light: theology is a matter of struggle, encounter, wrestling, confrontation—quite the contrary, one must say, to the reputation for sanctimonious tranquility which theology has (*somewhat* unjustly) acquired because it has so frequently insulated itself "professionally" from the battlefield of existence. But, more importantly, Luther's analogy points to the fundamental presupposition of engagement with the world if theology is to achieve the confessional stance, i.e., if it is to become theology.

This is no doubt the most difficult aspect of the theological discipline. By comparison with such engagement, the contemplation of past doctrinal struggles of the church, and the taking of positions with respect to them, is child's play—which may in part account for the fact that so much of what has the reputation of being theology is just that: the profession of the faith based upon some familiarity with the church's *past* acts of confession. The presupposition of confession is not only engagement in the present "battle," but the courage to risk decisions about the character of the battle, and to devise appropriate strategies on the basis of those decisions.

This is terribly difficult—perhaps it is impossible. For who can stand upon the battlefield of his or her own present moment and see with unquestioned accuracy even what the real issues are—the "little point

---

evolved only in a sociological situation of religious establishment, where systematic theology could seem to belong to the world of pure theory. It is inconceivable that such a statement might have been made by the early church "theologian" Paul—not to speak of Aulén's own hero, Luther!

53. *Luther's Works,* Weimar edition, letters, vol. 3, pp. 81ff. See my essay, "Die Vielgestaltigkeit christlichen Zeugnisses im Spannungsfeld zwischen Wortgebundenheit und Kontextbezug," in *Oekumenische Erschliessung Martin Luthers,* ed. Peter Manns and Harding Meyer (Paderborn: Verlag Bonifatius-Druckerei; Frankfurt-am-Main: Verlag Otto Lembeck, 1983), pp. 293ff. (English translation: Peter Manns, Harding Meyer, Carter Lindberg, and Harry McSorley, eds., *Luther's Ecumenical Significance: An Interconfessional Consultation* (Philadelphia: Fortress, 1984), pp. 247ff.

where the battle is raging." Being ourselves part of that tumult, we lack the height, the distance, the hindsight that might offer greater wisdom. Our involvement in a fast-moving historical pageant prevents us from taking up the stance of those who know absolutely who and where they are. But neither can we take refuge in our ignorance. In battles of the soul and mind, as in all battles, decisions must be taken and strategies employed. Perhaps it will turn out that, like Don Quixote, we have been fighting windmills, and not real evil. On the other hand, in our blundering way (and by sheer grace), we might sometimes have stumbled upon the very heart of the darkness—as in the last analysis the Don seems also to have done.

We are again coming close to the real *suffering* that belongs to the life of the disciple community. Thinking the faith implies suffering, if it is serious and committed thought. To avoid this intellectual suffering which belongs to the task of theology, many are glad enough to resort to *pro*fession and let it stand for their *con*fession. For what is required of a truly confessional theology is not only that it should participate in the struggles of its context, but that it should do so without the comfort of ready-made resolutions of those struggles in the form of accumulated traditions, dogmas, formulas, creeds, catechisms, and systems of doctrine. Not only is the disciple community called to enter the fray to discover, always anew, where the point of greatest peril lies, but in order even to locate this "little point" it must lay aside its practiced strategies and acquired insights and make itself vulnerable to "the enemy." Unless the disciple community *itself* exposes itself to that which is endangering the life of its world, it will be incapable of confessing the faith. It will be imprisoned in the professional mode.

The suffering of the theological community in its subjection to the changing structures of worldly *unbelief*, however, is the condition without which the confession of *belief* would be hollow, anachronistic, and merely formal. If the Spirit is to bring others "who are not of this fold" into the sphere of discipleship, it can only do so through the testimony of a community which itself must hear the gospel ever anew, must be made ever and again "to struggle for the answer" (Tillich).

To state this in terms of a metaphor already introduced: that the disciple community lives between the two "stories" means, not, certainly, that it is neutral or a calm mediator between the differing accounts of reality, but that the two stories *vie with each other within the soul of the community as such*. We have said that these stories meet and that their *meeting* is where theology happens, or may happen. But now we shall have to add: and their meeting is never placid! Unless, as those who try to hear God's story of the world, we find ourselves frequently almost persuaded of the truth of the other teller's tale—perhaps at times even won over to that other story—we shall not know how to articulate God's story when and where we are. What else does the temptation of the Christ mean if not this, that he could not bear witness to his "heavenly Father" unless he acquired familiarity also with "the father of lies" (John 8:44); that he could not be a convincing challenge to the world's disbelief and belief unless he also felt the pull of its religion and irreligion; that he could only become a healer of wounds if he were himself deeply, even mortally, wounded.

When it is said that theology is *confessional*, it is this that is meant. It is far from a merely rational comprehension of the tenor of one's times. It is real involvement in "the battle"—and there can be no guarantee of *personal* survival. Many of the most sensitive members of the disciple community in our own period have found, in the long run, that they *lacked* the courage to "go on." Many could not come to the point of confession, finally, having exposed themselves too closely to the poisons of the 20th-century dragons—dragons so much more potent than St. George's! Bonhoeffer himself seems almost to have succumbed; others, like his contemporary Kurt Gerstein, did succumb.[54] And no great Christian thinker of our epoch has made the confession easily, or with facility proferred the wherewithal to aid others in making it. For in our time (and in this we are noticeably different from the most formative Christian epochs of the past) the "little point" at which the battle rages is precisely the point of confession, that is, of belief itself. Other ages struggled over *what* was to be believed. Our struggle is to know *whether* belief is possible. So theology is as such today the point at which the disciple community is *most* susceptible to *Anfechtung* (temptation, abandonment).

4. The Dangers of Contextuality

4.1. The dangers are real! There is no theological method that excludes risk. The subject matter of Christian theology being what it is, the risks involved in this discipline are greater than in most. It was the

---

54. Gerstein is one of the most intriguing Christians of our epoch. He first came to the attention of the world as the Protestant S.S. officer in Rolf Hochhuth's play, *Der Stellvertreter (The Deputy)*. See his biography, *A Spy for God,* by Pierre Joffroy, trans. Norman Denny (Glasgow: William Collins, 1969).

knowledge of such risks that prompted the young Karl Barth to write that "the Word of God is . . . the impossible task of the preacher."[55]

This impossibility is however counteracted by another recurring theme of biblical faith, namely, the "necessity" of bearing witness to the Word of God. "The Word of God is at once *the necessary and the impossible task* of the ministers," declared Barth, and he added: "This is my ultimate conclusion. Further than this I have nothing to say."[56]

The fact that Barth went on to say a good deal should be considered under the rubric of this dialectic of necessity and impossibility. While theology always comes close to breaking the Second Commandment (or even the first one), the disciple community is under obligation to articulate its belief, and not only in ecstatic fragments and spiritual outpourings, but also in reasoned discourse. "Be prepared to give a reason for the hope that is in you" (1 Peter 3:15). If we may put it this way, combining the two sides of the dialectic in a single statement: "God permits theology." God makes God's self accessible in some measure to our minds, as to our spirits. To understand (to stand under) this permission is to experience the real meaning of freedom. "I have indeed become so free," wrote the old Barth in 1977, "as to be able to write dogmatics—which many notable theologians are afraid of doing."[57] But because this freedom is a matter of sheer grace, those who practice theology need always to be aware of the risks involved. Not only the general risks which apply to any who dare approach so near to the ark of the covenant, but the quite specific dangers associated with the particular methods and emphases that they adopt.

The danger implicit in any theology which takes seriously the contextual dimension is that it will give way to relativism, and may become too narrowly focused upon its own immediate social setting. Wishing to be witnesses to the Eternal within its own time and place, the disciple community may find itself the captive of currents and ever-changing trends within its host society. Because it seeks to respond concretely to these currents and trends, it may lose sight of long-range questions to which its greater tradition tried to speak. A tendency to permit the issues of the historical moment to determine its witness may emerge. Then the theological community ceases to recognize, not only that these issues may be

---

55. From Barth's essay, "The Task of the Ministry," in *The Word of God and the Word of Man*, pp. 212-213. The entire essay is still astonishingly timely.

56. Ibid.

57. Rolf Joachim Erler and Reiner Marquard, editors, *A Karl Barth Reader*, trans. Geoffrey W. Bromiley (Grand Rapids: Eerdmans, 1986), p. 113.

transient, but that matters of greater magnitude may be hidden by the surface concerns with which it has busied itself. Perhaps it will even go so far as to let its context, rather glibly conceptualized, become the touch-stone for any kind of theological "relevance," so that it retains out of the long tradition only what seems pertinent to the moment, and disposes of the rest as being *passé*. The logical end of this process is that theology will have nothing of its own to bring to the analysis of its host society or the resolution of that society's ills; that it will become indeed little more than a religious variation on existing opinions and mores.

Meantime, if the same procedure were being followed by theological circles in other societies, the outcome for the church catholic would be a fragmentation into theological provinces which are no longer capable of communicating with one another meaningfully, being so thoroughly identified with the problematic of their separate cultures.[58] Thus the ecumenical character of the church is destroyed, and its possibilities for worldwide witness forfeited—and just at a time in the history of the planet when both analysis and cure must be *global*.

Before we address these dangers, we should try to recognize something of their weight and seriousness. That they are not merely theoretical can be appreciated by anyone vaguely familiar with the history of Christian theology during the past two centuries. In some ways, liberal theology as it developed in the 19th century was precisely a struggle against the "timeless orthodoxies" of Protestant and Catholic doctrinal traditions, in favor of a Christianity in dialogue with its own social milieu. The world defined by the Enlightenment and (to some extent) the Romantic movement became the articulate center to which the Christian intelligentsia attempted to adapt the faith. Aspects of the tradition which did not correlate positively with this center were discarded as irrelevant. What was acceptable to modernity was retained, often in an exaggerated or one-sided form (for example, the liberal emphasis on love, which tended to degenerate into sentimentality because of its undialectical emphasis upon the "positive" side of that affection.) The *critical* function of belief was in this way greatly vitiated; so that when the high expectations of the age of progress were dashed by the outbreak of "the Great War" and other "impossible" occurrences, Christian theology in many quarters found

---

58. This danger is no longer hypothetical. Many Christians who are profoundly in dialogue with the particularities of their own societies can undoubtedly sympathize with an Asian theologian who recently announced to an ecumenical gathering of Western Christians: "The time will come when you and I can no longer talk to each other." That such a thing may indeed happen, has perhaps already happened in some circles, cannot be doubted; but surely it must be regarded with sorrow, and not as a desirable or even a normal state of affairs.

itself bereft of categories for understanding the situation. Having permitted its context (or what *seemed* to be its context) to play such a decisive role in its own thinking, theology had lost the best insights of the Christian tradition for comprehending the failure of the modern vision.

Some critics of theological contextuality would find in recent theological thought in North America a phenomenon in some ways reminiscent of the 19th-century liberal tendency to be influenced too uncritically by dominant social trends. For such critics, theological activity on this continent during the past two or three decades, apparently lacking any profound understanding of and commitment to established traditions of Christianity, has been captivated by a whole series of theologies addressed to various analyses of the human situation: the theology of secularity, the theology of the death of God, the theology of hope, the theology of liberation. To many—especially, of course, to those whose temperamental or hereditary loyalties make them sympathetic to *established* doctrinal conventions—it has seemed that theology has been "blown about by every wind of doctrine" during these years. Is this not the consequence of a kind of *working* contextualism, which places so much weight upon the situational realities that it is finally at the mercy of fads in a rapidly changing social climate?

In addressing these dangers, my intention is not to dispose of them. Real dangers cannot be dispelled by argumentation! These risks remain to be lived with by anyone taking up such a mode of reflection as we are here proposing. At the same time, it is not helpful to entertain these dangers as if they were either *inevitable* or present in the exaggerated forms in which they are regularly characterized by the opponents of this methodology. As I have already said, there are very real psychic and other reasons why any theology which attempts lively dialogue with its social context will be attacked. The person who adopts this theological approach should be prepared to defend it against its detractors, not in order to avoid the risks that belong to this method but in order to remind himself or herself of what these risks are. The following subsections will attempt to speak to the dangers we have named.

4.2. Dialogue, Not Monologue. Contextuality in Christian theology does *not* mean that the context as such *determines* what the theological community shall decide, say, or do, either with respect to its analysis of the situation or the confession that it seeks to make. Theology wishing to be contextual does not wait to be told by "the experts" within its social milieu what questions it should address, or what answers might be acceptable or relevant. Even with regard to *the questions*, theology cannot simply sit quietly by and hear what others identify as the character and concerns of the moment. For one thing, the "others" to whom the disciple community listens are seldom if ever unanimous in their assessment of their time and place. What one hears from the representatives of the dominant technocratic society today—for instance, from large corporations, governments, chambers of commerce, and the like—is very different from what one hears from countercultural elements within the society. For another thing, theology does not lay aside its own questions and presuppositions about the creaturely condition when it tries to formulate the character of the human situation within which it is commanded to make its testimony to truth. Even if no one in a given society asked any longer such questions as those implicit in the tradition of Jerusalem— questions about the meaning of existence (teleology), about the good (ethics), about truth and reality (ontology), etc.—Christian theology would still have to ask them, and would still have to incorporate them into its assessment of the human situation. Of such a society, indeed, the primary thing that the Christian theological community would have to note is that these kinds of questions had somehow been silenced, and it would want to know why. In any case, the point is that contextuality in theology does not refer to a method in which the context, interpreted by its own most powerful or vociferous elements, simply sets the agenda for theology. If theological liberalism in the 19th and early 20th centuries permitted this to happen, it was not because of a commitment to contextual methodology but because of a commitment at the level of *content*, namely, the propensity of so much theological liberalism *to endorse* the worldview espoused by the dominant culture with which large portions of the bourgeois church was identified. If liberalism had been *genuinely* contextual, it would have paid far more attention than it did to the movements within its historical purview which *protested against*, or *resisted*, the very goals and presuppositions of that dominant culture.[59]

In other words, contextuality in theology by no means implies accommodation to the main cultural trends. It may in fact mean the most persistent struggle *against* these trends. Indeed, if the prophetic tradition of ancient Israel, which for Christians achieved a certain recapitulation and flowering in the work of John the Baptist and Jesus—if *that* tradition

---

59. For this reason, a much better instance of authentically contextual reflection is found in that wing of the liberal movement which explored and identified itself with the plight of the *victims* of the dominant culture, namely, the so-called Social Gospel movement. See in this connection Walter Rauschenbusch, *A Theology for the Social Gospel* (New York and Nashville: Abingdon, n.d.; originally published by Macmillan, 1917). See also Richard Allen, *The Social Passion: Religion and Social Reform in Canada 1914–28* (Toronto: University of Toronto Press, 1973).

is our paradigm in this whole discussion, then we should have to conclude that the *normal mood of contextual theology would be one which is inherently suspicious of dominant values and trends*. What is important, however, is neither a priori approval nor a priori disapproval of society but (as we have put it in the foregoing) the *engagement* of society. It is dialogue that is called for—a dialogue in the course of which the disciple community may learn to "discern the signs of the times," and thus be able to bear testimony to a hope which both incorporates and transcends the possibilities and impossibilities inherent in the situation.

4.3. The Necessity for Historical Reflection. It is a caricature of contextual theology when it is portrayed as the kind of commitment to "the moment" which precludes any profound interaction with the Christian and human past. That it has happened that Christians concerned for the present have sometimes neglected the past can be granted. For example, that theological liberalism often manifested a disdainful attitude towards past formulations of the faith is true. So is the fact that North American ecclesiastical history demonstrates a fundamental weakness at the point of an ongoing, imaginative struggle with the tradition. But such admissions do not really touch contextuality in theological method, even if they show an unfortunate coincidence between preoccupation with the present and neglect of the past.

What is at stake here is of course the charge that contextualism courts the danger of historical relativism. But the supposition behind this charge needs careful examination. It is that the fixed or permanent component in Christian theology is its past expression. The fundamentals of Christian belief, it is assumed, have been articulated in the dogmatic traditions of the past. If these fundamentals do not themselves constitute absolutes from which there should be no deviation, they at least symbolize (for those making this charge) such absolutes. Therefore, not to feel beholden to this doctrinal past is to be at the mercy of the shifting sands of the present.

The fallacy of this assumption has been amply demonstrated by the whole discussion of the *development* of Christian doctrine, a discussion which has been in progress for a century or so. What the past history of Christian thought offers us is neither homogeneous body of teaching nor an early dogmatic tradition normative for subsequent theological thought. Rather, it offers us a great variety of doctrinal ideas which, far from exercising singular authority from the outset, evolved over a long period of time and show the marks of varying cultural (contextual!) influences.[60]

---

60. In his study of the nature and meaning of doctrinal change (*Historical Theology: Continuity*

This does not mean that the tradition leaves us bereft of guidelines. There *are*, as we have insisted in the foregoing, recurrent themes—a "common heritage" (R. M. Brown). But to construe this as *consensus* or to cast the tradition in the garb of theoretical finality is to fly in the face of all modern historical scholarship, secular and sacred. More significantly, it is to miss the really important thing that this doctrinal history has to teach us, namely, that the reason *why* we have this rich variety in the expression of Christian belief is that the confession called for under the many and changing circumstances that have pertained during these 2000 years has itself been diverse. Granting the probability that Christian thinkers frequently erred in their discernment of the signs of the times, it is hardly likely that the same emphasis would be called for from an Augustine working within the conditions of decaying Rome as from an Aquinas faced by the Aristotelian challenge to Christian belief or a Schleiermacher feeling the attack upon religion by its "cultured despisers." It would in fact be astonishing in the extreme if always and everywhere in our long doctrinal history we discovered the same sort of *confessio fidei*. It is perhaps remarkable that there are as many similarities as there are.

---

and Change in Christian Doctrine [New York: Hutchinson of London, 1971], Jaroslav Pelikan rightly calls attention to the service historical study of Christian doctrine has performed for the church during the past century. "The origins of historical theology in the Enlightenment's critique of the Christian tradition have helped to determine its role as liberator from the authority of monolithically defined orthodoxy. An explicit presupposition of the Vincentian canon was the existence of a dogmatic consensus in the tradition that was, if not quite unanimous on every issue, nevertheless clearly discernible in the documents of church history. It is the special calling of the history of doctrine to show that this presupposition is a simplistic reduction of a heterogeneous body of material to a single theological position, whether it be one of the several positions represented in that material or a later synthesis superimposed upon it. Harnack formulated this calling of the history of doctrine in his memorandum of 1888: 'Cardinal Manning made the frivolous statement: "One must overcome history by dogma;" but we say the opposite: one must refine dogma by history, and we as Protestants have the complete certainty that we do not thereby destroy, but build' " (p. 150).

While agreeing wholeheartedly with Prof. Pelikan's basic contention concerning the service historical theology has rendered, I am rather less convinced than he seems to be about the appropriation of this service by most theological communities. To be sure, not many responsibile theologians could be found today who would echo Manning's "frivolous" dictum. But even in places of high theological repute, it is rare to find persons who can take with full seriousness the implications of von Harnack's antithetical dictum. There is still among us a fear—an inordinate fear, I should say—of succumbing to historical relativism. Thus the plea of a minority in North America for a genuine indigenization of theological reflection is met by cries of parochialism, reductionism, even jingoism. Theological communities on this continent cling to dogmatic traditions offering certitude in a manner that would astonish not only Harnack and our liberal predecessors but also Karl Barth, who is not infrequently made to bear the fearful burden of endorsing this very need of Christian conservatives for proximity to the Absolute. Moreover, the quest for transhistorical finality is given an added boost today by that flight from history produced by the general apocalyptic conditions of our time. "Future shock!" The theological community increasingly becomes a haven from the storms of the age, and religion in general serves the human need for a fallout shelter. Thus the attempt of scholarship since Harnack to "refine dogma by history" is greatly inhibited by the growing demand of a confused and failing society for something permanent to which to cling.

What unites the different expressions of belief and makes of these many-colored fragments a cloak that the disciple community may still gladly put on, is not their similarity at the level of doctrinal content, however, but their effectiveness at the level of their intention faithfully to confess the Christ under the ever-changing conditions of historical existence. In short, what we learn from our own past, as we have already shown, is that in its greatest moments the church has always been contextual—indeed, that what made the Christian movement great, wherever that dubious adjective can be applied in any meaningful sense, was that it sometimes managed to overcome the natural human bondage to fixed conventions and found the wisdom and courage to say the thing that needed to be said, to address the "little point" (Luther) that was under attack. From the rich tradition of this de facto contextualization of the faith of the Christ, we are helped in our own attempts to speak from and to *our* historical context.

The practical consequence of such an observation is that genuine contextuality in Christian theology (as distinct from a concern for immediate "relevancy") implies a continuing dialogue with the tradition. Far from encouraging a dismissive attitude towards the doctrinal past of the church, the determination of the disciple community to speak from and to its own social context implies an equal determination to renew and deepen its dialogue with the Christian past.

Living in a dialogue with our tradition is, however, very different from the kind of traditional*ism* which would make of systematic theology little more than a linguistic updating of dogmatic conventions. In the first place a real struggle with "the" tradition precludes any unqualified use of the definite article! A theology which takes seriously its call to discipleship in the present will involve a continuous wrestling with the past, a struggle born, not of the need to escape from the complex realities of the here and now, nor yet of the attempt to avoid the risks of confession, but simply of the need for help. It is still the present, with its often strident demands and uncertainties, which sets the tone for our visitation of the past. Even the choice of what *aspects* of the tradition will occupy our thought is influenced by existential concerns derived from the present and impending future. Thus every impressive reformulation of the Christian faith involved on the one hand a break with the past, and on the other the establishment of new ties with the past. The break consists of a disentanglement from conventions which have dominated in the immediate background; the establishment is the discovery of different, often of *earlier*, traditions, which could provide insight for the present and could help the disciple community think its way into the future. In such a manner, Martin Luther returned to the tradition of Augustine over against the regnant traditions of the Schoolmen; Schleiermacher and the liberals found affinities with Abailard over against the entrenched atonement theology of Anselm; and Barth returned in spirit to Calvin for his criticism of theological liberalism. Similarly, many Protestants and Catholics today, in the face of nuclearism, turn to the historic peace churches whose Anabaptist and other forebears their own Protestant and Catholic progenitors rejected and despised.

This listening to and being driven back to the past will not *eliminate* the danger of arbitrariness or relativism; but it means at least that the disciple community feels an implicit responsibility to look beyond its own historical moment for aid in gaining the perspective necessary to making a faithful confession on its immediate "battlefield." Such listening to and being driven back to the past is not an option, which the disciple community may take or leave; it belongs to the faith that is to be confessed, whose hope is after all only the other side of its remembrance.

4.4. The Bible and Theological Contextuality. If our remembering as a theological community encompasses the whole dogmatic tradition, it focuses in a unique manner upon the earliest tradition, the Newer Testament, and upon that body of literature which the Christian Gospels and Epistles themselves presuppose as their primary tradition, the Sacred Scriptures of Israel. What has been said of the relation of the disciple community to the tradition at large can, much of it, be said to be the case with the Scriptures as well. There are, however, special questions to be discussed here; and while the more detailed treatment of these questions must wait until the second section and our consideration of the theology of *authority*, some aspects of this subject must already occupy our thought. In particular, we need to ask what the *sola Scriptura* of Reformation teaching has to say to the matter of contextuality in theology.

For many Christians on this continent, it is clear enough what would have to be claimed in this connection: the teaching of the reformers that "Scripture alone" is authoritative for belief and doctrine means that the message of the church is to be derived solely from its study of the Bible. The Bible is the "text" which is to be announced in our "context"—in *every* context. For such a mentality, the context itself contributes nothing to the message, either to the analysis of the culture or to the Christian witness within the culture. The Bible already knows what is the character of the human situation in every age and place; therefore it is not necessary for the disciple community to go beyond its pages in order to understand what sort of world it is in which the gospel is to be proclaimed. The Bible also knows what the proclamation must be, and we must be wary of putting alongside this one and only source of revelation anything additional. No doubt it is always necessary to "translate" the Bible, to find the right words, the appropriate metaphors and illustrations; but this is strictly a concern for the transmission of the biblical message, not a quest for its meaning as such.

But is that, in fact, what the Reformers' *sola Scriptura* really meant? Here we find ourselves straightway confronted by significant nuances in the variety of traditions we, as Protestants, have inherited. In the Reformed interpretation, there is perhaps a strong tendency towards biblical self-sufficiency—though it has always been easier to maintain this in theory than in practice, for those who consult the Scriptures for understanding can hardly rid themselves of the concerns, suspicions, presuppositions, and the like which have led them to "search the Scriptures" in the first place. Calvin himself did believe that the Bible was inspired, and in its entirety: "The apostles were only the sworn notaries of the Holy Spirit, so that their Scriptures might be held authentic; the successors have no other commission than to teach what they find contained in the Holy Scriptures."[61] Yet Calvin never affirmed the *literal* inspiration of the Scriptures, even though subsequent history has frequently presented him as the author of this concept:

> Although it is true to say that he thought one could find the word of God in the Bible, he nevertheless said that the word we possess in the Scriptures is a mirror which reflects something, but does not impart to us the thing itself. The Scripture itself is "an instrument by which the Lord dispenses the illumination of the Spirit to the faithful," but not to be identified with the Lord himself. Though the content of the Scripture is divine, inasmuch as it is the word of God, the form in which that content is clothed is not therefore divine. The authors of the books of the Bible wrote under the inspiration of the Holy Spirit; they were none the less liable to introduce human errors into it upon points of detail which do not affect the doctrine.[62]

For our present purposes, this means that at least Calvin did not conceive of the *sola Scriptura* principle in such a way as to *rule out* contextual reflection in theology. To what extent did he make positive room for

---

61. John Calvin, *Institutes of the Christian Religion*, IV, 8, 9.
62. Francois Wendel, *Calvin: The Origins and Development of His Religious Thought*, trans. Philip Mairet (New York: Harper and Row, 1950, 1963), p. 160.

contextuality? He himself was obviously deeply involved in his own historical situation. But did he make use of such involvement in his articulation of theological method?[63]

The answer, I believe, lies primarily in Calvin's theology of the Spirit. What precisely does he mean by "inspiration," both as it applies to the writing and the reception of the scriptural word? If it is the work of the Spirit to open the text of Scripture to us, or open us to the text of the scripture, then this presupposes an existential grasping of "us" in the midst of our life's circumstances. The human spirits with which the divine Spirit wrestles in this process of communication are not, after all, empty vessels, but historical beings like the original disciples, who must be convicted of this truth in all the particularity of their existence. The implications of his pneumatology upon his doctrine of Scripture seem, however, not to have been fully thought through by Calvin.

It is another matter with Luther. Luther is just as insistent as Calvin upon the centrality of the Scriptures in theology. Theology *is* for him the exposition of Scripture. "Abandon scripture," warns Luther, "and God abandons us to the lies of men."[64] But Luther, characteristically, has much more interest than has the Geneva reformer in the process of our *receiving* the Word to which the Scriptures bear unique witness. What is important for him is not that the Scriptures should be upheld and preserved against all attack (though he is capable of strong language against the "papist" and other detractors of biblical primacy). What is important, rather, is that the message contained in the Scriptures should be communicated, received, believed. Therefore, the *sola Scriptura* is not for Luther a *material* principle (something to be believed) but a *formal* (methodological) one, i.e., something to be used. The substance of belief, in other words, is not that the Bible is true, but rather that that towards which the Bible points us is true. The truth as such is incapable of containment in words, even the inspired words of the Bible. It is the spirit and not the letter of the text that we must hear; and this hearing can take place only if we, in all the explicitness of our personal existences, are caused by the Spirit of God to do so. Thus the situation of the hearer or the hearing community is a central dimension of Luther's concept of scriptural authority. The existential context and the biblical text are not separable; rather, in the process of faithful theological exegesis of the Scriptures, text and context

---

63. See David Kelsey, *The Uses of Scripture in Recent Theology* (Philadelphia: Fortress, 1975), p. 187.

64. E. Theodore Bachmann, introduction to *Word and Sacrament*, Part I, *Luther's Works*, vol. 35 (Philadelphia: Fortress, 1960), p. 116.

are made to encounter each other, and genuine understanding of the holy writ *pro nobis* may only occur through this encounter.

> This striving for a true understanding of the scripture, with its concern for the Spirit, *is of necessity concerned with the present existential situation.* For the Holy Spirit is a present and life-giving Spirit, by contrast to the letter, which owes everything to the past and consequently speaks of the past. Thus . . . the hermeneutic principle from which Luther starts, with its antithesis between the letter and the Spirit, also leads him to the realization that *the understanding of the scripture is not something that can be preserved and passed on.* As existential life continues, so the understanding of the scripture is a continuous task which can never be brought to a conclusion. *For there is a constant threat that an understanding once achieved will cease to be the Spirit, and return to being the mere letter, unless it is constantly attained anew and made one's own.* Thus unceasing progress is necessary in the understanding of scripture. The Spirit turns into the letter; but the letter must in its turn constantly become the Spirit once again. One state of understanding is always the letter from which the Spirit comes in the next stage.[65]

This, says its author, Gerhard Ebeling, "reveals an astonishing insight into the historical limitations of our understanding"; and he continues by citing Luther's exegesis of Ps. 119:125, "I am thy servant, give me understanding that I may know thy testimonies," as an instance of Luther's application of the insight:

> The Psalmist prays for an understanding against the mere letter, for the Spirit is understanding. For as the years have passed, so has the relationship grown closer between the letter and the Spirit. For what was a sufficient understanding in times past, has now become the letter to us. Thus at the present time, as we have said, the letter itself is more subtle in nature than before. And this is because of the progress of time. For everyone who travels, what he has left behind and forgotten is the letter, and what he is reaching forward to is the Spirit. For what one already possesses is always the letter, by comparison with what has to be achieved. . . . Thus the doctrine of the Trinity, when it was explicitly formulated at the time of Arius, was the Spirit, and only understood by a few; but today it is the letter, because it is something publicly known—unless we add something to it, that is, a living faith in it. Consequently we must always pray for understanding, in order not to be frozen by the letter that kills.[66]

---

65. Gerhard Ebeling, *Luther: An Introduction to His Thought* (Philadelphia, Fortress, 1972), pp. 97-100, emphasis added.

66. Cited ibid.

Taking Luther's interpretation of the meaning of the sole authority of Scripture as representative of Reformation teaching, we should have to conclude not only that the singular authority of the Bible for theology does not *exclude* contextual reflection, but that it positively *requires* it. For it would be no honest use of Scripture, according to this view, which was content to read the text *into* the context. Scriptural understanding presupposes that it is the heightened awareness of our context that gives to the text, under the impact of the Holy Spirit, its power and its wisdom.

Conversely, it would not be a genuinely contextual theology which left the scriptural text out of account in its quest for depth of engagement in the culture. What gives the disciple community the distinctiveness necessary for any such engagement is just its waiting for the Word which it hopes to hear in and through these Scriptures. There would be nothing in this community to be engaged with the culture—i.e., the community would be nothing more than a dimension of the culture itself—were it not for its always-renewed struggle to hear and understand this Word, addressed *to* the culture from beyond its own possibilities and impossibilities.

Biblical exegesis, like historical theology, is thus *necessary to* a genuinely contextual theology. The danger that Scripture and tradition will be forgotten or relegated to a place of relative unimportance does not lie within the logic of contextuality as such, but in an undialectical and reductive concentration upon the present.

4.5. Contextuality and Ecumenicity. Contextuality in Christian theology means not only caring about the *time* but also caring about the *place* in which one is called to give a reason for one's hope. Sensitivity to *place* is as vital to contextuality in theology as is sensitivity to "the times."[67] In fact, there is no experience of time which is not simultaneously an experience of place. The special concerns which have recently been labeled contextual in theological discussion have particularly to do with sensitivity to place—region, nation, "World" (e.g., "the Third World"). This has been a neglected dimension heretofore. Most theologians in the present century have been influenced by the historical (time) dimension in all theological reflection, even though in spite of this a remarkable degree of "timelessness" has prevailed. Few, however, have permitted the kind of particularity they have had to notice in connection with time

---

67. In this connection, see the thoughtful essay of Philippine theologian Oscar S. Suarez, "Theology of Struggle: Reflections on Praxis and Location," in *Theology, Politics and Struggle*, ed. Feliciano V. Carino (Quezon City: National Council of Churches in the Philippines, 1986), pp. 47ff.

to be carried over into their awareness of their particular *place*. Especially in the First World, it is often assumed that because we are *contemporaries* our situation—whether that means Scotland or Quebec, Dallas or Bonn—is essentially the same, at least for theological purposes. Certain minorities in our midst—especially those who are doing theology quite consciously from the perspective of women—have helped us to appreciate that the human condition has always to be spelled out in terms of such specifics as race, gender, power, and property. And Third World theologians have given us notice that the timely theologies we have been busy creating for our (First) world as well as theirs do not in fact *fit* in their place. What these groups have caused some of us to realize is that we, too, may have been all-too-willing victims of a theological method which might have learned a little about the times but still comprehends too little about the importance of location in theology. How submissively, for instance, have we North Americans given ourselves to textbook treatments of Christian doctrine which hardly ever take notice of any of our specific problems, our history, our scholars, our heroes, artists, writers?[68]

Place-consciousness also contains, however, some potential dangers. The danger of contextualism as it applies to time is that it will be too much influenced by the present and too little in touch with the past. Applied to place, it is the danger of being so thoroughly caught up in the life of one's own society (e.g., region, nation, language-world) that one tends to lose sight of the larger human community. That this has been a real danger throughout the history of Christianity, in fact, is testified to by the division of the church into greater and smaller segments, often based more upon geographic and ethnic factors than on genuine theological differences. Today we are inheriting the fruits of such divisions, and they are by no means only annoying ideological differences. The religious sanctioning of narrow, parochial loyalties militates against the development of a global consciousness of the type that is required for the survival

---

68. John Macquarrie's *Principles of Christian Theology* (New York: Scribner's, 1966) is a good example. It has been widely used throughout North American theological seminaries and colleges, and is in many respects a stimulating discussion of theology. Macquarrie, in the spirit of Tillich, has a fine appreciation for the role of the cultural factor in theology. But this is expressed almost consistently in terms of the time dimension and shows, for example, little comprehension of the distinctive differences between the British/West European and the North American societies. These societies, of course, share a great deal; but there are also many differences which are highly significant for theology as for other disciplines. It is not so much a matter of *knowing* the differences as it is of thinking and speaking and writing *from within the experience* of those for whom one is doing this. This is one reason why the importation of theologians from other contexts (for us, this has meant in particular from Europe) is problematical, especially if it is not countered by the cultivation of indigenous scholars and their appointment to positions in theological colleges and elsewhere.

of earth's peoples today. It is therefore incumbent upon theology, as upon every other responsible human discipline, to think carefully about any kind of *localization* of human reflection and concern which could contribute to the further alienation of peoples from peoples, worlds from worlds. In particular, because of the inherent concern of Christian faith for the oppressed, the disciple community must ask about the consequences especially for the Third World and for minorities in its own society, of any theologizing that it does. *Thought* is never ethically neutral. As a church thinketh, so it is! If the theological reflection of the church in the First World is wholly out of touch with what is happening in the Third and Second Worlds, it will in all likelihood be serving the interests of those who are helping to create problems in those other worlds.

Obviously, what this means for contextual theology is that its authenticity will depend upon an awareness, not only of its own immediate context, but of the greater context, the globe itself, of which its context is part. There is no reason why a theological community which is profoundly identified with its own regional culture should not at the same time be deeply aware of the greater context. Is it not reasonable, indeed, to suppose that anyone today who delves deeply enough into any specific locus of the planet's social "crust" *will have to* become involved in the totality? And while this may be difficult where individuals are concerned, or even individual congregations, we need to remember that theology in the church of Jesus Christ is a corporate undertaking. Given the worldwide character of the church and the marvels of contemporary communication, there is no reason why every Christian who is immersed in his or her own place ought not at the same time to be at least informed about many other places.

We may go even further: Not only is it reasonable to assume that contextuality with respect to the immediate context will lead to a more vital interest in the wider context as well; it is a matter of empirical observation that this is what happens. There are, of course, narrowly regional communities in the church, as in the world at large. But it is more often the case that those most profoundly committed to their own are at the same time those who are grappling with the greater issues of world society. For one thing, they cannot even comprehend their own place with any depth unless they know something of the influences brought to bear upon it by other places. For another, genuine attachment to the earth in one *locus* is the best guarantee of an all-embracing attachment to the earth. The gap today is not so much between regionalist and universalist orientations. It is between those who are content to live above the earth at the level of theory, whether of a sophisticated or a simplistic nature (e.g., unreflective nationalism), and those whose concern for God and neighbor lead them from theory to praxis.

The obvious antidote to a contextualism which ends in what we may term *localism*—beyond the hope that it might become more genuinely contextual—is an *ecumenical praxis-theology* which keeps building and repairing bridges between peoples and worlds. The emergence of a renewed interest in the specifics of "the context" thus provides the condition necessary to the creation of a new type of ecumenism. Ecumenism in the past has too consistently concentrated upon forging links between ecclesiastical confessions and denominations. No doubt this will continue to be necessary, but it should not be the normative form of ecumenism. The more important bridges that have to be built now are between "regions" or spheres (East/West; North/South; the three "worlds," etc.) and movements (women, blacks, economically depressed minorities, environmentalists, antinuclear groups, homophile organizations, etc.) In these "places," Christians out of many different ecclesiastical and theological backgrounds are involved. A working ecumenism (in the interdenominational sense) pertains among most of them. What is needed is an ecumenical cross-fertilization in terms of the regions and causes that they represent. It is not the business of Christians in the United States and Canada to be doing the same kind of theology as responsible theologians are doing in South and Central America. But a genuine ecumenicity in the ecclesia today must certainly mean that the theological community in North America will be made aware at some depth both of the character of Latin American liberation theology and the social matrix in which it is offered as the appropriate Christian witness. I cannot say this with equal authority, for obvious reasons, but I believe that it may also be important for Latin American theologians to know that in North America there are Christians who are attempting to come to terms with their context. If ecumenism is to work at anything beyond the ecclesiastical multinationalism it too frequently represents, then the various agencies of the *oikumēnē* will have to learn to serve the church at this level of cross-fertilization and mutuality of understanding. Given the confusing and often deliberately falsifying methods of secular communication in today's world, a church which made good its own claim to catholicity could have untold influence for good even in terms of the dissemination of accurate information. Beyond that, such an ecumenism could provide the appropriate climate, enabling regional and special-interest Christian groups to be thoroughly engaged with their own specific tasks, while offering them a continuing perspective on the church in the greater global setting.[69]

5. The Process of Thinking Contextually

In the first subsection of this chapter, we described the problem to which the quest for the contextualization of Christian theology on this continent must be addressed, namely, an entrenched doctrinalism, largely constructed outside the parameters of North American experience and history, which functions ideologically to prevent the Christian community from grappling in an original way with the realities of our First World society. From this point of departure, we moved through three subsequent stages in our attempt to understand Christian theological reflection as a contextual enterprise: (1) by stating a basic definition of contextuality as it applies to the discipline of theology; (2) by showing the internal rationale—the Why?—of this definition; and (3) by acknowledging and speaking to the dangers implicit in contextual method. In this final subsection, I should like to describe what I believe is involved in the thought-process of contextualization: What is it that impels the disciple community to think contextually about Christian faith?

5.1. The Text and the Context. In the concluding chapter of his learned discussion of theological method in the "postliberal" era, George A. Lindbeck defines the task of "descriptive (dogmatic or systematic) theology" as that of providing "a normative explication of the meaning a religion has for its adherents."[70] Especially in the case of religions possessing fixed canons of sacred texts, Lindbeck proposes, this task must involve interpreting all of existence in the light of the texts in question. His word for this process is "intratextuality." The picture of reality glimpsed through the window of the sacred text becomes the clue and basis for the interpretation of the world. "For those who are steeped in [authoritative texts that are the canonical writings of religious communities], no world is more real than the ones they create. *A scriptural world is thus able to absorb the universe.* It supplies the interpretive framework within which believers seek to live their lives and understand reality."[71]

---

69. An example of the kind of ecumenism alluded to here is the "success" of minority Christian communities in South Africa in alerting Christians throughout the world to the distorted interpretation of life—including religious life—in that context, and providing a stirring alternative perception. See, e.g., Allan A. Boesak and Charles Villa-Vicencio, eds., *When Prayer Makes News* (Philadelphia: Westminster Press, 1986).

70. George Lindbeck, *The Nature of Doctrine: Religion and Theology in a Postliberal Age* (Philadelphia: Westminster, 1984), p. 113.

71. Ibid., p. 117 (emphasis added).

This process, says Lindbeck, occurs as a matter inherent to the belief system as such; it does not depend upon an articulated methodology. Thus,

> Augustine did not describe his work in the categories we are employing, but the whole of his theological production can be understood as a progressive, even if not always successful, struggle to insert everything from Platonism and the Pelagian problem to the fall of Rome into the world of the Bible. Aquinas tried to do something similar with Aristotelianism, and Schleiermacher with German romantic idealism. The way they described extrascriptural realities and experience, so it can be argued, was shaped by biblical categories much more than was warranted by their formal methodologies.[72]

The "direction of interpretation," Lindbeck insists, is important: its movement is *"from the Bible to the world rather than vice versa."* "Intratextual theology redescribes reality within the scriptural framework rather than translating Scripture into extrascriptural categories. *It is the text, so to speak, which absorbs the world, rather than the world the text.*[73] Lindbeck does not, however, intend to confuse this primacy of the text with biblicist or fundamentalist claims; for these, he (rightly) believes belong to the modern era just as surely as do the liberal historical-critical interpretative procedures against which they protest. "In recent centuries," he contends, citing the work of Hans Frei,[74] the Scripture "ceased to function as the lens through which theologians viewed the world and instead became primarily an object of study whose religiously significant or literal meaning was located outside itself. The primarily literary approaches of the past with their affinities to informal ways of reading the classics in their own terms were replaced by fundamentalist, historical-critical, and expressivist preoccupations with facticity or experience."[75]

At this point in the discussion, one wishes that Lindbeck had devoted more time to the explication of "intratextual theology" as the movement from text to world. What precisely is involved in this movement? If it is not simply a matter of extracting from the text of scripture principles or dogmas containing a priori data applicable to all possible worlds, what part, if any, does one's "world"—i.e., one's apprehension of one's life situation or context—play in theological work? Is the movement from Bible to world all one-way? If this is Lindbeck's meaning, then it differs

---

72. Ibid.
73. Ibid., p. 118 (emphasis added).
74. Hans Frei, *The Eclipse of Biblical Narrative* (New Haven: Yale University Press, 1974).
75. Ibid., p. 119.

quite obviously from the characterization of theological method offered in the previous sections of this chapter. For while that discussion intends precisely to affirm that the lens through which Christian theology views the world is the tradition of Jerusalem (i.e., "God's story of the world" as it is apprehended, primarily, through the Scriptures of the two Testaments), it also insists that humanity's ever-changing conception of its world constitutes an active ingredient in the theological discipline; that the movement of interpretation, therefore, is not simply text to context but a dialectical interaction between the two, in which, being grasped by new and often unsettling factors in its sociohistorical context, the disciple community is compelled to rethink and reformulate the meaning of the story presented by its authoritative sources. In turn, the message derived through this process of interaction engages the context from the side of the text, and, in sometimes significant and sometimes inconspicuous ways, it becomes an agent in the alteration of its context. As I expressed it metaphorically, the theological community lives *between* the two stories; it is the place where the two stories encounter one another. Unless something like this approach is taken, the disciple community is apt to be regarded (and to regard itself) as little more than a vehicle for the transmission of the text. It is just because I consider the *koinōnia* to be more than such a vehicle that I am treating this subject under the larger heading of "The Disciple Community," and not "The Discipline." That the discipline (theology) of providing a normative explication of the faith is undertaken by human beings who are themselves immersed in time and place, and that these human beings bring to their continuing struggle with the text certain explicit concerns representative of their sociohistorical *context*—this is itself, I would insist, a lively and essential dimension of their vocation.

It is probable, I think, that Lindbeck's analysis would be able to incorporate this dialogical conception of what it would mean, in practice, to do theology intratextually. One (for me, quite decisive) piece of internal evidence for such a conclusion is Lindbeck's reference to Reinhold Niebuhr, who, he says, may have been "the last American theologian who in practice (and to some extent in theory) made extended and effective attempts to redescribe major aspects of the contemporary scene in distinctively Christian terms. . . ."[76] For Niebuhr certainly lived and thought

---

76. Ibid., p. 124. This interpretation of Lindbeck's intention is confirmed by his stimulating discussion, in another place, of Karl Barth's approach to Scripture. While he does not accept uncritically Barth's approach to Scripture, he clearly perceives Barth as one of the great exemplars of what he means by "intratextuality." He also recognizes (what is of paramount importance to the

as a contemporary American, thoroughly immersed in his social context, bringing to Christian sources the questions belonging to his historical moment, reinterpreting the tradition in the light of those questions, and at the same time confronting his context with the claims of the tradition. If anyone in our time and place has lived "between the stories," it is Reinhold Niebuhr!

Whether or not what Lindbeck means by "intratextuality" and what I have meant by "contextuality" are fully compatible, however, the aspect of his analysis upon which I should like to concentrate here—as a way both of introducing the concerns of this present section and of beginning to make a transition to chapter two—is his fear that the intratextual approach he describes will not be able to materialize under the present conditions of church and society. "Even if it were to become theoretically popular," he suggests, "the result might chiefly be *talk about* intratextuality rather than more and better intratextual practice."[77]

The practice of intratexual theology, Lindbeck avers, is hampered by several factors in our situation: one is the general "disarray in church and society," which makes it difficult if not impossible for those "who share in the intellectual high culture of our day" to be informed and articulate members of the religious community; another is the fact that "theology (in the sense of reflection in the service of religion) is being increasingly replaced in seminaries as well as universities by religious studies";[78] and, finally, it is difficult for contemporary cultures to grasp the "intrinsic sense" of religions.

> Religions have become foreign texts that are much easier to translate into currently popular categories than to read in terms of their intrinsic sense. Thus the fundamental obstacles to intratextual theological faithfulness may well derive from the psychosocial situation rather than from scholarly or intellectual considerations.[79]

He concludes his discussion rather wistfully, therefore, remarking that

> it remains an open question . . . whether the intratextual path will be pursued. There is much talk at present about typological, figurative, and

---

contextual thinker) that ". . . the worlds in which we live change," so that "they need to be inscribed anew into the world of the text"—a work which requires "constant reexplication, remediation, and reapplication." Then he adds: "Fortunately, one does not have to be a Barthian or a self-conscious intratextualist to do this. Reinhold Niebuhr was not, and yet he was a great practitioner of the art" ("Barth and Textuality," *Theology Today* [1986], p. 375).

77. Ibid., p. 124 (emphasis added).

78. "There are," he adds, "fewer and fewer institutional settings favorable to the intratextual interpretation of religion and of extrascriptural realities" (ibid., p. 124).

79. Ibid.

narrative theology, but little actual performance. Only in some younger theologians does one see the beginnings of a desire to renew in a post-traditional and postliberal mode the ancient practice of absorbing the universe into the biblical world. May their tribe increase.[80]

I confess that I share this concern. So much of the intellectual energy of the professional theological community in our time seems to be consumed by methodological preoccupations and the translation of primary faith into the categories of *Religionswissenschaft*. One is tempted to ask whether, besides the reasons given by Lindbeck, this situation is not in part prompted by a hesitancy on the part of First World Christians to apply to their context the critical canon of the tradition of Jerusalem. It is much less threatening for us to "talk about" the meaning of our authoritative sources than actually to apply them in a holistic and existential manner.

What Lindbeck fears might happen "even if" the intratextual approach were adopted, namely, that it would be co-opted by our methodological preoccupations, is equally true of contextualization. In fact it is truer of the latter, because in some real sense a kind of contextualism *has been* adopted by large numbers of Christians in our time; and it is precisely its co-optation by methodological concern that constitutes the most prominent feature of its use—to the extent that anyone wishing to employ the category in a serious way has to anticipate this handicap. Context and its derivatives have become "in" terminology, and where this terminology is not corrupted by its simplistic application to purely local and temporary situations[81] it too frequently becomes the subject matter of endless methodological speculation on the part of theological professionals. The point of contextuality in theology is not that it should become interesting in itself, but that it should be practiced. It should facilitate the thing that it purports to facilitate, that is, the actual *naming* of the context in its encounter with the text.

---

80. Ibid., p. 135.

81. As indicated earlier (introduction, note 34), contextuality in theology should be distinguished from mere *situationalism*. Too much of what goes by the name of contextuality is so entirely lacking in historical perspective that it cannot be considered anything more than narrowly regional or transient concern, superficially conceived. In the churches one speaks about "a theology for the 80s" or "the 90s" and calls it being contextual! It should be clear from the discussion of the first chapter that by context I am referring to a historical moment which, for all its specificity of time and place, is part of a continuum. Thinking by the decade may be interesting and even important for programmers of church renewal and involvement in society, but it is no substitute for the more demanding social and historical analysis that must be part of theological work.

5.2. Judging. Just that, however, is the aspect of the theological vocation that causes many to falter. To think our world theologically, to "absorb the universe" (Lindbeck) within the parameters of the story we have inherited, this, as we noted already in the foregoing, is probably the most difficult dimension of thinking the faith. Even where it is not further complicated by the repressive desire *not* to confront openly the realities of our situation, the need to "discern the signs of the times" is fraught with epistemological difficulty. Can one ever *know* one's own era? How can the disciple community determine "what time it is"? How, standing *within* the here and now, is it possible to say something true about the character of the here and now?

Yet the effort must be risked. If what we have claimed above about the nature of theological reflection is viable, then at some point the discourse of the theological community must turn from theoretical questions about method to the actual deployment of this method. Contextuality in theory only is self-contradictory!

The temptation to reside in the house of theory is particularly strong in our time and place. We have already mentioned one reason for this, perhaps the salient one: that for Christians in affluent societies like ours actually to engage their contexts requires a remarkable degree of consciously acquired knowledge, courage, and openness to self-criticism. But even apart from this psychosocial inhibition, the sheer daring of intellect, imagination, and will that is necessitated by this task is enough to discourage the wise and the modest. For immediately we think to move beyond contextual theory into contextual *praxis*, i.e., immediately we *implement* fully our decision in favor of the contextualization of theological thinking, we are confronted on every side by conflicting testimony and widely divergent readings of our culture. There are those within our society—and they are often vociferous in our mainline churches—who will insist that we North Americans are living in the best of all possible worlds; others, on the contrary, maintain with equal conviction that we are living on the brink of doom. The first group points to technological advances in communications, medicine, and the means of production; the second to the rampant encroachment of technology upon all areas of life, the breakdown of *real* communication between peoples and persons, and our society's overwhelming concentration upon technologies which are destructive of life. One segment lauds the capitalist system as having given us, after all, the most stable and comfortable society on earth; another announces the nemesis of capitalism, and finds more than enough evidence in our midst of the Marxist prognosis concerning the decadence of this system in its "late" stage. Between the most optimistic and the most pessimistic assessments of our civilization, an indefinite number of variations are presented in the great smorgasbord of contemporary research, opinion polling, think-tanking, and sociological pulse-taking. The average university campus houses so many heterogeneous opinions about who and what we are that the ancient nomenclature for these institutions, with its brave suggestion of the unity of truth, is daily betrayed by a thousand Babel voices, kept in geographic and institutional proximity to one another only by the segregation of disciplines and the comfort of lucrative employment.[82]

It is best, therefore, if we recognize immediately what in any case we should eventually have to admit, namely, that the disciple community attempting to discern the nature of its context is a community under obligation to *decide—indeed, to judge.* And this obligation originates, not with anything extraneous to the church's life and thought, but with the One whose disciple community it is.

> "When you see a cloud rising in the west, you say at once, 'A shower is coming'; and so it happens. And when you see the south wind blowing, you say, 'There will be scorching heat'; and it happens. You hypocrites! You know how to interpret the appearance of earth and sky; but why do you not know how to interpret the present time?
> "And why do you not judge for yourselves what is right?"
>
> (Luke 12:54-57)

Decision concerning the nature of "the present time" belongs, in short, to the condition of discipleship. It is our inheritance from the prophetic faith of Israel. Always, the prophet had to decide: to think this and not that, and to act accordingly. The prophet could not wait until all the evidence was in, and did not expect a consensus. It was a lonely business. It is still.

Habitually, we falsify the past by recounting it in terms which virtually eliminate the element of decision through the diminishment of ambiguities actually present in it. Thus the stand of Elijah against the prophets of Baal is made to appear clear necessity, and Jan Hus's struggle against a corrupt hierarchy becomes almost self-evident. Given our Anglo-Saxon propensity to regard the "German Christians" (*die deutsche Christen*) of the Third Reich as almost absolute in their evil and the "Confessing

---

82. See George Grant's essay, "Faith and the Multiversity," in *Technology and Justice* (Toronto: Anansi, 1986), pp. 35ff.

Church," correspondingly, as almost absolutely pure, the Barmen Declaration comes to seem an obvious necessity![83] But, in fact, in all of these and innumerable other situations of the kind, there was a high degree of ambiguity—to the point often (perhaps even characteristically) that those whom we now honor as saints and martyrs and heroes of the faith seemed, in their own contexts, precisely the opposite. *They* were the ones who were out of step, premature, one-sided, fanatical, etc. Not only were they so regarded by the majority of their contemporaries, but often (perhaps even characteristically) they were greatly tempted to regard *themselves* in this light. Thus, as we know, Luther was assailed almost beyond endurance by the prospect that he had begun "all that" for personal and ulterior reasons. Had a thousand years and more of Christianity been wrong? Was he then the very first to discover the truth? Bonhoeffer's decision to cast his lot with the conspirators against Hitler was for him an untold agony—difficult, especially for those of us who have not been reared in a culture which inculcates an innate respect for authority, even to comprehend; yet clearly, for him, a veritable hell on earth. Only afterwards could it seem the right decision—and perhaps only to those who survived him.

Nothing can or will alleviate the agony of discernment for the disciple community. Though it will sometimes be more excruciating and sometimes less, it will never pass from the valley of decision to the mountaintop of certitude. Never, under the conditions of time and space, will the church be in a position to say that it knows beyond the shadow of a doubt what is "going on" in its world. At the level of cultural analysis as at the level of its *kerygma*, with "the question" as with "the answer" (to use Tillich's methodological metaphor), it will be a matter of trust—*fiducia*. The *credo* stands at the head of *all* the activity of the disciple community, its apprehension of its world as much as its comprehension of the Word of God.

Are there then no tests of authenticity, no checks and balances, no criteria for distinguishing hasty, superficial analyses of the *Zeitgeist* from more profound discernment? And are we simply at the mercy of opinion—like John Godfrey Saxe's six blind men of Indostan and their elephant, each, in accord with his or her individual experience, determining what our context truly is?

---

83. See, however, Arthur C. Cochrane, *The Church's Confession under Hitler* (Philadelphia: Westminster, 1962); see also my essay, "Barmen: Lesson in Theology," in *The Toronto Journal of Theology* (1985), pp. 180ff.

5.3. Guidelines for Discerning the Times.   I believe that there are such tests of authenticity. They do not deliver us from the valley of decision, but they do deliver us from sheer arbitrariness and capricious-ness. We may consider four types of criteria for authenticity of discern-ment.[84] Articulating them in the interrogative form, they are: (*a*) Who are *the victims* of our society? (*b*) How is our society perceived and depicted by its own *most reflective members?* (*c*) How do the pursuits and values of our society compare with images of the human in *our authoritative sources?* (*d*) Within the *corporate dialogue* of the disciple community, what emerges as the problematic of our culture?

Before briefly expatiating on each of these categories, I should like to make an observation about all of them, namely, that they all rest upon the presupposition of the *credo* spoken of above, and therefore should be considered an *explication* of what Lindbeck, I believe, intends by "in-tratextuality" rather than an alternative approach. If the disciple com-munity asks about the victims, it does so on the basis of presuppositions about oppression which it derives from its scriptural sources. If it opens itself to the deliberations of sensitive persons within the larger culture, its selection is of course biased by assumptions supplied by its texts. The two final categories are explicitly intratextual, where the first two are only implicitly so. What I should like to suggest through attention to such guidelines, however, is a manner of considering the absorption of the universe by the text which does not bypass the universe in its rush to demonstrate the universal applicability of the text. In the North American context today, one cannot underestimate the capacity of a covert biblicism within *all* of our ecclesiastical communities to swallow the world whole!

(*a*) *The testimony of the victims:* While this "test" is certainly not *exclusively* objective, for it assumes a high degree of sensitivity and direct involvement on the part of the disciple community, it is all the same the most objective of all the criteria available to us, and this is part of the reason why it must be accorded a certain priority. The other part of the reason for its priority is the one named by the liberationists: the God of the tradition of Jerusalem has "a preferential option for the poor."[85] "The

---

84. In this part of the discussion it is necessary to anticipate some aspects of what must later be treated under the category of authority, but here we are reflecting on the question from a broader perspective; i.e., our point of departure in this section is the life of the disciple community within its worldly context, not the discipline of theology as such, which is the focus of the second section.

85. This ought not, however, to be turned into an ideological elevation of the poor as the locus of truth. Bishop K. H. Ting's recent writings on this subject are a needed corrective to some forms of liberationism, especially in the hands of its middle-class interpreters in First World contexts. Ting, who has been instrumental in building the new society of People's China and in the development of a Christian community and witness within that society, acknowledges many similarities between

poor," of course, refers to those who are literally poverty-stricken or deprived of the basic necessities of biological existence, and there should be no allegorizing of this term which would have the net result of causing us to neglect or minimize the hard, physical reality of poverty. Yet as Jesus' words about the "poor in spirit" and other allusions of the Scriptures make plain, poverty can and must also have reference to spiritual as well as physical deprivation. Those who are pushed to the edges of society, whose humanity is ignored or whose experience and suffering are bypassed, are also victims, in whose fate the prophetic tradition has a particular interest. That there will be victims of any human society is, perhaps, a given of the biblical understanding: under the conditions of a fallen world, there will be victims. This is how Jesus' much-misused statement, "The poor you have always with you" (Mark 14:7 par.), should be heard. It is part of the realism of the biblical view of the world. But it does not end in fatalism, because the question that is put to humanity is always: Who are these victims, and what will you do about them? Do the particular pursuits of your society create and even *need* victims—certain *types* of victims? Does your economic system *depend upon* the victimization of some? How do you deal with your poor, your unemployed, your marginalized groupings, your prisoners, your young, your aged, your ill and dying, the fragile persons in your midst who are most affected by your corporate instability? And what of those beyond your own borders? Do other peoples pay the price of your security, your prosperity?

The Christian church as a whole, and the church within the First World in particular, can no longer allow this criterion for the authenticity of its cultural analysis to function only at the level of practical or applied theology and ethics. It has to be taken up into our primary ("systematic") theological reflection; otherwise, that theological reflection almost certainly *legitimizes* the victimization of the victims—if not explicitly then implicitly and by default. While it is by no means without its own dangers (see the reference to K. H. Ting in note 85), liberation theology is in my

"the emerging theology of Chinese Protestant Christianity" and liberation theology, but he is disturbed by the latter's propensity to " 'absolutize liberation and make it the theme or content of Christian theology.' Ting grants that the poor have an 'epistemological advantage' in being able to perceive issues of injustice and domination. But he does not believe that all truth is necessarily in their hands. In fact, he argues that the cultural revolution was precisely a consequence of this idealized view of the poor. It pitted them against not only the rich but also against intellectuals, veteran revolutionaries, and all aspects of enlightened culture" (Don Browning, "The Protestant Church in the People's Republic of China," *The Christian Century*, March 4, 1987, pp. 218 ff.). See also Bishop K. H. Ting et al., *Chinese Christians Speak Out—Addresses and Sermons* (Beijing, China: New World Press, 1984).

opinion entirely justified in making the poor a test of theological authenticity. As for the theology of the cross, it is simply a betrayal of the whole tradition when Christians permit themselves to point to the "pathos of God" incarnated in the crucified one and then fail to give priority, in their *theological* reflection and analysis as in their general conduct of their witness in the world, to those in their own world who are being crucified by the economic systems, political structures, and dominant cultural mores with which, on the whole, the churches of the First World are clearly identified.

It surely belongs to the divine mandate of a church emerging at last from the Constantinian captivity of the faith[86] to elevate to the highest position in its criteria for discerning the character of its context this ancient prophetic test. "The voice of the poor is the voice of God" (Chrysostom).

It is threatening to all of us within the dominant cultures of First World societies today seriously to consider this mandate. For if it is contemplated in a truly *serious* way, and not simply at the level of "talk" (Lindbeck), it cannot mean anything else for those of us who are Christians within these situations than that we shall become witnesses against our own nations and classes. If we are Caucasian and male it probably must mean that we shall have to become witnesses against our own race and gender as well—though I do not think that this should be said in such a way as to imply that if, on the contrary, we are non-Caucasian or female (and still among the relatively affluent) we are exonerated from the mandate that belongs to the *whole* church of the First World and implies a judgment against ourselves and not only against others. By comparison with the oppression of the very poor of the earth, the oppressions of the nonpoor are almost luxuries.[87]

(b) The testimony of the sensitive: From the beginning, Christian theology sought out those within its orbit who could speak for the world. It did this for a number of reasons: because it was under compulsion to communicate with the world; because it could assume that its gospel, being intended as good news for humanity, might establish some point of contact with human wisdom, even though human wisdom could neither anticipate the good news nor fully comprehend it; because it was at base a respecter of human capacities for comprehension and repentance, etc. But it also *needed* these persons; for it needed to know what its own belief in ultimate meaning prevented it from knowing deeply, namely,

---

86. See the discussion of "The End of the Constantinian Era," chapter 3, §11.

87. In this connection, see Alice Frazer Evans, Robert A. Evans, and William Bean Kennedy, eds., *Pedagogies for the Non-Poor* (Maryknoll, N.Y.: Orbis, 1987).

what it meant to live both "in" the world and "of" it. It needed to find out what sort of story the world was telling; therefore it turned to those who were, so to speak, the amanuenses of the world's story.

This, for the greater share of the history of Christendom, has meant that theology sought its dialogue partner in philosophy. Stoicism, Platonism, Aristotelianism, idealism, existentialism—all have served the church in this capacity. And there will no doubt continue to be those with a vocation to philosophy who will be open to this special relationship to theology; for wherever human beings think profoundly about existence, wherever they still address the questions of being, of meaning, of good and evil, of beauty, they will give expression to the thoughts of many of their contemporaries who are not given to disciplined or consistent thought.

But in our era, and in the Anglo-Saxon world especially, formal philosophy—which has become a highly professional undertaking and, frequently, farther removed from everyday existence than academic theology itself—is for the most part no longer an *adequate* dialogue partner for theology. The direction of professional philosophy in the Anglo-American tradition has in fact been so much towards an empiricist-pragmatist approach to reality that the questions of being, meaning, goodness, etc., are frequently relegated to the realm of "mere poetry."[88]

It is not surprising, therefore, that theology has had to turn more and more precisely to . . . poetry! The artists, novelists, dramatists, poets,

---

88. This may be changing. In that connection, see Cornel West's excellent essay, "The Politics of American Neo-Pragmatism," in *Post-Analytic Philosophy* (New York: Columbia University Press, 1985), pp. 259ff.

I do not intend to suggest that philosophy can ever be dispensed with by the theologian, only that in its regnant forms in our particular contexts it is not adequate as a dialogue partner. It is of course still mandatory for responsible theology to remain philosophically informed. This is the point of Gerhard Ebeling in his discussion of "The Partnership of Theology and Philosophy," in *The Study of Theology*, trans. Duane A. Priebe (Philadelphia: Fortress, 1975), pp. 53f. While "the predominant tendency of contemporary philosophy certainly points . . . to an intensification of the contrast to the point of alienation, which impairs the possibility of conversation, if it does not make it altogether hopeless"; "theology would be poorly advised were it to neglect or completely abandon its previous partnership with philosophy in favour of phenomena of immediate interest." Ebeling adduces three reasons for this continuing orientation: (1) philosophy helps to prevent the theologian from "uncontrolled dependence" and sustains a spirit of "critical discussion" and "wrestling with the reasonableness of reason"; (2) it fosters the "disciplining of thought" and "a careful treatment of language"; and (3) it "represents its time" (and he quotes Hegel's definition of philosophy as "its time grasped in thought"). The third use of philosophy, however, is problematic today, Ebeling thinks, even in the continental European context, where it has not been so captivated by functionalism as in the English-speaking world. He therefore cautions his readers: "If, however, philosophy in its factual manifestation represents its time in a way that is all too hasty and lacking in distance, then it is all the more the case that theology cannot avoid falling into conflict with that philosophy as well" (pp. 64-66).

and musicians are more immediately helpful to the disciple community, because they are more apt to *represent* the *Zeitgeist*, and to do so in an unbiased and nonideological way. Though artists, too, can be ideologues with messages to communicate and axes to grind (George Bernard Shaw), they are more likely than are those who are committed to certain methodological and theoretical assumptions about existence to bring to the dialogue with the theological community the very thing that it needs to know: the story that humanity is now telling itself about itself and all things. The artists, as Marshall McLuhan insightfully stated it, are the DEW line of civilization.[89]

Among the sensitive, theology in recent years has also rightly numbered social scientists, anthropologists, historians, and (increasingly) physical scientists—especially from among the life sciences—who have their own irreplaceable skills and tools for attesting to the character of our context. Many of the most resourceful theologians of our time, for instance, have been moved to explore more deeply the tradition of Jerusalem on account of their exposure to Marxist economic analysis of society; and today there is a greater and greater need to seek out those who have the expertise to speak from the side of nonhuman nature, which is also seriously *victimized* by the goals of our civilization, and may indeed be the corporate victim whose fate ought to concern us most, since the future of our world depends upon our civilization's achievement of a better rapport with the natural order.

There is, literally, no way of circumscribing or prioritizing the lists of those human beings whose testimony to truth is important for the disciple community in countless ways, including its capacity to aid and authenticate the church's societal analysis. Certainly we would be remiss were we not to include in this category, as well, representatives of other world religions—and especially of our closest faith community, the Jews.[90] I should prefer, however, to leave this consideration to the fourth category, for I think that, at very least in terms of cultural analysis, Christianity today is obliged (*and privileged*) to regard itself as part of a much more inclusive community of faith, which in its inclusivity has far better chances of self-correction and mutual aid than do the religions separately.

---

89. The distant early warning line. Another, older simile is to think of the artists as being like the rabbits or canaries taken down into mines or (in the early days) submarines to monitor the supply of oxygen and, through their bodily reactions, which were faster, to warn the human beings present when that necessary commodity was running out.

90. Perhaps no contemporary non-Christian has been so important for developments within Western Christian consciousness and theology as Elie Wiesel. See in this connection Robert McAfee Brown, *Elie Wiesel: Messenger to All Humanity* (Notre Dame and London: University of Notre Dame Press, 1983).

(c) The direct testimony of the sources: In the foregoing chapter we have drawn attention to the fact that a contextual theology must guard against the danger of relativism by sustaining a disciplined and intensive dialogue with the tradition. Here, we ought simply to expand this observation by noting that the tradition—again, with special emphasis upon the Scriptures of the Older and Newer Testaments—contains certain recurrent themes in regard to the human condition. Contextual theology cannot assume, with traditionalists, that these themes are anything like inflexible laws to be applied without reference to the actual behavior of the human community; but, as part of the common heritage with which we have to work, the biblical and traditional teachings of the church concerning the human condition present, not only a "lens" (Lindbeck) through which we may view our own historical moment, but certain ideas which act as guidelines and tests in relation to our assessment of our context.

For example, the tradition of Jerusalem generally assumes that the human condition is not what it ought to be: it is fallen from the divine intention; its *existence* does not embody its *essence*; it exists in a state of "sin." This ought *not* to mean, and for the contextualist cannot mean, the kind of uniformity of degradation that is conventionally assumed by various orthodoxies. *Sin* is one of the most misunderstood words in the Christian vocabulary and its exposition cannot be entered into here; but it must at least be said in this place that the manifestations of sin are infinite, and therefore that neither in its hamartiology nor in its soteriology may the disciple community presume to know a priori precisely what must be said and done. Sin as pride is vastly different from sin manifested as sloth; and how varied are the faces of both pride and sloth!

What it means, however, that the tradition contains this analytical propensity to regard the human condition as "sinful," "fallen," is that this (from the modern point of view) "negative" assessment of reality will make its appearance *in some form* in every authentically Christian assessment of the world; and that Christians will not be surprised by the fact. Thus when the Jesuit liberationist Juan Luis Segundo insists that the point of departure for all honest theology today must be the recognition that "the world should not be the way it is,"[91] no Christians who have any rudimentary familiarity with their sources will be either surprised or offended. When Segundo then continues to explicate precisely what he

---

91. Quoted by Robert McAfee Brown, *Making Peace in the Global Village* (Philadelphia: Westminster, 1981. See Juan Luis Segundo, s. J., *Grace and the Human Condition*, vol. 2, trans. John Drury (Maryknoll, N.Y.: Orbis, 1973), "Introduction," pp. 3ff., 12.

means by this statement, there will in all likelihood be disagreement and dialogue, some of which (hopefully) will become the subject matter of our fourth test. But a Christian who objects to the statement as such would immediately disqualify himself or herself as representative of the tradition, and Fr. Segundo can at least be assured in this way that his premise has a foundation in "sound teaching."[92]

The same point could be illustrated in connection with other emphases of the tradition—for example, an assessment of the context which assumed or concluded that the situation was totally irredeemable would have to be tested against the tradition's teachings concerning divine providence and the doctrine of redemption. Let us, however, repeat: While the tradition provides us with very important guidelines and tests of authenticity, it does not remove from us the condition and necessity of decision. It has happened before, and it shall no doubt happen in the future, that even a disciple community wonderfully aware of its Scriptures and its best dogmatic traditions has erred gravely in its reading of the spirit of the times.

(d) The testimony of the body: It cannot be too emphatically stated that theology is the work of the disciple *community.* It is not merely the work of individuals, each one in her or his corner, providing what light he or she can. It is a dialogical and communal enterprise from first to last, and nowhere is the dialogue more needful than at this point of contextual discernment. Here the experience of one has to be tested against the experience of another. And fortunately there is, as Paul noted, a variety of gifts.

The variety is particularly significant where the ongoing decision concerning the character of the age is concerned. Protestants on the whole have not yet learned how to take advantage of this variety, and this is partly because much Protestantism, having never achieved its own vaunted "priesthood of *all* believers," has relied upon the theological experts too exclusively, i.e., it has given too much weight to the evidence from dogma, accessible to those professionally trained in Scripture, history, and dogmatics, and not enough to those whose closer involvement in the world and greater vulnerability to its movements (i.e., mostly laypersons) could have added immeasurably to the church's comprehension of its society.

Today, fortunately, we are beginning to witness the breakup of this professional monopoly on worldly discernment. And we are also being

---

92. See Frederick Herzog, *Justice Church: The New Function of the Church in North America* (Maryknoll, N.Y.: Orbis, 1981), pp. 140ff.

compelled to recognize that there is a great plurality of perspectives within the *koinōnia* from which our context can and must be assessed. Not only do laypersons frequently have quite different perspectives from professionals (clergy, theologians, and professional church workers) in their appraisal of society; but women, most of whom do not have the dubious benefit of "a view from the top," see the world in ways significantly different from most men; the marginalized old have yet another vantage point to bring, as do racial minorities, the victims of economic injustice, moral outcasts such as homosexual persons seem once more to have become, and many others whose opinions and experiences of the world have regularly been ignored by dominant forms of Christianity (one could well include here, for instance, many of those same persons who in our second test [above] were identified as the truly sensitive—artists and intellectuals who, as members of "the high culture," tend to be regarded with suspicion by bourgeois Christian majorities).

The breakdown of professionalistic monopoly in theology brings with it certain problematic factors, including perhaps a loss of historical and doctrinal rigor; but one of its great advantages is surely that it opens the disciple community to new forms of expertise which it has sorely needed. If these human resources are earnestly sought out and carefully nurtured, the church in our time could acquire a more profound (though of course not infallible) grasp of the character of its context. For if we add to the explicitly *Christian* resources at our disposal the testimonies of those who scan the world from the vantage points of other religious faith-postures, as we ought now to do and today *may* do, we shall find a rich dialogical matrix within which to undertake the awesome necessity of judging. While there are no doubt many, and perhaps permanent, barriers to interfaith communion at the level of answers to the human condition, there is certainly a greater potentiality for such communion at the level of social analysis than we have even begun to achieve. In the face of a world which seeks oblivion in a whole host of ways, the seriously faithful among all faiths can, if they will, discover certain common assumptions and goals, and in the process not only encourage one another in the difficult business of discerning the signs of the times, but constitute themselves a unified bulwark against humanity's more insane pursuits.

6. A Generalization: What Makes for Contextuality in Christian Theology?

It may be instructive for us to conclude our considerations of the nature of contextuality in Christian theology by asking what moves a disciple community towards such an approach. The dangers that we have observed (§ 4) may deter or inhibit this kind of theological praxis; I am nevertheless of the opinion that few Christians are kept from the conscious attempt to engage their contexts on account of these dangers. Conversely, what drives Christians to a contextual approach to theology in spite of the risks involved is seldom, I suspect, sheer intellectual daring. There is, I think, a strong element of historical necessity in it, and the logic of that necessity may be stated in this way: A disciple community is pushed into explicitly contextual reflection at the point where the societal-anthropological matrix that its theological heritage has *assumed* seems no longer confirmed by its actual experience. The community becomes aware that the context which has been unconsciously presupposed in its theological conventions is no longer in place, but has been or is being replaced by a different social matrix, in which different questions are present, different goals entertained, and different anxieties felt. At the point of such a discovery, *conscious* engagement of the context is no longer a matter of simple choice, but a "must" which presses in upon the community's intelligence and its will to believe and hope. At that point, the disciple community recognizes that apart from such a willed attempt to come to terms with its cultural context, its *doctrina* could exist only to reinforce a worldview whose time had passed. As such, it would undoubtedly serve certain interests. But it would not serve the interests of the God of the gospel, whose desire is to be *present*, to be "with us."

To elaborate: The history of the Christian church contains periods, some of them lasting for centuries, during which it was possible for Christian thinkers to assume—simply to take for granted—certain things about the nature of humanity, the possibilities of rational thought, the movement of historical time, the nature of the good, etc. These assumptions could be entertained without radical and regular examination, being generally and widely held within the culture at large. During such periods, it is not required of the church that it engage in active dialogue with the social milieu in order to discern the character of the situation and thus its appropriate witness within it. At least, such a requirement is not *felt* by the church. In fact, as Bernard Lonergan pointed out, the "classicist" notion of culture, which dominated throughout most of the church's history, assumed that culture did not change but "was normative . . . universal and permanent." Therefore, even if it were acknowledged that theology must be in dialogue with culture (and in the faith/reason dialectic, for example, medieval theology almost universally acknowledges this), this did not necessarily mean that theology had to be contextual in the sense developed in this study; for it could be taken for granted that the context in which theology was done remained in essence steadfast. Thus, alongside a static conception of culture, theology in turn could be "conceived as a permanent achievement" and the task of the theological community was to "discourse upon its nature."[93]

While Christian history tells of such periods, however, it also relates times and places where the smooth discourse between a permanently achieved theology and a normative social context was disrupted and thrown into confusion. These latter periods, moreover, are especially important for all critical theology, because they represent the times of greatest *creativity* in the church's thinking. I am thinking of such moments as the emergence of Augustinian thought at the close of the Roman Empire; the transition from Platonic to Aristotelian categories in the High Middle Ages; the fresh discovery of Scripture and the message of "justification by grace" at the outset of the Reformation. In such periods, what occurred—seen from the perspective of the present discussion—is that the contextual cultural assumptions presupposed by the previous period were thrown into disarray by the formative internal and external events of the present. In the confusion resulting from this loss, individuals and movements emerged whose destiny it became to find their way through the chaos to some new sense of their identity and their calling as Christians. They had to experience in themselves, as it were, the death of the old and the dubious birth of the new. But out of their extremities of mind and soul there emerged a new awareness of the world, and new possibilities of Christian dialogue with it.

Theology—as we may put it in perhaps a too facile way—is forced to become *contextual* where the universal *assumptions* of a previous age become visible *as assumptions*, where experience no longer conforms to familiar patterns, and where the "world" becomes a "strange land" calling for a new rendition of "the Lord's song."

This, surely, is what has happened to Western Christianity during the past several decades. Prior to the dramatic events which ushered in the 20th century, Christian theology had been able to presuppose a certain rather static cultural matrix. It was not the long-established culture whose characteristics could be assumed by the medieval scholastics; nevertheless, despite its relative youth, the "modern" worldview which informed this social matrix was astonishingly authoritative. With few exceptions (notorious among them, Søren Kierkegaard), theology after the earlier

---

93. Bernard J. F. Lonergan, *Method in Theology* (London: Darton, Longman and Todd, 1972), p. xi.

decades of the 19th century did not have to wrestle with its context, always trying to discover its real questions, fears, longings. The aims and suppositions of Western society were sufficiently entrenched that not only the theologian but also the scientist, the educator, the industrialist, and almost everyone else could take them for granted, build upon them, presuppose their *universal* applicability and, in fact, do all of this without a trace of skepticism but believing them to be laws of historical development.

It was only the obvious and (for Europeans) cataclysmic breakdown of this entrenched modern worldview which caused the theological community to recognize the extent of its own captivity by a particular way of conceiving of the world, and to go again to the marketplace in order to discover the truth about the matter. Whatever may be said about the *eventual* character of Karl Barth's "mature" theological position, there can be no question that in its first stages it was a thoroughly contextual undertaking. Barth and his contemporaries were thrust out of the happy and ordered household of liberal assumptions about the human condition and God's place in it, and made to experience the cold winds of their new century—the century that liberalism had determined would be "The Christian Century." It was a painful experience. It always is. But it is the very stuff out of which faithful and lively theology can be created—as well as art, literature, music, and other achievements of the human spirit and imagination.

For complex reasons, I believe, the contextualization of theology which occurred in European theology during this century and has lately occurred in Latin America and some other parts of the world, has not yet occurred significantly in North America. That it must occur here, if Christianity is to have any part in the future that is trying to be born among us, seems to me obvious enough. That it *could* occur here, and that its occurrence could be of ecumenical importance, is the hope that has engendered this study.

CHAPTER ▪ TWO

Discerning Our *Context*

I wish to show you the darkness
you are so afraid of.[1]

Having considered some of the basic principles of theological contextuality, we turn now to our own context. How, as Christians, can we assess the contemporary North American milieu, the situation in which we are called to do theology, the culture in whose midst we are to be a disciple community of the Christ?

Before we can justify any attempt to answer this question, however, we must address ourselves to a preliminary consideration. It has been anticipated to some extent in the previous chapter; but now we must make it our explicit concern. On what grounds may we speak, in the first place, of a "North American context"?

7. The Circumscription of Contexts

7.1. The World and the Worlds. We have assumed from the outset that a contextual theology addresses itself to a specific and identifiable sociohistorical situation, but does not such an assumption conceal what is in fact a very problematic aspect of this entire approach? Can contexts be so readily identified? Where does one context leave off and another begin? And within a given here and now are there not in fact many different contexts? Is there such a thing as a *North American* context?

---

1. Margaret Atwood, *Interluner* (Toronto: Oxford University Press, 1984), p. 102.

The question of the circumscription of contexts is all the more difficult at this time because of our consciousness of the unity of the planet and all life. We speak about spaceship earth, and from voyages into outer space we may actually view for ourselves what for our grandparents was still only known theoretically—the spherical character of our home. The earth has no more corners! At the same time, we have begun to realize the ecological interrelatedness of all forms of life. As human beings, we can no longer look into the faces of other creatures and find them utterly alien. We have learned to appreciate lines of continuity between our own species and species far less complex than monkeys, whose similarity to human beings so offended the sensibilities of our forebears under the impact of Mr. Darwin's theories. Ecologists have succeeded—probably better than they realize—in demonstrating to our technological society the terrible connectedness of things, and our consequent dependence upon sustaining delicate balances within the natural order. In short, the movement of human consciousness over the past century seems to have been towards a greater and greater sense of the reciprocity and comprehensiveness of all that is.

Given such a phenomenon, is it not altogether artificial, and perhaps retrograde as well, to divide the world into "contexts"? In particular, is not such a procedure questionable for Christians, since from the beginning the Christian message has stressed the unity principle: the unity of the divine Being; the unity of truth; the unity of created things, whose great variety should never conceal from faith the knowledge that they are, all of them, creatures of the one God; the unification through reconciliation of all that on account of sin has been divided; the pentecostal unity of the church, where persons of many languages begin to comprehend one another (Acts 2); the ultimate reunification of all creatures in "the peaceable kingdom"? If after centuries of parochialism and chauvinism the human spirit seems at last capable of grasping this integrating principle which is so important to our religious tradition, should not theology accentuate it as well? Instead of developing theologies which concentrate on specific contexts for their subject matter, therefore, should we not take advantage both of the apologetic climate and of our ecumenical reality as a worldwide faith and expend our creative energies constructing a *global* theology?

Such admonition is very compelling—until we remind ourselves of *the other side* of our contemporary consciousness and the stark realities upon which it is founded. At the same time that the knowledge explosion, widespread travel, and modern methods of communication have been providing us with a new sense of our global oneness, world events have made us exceptionally conscious of our dividedness. It may be that there has never been a time in history when human beings felt so threatened by divisions within the human community, and among the species. We may not be able to think of the earth as having corners, but we are very much aware of its "curtains." There are political and economic boundaries that are much harder to cross over than were any of the great walls erected by the ancients! We speak instinctively of planet earth and of the global village, but we also speak about "worlds." In the one world there are at least three "worlds." Their boundaries cannot be perceived from outer space, but these worlds are nonetheless so real and so tragically partitioned that their divisions may be responsible, finally, for the demise of life on the planet. Being unable to survive together, we may effect a common extinction.

Christian theology cannot afford to ignore these real divisions any more than it can overlook the contemporary intimations of unity. Nor is it necessary for it to do so. For while the theology of the cross places an emphasis upon the unity principle—not as principle, but as the new reality made possible by divine grace—it is at the same time well aware of the old reality of divisiveness and the threat to life that is implied in it. Christian hamartiology (its doctrine of sin) is indeed largely devoted to that theme.

Not that biblical faith espouses, as its *soteriology* (doctrine of salvation), a state in which all differentiation is overcome in an ontic unity. The quarrel of the Judeo-Christian tradition is not with *difference* (it celebrates difference!) but with divisiveness. Divisiveness or alienation is what happens when the principle of differentiation that is present in creaturely existence, and necessary to it, is distorted by the sinful impulse, i.e., the inclination towards the segregation and elevation—or, conversely, the denigration—of self. Against the historical reality of a pathetically divided creation, faith sets the reconciling work of God, who wills to break down all "dividing walls of hostility" (Eph. 2:14). But precisely the reality of that reconciling grace makes it mandatory for the disciple community to take with utter seriousness the reality of that with which the gracious, judging love of God wrestles, i.e., the brokenness and estrangement of the world. The biblical God does not ignore that negating reality, but rather seeks to engage and deflect its power from within. The theology of the cross describes the reconciling work of God in Christ as the negation of the negation: through self-subjection to the powers of alienation at work within history, the Christ turns their destructive energy

147

towards good and not evil. The point, after all, is not to obliterate distinction, but to eliminate from it the dimension of disaffinity and enmity which, under the conditions of sin, it inevitably courts.

Translating this into the terms of the present discussion, what it means is that the disciple community must enucleate a theological praxis which enables it to do justice, simultaneously, to two requirements of the Christian tradition which, outside the tradition, may appear antithetical or at least not easily harmonized: (a) while recognizing the immensity of the barriers to unity, we are required to satisfy the drive of prophetic faith towards the *universal* realization of God's reconciling work; (b) without losing sight of this universal impulse of the divine work, we are required to satisfy its quest for the fulfillment of the *particular*.

Precisely this, as I now hope to show, is the intention of contextuality in theological reflection.

7.2. Polarities within the Contextual Approach. It belongs to the process of contextualization, and is implicit in what has been claimed for this process in the previous chapter, that it contains two impulses which stand in a dialectical relationship with one another; that is to say, they imply quite different and even opposing emphases, yet in the end they do not contradict but complement and define each other. In fact, each requires the other in order to obviate the undesirable or destructive elements within it. We are dealing, in other words, with what are frequently called polar realities. Both are implicit within the concept of "the context," theologically understood.

(a) The impulse towards the particular: After what has been claimed already about Christian theology's need to engage the here and now, it will come as no surprise if we say that the contextualization of theological reflection means the determination to occupy itself with the particular. It cannot be satisfied with generalization. It cannot rest in doctrinal pronouncements which are supposed to apply always and everywhere. It does not question the belief that the gospel implies God's love for "the world" (John 3:16), but it needs to know: How does God's love for this world apply to *this* world, our world? It does not quarrel with the profession of a faith which dares to express itself in great eternal verities—God as creator of the universe; the ubiquity of sin; the mysterious providence of God; the significance of the sacrifice of Christ for all, etc.; but it wants to understand: How are we to *confess* this faith?

That the faith must be contextualized means that it must be made specific in relation to what is "there." Jesus commands his disciples to "love your neighbor." The Torah, which Paul claims (Rom. 13:9; Gal.

5:14) is summed up in this one commandment, is as explicit as the one next door! Was it only dullness of mind that prevented Jesus' original disciples from understanding that this commandment has a universal application? Or was it something more complex than mere lack of imagination? Was it not perhaps the fact that the universal always eludes us until we can glimpse its meaning, its radicality, through the particular? The love of neighbor as a "general" law has as frequently been used to *avoid* the (disturbingly specific) neighbor as to love and serve him or her. The point of Jesus' familiar parable of the good Samaritan is lost if it is turned into a mere *exemplification* of the commandment to love the neighbor. If it is to achieve its intended end, the parable must function for us as a radical particularization of the commandment: love is not a principle which we apply, but an event in which we are involved, person with person, creature with creature.

This explains, at least in part, the prominence of story (especially of parable) in the Synoptics, and of narrative history in the scriptural tradition at large. With story and history, it is never quite possible to extract the universal from the particular—not, at any rate, in such a way that the universal can become, in turn, the type of theory which *insulates us from particulars*. Conceptualization easily ends in generalization. It is perhaps the primary crisis of theological thinking in the Western world that it has been so consistently reduced to conceptual thought that it is no longer capable of imaginative encounter with the particular. Theology, Christology, anthropology—all are turned into ideas, into whole networks of ideas. The ideas are given a nomenclature and they achieve a life of their own. The practitioners of the discipline are those who familiarize themselves with these ideas and this nomenclature and are able to converse with one another using the language of this "science." But many of them are not able to converse with anyone outside the discipline, and frequently their encounter with Christians who use another language (for instance, the language of Asian experience and metaphor)[2] is frustrating in the extreme.

This criticism of theological theory should not be read as if it implied a rejection of conceptualization as such. Our purpose here is to consider the nature of Christian *thinking*—thinking the faith. Theological thought certainly involves the formulation of concepts. But the question that must always be put to concepts and to those who formulate them is, What end do these ideas serve? If they serve the end of an intellectual detachment

---

2. See C. S. Song, *The Compassionate God* (Maryknoll, N.Y.: Orbis, 1982).

from time and place, then they must surely be called into question. With theoretical concepts as with any other product of the human imagination it is true that "by their fruits you shall know them." The proper end of the concept—which is an abstraction from particularity—is to return its creator to the particular, with a more profound comprehension and commitment. Let us say it more concretely still: with love! Any thinking the faith which remains at the level of abstraction is like any other manifestation of "faith without works": it is "dead" (James 2:17). One may "understand all mysteries and all knowledge," yet come to "nothing" (1 Cor. 13:2). If our theology does not bring us at last to the threshold of the neighbor—notably, the one who "fell among robbers"—it has remained at the level of theory. Contextualization of the gospel means the inherent and persistent drive of faith in the Christ towards the particular, the neighbor.

(b) The impulse towards the whole: While contextualization immediately suggests the particularization of theological reflection, it does not do so in a narrow or isolationistic manner. A context implies both the particular and that by which the particular is *surrounded*. This is implied when one says, for instance, that an event should be seen within its context, or that an historical figure cannot be understood apart from his or her context.

It is here that contextual thought is most conspicuously different from what has made its appearance in Christian theology and ethics since the 1960s—situationalism. "The situation," as in the thought of Joseph Fletcher and others,[3] is a thing in itself and interesting for itself. It is sufficiently isolable from its surroundings to constitute a case to which certain moral principles can be applied. In distinction from this, the context, while remaining rooted in particularity, positively needs its surrounding reality for any adequate comprehension of its own reality and meaning.

And what *is* its surrounding reality? Where will one stop in one's attempt to discern any entity in its context? As Max Stackhouse has put it: "How big is a 'here' and how long is a 'now?' "[4] What will satisfy the drive, implicit within the thought of contextuality, to set the particular object of investigation properly within its total environment?

The answer is that this drive cannot be satisfied, really, until *the whole* environment of the particular has been penetrated and accounted

---

3. See Joseph Fletcher, *Situation Ethics: The New Morality* (Philadelphia: Westminster, 1966).

4. Max Stackhouse, "Contextualization and Theological Education," *Theological Education* 23 (1986): 80.

for. In practice this cannot be successfully achieved, for no one is capable of grasping the entirety. But the point is that the *impulse* to do so is present in the contextual process. It is comparable to the child, who at the age of eight or nine is suddenly overtaken by the thought of its particularity, but at the same time by the vastness of the universe to which it belongs. What child has not amused itself with such an address as: Jean Smith, Apartment 4, 1000 Front Street, Mytown, U.S.A., North America, The Earth, The Galaxy, The Universe . . . ? Innately we seem to understand that we cannot identify ourselves *truly* unless we can see ourselves standing within the totality of our environs. We cannot know this totality, and just that agnosticism may be the seat of a certain kind of religious proclivity—for "only God knows" the totality, and therefore what and who and where and why we, individually, are. But the drive to understand the nature and meaning of the totality is never far removed from the existential discovery of our particularity.

Like the child, the theological process which begins by taking very seriously the particular cannot be satisfied until it has gone as far as it possibly can go towards seeing this particular within the totality of its environment—its context. How, for example, would it be possible to understand the neighbor unless one understood the social environment of which the neighbor were part? It was just this need to see the individual within the larger social context that drove that branch of theological liberalism which came to be known as the Social Gospel away from the narrow individual*ism* of bourgeois liberalism. One cannot even do justice to the individual if one concentrates on nothing *except* the individual. Too much liberalism ended in an arid and sentimental personalism. The advocates of the Social Gospel were grasped by the other polar impulse, the impulse towards the whole, which cannot be avoided by anyone who is concerned seriously enough about the particular.

It is this same interconnectedness between the particular and the totality which led the tradition of Jerusalem from its profound contemplation of its own quite specific history to an intensive feeling of involvement in the history of the whole of creation, a feeling which expressed itself in its theologies both of creation and redemption. Unlike countless other peoples, the main stream of Judaic thought did not become ensnared in its own story. Israel saw its history as a medium through which God was dealing with *the whole* creation: "by you, all the families of the earth will bless themselves" (Gen. 12:3). Israel's sense of the universal significance of its covenant with God saved it from the elitism of other religious and philosophic traditions, which could not get past their own particularity. While the concept of election sometimes led to elitist pretentions, it could only do so through a distortion of its manner of concentration on the particular. Election, like the idea of an elite, singles out a few; but in radical distinction from every form of elitism, the few exist (and suffer!) for the sake of the many. In other words, there is a thrust towards the universal within the particular as such, *whenever the particular is considered within a framework of the universality of the divine love.*

Through Israel, the Christian movement received this same sense of the paradoxical nature of the particular. The divine love had expressed itself fully in this one life. There could be no more intensive concentration upon the particular; nor could there be any circumventing of the "*scandal of particularity.*" Yet precisely in this one life God had extended the divine *agapē* to *all*.[5] Truly to contemplate this one life and death was to be led to the life of the totality, truly to enter into baptismal solidarity with this one life and death was to be raised from the deadness of a futile search for personal autonomy to the knowledge of solidarity with all.

What this juxtaposition of the two poles of contextuality demonstrates is that contextual theology and global theology—contextualization and globalization—are not *alternatives* but two sides of the same coin. If the disciple community probes its own context deeply enough, it will be moved towards the totality by the internal logic of its own existence and calling.

7.3. Critical Contexts.   Before pursuing this more explicitly, however, we must consider an aspect of the topic which we have left behind for purposes of clarity. We noted that when one asks about the limits of the context of a specific entity, there is literally no end to the speculation to which this leads. From the immediate surroundings of the entity in question one is carried to ever widening circles of temporal and spatial environing.

Yet there are stages and degrees in this process of reflection on the context. One way in which we regularly acknowledge these stages (it is present in the example of the child's address) is by moving from the more restrictive to the more inclusive. An individual's context may thus be considered first from the perspective of family, then neighborhood or district, then region, then nation, family of nations (e.g., the British Commonwealth), planet, galaxy. . . . Or again, one may consider the

---

5. See Karl Barth's sermon, "All!" (September 22, 1957) in the collection of his prison sermons, *Deliverance to the Captives*, trans. Margaret Wieser (New York: Harper and Row, 1959), pp. 85ff.

particular in relation to similarities—its participation in smaller or larger classes of things. Thus a person's context may be designated by racial, linguistic, sexual, economic, political, or generally cultural distinctions. Another obvious way of acknowledging the stages of contextual identification is chronological: an anxiety belongs to the Middle Ages, or an event occurs in the 18th century, the high point of the modern epoch of Western civilization.

In acknowledging these stages or degrees of the total environing of the particular, we are implicitly recognizing distinctions. All events happen in time and space, and therefore no one entity (event, person, nation, concept, etc.) can be isolated from the totality. Historical time and materiality bind every particular to every other. Yet the relation of a given phenomenon to some particulars is always obviously closer than to others. Without vitiating the *universal* thrust of contextual thought, we may nevertheless recognize important contexts within the larger context: I am a 20th-century Canadian, middle-aged, mainly Caucasian, and male, and while this does not (I trust!) cut me off from the *whole* human species, past, present, and future, it does identify me with certain groupings of the species and, concomitantly, distinguish me from others.

Let me propose that another way of designating such contexts-within-the-context would be by grouping the smaller contexts around the existence of *shared crises*. This is not really an arbitrary designation, so far as Christian theology is concerned, since the notion of crisis belongs very much to our tradition. It is to those who participate in common crises that the prophets address themselves—Amos, for example, or the author of the Apocalypse with his different letters to the different churches, or Paul with his word (in the opening chapters of Romans) for the Gentiles on the one hand and the Jews on the other. It is likely that those who share crises also share other things as well—perhaps language, culture, history, natural environment, economic situation. At the same time, critical contexts are not immediately synonymous or even necessarily continuous with other types of contexts. One may share the same geographic location with thousands of other persons but, being of another race (for instance, an American "Indian"), one's most decisive context is by no means simply geographic. In that case one would not be able to extricate oneself totally from the problematique of one's specific region or nation, yet neither would nor should one feel as implicated in the crises of that geopolitical unit as one would do were one a member of the dominant culture. As a member of an economically and culturally oppressed minority, one is indeed more nearly a victim of the crises of the dominant culture than someone who bears immediate responsibility for them.

153

This method of designating contextual distinctions has a number of advantages theologically: (1) It allows us to keep in view the universal impulse of contextual thinking: the crisis of a given society—e.g., of the economically depressed majorities in the Caribbean—can only be understood fully when it is seen in relation to the crises within other societies. (2) It allows us to take seriously the important distinctions within the larger whole: the three "worlds" may not be separable either in their socioeconomic interrelatedness or in their geopolitical reality, yet they are significantly different in terms of the crises that they confront. (3) It allows us also to recognize distinctions *within* geographically or historically defined contexts. For instance, to be a woman in a male-dominated society, to be black in a society whose population is predominantly white, to be French- or Spanish-speaking in an overwhelmingly Anglophone culture, to be poor in a society whose values and mores are determined by the middle class—all of these and similar distinctions must be taken seriously by a faith which manifests a special interest, not only in the particular as such, but in oppressed particularities.

7.4. North America as Context. Let us now ask how these distinctions help us to answer the questions with which we began this subsection, i.e., whether it is either right or possible in the first place to circumscribe contexts; whether, and under what conditions, we can designate, in particular, a North American context.

In the first place, our discussion of the polar relationship between the particular and the universal in contextual thinking enables us to affirm the pursuit of explicit contexts while at the same time upholding the necessity (which is both implicit in the gospel and made mandatory by the current world situation) of a global theology. Indeed, it would be hard to envisage a responsible global theology which did not root itself in the particularity of one's own culture. Conversely, it would be impossible, on the basis of our argument above, to pursue a theology that was responsible to one's own culture which did not lead inevitably to the contemplation of the whole. Therefore, as was said earlier, it should not be insinuated that contextual theology and global theology are mutually exclusive alternatives; they are in fact correlates, each requiring and helping to define the other. The universal thrust of the gospel prevents theology from becoming parochial; and the particularistic concentration of the same gospel prevents theology from becoming transhistorical, supramundane, and merely theoretical.

It is almost palpably demonstrable today that the most responsible *global* act on the part of the North American disciple community would be its serious attempt to come to terms with the realities of our own context. In a planetary society held hostage to the economic and military pursuits of two mutually suspicious superpowers, one of which *is* our context, it is required of *all* disciples of One who came "that the world might be saved" that they devote their spiritual and physical energies to the amelioration of these hostilities. How much more is this demanded of those disciples of the Christ who dwell *within* those empires—and especially within the sphere of *that* empire which daily proclaims its Christianity.

Second, our discussion of the distinguishing of contexts on the basis of shared crises enables us to concentrate on a larger context while acknowledging distinctions within it. Specifically, we can identify the dominant culture of North America as a context without overlooking the fact that within this large geographic and sociohistorical grouping there are significant minorities which do not conform, or conform only partially, to the dominant pattern, and ought not to be presented as though they were simply part of an homogeneous whole.

To begin with, to speak of the "dominant" culture of this society is almost at once effectively to eliminate Mexico, though it belongs to the geographic entity called North America. It is also possible on the basis of such a distinction to recognize that Canada and the United States, while sharing a common crisis (as well as important aspects of history, a common geographic space, a majority language, etc.) manifest certain significant differences (political, economic, historical, geographic, linguistic, and broadly cultural). And within each of these geographically larger nations of the continent there are also important geopolitical and other distinctions: Quebec, Western as distinct from Eastern mentalities, urban as differentiated from rural and suburban life, etc. Again, within the larger or dominant grouping there are also other distinctions based on race, gender, age, etc., all and each of which may require treatment different from the majority culture at important points. Contextual reflection will drive us always towards the specific; but it will also require us to observe the specific in relation to the larger entity by which it is surrounded. None of the specifics (e.g., Northwest Territories, the American South, women, native peoples, the unemployed, senior citizens) is independent of the whole—even if that means only victimization by the dominant culture.

This last observation brings us to an aspect of the topic which has vital importance for what follows. In the light of the foregoing discussion, it is surely more than a matter of passing interest that so much of the creative indigenous theological thought which has been undertaken within the North American context over the past three or four decades has been the work of minorities or those representing minorities: blacks, women, the poor, victims of social injustice, advocates of peace, and others. Given the suggestion of the generalization articulated at the end of the previous chapter, namely, that spirited theology is likely to occur only where there has been some shaking of the foundations, it is not surprising that this is so. The critical character of the contexts shared by these groups has caused persons within them to rethink the meaning of the faith. Their crises could not be repressed or ignored—at least not by *all* of those concerned. In a society whose every other word was "freedom," someone had to speak out of the unfreedom of the black population of this continent. In a world which did not grant equal opportunity and respect to women, its rhetoric notwithstanding, a few women were impelled to give expression to their rejection and to ask about the role of empirical Christianity in the history of that rejection. Oppressed minorities are driven by their very oppression to become "original," and anyone who cares for the church and its message will be grateful for it—even when it makes itself felt as a judgment which begins at the household of God (1 Peter 4:17).

There is, however, a problematic aspect of all this which is frequently overlooked. It is that when theology is concentrated upon the oppressive contexts of minorities there is a tendency to neglect or camouflage the crisis of the majority culture. Or else the latter crisis is perceived in terms of its criticism by the minorities who are its victims, and not in terms of its own internal dynamics. As we have insisted earlier, the testimony of the victims is an important guideline for authenticity in the theological analyses of cultures. The victims *are* able to see dimensions of societal malaise which only they have experienced in sufficient depth to comprehend. Yet the crisis of a culture is not wholly visible in or through the testimony of its victims, invaluable as that testimony is to theology. The crisis of the dominant culture of North America is not to be equated with any of the things that it does to its minorities—to any of them or all of them together. To the perceptive mind, the crises of the dominant culture may become especially *visible* in the plight of the minorities, and some of the spokespersons for minorities will likely bear witness to this. But too often the message that is conveyed through the testimony of the minorities, unless it is supplemented by other studied reflection, is that what is wrong with the dominant culture is that it oppresses these minorities; that, therefore, its restitution would mean the cessation of that oppressive behavior. Such a message sometimes translates itself into very important concrete emendations of the status quo (equal rights, economic justice, toleration of difference, etc.), but it may also serve to deflect further, deeper probing of the larger crisis. For the truth is, surely, not that majority cultures set out to oppress certain elements but rather that, pursuing particular goals and upholding particular values, they necessarily end by jeopardizing those who are handicapped in relation to those goals and values. The analysis of the crises of such societies, therefore, is bound to ask about the nature of the goals and values and to attempt to comprehend the crises of such societies in the light of the same.

Christian theology, even when it recognizes (as it has again begun to do in our time) its own minority status in society, is obligated to attempt to come to terms with the crises of the dominant culture that is its host. It cannot afford to let power go its own way, choosing instead to identify itself only with the powerless. It has inherited the prophetic task of dealing with kings and potentates and rulers of the people—a task which it could scarcely perform while it was content to play the role of chaplain to power! Today it is able, where it is willing, to resume the prophetic role. And until it does resume it, it will not serve the victims either, in any deep-rooted sense, though it may certainly bind some wounds—and that is an honorable thing. The situation of oppressed minorities will not be altered greatly, however, until the crisis of the majority has been confronted. For it is that crisis which makes necessary and even inevitable the various forms of oppression felt outside the gates of the ruling classes.

The analysis of our context which follows is informed by this concern. If it does not speak directly to minorities (about whose destiny its author certainly cares), it is because its primary goal is to uncover whatever can be uncovered of the far more subtle, largely unacknowledged unfreedom of the dominant middle-class majority—the rich who look for salvation in the building of greater barns and the "well" who say they do not need a physician and the religious who provide cultic foundations for these illusions. If there is to be any liberation of these rich, these well, and these complacent ones—the "Establishment" of our society—it has to be a very artful affair, and perhaps only time itself will make the necessary transformation possible. But for the sake of life theology has to anticipate time's possibilities, in the hope that it may be a little gifted with foresight, if not with insight.[6]

---

6. In "Contextualization and Theological Education," Max Stackhouse laments what he calls "contextual*ism*": "It is frequently implied by some committed to a liberationist approach to theology and ethics that truth emerges from the actual material needs and interest of oppressed peoples, *and that that alone is what theology is all about*" (p. 76). There is considerable justification for such a warning. I have developed the thought of the preceding chapter, as well as the introductory subsections of the present chapter, in the full consciousness of such a potential distortion. But Stackhouse evidently

8. Prisoners of Optimism

8.1. European and American Responses to the Crisis of Modernity. How, then, shall we characterize the dominant culture of the North American context? Obviously enough, such an undertaking could be endless, and therefore limits have to be established. Our interest in discerning our context are theological, so it follows that our discussion will manifest a special concern for the role that religion and theology have played in the evolution of the present situation.

The thesis that I shall develop in response to this question can be stated fairly succinctly as follows: *The crisis of the dominant culture of North America is a particular species of the failure of the modern vision.* Since mainstream Christianity on this continent permitted itself to be absorbed into modernity, it has been helpless, for the most part, to come to terms with this failure. Nevertheless, there exists for us a persistent and increasingly urgent call to originality as a disciple community at the nerve center of the First World; and there are signs that this call is being heard.

The failure of modernity has been the common experience of all the (chiefly Western) societies which were captivated by the modern vision; but some of these societies were better equipped to cope with the failure than were others. North America was and is the most vulnerable to the devastations inherent in this failure; and to grasp something of the nature of that vulnerability we may compare American and European responses, with special reference to theological responses.

To begin somewhat obtusely, but for reasons that will shortly become obvious, it is instructive to recall what has been said earlier about the genesis of contextuality. Theological communities, I have claimed,[7] *become* contextually engaged at the point where the world they actually experience calls in question the presuppositions of the *worldview* they have inherited. Such communities are driven into active dialogue with

---

is among those who have intellectual qualms about contextualization generally: "Every choice that we make in these areas is freighted with lopsided interpretations of contextuality and leads us inevitably to contextualism. Even if we found some way of combining all these theories and interpretive periodizations in a 'unified' theory, it is not certain that we would 'know' any context exhaustively, or know how to respond to them theologically" (ibid., p. 82). To such scrupulous hesitancy, it needs to be pointed out that the only *alternative* to decision concerning contexts ("judging") is a permanent residency in the house of theory and the (no doubt tacit and unacknowledged) determination to keep one's theology professional—not to embark on the eminently perilous journey of the *confessor fidei*. *Of course*, "the best we can do is . . . make it clear that when we say the word 'context' we are using it provisionally" (ibid.). In theology, provisionality is (to employ a current expression) the name of the game.

7. Chapter One, §6.

their cultures because the human condition as it is assumed in their received traditions begins to appear contrived—a theoretical construct which
can no longer stand the test of ordinary experience. Under such circumstances, some Christians within the larger body of the church feel constrained to leave their doctrinal sanctuaries and return to the marketplace,
opening themselves in a less biased way to those who are telling the
world's new story of itself, and learning, as if they were novices, how
to interpret God's story of the world in the light of existing cultural
questions, insights, anxieties, and hopes. They sense that apart from this
encounter with the altered social context, Christianity could exist only as
representative of a bygone age, with its no-longer-vital metaphysical and
moral assumptions. They also sense that such a religion is easily used by
repressive and dangerous forces in the society to distract the general
consciousness from existing circumstances.

European theology in the 20th century, beginning with the "theology
of crisis" inspired by Karl Barth's early writings, has frequently derived
its originality from just this kind of fresh, unsettling, and risky exposure
to the new, postmodern, post-Christian world. This fact, I should say,
rather than the alleged superiority of European scholarship, is what has
made European and especially Germanic theological work stimulating
during the past century. In other words, at its best European theology
during this period has been the consequence of a radical process of *contextualization*. It was the work of a disciple community shocked by dramatic world events into a new awareness of its real *Sitz im Leben*. Wars,
the failures of governments and all social institutions, economic depres-
sions, and mass exodus from the churches have all served to drive reflective segments of this community from the comfortable sanctuary of
its established theory and made the community face the bankruptcy of its
own and its society's official assumptions. Having experienced the eclipse
of the light it fancied itself to possess, having been made to dwell in the
thick darkness of two horrendous wars, this community has exemplified
the truth of Hegel's famous dictum that "the owl of Minerva takes its
flight at evening." While darkness is not to be admired or sought after
by Christians, biblical faith has always known that the true light can be
perceived only by those who have found the courage to enter the darkness
of their hour. "The day of the Lord is darkness and not light" (Amos
5:18,20). It is not, I think, that European thinkers have had more native
courage than Christians and others on this side of the Atlantic. They have
simply been pushed into their darkness in spite of themselves, driven
there by unavoidable events—or by that same Spirit who took Jesus of
Nazareth to the wilderness to be tempted, and to Gethsemane.

THE DISCIPLE COMMUNITY

Our fascination with continental 20th-century European theology is to be explained, on its positive side, chiefly on these grounds. It is impossible to read the letters of Bonhoeffer, or the essays of Bultmann, or the theological treatises of Barth, Niemöller, Visser 't Hooft, de Dietrich, Hromodka, Tillich, Rahner, Ellul, Mehl, Casalis, Küng, Metz, Moltmann, Sölle, Hamel, Falcke, and many others without sensing intuitively that one is listening in on the testimony of a Christian disciple community which has descended into the particular hell of its own epoch—"the decline of the West" (Spengler), "the eclipse of meaning" (Horkheimer), "the death of God" (Nietzsche), "the death of Man" (Wiesel), or by whatever name it may be called. The source of our *fascination* with these testimonies is not, I think, tied to our agreement with the ideas contained in them, so much as it is our instinctive recognition that the root experience out of which they have been born is a rather naked encounter with *reality*. Certainly it is real for *them*, this world of Nazi concentration camps and military brutality and direct confrontation with powerful nontheistic alternatives to religious meaning and secular *ennui*. For the most part, we have not been able to bring ourselves openly to think that it is also real for us in some form; nevertheless, we know at the subconscious or semiconscious level of awareness that it is also in some way *our* civilization that these commentators on the state of the world's autobiography are describing, and we have been enthralled, some of us, by their imagination and courage in the face of such a battle. We sense that this fight is being fought very near to that "little point at which the world and the devil are striking" (Luther).

To state it in a word, theology in continental Europe in this century has come closer to being *confession* than what has been offered by the Anglo-Saxon ecclesiastical world in general and by the North American church in particular. Our captivation by Bonhoeffer and the Confessing Church pinpoints this general phenomenon. What confession of faith in the modern world has received as much attention as the Barmen Declaration? However we may sometimes distrust its one-sidedness, we are nevertheless strangely drawn to this European witness; and while there are very questionable explanations for this phenomenon, as we have already intimated, the more commendable reason for our continuing attraction to this theological work is that there is among us, as an inherent and indelible trait of our religious heritage, the remembrance that theology is alive—is theology—only when it achieves the character of confession; that when it is just the *pro*fessional recollection and rearrangement of dogma it is not really what it is called to be and do. It excites us when we perceive a disciple community which has the fortitude and wisdom to take on the world in all the nakedness of its 20th-century technological pomp and moral decay, and to produce confessions of belief and hope which seem categorically impossible in the face of such crises. We are moved by this testimony, as we are (more recently) moved by the confessional character of Third World (Latin American, black South African, Philippine, etc.) theologies; and, as the church throughout the ages has always taken to itself the results of the struggles of its saints and sages, without, however, exposing itself greatly to the enormous sufferings by which they were won, so we latch on to the most portable aspects of this contemporary witness.

But to what end? While we have been drawn to European expressions of Christian belief on account of their confessional quality, North American theology on the whole has not been able to emulate them in the one thing that makes them confessional, viz., their engagement with the real crises of their world. The reason for this is complex, but I believe that it has primarily to do with the fact that, up until the present time at least, North American Christianity has been consistently beholden to a worldview which rejects a priori exactly the *kinds* of crises that continental European theology has *had* to contend with. To be more precise, while this worldview may allow us to grant the occurrence of radically negative realities *within the European context*, it prevents us from entertaining the prospect that such evil could be native to the human condition as such, and therefore could be found in some form also in *our* social context. (The popular assumption that neither Hitler nor Auschwitz could happen on this side of the Atlantic mirrors this general sentiment.) For the worldview which has been our foundational philosophy taught us to expect continuing manifestations of darkness in that Old World, but to look upon this continent as "mankind's great second chance."[8] As such it was not only geographically but *ontically* discontinuous with the old European motherland. It was in fact a New World, a second Garden of Eden in which the new Adam contrived by Renaissance and Enlightenment visionaries and sanctified by post-Reformation Christianity would play his enlightened role.[9] This "American Dream," explicitly the foundational

---

8. Sydney E. Ahlstrom, *A Religious History of the American People*, vol. 1 (New York: Doubleday, 1975), p. 34.

9. See in this connection Henry Steele Commager, *The Empire of Reason: How Europe Imagined and America Realized the Enlightenment* (Garden City, N.Y.: Doubleday, 1977). "The thesis of this book," writes Commager, "can be stated quite simply: The Old World imagined, invented, and formulated the Enlightenment, the New World—certainly the Anglo-American part of it—realized it and fulfilled it" (p. xi). It belongs to Commager's main hypothesis, which he carefully documents,

mythos of the United States of America but entertained in a pale copy by Canadians as well,[10] is our continental birthright. We have conceived of existence almost exclusively along the lines of this modern Weltanschauung, and, as the recent mood in American politics, economics, and foreign policy makes abundantly plain, we are determined to claim the promises of this birthright even today, when the evidence for its viability has been all but obliterated.

That a people should cling so tenaciously to such a worldview may seem a mystery to those who have never participated in this dream; but our tenacity is not without a rationale. In the first place, the dream makes no provision for failure. Therefore, the world which has in fact come to be around us and within us is a world whose character is fundamentally inaccessible to our public understanding. For, from the standpoint of what we dreamed and still desire to dream, what has come to be *is* a failure. We lack the intellectual and spiritual wherewithal to "take in" the darkness that has descended upon humanity during this present century. Even more pathetically do we lack the capacity to think that our own pursuits might have had something to do with the descent of the darkness. Cartographers of such a night must have access to categories of measurement of which we know little or nothing—categories that were denied us by the very assumptions of the age of light that brought us into being. How could we know the darkness, or even admit its presence, when we had been assured from the beginning that it would grow ever lighter (Buber)?

By contrast, the Europeans who were propelled into the 20th century, however innocent of the knowledge of good and evil modernity had made them, were not so bereft as we are of a vantage point from which to contemplate the failure of the modern vision. It is true (as Tillich, Barth, Bonhoeffer, and many others have amply testified)[11] that the experience of immersion into the cold waters of what the European W. H. Auden dubbed the "age of anxiety" was for European Christians a humiliating loss of the hopes their liberal mentors had taught them to cherish. But

---

that this European vision could seem to incarnate itself only in a context that could appear discontinuous with the past: "Only rarely, and sporadically, could Old World philosophes turn their energies to the tasks of improvement and reform. But in America, where there were no ancient tyrannies to overthrow, no barriers of tradition or poverty or ignorance to surmount, and few iniquities—except the prodigious iniquity of slavery—to banish, the philosophes could devote their energies to realizing the program of the Enlightenment" (p. xii).

10. See my book, *The Canada Crisis: A Christian Perspective* (Toronto: The Anglican Book Centre, 1980); also, *More Than Survival: Viewpoints toward a Theology of Nation,* ed. Graham Scott (Don Mills: Canec Publishing, 1980).

11. See, e.g., Paul Tillich's "Autobiographical Reflections," in *The Theology of Paul Tillich,* ed. Charles W. Kegley and Robert W. Bretall (New York: MacMillan, 1952), pp. 3-21.

the loss of the modern vision is one thing for those who can still count on a modicum of access to premodern conceptions of the world, and something else when the modern conception is all one possesses. For all its capitulation to the spirit of modernity, European theology has usually given evidence of knowing ancient secrets about the world and humanity that have not been remembered by the leading lights of the brave, new world.

Thus, threatened with exclusion from the ranks of the intelligentsia, Schleiermacher and his colleagues learned how to confess that faith by exploring a dimension of rationality too soon despised by the denizens of the *Aufklärung*, namely, "feeling" (*Gefühl*). This was a dimension of human *thinking* (not emoting) that Schleiermacher *could* recall and many of his contemporaries *could* respect because they had not been wholly cut off from the medieval world, which knew better than the modern world that the heart and head cannot be conveniently segregated. Similarly, a Tillich deprived of his illusions on the ghastly battlefields of Kaiser Wilhelm II could turn in spirit to alternative conceptions of existence, conceptions in which the devastation and death he experienced on those battlefields could at least be accounted for, if not accepted. These older thoughts about the world, which Tillich imbibed (he sometimes said) "by osmosis" through the very buildings that surrounded him in childhood, could never be finally eradicated by the progressive assumptions of the age that educated him. After the collapse of those assumptions, therefore, Tillich, and many other Europeans, did not have to go on believing in modernity despite its manifest failure. Though shaken to their roots, they could still contemplate the demise of the 19th-century liberal utopia from the perspective of other, earlier worldviews, and thus go on to build their hope where real hope must always be built—"on the far side of despair" (Keats).

For Tillich's American contemporary, Reinhold Niebuhr, the devastation of modernity, if not less brutal in its effects on the human spirit, was decidedly less obvious. It takes a more determined, if not a more original wisdom, as well as a more imaginative type of solidarity with the victims of modern industrialism to perceive the lie in the modern vision from a point within Henry Ford's apparently progressive Detroit than from the perspective of Kaiser Wilhelm's luckless Reich.[12] Niebuhr,

---

12. In his essay "On Keeping Theological Ethics Theological," Stanley Hauerwas questions Reinhold Niebuhr's rejection of modernity. His argument seems to be that although Niebuhr imbibed the Augustinian-Lutheran tradition of the ubiquity of sin, he still assumed that Christian ethics had to be addressed to, and in some sense accessible to, secular modern society, particularly democratic

however, was far better equipped than most North Americans for coming to some informed awareness of the crisis of the modern worldview; for his heritage encompassed that intuitive sense of the absurdity of human pride and the pathos of human history that is present particularly in the Reformation's Lutheran side.[13] By contrast, the *characteristic* forms of Protestant Christianity in North America were as ill-prepared to admit "the encircling gloom" as were most other institutions of our society.

It is still unbelievably hard for most North Americans to question the positive outlook in which our whole experiment has been steeped. We are imprisoned in the very brightness of this vision, its sheer, daring optimism. The power of doctrinaire optimism should not be underestimated. Its doggedness is testified to not only by the fact that it has risen again in a very militant form in this last quarter of the 20th century within our own part of the First World, but that since 1848 the Western world has seen the birth, late in time, of another, still more determined and more militant version of this same highly positive version of human destiny. It gives one cause to wonder when one considers that, today, this same insistent and official optimism about the future of the species informs *both* of the great empires on account of whose grave insecurity and striving for the control of that future the world is dangerously imperiled.

We are dealing with a heady vision. It robs its adherents not only of the axiological norms necessary to assess its failure, but it conditions them to spurn any view of the world which offers failure a place in the scheme of things. Disappointment and setback there may be. But the movement of time is irrevocably set towards the positive unfolding of purpose, the enhancement of all life, the fulfillment of the dream. These heights once visited, every other view of the human prospect is bound to seem a concession to gloom. The religion of progress does not lend itself to being succeeded by any other faith. If it must be forfeited, the alternative

---

America; therefore Niebuhr did not really part company with the social gospel that he criticized, and with its advocates did not yet realize how thoroughly Christian ethics is dependent upon Christian theology and faith (*Truthfulness and Tragedy: Further Investigations in Christian Ethics* [Notre Dame and London: University of Notre Dame Press, 1978], pp. 22ff.).

Besides begging many questions about the program of Hauerwas himself, this seems to me a particularly circuitous argument. It was precisely Niebuhr's grasp of the hamartiological core of Christian anthropology that set him at odds with modernity, for modernity *was* and *is* the rejection precisely of that dogmatic tradition. The fact that Niebuhr *and* the advocates of the social gospel continued to believe that modern socity—and particularly their own society, America—had to be addressed, and could be addressed, does not imply that their critique of modernity is less than serious. It is absurd to equate the critique of modernity with the adoption of a fideistic, church-and-belief centered theology which embraces a strict discontinuity with any worldly wisdom.

13. See my essay, "The Cross and Contemporary Culture," in *Reinhold Niebuhr and the Issues of Our Time*, ed. Richard Harries (London and Oxford: Mowbray, 1986), pp. 183ff.

that remains—for most—is not faith of any variety but cynicism. A significant number of people in our society have followed that course. A much greater number cling blindly to the dream, refurbished with whatever tidbits of evidence they are able to discover, because forthright cynicism is abhorrent to them. It is no doubt better that they should do so; for our public and private morality is already too much colored by the cynicism of those who no longer believe in anything or hope for anything.

8.2. The Amalgamation of Protestantism and Americanism.   A critical theology is bound to ask about the role of Christianity in the making of such a society. It could be supposed on the basis of the biblical story that Christianity, of all systems of meaning, might have wanted to resist the writing-off of the past as well as the pride of future informing the modern vision. It could be supposed, in short, that Christianity in the New World context might have told a story very different from the triumphant tale of historical progressivism. This did not in fact occur. Or let us say that its occurrence—as in French Canadian Catholicism, or ethnic strands of Lutheranism, or among black and other minorities—did not materially influence the general direction of North American civilization. The most influential expressions of the Christian faith in North America were those which could provide a spiritual buttress to the secular mythology of progress and mastery, or which at least did not throw up serious barricades against the advance of that ideology.

So far as the earliest and most permanently formative traditions of European "Christian" civilization on this continent are concerned, that means, above all, Calvinism.[14] For the peculiar brand of covenant theology in the Calvinist tradition *could* lend itself to the sense of its divine election and destiny which captured the heart of the New World's citizenry almost from the outset. As Sidney E. Mead has written,

> The keynote of the American idea of destiny was struck by John Winthrop in his address "Written on Boarde the Arrabella" in 1630. He said:
> As "for the worke wee haue in hand, it is by a mutuall consent through a speciall overruleing providence, and a more than ordinary approbation

---

14. "If one were to compute (a percentage of Calvinist heritage) on the basis of all the German, Swiss, French, Dutch, and Scottish people whose forebears bore the 'stamp of Geneva' in some broader sense, 85 or 90 percent would not be an extravagant estimate" (Sidney E. Ahlstrom, *A Religious History of the American People*, vol. 1, p. 169.) Canadian history differs from that of the United States chiefly on account of the French Catholic heritage; yet the Calvinist influence has been powerful in Canada as well, as is attested by the novels of Robertson Davies, Hugh MacLennan, and many others.

of the Churches of Christ to seeke out a place of Cohabitation and Consorteshipp vndèr a due forme of Government both ciull and ecclesiasticall."

If we are faithful to our covenant with him, Winthrop continued, "wee shall finde that the god of Israell is among vs . . . when hee shall make vs a prayse and glory, that men shall say of succeeding plantacions: the Lord make it like that of New England; for wee must Consider that we shall be as a Citty vpon a Hill, the eies of all people are vpon vs."[15]

While the sense of advancing towards a high and noble destiny could derive from the Calvinist doctrines of election and divine providence, the Reformed emphases upon obedience, thrift, and the triumph of the righteous could inspire a work ethic which contributed immeasurably to the other mainstay of the positive outlook: human mastery over history and nature. Incongruous as they may appear when considered in their original forms, Calvinism and Renaissance/Enlightenment humanism became copartners in the formation of the North American spirit. While the triumphalism of later Calvinism was based upon an interpretation of the sovereign deity of the Scriptures and the triumphalism of humanism found its rationale in the "laws" of nature and history, both of these chief inspirational sources of the North American experiment shared a highly positive view of human meaning.[16]

Subsequent religious traditions added their peculiar insights to the basic vision. The Methodist doctrine of perfection could certainly find a place in such a social scheme; besides, Methodism, like its parent body, Anglicanism, lacked a searching doctrine of human sinfulness, on whose basis it might have been more skeptical of anthropocentric pretension. While Catholicism, apart from ethnic groupings and French Canada, did

---

15. Sidney E. Mead, *The Lively Experiment: The Shaping of Christianity in America* (New York: Harper & Row, 1963), p. 151.

16. "It is particularly remarkable that the two great religious-moral traditions which informed our early life—New England Calvinism and Virginian Deism and Jeffersonianism—arrive at remarkably similar conclusions about the meaning of our national character and destiny. Calvinism may have held too pessimistic views of human nature and too mechanical views of the providential ordering of human life. But when it assessed the significance of the American experiment both its conceptions of American destiny and its appreciation of American virtue finally arrived at conclusions strikingly similar to those of Deism. Whether our nation interprets its spiritual heritage through Massachusetts or Virginia, we came into existence with the same sense of being a 'separated' nation, which God was using to make a new beginning for mankind. We had renounced the evils of European religious bigotry. We had found broad spaces for the satisfaction of human desires in place of the crowded Europe. Whether, as in the case of New England theocrats, our forefathers thought of our 'experiment' as primarily the creation of a new and purer church, or, as in the case of Jefferson and his coterie, they thought primarily of a new political community, they believed in either case that we had been called out by God to create a new humanity. We were God's 'American Israel' " (Reinhold Niebuhr, *The Irony of American History* [New York: Scribner's, 1952], pp. 23-24).

not exercise a strong influence in the continent as a whole, Catholic ecclesial triumphalism was used to accommodating itself to national ideologies, and through long experience the Church of Rome had learned to make the most of a great variety of social visions. As for sectarian Christianity, some denominations would continue to hold up to proud, modern Homo sapiens the provocatively antithetical reminder of human mortality, sin, and degradation; but since most sects did not develop the *social* consequences of this doctrine, and at the same time projected unto the heavenly afterlife a utopian goal only linguistically different, often, from the evolving secular dream, sectarianism did not offer significant oposition to the evolving society's determined "pursuit of happiness." Besides, other aspects of sectarian religion were more than amenable to the optimism of the New World, including such emphases as the deuteronomic sense of reward and punishment, the insistence upon obedience to governing authorities, and, withal, the general approbation of "success." Those Christians whose traditions contained hues that were darker and ideas that were out of step with modernity (I am thinking particularly of denominations stemming from the Lutheran Reformation) confined themselves for the most part to the ethnic minorities which had brought them to these shores, and to "religion." They did not—perhaps they could not—enter the mainstream of North American life at the level of their ideas, so they learned how to think on two levels (a thing frequently aided and abetted by the popular misapprehension of Luther's concept of the *Zwei Reiche* [the two-kingdoms theory]).

To crown these efforts, liberalism in the 19th century completed the work of making the Christian faith into a stained-glass version of the dream by ridding the faith of its most glaringly "negative" elements: original sin, with its reminiscence of "the tragic dimension" (Tillich); the cross, which now became an ultra-Abelardian exemplification of divine forbearance; the wrath and judgment of God, which was now replaced by the idea of a soon-to-be-realized kingdom of God on earth, etc.

It was in fact the thesis of the church historian Sidney Mead that "during the second half of the nineteenth century there occurred an ideological amalgamation of . . . Protestantism with 'Americanism,' and that we are still living with some of the results."[17] In the first place, he notes, "the whole grand dream of American destiny . . . while its tangled roots drew nourishment from many different soils in past centuries, was nevertheless profoundly religious in origins and conception." The potentiality

17. *The Lively Experiment,* p. 134.

for criticism of the dream was therefore never very great, so far as Christianity in North America is concerned. But with the merging of denominational Protestantism and "Americanism" in the latter part of the 19th century, whatever possibilities of prophetic faith were latent in Christianity were effectively forfeited. Mead continues:

> Grant all this, plus the prevalence of a fuzzy and amorphous intellectual structure in the religious groups, and the way is left open for the uncritical adoption of whatever standards do actually prevail in the society. Hence, as noted, the American denominations have successively lent themselves to the sanctification of current existing expressions of the American way of life.
>
> John Herman Randall, Jr., by taking a more theoretical route as befits a philosopher, arrives at the similar conclusion that "Protestantism left the way open for the assimilation of any pattern of values that might seem good in the light of men's actual experience . . . [and] has thus tended to become largely an emotional force in support of the reigning secular social ideals."[18]

In the decades since World War II, much professional theology in North America has learned how to criticize the liberal exaggeration of the positive; and we have seen a return to serious discussion of human sin, divine judgment, the reality of evil in persons and society, the inadequacy of rationality, and other aspects of Christian tradition that had been set aside by 19th- and early 20th-century enthusiasm for modernity. But it is one thing to reintroduce neglected doctrines and something else to live with and under a *kerygma* of which such doctrines may only be, after all, superficial theoretical tokens. While individual Christians and clusters have made the transition from doctrine to theology in this connection (or as Mead would call it, the transition from *pre*-theology to theology), it seems true of the churches at large that these older, more biblical concepts exist at a highly theoretical level. In order to get beyond the doctrinal tokens of a gospel that admits of the night, it is necessary to live for a while in the quite specific darkness that pertains to our social context. We shall not recover the meaning of sin, judgment, evil, the demonic, or the cross simply by reading them back into our theory. We shall regain their deeper significance only when we have unlearned the habit of submitting these "negatives" forthwith to the power of the overwhelming positive. Like the original disciple community, we shall have

18. Ibid., p. 141.

to learn that we cannot rush to the glory before we have tasted the humiliation. It is as least as hard for us to appropriate that lesson as it was for them—harder, I suspect, for "solutions" are endemic with us.

Perhaps *theology* will become possible only when we have developed a distaste for answers, i.e., when we have come to know better the depths of the questions. Yet for those who are prepared for such an exposure to our context, there exists today—and in a way unique in our history—not only a summons but also an invitation to theology.

9. Invitation to Theology

9.1. Social Extremity/Theological Opportunity. The old adage that "man's extremity is God's opportunity" has been applied in questionable and even despicable ways—for instance, by "evangelists" who operate on the principle that you must first break the human spirit and then offer it the "balm of Gilead." If the proverb is understood in a descriptive rather than a prescriptive sense, however, it makes considerable sense. It is the same kind of sense Jesus made when he said, "Only the sick have need of a physician." Those who are in good physical and mental health, with money in the bank, a promising career, and two lovely children, may have some additional comfort from the "consolations of religion"; but they are not likely to cry out for help, forgiveness, salvation! The same thing may be said of societies. Surely the reason why Christianity has operated in our society primarily as a "culture religion" (Peter Berger), a blend of religious denominationalism and nationalism, is that few have needed it for what it really is—a religion of radical grace. The dominant culture of our society has felt no overwhelming need for the drastic reading of the human situation that is presupposed by a theology of radical grace.

It does not lie within the power of the disciple community to *engineer* such need in its host society. However fervently prophetic spirits within the disciple community may wish for the kind of depth and vitality of faith and theology that great social transitions have often evoked, they cannot cause such transitions to occur. All the admirers of the pivotal Christian figures of such epochs (Augustine, Aquinas, Luther, the young Barth), who want the world always to be ready for such ringing messages as those epochs called forth—all such persons are frustrated, because the world will move at its own pace. Its crises cannot be ordered up by prophets! In this sense, theology is dependent upon society, upon the world. It has to take what is there, what is given in the moment, including

169

what may indeed be hidden and should be brought to light. It cannot manufacture shakings of the foundation.

But when such shaking occurs; when in the course of society's unfolding the thinly veiled chaos that its "culture" just managed to cover begins to show through and the ancient unrest of Homo sapiens is no longer contained by the careful conventions of the ages, *then* the disciple community must prepare itself to wake from its dogmatic slumbers, reach more deeply into the resources of its tradition than it has been accustomed to do, and see what can be found there for the healing of the nations. In *this* sense, the *extremity* of a human community is the *opportunity* for a new attempt at telling *God's* story of the world.

9.2. The Situation. This, I believe, is how we should regard the context in which we find ourselves on this continent today. The worldview out of which our society has evolved has reached its extremity. It is a theologically evocative situation, and for our province of the universal church it is the first situation of this kind that we have experienced. For that reason alone it is difficult enough, of course. Christians in North America have known hardships—for instance, the hardship associated with the settlement of this vast continent. But on the whole ours has been one of those "peaceful" epochs, during which a certain domestication of the faith occurs. Religion has been a comforting and comfortable thing, imbibed in the quietness of small-town Sunday mornings.

Moreover, we are the products of an age which thought that upheavals of the kind that is now brewing in our midst were things of the past. There are, to be sure, tens of thousands who would be content to have us play our conventional role as pacifiers and alleviators of the little pains of existence. The disciple community is always under this temptation in such times—to preach "peace, peace, where there is no peace" (Jer. 6:14; 8:11). But, on the other hand, there are problems of such enormous proportions that no amount of pacification will make them disappear: the crisis of resources and the environment, of population, of economic and social injustice, of violence, of the threat of nuclear war, and other specific issues whose significance for theology we shall discuss in the subsequent chapter. And beneath and in them all there is a monumental shift in the *mood* of our society at large which, if we have ears to hear, sounds like the clear announcement of human corporate extremity.

This mood is articulated, not only by historians, anthropologists, and political philosophers, but in widely circulated literature and the most accessible forms of art. Even Hollywood movies are no longer "Hollywood." A popular journalist describes the mood shift in the following provocative statement:

> The entire American proposition has been built upon the premise of ever expanding opportunity, upon a vision of the future as a territory open-ended and always unfolding, upon ascendant history. "We are the heirs of all time," said Herman Melville. What happens if the future seems to be closing down, to be darkening? If nature, first an enemy to be subdued and then a resource to be exploited, is now an endangered victim of technology? The classic American salvation (clear the land! build! disembowel the mountains!) threatens to invent damnation. . . .
>
> All the furniture of the American myths is being dismantled and stored. Psychologically, if not yet financially, a stale air of foreclosure has wafted around. . . . *Americans feel themselves sliding towards triviality, and beyond that toward an abyss that might swallow the whole experiment like a black hole. . . .*
>
> . . . Many of them remain sunnily confident. But the old interpretations, *the old American theology, no longer works very well.* Americans invented themselves in the first place, and then were interminably reinvented by the rest of the world. Perhaps more than most peoples, they need to possess an idea of themselves, a myth of themselves, an explanation of themselves. It is time for them to start inventing and imagining again.[19]

The sense of dislodgment is also the tone adopted by Sydney E. Ahlstrom in the final chapter of his monumental work, *A Religious History of the American People.* "The Turbulent Sixties," he writes, witnessed "the sense of national failure and dislocation (which) became apparent to varying degrees in all occupational groups and residential areas."[20]

> Americans, whether conservative, liberal, or radical, found it increasingly difficult to believe that the United States was still a beacon and blessing to the world. . . . One could only be assured that radically revised foundations of belief were being laid, that a drastic reformation of ecclesiastical institutions was in the offing, and that America could not escape its responsibilities as the world's pathbreaker in the new technocratic wilderness.[21]

For a historian of American religion and life, Ahlstrom concludes, to

---

19. Lance Morrow, "On Reimagining America," *Time,* March 32, 1980, pp. 38-39 (emphasis added).
20. Sydney E. Ahlstrom, *A Religious History of the American People,* p. 609.
21. Ibid., p. 617.

contemplate our society in the sixties and beyond is to consider "a time of calamities."[22] To reflect on the American experience in such a time, "whether as amateur or as professional," is to know oneself to be "a pioneer on the frontiers of post-modern civilization."[23]

The question that this situation poses for thoughtful participants in it is whether the "postmodern" society that may come to be will be worthy of the lofty term "civilization." Many of our contemporaries have already concluded in their hearts, if not openly, that we are witnessing the inauguration of a new barbarism in the Western world generally.[24] There is indeed a growing feeling among us—almost a popular expectation—that neither the meek nor the strong will inherit the earth, that "of these cities, all that will remain is the wind that blew through them" (Bertolt Brecht). For the extremity of modernity is not like the extremities of earlier civilizations. We can pull down the whole world along with us into the abyss.

Apocalyptic, it has been said, is the mother of religion.[25] Christianity not only finds human endings evocative, but it dares to announce that real *beginnings* are made only at the point where endings are experienced, or anticipated. Can this "logic of the cross" (Reinhold Niebuhr) apply also to the extremity of our civilization? Let us attempt to explore that possibility, and to see what it may hold for us by way of detailing the character of the invitation to theology implicit in our context.

9.3. Alternatives for a Society in Despair. The life of a society undergoing the collapse of the system of meaning upon which its laws, institutions, moralities, and unspoken values have been based presents to those within it a choice among three rudimentary *types* of response: they can capitulate to the hopelessness entailed in such an event; they can refuse to admit its occurrence; or they can look for ways to be realistic without becoming immobilized.

---

22. Ibid., p. 618.

23. Ibid., p. 620. See also Harvey Cox, *Religion in the Secular City: Towards a Postmodern Theology* (New York: Simon and Schuster, 1984).

24. E.g., Alisdair MacIntyre concludes his book, *After Virtue: A Study in Moral Theory* (Notre Dame: University of Notre Dame Press, 1984), p. 263, by noting that in many respects there are parallels between our society and the decline of Rome. "What matters at this stage is the construction of local forms of community within which civility and the intellectual and moral life can be sustained through the new dark ages which are already upon us. And if the tradition of the virtues was able to survive the horrors of the last dark ages, we are not entirely without grounds for hope. This time however the barbarians are not waiting beyond the frontiers; they have already been governing us for quite some time." See also Jacques Ellul, *The Betrayal of the West*, trans. Matthew J. O'Connell (New York: Seabury, 1978).

25. In this connection, see J. Christiaan Beker, *Paul's Apocalyptic Gospel: The Coming Triumph of God* (Philadelphia: Fortress, 1982).

(a) The first alternative is the most fearful, and for that reason is less common a response than the second. For it means the more or less conscious abandonment of hope. At least hope *for the society* is abandoned, and whether personal hope can be sustained without the support of a system of meaning which transcends the individual is a matter of grave doubt. That a significant number of people in our society have found it impossible to maintain hope for their personal destinies is borne out by recent statistics concerning suicide (especially the rate of suicide among the young) and mental collapse.[26] That the line between personal and social hope is at best a fine one is verified by the necessity of regarding very private matters like suicide and mental health as special *social* phenomena on account of their frequency. The resort to self-destruction, whether through deliberate acts or in more subtle ways, is only a final resort—the tip of a very large iceberg. It must be assumed (and most social analysts do assume) that a much larger number of persons in our society experience the same symptoms which lead their contemporaries to such drastic "solutions," though not in as acute forms. A "Time Essay" speaks about "The Burnout of Almost Everyone."[27]

Hopelessness of an advanced and pathological sort also expresses itself in the violence and vandalism marking our cities, highways, and entertainment world. But the most common and most fearsome dimension of this phenomenon is neither overt self-destruction nor the spoilation of the environment, but a pervasive cynicism.

Cynicism can be adopted by the respectable citizen who would not go in for graffiti on the surfaces of public monuments, and for whom madness and suicide are constitutional improbabilities. The cynic does not even have to voice his or her cynicism. The cynic can carry on nicely within the officially optimistic society, mouthing the necessary platitudes and going through the motions of business, professional, and social life.

---

26. Thirty years ago, in a book with the suggestive title, *Mirage of Health* (New York: Harper & Row), reprinted in John G. Burke, *The New Techology and Human Values* (Belmont, Calif.: Wadsworth, 1966), p. 309, scientist René Dubos wrote: "In the United States during 1956, close to one million persons were hospitalized for mental disease, more than ten million were thought to be in need of psychiatric treatment, and there was reason to believe that a good percentage of the total population would spend at least part of their lives in a mental institution. In 1955, 16,760 persons were known to have committed suicide, and not a few of those who had died a violent death had directly or indirectly been victims of abnormal or antisocial behaviour. On the other hand, it was considered a great medical advance that tranquilizer drugs had become available to all. Three out of ten prescriptions were for these drugs in 1956, and more than a billion tablets of meprobamate alone were sold in a year." Far from abating, the tendencies tabulated in these statistics have increased in the time that has elapsed.

27. *Time,* September 21, 1981 (European edition), p. 60.

An unspoken convention in the public realm anticipates and even en-courages these attitudes in persons. The open articulation of cynicism is contrary to the social code. But the *living* of cynicism is a well-docu-mented phenomenon in North America today. Its most familiar garb is shallow hedonism: the jogger who concentrates on physical well-being and whose devotion to the cult of the body has the convenient bonus of squelching persistent questions of the mind; the tourist who is able to find Calcutta and Mexico City "interesting"; the spectator who can ob-serve life's pathos with eyes as dry as the protective glass covering of his television screen. It is very difficult to gauge the extent and the conse-quences of the covert cynicism in our society, for we have come to expect so little.[28] One can glimpse something of its hold upon us, however, if one compares a typical Hollywood film of the 1940s or 1950s with most films produced in North America today.

(b) Overt hopelessness, however, requires a certain daring, and there-fore the second alternative open to persons in communities whose foun-dational beliefs are being eroded is without question the more common among *us*: repression and the nurture of false hope.

Repression, as psychiatry since Freud has shown, is an automatic defense mechanism of the human psyche. The subconscious intuits di-mensions of reality that the conscious mind cannot bear, and stifles them. It is natural and necessary.[29] We could not bear "naked exposure to anx-iety," said Tillich (in the context of his discussion of the Christ's cry of dereliction from the cross).[30]

---

28. In his disturbing book *The Culture of Narcissism*, the subtitle of which ought to be taken as seriously as the title (*American Life in an Age of Diminishing Expectations*), Christopher Lasch writes: "After the political turmoil of the sixties, Americans have retreated to purely personal preoc-cupations. Having no hope of improving their lives in any of the ways that matter, people have convinced themselves that what matters is psychic self-improvement: getting in touch with their feelings, eating health food, taking lessons in ballet or belly-dancing, immersing themselves in the wisdom of the East, jogging, learning how to 'relate,' overcoming the 'fear of pleasure.' Harmless in themselves, these pursuits, elevated to a program and wrapped in the rhetoric of authenticity and awareness, signify a retreat from politics and a repudiation of the recent past" (New York: W. W. Norton, 1978), pp. 4-5.

29. "We cannot repeat too often the great lesson of Freudian psychology: that repression is normal self-protection and creative self-restriction—in a real sense, man's natural substitute for instinct" (Ernest Becker, *The Denial of Death* [New York: The Free Press, 1973], p. 178). Humanity, whose nature and destiny it is not only to *be* mortal but to be vulnerable to the debilitating consciousness of mortality, must repress a great deal simply in order to function. "The animals don't know that death is happening to them. . . . They live and they disappear with the same thoughtlessness. . . . But to live a whole lifetime with the fate of death haunting one's dreams and even the most sun-filled days—that's something else. . . .

"I believe that those who speculate that a full apprehension of man's condition would drive him insane are right, quite literally right. . . . 'Men are so necessarily mad that not to be mad would amount to another kind of madness' [Pascal]" (ibid., p. 27).

30. Paul Tillich, *The Courage to Be* (New Haven & London: Yale University Press, 1952), p. 39.

Yet the repressive mechanism, however necessary, can never be utilized without cost; and when it is adopted as a way of coping with very sizable segments of experience, perhaps even the most decisive segments, then the cost is very great. A person or a collectivity that draws upon the repressive mechanism consistently and deeply is probably expending more emotional energy in this activity than in any other. For it requires a great deal of psychic energy to blot out unpleasant or unbearable realities.[31]

Part of this psychic energy is expended on exaggerated tokens of belief in that which is not spontaneously believable, but which must be believed in order to reduce the threat of what *is*. The cost of such an exercise is not just the draining of personal and public resourcefulness which it necessarily entails. It is also the forfeiture of the quest for truth, and the suppression of things (and persons) through whose presence unwanted truth continues to assert itself.

This alternative is the apparent choice today, not only of a vociferous minority in our society—persons and groups whose noisy insistence upon the retention of old values and ways is too ostentatious to be true; it is the pattern of many who are less demonstrative—perhaps, indeed, "the silent *majority*." It is not accidental that observers representative of a wide variety of expertise have dubbed our society "the repressive society." Nor is it accidental that this alternative becomes more popular the more conspicuously the "old" values and ways are harried by events. The advocates of this path have become increasingly defensive, one-sided, and militant. Repression under intense pressure expresses itself in *sup*pressive activities. The consequences are seen today in the face of governments that promise a speedy return to rhetorical virtues and verities, are elected to office on the strength of these promises, and then can make their promises appear practicable only by adopting economic and international policies that further victimize oppressed minorities and endanger the peace of the larger human community.

And by outright lies! The way of repression pursued *as a way*, especially on the part of a collectivity, is the tacit decision that false hope is better than no hope. And in theory this may be so. But false hope defending itself as true can be as dangerous as cynical despair in retreat from public life. It is in fact only so far removed from cynicism as the subconscious is from the conscious mind. As a temporary measure, it

---

31. "We know very well that to repress means more than to put away and to forget that which was put away and the place where we put it. It means also to maintain a constant psychological effort to keep the lid on and inwardly never relax our watchfulness" (G. Zilboorg, "Fear of Death," *Psychoanalytic Quarterly* 12 [1943]: 467).

may seem to succeed. But under continued and prolonged duress, its truly cynical aspect will become increasingly visible.[32]

(c) Neither of these alternatives commends itself to a reflective and responsible Christian faith. The Christian can recognize in certain types of hopelessness (for instance, in the classical pessimism of a Camus) the advantage of a preference for realism. But because the realism of the pessimist or the cynic is no longer goaded by any persistent vision of the good, its honesty about evil is finally, literally, meaningless. The second path—repression and the pursuit of unworthy hopes—wards off the threat of meaninglessness and despair temporarily, but only at the expense of truth. The faith it saves is "bad faith" (Sartre), and its hope is cheap hope—hope as a shield from life. The first alternative makes it necessary to dispose of the questions of being and meaning which *will* assert themselves and can be silenced only through prolonged and concentrated effort; the second makes it necessary to lie about the world in order to believe in "the System." The one courts the night, the other throws up artificial light before it has really experienced real darkness.

This leaves a third alternative, and we can infer from the analysis of the first two, *via negativa*, what requirements it has to meet: It must provide the possibility of being truthful about what is happening in the world, to the self, to society. Persons must be able to feel a certain permission to orientate themselves towards the truth. At the same time it must hold out the prospect of a good which transcends this present reality, and permits the spirit to explore it without falling victim to ultimate despair.

Both of these things are necessary: The human spirit needs, on the one hand, the freedom to be truthful about the perceived realities of its condition. Not only for our intellectual integrity, but for our mental and moral sanity, "we have to be as hard-headed as possible about reality and possibility."[33] Without this capacity, the spirit soon finds itself mired in the constraints of self-deception. Wisdom, as we have already agreed, admits the necessity of repressing some of the truth for the sake of health, even for survival. But if repression becomes the habitual manner of coping with the most conspicuous realities of one's world, then it destroys the self whose happiness it has been invoked to protect. This, surely, is as true of the macrocosm as of the microcosm. A society which silently commits itself to a kind of programmed indifference towards the sorts of

---

32. There is no better demonstration of precisely this sociopsychic fact than the behavior of the Reagan administration in its relation to the situation in Central America, especially Nicaragua.
33. Ernest Becker, *The Denial of Death,* p. 280.

life-and-death issues confronting us today in the Western world is engaged on a course of self-destruction. "A society based on happiness cannot survive; only a society based on truth can survive."[34]

On the other hand, the human spirit cannot survive either on sheer unalloyed honesty about the world—especially when "the world" presents bleak and futureless images of itself. In times of social extremity, such truth as thrusts itself into our conscious or subconscious minds can more readily be oppressive and damning than liberating. "There are ultimate problems of life which cannot be fully stated until the answer to them is known. Without the answer to them, men will not allow themselves to contemplate fully the depth of the problem, lest they be driven to despair."[35] The human spirit, then, needs not only the freedom truthfully to contemplate what *is* then, but the courage to believe that such contemplation can help to bring about a better state. Indeed, unless they are able to trust that something good can come of truthfulness, most men and women will always prefer half-truth or downright falsification—not, of course, as a conscious ploy, but intuitively, recognizing that the truth which under certain conditions "makes free" under other conditions makes one infinitely sad, or simply terrified.[36]

Thus the invitation to theology sharpens itself and becomes more explicit. It becomes a kind of echo of Job's invitation to his religious advisors, "Oh, that I knew where I might find him!" (Job 23:3). Is it possible to find in this faith-tradition a foundation for the spirit and mind to discover the courage to be open to the negating and overwhelming realities of our societal extremity—but without despair? How, under the conditions of a society sliding towards triviality, shall we sustain an orientation towards the truth (*Wahrheitsorientierung*) that is also in some authentic way a theology of hope?

10. Visions in the Night

10.1. The Search. It would not, I think, be an exaggeration to say that all creative and responsible social thought today is a search for

---

34. C. F. von Weizsäcker; see *Die Zeit drängt: Eine Weltversammlung der Christen für Gerechtigkeit, Frieden und die Bewahrung der Schöpfung* (Munich and Vienna: Carl Hanser Verlag, 1986).
35. Reinhold Niebuhr, *The Nature and Destiny of Man*, vol. 2 (New York; Scribner's, 1964), p. 75.
36. "Why are groups so blind and stupid?—men have always asked. Because they demand illusions, answered Freud, they 'constantly give what is unreal precedence over what is real.' And we know why. The real world is simply too terrible to admit; it tells man that he is a small, trembling animal who will decay and die. Illusion changes all this, makes man seem important, vital to the universe, immortal in some way. . . . The masses look to the leaders to give them just the untruth that they need" (Becker, *The Denial of Death*, p. 133).

answers precisely to the question, How can one be truthful and at the same time hopeful? Perhaps such thought is always that kind of a search. Perhaps what makes thought creative is precisely this daring to overcome the apparent contradictions between truth and hope, honesty about perceived reality and the affirmation of existence despite the negations that are always unearthed by such honesty. Human thought is never a creation *ex nihilo*, for we think after the fact and gift of being. Yet, profound thought always seems to occur in the nether regions of the Nihil, as if the Creator had ordained that those who are privileged to contemplate the wonder of being should have to participate in the divine struggle to wrest being from oblivion.

Such a search is perennial, because the suspension of human life between death and illusion is perennial. But the search for a "hope that does not disappoint us" (Rom. 5:5) intensifies itself during periods of widespread upheaval and negation. For whatever may be the immediate crises during those periods, the underlying crisis—the fundamental *krisis*—is that the "Answer" provided by a former age has been weighed in the balances and found wanting. At such times, besides those who capitulate to the general hopelessness and those who retreat from reality, there will be others who try to hold together an honest assessment of the situation and a quest for the meaning there could be in and beyond it. If the apocalyptic period produces despair and cynicism and cheap hope, it also produces persons who, like the prophet Daniel, are vouchsafed "visions in the night" (Dan. 2:19; 7:1; etc.).

Our time has had more than its share of such visionaries. Not unpredictably, if the argument of this essay is accurate, a great many of them have been persons who were subjected to the worst torments of our tormented period—the death camps and gulags, political and economic oppression, and the torture chambers of the electronic age. Most of these persons have been—or at least have ended as being—profoundly religious, though few of them have been so conventionally, and fewer still have been explicitly Christian. It is by no means a foregone conclusion that this should have been the case; for while, as we have noted, dire human need has frequently induced the will to believe, it ought not to be forgotten that 20th-century humanity entered into its night as a species of thinking animal which had lost not so much the *will* to believe as the *possibility* of belief, humanly speaking. That is to say, those who were most sensitive to the moods and influences of modern Western civilization, unlike medieval men and women, were not predisposed towards belief; they were predisposed towards unbelief. Even those who in time became the greatest spokespersons for *Christian* faith—Barth, Tillich, Bonhoeffer, Niebuhr, and Karl Rahner, for example—did so only through a continuing existential struggle with the impossibility of belief. Belief was for them an "impossible possibility" (Reinhold Niebuhr). Yet there is an unmistakably numinous dimension in the thought even of many who continue to deny the possibility of belief—Camus, for example, or Beckett, or even Sartre. And one may infer from their witness that a consistent atheism is particularly hard to sustain in a time of felt human abandonment. Stark atheism—the atheism that most of us still have in mind when we speak of this phenomenon, the atheism that boasts of its achievement—belongs to the 18th and 19th centuries, that is, precisely the moment in Western history when many intellectuals and prominent persons could sense no universal *Angst*. In the age of light, they felt no need for the little light which shines in the darkness. "The day of the Lord is darkness and not light." The day produces its own grand schemes, but they are very different from the visions that are born in the night.

A contextual theology has particular interest in the search for human hope as it develops within the worldly context itself. It does not seek heteronomously to impose forms of hope upon its context; rather, it tries to formulate its own, Christian hope in the light of the "visions" that are vouchsafed to persons and movements within its context. These visions are theologically significant, even when they are not explicitly religious, because they represent the creaturely instinct for life against the pull of oblivion.[37]

One of the most profound statements of the search for our third alternative has been articulated in our period by the American/Canadian anthropologist, the late Ernest Becker. I have been referring to his work in the notes of this chapter. At this point, I should like to treat his analysis in *The Denial of Death* more explicitly.

In this particular work, Becker was more concerned than I am in the present discussion about the individual; and his categories and terms are not in all cases the ones that I should have used. Yet the statement that he made is in many respects a nontheological parallel to the one that I should like to put in more directly Christian terms. Moreover, as we shall see, it is not even strictly accurate to call his statement nontheological, for not only does it contain allusions to religion in general and

---

37. In support of the argument of this section, see Paul Tillich's discussion of "Aspects of a Religious Analysis of Culture," in *Theology of Culture*, ed. Robert C. Kimball (New York: Oxford University Press, 1959), pp. 40ff.

the Judeo-Christian tradition in particular, but it further sharpens the invitation to theology and almost provides us with concrete reminders of what, as Christians, we might have to offer in such an age. Even so, Becker's statement is not that of a lone voice in the wilderness. It has sufficient similarity with many other "visions" in our particular night that it can be considered somehow representative of what our context— or rather, the Spirit who broods over the face of our as yet rather amorphous context—may be seeking to evoke from us.

One of the elemental urges of the human creature, says Becker, is *heroism.* What we call "society" is "a symbolic action system, a structure of statuses and roles, customs and rules for behavior, designed to serve as a vehicle for earthly heroism. Each script is somewhat unique, each culture has a different hero system."[38] The need to be heroic—the "ache of cosmic specialness"[39]—has both a "mean" and a "noble" side. The former aspect is seen in our "hopeless absorption with ourselves. . . ."[40] He continues:

> Everything painful and sobering in what psychoanalytic genius and religious genius have discovered about man revolves around the terror of admitting what one is doing to earn his self-esteem. This is why human heroics is a blind drivenness that burns people up; in passionate people, a screaming for glory as uncritical and reflexive as the howling of a dog. In the more passive masses of mediocre men it is disguised as they humbly and compliantly follow out the roles that society provides for their heroics.[41]

Yet there is a noble aspect also: people will give their lives for others, will deprive themselves of many things for good causes—provided they can believe that what they are doing is "truly heroic, timeless, and supremely meaningful."[42]

The question that has to be asked of societies, Becker claims, is whether the "cultural hero system" they embody is capable of eliciting belief. "How *empirically true* is the culture hero system that sustains and drives men?"[43]

Applying this test to our society, Becker finds that our "cultural hero system" is no longer credible. The young, who are in the first instance

---

38. *The Denial of Death,* p. 5.
39. Ibid., p. 4.
40. Ibid., p. 2.
41. Ibid., p. 6.
42. Ibid.
43. Ibid.

those to whom any cultural hero system must appeal spontaneously, are frankly "turned off":

> The crisis of modern society is precisely that the youth no longer feel heroic in the plan for action that their culture has set up. They don't believe it is empirically true to the problems of their lives and times. We are living in a crisis of heroism that reaches into every aspect of our social life: the dropouts of university heroism, of business and career heroism, of political-action heroism; the rise of anti-heroes, those who would be heroic each in his own way or like Charles Manson with his special "family," those whose tormented heroics lash out at the system that itself has ceased to represent agreed heroism. The great perplexity of our time, the churning of our age, is that the youth have sensed—for better or for worse—a great social-historical truth: that just as there are useless self-sacrifices in unjust wars, so too is there an ignoble heroics of whole societies: it can be the viciously destructive heroics of Hitler's Germany or the plain debasing and silly heroics of the acquisition and display of consumer goods, the piling up of money and privileges that now characterizes whole ways of life, *capitalist and Soviet.*[44]

Just here, Becker makes an incisive comment about the *church* in such a society—a comment which, taken together with a number of others that we shall note, represents the special challenge to Christians of this whole analysis:

> The crisis of society is, of course, the crisis of organized religion too: religion is no longer valid as a hero system, and so the youth scorn it. If traditional culture is discredited as heroics, then *the church that supports the culture automatically discredits itself. If the church on the other hand chooses to insist on its own special heroics, it might find that in crucial ways it must work against the culture, recruit youth to be anti-heroes to the ways of life of the society they live in.* This is the dilemma of religion in our time.[45]

Against the backdrop of this social analysis (which Becker developed more completely in other works),[46] the author of *The Denial of Death* now turns to the special concern of his present work. In order to show "what gives human heroics its specific nature and impetus," one has, he

---

44. Ibid., pp. 6-7 (emphasis added).

45. Ibid., p. 7 (emphasis added).

46. See Ernest Becker, *The Structure of Evil* (New York: Free Press, 1976); idem, *Escape From Evil* (New York: Free Press, 1975).

says, to consider it in relation to death and the "terror of death." The creature who seeks to be heroic does so in and over against the knowledge that it will "surely die." It is not merely our finitude that makes us "impossible creatures," but our awareness of our finitude. Other animals live by instinct:

> An instinct is a programmed perception that calls into play a programmed reaction. It is very simple. Animals are not moved by what they cannot react to. They live in a tiny world . . . . But look at man, the impossible creature! Here nature seems to have thrown caution to the winds along with the programmed instincts. She created an animal who has no defense against full perception of the external world, an animal completely open to experience. Man not only lives in this moment but expands his inner self to yesterday, his curiosity to centuries ago, his fears to five billion years from now when the sun will cool, his hopes to an eternity from now. He lives not only on a tiny territory, nor even on an entire planet, but in a galaxy, in a universe, and in dimensions beyond visible universes. It is appalling, the burden that man bears, the *experiential* burden.[47]

It is in fact a burden that we cannot bear. Early in our lives we realize this, and we teach ourselves to blot out the pathos and "terror of creation" that we experience: "Most of us—by the time we leave childhood—have repressed our vision of the primary miraculousness of creation."[48]

> Sometimes we may recapture this world by remembering some striking childhood perceptions, how suffused they were in emotion and wonder—how a favorite grandfather looked, or one's first love in his early teens. We change these heavily emotional perceptions precisely because we need to move about in the world with some kind of equanimity, some kind of strength and directness; we can't keep gaping with our heart in our mouth, greedily sucking up with our eyes everything great and powerful that strikes us. The great boon of repression is that it makes it possible to live decisively in an overwhelmingly miraculous and incomprehensible world, a world so full of beauty, majesty, and terror that if animals perceived it all they *would be paralyzed to act.*[49]

Repression ("lying to ourselves about ourselves"[50]) enables us, then, to live. It is "man's natural substitute for instinct."[51] But it also robs us

---

47. *The Denial of Death*, pp. 50-51.
48. Ibid., p. 50.
49. Ibid., emphasis added.
50. Ibid., p. 51.
51. Ibid., p. 178.

of the *depth* of living. "The irony of man's condition is that the deepest need is to be free of the anxiety of death and annihilation; but it is life itself which awakens it, and so we must shrink from being fully alive."[52] (One is reminded of the beautiful dictum of Irenaeus: *Gloria Dei vivens homo*—the glory of God is humanity fully alive.) How is it possible to be fully alive, though, if in the very fulfillment of life one is brought to the unbearable realization of life's beauty and terror?

The *successful* repression of the terror of life and death is greatly dependent upon a social context which, even if it is not perfectly stable, at least provides a credible "cultural hero system" to support individuals in their quest for purpose. The cultural hero system is the proffering of an illusion of purpose.[53]

Becker, as we shall see, did not use the term "illusion" in Freud's negative sense, but wanted to retain for it a highly positive interpretation. Yet he was well aware that when an illusion becomes visible as *mere* illusion it is incapable of serving the end for which it came to be. This was the historic fate of the medieval Christian worldview. It had constituted an astonishingly effective "heroic denial of creatureliness":

> When man lived securely under the canopy of the Judeo-Christian world picture he was part of a great whole; to put it in our terms, his cosmic heroism was completely mapped out, it was unmistakable. He came from the invisible world into the visible one by the act of God, did his duty to God by living out his life with dignity and faith, marrying as a duty, procreating as a duty, offering his whole life—as Christ had—to the Father. In turn he was justified by the Father and rewarded with eternal life in the invisible dimension. Little did it matter that earth was a vale of tears, of horrid sufferings, of incommensurateness, of torturous and humiliating daily pettiness, of sickness and death, a place where man felt he did not belong, "the wrong place," as Chesterton said. . . . In a word, man's cosmic heroism was assured, even if he was a nothing. This is the most remarkable achievement of the Christian world picture; that it could take slaves, cripples, imbeciles, the simple and the mighty, and make them all secure heroes, simply by taking a step back from the world into another dimension of things, the dimension called heaven. Or we might better say that Christianity took creature consciousness—the thing man most wanted to deny—and made it the very *condition for* his cosmic heroism.[54]

Modernity dissolved this secure view of the world. It tried to substitute a great many other things (in particular romantic love and sex) as

---

52. Ibid., p. 66.
53. See the quotation in note 36.
54. *The Denial of Death,* pp. 159-160.

bearers of ultimate meaning; but none of these things is really capable of such an office. "No human relationship can bear the burden of godhood . . . ,"[55] and sex, which can finally only remind its devotees of their mortality, makes a very bogus divinity, a "disappointing answer to life's riddle."[56]

The breakdown of the religious worldview therefore introduces a vast complication into the necessary business of repression. Postreligious *anthrōpos* is for Becker a pathetic figure, because the human creature is by nature religious. A religious being without a proper god, contemporary humanity has had to create wars and revolutions to serve as the context for its misplaced heroism. "That is the price modern man pays for the eclipse of the sacred dimension. When he dethroned the ideas of soul and God he was thrown back hopelessly on his own resources, on himself and those few around him. Even lovers and families trap and disillusion us because they are not substitutes for absolute transcendence. We might say that they are poor illusions in the sense that we have been discussing."[57] The human spirit cannot settle for that which is patently less than ultimate. Becker quotes Otto Rank, whom, along with Kierkegaard, he claims as his own mentor: "The need for a truly religious ideology . . . is inherent in human nature and its fulfillment is basic to any kind of social life."[58] And again: "Man is a 'theological being,' . . . and not a biological one."[59] "In all of this," Becker comments, "it is as though Tillich were speaking and, behind him [Rank], Kierkegaard and Augustine; but what makes it uncanny in the present world of science is that these are the conclusions of the life-work of a psychoanalyst, not a theologian."[60]

Still following Rank, Becker affirms that the consequence of a situation in which innately religious beings are deprived of a social climate in which theistic belief is supported is pervasive neurosis. "Neurosis is the modern tragedy of man; historically he is an orphan."[61] Neurosis is of course a private response, differing in each individual; but the unique contribution of Rank, Becker says, is that he realized that neurosis is also "*historical* to a large extent, because all the traditional ideologies that disguised and absorbed it have fallen away and modern ideologies are just too thin to contain it."[62]

---

55. Ibid., p. 168.
56. Ibid., p. 164.
57. Ibid., p. 190.
58. Ibid., p. 174.
59. Ibid., p. 175.
60. Ibid.
61. Ibid., p. 200.
62. Ibid., p. 177.

To protect itself from the pain of existence, contemporary humanity trivializes experience and reduces the world to manageable proportions:

> What we call the well-adjusted man has just this capacity to partialize the world for comfortable action . . . : the "normal" man bites off what he can chew and digest of life and no more. . . . As soon as a man lifts his nose from the ground and starts sniffing at eternal problems of life and death, the meaning of a rose or a star cluster—then he is in trouble. Most men spare themselves this trouble by keeping their minds on the small problems of their lives just as their society maps these problems out for them. These are what Kierkegaard called the "immediate" men and the "Philistines" [Nietzsche was crueler: he called them "the last men"]. They "tranquilize themselves with the trivial"—and so they can lead normal lives.[63]

Neurosis, by contrast to "normality," is what happens when the techniques we have developed for repressing the depths of life and death fail. "This is neurosis in a nutshell: the miscarriage of clumsy lies about reality."[64] To insulate themselves from the more torturous consequences of this psychic malaise, our contemporaries will enage in activities, "compulsive routines," "utopian" political systems, and other activities which in fact constitute "obsessive denials of reality."[65] But while they may in this way avoid being hurt themselves, "somebody around has to pay for it":

> We are reminded of those Roman portrait-busts that stuff our museums: to live in this tight-lipped style as an average good citizen must have created some daily hell. Of course we are not talking only about daily pettinesses and the small sadisms that are practised on family and friends. Even if the average man lives in a kind of obliviousness of anxiety, it is because he has erected a massive wall of repressions to hide the problem of life and death. His anality may protect him, but all through history it has been the "normal, average men" who, like locusts, have laid waste to the world in order to forget themselves.[66]

What, according to Becker, is the answer to this dilemma? It is *not*, he says flatly, Freud's. Freud, the Stoic,[67] wanted to eliminate illusion in favor of realism. His "orientation towards reality" is to be lauded;[68] but

---

63. Ibid., p. 178.
64. Ibid.
65. Ibid., p. 186.
66. Ibid., p. 187.
67. Ibid., p. 267.
68. Ibid., p. 102.

carried to the lengths he practiced it became *his* neurotic weakness: "He lacked the capacity for illusion, for a creative myth about the possibilities of creation. He saw things *too* 'realistically,' without their aura of miracle and infinite possibility."[69]

But the answer is not that given by the advocates of "unrepression," either. The person who becomes totally unrepressed *a la* the "prophetic message" of Norman Brown—even if such a feat were possible in the first place—would be "a subhuman creature, not a superhuman one."[70] It is not possible to live without repressing some dimensions of our experience. "If repression makes an untenable life liveable, self-knowledge can entirely destroy it for some people."[71] In fact Becker denounces all the "modern" solutions—the silly ones which announce that death itself can be done away with, or postponed greatly (as if that would answer the problem of the *fear* of death), and the more profound ones, like Marcuse's, which offer an immortal *society* in place of our personal mortality (as if that were possible). All such "solutions" end by overlooking or trivializing the real dilemma of existence, the dilemma of the "mortal animal who at the same time is conscious of his mortality."[72] The test of the authenticity of any system of meaning is whether it can keep this primary data to the fore, and not cover it up with non sequiturs at the end of the analysis, as both Brown and Marcuse do, according to Becker. "Whatever man does on this planet has to be done in the lived truth of the terror of creation, of the grotesque, of the rumble of panic underneath everything. Otherwise it is false."[73]

This gives one the clue to Becker's own "answer" (one must say that it is an answer without being a solution). What is needed for "mental health," for life itself, is a "creative illusion," that is, a *mythos* which can permit a maximum of realism about the world and at the same time point beyond the terror of existence towards transcendent meaning.

Several things need to be said at once: First, by "creative illusion" Becker does not mean that the thing he has in mind would be by definition *untrue*. A "mere illusion" would never contain the potentiality for lifting human beings beyond the dilemma of their existing. Some of the other

---

69. Ibid., p. 257.
70. Ibid., p. 263.
71. Ibid., p. 269.
72. Ibid., p. 268.
73. Ibid., p. 284. Hans Küng has made a similar observation: "Coping with the negative side of life is the acid test of Christian and non-Christian humanisms" (*On Being a Christian*, trans. Edward Quinn [Glasgow: Wm. Collins, 1978], p. 571).

terms Becker uses to describe the same phenomenon are instructive: human beings, he says, require a "metaphysic of hope,"[74] a "dream,"[75] a sense of transcendence,[76] of "mystery,"[77] the suspicion of a "plenitude of meaning,"[78] a "vision,"[79] a "myth of heroic transcendence,"[80] a "creative myth." "A creative myth," writes Becker, "is not simply a relapse into comfortable illusion";[81] on the contrary, it is that which enables the human spirit to open itself to reality in a new and "bold" way, to face the negating dimension of existence.

This already anticipates the second point that requires clarification: The *purpose* of the "creative illusion" is not only to encourage, provide hope, joy, peace, and "all things lovely and of good report." This is what the purveyors of cheap hope do, the prophets of "peace, peace, where there is no peace." The adjective *creative* is important here. An "illusion" is "creative" only if it is able to take in the impossibility, the nothingness, over against which it pits itself heroically—the test we have already mentioned. Says Becker: "We need the boldest creative myths, not only to urge men on but also and perhaps especially to help men see the reality of their condition. We have to be as hard-headed as possible about reality and possibility."[82] As I have expressed it in the earlier part of this chapter, human beings need *permission* to explore their darkness, and they can feel that they have such permission only if and insofar as they can believe that there will be some light at the end of the dark tunnel. In Becker's words, the test of the authenticity of any truly creative "metaphysic of hope" is its capacity for taking into itself "the maximum amount of nonbeing."[83] He cites with approval Paul Tillich's *The Courage to Be*, and comments that

> the bold goal of this kind of courage is to absorb into one's own being the maximum amount of nonbeing. As a being, as an extension of all of Being, man has an organismic impulse: to take into his own organization the maximum amount of the problematic of life.[84]

---

74. Ibid., p. 275.
75. Ibid.
76. Ibid., p. 200.
77. Ibid.
78. Ibid., p. 153.
79. Ibid., p. 284.
80. Ibid., p. 285.
81. Ibid., p. 279.
82. Ibid., p. 280.
83. Ibid., p. 279.
84. Ibid.

It is only as that which negates life is itself faced, accepted, taken in, that it can be transformed by "grace" (his word) and become the very stuff out of which hope is made. (Those who are familiar with the Christian teaching of *creatio ex nihilo* as well as the related concepts of the justification of the sinner and the resurrection of the dead, will recognize the parallel.) Thus, says Becker in a key passage to which we shall return, "The creative person becomes, then, in art, literature and religion the mediator of natural terror and the indicator of a new way to triumph over it. He reveals the condition and fabricates a new symbolic transcendence over it. This has been the function of the creative deviant from the shamans through Shakespeare."[85]

But where can such a "creative illusion" be found? How do "myths of transcendence" come to be? Certainly they cannot be produced at will. Neither individuals nor societies sit down and deliberately map out "myths of heroic transcendence." The folly of such attempts Becker sees not only in scientism, romanticism, and various political ideologies, but also in the attempt of Western people to solve their dilemma through the adoption of Eastern religions. The absence of any transcendent "vision," however, *is* the death of contemporary Western society: "Modern man is drinking and drugging himself out of awareness, or he spends his time shopping, which is the same thing. As awareness calls for types of heroic dedication that his culture no longer provides for him, society contrives to help him forget."[86] Clearly, for Becker himself as for his mentor, Rank, biblical faith produced one of the most profound heroic myths humanity has ever uncovered:

> What is the ideal for mental health [read, "for life"], then? A lived, compelling illusion that does not lie about life, death, and reality; one honest enough to follow its own commandments: I mean, not to kill, not to take the lives of others to justify itself. Rank saw Christianity as a truly great ideal foolishness in the sense that we have been discussing it: a childlike trust and hope for the human condition that left open the realm of mystery. Obviously, all religions fall far short of their own ideals, and Rank was talking about Christianity not as practiced but as an ideal. Christianity, like all religions, has in practice reinforced the regressive transference into an even more choking bind: the fathers are given the sanction of divine authority. But as an ideal, Christianity, on all the things we have listed, stands high, perhaps even highest in some vital ways, as people

---

85. Ibid., p. 220.
86. Ibid., p. 284.

like Kierkegaard, Chesterton, the Niebuhrs, and so many others have compellingly argued.[87]

What Becker does not tell us straightforwardly is whether he thinks Christianity is still a candidate for the role of "creative illusion." In his concluding paragraph he rightly notices that the creation of heroic myths is "not even in man's hands to program."[88] But he also knows that life is stronger than death; that it "seeks to expand in an unknown direction,"[89] and that one cannot know "what form the forward momentum of life will take in the time ahead or what use it will make of our anguished searching."[90] Then he concludes with the poignant statement,

> The most that any one of us can seem to do is to fashion something—an object or ourselves—and drop it into the confusion, make an offering of it, so to speak, to the life force.[91]

He knew himself to be dying when he wrote this sentence. He was not yet 50 years of age.

10.2. Mandate to Theology.   I believe that we must hear this *kind* of cultural analysis (and it is only one of many which bear the imprint of similar influences)[92] as an insistent and compelling mandate to theology. Many other challenges to Christians are indirect, cloaked in secular or even atheistic language, implicit. This one is explicit. It puts very pointed questions to contemporary Christians: Can you be "for real"? Can you leave off proferring Christianity as a bourgeois affair, an aid to the neurotic repression of reality? Can you be "serious?" ("I think that taking life seriously means something such as this: that whatever man does on this planet has to be done in the *lived truth* of the terror of creation, of the grotesque, of the rumble of panic underneath everything. Otherwise it is false.")[93] Have you anything to offer to "the life force"? Have you a hope that does not have to lie about the hopeless things that are really present in our world today? Is there in your tradition that which can at the same time "reveal the darkness" and "fabricate a new symbolic

---

87. Ibid., p. 204.
88. Ibid., p. 285.
89. Ibid., p. 284.
90. Ibid., p. 285.
91. Ibid.
92. Among whom I would list such names as Hannah Arendt, Maurice Friedman, Lewis Thomas, Elie Wiesel, Simone Weil, Loren Eiseley, Konrad Lorenz, George Grant, and many other analysts of the age, as well as a great many of the novelists and artists of our culture.
93. Ibid., p. 284.

transcendence over it"?[94] Are you able again to bring off the thing that, from time to time in its history, the church managed: to keep human beings truthful and at the same time hopeful?

Here the invitation to theology is not merely a general one. It is a mandate to recover and rethink dimensions of our tradition that we have permitted to disappear, or have hidden beneath the bright concepts that were more acceptable to modernity. With Becker and his ilk one is reminded of the statement of Jesus to his disciples: "If these were silent, the very stones would cry out" (Luke 19:40). He goads a silent church into remembrance of the treasures that it has buried. The tradition of Jerusalem has sometimes in the past provided the very frame of reference required by persons and societies in their extremity. Truth which merely delineates the wretchedness of the human condition—Freud's kind of truth—ends in bitterness and cynicism, no matter how preferable it may be to lying. On the other hand, hope which sustains itself through sheer unthought *denial* of the wretchedness ends in superficiality and the infliction of the thwarted pain of existence onto others, and eventually, in all probability, onto oneself or those nearest one. But historic Christianity has had the capacity to take the very insignificance and impossibility of our human condition ("All our goodness is as filthy rags" [Paul]; "We are beggars!" [Luther]) and "make it a condition of hope."[95] "My grace is sufficient for you, for my power is made perfect in weakness" (2 Cor. 12:9).

Did this magic die with the death of the Middle Ages or the earlier stages of the Reformation? Is the modern church condemned to perpetuate a "*mere* illusion," a no-longer-credible mythology, which may serve the surface needs of the affluent and unthinking but cannot appeal to the sensitive young or to those who are unable to avoid . . . "death"? Is the role of Christianity in the postreligious world nothing more than the vapid repetition of yesterday's myths of heroic transcendence, serving only the interests of those who want to avoid today? Or can the faith of the Christ be rethought, reformulated in the light of "our darkness"? Can the disciple community exercise the function of the "creative person"—revealing the truth of our problematic and constructing out of the exposure to that crisis a new and credible symbolic transcendence over it?

Becker and others like him seem almost to believe that it could be done. They shame us, for they appear to have more trust in our tradition than many of us ourselves have. We hold back from the exploration of

94. Ibid., p. 220.
95. Ibid., p. 204.

190

our societal extremity because we fear we have neither the courage nor the wisdom to comprehend it, let alone the audacity to turn it into "God's possibility." But the stones who cry out may help the children to find voices for their hallelujahs.

10.3. The Possibility.   In the introduction, I made what may have seemed to some the strange or even distasteful comment that I found the most hopeful sign in our contemporary North American experience to be our growing *disillusionment*. While agreeing with the formulators of the Detroit statement concerning the significance of "the tradition of idealism and struggle against oppression in our own history," I cautioned that the pursuit of that line on the part of persons wanting to become theologically contextual in North America today (apart from minorities) could be a grave error. Instead, I claimed, we should reflect carefully on our nascent disillusionment: "In the disillusionment of those who have given themselves so long and so wholeheartedly to the modern illusion, a foothold might be found for a gospel that believes real hope can begin where illusion ends. . . ."[96] Through his use of the language of illusion, Becker has helped to clarify the meaning of such a statement.

The "creative illusion" that informed the Middle Ages (the "ideal foolishness" of Christianity) gave way to a new illusion. This had to be, of course, because the Christian illusion in its medieval form proved in the long run too scant to absorb into itself a whole constellation of new experiences, including new forms of negation, which came to be with the Renaissance and Reformation. For vast numbers of human beings, medieval Christianity increasingly showed itself to be "mere illusion." They could wish to keep hold of it—as the Romantics did; but they could not believe it. Nor could the church, for all its efforts, make the old mythology credible. In some parts of the world (in much of Latin America and in Quebec prior to World War II, for example) the old myth of transcendence could be shored up by ecclesiastical authority, poverty, and legislated ignorance of the modern world. But because it had ceased to take into itself the contemporary *threat* to the heroic vision, the medieval illusion could sustain itself only where the modern world had not yet quite achieved its ostentatious victory. Even in these societies, that possibility is by now finished—and, not infrequently, with a vengeance! Wherever Christianity is offered today in *our world* without reference to Darwin, Freud, Marx, Nietzsche, technology, the bomb, and the whole eclipse of God and meaning that has come upon us with the unfolding

---

96. Above, introduction, §4.

191

of modernity, it fails as a creative myth—even when (as in North American "evangelicalism") it attracts considerable numbers to itself.[97]

But what of the illusion that replaced "Christendom"? It seemed to countless of our progenitors the very essence of the heroic: "Man" as the Promethean steersman of the bark of history, the lord and master of nature! But, as Becker said early in his study, illusions have to be tested. "Cultural hero systems" always live under the threat of the question, How empirically true? The modern hero system based its appeal on a highly positive estimate of the world, nature, and history, and, above all, of the human species itself. What has shown up at last (for some, like Kierkegaard, it was already visible at the height of industrial heroics) is that this hero system has no real capacity for taking into itself the experience of negation ("death"—by which Becker, like the Bible, refers not so much to the biological phenomenon as to the whole quality of finitude, vulnerability, littleness, and failure which is made both symbolically and literally poignant by the fact of our physical mortality.) The modern heroic illusion has at last manifested itself as "*mere* illusion"— indeed, as one of the *least adequate* of the illusions by which human beings have lived; for it built itself on an exaggerated estimate of our capacities for life and ignored our fear both of life and of death. The failure of the illusion has been pathetic in the Western world at large; but it is most pathetic among the people who gave themselves to it most uncritically, the North Americans. We are a disillusioned people, a people whose rudimentary *mythos* has proved unworthy, but who as a people remember no alternatives.

And I claim: It is just in our disillusionment that it is possible to discern the truth that *could*—with the grace of God—fashion itself in time into a more genuine approximation of human hope ("creative illusion"). This, I would repeat, is *possible*. But it is by no means inevitable.

The state of disillusionment is a highly provocative one, whether one considers it in ordinary human terms or within a specifically Christian framework. Humanly speaking, it signifies a condition of crisis and, at the same time, of a reflective sensitivity to reality. The crisis is serious, because that upon which life has been based (the foundational "illusion") has been shaken. Yet by this same token there is an unusual openness to reality; for the worldview which has cushioned our perception of our condition has been or is being removed. Whether this susceptibility to reality will become the occasion for a new wrestling with the primary

---

97. See George Grant, *Technology and Justice* (Toronto: Anansi, 1969), pp. 76-77.

data of experience and a new search for meaning and hope, or whether on the other hand the crisis will simply deepen into catastrophic forms depends in large measure upon how the disillusionment is dealt with. A disillusioned lover can be driven to despair and irrationality if he or she is granted no perspective from which to regard his or her condition as potentially meaningful. On the other hand, provided with some reassurance of ultimate worth and a friendly arm to lean upon, the period of disillusionment may prove the most important and maturing experience in the lover's life. It may be a time of deepening and growth, the passage from adolescence to adulthood. Surely something of this nature applies to societies as well as to individuals.

Another aspect of the state of disillusionment is provocative for our present considerations: the disillusioned one is still close enough to the state of living within an illusion to be open to new illusions—if compelling ones can be found. By contrast, those who have never dreamed dreams or seen visions, or who long ago became cynical about such things, are poor candidates for any compelling vision. Often I have had occasion to think of the differences between Europe and North America in such terms. The old societies of Europe, more particularly (in my experience) the Germanic societies, have been so victimized by dreams and dreamers of one kind and another that they are almost incapable of hope. One reason why the Marxist mythology has such a hard time achieving a positive foothold in the Eastern European block (besides the obvious problem of being laid on from above) lies in just this pervasive skepticism about illusions. It is not accidental that the quintessential European, Sigmund Freud, looked for salvation in the destruction of illusions. By contrast, the North American (like Becker) remembers the power of the illusion, and even in his or her disillusionment is still capable of being aroused by dreams and dreamers. This, of course, is not an unmitigated boon; for it means that North Americans even on the point of despair, and perhaps especially then, too easily give way to new schemes and dreams, or to promises of reviving the old dream—and in even more grandiloquent and simplistic forms! Yet there is in the state of disillusionment a certain advantage, in that proximity to the illusion makes for openness to new and compelling visions as well as to bad faith and cheap hope. No doubt this is where it is right to see a certain point of contact for creative theology in the "tradition of idealism and struggle against oppression" in our history. But a *direct* appeal to that tradition would not, I think, achieve the depth of self-knowledge and critical reflection that is required of us as a people today.

The practical implication of these human observations about disillusionment is, it seems to me, that we are given a little time, a certain period of grace, during which we may enter meditatively into our experience as disillusioned followers of the modern illusion, and attempt to come to terms with our failure creatively. Patterns of history suggest that disillusionment is a relatively brief period in the cycle of civilizations, as in personal life. The mood of disillusionment is one of suspension, and human beings are not very adept at living *between* more decisive points of view. There is a kind of impulse within the state of disillusionment to move one way or another, either towards a new and credible "illusion" or towards cynicism and despair. In addition to this natural haste, the apocalyptic conditions of our present world contribute an *un*natural dimension. All the old, natural cycles of individual and corporate life are telescoped. There is an urgency about the situation. One senses that disillusionment in our society could rather quickly go over into moods ranging from bored resignation to crass and overt nihilism. Perhaps this has already happened. With well-known protectionist economic, military, and other policies appended to such moods, the situation does not augur well for the security either of our own society or that of the world at large. It belongs to whatever humane and life-affirming impulses there are in our culture to seek alternative ways of directing our disillusionment.

Under such circumstances, Christians *ought* to be able to offer something to "the life force." For if, humanly speaking, the period of disillusionment in the life of persons and of peoples is at least potentially life-affirming, disillusionment is even more provocative *as a religious concept*. It would not be too much to say that all profound religious experience presupposes, or occasions, or both, some degree of disillusionment. Disillusionment with his Pharisaic devotion to law left Saul of Tarsus open to the gospel of the Christians he was persecuting. Disillusionment with the thought-forms of his age made Justin Martyr regard Christianity as "the only safe philosophy." Disillusionment with the various "isms" to which he had given himself led Augustine of Hippo to his discovery of the Christ of the Newer Testament. Disillusionment with medieval systems of penitence was the condition without which Martin Luther could not have been prepared for the message of "justification by grace through faith." Most of the early European inhabitants of the North American continent came to these shores because of their disillusionment with the Old World and its religious as well as its civic prospects. It is indeed hard to conceive of a penetrating religious experience which does not entail a high degree of disillusionment—with "the world," "the flesh," "life," "society," one's class or peer group, and above all with one's self. Theology, one could even say, begins with the experience of disillusionment, and it consists in considerable measure of reasoned reflection upon that experience, the causes of it, the meaning in it, the thrust beyond it.

If the disciple community were willing and able to cease lending its support to the *modern* illusion; *if*, instead, it were to concentrate its considerable powers of analysis and understanding upon the experience of a society which has become disillusioned with the promises of modernity, *then*, I believe, a truly creative theology could occur in our context, and in a way that is sorely needed. This is what the invitation to theology means in North America today. Living in a situation of growing but largely incoherent and chaotic forms of disillusionment, the disciple community has the vocation of exploring the failure of the illusion that is passing, and of articulating a new expression of the faith which can absorb this failure and point towards a new symbolic transcendence of it. In other words, the disciple community is called to fulfill the function of Becker's "creative person": that is, to enter and illuminate the meaning of the "natural terror" as it comes to us in our time and place, and to point to a way to pass through and beyond it.

But the *condition* for this vocation is also the one that Becker names with great precision: The church can only offer "its own special heroics"—the triumph of *the cross*—only if it dissociates itself from its past functioning as the cultic supporter of the dominant social illusion. To achieve the opportunity for its gospel which is present in the extremity of its civilization, Christianity will have to find a quite different way of being vis-à-vis the dominant classes, the public goals, and the private values of its host society. A truly contextual theology will be a critical theology; for it can serve the biblical God in its social context only by naming the inadequacy and the dangers of the illusion its society tries still to cling to. Its task is not to buttress that illusion but to explore the depths of truth present in our real disillusionment, so that the new metaphysic of hope which may come to be shall be constructed out of God's Word, and not only out of our own desperate need.

We are engaged—as one might say in the spirit of Becker's terminology—in a work of *re*-illusioning (Tillich would say re-mythologizing). For those who want theology to be "the whole truth," and in a very straightforward manner, such language will no doubt seem blasphemous; for others, futile. But from another point of view (the one, namely, which informs not only this but any attempt at theology which remembers that

195

it is by definition a "modest science"—Barth), the only great blasphemy would be to consider any historical version of the Christian gospel "the whole truth."[98] The whole truth cannot be put into words, and it need not be. The whole truth is there only in the one who said, "I *am* the truth." In relation to this one Word, all of our words are relative—mixtures of truth and error, fact and fantasy, myth and longing. The task of the disciple community is to find for its here and now the appropriate mix, the right "illusion." Behind and above all our illusions there is, we believe, One who is utterly real, in whom there is neither shadow nor turning, whose ways are elusive but not illusory. All that our theology can hope to achieve is the statement of a momentary illusion so compelling in its timeliness that it will point to the reality that transcends every illusion, that is eternal. But that reality is no system of theology. It is no "it." It is Thou.

---

98. In his recent book, *What Is Living, What Is Dead in Christianity Today: Breaking the Liberal–Conservative Deadlock* (San Francisco: Harper & Row, 1986), Charles Davis employs a different language from what I have adopted here, but he seems to intend a similar meaning. Instead of "illusion," Davis employs the more conventional language of "myth." He contrasts "myth and metaphysics" and claims that "not much is left of the metaphysics" of Christian tradition, and "the doctrinal elaboration" which derived from Christian metaphysics "needs to lose its rigidity." But has mythical Christianity in any sense survived? In a way reminiscent of Becker's discussion of "illusion," Davis insists that "a myth must relate to the deepest challenges posed by human existence in this world if it is to live as myth and not survive merely as a piece of folklore" (p. 34). For Davis, as for many of us, "the deepest challenges" include in a very existential way the prospect of global catastrophe: "There is . . . a dark element in my own consciousness. The probability that in a decade or so any of us who survive will have entered into the hell following a nuclear war makes it impossible for me to treat rationally elaborated worldviews with solemn seriousness. Our sanity is preserved in this present world not by rational argument or appeal to invariant structures but by rejoicing in the sheer unexpectedness, the ungrounded giftfulness, which characterizes the game of human existence and which might yet save us" (p. 77). Davis seems to me less than lucid about the manner in which this "unexpectedness" and "giftfulness" (grace?) relates to the continuing reflection of the community of faith on its gospel and tradition, but he does suggest that the mythical form of Christianity contributes to it: "What is of continuing validity in mythical Christianity is the understanding of religious language as metaphorical or poetic language and the acknowledgment that goes with this of the indispensable function of the imagination and feeling, of tradition and community" (p. 77).

CHAPTER · THREE
Components of Our Context

Humankind is currently in a state of manifold crisis, the catastrophic climax of which probably still lies ahead.

—*Carl Friedrich von Weizsäcker*[1]

Introduction: Contributing Crises

We have said that noncontextual theology tends to function in church and society to insulate people from the real issues of their historical moment. This is not designed. It is a matter, largely, of unconscious avoidance. A theology which determines quite deliberately to engage its sociohistorical context, on the contrary, must be prepared to expose itself from the outset to the actual exigencies of its time and place, and without an advance guarantee that it will be able either to comprehend or to meet, with "answers," the "questions" implict therein.

In the preceding discussion, we have identified the *underlying* crisis of our culture as the breakdown of the modern worldview which is our foundational *mythos*. We have come to the end of an age, and it is an especially painful experience for North Americans because as the pilot project, so to speak, of the "illusion" (Becker) which fired that age we have been deprived of categories on the basis of which to comprehend its failure. Our crisis is the crisis of the disillusioned who have no frame of reference for the experience of disillusionment.

Any delineation of the crisis of modernity in less stark and encompassing terms must, it seems to me, be regarded as an exercise in reductionism. What has failed is not just capitalism, or humanism, or technology, or democracy. The cause of our societal malaise cannot be laid

1. "Die Menschheit befindet sich heute in einer Krise, deren katastrophaler Höhepunkt wahrscheinlich noch vor uns liegt," Carl Friedrich von Weizsäcker, *Die Zeit drängt* (Munich and Vienna: Carl Hanser Verlag, 1986), p. 25.

197

at the doorstep of "big government," or "the welfare state," or "the failure of the educational system," or "patriarchy," or "the laziness of the work force." Nor can everything be set right again by replacing private with state ownership, or vice versa, or by destroying all complex machinery, or inventing still more complex machinery, or returning to the land, or putting more women into positions of authority, or waging all-out battles against such things as corruption in high places, pornography, and organized crime. Our kairotic moment is nothing less than the bankruptcy of the worldview which brought us into being and sustained us for some centuries. This conception of humanity and the world has proved incapable of absorbing the negating factors which it has itself helped to produce. Until we are prepared to examine critically and openly this *fundamental* failure, our concentration upon less ultimate problems will only confuse the issue and deepen the real problem. The raw flesh of humanity has been exposed in our time. The protective blankets of culture and convention which allow human beings in less critical epochs to address themselves to less rudimentary problems of existence have been snatched away, and we are left naked and vulnerable to impersonal forces and fates in what seems an "indifferent" universe (Camus). If Christian theology cannot address itself to the rudiments of this predicament, then it had better exercise caution in respect to the external manifestions of the root crisis. Theology, if it has any cultural justification at all, must concern itself with *basic* realities, including both their analysis and their cure. Too much religion in our time has busied itself with the symptoms of our malaise, treating them as if they were the disease as such.

It is true, however, that the underlying malaise of our society expresses itself in, and is complicated by, a great variety of more specific and tangible problems. As in the breakdown of an organism (the human body, for instance) many apparently separable things go wrong, so with the breakdown of a society there are numerous visible areas of dis-ease. These should not be regarded with greater seriousness than they deserve: they are symptoms. At the same time, the less visible dimensions of the malaise cannot be comprehended or tackled unless some attention is given to the symptoms. For they are in their way contributing crises. They aggravate and exacerbate the climacteric as in a vicious circle of cause and effect. With some of them, in fact, the primal crisis is almost transparent—one thinks in particular of the nuclear issue, which is no mere "issue" but in a real sense is parabolic for the whole as well as being in its own right a critical dimension of society. (The contemporary plague designated AIDS might also be regarded as parabolic in this sense, symbolizing the internal and personal as distinct from the external, political threat to the life of our civilization.) In the case of other symptoms, such as those which have in a specific way to do with the state of religion, the connection with the fundamental problematic of the society is perhaps less immediate, or at least more subtle. Yet all of these components (and more, certainly, than we can adequately treat in this discussion) have to become the concern of a theology which tries to think the faith in context; and in each case it will be necessary for such a theology to attempt to understand, not only what significance these contributing crises have for society at large but also what they mean for the thought and life of the disciple community within that society.

In seeking to describe these contributing crises, theology necessarily crosses and re-crosses the invisible line between dogmatics and ethics. A contextual theology is barred a priori from honoring the division which academic conventions have created between these two dimensions of faith's rational reflection. From the perspective of contextuality in theological thought, the division is not only theoretically suspect, but it has revealed itself in our own time to be completely unworkable.

An incident from recent ecclesiastical history illustrates the point. A European faculty of theology was choosing a successor for its most renowned theologian, a man who had at once stimulated and irritated the church as well as the state, because he would not honor the theology/ethics distinction, but kept inserting disturbing "ethical issues" into his work as a dogmatician. One of the candidates for the vacant chair was asked his opinion on the relation between the two theological sciences. He responded in a metaphor (no doubt it seemed a clever one to many who heard it): "What has the Cologne Cathedral to do with the Ruhr district?" What neither the candidate nor the majority of his hearers seemed to realize (he was offered the position!) was that the beautiful and historic cathedral is today being systematically eroded and ravished by noxious air originating, in large part, from the industrial Ruhr valley!

Theology does not exist in a sociological/ethical vacuum any more than the great cathedrals of the West exist in an atmosphere unaffected by industrial pollution. Theology which attempts to segregate itself, even temporarily, from the issues of its total environment will be rendered irrelevant (and perhaps finally extinct) by those same issues.

Today, specialization in every field of human endeavor is called into question by the reality of a global *problematique* which requires interdisciplinary discourse *even for its comprehension*. The era which produced specialists was, first, one of relative peace and, second, one which could still assume that the specialists would talk to one another, as civilized and universally concerned persons of learning. In the present "manifold crisis" of humanity, the division of the learned into mutually exclusive elites is part of the problem; it is indeed one of those almost transparent manifestations of the *rudimentary* problem.

Christian theology, all too famous in the modern epoch for its imitation of worldly trends, allowed itself to be siphoned off into specialties along with most other disciplines, and it has not been more diligent than the others, on the whole, to sustain any depth of *inter*disciplinary dialogue. But this is a luxury of our immediate past which we cannot afford to continue. It was always, potentially, a betrayal of the inner logic of biblical faith, with its drive to comprehend a mysterious whole; today it is a betrayal of the unity (i.e., the survival!) of the world as well. No less than any other attempt of humanity to comprehend its real situation, and indeed with greater inherent urgency than most sciences, theology is called to put aside the extravagance of examining the parts in order that it may come to the aid of the whole. There can be no place for *Fachidioten* in the disciple community.[2] As Ernest Becker has written, "Someone has to be willing to play the fool in order to relieve the general myopia." One has to "run the risk of simple-mindedness in order to make some dent in the unintended imbecility brought about by overspecialization and its mountains of fact."[3] (Is this what being "a fool for Christ" must mean for Christian academics today?)

As I have intimated, the critical components of our context which I shall discuss in this chapter are in some cases explicitly related to Christianity while others are of a more public character. None of them, however, permits classification into purely secular or purely sacred categories. All represent issues posing particular difficulties and challenges—including highly positive *opportunities*—for Christian belief and theology in our context. The list is far from exhaustive. I have concentrated on what appear to me especially crucial areas.

11. The End of the Constantinian Era

The extremity within which the disciple community in North America finds itself today is not only the end of an age, it is also the end of a

---

2. I.e., persons who, while knowing a great deal about some particular (and often remote) subject or area of investigation (*Fach*), are wholly uninformed about most of life, including the relation of their own academic pursuits to the larger society, and who, literally, are "idiots" when it comes to the world at large.

3. *The Denial of Death,* p. 209. (It was in part under the impact of such reasoning that I abandoned the temptation to designate the present work a "Systematic Theology" and chose instead to name it, simply, "Christian Theology." My reasoning also took into account the reality of religious pluralism which, among other things, means that we are no longer permitted to speak of theology as if it automatically meant Christian theology.)

long and deeply entrenched form of the church. The single most far-reaching *ecclesiastical* factor conditioning theological reflection in our time is the effective disestablishment[4] of the Christian religion in the Western world by secular, political, and alternative religious forces.[5]

Christianity began as a minority religion, and for the first three centuries it was ignored, despised, or openly persecuted by the society within which it developed. The Newer Testament's writings, as well as other important documents of the early church, assume this *exclusion* as their most salient sociological presupposition. The extent to which this presupposition conditioned their *theology* has been largely overlooked by historical and systematic theology until recent times. It is probable that secular historians and essayists have been less myopic than theologians when it comes to perceiving the subtle connections between empire and ideology in this connection.[6]

---

4. I should like to accentuate the adjective "effective." It is true, as William H. Willimon notes in "Answering Pilate: Truth and the Postliberal Church" (*The Christian Century*, January 28, 1987, pp. 80ff.), that "Christians are in an awkward stage in Western culture" because "having once been culturally established, they are not yet clearly disestablished." Not *clearly*, but effectively nonetheless. While in certain regions of the United States (notably the South) the "cultural establishment" can still *seem* real, the continent as a whole does not reflect Constantinian assumptions. The very defensiveness which attends the most "Christian" regions betrays an underlying consciousness of the unreality of the basic religious assumptions. A noisy and promotional Christianity is in a real sense the best illustration of the demise of Christendom.

5. I have devoted two previous books to this subject, and therefore I shall not attempt to develop it broadly here. It cannot be passed over, however, because it makes all the difference in the world if the disciple community knows that its own *status* in the world has been greatly altered. The difference is visible not only in regard to the *living* of the faith (vol. 3) but also at the level of our *thinking* the faith. For one thing, Christians who are conscious of the new contextual circumstances *of the church itself* tend to be more critical of many doctrinal traditions in view of the fact that they were created under the conditions of establishment. It is impossible to divorce the triumphalism of much Christian doctrine, and the concomitant neglect of the "theology of the cross," from the fact that Christianity for the greater share of its history has served as handmaiden to successive empires. (See my analysis in *The Reality of the Gospel & the Unreality of the Churches* [Philadelphia: Westminster, 1975], and *Has the Church a Future?* [Philadelphia: Westminster, 1980]).

6. It is not surprising that historians should have had better insights into this connection; it would be hard to be a historian and miss the significance of contexts. G. P. Baker, writing his study of Constantine in the early 30s of this century, notes the significance of the sociopolitical condition of the church for its pre-Constantinian message and image: "It is interesting to reflect," he writes, "that there was a time when the Christian Church could be instanced as a foe of law and order, and an enemy of good government and social safety." This remark is by way of a commentary on the fact that when the Emperor Galerius came to Nicomedia around 302 C.E. in order to instruct Jovius that the foes of order and good government had not as yet been fully suppressed, he named the Christian church as such a foe. Baker continues: "In theory—or at any rate in principle—the Church had not even the right to exist. It was an illegal body, whose creed had only to be stated in order to demonstrate its unlawful nature. It acted as a corporation, though it was no corporation. It owned money and other chattels; it exercised power and influence; it was an alien and intrusive body, an *imperium in imperio*, counteracting the legal influence of properly constituted authorities, drawing away the obedience of citizens to a code of conduct and a scheme of ideas not endorsed by the government—imposing a law in supersession of the constitutionally valid law of the sovereign state. It was a seditious body. It was a conspiracy, a treason, and a revolution" (*Constantine the Great and the Christian Revolution* [New York: Barnes and Noble, 1931], pp. 72-73).

Whether the great change occurred rather suddenly or gradually, it is clear *that* it did occur: after 313 C.E., the whole *modus vivendi* of Christian faith and life was dramatically altered, and by 394 the once-illicit Christian minority had become *the only legal religion* of the empire. While there is no reason to minimize the role of the emperors themselves in this transformation, notably of Constantine and Theodosius I, it is evident that even very powerful individuals do not single-handedly cause such shifts in the destinies of historical movements. If the imperial figures who were the most prominent actors in this drama were able to see in the Christian phenomenon certain prospects favorable to their own cause, it must be supposed that such dimensions were present in Christian teaching and behavior prior to its adoption by empire.[7] Clearly, the philosophic emphasis upon "oneness," both as applied to the Deity and to the creation, appealed to Constantine, whose plan for the unification of the empire needed just such a transcendental undergirding. Moreover, as the writings of the second-century Apologists demonstrate, there were many in the church itself who, if they did not strive after establishment as such, were keen to have the movement recognized.

Our present purpose, however, is not to sort out the complex details of the transition from diaspora to establishment, but rather, in the first place, to notice the consequences of this transformation for the theology of the Christian movement. A growing segment of contemporary Christians of all confessional backgrounds is today open to the prospect that these consequences were both extensive and deleterious to the gospel. "There is a legend in the life of Sylvester who was pope [at the time of Constantine]," writes Alec R. Vidler. "It says that at the moment when Constantine bestowed large endowments on the church a voice from heaven was heard to say, *'Hodie venenum effusum est in Ecclesiam,'* 'Today is there poison poured upon the Church.' "[8]

One consequence of the establishment for Christian thought has already been alluded to: the emphasis on oneness or unity (the ecumenical or catholic dimension) could never be regarded in purely theological terms after the adoption of the faith by imperial Rome. For now it was bound up with quite specific political aspirations and concepts. When we confess belief in "one, holy, catholic, and apostolic church" in the Nicene Creed, it is well to remember that fact. On precisely such grounds, Theodosius

---

7. See Roland Bainton's discussion of this subject under the heading, "The Christian Roman Empire," in his *Christendom: A Short History of Christianity and Its Impact on Western Civilization,* 2 vols. (New York: Harper & Row, 1964), vol. 1, chap. 4, pp. 89ff.

8. Alec R. Vidler, *Christian Belief and This World* (London: SCM, 1956), p. 16.

outlawed all forms of Christianity but the "Catholic" (i.e., the imperially recognized majority) form, at the same time (394 C.E.) as he outlawed the non-Christian religions. Unity, under the conditions of Constantinianism, is defined by secular authority and/or standards of assessment, and it is therefore likely to mean something closer to *uniformity* than to the oneness for which Jesus prayed in the Garden of Gethsemane (John 17).

A still more provocative consequence of the establishment for the theology of the church is implied with the mention of Nicaea. *Both* the councils of Nicaea (325) and Chalcedon (451) took place under the conditions of Christian establishment. Concretely this means: the church's doctrinal decisions about (a) the nature of the Godhead (that God is triune) and (b) the person of Jesus (that he is God and man in one historical person) were taken by a church which now conceived itself in the role of official cult to the empire. Indeed, Nicaea was convened by Constantine personally, with the express purpose of putting a stop to Christian differences which could only further divide an already disunited empire. The decisions arrived at in these two pivotal councils were to determine orthodoxy in Theology and Christology up to and including our own time. This is a staggering observation, and from our present perspective we must ask: How would it have influenced the Christian church's conception of God, and even more explicitly its Christology, if decisions in these key areas of belief had evolved under the conditions of diaspora and persecution rather than those of establishment?

Such questions have become mandatory for the disciple community today because there is a growing consciousness among the remnants of the churches of the older denominations that *our* sociopolitical condition may resemble the preestablishment situation of the early church more than it does that of later, settled forms of the church. Particularly with respect to ecclesiology, though also in many other areas of Christian belief, we find ourselves wondering whether much that has been held sacred in the Christian tradition does not emanate more directly from the birth of *Christendom* in the 4th century C.E. than it does from the *Pentecostal* beginnings of the church variously described in the Newer Testament, especially Acts 2. Indeed, to what extent is our very reading of these beginnings—and of the Bible as a whole—conditioned by presuppositions that were first awakened by the marriage of church and empire, and then nurtured by 16 centuries of culture-religion?

These are no longer the questions of a handful of critics within and outside the churches. Few reflective Christians today are capable of the purity of Søren Kierkegaard's mid-19th-century *Attack upon Christendom*,[9] and fewer still are prepared to go so far as Franz Overbeck, the contemporary and friend of Nietzsche, who at the end of the 19th century suggested that "Christendom" had been a mistake, a gross misunderstanding of the message of Jesus.[10] Only a few scholars even bother themselves with the anti-Christendom "rantings" of these earlier critics. Yet, particularly since the 1960s and the association of countercultural movements with the early forms of the Christian movement by commentators like Theodore Roszak and others,[11] there are significant minorities within all the churches which suspect that biblical faith is somehow fundamentally incommensurate with empire. These minorities, moreover, are strongly represented in theological colleges and seminaries, and the consequences of that representation are already being felt in the churches. It can be assumed, I believe, that the contrast between imperial Christianity and diasporic forms of the church will become increasingly significant in the ensuing decades, not only for the practical "life-style" of the church but for its theology as well. What we are witnessing (and to some degree participating in) is nothing less than a radical re-formation/ purification of Christianity, comparable in magnitude only to the alteration which occurred at the other end of this same process, when the church moved into Caesar's court. "We are living at the end of the Constantinian era."[12]

The results of this shift in ecclesial models cannot yet be predicted, though one is given intimations of its meaning in places (like East Germany, Czechoslovakia, Cuba,[13] and elsewhere) where the "natural" process of secularization has been accelerated by the emergence of new

---

9. E.g.: "This whole thing about 'Christendom' is . . . a criminal case, corresponding to what ordinarily is known as forgery, imposture, except that here it is religion which is thus made use of . . ." (*Attack upon Christendom*, trans. Walter Lowrie [Boston: Beacon, 1944], p. 117).

10. See Martin Rumscheidt, *Revelation and Theology: An Analysis of the Barth–Harnack Correspondence of 1923* (Cambridge: At the University Press, 1972), pp. 134-139.

11. Theodore Roszak, *The Making of a Counterculture: Reflections on the Technocratic Society and Its Youthful Opposition* (Garden City, N.Y.: Doubleday, 1969).

12. The statement was made by Günther Jacob of Cottbus in the German Democratic Republic, and it is quoted by Karl Barth in *How to Live in a Marxist Land*, trans. Thomas Wieser et al. (New York: Association Press, 1959), p. 64.

13. It is not to be assumed, however, as First World Christians are wont to do, that such societies are simply anti-Christian. As the existence of lively Christian communities in Russia and all the Eastern bloc countries indicates, together with such phenomena as the "unofficial" peace movements in these societies and a growing recognition of humanizing elements in nontriumphalistic expressions of Christian faith, it can be argued, as Milan Opocenski of the Comenius Faculty in Prague has stated it, that the situation of the church in such contexts is the "normal" situation, and that Christian establishment is "abnormal." See also in this connection the best-selling book about Fidel Castro's view of religion, *Fidel Y La Religion: Conversaciones con Frei Betto* (Havana: Oficina de Publicaciones, 1985).

societies hostile to or critical of established religion or, in another sense, in places (like South Africa, Central America and the Caribbean, and South America) where countercultural Christian communities have presented live alternatives to the *officially* Christian power-groups.[14] One thing appears certain: what is occurring in this transition is more decisive and vast than most of us, conditioned as we are by the theological and ecclesiastical conventions of the past, are capable of taking in. It is possible that by comparison with this re-forming of the Christian movement, the Reformation of the 16th century will prove less dramatic than it has heretofore seemed. For, excluding the later Wycliffe, Thomas Münzer, and various elements of the Radical Reformation, the 16th-century reformers still assumed the Constantinian form of the church in a fundamental sense. This assumption is observable not only in their ecclesiologies but in other aspects of their doctrine as well.[15]

The present transformation of the disciple community, of which in some respects the 16th-century Reformation may be an early expression, is calling for far more radical changes, both in the form of the church and in its thinking. One seriously doubts that the extent of these alterations have been glimpsed by more than a few of our contemporaries. Most of us are still throughly influenced by Constantinian assumptions, so that even when we are able to transcend them intellectually they are effective at the emotional level and fully operative in terms of our unspoken assumptions. This applies to both Protestant and Catholic branches of Western Christianity. As Gustavo Gutierrez has warned concerning "the Christendom mentality" in his *A Theology of Liberation:*

Let us not too easily dismiss this mentality as extinct. It survives today implicitly or explicitly in large and important sectors of the Church. It is

---

14. Intimations of the Christian future can also be glimpsed, I believe, in the United States and Canada, where what has conventionally been called "mainline Christianity" has been virtually ignored, recently, by the governing authorities. It is perhaps parabolic of the new status of classical forms of Protestantism in particular that it is called upon less and less frequently to represent cultic proximity to or approval of officialdom. When the Inter-Church Center in upper Manhattan was officially opened some two decades ago, the President of the United States himself presided over the occasion. Today, when the White House desires a visible Christian presence (which, of course, it frequently does!), it calls upon representatives of a very different form of religious commitment. (I owe this illustration to Dr. Burgess Carr, Episcopal priest and officer in the National Council of Churches.)

15. Von Harnack considered Luther's "weakness" to be his failure to apply critical reformation standards to his doctrines of ministry and sacraments, thus creating a church which "threatens to become a scrawny twin of the Catholic Church" (*Outlines of the History of Dogma*, trans. Edwin Knox Mitchell [Boston: Beacon, 1957], p. 567). The comment is seriously dated; but it points to the larger and more permanent truth that the main reformers did not entertain a radically different conception of the nature and mission of the church in society.

the cause of conflict and resistance to change in the Church today which cannot otherwise be explained. The conciliar debates and perhaps above all the postconciliar era provide sufficient proof of this.[16]

This is inevitable. A phenomenon as thoroughly entrenched as "Christendom" does not disappear or devolve overnight. The tokens of establishment will be with us, no doubt, for decades still, perhaps for centuries. *But this does not mean that the social and religious climate which made the establishment possible in the first place, and sustained it for many centuries, still pertains.* Attempts to reaffirm or reinstate Christendom (for instance, those of the Moral Majority and various "missionary" movements in the United States and Canada) flounder on the rocks of reality. It is simply not possible to perpetuate a religious atmosphere which ignores or denies the impact of the secular mentality upon *all* contemporary life, even the most "primitive." The end of the Constantinian era "begins to show itself everywhere," but "very sharply" in some parts of the world.[17] Charles Davis writes:

> *Now*, in my opinion, the ethos of our present society is unchristian. Christianity is no longer functioning as an ethos, even though elements, often distorted or enfeebled, continue to have some impact from our common Christian past. The situation of Christians today is that they are immersed in an unchristian ethos which, willy-nilly, pervades their day-to-day lives. They can live as Christians only by resisting the prevalent ethos and finding in their Christian convictions a transformative and critical principle.[18]

The attempts of militant Christians to Christianize the world[19] must carefully shut out every reminiscence of agnosticism and skepticism in order to seem credible even to the committed.

The future of the church does not lie in that direction, and students of the Bible ought to be the last persons to find it there! Historical providence is demanding of the Christian movement a different role—but not an entirely new one. It is the role of a minority—potentially, a significant minority—whose significance does not lie in quantitative considerations but in the quality of the alternative vision it represents. If we are attentive

---

16. Gustavo Gutierrez, *A Theology of Liberation,* trans. and ed. Caridad Inda and John Eagleson (Maryknoll, N.Y.: Orbis, 1973), p. 53.

17. Karl Barth, "Letter to a Pastor," in *How to Serve God in a Marxist Land*, p. 64.

18. Charles Davis, *What Is Living, What Is Dead in Christianity Today*, p. 56.

19. The program, not only of many "interdenominational" movements on this continent but also of some denominations (including the largest Protestant denomination in the United States)—often inspired by the approach of the year 2000.

to the Scriptures and teach ourselves how to read them without Constantinian presuppositions, we may discover that such a role has much in common with the one envisaged for the disciple community in its *first* formative stages. There is therefore no justification for despair or discouragement. "When we say that we have the right to make a cool, dispassionate reckoning with the fact that the Church is a *diaspora*, we mean, understanding it rightly, the very opposite of resignation and defeatism."[20] The task of theology today is not to avert or camouflage the humiliation of Christendom but to give direction to this critical re-formation of the church. Only as the church itself willingly undergoes this "decrease" (see John 3:30!)—this crucifixion of Christendom—can it be prepared to absorb into its message of hope other, worldly aspects of the crisis of our social context. What Rosemary Ruether has said of the Roman Catholic church is appropriate to all branches of Christianity today: "If the Catholic Church is really to be reborn from its past, it must be willing to do a lot more dying."[21]

12. Religious Pluralism

One of the consequences of the breakdown of Christendom in the Western world, combined with the global diversification of peoples and cultures, is the plurality of religious and quasi-religious groupings within the formerly "Christian" world. Even during the past two or three decades, this phenomenon has become a conspicuous aspect of what social scientists have named rapid social change. It is a visible phenomenon in North America, especially in metropolitan areas; but its invisible aspects are more profound than the obvious (e.g., objective, statistical) factors associated with it.

To be appreciated for what it is, this religious situation has to be contrasted with the circumstances pertaining in our society in the immediate past. It may facilitate communication if I express these autobiographically. As a child growing up during the 1930s and 1940s in a small southwestern Ontario village, I had absolutely no contact with members of other religious traditions.[22] Until a few Eastern European Roman Catholics began to move into the area, purchasing supposedly poor farmland

---

20. Karl Rahner, *Mission and Grace*, vol. 1 (London, Melbourne, and New York: Sheed and Ward, 1963), p. 50.

21. "Is Roman Catholicism Reformable?" *The Christian Century*, September 22, 1965.

22. The novels of Alice Monroe, and in particular her *Lives of Girls and Women* (Scarborough: McGraw-Hill Ryerson, 1971), present an accurate and insightful account of the general ethos of the context in question, including its religious situation—as do the novels of Robertson Davies.

which they quickly turned into lucrative tobacco farms, even Catholics were more theoretical than real for us. Nearly every person of my acquaintance was either Presbyterian or United Church of Canada. There were a few families of Anglican and Baptist persuasion, though they did not have church buildings in the village; but I cannot recall more than a half-dozen homes where agnosticism had a hearing, and my father's particular variety of skepticism was an embarrassment to us as children in this church-centered environment. I knew no Jews. We heard people speak sometimes of Jewish merchants in the nearby county-town, and the all-too-common image of the Jew prevailed (one spoke freely, for instance, of being "jewed"). As for Muslims, Buddhists, Hindus, and members of other religious traditions, they were as remote for us as were the lands in which (we might have read) they were dominant. Missionaries from India or China who appeared among us periodically provided our only relatively personal entree into such strange places, and their stories—at least as they were received by us—almost invariably accentuated the need to rescue souls and bodies from such benighted heathendom.

This experience could be duplicated all over the North American continent, with the appropriate alterations in nomenclature (e.g., in rural Quebec it would be Protestants who were rare beings, and in the South of the United States, Baptists rather than Presbyterians would no doubt dominate the scene).

All of that has changed—radically, and very quickly. The change is to be seen statistically and in the variety of religious traditions represented in our cities, towns, and even hamlets. The more significant aspect of the change, however, is qualitative: there is a new *mentality* with respect to religion and religious decision making. Indeed, the very fact that religious belief *has become a matter of decision and choice among alternatives* is itself indicative of the transformation in question. Another indicator of that change is the relative ease with which members of nominally or even committed Christian families adopt novel religious positions which, in former times, were either unheard-of or condemned out of hand. This situation is caused partly by the phenomenon of secularism, which no longer values religious loyalty and is therefore tolerant of or indifferent towards such "backslidings" (as they would formerly have been called). But it is also partly an openness to other religious traditions or spontaneous expressions of belief, an openness which could not have existed in the "Constantinian" situation.

The significance of this phenomenon for our present purposes is its critical meaning for Christian theology. At a very obvious, though still frequently ignored, level, it means that everything we think, say, write, sing, and pray as Christians must now be done in the lived recognition that ours is a particular religious tradition, a choice we have made and (if we are to continue Christians) must continually reaffirm. We do our theology from now on in the midst of many others "who are not (but decidedly not!) of this fold." Our own *faith*, if only we are aware of it, is a constantly renewed decision, taken in the knowledge that other faiths are readily available to us.

At another level of concern, the reality of religious pluralism means that we are given today the formidable chore of rethinking our relation to these "others." This entails not only asking with new seriousness about the actual nature and content of the belief systems they embrace, of which most of us are sublimely ignorant; it means also something much more personal and more difficult: to what extent does coexistence with other religious traditions make it necessary for us to alter our own belief, perhaps radically?

What about the Christian *mission*, for example? Is it our calling as Christians to convince all others that *we* possess the truth, or at least have access to the highest religious expression of the human spirit? Should we frankly seek to "christianize" all the others? Is that what the Great Commission at the end of Matthew's Gospel means? If not, what *is* our Christian mission? It is clear enough how it has been understood by the vast majority of Christians in the past, whether Catholic, Orthodox, or Protestant. Approximately 1500 years ago, as we have noted, the Emperor Theodosius the Great forbade the practice of any religion other than the official Christianity of his court. The church quickly adapted itself to this apparently fortuitous, nay providential, victory. Its whole language—its *theology*—reflects this religious monopoly on the souls of human beings and whole nations.[23] This language, and the attitudes and actions that it engenders, have characterized almost the entire history of the church in the West. What I have described of my own childhood was approximately the same religious situation of the boy Augustine in the fourth century C.E. Apart from the intrusion of Islam into the European Middle Ages, only the Jews stood consistently for a religious alternative to Christianity throughout the most formative years of Christian doctrine-making. And it is well known what we Christians did about that alternative!

---

23. For example, the mission to the native peoples of this continent. For a moving presentation of one segment of this historic drama, see Brian Moore's novel, *Black Robe* (Markham, Ontario: Penguin Books, 1985); see also Francis X. Talbot, s.j., *Saint among the Hurons: The Life of Jean de Brebeuf* (Garden City, N.Y.: Doubleday, 1956).

Individual Christian theologians here and there have begun to reflect seriously on this component of our context. "If religion is to regain public authority," writes Wolfhart Pannenberg,[24] "it has to appropriate the spirit of pluralism without losing its identity." "Christ did not ask us," says Kosuke Koyama of Union Theological Seminary in New York,[25] "to behave as a prima donna among the other religions." But in what manner are we to behave? This must become a concern of all Christians who are serious about their belief, who respect its doctrinal past, but respect as well the faith of others. How can we revisit our doctrinal heritage with genuinely critical and self-critical insight in such a way as neither to end in sheer sentimentality and religious relativism on the one hand nor, with certain militant forms of Christianity in North America again today, with an attempted and (surely one must recognize it!) a violence-prone return to the monopolistic situation?

13. The Theological Impact of "Auschwitz"

We have not been able to consider other religious alternatives to Christianity without mentioning *that* religious tradition which, in a way that is surely full of the deepest mystery, has never been willing to let the Christians assimilate it, has never allowed them to forget their indebtedness to it, has never left them alone to rule the Western soul: Israel. This theme by itself deserves a volume; for it is one of those transparent specifics, mirroring the crisis both of the "Christian" West and of Christianity as such. Understandably, several volumes have been devoted to it in recent theology.[26]

---

24. Wolfhart Pannenberg, "Freedom and the Lutheran Reformation," *Theology Today* 38 (1981): 287ff.

25. In a lecture in the Faculty of Religious Studies, McGill University, 21 March, 1985.

26. The following works are representative of some of the better Christian reflection on this subject: Gregory G. Baum, *Christian Theology after Auschwitz* (London: Council of Christians and Jews, 1976); Alan T. Davies, *Anti-Semitism and the Christian Mind: The Crisis of Conscience after Auschwitz* (New York: Herder and Herder, 1969); Alan T. Davies, ed., *Antisemitism and the Foundations of Christianity* (New York, Ramsey, and Toronto: Paulist, 1979); Franklin Littell, *The Crucifixion of the Jews: The Failure of Christians to Understand the Jewish Experience* (New York: Harper & Row, 1975); Paul M. Van Buren, *Discerning the Way: A Theology of the Jewish-Christian Reality* (New York: Seabury, 1980); World Council of Churches, *The Church and the Jewish People* (Newsletter No. 4, 1975; Newsletter No. 2, 1977) (Geneva: World Council of Churches, Consultation on the Church and the Jewish People); Rosemary R. Ruether, *Faith and Fratricide: The Theological Roots of Anti-Semitism* (New York: Seabury, 1974); Evangelische Kirche in Deutschland, *Christen und Juden: Eine Studie des Rates der Evangelischen Kirche in Deutschland* (Gütersloher Verlagshaus Gerd Mohn, 1979); James Parkes, *The Conflict of the Church and the Synagogue: A Study in the Origens of Antisemitism* (New York: Atheneum, 1969); Reinhold Niebuhr, "The Relations of Christians and Jews in Western Civilization," in *The Essential Reinhold Niebuhr: Selected Essays and Addresses*, ed. Robert McAfee Brown (New Haven and London: Yale University Press, 1986), chap. 13, pp. 182ff.

What is called for here is enormously complex, and it will require generations of careful scholarship and profound spiritual reflection to meet the challenge. It is not simply a matter of discovering, as Christians, our lack of Christian *caritas* with respect to the Jews. It is a matter of becoming exposed to the *essential*, i.e., theological, roots of our centuries-long ambiguity about the Jews. The problem lies not so much in our deeds of violence or our doctrinal narrowness and neglect as it does in the *positive* affirmations of our theology, especially our Christology.[27] We could not have presented the Christ in the way that we have, through centuries, presented him; we could not have worked out our ecclesiologies in the way that we have worked them out, and lived them; we could not have devised the sorts of eschatologies that we have in fact devised, without it all preparing the ground for something like . . . Auschwitz.

This is not to indulge in the simplistic (and possibly masochistic) claim that Christians were directly responsible for the Holocaust, though they were certainly responsible for the pogroms and centuries of victimization which preceded the Nazis' "Final Solution." Still, other conditions had to be met before that "Solution" could be adopted by some of the most civilized peoples of Western history. A kind of working nihilism had to be evolved, which even the most decadent forms of Christianity could not manage single-handedly. Yet, as Gregory Baum has put it in his introduction to Rosemary Ruether's important book, *Faith and Fratricide*, "The Church has produced an abiding contempt among Christians for Jews and all things Jewish, a contempt that aided Hitler's purposes."[28] At the heart of this "abiding contempt" there lies, not the (after all) rather uncouth charge against the Jews as "Christ killers," but the monopolistic implications of our "high" Christology:

When a Church that has become culturally dominant proclaims Jesus as the one mediator between God and man and regards him as the one way, invalidating all other ways of salvation, it creates a symbolic imperialism that no amount of personal love and generosity can prevent in the long run from being translated into social and political realities. The symbols of exclusiveness belonging to a religion that has become culturally successful are objective factors that will affect the consciousness of a people and promote their cultural and/or political domination, a trend that no subjective factors, such as love and generosity, can overcome. A religion

---

27. See my essay, "Rethinking Christ," in *Antisemitism and the Foundations of Christianity*, pp. 167ff.
28. *Faith and Fratricide*, p. 7.

that has achieved cultural success, therefore, must be willing to submit itself to an ideological critique.[29]

Not only the centuries of blatant anti-Judaic preaching and religious symbolism[30] but, even more, the centuries of a triumphalistic gospel created a social atmosphere in which it was possible for such a thing as the Holocaust to occur without great opposition even from the side of serious, believing Christians.

If it is indeed our theology that has contributed so significantly to the social atmosphere favorable to such an unspeakable event, then this represents a crisis of *theology* and not only of the church or of Western "Christian" civilization. It calls for a rethinking of *our belief* along lines that may be more agonizing than most Christians have yet envisaged.

The consequences of such a rethinking are of vital importance for many others in addition to the Jews and Christians. For the Christian treatment of Judaism is paradigmatic for its treatment of other religious traditions as well—for example, the religions of the native peoples of this continent, whose gods were banished by European Christian missions. The basic theological question implied in all this is one that will have to occupy our attention in many places throughout this study. Does the triumph of God in Jesus as the Christ mean that the God of the *living community* of Israel and the Manitou of the "Indian" peoples must be reduced to failure and shame, and their worshipers destroyed, physically or spiritually? Is this what the Easter triumph of the Christ means? If not, what can it mean? The question is: What *do* Christians mean by Christ's "triumph"?

The positive side of this same concern is potentially even more important. For the "Final Solution" has caused thinking Christians to realize not only that our assumed monopoly of truth has to be questioned but that our own original roots are inextricably intertwined with the religion of the Jews. For a long time, representatives of the best Christian scholarship have been telling us that, early in its history, Christianity lost touch with its Judaic origins and adapted itself to the religious and philosophic traditions of the Hellenistic world. Adolf von Harnack believed

---

29. Ibid., p. 7.
30. The symbols of Christian triumph over Israel are perhaps more powerful—especially in the preliterate society—than the verbal declarations. For example, in almost every cathedral in Europe one may discover sculpted representations of "The Synagogue" and "The Church." Both are depicted as women, queens; but the former is a deposed and dejected queen, her crown askew, her staff broken—often she is blindfolded—while the figure representing the Church resembles no one so much as Elizabeth I of England, haughty, commanding, in charge. It is a stunning representation of Christian supersessionism.

that the early church had completely succumbed to Hellenism—although at the same time he drew conclusions about the relation of Christianity and Judaism which are less than consistent with this insight.[31]

By itself, such scholarship made little impact upon the church at large. In the wake of the Holocaust, however, which so dramatically highlighted the alienation of Christianity from its own Judaic origins, the theoretical questions that earlier scholarship raised have become questions of life and death for sensitive Christians. Since World War II, Christian biblical and theological scholarship has manifested a new concern for dialogue with Judaism—with the living community of Jewish believers, and not only with "the Old Testament." Among those who have most influenced *Christian* scholarship during the past four decades are many Jewish thinkers—Buber, Heschel, Fackenheim, Wiesel, Lapide, and many others.[32] It is my conviction that the new *kind* of dialogue with Judaism, represented by such works, has only just begun. As Christians are brought to face more directly questions posed by the circumstances of the world and the place of the disciple community within it, we will be drawn more and more towards Judaism. For one thing, it is from Israel as from no other living source that we may learn again what it means to be a Diaspora. For another, we shall need to ask of the Jews the implications of the kind of worldly commitment that has been present in their history and ethos in a way that, under the Hellenistic influence, has been lacking in our historic pilgrimage.[33] In this manner, the crisis of Christian theology provoked by Auschwitz may in the long run result in a Christian authenticity heretofore unrealized.

14. Marxism and the Revolution of the Oppressed

The most compelling as well as the most critical alternative to Christianity in the contemporary world is not any of the traditional religions of humankind but what may from one standpoint be called a nonreligion or even an antireligion and from another a quasi-religious system of meaning: Marxism.

Marxism of a doctrinaire stamp has not existed as an explicit alternative for North American Christians as a whole; yet, as is demonstrated

---

31. See Adolph von Harnack, *Outlines of the History of Dogma*, "Prolegomena" and "Presuppositions," pp. 1-38.

32. See in this connection Michael Oppenheim, *What Does Revelation Mean for the Modern Jew?* (Lewiston/Queenston: Edwin Mellen, 1985), and Hans Küng and Pinchas Lapide, *Brother or Lord? A Jew and a Christian Talk Together about Jesus*, trans. Edward Quinn (Glasgow: Collins, 1977).

33. Cf. chap. 1, §3.2.

both by the existence of minorities with sensitized social conscience in all of the older denominations and by the influence of liberation and other schools of theology that have learned from "the Left," no thinking Christian today can ignore, or simply discount, the Marxist challenge. At the very least, it defies the identification of Christianity with capitalism and prompts the disciple community to ask after a new economic order.

Marxism is a nonreligion insofar as it denies any transcendental framework or guarantee of meaning outside the material universe. It is a quasi-religion, however, insofar as it finds meaning built into the historical process as such. From the standpoint of a consistent secularism, the belief in historical meaning must be regarded as a type of faith, for it cannot be objectively demonstrated. Yet Marxism intends to have this *credo* without any supramundane frame of reference, and therefore it vigorously denies that it is a religion.

Variously interpreted, Marxism has been the primary 20th-century alternative to an explicitly *theistic* faith. It has had particular appeal to the religions of the Abrahamic tradition (Christianity, Judaism, and Islam). For many it has proved to be the type of this-worldly humanism which can be adopted without letting go of the historical *telos* present in biblical faith. One is able to embrace the purposefulness of the human enterprise even when the transcendent Guarantor of this purpose has been "edged out" (Bonhoeffer) of the system. This, at least, is the *promise* of Marxism. Marxism is thus a direct assault on the Christian conception of God. While it is in practice sometimes also a violent attack on empirical Christianity, its basic critique of Christian faith is in reality more subtle and more poignant. For it suggests that we may have all the *teleological* and *ethical* benefits of biblical religion without the burden of supranaturalism. We may even retain Jesus and the prophetic tradition out of which he comes. Indeed, the point which the learned Marxist philosopher of Prague, Milan Machoveč, makes in his book, *A Marxist Looks at Jesus*,[34] is that it may well be that Marxists are the true inheritors of the Jewish and early Christian gospel:

> One may even wonder whether the disciples of Karl Marx, who 1800 years after Jesus set in motion a similarly far-reaching and complex process with as yet quite unforeseeable consequences but similar aspirations to a radical transformation of social relationships and a future conceived in a radically

---

34. Milan Machoveč, *A Marxist Looks at Jesus*, with an introduction by Peter Hebblethwaite (London: Darton, Longman & Todd, 1977). (The original German title seems to me a superior rendering of the basic thesis of the book: *Jesus für Atheisten*.)

different way, have not in fact the greatest right to regard themselves as the authentic perpetuators of Old Testament messianism and early Christian desires for radical change. Many Marxists, but also many self-critical modern theologians, are aware of the fact that concern for the future— that longing for liberation and radical change once found in Christianity— has been taken over in the modern period almost exclusively by Marxism.[35]

Christianity, says Machoveč, so spiritualized the message of Jesus that there is a "shocking disproportion" between "the ideal which brought Christianity into existence and the results"—a discrepancy which "ought to disturb Christians more than it does."[36] The dogmatized, "sublime" Jesus of historic Christianity, he claims, represents a victory of docetism. Christian *theology*, in other words, has not only failed to provide a raison d'être for the Christian ethic; it has had the opposite effect of destroying the radicality of the prophetic tradition, which clearly identifies itself with the oppressed and intends to change the world on their account. A more aggressive critic than Machoveč might ask: "Isn't it just your *theology* that you must have done with, you Christians, if you are ever to grasp the real message of your Christ?"

The negative side of the Marxist critique is of a piece with the foregoing, but it turns more directly on the consequences of spiritualistic religion for the Christian attitude towards this world. It is given classical expression in the famous dictum of Marx that religion is the "opiate of the people." It is important to notice that Marx's formulation of this thesis makes religion a form of *re*pression, not *sup*pression. As we have established in the discussion of the preceding chapter, repression is a subconscious activity of the psyche, which fears conscious confrontation by an inadmissible reality. Thus religion for Marx is a repressive movement of the subconscious—something that human beings "arrange," so to speak, for themselves, not, in the first instance, something superimposed upon them from above. In Lenin's reinterpretation of this article of Marxist doctrine, religion becomes more unambiguously a matter of suppression: "opiate *for* the people." This is a much less sophisticated view which, while doing justice to the *use* of religion by oppressive regimes, does not account for the all-too-willing capitulation of human beings to such authorities. It is particularly the Marxist rather than the Leninist formulation with which theological reflection has to wrestle.[37]

---

35. Ibid., p. 193.
36. Ibid., pp. 194-195.
37. V. I. Lenin, "Socialism and Religion," in K. Marx, F. Engels, V. Lenin, *On Historical Materialism* (Moscow, 1972), p. 411. Karl Marx, *Early Writings* (Penguin, 1975), p. 244. See also Nicholas Lash, *A Matter of Hope: A Theologian's Reflections on the Thought of Karl Marx* (Notre Dame: University of Notre Dame Press, 1982), pp. 158ff.

This criticism of religion in general represents an especially weighty challenge to the Christian religion. There are, after all, religions which could without any qualms admit to functioning as deliverance from historical existence. Few of them would accept the connotations of the term "opiate," to be sure; for the majority of such religions, the flight from the world is regarded, not as mere escapism, but as the beginnings of the soul's journey towards the real. These religions perpetuate the long tradition of philosophic and theological reflection which finds this world— this daily round, this eating and drinking and propagating and working— to be the essence of *un*reality. The journey to the real, in such traditions, entails the sloughing-off of our human entanglement with "matter" and with time. For religions of this genre, the Marxist criticism of religion as the spiritualization of reality contains little bite, even though they may exemplify the point of the Marxist critique of religion more consistently than any other historic faiths.

But in the formative traditions of *Christian* belief, there is a decisive, if too seldom owned declaration of concern for, and commitment to, this world which is not only one dimension of Christian belief, but the very core of it.[38] Even that Gospel which (as Machoveč notes) more than any other understands Jesus' message as a "programme for the reform of the heart" ("my kingdom is not of this world," John 18:36)[39] still has sufficient memory of the original *kerygma* that its writer must attribute the whole work of God in Christ to God's love *for the world* (John 3:16).

Nor is this emphasis something new. While the incarnation may indeed represent the introduction of a new tactic, as it were, on the part of the biblical God, that which it is intent upon achieving has been there from the first chapter of Genesis onwards. The Hebrew Scriptures insist that this world, for all its pain and ambiguity, is "good," and is the scene of God's redemptive activity. In the line of that Hebraic faith, the explicitly Christian Testament too, despite its waverings under the impact of Hellenistic religion, clings to the worldliness of Yahweh's orientation. It cannot conceive of God in abstract terms, but only as a God who relates to creation. Any expression of faith *in God*, therefore, which ends by

---

38. E.g. "Through increasing and ever new witnesses the world must be given the intimation that God has espoused its cause, that God has aided it, that it is not a world left to itself but a world which He has loved and saved and which He preserves and rules and conducts to its salvation, and that everything that takes place in it, the whole of human life in all its confusion and affliction and sin and guilt and trouble, indeed, the whole of creaturely life in its subjection, hastens to meet the revelation of what God has accomplished in its favour" (Karl Barth, *Church Dogmatics: Selections by Helmut Gollwitzer*, trans. G. W. Bromiley [Edinburgh: T. & T. Clark, 1961], p. 65).

39. M. Machoveč, *A Marxist Looks at Jesus*, p. 202.

functioning as an escape-hatch from God's beloved world must be regarded as a contradiction. Thus the Marxist critique of religion is necessarily experienced by *biblical* religion, whether Judaic or Christian, as a very serious one—so serious, indeed, that it has fostered a radical rethinking of Christianity that today cuts across denominations and continents and has produced, among other things, varieties of "Marxist Christianity."

It becomes the mandate of Marxist Christians, and of many other Christians who would not accept that particular designation but nevertheless feel the force of the Marxist critique, to "reread history from the viewpoint of the rejected and humiliated."[40] Such a task brings to the surface the extreme ambiguity of Christian practice in relation to this world, and especially those who are not *able* to avoid the pain of this world through spiritualistic flights and sublime preoccupations. Reading our own *Christian* history from the standpoint of the oppressed, Marx's criticism of religion fits historical Christianity all too well. The "contradiction" referred to above is a contradiction at the very heart of Christian historical experience. Proclaiming God's immeasurable love for the world and God's passionate concern for its healing, the church has more often than not acted as if the only solution to life were to abandon the world as soon and as wholeheartedly as possible. Partly because of its early admixture with otherworldly religions and philosophies; partly because of its use by oppressive empires (Lenin's point); partly, no doubt, simply because it was the only (or the dominant) religion of a whole civilization and was obliged by the innate requirements of human anxiety to play this role—in short, for a variety of reasons—Christianity has *rather characteristically* fostered a world-denying, "religious" orientation to life.[41]

---

40. Gregory Baum, reporting on Gustavo Gutierrez's contribution to the Detroit discussions referred to in the introduction. The passage bears quoting: "Normally history is written by the victors. The successful classes mediate their self-understanding to the entire nation through lore, culture, and the telling of history. But what would happen, for instance, if Canadians were willing to re-read their history from the viewpoint of the native peoples? . . . One does not have to be a Christian to reconsider one's cultural self-understanding in terms of the oppressed communities. But Christians ought to do this . . . in fidelity to the humiliated and crucified Jesus. . ." (in *Theology in the Americas,* ed. S Torres and J. Eagleson (Maryknoll, N.Y.: Orbis, 1976), pp. 419-420.

41. H. Paul Santmire, in his excellent discussion of Christian attitudes towards the extra-human creation, *The Travail of Nature: The Ambiguous Ecological Promise of Christian Theology* (Philadelphia: Fortress, 1985), pp. 210ff., demonstrates the "ambiguity" of biblical and traditional doctrine as it relates to nature: there *is* an "ecological motif" in this tradition but it "does not represent the dominant thinking" of the church, which he characterizes as a "spiritual motif," a "metaphor of ascent," which conceives salvation in terms of "the removal of believers from this world to some higher heavenly sphere. . . ." What Santmire demonstrates about Christian "ambiguity" vis-à-vis nature is surely, unfortunately, only an aspect of a greater ambiguity which includes history as well. Perhaps in our time, and especially in our *place*, the ecologically unsatisfactory character of so much of what we have inherited as Christianity is achieving a clearer profile; but it points to a larger area of concern: What *do* Christians think about *this* world?

In any case, it has by no means commended itself to the world as unambiguously world-affirming! The incarnation itself—perhaps already with *some* Newer Testament backing—has been taken, not as the supreme act of the divine *commitment* to creation and the means through which the faithful are *incorporated into* that commitment, but as the way out: Jesus providing his disciple community with the mode of escape from an impossible and doomed situation. By dying to the world, with and "in" him, the faithful are led to eternal paradise. . . .

Given such a view of the goal of the gift of "new life," it is not strange that empirical Christianity has been able to offer an "opiate" to very tangible forms of human suffering throughout the centuries. Slaves could be counseled to endure their slavery as God's will for them, under the belief that they would at last be "carried home" in God's "sweet chariot."[42] Armies could be urged on to "just wars" and holy crusades in the belief that death in battle would ensure one a place in paradise: wars, which in the light of subsequent history must certainly (with Marxist analysis) be forthrightly acknowledged as "class wars"; wars which featured soldiers fighting against their own kind in behalf of lordlings in whose glory and properties they had no portion whatsoever. Women could be kept in their places by the same "opiate" of a Christianity which assured them of their natural inferiority while holding out the promise of (almost) full citizenship in heaven as a reward for earthly obedience to God and their husbands, fathers, and brothers.

There have been exceptions to such practice, of course. Fortunately, "the dogmatised image of Jesus Christ has never been able thoroughly to banish the image of the man Jesus of Nazareth."[43] Thus attempts have been made throughout this long history (the Franciscan movement in its early stage; Zinzendorf's community, "Herrnhut"; the Social Gospel movement; etc.) to bring the promises of the kingdom nearer earth, to make peace and not war normative, to acknowledge the full humanity of women and children, and so on. But historical honesty makes us ask why these *exceptions* have not been normative, given the original vision. In the main, empirical Christianity falls no less under the pall of the Marxist

---

42. The otherworldly language of much black Christianity, however, frequently cloaked very *this-worldly* hopes, thus foiling the intentions of those who used this language to bring about in their slaves an attitude of resignation. In his introduction to Barbara Smucker's *Underground to Canada* (Harmondsworth: Puffin Books, 1978), p. 7, Martin Luther King writes: "Our spirituals, now so widely admired around the world, were often codes. We sang of 'heaven' that awaited us, and the slave masters listened in innocence, not realizing that we were not speaking of the hereafter. Heaven was the word for Canada."

43. M. Machoveč, *A Marxist Looks at Jesus*, p. 203.

critique of religion than do other religious traditions. But for Christianity the criticism is decisive; for it can only serve to make visible a *krisis* of the church which comes, not from Karl Marx, but from the God of the prophets, of Abraham, Isaac, and Jacob, of the "Father" to whom Jesus Christ prayed. Christians who have heard that this *krisis* "begins at the household of God" (1 Peter 4:17) should hear echoes of *God's* judgment in Marx's.

What I mean is that the question posed by Marxism is nothing less than a question about Christian earnestness with respect to *our own confession of faith*. Does it, or does it not, commit us in some ultimate sense to this world?

We shall presently observe that this same question is hurled at the Christian community from numerous other quarters in the contemporary situation—notably and most dramatically from the prospect of a nuclear catastrophe. It is as if all the forces both of nature and history had conspired in this historical moment to put the church to the test, to catechize us. Is *the world* encompassed in our "ultimate concern" (Tillich)? Or is history, being less than ultimate, only a dress rehearsal for reality, a stage along the way—perhaps even just something to be "gotten through"? Whenever Christians are prevented by an otherworldly allegiance from behaving in this world as though it mattered supremely, we beg the question of *our own foundational Event*. Why, unless the world mattered supremely *to God*, would our gospel insist upon the cross at the center?[44] All religion from Marx onwards lives with the charge that it functions as a palliative, a happiness-drug against reality. But, for the Christian religion, the roots of this criticism go much deeper than Karl Marx.

15. The Rebellion of Nature

A fifth critical component of our context having particular significance for the theological task is what has been termed the rebellion of nature. It is possible that North American Christians, more than those in any other province of the ecumenical church, have a background of experience for the investigation and confrontation of this aspect of our global problematic. For we are a people which not only conceived itself in terms of nature's mastery but also found itself the inheritor of a natural environment of immense proportions—and we have played our role on that stage unreservedly! Now we are experiencing some of the consequences of this

---

44. See "The Point of View," introduction, §2.

manner of conducting the human project. Awareness of the crisis of nature has spread to large segments of our population and has achieved priority in many ecclesiastical as well as secular agencies.[45]

"The rebellion of nature" refers to a many-sided problem so complex as almost to defy description. The investigations of many sciences are needed to probe the parameters of the situation. To begin with, it is a matter of the discovery that nature has *limits*. For a society based upon the supposition of a limitless and infinitely resilient natural world, this discovery is often traumatic. At the same time, it refers to the growing recognition of the human *spoiliation* of nature, and here demographers point to the quantitative factor, that the greater earth's population becomes the more conspicuous the problem of pollution, while social scientists and others remind us that the problem of pollution relates as much to attitudes as to numbers of people. At yet another level, the rebellion of nature is seen in the *dysfunctioning of natural "systems" and the disappearance of species*. It is estimated that we are losing one plant or animal species daily, and that in less than a decade the loss will be hourly. If it is not curbed, 100 species per day will be disappearing by the year 2000.[46] In short, the combined testimony of a great variety of researchers suggests that there is a considerable danger that our planet will reach a stage in the not-distant future in which its capacities for supporting life will be crippled or greatly impeded. This phenomenon, we are advised, is already visible even in the still-affluent West.

While the consequences of nature's rebellion are difficult to chronicle, being diverse and often subtle, the causes are perhaps more obvious. Certainly, as the term "rebellion" in this subhead connotes, it has something to do with the attitudes and expectations of the human community. If human beings insist upon pressing nature beyond its capacities to produce; if human societies value standards of living more grandiose than their natural habitat can consistently sustain; if for the sake of its own (short-term) survival the human species is ready to "sacrifice" other species and ecological systems on which its (long-range) survival is dependent, then, surely, one can expect nature to respond to these inordinate demands in a manner suggestive of a rebellion.

But while the cause of the crisis of nature has evidently to do with

---

45. Recent statistics in Canada indicate that between 70% and 80% of Canadians consider environmental issues the *primary* social problem, outranking nuclearism, economic problems, unemployment, and others.

46. These statistics are given by Elizabeth Dobson Gray in an article entitled "Watchman! Tell Us of the Night, What Its Signs of Promise Are" (*The Churchman*, July 20-24, 1980). Gray is commenting on Norman Myers' *The Sinking Ark*.

questionable human attitudes towards nonhuman species, the problem becomes more complicated as soon as one asks: And what is the source of these problematic attitudes? Does it simply belong to "human nature" to struggle against the natural world? Is it "natural" for the species loftily named Homo sapiens to foul its own nest? There may be some truth in this insinuation. Yet there have been and still are societies, many of which *our* society regards as "primitive," that do not manifest these same attitudes and have been able, consequently, to live more amicably with their environment. Some of North America's indigenous peoples may be among the best representatives of such societies.

For this reason, many of the students of the present situation who are most familiar with the attitudes of past societies have insisted that the problem of a rebelling natural world must be traced to the emergence in the Western hemisphere of a technocratic mind-set.[47] This mind-set stems in turn from a conception of humanity which places our species "above" nature, and reduces the extrahuman creation to an objectivized status ("things"). Denied any inherent rights, and having no appeal beyond the human court, a bruised and battered natural world rebels; that is, the laws of survival inherent within the natural process assert themselves in the face of the threat. The ground does not give up its increase (Lev. 26:20).

The historical question must then be put: What are the sources of such a conception of humanity and its relation to nature? Just here is where Christian theology is again put to the test. For many analysts in recent years have been led to the conclusion that the most decisive influence in this *imago hominis* (image of the human) has been biblical religion. With its elevation of the human creature, its relative lack of interest in nature as such and, above all, its depiction of the human vocation in terms of "dominion" over the natural universe, the Judeo-Christian tradition, according to the critics,[48] has abetted the rise of a technocratic society which knows no limits to human use and misuse of natural resources. The ecological crisis must therefore be laid at the doorstep of the Judeo-Christian religion, its spiritual progenitor.

---

47. Particular attention should be drawn to the work of Jacques Ellul, especially his major work, *The Technological Society.* So far as North Americans are concerned, however, a more cogent articulation of this position is provided in the works of George P. Grant (see my essay "The Significance of Grant's Cultural Analysis for Christian Theology in North America," in *George Grant in Process: Essays and Conversations,* ed. Larry Schmidt [Toronto: Anansi, 1978], pp. 120ff. See also Carl Mitcham and Jim Grote, eds., *Theology and Technology: Essays in Christian Analysis and Exegesis* [New York and London: University Press of America, 1984]).

48. The initial study leading to this conclusion was that of Lynn White Jr. in an essay entitled "The Historical Roots of Our Ecologic Crisis," which first appeared in *Science* 155 (March 10, 1967), pp. 1203-1207. Many others have followed White's lead.

Christians have protested this accusation and continue to do so. It is no doubt a simplistic explanation, lacking in nuance. It seems particularly unaware of mitigating factors in the Christian view of human nature which, had they not been lost sight of in the modern era, would certainly have militated against the attenuation of the emphasis upon human *creaturehood* which informs the biblical *imago hominis*. Yet no Christian *apologia* can be wholly convincing in relation to this charge; for even if such qualifying factors are present in the biblical conception of the relation between humanity and nature,[49] the question must be raised why they did not surface more consistently. How did it happen that the Christian religion, by all accounts the chief spiritual force in the Western world, offered so little resistance to the modern image of Homo sapiens in terms of technocratic mastery (*Scientia est potestas* [Science is power])? Was there not a sufficiently critical view of such a conception of humanity in the biblical idea of *sin*, for example, with its insistence that the human bid for mastery is a direct affront to the lordship of Yahweh? What happened along the way to the Bible's own exegesis of the meaning of *dominion* in terms of human *stewardship* of the creation? The image of humanity contained in the metaphor of the steward[50] is, after all, very different from the one which actually developed in Western industrial society, which has perhaps capitalized on one side of the dialectic of stewardship (i.e., human responsibility) but has neglected almost totally the other side (i.e., human *accountability*).

The meaning for theology of this very significant critical dimension of our context is manifold. It will have to occupy our reflections at many points in this study. It has implications not only for the doctrine of creation in general and the human creature in particular, but it requires, as well, a serious rethinking of the meaning of *redemption*. To what extent is the redemption envisaged in the Newer Testament's message also a redemption of *"fallen" nature?* What would reconciliation mean if we kept in mind (as in the light of this critical aspect of our context we are bound to do) the alienation between the human species and its *natural* environment? Too much theology has left this out of account in its eagerness to speak of the reconciliation between God and humanity, and of human being with human being.

Above all, this dimension of our total crisis requires us to ask whether

---

49. I, for one, have insisted that they are. See my study, *Imaging God: Dominion as Stewardship* (Grand Rapids: Eerdmans, and New York: Friendship Press, 1986).

50. See my discussion of this metaphor in *The Steward: A Biblical Symbol Come of Age* (New York: Friendship Press, 1982).

redemption is itself creation-orientated.[51] Does salvation imply the healing of *creation*, or have we in Christian soteriology especially a statement about the final transcendence of creaturely existence, the emergence of a "new creation" in which the world of our present experience is set aside in favor of something else? Once again, we are brought by our reflections upon this aspect of our contextual crisis to the question concerning Christian attitudes towards *this world*.

16. The Nuclear Crisis

The most solemn statement of that question, however, and what may even be regarded as its ultimate expression, appears in the form of "the nuclear madness" (Heschel). At one level, this madness of late 20th-century humanity is simply an extension of the bid for mastery over nature, the subject of the foregoing observation. But it cannot be discussed in that connection only, because the immensity of the powers that have been unleashed by nuclear experimentation, exploration, and deployment is such that it requires a different set of categories for its contemplation. "Lenin's law" certainly applies here: There is a point where a change in quantity introduces a qualitative change.[52] The methods and the motives governing nuclear experimentation are continuous with those which have informed the whole modern experiment: "Science is power" (Bacon). But the *consequences* of the nuclear quest are so vast, so far beyond the results of previous scientific and technological pursuits that they catapult us into another epoch: the nuclear age.

What is new in this age is not just our species' heightened power over nature. We were convinced of that power long ago—and far more pleased with ourselves than we can be now! What is new is the realization

---

51. One way of redressing the denigration of creation implicit in so much of the tradition is the development of forms of "concrete" as distinct from "abstract" (Tillich) mysticism which locate the dimension of transcendence in the created order. The work of Matthew Fox is important in this connection (see especially *Original Blessing: A Primer on Creation Spirituality Presented in Four Paths* [Santa Fe, N.M.: Bear, 1983]). It is not, however, the only way to turn Christian belief towards world-affirmation, and there are some aspects of the mystical tradition about which an informed Reformation theology must be wary. See in this connection the recent study document of the Church and Society Division of the World Council of Churches, *Reintegrating God's Creation: A Paper for Discussion* (Geneva: Church and Society Documents, September 1987, No. 3).

52. Such quantitative data as the following, for example: the standard bomb (1 megaton) contains 70 times the power of the bomb dropped on Hiroshima, i.e., the equivalent of one million tons of TNT. If you put that much TNT into box cars, the train would be 200 miles long. Ten megatons is more than all the explosives used in World War II. Twenty megatons is more than all the explosives *ever* used.

that we could destroy our environment and ourselves in the very process of *achieving* mastery.

> We had imagined that the very technics that finally produced atomic destruction would make us the masters of history. But they merely produce an increased amount of power over nature that has a dubious role in the affairs of men. When we confront the problem of bringing the destructive possibilities of this power under moral control, the whole ambiguity of the human situation is more fully revealed.[53]

When it is realized that the "destructive possibilities of this power" do not refer only to the use of nuclear weapons but also to the "peaceful" deployment of this force, with all the unsolved problems thereto pertaining,[54] then the full irony and terror of this aborted bid for human control presents itself.[55]

That the nuclear situation poses a whole spectrum of questions for

---

53. Reinhold Niebuhr, *Love and Justice: Selections from the Shorter Writings of Reinhold Niebuhr*, ed. D. B. Robertson (Cleveland and New York: World, 1967), p. 235.

54. See the CBC series, (1) "At Work in the Fields of the Bomb" (D086) and (2) "Radiation and Regulation" (D112); Montreal: CBC Transcripts. The series is also available in book form: Robert Del Tredici, *At Work in the Fields of the Bomb* (San Francisco: Harper & Row, 1987).

55. The practice of making distinctions between the peaceful and violent uses of nuclear energy is still often indulged in. This is partly a rationalization of the affluent peoples of earth, who will run many risks to retain their present standards of living. It is also partly an example of the modern mystique of freedom, which imagines that technology is something neutral, and that society and its institutions are free to "use" technology for either good or evil ends. Jacques Ellul and many others have demonstrated that this is a naive and dangerous assumption. The problematic character of the technological society does not lie in the machinery that such a society produces but in the mentality which makes the production of such machinery "necessary." "We *are* technique," says George Grant, thus establishing in a single, simple theorum the character of our problematique (*Technology and Empire* [Toronto: Anansi, 1969], pp. 137ff.) The mind-set which insists upon mastery over our environment has driven us to the production of instruments, some for peaceful, some for purely aggressive employment, which contain the potentiality for annihilating the inventors. What must be altered, if life is to be preserved, is the mind-set, i.e., the very thing that makes us so sure we have unlimited freedom to use the machinery for happy ends.

Another aspect of the naïveté which draws easy distinctions between peaceful and violent uses of nuclear power is related to sheer ignorance concerning the facts of nuclear energy. People imagine that they can opt for nuclear energy while declaring themselves opposed to nuclear weaponry and the arms race. No one would deny that there are differences to be made between these two expressions of our technical know-how. Nuclear war cannot be prepared for without confronting the most basic questions of survival and the meaning of the whole human experiment. The development of nuclear energy on the other hand can seem to lend itself to "pro-life" thinking, and therefore can commend itself to many who have no doubt at all about the evils of nuclear armaments.

It is for this reason perhaps the more dangerous of the two prongs of the nuclear industry. For in fact the same questions are implicit within the "peaceful" as within the violent use of nuclear power. "Peaceful" here must be interpreted to mean: seemingly harmless so far as our immediate safety is concerned; quite possibly deadly for *future* generations.

The truth is that there is no clearly nonviolent role for nuclear energy as it is currently understood; and it would take enormous strides in human ingenuity and charity to ensure a situation of nonviolence

Christian ethics has long been recognized. What lifts it out of the "merely" ethical into the center of contemporary theological meditation is the recognition that the destruction which nuclear power makes possible, together with the picture it paints of Homo sapiens in the role of destroyer, raises questions of an ultimate character. The nuclear reality exists for us, not only as a series of data, phenomena, experiences, and probabilities about which moral as well as other kinds of thinking could be engaged in, but, beyond this, it confronts us with questions about the world, history, nature, and ourselves which immeasurably transcend its facticity. Indeed, it takes a special kind of conditioning—the conditioning of the *apparatchik* (technocrat-bureaucrat)—to deal with this issue even at the factual level without being plummeted into metaphysical thought in spite of oneself. For we are faced here, not only with yet another extension of technical mastery, but with a flirtation with Nothingness so profound that the residual wisdom of our thought-impoverished civilization is scarcely capable of taking it in.

At the heart of this symbolic confrontation is the question whether the human spirit may not actually be *seeking* oblivion. Is there a logic of death, a collective *Todestrieb* (death wish), at work in humanity today? Is our civilization imbued with a will to self-destruction? Dorothee Sölle writes:

> I am afraid . . . that human beings today are a part of nonbeing, that our unrelatedness is catapulting us into undoing creation and all that lives on the small planet earth. I fear that nothingness will supersede being, that the bomb is in our hearts as well as in our hands, and that we hate creation because we have chosen to live under the bomb. No generation in history was ever able to say no to creation as we can. No generation has heretofore been able to kill not just Jesus Christ again and again but God the creator, the Being-in-relation. We may fool ourselves with superficial Christian

---

for the use of this energy source in the future. So long as we do not know how to control the wastes from nuclear energy sources, we are condemning our children's children and all earth's progeny to millenia of humiliation and suffering. As E. F. Schumacher has stated the matter, "No degree of prosperity could justify the accumulation of large amounts of highly toxic substances which nobody knows how to make 'safe' and which remain an incalculable danger to the whole of creation for historical or even geological ages. To do such a thing is a transgression against life itself, a transgression infinitely more serious than any crime ever perpetrated by man. The idea that a civilization could sustain itself on the basis of such a transgression is an ethical, spiritual, and metaphysical monstrosity. It means conducting the economic affairs of man as if people really did not matter at all" (*Small Is Beautiful: Economics as if People Mattered* [New York: Harper & Row, 1973], p. 145).

slogans about the "Eternal God," but there will not be any heavenly father or mother or creator after the nuclear holocaust, after the final solution.[56]

Christian and other forms of liberalism, combined with certain gleanings from 19th-century social evolutionary thought, has conditioned bourgeois society to assume that, whatever disquieting events may be occurring on the surface of history, the great subterranean movements of time are always "pro-life." This highly positive doctrine helps to insulate us against many dangerous realities present in our contemporary society, including the nuclear menace. There are, however, dimensions of the nuclear madness which not only defy this progressive philosophy of history, but for their explanation require less complimentary assumptions about the bent of human nature. The great "misevangelists" (Rosenstock-Huessy) of the 19th century (Freud, Marx, and Nietzsche) already offered suggestions along these lines. Freud reminded us of a "death wish" which will seek oblivion rather than truth; Marx detailed the "decadence" which develops in capitalist societies in their later stages; and Nietzsche spoke about the revenge of "the nihilists," who hate the world because it is meaningless, and the "last men" who close their eyes and tell each other, " 'We have invented happiness,' . . . and they blink."[57]

Theology today has the task of attempting to comprehend this madness. What can Christians know—from their own story—of the human need to destroy? of the will to corporate suicide? of the function of "the enemy" in personal and social life? What resources may be found for the comprehension of this madness in the Christian traditions concerning the demonic?

And what of redemption? In the presence of machinery which could destroy planetary civilization, with every major city targeted, can Christians finally overcome their long-standing ambiguity about this world? The present religious climate in North America would suggest that nuclearism only *deepens* our ambiguity. Not only in circles of "evangelistic" enthusiasm, where the motif of Armageddon has again come to the fore,[58] but also in more sane, academic quarters there is what could be construed to be a certain hesitancy about deliberate world-affirmation. James Gustafson's *Ethics from a Theocentric Perspective*, for example,[59] insists that

---

56. Dorothee Sölle with Shirley A. Cloyes, *To Work and to Love: A Theology of Creation* (Philadelphia: Fortress, 1986), pp. 162-163.

57. "Thus Spake Zarathustra: First Part," 5; in *The Portable Nietzsche*, ed. Walter Kaufmann (New York: Viking, 1954), p. 129.

58. See A. G. Mojtabai, *Blessed Assurance: At Home with the Bomb in Amarillo, Texas* (Boston: Houghton Mifflin, 1986).

59. James Gustafson, *Ethics from a Theocentric Perspective* (Chicago: University of Chicago Press, 1981, 1984).

God's purposes must not be too closely associated with the fate of the earth and of the human species. A "theocentric" ethic rejects the anthropocentrism of so much of the God-of-history thinking of modern Protestantism, Gustafson announces. But what about the *Christo*centric basis of our faith? John C. Bennett writes:

> I do not think that he [Gustafson] does justice to the revelation with Christ as the Center, within this human experiment, of the character of God and of values that God seeks in whatever worlds there are. Whatever interpretation of the incarnation we may hold the denial that it has any meaning for history—and I do not say that Gustafson denies this but only that he threatens it—would seem to me to be a denial of Christian faith itself.

According to Bennett, therefore, the future of God as biblical faith conceives of God *is* bound up with the future of the earth:

> There are those who try to play down the significance of such a prospect [as the destruction of planetary life] by saying that cosmic events will make this planet unable to support the human experiment in the far distant future anyway, so the present threat is merely a matter of timing. An end of history that humanity brings on itself would produce such intense human suffering on so vast a scale that it is the height of callousness to try to belittle it. More important, when we consider how short the conscious history of humanity has been, how short the period of its spiritual, moral and cultural achievements compared with the eons of preparation for human awareness of this planet, a self-inflicted early end of the human adventure would be an unbelievable tragedy. It would be a defeat of God's own purposes.[60]

It seems probable that the position represented by John Bennett is a minority one so far as the North American churches are concerned. The majority of Christians, influenced on the one hand by a repressive credulity which refuses to entertain the possibility of a nuclear holocaust and on the other by a fanatical apocalypticism which courts it, are in no mood to embrace the type of action taken in some Western European ecclesiastical camps—for instance, by the *Moderamen* of the Reformed Church in the Federal Republic Germany, which declared peacemaking in a nuclear age to be a matter of primary faith (*status confessionis*).[61] Yet, as

---

60. From an unpublished paper, "Christian Hope in the Face of the Possibility of Nuclear Death," given at the meetings of the American Academy of Religion in Anaheim, California, November 1985. An earlier version of the paper was published in *The Christian Century*, May 29, 1985, pp. 554f., under the title, "Divine Persuasion and Divine Judgment."

61. See *Das Bekenntnis zu Jesus Christus und die Friedensverantwortung der Kirche: Eine Erklärung des Moderamens des Reformierten Bundes* (Gütersloh: Gütersloher Verlagshaus Gerd Mohn, 1982).

disciples of Jesus Christ in the midst of one of the two major powers which are locked into a *Logik des Wahnsinns* (Logic of Madness), we can hardly ignore the colossal questions that this situation raises for us. Is it not possible, in fact, that precisely this is the "little point where the battle rages" (Luther)—the issue in relation to which we must learn to make our *confession*? Not that nuclearism alone constitutes our condition, but because in this one issue all the other theoretical and practical crises of our context gather themselves symbolically and materially, this may be the most explicit test of our faith and our theology.[62]

17. Apocalyptic Consciousness and the Rise of Religious Simplism

In Walter M. Miller's brilliant novel *A Canticle for Leibowitz*,[63] the nuclear holocaust which is presupposed at the story's opening has been followed by an "age of simplifiction." This is a period during which the few survivors of the deluge, many of them maimed or the products of genetic mutations, set to work to destroy all the remnants of the complex civilization which produced, at last, the means of its own destruction.

The urge towards simplicity can as easily occur in prospect as in retrospect.[64] The prospect of a dread and tragic ending calls forth in many the strong desire to eliminate all the complex, ambiguous, and dangerous elements by which life is threatened, and to "return" to the primitive roots with their real or imagined verities, their uncomplicated goals, their simple virtues. In these past decades, the Western world in general and North America in particular have seen the emergence of many and various movements fueled by this impulse. It is particularly strong in our society because, as we argued in the previous chapter, we possess so few intellectual and spiritual resources for the contemplation of negation.

The antecedents of the drive towards simplification are present in

---

62. See in this connection *A Covenant Challenge to Our Broken World*, A Study Carried Out by the Committee on Theology, Caribbean and North American Area Council, World Council of Reformed Churches, ed. Allen O. Miller (Atlanta: Darby, 1982); Arthur Cochrane, *The Mystery of Peace* (Elgin, Ill.: Brethren Press, 1986), and Gordon D. Kaufman, *Theology for a Nuclear Age* (Manchester: Manchester Unversity Press, and Philadelphia: Westminster, 1985); James Garrison, *The Darkness of God: Theology after Hiroshima* (London: SCM, 1982); Charles Davis, *Christian Hope in a Nuclear Age*, R. T. Orr Visiting Lecture, 1983/84 (London: Huron College).

63. Walter M. Miller, *A Canticle for Leibowitz* (New York: Bantam, 1959).

64. A more recent work of fiction, Margaret Atwood's *The Handmaid's Tale* (New York: Fawcett Crest, 1985), assumes precisely this. In Atwood's work, which is obviously inspired by the current wave of religious enthusiasm on this continent, the simplification of existence in the face of contemporary complexity is achieved by fascistic Christians.

the Romantic movement of the previous century. Romanticism protested against the spirit of industrial society, with its rationalistic and mechanistic reduction of life, and sought to return to a premodern sense of communion with "nature." While it frequently engendered a contrived conception of the natural, and while it sometimes courted the irrational all too uncritically, Romanticism was a religiously significant movement on account of its undergirding commitment to life and its sensitivity to the threat to life contained in ideologies which attempted to eliminate the nonrational. In a real sense, *all* responsible thought and activity in our time represents something of this Romantic attempt to head off civilizational disaster caused by demonic forces within the technocratic mind-set. Through the recovery of visions, wisdom, and crafts which have been forfeited by our civilization's capitulation to the spirit of mastery, the Romantic spirit endeavors to keep alive an alternative conception of the human. In this sense, all are involved in a quest for *simplicity* who perpetuate this alternative, and who bear witness to the dangerous duplicity of our dominant pursuits and institutions.

But the quest for simplicity is not yet *simplism*. The quest for simplicity devolves into simpl*ism* when the threat to life is objectified and victory over this "enemy" no longer involves self-struggle and inner turmoil of spirit. This readily occurs in times of great peril. In anticipation of catastrophe, or in its wake, people revert to that type of irrational and plainly paranoid behavior which strikes out at the supposed cause of experienced evil, simplifying both the evil itself and their own ("good") motives. Thus with the increase of anxiety in the face of nuclear and other crises today, the drive towards simplicity easily transmutes into simplism, and often a hysterical simplism. Hysterical, militant simplism sets out to destroy every trace of the things it believes have led or are leading to destruction, or it expresses itself in escapist forms which leave the hell-bent society to its own devices while seeking sanctuary for itself in secondary worlds.

It is no doubt inevitable that religion should again and again become the vehicle for such simplism. We have already drawn attention to the thesis that religion originates in apocalyptic consciousness,[65] that the sense of an ending inspires the human soul to seek transcendent refuge.

> As the battle of Armageddon reaches its awful climax and it appears that all life will be destroyed on earth—in this very moment Jesus Christ will return and save man from self-extinction.

---

65. Above, Chap. 2, §9.2.

As history races toward this moment, are you afraid or looking with hope for deliverance? The answer should reveal to you your spiritual condition.

One way or another history continues in a certain acceleration towards the return of Christ. Are you ready?[66]

Throughout the ages, religion has functioned as a fire escape from history, and the Christian religion is by no means immune to this usage. Perhaps from the beginning, but certainly at critical moments throughout history, Christianity has been the medium for that mentality I have designated hysterial and militant simplism. The mobs which destroyed all the art of Christendom on which they could get their hands at the time of the Reformation are, I have no doubt, Walter Miller's model for his postnuclear "simplifiers." Some monastic communities, separatist movements, anti-intellectualist and spiritualistic enthusiasts (Luther's *Schwärmer*)—all have frequently chosen to solve the duplicity of the human soul and the complexity of the world by reducing it conceptually to a doomed and damned object whose inevitable end they could feel. And it would seem that such a will can always discover biblical warrant!

In the North American context, it could be argued, religious simplism has always been the majority expression of the Christian faith. If millions subscribe to Lindsey's neoapocalyptic "gospel," they cannot easily be distinguished from the spectrum of believers ranging all the way from the ultraliberal cults of "positive thinking" to the lately respectable conservatism of the older mass evangelists. In his 1957 analysis of religion in America, Reinhold Niebuhr remarked that Billy Graham's "simple version of the Christian faith" was even more simplistic than the liberalism that Graham attacked.

> It gives even simpler answers to insoluble problems than they. It cuts through all the hard antimonies of life and history by the simple promise that really good people will really be good. It does this at the precise moment when secularism, purged of its illusions, is modestly ready to work at tasks for which there are no immediate rewards and to undertake burdens for which there can be no promise of relief.[67]

The wild abandonment of earth encouraged by current expressions of

---

66. Hal Lindsey with C. C. Carlson, *The Late Great Planet Earth* (Grand Rapids: Zondervan, 1970), p. 168.

67. Reinhold Niebuhr, *Pious and Secular America* (New York: Scribner's, 1958), pp. 21-22.

nuclear-inspired End-thinking is at least prepared for by our indigenous biblicism, with its very *un*biblical disregard for earth-keeping.[68]

For, despite its apparent willingness to provide fuel for the fires of history's simplifiers, the Bible contains in its *major* strains the most telling critique of precisely this propensity. Against the simplistic objectivization of evil, the Scriptures continually remind their readers of the evil of the righteous: "first take the log out of your own eye" (Matt. 7:5); "all our *righteous* deeds are like a polluted garment" (Isa. 64:6). Against the simplistic identification of wickedness with its most obvious forms, the Bible speaks about the subtle evil of those who "do the right thing for the wrong reason" (Eliot—see Romans 7). Against the promotion of easy solutions to difficult human questions, the Bible offers the cross: that is, *God* involved in the ambiguity of existence, broken by alienation, powerful only in the weakness of love.

While our Christian past, with its strong influences from post-Reformation Calvinist and Catholic forms of scholasticism, contains elements of a more intellectually complex approach to religious questions, it belongs to our North American context today that simplistic deployment of Christian precepts and piety has become the faith's most vociferous expression. In his survey of the state of religion in the United States, Jeremy Rifkin notes that "the two overriding reasons for [the] renewed interest in religion according to Gallup are: 'The general turning inward to seek refuge from everyday pressures,' and 'a search for non-material values in light of the fading American Dream.' "[69] The "eye of this spiritual storm," Rifkin reports, "is the Christian Evangelical Movement"—"There are currently around 45 million evangelical Christians in the United States. . . . One in every three Americans now claim to have been 'born again'. . . ."[70] These statistics indicate, in Rifkin's interpretation, that "already, the evangelical renaissance has eclipsed the once powerful liberal-oriented mainline denominations represented by the National Council of Churches."[71] Moreover, the "evangelical" variety of

---

68. The truth is, of course, that biblicism *is* a pious ruse for avoiding the actual content of the Bible while seeming to honor it above every earthly authority. Knowing this, Atwood in her novel cleverly depicts her fundamentalist Utopia as a society whose citizens are never allowed actually to read the Bible for themselves: "The Bible is kept locked up, the way people once kept tea locked up, so the servants wouldn't steal it. It is an incendiary device: who knows what we'd make of it, if we ever got our hands on it? We can be read to from it, by him, but we cannot read. Our heads turn towards him, we are expectant, here comes our bedtime story" (Margaret Atwood, *The Handmaid's Tale* [New York: Houghton Mifflin, 1986]).

69. Jeremy Rifkin, *The Emerging Order: God in the Age of Scarcity* (New York: Putman's, 1979), p. 99.

70. Ibid., pp. 100-101. A later poll, conducted by *U.S. News and World Report* ("Christian Right Aims Votes at New Targets," November 4, 1985, p. 70) sets the figure at 40% of the adult population.

71. Rifkin, *The Emerging Order*, p. 101.

Christianity easily dominates the communications systems of the continent:

> Today, 1300 radio stations—one out of every seven in America—[are] Christian owned and operated. Every seven days a new Christian-owned radio station is established. Together, these stations reach a listening audience of 150 million people. At the same time, Christian broadcasters are adding one new owned and operated television station to their arsenal every thirty days; presently these stations claim a viewing audience of thirteen million households, or nearly 20 percent of the entire United States viewing public.[72]

The character of the Christianity in question is accurately described in this statement of an advertising consultant for one of the Christian networks: "We are trying to sell a product, and that product is Jesus Christ."[73]

The selling of Jesus Christ involves two seemingly contradictory tactics. On the one side, the evangelicalism in question seeks to "win the world for Christ"—often with the typical millennialist-apocalyptic addendum, "by the year 2000." Thus one spokesperson for this approach, Bill Bright, founder of Campus Crusade, announces: "I am involved with thousands of others in a conspiracy to overthrow the world."[74] At the same time, much of the effort of the Christian simplifiers is devoted to the creation of "an alternative Christian environment in which materialist values would be replaced by spiritual beliefs."[75] Different emphases are found in various groupings, but the common denominator would seem to be a decision that the Christian gospel is incompatible with life in this world: either believers must make the world over into a wholly Christian world, or else they must create within it pockets of true belief which insulate believers against the temptations of the world. The latter thrust has led to the production, not only of such things as the "Christian Business Directory" and the "Christian Yellow Pages," with their blatantly racist biases, but of whole complexes of living which ensure that believers can conduct most of their lives without contaminating contact with secular society. What characteristically emerges from such attempts, however, is what may be termed a stained-glass version of the same middle-class conception of the good life from which the believers are supposed to be fleeing: night-clubs without liquor, slick magazines without *overt* sex,

---

72. Ibid., p. 105.
73. Ibid., p. 105.
74. Ibid., p. 119.
75. Ibid., p. 231.

television talk-shows whose religious banter differs only linguistically from their secular counterparts, homes featuring the same aesthetic tastes and economic pursuits as those mirrored in *Good Housekeeping* but with prayer at mealtimes, and churches which prefer gospel hymns and "charismatic" sermons but offer no real alternative to the credo of the dominant culture.

Rifkin approaches his subject matter as a sociologist and journalist, and his aim is to discern the broader cultural/political meaning of this movement. It is his thesis that the new evangelicalism could represent a religious response to the new circumstances of "scarcity" in our society. As the 16th-century Reformation and its liberal progeny represented a religious response to the expanding and growth-oriented worldview introduced by the Renaissance, so the new religious trend represents a human endeavor to come to terms with the limits to growth, the nuclear threat, and other crises which have narrowed our present-day horizon. In my view, while his warning to "mainline" Protestant Christianity must be taken very seriously,[76] his thesis with respect to those whom he refers to as "evangelicals" and "charismatics" rests on very shaky ground. I do not doubt that this type of Christianity is a response to the world grown old and jaded; but I greatly doubt that it can provide a way into the future for our society. For one thing, too much of its supposed "antimaterialism" is just another, pietistic type of consumerism and collective egotism, all too typical of First World societies. For another, apart from minorities within this movement,[77] it is on the one hand too apolitical and on the other too clearly identified with reactionary politics to offer any genuine alternative either economically or spiritually.

Above all, it fails to meet the test of authenticity that we have established in the earlier discussion. That is, it will not (I would say that

---

76. "Of one thing there is little doubt: The Protestant Reformation theology of Luther and Calvin and the liberal ethos which grew out of it will not outlive the age of material growth with which it has been so intricately bound up" (ibid., p. 272).

77. Rifkin is naive about the influence of more politicized elements which he regards as belonging to "the new evangelicals," such as the Sojourners community. He sees in the emphasis of stewardship over against dominion on the part of such groups a relevant response to the limits to growth. But in the first place it is simply unwarranted to identify such groups as Sojourners with the "movement" that Rifkin analyzes in this study. It is well known that Sojourners is not at all trusted by the leading evangelists of that movement, even if there are some points of mutual concern. For in distinction from Sojourners and similar groups within a broadly evangelical tradition, the message and lifestyle of "the new evangelicalism" is radical neither politically nor spiritually. Its support of the most conservative (indeed, right-wing) political forces on the continent, as well as its oblique sanctification of the *basic* moral, cultural, and economic goals of the dominant culture, indicate just how thoroughly *representative* it is of the spirit of our society. While it rejects superficial aspects of the secular city, it is as much committed to the *fundamental* pursuits of the First World as any crassly secular dimension of North American society.

it cannot) take into its life and thought the truly negating factors by which the human spirit is besieged in our sociohistorical context. In fact, its energies are expended chiefly in much the same way as the energies of the simplifiers have always been expended: in denying, ignoring, and fleeing from the most devastating scourges of the age. Its edifice is erected on an ideological rock high above the shifting sands of late 20th-century civilization, and its appeal is the appeal of a powerful aid to repression—therefore it does not lack worshipers. It capitalizes on the apocalyptic atmosphere of the times without ever confronting, in a responsibly human and worldly way, the things which make for the secular apocalypse.

Therefore if the world does end, its end will have to be attributed in part to these simplifiers, who were more concerned for their own personal salvation than for the healing of the creation. Because they wanted above all to shield themselves from the world's brokenness, they could have no part in its mending. Their winning of the world for their Christ—even if it could be accomplished—would amount to a travesty of the cross, salvation through escape. Jesus uttered a final no to all religious oversimplification of existence when he refused the final temptation, to come down from the cross.

Religious simplism in an apocalyptic age is a *reflection* of the crisis, not a cure. It represents a flight from truth in the name of security. Yet, for thinking faith, it constitutes a particularly frustrating dimension of the total problematique of our times; for if Christianity in North America is increasingly defined by this truncated version of itself, how can the disciple community in its embodiment within mainstream churches provide a distinctive confession in the face of the expectations and presuppositions established by this powerful form of the Christian religion? It is one thing to do spiritual and intellectual battle with unbelievers and with non-Christians. In our context, however, the most de-energizing struggle of the disciple community must be with those who have claimed for themselves (usually for themselves *exclusively*) the name "Christian." It means that the identity of the disciple community is confused and challenged, not only by secular nonreligion (such as Marxism), and religious pluralism, but also and perhaps most devastatingly by *the Christian religion!* And I think that we who are the inheritors of classical Protestant traditions of Christian belief have yet to demonstrate convincingly, either to the world or to ourselves, that our manner of *being* and *thinking* is either distinct from the simplifiers' modus operandi or a positive alternative to their interpretation of the Christian tradition. In the realm of *doing* we have perhaps given notice, here and there, of our difference. But until this is translated into terms of faith and life, until we can give *the reason* for our deeds and our hope, we shall live in the vast and lengthening shadow of Christianity's simplistic forms.

This is especially true of the North American province of the church, and the primary reason for it is precisely the concern that lies at the heart of this study, namely, our failure to become purposively and profoundly contextual in our thinking. Throughout our history, we have been victimized by religious simplism. Sidney Mead quotes A. N. Whitehead's aphorism, "Seek simplicity and distrust it," and, as one of America's foremost ecclesiastical historians, he comments: this aphorism "makes an appropriate motto for the historian of religion in America."[78] The threat of the present new wave of simplistic religion, greater than all the others because the contextual conditions are more favorable to it and the potential consequences more terrible, can be averted only by a *widespread attempt* within the remnants of formerly "established," "classical" expressions of Christianity to bring doctrine into the streets—not, certainly, *as doctrine*, but as a struggle to know ourselves in the light of a gospel that penetrates *our* darkness.

---

78. Sidney E. Mead, *The Lively Experiment* (New York: Harper & Row, 1963), p. xi.

Conclusion and Transition

Our subject is thinking the faith. Theological thinking is never purely abstract or detached. It is the thinking of human beings—of quite specific men and women who dwell within quite specific social contexts. It is the thinking of sentient creatures who live under the conditions both of nature and of history.

Theological thinking need not be embarrassed by its necessary participation in finitude. Much human thought, including, to be sure, much that has been undertaken in the name of Christian theology, conducts itself as though it could achieve its desired end only by transcending its natural and historical limits. With the thought of the disciple community of Jesus Christ this should not be so. Here, if anywhere in the realm of human reflection, one is enabled to affirm one's being as a child of nature and history. One may aspire to comprehend "things eternal" (2 Cor. 4:18)— but as one stands within time, accepting its reality and its essential goodness, and opening oneself to the eternal *in* the temporal. One does not have to play the pseudo-intellectual's game of pretending to be pure mind. Quite the contrary, the affirmation of creatureliness is the condition without which theological thinking in the Christian mode is not possible. For the *Theos* whose person and presence is the *Logos* of this thinking has graciously entered the temporal condition, accepting its limits and adapting to its possibilities. It is possible to reflect upon this God and the things pertaining to this God only insofar as we ourselves, willingly and consciously, *become* the creatures that we in fact are. The path to understanding in *this* science is not attained by trying to rise above our lowly circumstances as "frail creatures of dust," setting aside our personal identities and cares, and dispassionately seeking "pure truth." Precisely as "frail creatures of dust," we have vested interests in our subject! It is a matter of life and death to us. Thus, "a person becomes a theologian by

237

living, by dying and by being damned, not by understanding, reading, and speculating."[1]

In penning these words, Luther, of course, did not mean that "reading and speculating" are to be shunned. He intended only to assign priorities. Study—even exhaustive study—is necessary. A faith which depends upon historical traditions as thoroughly as does Christianity cannot afford to scoff at scholarship. Yet (and this is Luther's meaning) real *understanding* (standing under!)[2] begins only where we find ourselves more—not less— conscious of ourselves and our environs more—not less—deeply involved in our world. Concentration upon the "object" of theology implies at once—not even as a second step—an intensified awareness of ourselves as the subjects engaged upon this search. This is not an exercise in egotism, though the temptation to an *inordinate* self-consciousness is as present to contemporary disciples of the Christ as it was to the original twelve; it is the process the Scriptures name *metanoia* seen in relation to the mind. Contemplation of the Lord of creation engenders a growing consciousness of and curiosity about our own existence as creatures, dwellers in God's world. Necessarily so, because it is precisely our fleshly reality, meaning and mystery that the Word-become-flesh intends to illumine and to sanctify.

Accordingly, in Part I of our study we have been attempting to understand ourselves and our *Sitz im Leben*—latter-day disciples of the crucified one, living within the conditions of a New World grown older and wanting wisdom. Who are we, the ones engaging in this thinking, Christians living many centuries after the beginnings of this story and in a "strange land" whose pursuits and whose speech would have been foreign to all who participated in those beginnings? Who and what are we, and what do we bring to the story that we, in turn, are to rethink and relate to our world?

The pursuit of this question should be considered an aspect of "the scandal of particularity." The scandal of particularity (a term coined in the earlier theological discussions of this century) does not refer only to

---

1. Martin Luther, WA 5.162.28. "Vivendo, immo moriendo et damnando fit theologus, non intelligendo, legendo aut speculando."
2. Referring to a sentence of Mozart, in which the composer describes the way that musical compositions come to him ("I understand them altogether at one moment"), George Grant points out that "it is worth remembering when Mozart speaks of understanding (in German the very similar word *verstehen*) he did so at a time when Kant was exalting reason above understanding, in the name of his account of human beings as 'autonomous.' This was to place on its head the teaching of Plato in which understanding is the height for human beings: Indeed the English 'to understand' and the German *verstehen* were in their origins filled with that very sense of receptivity which Kant lessens in the name of our freedom" (*Technology and Justice* [Toronto: Anansi, 1986], p. 49).

the particularity of Israel, or of Jesus (Why not Socrates? Gandhi? Schweitzer? etc.); it refers also to the particularity of Peter, Mary, Mark—and of Augustine, Hildegaard, Francis, Jean de Brebeuf, Dietrich. It refers to the radical historicity which runs through the length and breadth of the tradition of Jerusalem, insisting upon the uniqueness of each epoch, each situation, each individual.

In faithfulness to this concentration of biblical faith upon the particular, a concentration which is rooted in the Bible's understanding of the divine *love,* we have begun with an attempt to characterize our own particularity. We might instead have begun immediately with a discussion of the discipline, assuming, as is usual, that it carries with it its own interpretive codes and laws, binding upon all who wish to make it theirs. But besides the historical fact that the discipline has evolved in response to the particularities of its practitioners, we have begun to know ourselves called, as were the best of our forebears, to a task which requires soul-searching—"living, dying, and being damned!" The specific, unique, and unrepeatable circumstances of an age and a people call forth nuances both of content and method; and while we may and must learn from the past we cannot expect the Christian past to provide our theology ready-made, or even to hand over to us the tools that it used. No previous disciple community had to think its discipline under the threat of nuclear annihilation. That one dimension of our context, to mention none of the others, should bring us face to face with the scandal of particularity as it applies to our vocation as disciples of the Christ. Theology is always a *present* undertaking conducted by a *living* community of belief.

It is the contention of this study that the disciple community in North America has for too long been a dependent community—that we have permitted ourselves to live from the inheritance of an ecclesiastical-doctrinal tradition which is curiously lacking in originality of thought despite the persistent claims of freedom and daring made by our host society. In the foregoing, we have considered some of the reasons for this—our captivation by the spirit of modernity; our incapacity to entertain failure; our repression of the 20th-century experience of negation. We have reminded ourselves (our study did not have to demonstrate this; it is demonstrated by every news broadcast) that we are members of a civilization which feels itself to be on the brink of peril, but is poorly equipped to cope with any peril, let alone so abysmal a "catastrophe" (von Weizsäcker) as may be awaiting us. We have considered, also, some of the specific crises which contribute to or are consequent upon this underlying spiritual malaise: the crisis of an ecclesiastical superstructure which for most of its long history pursued the way of power but is now humbled; the crisis of conflicting religions and quasi-religions, and the religion of no religion; the crisis of guilt in a "Christian" culture which transferred its own unacceptability to a scapegoat race and tried to purge itself, but was in the end only rendered more unworthy still; the crisis of a civilization seemingly bent on oblivion. We might have gone on to detail the crises of authority, the breakdown of institutions, the loss of individuality, the eclipse of public meaning, and so on. But enough has been said to establish an impression of who—in the view of at least one observer—we are, and what we bring to the contemplation of our tradition.

Needless to say, I cannot assume that this personal statement will be universally acceptable. Many will find it bleak, one-sided, and pessimistic.[3] With them, I should want to engage in certain discussions about the important distinction between the "childish categories" (Heidegger) of optimism and pessimism and, on the other hand, the biblical categories of sin and hope. But if in the meantime I have caused such persons seriously to reflect upon "us"—disciples of Jesus Christ in the North American context circa the ninth decade of the 20th century c.e.—then I shall have accomplished all that I hoped to do. For the point is not to achieve universal *agreement* about our context. Peter and Paul did not agree what time it was! The point, rather, is to begin seriously to work with that question, and to leave off behaving as if the circumstances in which theology is thought and the identity of the thinkers have nothing to do with the thinking!

As for the possible bleakness of this analysis, I should want to remind my critics of a certain characteristic paradox of biblical faith. In that "strange, new world within the Bible" (Barth), things are seldom what they seem. Not only is apparent righteousness judged "filthy rags," and apparent wisdom folly, but apparent strength is perceived as weakness. Those who think they stand are warned to take care lest they fall; the humble and meek are exalted, the poor blessed, and the failed and the dead are raised up to newness of life. It is not the end of the story if, in this tradition, one speaks of human crises and failure and even death.

As a citizen of this "New World," one, moreover, who loves it as his own, his ancestral home, I am not able to avoid the impression of loss. I think that I sense a fallenness. There are "intimations of deprivation" (Grant) which those who remember our hopes cannot ignore. A

---

3. But see Reinhold Niebuhr's essay, "Optimism, Pessimism, and Religious Faith," in *The Essential Reinhold Niebuhr: Selected Essays and Addresses,* ed. Robert McAfee Brown (New Haven and London: Yale University Press, 1986), pp. 3-17.

mood of bravado and self-righteous revenge has supplanted the idealism of our earlier images to ourselves, and it is not convincingly cloaked by the continued commercialized rhetoric of the Dream. Republic has become imperium, and bombs have replaced persuasion in our dealings with our critics. (I am writing this on the day following the United States bombing of Libya. I am reviewing it on the day after the United States resumed nuclear testing. If I re-read these words a decade hence, I hope that I shall have reason to qualify them!)

In his moving one-actor play, *Krapp's Last Tape,* Samuel Beckett has his nonhero sing the familiar evening hymn, "Now the Day Is Over"—a hymn which brought comfort to generations of 19th- and early 20th-century worshipers; only, in the context of Beckett's tale of a life that has run its course, pursued its dreams, and failed to make good the meaning it sought, the hymn takes on a somber and ironical hue:

> *Now the day is over,*
> *Night is drawing nigh;*
> *Shadows of the evening*
> *Steal across the sky.*[4]

The disciples of the Christ in North America towards the end of what was to have been "the Christian century" find themselves on the edge of a cultural night for which our intellectual and spiritual conventions have not at all prepared us. One suspects that this night is not yet fully with us, that it will grow darker still—that the "catastrophic climax" of our "manifold crises" still lies in the future. Many of our fellow Christians, along with their no-longer-religious counterparts, have sought sanctuary from the night. They attempt to perpetuate the illusion of light with which our society was endowed from its inception. Had they stood in the darkness at noon around Golgotha, they would probably have done the same thing, incapable as we all are of waiting for the third day.

It is better for us to go into the night. Not "gently" (Dylan Thomas), not heroically either, like the dying Goethe, and certainly not as if we enjoyed it! But as it is darker, let us see what meaning the darkness might contain for us. Instead of attempting, vainly, to prolong the modern illusion of Light, we might profitably explore the significance of our present disillusionment. It is possible—given the "strange" logic of biblical faith—that there could be more honest hope in our despair, more good

---

4. Samuel Beckett, *I Can't Go On, I'll Go On: A Selection from Samuel Beckett's Work* (New York: Grove, 1976), p. 488.

in our experienced evil, more strength in our hard-to-admit weakness, more life in our dying than in all the pathetic attempts of a disintegrating Babylon to appear young and vigorous.

At the end of the second novel of his well-known trilogy, Robertson Davies has his heroine, the Swiss woman Liesl, take her Canadian friend David Staunton, a self-conscious and rather cynical young lawyer, into a cave high in the Alps where primitive cave-dwellers once performed liturgies to their god, the bear. The Canadian is afraid and is desperate to leave—

"But for the love of God let's get back to the light!"

"For the love of God [Liesl responds]? Is not God to be found in the darkness?"[5]

■   ■   ■

"Thinking," wrote Hannah Arendt, "calls not only for intelligence and profundity but above all for courage."[6] In our activist society and religious milieu, courage is nearly always associated with deeds. Perhaps this is because most of the thought in which we have been called, until now, to engage has not been existentially taxing. Anything deserving of the name of thought in North America today, however, presupposes courage.

Courage in the Christian vocabulary is a gift. It is not self-achieved, it is a matter of grace. But the gift is neither painless nor once-for-all given. It makes continuous and stringent demands upon the human intellect and will, demands to which none of us ever becomes quite accustomed. Whether we are speaking of the courage to love, or the courage to believe, or the courage to think and to confess our faith, it is the same thing. It is never effortless. Beginners in theology frequently expect to read works of Christian thought as if they were reading Agatha Christie. It may require wit to read Ms. Christie, but it does not require courage. Theology requires courage.

That is why we may say that the mode in which the gift of the courage to think is given to Christians is called a "discipline." The *discipline* of theology. What this means concretely is that the grace which is the precondition and impetus for this thought grasps, turns, and schools us to concentrate upon a certain frame of reference. We are neither "enlightened," simply and suddenly (that is not discipleship but magic), nor

---

5. *The Manticore* (Harmondsworth: Penguin Books, 1976), p. 86.
6. *Men in Dark Times* (New York & London: Harcourt Brace Jovanovich, 1955), p. 8.

are we given general freedom to inquire where we will—a sort of carte blanche to the universe. Rather, we are led to a particular set of events, to a tradition, a story. Our minds are turned towards this center and instructed to think ourselves and our world in relation to it. On the one hand we are denied the instant understanding offered by all the cults (including Christian cults!) which bypass *human thinking*. On the other hand we are denied the absolute freedom to wander where we will, the freedom coveted by an uncommitted intelligentsia. It is a matter of *discipline* to accept the gift of this courage, because it means renouncing the alleged liberty to wander and wonder, and focusing our attention upon a particular point. Paul's formula for this point was: "Jesus Christ and him crucified."

Yet the discipline by no means bypasses our human mental processes, because, far from being offered all truth in this concentration upon the Christ event, we are left to discover what meaning this event contains for us here and now. "Work out your own salvation with fear and trembling; for God is at work in you. . ." (Phil. 2:12-13). God works *within* our minds. In the biblical tradition, God does not replace our minds; God renews them—that is, pushes them to the limits of their potential.

We are to turn now towards this place of concentration. *We* are to turn there. *Our* minds, *our* questions, *our* darkness, *our* need are to be focused upon this center. We submit ourselves to this discipline, not as Everyman/Everywoman, but in all the specificity of our existing. We come to this story with our story.

In some ways, therefore, one wishes that it were possible to move directly to the central content of the gospel story—the subject matter of our second volume: Theology, anthropology, Christology. But two considerations prevent this. The first is an apologetic factor: despite what may constitute a new openness to theological thought in the immediate past and present, we know ourselves to be disciples in a time when faith, however desirable, is by no means easy or natural. We know this because we know *ourselves,* not merely because we find disbelief in others round about. The question, How is belief possible? lives within the community of belief, and more existentially there, perhaps, than elsewhere. The question, What *is* theology, really? is not only a question of worldly and curious persons; it belongs to the life of the disciple community in our time. We are not at liberty, then, to go at once to the central doctrines of our tradition, but we must first address these issues relating to epistemology and the nature of the theological discipline.

The second reason why it is necessary to think further about the *thinking* of the faith is that the discipline into which we are being initiated is already old and well established. It has as it were, a life of its own. Disciples and disciple communities have been there before and have devised certain patterns and connections and relationships and problems in relation to which all who take up this discipline must clarify their own positions. We cannot simply take over the *methods* of our predecessors any more than we can merely copy their *content;* all the same, neither can we ignore their ways of approaching this discipline. For the content upon which we want (in the succeeding volume) to focus is inseparable from the methods which have been employed to delineate it. *We ourselves* must think the faith; but the thinking of *the faith* involves a necessary continuity with the past.[7] Our own thinking lifts us beyond our immediate experience and puts us in touch with the ages which have thought the faith before us. We shall come to our own confession only as we wrestle with theirs.

This too is part of the discipline of theology. There is not only a message, an event, a story upon which faith focuses; there is also an extensive tradition of those who have focused upon this message. We are not beginning de novo, but as pupils of a *schola,* a school. We are entering a room where a conversation has been going on for a very long time. We do not attempt to intrude upon this conversation immediately. We listen; we try to catch the drift of the discussion; we acquaint our ears and minds with the language, the recurring concepts, the unspoken presuppositions: reason and revelation, spirit and letter, authority and freedom. Thus we orientate ourselves to the discipline which is to be the vehicle of our courage to think the faith, and train ourselves to hear what wisdom there may be for us in this divine and human "foolishness."

---

7. Cf. above, "The Dangers of Contextuality," chap. 1, §4.

PART II
THE DISCIPLINE

CHAPTER · FOUR

Elements of the Discipline

The freedom of theology—which it, like all thinking, requires—has its foundation precisely in the fact that we must ever anew ask for the message, for its authentic content and meaning, and consequently can come into conflict about it ourselves, and in the fact that we have nothing under our control from the beginning.[1]

Introduction

One way of coming to a better understanding of the nature of any discipline is by considering its parts. There are certain components which, though they themselves do not constitute Christian theology either singly or together, are nevertheless invariably bound up with theological thought. If we inquire about the roles that they play in the work of theology, we shall acquire, gradually, a more comprehensive conception of the whole subject.

The actual naming of such elements or ingredients, including both the order of their treatment and *what* is said about them, of course involves many decisions. The arbitrary factor in these decisions cannot be wholly avoided; but it will minimize that factor if the contextual nature of what we are about here is borne in mind. The seven elements of theology that I shall treat in this chapter are thus determined not only by the conventions of the discipline but also—and perhaps more importantly—by the realities, ecclesiastical and secular, of our context, to which the first part of this

---

1. Helmut Gollwitzer, *An Introduction to Protestant Theology*, trans. David Cairns (Philadelphia: Westminster, 1982), p. 32.

study has been addressed. While other elements might have been added or while the ordering of the various categories might have been different under other sociohistorical conditions, the discussion of our own situation as a disciple community seems to me to warrant the choices and priorities that are presented here.

18. Theology and Faith

18.1. Defining Faith. Clearly, faith is an important component of theology. We implied this when we said earlier that theology is *confessional*. One *thinks* the faith because one believes, or is at least curious about belief. But what *is* belief? What is *faith*?

It is necessary, given our North American context in general and the ecclesiastical-religious dimension of that context in particular, to distinguish faith from two distorted conceptions of it. The one is objectivistic and intellectualistic; the other subjectivistic and experiential.

For certain Christian groupings on this continent, to "have faith" means to accept a body of doctrine. One assents to the truth of this doctrine on the authority of the church, or of a creedal tradition, or of the Scriptures, or of some less easily defined (perhaps charismatic or "spiritual") authority. The doctrine may be called "revealed truth"; it may be quite explicitly stated in propositional form; or it may be expressed more nebulously in symbolic, liturgical, or moral practices. Some of those for whom faith means the submission of the mind to established *doctrina* are able to express the content of their belief verbally in almost mathematical formulas and theory; for others, the acceptance of Christian teaching is articulated in more symbolic ways, indicative of a readiness to accept the authority of an impressive tradition and the guardians thereof. The first type is more characteristic of the Protestant and the second of the Catholic appropriation of this interpretation of what faith means. Both, however, share the assumption that faith is assent (*assensus*) to religious truth.

At the opposite extreme, faith is conceived in terms of a subjective mood, a belief-ful attitude. It is not *what* one believes that is important here but the posture of believing as such. President Eisenhower was exemplifying this view of faith when he said, "I don't care what a man [*sic*] believes, only that he believes." If the former type of faith is associated with doctrinal and ecclesiastical "orthodoxy," the latter belongs to circles of less doctrinaire pietism, especially the vaguely liberal and often sentimental sort of pietism which is so prevalent in North American neo-Protestantism.

Against both of these popular conceptions, I am assuming here that faith is a category of relationship. It means in the first place "faith *in.*" It is fundamental trust (*fiducia*). At least at the linguistic level, both of the classical ecumenical creeds of the church (the Apostles' and the Nicene) assume this relational posture when they begin with the words, *Credo in. . . .*

There is a subjective as well as an objective component in the relational understanding of faith. It is objective in that the "object" of one's *credo* lies outside the self: *Credo in Deum.* It is subjective in the sense that belief involves the decision and commitment of the self: *Credo—I* believe. Faith is what occurs, from the human side, when we know ourselves to be encountered, judged, and accepted by the gracious God. While the object of our faith (God) is different from the objects of ordinary human faith in other persons who have shown themselves trustworthy, the faith itself is not essentially different. When I say that I have faith in my wife, or my friend, or my lawyer, I am using the word "faith" in basically the same way as when, as a Christian, I say that I have faith in God. What is intended is simply: *trust.* Luther would only use the German word *vertrauen* (to trust) as a synonym for faith (*glauben*).

18.2. Whether Faith Is a Prerequisite for Theology. The question posed by the juxtaposition of faith and *theology* is whether faith is a necessary *prerequisite* for the doing of theology. The answer to this question depends a good deal on one's preunderstanding of faith, and therefore we have tried first, in a preliminary way, to establish the typical alternatives present in our context. If faith means assent to a body of doctrine, whether in explicit propositional form or more symbolically conceived, it will almost certainly follow that faith will be regarded as an indispensable prerequisite for theology; for in this view, apart from such assent one does not have access to the truths he or she is to explicate, or one's apprehension of those truths would be by definition false or incomplete.

At the other extreme, where faith does not refer to religious data but to a mood or posture (belief-ful-ness), faith may or may not be regarded as a prerequisite to theology; for those assuming this mind-set, theology is usually of only secondary importance, and therefore the tendency of communities embracing such a position is to be very open with respect to conditions requisite to the doing of theology.

But what if one insists that faith refers neither to religious data nor to a spiritual attitude, but to a response of trust within the context of relationship with God? How does such a view of faith relate to the theological enterprise as such? We may best arrive at an answer to this question if we proceed *via negativa*. Two alternatives should be avoided:

(a) Fideism: The suggestion that theology can be undertaken only by believers, and at every level of analysis, is an aspect of Christian fideism, i.e., the assumption that the human intellect is incapable of attaining true knowledge of God. While this position may sometimes be found intermingled with a relational understanding of faith (*fides*), as in the Barthian school, it is normally heavily informed by the dimension of knowledge (*gnosis*). A strict discontinuity is perceived between those who are recipients of revealed truth and those who are not. Without the *gnosis* which is the primary data of theology, it is naturally impossible to do theology.

But if faith is not the acceptance of revealed truth but trust in the revealing God, the matter comes out differently. For then the lines of demarcation between belief and unbelief, believer and disbeliever, are at least more fluid than fideism supposes.

And, in the post-Christendom, religiously pluralistic situation of our present context, must we not in fact conclude that these lines *are* fluid? On the one hand, the demise of imperial Christianity has left Christians in a state of continuous decision making. It cannot be assumed that one is Christian by birth, or even by a dramatic and once-for-all *re*birth. Again and again the line between belief and unbelief is traversed. It is indeed for most of us an invisible line. Absolute distinctions between the states of belief and unbelief are no longer convincing. No biblical verse is more existentially meaningful to post-Constantinian disciples of the Christ than the prayer, "Lord, I believe, help my unbelief!" (cf. Mark 9:24). And while we may sometimes lament the fact that a pure, unalloyed, and childlike belief seems impossible for us, we are on the whole grateful that such a model of belief is no longer mandatory—is no longer, at any rate, the measuring stick by which authenticity of membership in the disciple community is tested. For not only does it seem beyond us in a world "come of age" (Bonhoeffer), and perhaps beyond mature humanity under any conditions, but it appears indistinguishable from mere credulity.[2] What we encounter in the Scriptures, both in the long saga of ancient Israel and in the story of the Christ and his original disciples, is not credulity. It is a trust which struggles with existential distrust and a faith which is in dialogue with doubt. It is faith and not sight (Heb. 11:1).

---

2. See my article in *The Princeton Seminary Bulletin* 6/3, New Series (1985), pp. 201ff., "Beyond Cynicism and Credulity: On the Meaning of Christian Hope."

There is a Judas in Peter, too. Knowing, therefore, something of unbelief within ourselves, and of the strangely *positive* contribution of such unbelief to the life of belief, we are skeptical of a fideism which assumes unquestioning assent to allegedly revealed knowledge as the precondition for authentic theological reflection.

At the same time, the plurality of religious, quasi-religious, and humanistic alternatives present in our context also contributes to this experiential refutation of the fideist position. We no longer exist in a world where "Christianity," whether genuine or merely official, holds almost exclusive sway; where concepts and concerns can be identified as "Christian" only because people lack knowledge of the beliefs and practices of other religious traditions; and where "non-Christian" is itself a category defined by Christians. Daily we encounter ideas and deeds, persons and movements, whose ethos lies outside the Christian fold, but whose reality is unmistakably reminiscent of our own. As we find disbelief and doubt within ourselves, so we are apt today to find something akin to what we mean by belief and depth of understanding within others who do not profess *our* creed.

We may find such in those who do not, some of them, profess *any* overtly religious creed! Many of the persons whose ideas we have employed in the preceding section of this study, for example, either claim not to be believers in God or are more or less silent on the matter of theistic belief. Yet we have learned much from them—from Becker and Arendt and Machoveč and many others—not only about the truth of our common human condition, but also about matters expressly associated with Christian teaching: Jesus, the meaning of suffering, courage, hope, and so on. Can one really draw hard and fast distinctions between theological work emanating from an explicit faith in the triune God and less intentional but perhaps more profoundly theological work? One of the more neglected parables of Jesus might be helpful here: quite possibly there are Christians who assert their willingness to work in the theological vineyard of their Lord but do not actually *do* the work; and perhaps there are also others who refuse to hear any specifically Christian command, yet in the end perform what is in a real way theological work (see Matt. 21:28-32). Such parables should not be confined to the realm of deeds only!

This is not to say that faith—an explicit faith in Jesus Christ—is *un*necessary to theology. It is simply to warn against a false way of making the distinction. Confining relevant theological workmanship to those who confess belief in the Christ means ruling out a great many persons who throughout the history of the church as well as in our own time contribute very substantially to our understanding of the faith, though they themselves remain outside or on the periphery of the community of belief. All of us who confess the name of Jesus as Christ do so in language that is full of indebtedness to persons who did not or do not believe in Jesus Christ. One name alone is enough to secure the point: Plato.[3] Instead of making the distinction in such a way as to eliminate a priori this whole company of co-workers, let us say that theology done from within a specific faith stance within the disciple community differs from the theological or paratheological work of the co-workers in that it involves the decision to commit oneself to an explicit confessional posture, and to attempt to interpret the world from the perspective of that commitment.

It is in this sense, I believe, that we should understand the famous dictum of St. Augustine, *Credo ut intelligam* (I believe in order that I may understand). Belief here means trust in God, in the sense discussed above. But it is not simply a vague openness to deity or transcendence; rather, it is a trust directed towards *that* God who has been revealed in the Christ and is testified to by the Scriptures and the apostolic tradition. *Trusting* God is the prerequisite for the disciplined attempt to understand the meaning of this God's self-manifestation. When Augustine goes on immediately to say, "Indeed, unless I believed I should not understand," he is not intending to assert (as fideism is wont to do) that nonbelievers can understand nothing of God or the things of God. That would be wholly inconsistent with Augustine's essentially Platonic epistemology. He is saying, rather, that apart from belief—that is, apart from the relationship of faith *in* God—fullness of comprehension is impossible; for this relationship, and the trust that characterizes it, is the existential basis of all theology. It would be at least as impossible to achieve depth of understanding outside the relationship with God as it is to achieve such depth apart from personal relationship with another human being about whom "knowledge" is claimed. (We shall return to this comparison when we treat the knowledge of God in a subsequent chapter.)

(b) Subjectivism: The second position that should be avoided in the attempt to understand how theology and faith are related may be called subjectivism or religious introversion. It consists in the supposition that faith *by itself* is sufficient for the theological task, or that theology is

---

3. Many Christians from Augustine to C. S. Lewis are conspicuously Platonic in their articulation of what they believe. George Grant, whom I have quoted frequently in these pages, describes himself as being "above all a lover of Plato within Christianity" (*Technology and Justice* [Toronto: Anansi, 1986], p. 90).

essentially if not exclusively the articulation of personal religious feeling. In reality much more is involved in the discipline of theology than my personal belief. Belief is, we have said, requisite for depth of understanding: to understand is to stand under, to know oneself to be dependent upon the outcome of that which one beholds. A sustained concentration upon the claims of the tradition requires the kind of struggle of spirit and intellect which can occur only if the outcome truly matters. But faith is oriented towards something, Someone, beyond itself: it is faith *in*. A faith which manifests an inordinate interest in itself is a contradiction in terms.

All the same, precisely this contradiction is a conspicuous factor in our particular context. Traditional forms of pietism, aided and abetted by modern psychologism and the flight into subjectivity on the part of generations doubtful of objective meaning, have ensured that Christianity in our society should become a popular vehicle for a type of self-preoccupation. The narcissism that secular persons manifest in the care of their bodies or their houses is equally evident in the religious whose attention is devoted to the cultivation of their own private spirituality.

In such subjectivistic circles of Christian spirituality, it is faith itself that is celebrated: the fact of faith, the experience of faith, the ecstatic or agonizing moods and emotions belonging to the life of faith. Theology then becomes the articulation of "my" or "our" faith—our spiritual ups and downs, our religious feelings, our prayer life, our fellowship, our life "with Jesus" or "in the Spirit," etc. Everything is centered in the believing subject or subjects.

It is interesting to note that St. Paul, who has more to say about the meaning of faith than any other writer of the Newer Testament, never speaks of faith in the first person, except rhetorically. Nor does he ever tell his readers about his famous "Damascus road experience," the subsequent model for so much that has transpired along these lines! The account of the "conversion" of Paul comes to us from the Luke-Acts tradition. Only once does Paul himself give himself as it were the luxury of personal religious reflection—and that in a cloaked way and in a context full of irony (2 Corinthians 12). Similarly, John Calvin never provides any detail about his "sudden conversion." This is because faith, for Calvin as for Paul, however indispensable, is no end in itself but only a means. It is that gift of God which enables us to see—to *glimpse*, rather, "as through a mirror dimly (1 Cor. 13:12)—what is infinitely more worthy of contemplation than our own selves, and apart from which our self-knowledge is stunted and neurotic.

The habits of doctrine impel us to name that upon which faith opens the human spirit to God, but that convention does not do justice to Paul or to biblical religion generally, because, while faith is *in* God, what this existential trust enables us to "see" is much more inclusive than what the word *God* normally signifies. Trust in God opens us to a whole new world. It is a window onto all of reality. Everything appears in another light—our own kind, the other creatures, nature, work, time, and (yes, of course!) God.

Precisely this *end* of faith, namely, its reorientation of the human spirit *towards the other*, is why a faith which finds *itself* interesting is a contradiction in terms. The intention of that grace which makes faith possible is exactly to *free the self from preoccupation with itself and to turn it towards the other*—God, the neighbor, the world. *Theology*, which faith enables and which can only, at depth, be enabled by faith, is the attempt of the mind that is being liberated from the prison house of self to give expression to the great universe of meaning that through the grace of belief in God it has begun to intuit. Subjectivistic theology has mistaken the means for the end, the window for that upon which the window allows us to fix our gaze.

18.3. Faith as Love in Understanding. To say that faith "opens us" to the other is in reality not yet linguistically strong enough. It would be more accurate to say that faith *drives us* towards the other—or, to state the matter still more accurately, that faith expresses itself *in love*.

In a rudimentary and halting way, we know what this means at the level of Christian ethics: "Faith without works (of love) is dead" (James 2:17). As Luther put it, "Faith is a living, restless thing. It cannot be inoperative. We are not saved by works; but if there be no works, there must be something amiss with faith."[4] But, especially in our North American context, where knowledge and its pursuit has been conceived in almost exclusively instrumentalist terms, we hardly ever think of applying the dictum that faith expresses itself in love to the human quest for understanding—for *sophia* (wisdom). To theology! Yet precisely that is what we shall have to discover if we are to meet the challenge and invitation to theology implicit in our context. What *theologia* and *philosophia* have in common is love—the love of truth.[5]

Unlike the word *philosophy, theology* does not contain within itself, etymologically, the idea of *loving* wisdom or truth; but the reality which

---

4. Quoted by Roland Bainton in *Here I Stand: A Life of Martin Luther* (New York: Abingdon, 1950), p. 331.

5. On the relation of faith, love, and truth, see Emil Brunner, *The Divine-Human Encounter* (London: SCM, 1944).

for Christians lies behind the word *theology*, namely, the God whose love liberates humanity for newness of life, is as insistent upon the quest for understanding as were the ancients who coined the term *philosophia*. In this, Jerusalem and Athens are at one. Their ways of understanding are different, and what is understood is different, but for both of these founding traditions of our civilization the quest for understanding is of the essence—is a matter of love. Both therefore stand in fundamental opposition to modernity, for which the goal of understanding is not love of truth but mastery of the world.

Faith in the God who "is love" (1 John 4:8) moves us to love the other—namely, everything upon which the window of faith opens. The same faith which expresses itself in the love of God and the neighbor impels us to embrace the totality in our understanding. It is this desire for consummate understanding that informs the theological quest—and often, because the desire ceases to be nurtured by love and becomes instead the product of concupiscence and pride, turns to pretension. Theology as the Queen of the Sciences! Yet these distortions are distortions of an impulse that inheres in Christian theology as such—the impulse to know what is loved; and no false modesty should deter the disciple community from exploring that impulse, especially not when such assumed modesty is a cloak for intellectual sloth or plain anti-intellectualism, which is too frequently the case in ecclesiastical circles in our context.

Faith expresses itself in the will to comprehend just as insistently as in the will to perform good deeds. The intellectual impetus emanates from the same love, the same thrust-beyond-self, as does the ethical. In fact, the one without the other is inevitably a reduction of itself. It is this insight that has again surfaced in the language of *praxis*, where the deed and the thought are inseparable.

That faith manifests itself in the love of understanding is the meaning of Anselm of Canterbury's famous phrase, *fides quaerens intellectum*, faith seeking understanding. *If it is truly faith*, Anselm insists, it will seek to understand what is believed. We ought to hear the verb "to seek" here in an almost aggressive sense. Like the defiant boldness of a lover, the doing of theology entails a search that will not be deterred by the many obstacles that are certainly in the way of it. The quest into which, by faith, we are initiated is no mild inquiry ("research") but a determined and unquenchable passion to comprehend. It *will know*! It will not be satisfied with simplistic answers to difficult questions. It will be like Jacob wrestling with the angel until dawn, until he is blessed and limps away from the encounter. There is a drive towards understanding built into faith itself, if it is really faith and not just sentimentality.

255

Of course it will never be fully satisfied! This is Paul's point about the distinction between faith and sight. Faith will not be sated until it has been replaced by sight. That is the eschatological dimension in faith, the hope that keeps the disciple community striving for genuine wisdom and makes it forever dissatisfied with whatever wisdom it thinks it finds— though this eschatological dissatisfaction (we must immediately add) is held in a dialectical tension with the contentment to which we drew attention earlier, the calm of a discipline which knows from the outset its finitude.

To make fully contextual the point that theological inquiry belongs to the love into which faith leads us, we need to recall once more what was said in Part I concerning the demise of Constantinian religion. The greater share of those who have been designated Christians throughout the 16 centuries during which Christianity has served successive empires as their official cultus have not found it necessary resolutely to strive for understanding. Even clergy could be found (in pockets of Christendom they still exist) who could boast that they had no interest in theology. Let us be forthright: what calls itself faith, under the conditions of culture religion, does not necessarily drive to understanding. On the contrary, it may well function to quell ordinary intellectual curiosity and offer people thought-free tranquility! Given the formative character of such a long history, it is not surprising that still today theology can be regarded by many Christians as an esoteric and merely professional activity, conducted on the periphery of the religious life.

But in the diaspora situation in which the earliest Christians lived, which (as we have seen) has again become the norm in many parts of the *oikoumēnē,* and which promises to become the standard form of the church of the not-distant future everywhere, the situation is very different. In that situation, people are not pushed into the Christian community by unthinking forces of social custom, and faith is no merely "natural" response to existence. It is gift and struggle. It is a matter of decision— not a once-for-all decision, but one that must in a real sense be renewed daily, and in the presence of much evidence to the contrary.

Such a context brings us once more to the authentic character both of faith and theology. To commit oneself to the God of the gospel in our present context is to know from the start, and to be made to know again and again, that *the discipline of understanding is inherent within the faith decision.* Without theology, that is, without a continuous, determined, and studied quest for comprehension on the part of the whole people of God, the church of the future will not be able to subsist. In the society whose situation we sketched in Part I of this study, the disciple community does not have a choice between faith-by-itself and faith-with-theology. If there is faith in such a context there will be a disciplined passion to understand; and the age-old distinction between "theologians" and "ordinary Christians" will be terminated at last, or at least interpreted in strictly functional terms. For in that context *all* Christians must in some measure become theologians. How else could they give a reason for the hope that is in them (cf. 1 Peter 3:15)? Why else would they remain?[6]

19. Theology and the Bible

19.1. *Sola Scriptura.* Unlike some varieties of religious belief, Christianity contains a vital and indispensable historical component. The character and will of the God in whom Christians' trust is manifested,

---

6. I am in complete agreement with Edward Farley when he writes that "Education in the truest and most serious sense of that word (*paideia*) needs to be introduced into the church" (*Theologia* [Philadelphia: Fortress, 1983], p. 196). Behind this assertion lies Farley's profound analysis in an earlier work, *Ecclesial Man: A Social Phenomenology of Faith and Reality* (Philadelphia: Fortress, 1975), of what he calls the "reality-loss" in present-day manifestations of Christian faith, which he identifies "largely" as "an *intellectual* problem." "Faith's realities have not simply flown away; they have been obscured by the emergence of a certain kind of human being, civilization, historical consciousness, all of which are attended by an insistence on playing the games of intellectual inquiry by some very narrow rules." This "reality-loss," he avers, cannot be overcome by theological education alone, for the realities of faith cannot be established by theology, only by "participation in the community itself." Yet the community of faith will wither and die—or suffer still more questionable fates—unless it is continuously nurtured by *theologia*. By *theologia*, however, Farley does not mean what has all-too-consistently been identified as "theology" in institutions for the training of professionals, which in his view represents a functionalistic-professionalistic truncation of *theologia* in the classical sense. *Theologia* is, rather, a *habitus*, i.e., a "disposition" of spirit and mind, which "originates partly from a supernatural gift and partly as an effort of inquiry" (*Theologia*, p. 44). It refers to "theology as wisdom and theology as discipline"—not something that can be easily broken down into "independent disciplines whose end and unity is training for ministerial tasks" and whose character is marked by its association with "strategic, technical knowledge."

Theologia in this sense of a *habitus* of faith belongs, Farley insists, to the *whole community of faith*. But he does not wish this to be interpreted as a call for more "Christian education," which (as he rightly says) suffers from "a certain ambivalence" on account of the fact that what we designate "theological education" is largely reserved for the clergy, leaving only "the crumbs spilling over from the hearty meal enjoyed by" the latter for the laity to digest. Christian education is "education and yet is not education"—it is usually "a small educational moment dropped from a clergy course of study which itself lacks unity and coherence." At the end of the Constantinian era, a diaspora church requires a full and serious "educational enterprise . . . in the churches." Indeed, Farley thinks, until *theologia* in the deepest sense becomes the disposition of the whole church, not only the church at large but also "professional" theological education itself will be impoverished. "If a Christian *paideia* is introduced into church education, it will involve the recovery of theological understanding. The reason is simply that *theologia*, a dialectical reflection which presides over faith's self-conscious and critical responses to the world, is the heart and soul of any Christian *paideia*" (p. 196). Thus, in this view, the very "reality" of the Christian enterprise is dependent upon a faith which "drives to understanding." (See also my book, *The Reality of the Gospel and the Unreality of the Churches* [Philadelphia: Westminster, 1975].)

first of all, not in individual religious experience but in a sequence of historical events, the culminating moment (*kairos*) of which, for the *Christian* side of biblical faith, is the event of the Christ. In the sequence of occurrences surrounding this central *kairos*, including the long march of the people of Israel, the God in whom the disciple community believes is self-revealed. All subsequent revelation is "dependent" in relation to this "original revelation";[7] that is, so long as a community designates itself "Christian," it is beholden to the scriptural testimony to the foundational historical events which establish the fundamental character of Christian belief. If we have treated "faith" prior to our consideration of the Bible as an element of theology, it is not because the revelatory history testified to in the Scriptures is secondary to the belief of the existing disciple community, but only because the existential significance of the biblical testimony for the community of belief depends upon faith. What we have in the Scriptures of the two testaments is itself the product of faith. Like all history, the biblical record consists of event plus interpretation; and here the primary interpretational element or hermeutic is faith—faith in God as the one acting in and through this history for the world's redemption.

For the Christian theological task, the Bible is of immediate and primary significance, then, because it is for all intents and purposes *the sole witness* to this foundational history. The awareness of these events and their salvific meaning is not given to us automatically at birth, nor is it miraculously imparted at "the second birth," as Christian conversion is sometimes called. It has to be learned. We may of course assume that there would be no conversion to an explicitly Christian faith apart from an initial hearing of some aspect of the scriptural message, whether directly or indirectly. But theology goes beyond the initial hearing involved in the experience of coming to faith. It assumes an ongoing dialogue with the biblical record.

This dialogue is what the Reformers meant by the teaching, *sola Scriptura*. Only the Scriptures of the Older and Newer Testaments are given a place of supreme significance in the theological discipline. The *sola fide* by itself could easily end in a babel of religious convictions and communities. Faith which intends to be Christian must be prepared to listen to and submit itself to the authority of the Scriptures. Only of the canonical Scriptures of the two Testaments were the Reformers willing

---

7. Paul Tillich, *Systematic Theology*, vol. 1 (Chicago: University of Chicago Press, 1951), pp. 126ff.

to say this. They did not intend to minimize the significance of nonscriptural tradition (to which we shall turn next); but in order to establish methodologically their main theological point, namely, that the God with whom Christian faith has to do is the one who is revealed in the events testified to in the Bible, they placed their *sola Scriptura* alongside their *sola fide*.

19.2. Attitudes towards the Bible Prevalent in Our Context. We shall have to discuss the nature of scriptural *authority* later, but already in connection with the role of the Bible in the theological discipline we encounter aspects of this question. It cannot be circumvented, because as soon as the Bible is mentioned in the North American setting today one is conscious of two attitudes towards this collection of writings which are strongly present in our midst, and which handicap further discussion. It is necessary to clarify our position with respect to these prevalent preconceptions.[8]

On the one hand, secular thought insists that the various writings that constitute the Bible are the products of human beings like ourselves, and therefore should not be singled out as if they contained ultimate truth. On the other hand, it belongs to the religious simplism described in the previous section that it invests these writings with precisely the absoluteness which secularity deems impossible and fanatical. This polarized situation with respect to the sacred writings of Judaic and Christian faith makes it very difficult for anyone to communicate the kind of nuanced historical-theological thinking that belongs to the best biblical scholarship of the past hundred years. Moreover, the increasing power and popularity of American biblicism, with its only slightly camouflaged fascistic political overtones, makes it more and more difficult for responsible Christian scholarship to embrace a theology of biblical authority without appearing to endorse biblical literalism and much besides.

Let us be clear that both secular and biblicistic views of the Bible must be rejected. But the charges of both against any avowedly Christian rejection of them must be answered. On the one hand we have to justify

---

8. For an informative discussion of the ways in which contemporary theologians have employed the Bible in their expositions of the Christian faith, see David H. Kelsey, *The Uses of Scripture in Recent Theology* (Philadelphia: Fortress, 1975). Kelsey sets out to answer three questions suggested by the words "text, con-text, and pre-text":

"When a theologian takes biblical texts as scripture authoritative for theology, what decisions does he make about these *texts*? What decisions does he make about the *setting* in which the texts will be used? And what decisions does he make *before* ever turning to the text at all?" (p. ix).

The pertinence of this study to our present enterprise will be evident to the reader.

theology's use of the Bible over against the secular charge of relativism; on the other hand we must explain why, unlike biblicism, we cannot treat the Bible as if *it* were absolute.

(a) The answer to the secularist charge of relativism, while it cannot be held up as a convincing response so far as secularity itself is concerned, is nevertheless not totally inaccessible to ordinary common sense. If you confess that the God in whom you believe is specially revealed in certain historical events and persons, then you must have access to the most reliable witnesses to those events and persons. You cannot demonstrate objectively that God has "spoken," through these persons and these events; and you cannot demonstrate either that those who recorded these things or commented upon them were either faithful to "the facts" or perceptive in their interpretation. But at least you can insist that the Bible, being the only or the primary testimony to occurrences which you believe to be ultimately significant, is indispensable to your discipline. The secular thinker may reject your belief as such, but, given the nature of what you believe, he or she cannot reject the logic of your need for the Scriptures.

(b) To the charge of literalist or biblicist faith, which demands that the Bible be accepted uncritically and that theology must be nothing more nor less than the faithful exposition of the Scriptures, the first answer must be that which comes from the Bible itself, namely, that for these witnesses, the Truth is God in person, the living God, the speaking God, the *incarnate* Word, who transcends all description and expression. That the Bible too, and all who honor it, must live with this relativization of everything that claims to be absolute is, after all, one of the teachings of the Bible! It is present within the First Commandment; it is explicit in the Second and Third. It is expressed in a multitude of ways through these sacred writings.

Therefore Christians who elevate the Bible to the level of the absolute are just as guilty of idolatry as other Christians (whom the biblicists invariably berate) who absolutize holy objects, or saintly persons, or ecclesial authorities. Biblicists are perhaps even more susceptible to the charge of idolatry, because their idol, the Bible, frankly warns them against any such elevation of itself. The Newer Testament is even more adamant on this subject than is the Older. Jesus repeatedly rejects the primitive biblicism of many persons whom he encounters. He admonishes against literalism especially, for its rigid adherence to the letter precludes spiritual perceptiveness and imagination. But even more important for this subject is the fact that when the writers of the Newer Testament want to identify the ultimate, the one Word of God that (as Barmen put it) "we must obey in life and in death," they do not point to *any* words, and certainly not to their own, but to Jesus himself. According to this record, not even the words *Jesus* speaks, which these writers may or may not have transcribed accurately, can command our ultimate loyalty, but only the Word that Jesus *is*. *He* is "the Truth" (John 14:6), and the world itself could not contain the books that would have to be written to describe the Truth that he is and does (John 21:25).

19.3. The Bible and the Protestant Principle. Classical Protestantism is ill-represented on this continent today, and nowhere is this more conspicuous than in connection with our present topic. We have already noted the high esteem in which the Reformers held the Scriptures. *This* aspect of classical Protestantism has been grasped by the simplifiers, but without the other aspect—about which we have just now been thinking— the *sola Scriptura* is a hollow and a superficial dogma, which invariably ends by giving the authority, not to the Bible, but to those who make the Bible their own. (Whenever the statement "I've got it right here in the Bible" is heard, one can be absolutely certain that the real emphasis, as distinct from the rhetorical one, is on the first word of the sentence— "I've"!)

That neglected aspect of classical Protestant teaching about the Bible is the qualification of the authority of the written word that is made mandatory as soon as ultimacy is given to the *living* Word, the Word Incarnate, the Word which remains person and Spirit and cannot *be* made one's own, does not admit of possession. And that is where ultimacy is placed in classical Protestant expressions of the faith. To God *alone* belongs the glory (*Soli Deo gloria*—Calvin).

The *relativization* of the Bible that results from the Reformed teaching concerning the sole sovereignty of God and the Lutheran teaching concerning the Spirit and the Word is no small matter for Protestantism; it is really at the heart of the whole "protest." It is perhaps not surprising that only a few so-called Protestants seem to have grasped this in a profound way, for it belongs to that "religious heresy" to which we drew attention earlier that it is satisfied only with possession ("I've"!). Religion wants to have something quite concrete—something that can be *had*. Observing the way in which television evangelists hold their Bibles is very instructive in this connection (I am told that courses are offered in certain seminaries on Bible-holding!). The Bible appears a veritable extension of their persons—and that is precisely what is intended.

For perhaps the majority of those who came through the upheavals of the 16th century on the so-called Protestant side, what had happened was that an authoritarian church with concrete regulations and practices and rites was replaced by an authoritarian book which could also convey the impression of concreteness and certitude—which even had the advantage of being portable, of being subject to ownership, of adorning one's home, one's meal table, one's bedside.

In other words, a great deal of Protestantism probably never appropriated what Paul Tillich (rightly, so far as classical Protestant expressions of faith are concerned) named "the Protestant principle," the insistence that the absoluteness of God alone, when sincerely confessed and lived, absolutely precludes the attribution of ultimacy to anything else.[9] *Anything* else! This belongs to the heart and soul of the Protestant protest, for the Reformation was a revolt against all pretensions to absolute truth, and the inordinate authority claims to which such pretensions inevitably lead. It was a gospel of liberation from the oppressive authority of finite and conditioned authorities parading as infinite and unconditioned. It beckoned men and women away from these pseudo-authorities whom, to control or ameliorate, they had always to placate. It offered them an Authority who had their welfare, and not its own, at heart—but who could not be possessed or manipulated, but only . . . trusted (*sola fide!*). And it offered them a witness and guide to this living Authority—which, alas, they frequently substituted for the Authority as such.

19.4. The Bible as Primary Source for Theology: Information and Inspiration. Theology lives with and from the Bible, not as a pupil of primary school mathematics lives with a set of "correct answers" but as a storyteller lives with what seems the original and most authentic version of the story he or she is trying to tell, now, under different circumstances. For the disciple community, in other words, the Bible exists as its fundamental source of imagination and courage.

It is also of course the fount of *information*. We have already insisted upon that: it describes "original revelation," in relation to which the revealing that is the ongoing source of Christian faith and understanding is "dependent" (Tillich). But the informational function of the Scriptures, important as it may be, is secondary and subservient to its inspirational function. If only information were given, or sought, then theology could be content to be biblical exegesis pure and simple. But the Bible apparently

---

9. There are numerous references to this concept in Tillich's works. See especially *Systematic Theology*, vol. 1 and vol. 3 (1963). "Protestant theology," writes Tillich (vol. 1, p. 37) "protests in the name of the Protestant principle . . .against the identification of our ultimate concern with any creation of the church, including the biblical writings in so far as their witness to what is really ultimate is also a conditioned expression of their own spirituality."

wants to give, and is able to give, more than information—and faith certainly needs more.

What those who pursue the theological discipline attempt, therefore, is so to expose themselves to the biblical witness and story that what is present in it, or rather what through the testimony of the divine Spirit can be evoked from it, can illumine the life of the disciple community in the world here and now.

To do this, theology must attempt to be faithful to what is really present in the biblical writings, and therefore systematic theology, without being slavishly dependent upon it, must nevertheless be in serious and continuous dialogue with biblical scholarship. But theology must also be in touch with life in the here and now, and so the questions and concerns which it brings to the Scriptures are not identical with those of the exegetes. What theology needs from its ongoing discourse with the biblical text is determined in large measure by its worldly context. It seeks from the scriptural testimony the inspiration and the courage to address its world from the perspective of faith in the God of Abraham, Isaac, and Jacob, the God whom Jesus addressed as "Abba." It would be difficult, given such a need, to improve upon the *bon mot* of Karl Barth, applying it not only to preaching, as he did, but to the whole task of theology: the theologian must have the Bible in one hand and the newspaper in the other.

20. Theology and Doctrinal Traditions

20.1. The Dynamic Character of Tradition. A third basic element in the discipline of Christian theology is tradition. It would be better to say tradition*s*, because, as we have already had occasion to notice, the past articulations of Christian belief with which the disciple community lives are not sufficiently unified or congruent to constitute a single entity. There is in fact great variety in the doctrinal self-expressions of the church's past, just as there is variety in its present.

Moreover, far from being a fixed or static thing, the debates and councils and decisions and counterdecisions which constitute this vast theological heritage continue to engage one another in the ongoing dialogue of the church. Of course, I do not mean that documents like the formula of Chalcedon or historically important works like the *Sentences* of Peter Lombard are themselves altered. Nevertheless, the church's assessment of such products of the past struggles of Christians to understand what they believed is in a constant state of flux, so that sometimes quite radical alterations in the significance of traditions for faith and theology can be noticed by the student of church history. A particular tradition which may have been important for one age is replaced, in the next epoch, by a different—not infrequently by a radically different—tradition. A Christian thinker taken up by this era and made, as one may say, almost the patron saint of the theologians, is dropped by the next. An obscure scholar of the distant past suddenly becomes particularly authoritative for the present disciple community, or some segment thereof.

Dramatic shifts in the evaluation and meaning of doctrinal traditions occur, especially, in periods of radical transition in church and society.[10] Indeed, part of what is meant by a term like "radical transition" is precisely this diversification in the search for authorities within the abundant traditions of the faith. At the time of the Reformation, for example, there was a sudden resurgence of interest in Augustine, who, during the High Middle Ages, had been caused to retire into the background on account of the high scholastic preference for Aristotelian categories rather than the Platonic views of the Bishop of Hippo.

We have acknowledged in Part I that our own age is also an age of radical transition. It is not surprising, therefore, that this dynamic character of the role of tradition in theology is again conspicuous. Charismatics have found new meaning in ancient movements like Montanism and the spiritualistic "sects" of the 16th century—movements generally rejected heretofore. Liberationists are critical of the substitutionary atonement theology which has dominated Western Christendom and turn to accounts of the work of Christ which accentuate his victory over oppressive powers. Political theology manifests a special interest in minority movements of the past which were denounced more on account of their radical views about the nature of human community than their theologies: the so-called left wing of the Reformation is approached in most progressive seminaries and graduate schools of theology today in a way completely different

---

10. James Gustafson writes that "theologians tend to hold the tradition and what is received with a greater degree of reverence and respect than do scientific investigators. . . ." Nevertheless, the history of theology is marked by "radical changes" in the reception of biblical and postbiblical traditions. "Abandoning and discarding are part of theological development. . . . Selection of what is to be retrieved or sustained is relative to knowledge and understanding present in the culture that pertains to matters of concern to theology." Such development can be seen both in great issues of belief, such as the readiness of the reformers to "discard a great deal of the philosophical apparatus of the tradition they inherited" and in more explicit issues such as ethical teachings of the church (Gustafson cites homosexuality, "long judged to be a moral sin against nature," but "now interpreted by some Roman Catholic moral theologians as an excusable act in those instances in which the agent cannot be held accountable for the conditions which disposed him or her to act in this way" (*Ethics from A Theocentric Perspective* [Chicago: University of Chicago Press, 1981], pp. 140f.).

from the largely unsympathic treatment that it received in such institutions three decades ago. All who are conscious of the end of the Constantinian era have a newly emergent concern for *pre*-Constantinian forms of the church, and look upon post-Constantinian developments in theology differently because of their awareness of the consequences for doctrine of the sociopolitical status of the church in the situation of establishment. Perhaps most conspicuously of all, especially in the North American context, feminists have returned to the history of the church and its doctrinal traditions with a whole new perspective on what was transpiring in that long past. They pose for the disciple community at large awkward and provocative, but very basic questions about the influences of sexism and patriarchy upon the *thought* of the church as well as its deeds. And they discover "new" authorities, many of them women (e.g., Julian of Norwich, Hildegard of Bingen), who were obscured or purposely ignored because of the masculine domination of the tradition.

All of this demonstrates the flexible and lively nature of the role of tradition in theological work.[11] It tells us, besides, something about the reason for this dynamism. Theology always requires a past—roots! A Christian theology lacking any past would be an anomaly. For Christianity is, as we have already noted, a historical faith, and no theologian of this faith, even the most charismatic, can be content to spin theology out of his or her own entelechy. At the same time, theology that is sensitive to its context cannot be satisfied with any and every past articulation of belief. It will not simply accept what is "there," i.e., the particular tradition(s) which ecclesial convention has for the time being baptized. It needs a past which can be truly foundational for what it feels must be said and done here and now. This need is built into the theological discipline as such, it is not imported to it by restless persons who are not content with the *assumed* traditions. The rejection of regnant traditions and the search for new ones has been a feature of Christian theology throughout the ages. What is happening all around us today in this regard is simply a heightened application of a very ancient (and honorable) practice of this discipline—the quest for relevant and supportive traditions.[12]

---

11. In the conclusion of his insightful book on the subject of tradition, Brian Gerrish writes: "What the theologian receives from the past as 'tradition' is not a fixed, external authority, but the constantly changing expression of the church's interior life. In other words, tradition . . . , while no substitute for thought, is the occasion for thought; and precisely because it is something mobile, it requires to be transmitted, not passively or mechanically, but by a conscious, creative act" (*Tradition and the Modern World: Reformed Theology in the Nineteenth Century* [Chicago and London: University of Chicago Press, 1978], p. 181).

12. See Farley, *Ecclesial Man*, p. 232.

20.2. Contra Modernism *and* Traditionalism. The word *tradition* comes from the Latin *tradere*, "to hand over," "to deliver." We have noted that the Christian faith is a historical faith. It is this, not only in the sense that its origins are inextricably bound up with historical events, moments of high revelatory significance (*kairoi*), as we saw in our reflections on the Bible; it is also historical in the sense that we receive from the past generations of Christians certain interpretations, concepts, dogmas, formulas, and the like, with which we must somehow come to terms.[13] We cannot take lightly these counsels that are delivered to us from our forebears. For one thing, whether we like it or not, we are ourselves always in some measure products of these traditions. There is no Christian alive, regardless of her or his specific intellectual background or ecclesial allegiance, whose belief has not been influenced by thousands of Christian thinkers of the past. Even persons who imagine that they can go straight from the present to the Scriptures (of whom there are a great many in North America) bring to their reading of the Scriptures countless presuppositions that they have gleaned, consciously or unconsciously, from the centuries of evolving Christian tradition.

We have spoken in an introductory way about the dynamic character of the role of tradition in theology, but we are left with a number of questions: How ought theology to be informed by tradition? What responsibility does the disciple community have towards what is "handed over" by previous generations of Christians, including aspects of the tradition which it cannot or will not itself appropriate? What *attitude* towards tradition should the theological community adopt?

As was the case in our discussion of the two previous elements (faith and Scriptures), so with tradition it may be that the most instructive method of responding to such questions would be to formulate our answer over against two alternatives which present themselves to us in our North

---

13. In this sense, George Lindbeck is right when he castigates the condescending attitude towards tradition on the part of many Protestants and Catholics who view Christian faith in what he names the "experiential-expressive" manner: "The very words 'doctrine' and 'dogma' have the smell of the ghetto about them, and to take them seriously is, it seems, to cut oneself off from the larger world. One way to escape from this dilemma is to argue that the (from the modern perspective) absurd doctrines of the past never were important in themselves, but were only expressive symbolizations of deeper experiences and orientations that ought now to be articulated in other and more contemporary ways" (*The Nature of Doctrine* [Philadelphia: Westminster, 1984], p. 77). (I feel constrained to demur, however, when Prof. Lindbeck proposes that my colleague, Gregory Baum, is "a Roman Catholic example" of this approach (ibid., p. 89). Prof. Baum lives with the tradition in an earnest and responsible way, and while he shares with most of us the conviction that the past must not be allowed to dominate the church or determine its manner of confessing the faith, he is a very long way from the kind of "religious privatism and subjectivism" that Lindbeck [rightly] laments.)

American religious context—what we may name (without being too committed to the nomenclature as such) modernism/individualism and traditionalism.

(a) Modernism or, as one might say more accurately, the modernistic dimension within most forms of theological liberalism, seeks to minimize—and, in extreme expressions, to eliminate—the regulative role of tradition in theology. In the name of what is—or seems—relevant to the present, the modernist spirit feels quite free to dispense with whatever it receives from the past that does not relate in any obvious way to present spiritual needs. This approach generally assumes that *most* of what has been handed over from the long Christian past is in fact irrelevant to the present, and that much of it constitutes a downright impediment to the Christian apologetic.

It is, in other words, the present situation with its most conspicuous ("felt") needs that constitutes for the modernist the touchstone of authenticity. But this concern, laudable in itself, can be problematic—to the point of a betrayal of itself—when it is not accompanied by a perspective that is gained from a dynamic relation to the past. The case of early 20th-century modernism exemplifies the point:

A time came when modernist forms of Christian liberalism, having so thoroughly identified themselves with the modern project, had nothing to say to the society that had bought into that project. With the year 1914 and following, the present to which modernism attached so much importance began to cast up questions and experiences which the architects of modernity had assumed no longer belonged to advancing history. Like its secular counterparts, religious modernism was so certain that the world was progressing towards the realization of the good that it could only be chagrined and embarrassed by the "primitive" and "medieval" associations of historic Christianity. In the name of adapting the Christian message to the times, the modernists discarded whole segments of tradition which did not, in their estimation, measure up to the enlightened standards of the new era. But in the end many who were influenced by this trend realized that they had thrown out the baby with the bathwater. For when the world began to show signs of growing darker instead of lighter, there were no categories left in the modernist vocabulary to name such phenomena as were once designated sin and the demonic and spiritual death and transcendent evil, etc. To comprehend their world, the successors of modernism had to return to earlier, "orthodox" language (hence "neoorthodoxy"[14]), and to take up traditions which the generations of their teachers had consigned to the dark ages.[15]

The modernist mentality has nevertheless persisted in North America, despite the fact that many or even most of those who have been exposed to the formal study of theology in the past half-century have learned from their teachers to distrust it. For modernism on this continent has been able to depend upon a powerful ally not found to the same extent in the European situation—individualism. The truth is, tradition has never appealed to the North American spirit, especially to the middle classes, even though (as we shall see in a moment) this same phenomenon begets a traditionalistic reaction. As Bellah and his associates report in *Habits of the Heart*,[16] "the very freedom, openness, and pluralism of American religious life makes [the traditional pattern of Jewish and Christian religion] hard for Americans to understand. For one thing, the traditional pattern assumes a certain priority of the religious community over the individual." What comes naturally to most North Americans who have "found themselves" associates of the more established denominations of Christendom is not adherence to inherited dogma and ritual, but a sense of the rectitude of self-determination in matters of belief. Before the tribunal of the self, the most sacred and time-honored teachings of religious communities are nothing but matters of taste and opinion. Every young clergyperson, straight from seminary classrooms where he or she has been inspired by some fresh introduction to the beauties of some great tradition, knows how powerless such messages are in the face of the omniscient souls of self-directed parishioners. Moreover, the same spirit frequently invades the theological communities themselves, which on this

---

14. It has largely been forgotten by history that Karl Barth and others were *embarrassed* by their association with "orthodoxy," and that (therefore) the term "neoorthodox" is hardly one that accurately describes what they felt they were doing. To Eduard Thurneysen on February 1, 1924, the young Barth writes: "To me the shadow of orthodoxy in which we necessarily stand for the moment presents the most painful problem of the situation. I was overjoyed in Bern at the citation of Overbeck which I had introduced at one point and which saved me from an all too unconditional approval by Hadorn. Also Hormann had to concede that 'our' position is not simply a return to 'conscience-enslaving' orthodoxy. In this connection the liberal resistance concerns me far less than the fact that one necessarily finds himself in a certain remoteness in relation to the humanists and the socialists, i.e. in relation to the ethical problem that is certainly pressing enough" (*Revolutionary Theology in the Making: Barth-Thurneysen Correspondence 1914–1925*, trans. James D. Smart [Richmond: John Knox, 1964], p. 165).

15. This happened in Europe long before it happened on this continent—for reasons we have already discussed. It is said that when the European student of theology, Dietrich Bonhoeffer, as a graduate student in Union Theological Seminary, New York, in the early 1930s invoked the names of Luther and Calvin, his classmates were astonished that he would turn to such outmoded authorities.

16. Robert Bellah et al., *Habits of the Heart* (Berkeley, Calif.: University of California Press, 1985), pp. 227f.

continent easily move from one consuming cause to another. Nothing is immune to the winnowing of individual preference—a preference containing, of course, a generous portion of peer and group pressure, and therefore readily giving way to faddism. "God himself becomes a discardable item, as for some 'death of God' theologians of the 1960s, even among those who continue to think of themselves as Christians." [17]

(b) Traditionalism: There is an opposite response to tradition that is equally questionable. I am referring to the tendency to conceive of the real task of theology as preserving intact, without blemish from the side of the world, the corpus of Christian teaching handed over by the past. In practice, of course, this always means the preservation of *some particular doctrinal tradition*, although the selectivity (not to say arbitrariness) involved in this procedure is seldom acknowledged by those who engage in it.

Modernism at least concerned itself with the present and future, and from the standpoint of a theology committed to contextuality this must be judged commendable. Its weakness was that it misconstrued appropriateness to the present, identifying pertinence with acceptability. Contextual theology does not seek to be acceptable; its goal is to be appropriate. Appropriateness may well mean confrontation and opposition to the major trends of its social context, and support for this opposition may well come from the tradition. But the contextualist regards the tradition as a resource for addressing the present, not as an end in itself. Traditionalism, on the contrary, is not primarily interested in speaking to the realities of its present historical moment; rather, it aims to preserve ideas and practices whose definitive articulations were given in the past. It would not be accurate to say that traditionalism is *dis*interested in the present—this is to caricature the traditionalist; but its primary intention is to cause persons and institutions in the present to accept as true the traditions to which it has given its loyalty. It will certainly be ready to *interpret* these traditions, and many of those whom I would include in this category are willing to devote great energy to the task of demonstrating the applicability of their traditions to the present. But traditionalism rejects (what is essential to contextuality in theology) the notion that the context provides the mold—"the question" (Tillich)—which theology must allow to shape its articulation of the faith. For the traditionalist, where a *consistent* traditionalism can be assumed, both the form and the content of Christian teaching are provided by the tradition. [18]

---

17. Lindbeck, *The Nature of Doctrine*, p. 77.

18. In his article, "Answering Pilate: Truth and the Postliberal Church" (*The Christian Century*,

What is really happening in traditionalism is the same thing that happens with biblicism, only now the subject matter is not the Bible but some fondly held doctrinal orthodoxy. What is not recognized or taken seriously in this way of responding to the tradition is that the traditions which are thus fondled and preserved are themselves *historical* expressions, ergo *contextual* expressions, of Christian belief—ideas and systems thoroughly influenced by the particularities of their times and places. So that what is frequently transpiring in this type of attitude towards tradition (as in biblicism) is that the worldview of another epoch, or another clime, is being substituted for original reflection upon the present context. Such usage is almost by definition repressive. It functions, that is to say, as an ideational *alternative* to the actual present, a sanctuary from the always unknown land that is Now and Here.

It is enormously tempting for *all* religion to perform in this way, because it is far more comfortable to live with the questions of the past, and the Christian responses to them, than to be open to the unresolved, and even unknown, or only half-understood anxieties of the present. Much of the renewed interest that can be found today in past expressions of Christian belief comes from this (entirely understandable) need to escape from a particularly anomalous and agonizing present. It is the religious equivalent of the current vogue in Victorian antiquity. On the one hand the problematique of the age *drives* faith to search for a "usable past"; on the other, the same problematique *tempts* faith to take refuge in the past. It is always in practice difficult to distinguish the one motive from the other.

20.3. Developing a Dialectic of Dependence and Independence. These reflections on two questionable attitudes towards tradition help us to formulate a positive response concerning the relation between theology and doctrinal traditions. Over against the impulse to free ourselves from the past, it must be said that the discipline to which Christ's disciples are

---

January 28, 1987, pp. 82ff.), William H. Willimon accuses Paul Tillich of "setting the agenda" for subsequent theologians by being too concerned about the "cultured despisers" of his day. This is a superficial—if common—accusation. As an apologist, in the long line of Christian apologists, Tillich naturally wished to be in dialogue with his epoch, and especially with those whom he regarded as its primary representatives and spokespersons. But the same Tillich, who sought ongoing converse with the present ("the situation"), maintained throughout his lifetime an active dialogue with the Christian theological tradition—in fact, during most of his years at Union Theological Seminary he taught the history of Christian thought as well as systematic theology. Possibly more than any other teacher of theology on this continent, this man, trained in the rigorous scholastic traditions of pre-World War I Germany, valued *the whole* (Catholic and Protestant) past of the church, and taught his students to develop a sympathetic and listening attitude towards even those aspects of the tradition with which neither he nor they could immediately identify.

called necessitates a greater attentiveness to the past—indeed, a new alertness to the past as a whole, since it is for faith the unfolding story of God's good creation, but a concentrated and cultivated awareness of the Christian theological past in particular, since it is faith's mode of communication with the faithful of the ages. The community of faith needs this past, and it belongs to the gift of grace that the disciple community is given access to it. Because it has such access by grace, as *God's* gift, it is less tempted to regard the past as an oppressive authority to which it must do obeisance. Only God, the giver of the gift, is ultimately authoritative; therefore God's gift of a tradition can be received in a spirit of gratitude, as a support and a source of courage.

At the same time, this gift of tradition has a humbling effect on those who receive it. It causes them to realize that they stand along the moving edge of a lengthy process. They did not invent the gospel. They have come upon the scene, late in time. Today as we approach the year 2000 we think of two millennia of *Christian* tradition, not to mention the even longer Judaic past into which we have been "grafted" (Rom. 11:17f.). We are inheritors of a precious depository of thought. We do not begin de novo. It would be nothing short of crass arrogance and ignorance for us to imagine that we had nothing to learn from this treasury of meditation. If we are wise enough and humble enough, we shall realize our dependence upon this foundation. There is hardly an idea in our minds which does not have a hoary history! To acknowledge this, to admit our dependence, is not a mark of weakness but of maturity. The need to flee from the past belongs to adolescence. Perhaps it is a necessary stage, also within the disciple community. But as a permanent response to the past it is just as immature as adolescent rebellion carried into adulthood.

On the other hand, there is an equally immature type of dependence upon the past. Against the traditionalist impulse which is found, in some measure, in nearly everyone, it must be said that the process depicted within the Christian tradition itself, rightly understood, is an unfinished one. To fix the end, or the apogee, of this process at any point in the past is not only questionable ontology and eschatology (and an affront to the Holy Spirit!); it is also a failure to notice the most obvious thing about that past, namely, that *each generation has to do it all again, has to think the faith all over again.* Faith itself cannot be transferred from one generation to another, nor does time stand still. Therefore each new cohort of the disciple community has once more to expose itself to the basics, to think the faith for itself, under the conditions of its total environment. As we put it earlier, humanity's story of itself is never quite the same today as it was yesterday; those therefore who intend to bear witness to God's story of humanity must submit to a discipline which demands of them the most *original* thought, no matter how ancient the antecedents of this thought.

To be dependent upon the past after the manner of doctrinal traditionalism is to confuse profession with confession, preservation with conservation, doctrine with theology. On the other hand, to boast of independence from the past is to equate the liberty of the Spirit with arbitrariness. Between these two attitudes lies a third, which knows how to be grateful for and responsible towards the authority of the tradition without using it as a refuge from intellectual and spiritual struggle. Anyone who has subjected herself or himself to the task of seeking to know, deeply, any of the great thinkers of the Christian past will realize how inconceivable it is for her or his generation to dispense with such testimony. But neither Augustine nor Aquinas, Calvin nor Luther, Barth nor Niebuhr can tell us what we have to understand, as Christians today, as we face nuclear war and continental famine and racial strife and sexual tensions whose precise character none of these persons could have anticipated. From them, as from the Scriptures, we can receive inspiration and courage without which our own thought is impoverished, trivial, and literally impossible. But in the end it is we ourselves who must do theology.

21. Theology and Experience

21.1. The Liberal Background of the Category. Experience can be considered the polar category in relation to tradition. If tradition refers to that which is "handed over" to us, then experience indicates that which we did not receive from others but were ourselves granted in a firsthand way.

By *experience* in this context I am not thinking of explicitly religious experience (about which something will be said later), but of human experience in general, in all of its variety, inclusive of nonrational as well as rational dimensions. Such a category has to be included among the elemental ingredients of the theological discipline, not only because it is obviously present whether it is or is not acknowledged,[19] but expressly

---

19. "Human experience is prior to reflection. We reflect on human experience itself, and on objects perceived, interpreted, and known through our experiences of them and through the experiences of others. Religion and morality are aspects of human experience; theology and ethics are not only articulations of ideas in relation to the ideas others have expressed but are ideas about aspects of experience. . . . If there is knowledge of God it is human knowledge of God; it is knowledge of God mediated through experiences, either of one's own, or a community in which one participates, or of another person (and particularly those 'paradigmatic' persons whose experiences and teaching is deemed to give authentic knowledge of God" (James Gustafson, *Ethics from a Theocentric Perspective*, p. 115. See also pp. 134, 153-154, 158-159, 165, 176-177, 190, 236-237, 277).

because one of the prominent *traditions* by which Christians in North America are most immediately influenced made experience *the fundamental ingredient* in theological reflection.

While the experiential component has been powerfully present in almost all expressions of Christian faith among us, it has been particularly prevalent in the various forms of religious liberalism. In fact, what unites these often diverse manifestations of the liberal Christian spirit and method is their common assumption that religious faith, whatever its extraneous sources, must relate in a positive manner to human experience. Since human experience is both a very broad category and one which lends itself to an indefinite variety of descriptions and classifications, it is not surprising that a theological posture which makes such an assumption should give rise to numerous and often incompatible forms of Christian belief and community. Thus some strands of liberalism have been able to retain almost all of the central emphases of Christian orthodoxy, though cast in another mode on account of their need to correspond with the common experience of those concerned, while other strands have found it necessary to dispense with nearly every conventional dogma (modernism). And, of course, a whole spectrum of possibilities exists between the two extremes.

That human experience should have come to play such a significant role in faith and theology is a matter not readily understood apart from a prolonged and serious study of Western civilization from the Reformation onwards, with special reference to the 18th and 19th centuries. Obviously we cannot undertake such an investigation here. Two general observations can, however, be introduced by way of background:

(a) The breakdown of external authority and the emergence of the individual: With the demise of the medieval vision, European Christianity lost not only a more or less consistent and authoritative image of the divine but (what may be more consequential) a constant and preeminent image of the human. The piety of the Middle Ages did not occupy itself greatly with the question of basic human identity and destiny. Indeed, the so-called doctrine of man is a latecomer in the family of theological classifications; and the reason is that the character and destiny of the human creature could be accepted, prior to the modern epoch, as a given of Christian teaching, inseparable from the major doctrines of creation, redemption, and sanctification. Even the reformers, who modified, certainly, many of the anthropological presuppositions of Christianity, continued to assume that what humanity *is* and what it *should be* are aspects of revelation, corresponding at least with a rationality which has been

illumined by faith. For them, as for their medieval precursors, there are predictable patterns, types and "laws" of human behavior. These can be discussed under the rubrics of creation, fall, and redemption, and all human beings, regardless of their particular histories, are accounted for in these rudimentary categorizations. Experience *is* assumed as a necessary correlate of grace: grace must be received, the human spirit must be addressed by the divine Spirit, externalities and ritual observances are not enough. The centrality of *faith* in Reformation teaching makes it evident that personal religious experience is vital to the Christian life. But it is equally evident that human experience as *we* automatically think of it—the experience of individuals in all of their uniqueness—is not, for the reformers, an element in the sorting and discernment of theological authenticity. It cannot be, because for them the nature of humanity is a correlate of revelation, joined to the primary data of belief. To be sure, the reformers define this primary data on the grounds of biblical rather than ecclesiastical authority, and this introduces a dimension of individuality which eventually contributes to the transfer of significant authority to experience; but neither Luther nor Calvin seem prepared to entertain personal experience as normative for theology, and in fact the notion is not congruous with the milieu in which they moved. Experience as an independent element in theological reflection can only emerge in a society which has seen the displacement or qualification of external authority by a more autonomous conception of reality and truth. So long as there is a general willingness to assume that what is fundamental to the human condition, variations notwithstanding, is what is described in ecclesiastical dogma or the sacred text, experience cannot play an independent and regulative role in theological thought, for its essential form is predetermined by the same gospel that persons are asked to believe.

While the mainstream of the Reformation did not introduce experience, in a direct way, as a detached component in theological reflection, and while its critique of human rationality even had the effect of contributing additional reasons to *distrust* experience (as Karl Barth never failed to insist), its transfer of authority to the Scriptures meant that a door was opened to personal reception and interpretation of the primary data of belief; and this door soon became a very wide access to a new religious situation. The established or classical anthropology of the medieval Western world gave way to a variety of views concerning the human being's essential character and possibilities. The universalistic approach to the understanding of the human condition was replaced by a more empirically based mode of conceptualization. This was bound up with the transition from Platonic and Aristotelian to a nominalistic orientation towards reality—the new significance of the particular. But it also implied the growing recognition of the variety of experience on account of geographic, economic (class), and other factors, which, when taken seriously, militate against monolithic descriptions of the human condition and introduce the experiential element as a distinctive ingredient in all thought, including theological thought. After the advent of an historical-inductive approach to reality, it is simply not possible for theology or any other science to *deduce* its anthropology from an a priori metaphysic or ontology. Christian theology cannot avoid the positing of *preconceptions* concerning human nature and destiny, nor should it. But neither can it any longer assume that its anthropological preconceptions will, or should, go unchallenged by concrete data emanating from actual human experience of every sort. If it does not permit this data to enter into its discourse, and as a vital component of the discipline, theology will soon devolve into a type of doctrinal isolationism which, to maintain itself, must present and defend a system of meaning which claims to be self-authenticating at the anthropological as well as the theological level. And this of course is precisely what happened to modern theologies which resisted the "incursion" of human experience into the realm of theology and faith.

(b) The truncation of rationality and faith's appeal to "the heart": A second reason for the emergence of experience as a distinctive theological category has to do with the fate of reason in the modern Western world. This will become a more explicit concern in our later discussion of revelation and reason, but aspects of that discussion must be anticipated at this point in order to explain why experience, for better or worse, entered the theological vocabulary in the modern epoch—and prominently so within the North American context.

Reason belonged to that vocabulary, of course, almost from the outset. Already in the Newer Testament it is assumed that faith has some kind of discourse with human rationality. The term *logos* incorporates this assumption, and in Paul's address to the philosophically minded on Mars Hill (Acts 17) we have what appears to be a highly positive sense of correlation between reason and faith. This positive assessment of the relation does not go unchallenged by the New Testament itself (e.g., 1 Corinthians 1–2) or by the church fathers (e.g., Tertullian); but it is a prominent assumption of the second-century Apologists, and of Augustine, who in this respect remained consistent throughout his life, positing what has been described as "a concordat between faith and reason."[20] Indeed, a largely Augustinian conception of the role of reason in faith and theology dominates the scene until the High Middle Ages, when Albertus Magnus and his more famous pupil, Thomas Aquinas, reinterpret the faith using Aristotelian categories instead of the Platonic and Neoplatonic ones which had been baptized by Augustine.

It would be possible to say that the beginning of an independent experiential component in theological reflection dates from this introduction of Aristotelianism; for, unlike the Platonic-Augustinian synthesis, where rationality and belief are so continuous that it is virtually impossible to tell where one leaves off and the other begins, the Thomistic synthesis of reason and faith gives human rationality a distinctive, autonomous role in theology: beginning with the evidence of the senses (*principium cognoscendi est a sensu*), "unaided" reason derives theologically significant data which support the truth that has been revealed. Already with Thomism, then, the human being brings something to theological work besides the drive to understand (Anselm).

But with Thomas we are still limited to *rational* experience, and, moreover, to a rationality which is universally applicable. Something has to occur before experience can connote what it does connote for us—i.e., the extrarational and the personal. This development began to appear in Western experience very soon after Thomas. With the advent of nominalism in Duns Scotus and Ockham we have the first stage of the process: rationality has to do with particulars, not universals. Universals are only classifications (*nomen*) that we assign to particulars which have common characteristics. As for what can be known directly by human reason, it is limited to particular things.

This approach to reality marks, to be sure, a rather dramatic movement towards empirical thought which is important for the development of the category of experience in theology. But the more significant dimension of what is occurring here, so far as our present theme is concerned, is the narrowing-down of rationality. Without access to universals, reason is rendered inadequate for theological knowledge. The earlier nominalists, still being staunch believers (both Duns Scotus and Ockham were Franciscans), turned to religious *authority* for their theological sources—in Ockham's case particularly, to Scripture. The process which they introduced, however, could not guarantee that reason and faith would continue to live side by side; and in fact with the Renaissance and Reformation

---

20. David Roberts, in *A Companion to the Study of St. Augustine*, ed. Roy W. Battenhouse (New York: Oxford University Press, 1955), p. 97.

their divorce becomes visible, until, in the 18th century we have the emergence of a form of human rationality which is, or claims to be, sufficient unto itself. It does not need revelation, faith, or the God "hypothesis" (Voltaire).

What seemed to the Enlightenment a grand liberation and expansion of rationality and the life of the mind, by the end of the 18th century appeared to many sensitive thinkers and artists an unwarranted absolutizing of the intellect, reducing essential humanity to sheer mind. The Romantic rebellion against a confining and potentially oppressive rationality is the seedbed of the liberal Christian exposition of *experience* as a theological category. If Friedrich Schleiermacher can rightly be designated the father of liberalism, it is because it was he who first articulated— over against religion's "cultured despisers"—a faith which gave extra-rational experience a key position in religious knowledge. The point of departure for faith, he insisted, is neither reason, narrowly conceived, nor authority, but experience—specifically the feeling (*Gefühl*) of contingency, or "absolute dependency."[21]

Schleiermacher used the term *Gefühl* in order to designate that whole area of mystery in the human spirit which is not *non*rational but, given the reduction of reason to empiricism, must be regarded as suprarational. With the victory of empiricism and pragmatism in the age of science, the suprarational became increasingly significant for religion. While faith could not be justified on purely reasonable grounds, it could be explained as a consequence of a larger-than-rational experience; and this is in fact how the majority of "mainstream" Christians on this continent have been taught to regard their faith. What we bring to reflection upon matters of faith, therefore, is not disciplined rational thought, but broad experientially based intuition or "feeling"—to the point, sometimes, that disciplined thought is suspect among us, and "theology" itself is disavowed in favor of a more affective approach to religious belief.

Given both of these factors in our history—and both the emergence of the individual and the association of faith with suprarational feeling are very much part of *our* history—it is obvious that we must regard experience as an important ingredient in theology; but it is equally obvious that it is a problematic ingredient *for theology*, for there is that within

---

21. "The common element in all howsoever diverse expressions of piety by which these are conjointly distinguished from all other feelings, or, in other words, the self-identical essence of piety, is this: the consciousness of being absolutely dependent, or, which is the same thing, of being in relation with God" (Friedrich Schleiermacher, *The Christian Faith*, ed. H. R. MacKintosh and J. S. Stewart [Edinburgh: T. & T. Clark, 1928], Proposition 4, chapter 1, p. 12).

the category, understood in its historical setting, which is suspicious of theology and of which responsible theology must in turn *be* suspicious. How can we regard this category, then, in such a way as to retain its justifiable protest against the truncation of rationality and to avoid, at the same time, its proclivity to personalism and the elevation of the irrational and the purely emotive?

21.2. A Critique of Experience.   As with our discussion of the three previous elements of theology, we shall develop our understanding of the role of experience in theology in juxtaposition with two alternative positions, both of them present in our sociohistorical context.

(a) Experience as touchstone of truth: The first is a highly positive assessment of experience, coming from the history that we have just now traced in outline. Inheritors of liberal theological influences in our midst tend to make experience the touchstone of theological truth. What corresponds with human experience is acceptable, what does not should be discarded as irrelevant. If, for example, it can be shown that there is that in our experience which corresponds to the traditional conception of the deity in triune terms, then it is permissible to retain, in some form (probably in an "economic" form)[22] the doctrine of the Trinity. Or if the concept of "sin" can be spelled out in ways which correlate with our experience of life, then it is meaningful to employ this concept still. But where no fairly clear correspondence can be found between what human beings generally go through in the course of their lives and what has been passed on to us as dogma, then it is the latter that must give way. Either it should be adjusted to experience (e.g., through demythologization or psychological interpretation, etc.) or dispensed with.

The doctrine of atonement is a special test case here, as might be expected, given the existential character of this doctrinal area. Liberalism as a whole discarded the powerful and established substitutionary-sacrificial atonement theology classically developed by Anselm and refined, for Protestant sensibilities, by Calvin. Liberalism did not find the necessary correlate in human experience for a theory which made it necessary for God to abandon and deliver to death the innocent Christ. The liberals read the human condition in a less drastic manner: humanity was not so much guilty as it was ignorant—specifically, ignorant of the extent of the divine mercy, and therefore *morally* ignorant. Liberal theologians and preachers learned, consequently—with some help from Abelard and others—to depict the death of Christ as a demonstration of the immense love

---

22. I.e., what has been termed "the Trinity of experience" in contradistinction from the "immanent trinity."

of God, a God who would "lay down his life for his friends" (John 15:13). And while it is virtually impossible to eliminate all references to the thousand-year-old tradition of Anselmic soteriology (in hymns, prayers, and folk wisdom), it is obvious that the atonement theology which dominates mainline Protestantism (as distinct from Fundamentalism and self-styled Evangelicalism) on this continent is still some variation on the theme of the "moral influence theory."

Another and somewhat different indicator of the prevalence of an experientially orientated faith in North American Protestantism is the predominance of "topical" preaching in our churches. Topical preaching addresses itself to topics (issues, concerns, attitudes, and so on). drawn from personal or societal experience. The whole approach to homiletics is antithetical to classical homiletical traditions (still practiced in the more liturgical churches, though more in name than in actuality). The sermon in classical Protestant homiletics, in particular, is "address" (*sermo*) from the perspective of the Scriptures.[23] It is understood to mean proclamation of the Word, and therefore it is normally heavily informed by the exegesis or exposition of the Bible. This pattern still informs most of European Protestantism, even where it has been influenced by liberalism. In contrast, North American preaching within the mainline Protestant milieu begins, characteristically, with what can be regarded as common experience, and conveys whatever scriptural or doctrinal points it intends to make by building upon that experience. It is interesting to note that whereas North American *theology* has been beholden to European patterns, as we have pointed out, *preaching* on this continent has been very much attuned to our own situation, popularly understood. Indeed, there is that in the convention of topical preaching (to admit the *beneficial* side of it) which contains a certain predisposition towards contextuality. But two things have prevented this church practice from becoming a genuinely contextual approach to faith and theology. One is the personalism of so much of our preaching; the other is the failure to develop a serious biblical and theological scholarship which could *engage* the "topics" under discussion, and not simply provide a pious backdrop for popular themes.

This latter observation already indicates the greatest weakness of the liberal use of experience. When experience becomes the primary canon of authenticity in theology, the disciple community is robbed of a vantage point from which to reflect critically upon . . . *experience*. What happens

---

23. The best—in many ways exceptional—exposition of the sermon along these lines is nevertheless by an American theologian-preacher, Paul E. Scherer; see especially *The Word God Sent* (New York: Harper & Row, 1965).

in practice is that "experience" is stereotyped, i.e., the term comes to stand for this or that construct, derived from the experiences of this or that class, age group, gender, race, etc. The construct is elevated to the level of a universal or common denominator, norms are derived from it, and it becomes *the* decisive criterion of authenticity. Those belonging to the group within which this occurs (e.g., white Anglo-Saxon Protestants) can of course accept with alacrity such a gratuitous apotheosis of their own values. If it also happens that the group in question is dominant in the society at large, it can even impose its experiential norms on many whose experiences are significantly different. But the consciousness of difference will immediately weaken the hold of this particular experiential construct, and of the mores that it enshrines, upon the broader society.

This is precisely what has occurred in our time. With the emergence of a pluralistic cultural and religious situation, the liberalism that was formerly identified with mainstream North American culture has had to face the fact that when experience is made the touchstone of religious truth it is a criterion inaccessible to, and exclusive of, many whose experiences are vastly different from the "normal" life of white, middle-class, cultural-Protestant males, living under what can be regarded as progressive conditions in an affluent society.

I should of course want to argue that it has been very beneficial for bourgeois liberalism to make this discovery, and if the experiential basis has contributed to this eventuality, then that alone has justified it! At the same time, it is obvious that when experience is made the ultimate court of appeal for "sound teaching" (Herzog) the disciple community finds itself in a situation where no clear note can be sounded as gospel and no real communality of faith is possible.

(b) The rejection of experience: It was just the recognition of this impossibility, dramatized by the events surrounding World War I, that brought into being another, antithetical attitude towards experience which, in albeit minority situations or distorted applications, has influenced our immediate context. Neoorthodoxy carried with it a new distrust of experience which it could relate to the historic distrust of rationality informing Christian history from Paul to Tertullian to Luther and Kierkegaard. What lies behind the neoorthodox return to something vaguely reminiscent of old forms of orthodoxy[24] is in fact not so much a matter of theological content as it is of theological method: serious attention must be paid to what is *given*—given by revelation, given by the Spirit, given

---

24. But see note 14, above.

by Scripture and the proclaimed Word. Theology must not be allowed to become a mere religious variation on the everyday pursuits and values of a people, class, or gender raised to the level of universal experience.

There were very good historic reasons why such an uncompromising theology of revelation had to occur at that time. It was in its way a highly responsible type of *contextual* theology. In a context which had identified God with the supposedly high achievements of Western civilization, it was necessary for someone to say very explicitly and loudly (as Karl Barth did), "God's ways are not our ways, nor God's thoughts our thoughts" (cf. Isa. 55:8-9).

But when this contextual insight is turned into a permanent truth of theology, so that human experience is rejected on principle and not because of the elevation of specific types of human experience and the presuppositions thereof, then the theological community destroys the very brilliance of the insight into its context. The "theology of crisis" under whose banner the younger Barth and his companions found the courage to call in question the pretensions and assumptions of their society and to become in the subsequent years a prophetic voice in the Nazi wilderness, gave way in time to a whole theological worldview, with its own language, its own rules, its own systematic appeal. Everything could be understood from *within* the circle of faith, it was no longer necessary to go into the marketplace; or, if one went there, one knew pretty well in advance what one would find. Again the anthropology is deduced from the theology. Experience is not only untrustworthy; it is unnecessary. Everything that needs to be known about it is already known a priori, from within the sphere of the revealed Word.

21.3. Experience and Theological Contextuality. Juxtaposing our own thought on this subject with these two opposing attitudes towards experience, we may draw the following conclusion: It is evident that a theology which intends to be *contextual* must respect (by whatever name) the category of experience. Such a theology will be wary of the propensity of a *Dogmatik* which feels no compulsion to test itself in relation to the ongoing human experience to devolve into ideology. It is the sad fate of much excellent and timely theological work, such as that of Karl Barth, to function ideologically in the hands of those who receive it uncritically. It becomes a bulwark *against* experience, particularly useful to all who fear, for whatever reason, profound exploration of their own and their society's real condition. Contextual theology is bound by its fundamental tenets to take seriously specific human experience, both its personal and its public aspects.

Yet the propensity to ideological obfuscation of theological work does not reside in conservative religious circles only. As we have seen, it is just as easy to turn "experience" into an ideology as to do so with established religious doctrines and mores. Against stereotypical constructs of the meaning of human experience, it is always necessary to sustain an existential awareness of the *variety* of experiences actually present in a society, especially a pluralistic one. In the wake of black, feminist, "gay," and other critiques of liberal ecclesiasticism, it is doubtful whether the Christian churches will ever be quite so tempted to elevate a particular *type* of experience as was done in the past with bourgeois liberalism. At the same time, *every resort to experience as normative contains within itself the danger of ideology*, and this danger can be averted only if experience as a category of theological investigation is counterbalanced by other sources of authority, as well as by other forms of human experience.

While contextual theology is bound to give a prominent place to experience, then, since the context is after all comprised of a constellation of human experiences, it will not simply become an experientially based theology in the liberal sense. For its object is not to mesh harmoniously with experience, or to undergird as valid or "normal" certain specific types of experience, or to foster this or that prototype. It is rather to engage in dialogue with the existential realities of a society and the persons within it.

As we have seen earlier, such engagement means both a sympathetic and participatory understanding of experience *and* a point of view from which a prophetic critique of experience can be derived. This means that, contrary to liberal tendencies, theology does not abdicate its position as listener to Scripture, tradition, and Spirit in favor of a neutral or noncritical auditing of social and personal experience. Rather, the more faithfully it opens itself to its context and the *multitude* of experiences which constitute its context, the more forcefully it will be driven to the extraexperiential sources of its discipline in order to interpret for itself the meaning of present and future.

There is not a choice between experience and tradition, then, or between the honoring of human experience and the rejection of it as having any place in theology. Experience and tradition are both evoked within the parameters of a contextual theology, and the one by the other.

22. Theology and Prayer

22.1. Theology as a Form of Spirituality. In the immediately foregoing text, I described the theologian as listener to Scripture, tradition, and Spirit. Enough has been said of the first two categories to indicate what such a claim might mean for them. But what could it imply for theology that it is also a disciplined listening to the divine Spirit?

Obviously we cannot speak (without blasphemy!) of the Spirit of God as "an element" in theology. We can and must, however, speak of that attitude, or posture, or speech (language) which presupposes the reality and presence of the Holy Spirit as such an ingredient, i.e., what is usually called prayer.

Theology is a *spiritual* discipline in the sense that it assumes the stance of listener, not only to the various tangible sources that we have described in the preceding sections, but also to an intangible, transcendent, but nonetheless *present* reality named by our tradition *Spiritus Sanctus*. This pneumatic (from *pneuma* = spirit) element in theology is what differentiates the discipline from the historical study of doctrine, philosophy of religion, psychology of religion, *Religionswissenschaft,* etc. All such disciplines can claim, more or less convincingly, that they are "scientific" in nature and that knowledge (*scientia*) is their primary goal. Theology does not (or should not) wish to claim this for itself. It may possess scientific *aspects*—certainly it does have to do with specific data, in the form of historically verifiable ideas, doctrines, creeds, formulas, etc.; but it is not a science and cannot pretend to be such, for the *primary* object of its inquiry is radically nonobjectifiable, is Subject . . . is Thou! As soon as it reduces this Thou to knowable data it has destroyed—or ceased to be in touch with—its primary subject matter.

> The eternal *Thou* can by its nature not become *it*; for by its nature it cannot be established in measure and bounds. . . . And yet in accordance with our nature we are continually making the eternal *thou* into an *it*, into some thing—making God into a thing.[25]

One could even say that it is the basic function of the Spirit in theology to prevent precisely this reductionism. That, we may claim, is at least the "negative" (alien?) work of the Spirit in relation to theology. Being a product of human hands, a work of the intellect, theology, like every other achievement of human beings, is constantly tempted to raise itself above its actual status and worth. Who would not like to utter the definitive word about the Word! Anyone who imagines that theologians are essentially modest persons, humbled by the infinite and unreachable

---

25. Martin Buber, *I And Thou*, trans. Ronald Gregor Smith (Edinburgh: T. & T. Clark, 1937), p. 112.

truth of their subject, has had very little to do with the practitioners of the discipline. Even at the end of the Constantinian era, even in the midst of an intellectual environment which for centuries has humiliated the former "queen of the sciences," the discussions of theologians are as prone to *hubris* as those of any other academics, and perhaps more so on account of their frequent defensiveness! The pneumatic dimension of theology is abhorrent to no one as much as to theologians themselves, for it means that a mere sigh of the divine Spirit—perhaps in the form of a chance remark of some physicist, or some child!—can blow away all the certainties of the most dearly held system.

Yet there is also a *positive* benefit in this spiritual genesis of theological *eros* (though who would deny that the above-named negative is also highly positive in its effect upon the discipline?): it implies, namely, a certain freedom, an openness to what may be given—a freedom and openness also in relation to the past, including one's own previous theological work. If one considers the life of a great theologian like Augustine, for example, one notices this freedom as a quality that the thinker Augustine seems increasingly to have been able to make his own. Looking on, those who demand of their mentors that they should always be consistent with their own past are properly astonished at the great variety of opinions advanced by the Bishop of Hippo—his movement from Manichaeism to Neoplatonism to catholic Christianity; his apparent uncertainty whether the body should or should not be celebrated; his willingness in old age to "retract" a great many of the views he formerly and vigorously held. Granted, there are lines of continuity as well (the "concordat between faith and reason," for example). But, like Luther, like Niebuhr and Barth, Augustine could sit rather lightly to his own past pronouncements. For his aim—which of course he did not consistently manage to achieve—was to be faithful to God, not to his own images of God.

In academic circles of theology in North America, it is perhaps as much the consequence of our failure to embrace this gift of spiritual freedom as it is our undue adherence to the theological traditions and movements of the parental culture that we have failed to become genuinely contextual in our thinking. And these two are inseparable. Karl Barth, whose freedom for theology we noted earlier, diagnosed our New World theological situation in precisely these terms when, at the end of his only visit to North America, he offered the "advice to young theologians" cited at the beginning of this volume.

It is possible, of course, with this freedom as with any other, to exchange it for license, to practice fragmentary and episodic thought as if it were a virtue, to eschew the quest for the unity of truth. But then there is no nondangerous theology, and it is perhaps a greater temptation for those who take up this discipline to make too much of their "systematic" quest for truth than to make too little of it. The divine Spirit, like a holy wind, "scatters the proud theologians in the imaginations of their hearts"; but this same Spirit grants to the theological community the courage to do theology in spite of the impossibility of the undertaking, in the knowledge that it is possible as gift, and that the gift will always exceed its appropriation.

22.2. Praying and Thinking. Prayer is the nomenclature that we assign to our activity as listeners to the divine Spirit. As such, it is indispensable to theology—just as indispensable as is imagination and inspiration to the artist or musician.

But, even so, one hesitates to introduce the term into this discussion—and with good reason. Especially in our particular context, prayer too often conjures up a kind of pious mindlessness. In a volume called *Thinking the Faith*, we could hardly ignore the fact that prayer, in North American religious circles, is seldom associated with thought, especially the most rigorous and disciplined thought. There are thinkers, and there are pray-ers. Thinking persons are liable to regard prayer as a form of escape from thought; conversely, praying Christians seem frequently to consider theology an intellectual camouflage for virtual unbelief.

What this mutual suspicion indicates is that both prayer and thought have been impoverished. The impoverishment of *thought* is related to the discussion of the previous theological ingredient, experience. With the reduction of human rationality to pragmatic and functionalist conceptions of reason, there occurred a diminishment of the quality of depth or mystery which belongs to the understanding of reason in both the Hellenic and Hebraic traditions. For the technological society, serious thought is almost entirely limited to the calculation and manipulation of data. An epoch which can even raise the question whether computers may not be more capable of "thinking" than are human beings, hampered as the latter are by emotions, value judgments, and various distractions, has quite lost touch with the meditative process that the classical traditions refer to as reasoning.

Thinking—as, for example, it is graphically depicted in Auguste Rodin's famous sculpture "The Thinker"—connotes for these older traditions an entry into the hidden depths of the self, a pondering, a contemplative self-forgetfulness that is a far cry from anything that goes on in the electrical interior of a computer, howsoever intricate.

Would it not be possible to say that thinking so understood is already *prayer*? Or at least that the line between such thinking and prayer must be a quite indistinct one?

It would, of course, be prayer in a sense quite different from the way in which that term is used in most religious circles. But has not *prayer*, too, been severely truncated by pietistic misuse? As thought requires reclaiming on account of its captivation by empiricism and technologism, so prayer must be reclaimed by theology on account of its captivation by manipulative religious technique.

At very least, prayer should not be confused with the language or postures through which it has conventionally been expressed or with which it is associated. The Psalms, which are the prayers of ancient Israel (and which contain some of Israel's best theology), provide models of prayer which are very different from the formal addresses to the deity, with their mood of pious acquiescence, so typical of Christian piety on this continent. There are elements of formal address in these prayers, as there are in ordinary speech; and there may be moments, as well, of resignation. But for the most part the paradigm of prayer we are given in the Psalms and in other parts of the Bible suggests a spontaneous and utterly honest wrestling of the human spirit with the Spirit of God.[26]

22.3. Prayer as Thought-in-Relationship. With the notion of prayer as *struggle*, we come closest, perhaps, to the distinction between thought as it is ordinarily understood today and the kind of thought that belongs to the theological discipline, prayerful thought. The presupposition of the latter is that there is One—a co-respondent—in whom wisdom, meaning, and coherence are to be found, and from whom the courage to seek these qualities can be gained by the persistent. Thought does not necessarily presuppose a transcendent partner; but the thinking which belongs to Christian theology necessarily does so. It is thought-in-relationship.

This does not mean, however, that there are no parallels to such a view of thinking in the non-Christian world. Both in most other religious traditions and in classical philosophy one encounters the belief that true thought is *response*. It may not be response to an identifiable being, an

---

26. Kenneth Leech is one contemporary writer on the subject of prayer who has grasped this point. "Struggle is viewed by Leech as a positive, active force which liberates individuals and societies in the search for transformation and healing. Central to this positive evaluation of the role of struggle is Leech's contention that 'much Christian writing and thought exalts peace and harmony at the expense of justice' " (Andrew Taylor, "The Social Dimensions of Christian Spirituality in the Thought of Kenneth Leech," unpublished dissertation, Faculty of Religious Studies, McGill University, 1985, p. 58).

Other, a Thou; that is, it may not have the same personal or relational connotations as are contained in biblical meditations like the Psalms or the prayers of Jesus. Yet in philosophical traditions like Platonism and Stoicism the sense of *participation* in what is infinitely greater than the self and its determinations is marked.

This implies something very important for all such thinking, namely, *its essential receptivity.* The one who thinks knows himself or herself to be "on the receiving end" of something. Without being merely passive, the thinker is conscious of the fact that he or she is not the sole, active agent of thought. Such a one is responding, rather, to an impulse that is both internal and external to the self. Thought is *occurring within* the self; the self is "taken up into" a process which it did not, in the strict sense, initiate, and over which it is not simply in control. ("We have nothing under our control from the beginning.")[27]

While such a conception of thinking is given a particular, personal referent in Hebraic-Christian tradition, it is also basic to the classical philosophic traditions of the Greeks. It is, in fact, only in the modern world, with its near restriction of reason to the empirical and technical, that there has come to be a view of thought in which the human agent considers itself the prime mover. In such a world, it is not surprising that prayer, too, as popularly conceived, has devolved into a technique, variously devised, through which the human agent attempts to achieve certain results beneficial to himself or herself ("lobbying in the courts of the Almighty," as William James put it).

22.4. Theology as *Persistent* Prayer. The fact that theological thought involves a fundamental dimension of receptivity ought not to be taken to mean that the theologian or theological community acts merely as recipient, playing a purely passive role in the acquisition and articulation of theological truth. Such a view does not even apply to the inspiration of the scriptural writings, except as this is explained by literalists who regard the scriptural authors as mere amanuenses of the Holy Spirit. We have used the word "struggle" to elucidate this process, and no effort to do justice to the importance of the element of receptivity in theology should in effect nullify the dimension of contest in this discipline—a dimension without which, indeed, the whole idea of its being a *discipline* is lost.

Reception and contest are not contradictory states, but polar qualities in a unitary relationship. As we shall have occasion many times in this

---

27. Gollwitzer (see the epigraph to this chapter).

study to notice, Christian theology is thoroughly relational throughout; and the relationship which is primary to it, i.e., the divine–human relationship, as well as the relationships which are conditioned by this primary relation (human to human, human to nature, etc.) honors the otherness of both partners. The human partner is not intended to be a mere vessel for the reception of the divine. The personhood of the human being depends upon its separation, its distinctiveness. The ideal, so far as this relationship is concerned, is not that the otherness of the human counterpart should be overcome, so that an ontic or mystic union with the divine is achieved. This is not how the tradition of Jerusalem conceives salvation. The ideal is rather the coming to be of a mutuality, a face-to-face respect and acceptance, in a word: love.

Love, in the biblical understanding of it—for instance, in the well-known passage 1 Corinthians 13—does not imply the loss of personal identity, but its gain. In loving and in being loved by God I *become* myself, I find authentic selfhood. Too often, especially in sentimentalistic circles of Protestantism on this continent, this is not understood, and, following the patterns of rhetorical sentiment which govern their personal lives, Christians think that *God's* love and our love for God ought to indicate a relation in which there is no element of contest, especially from the human side, but only acquiescence. In consequence, an aura of unreality surrounds the entire notion of the love of God, since even the most loving human relationships *do* contain a dimension of contention, and indeed must do so if they are not to degenerate into forms of docility or the domination of one partner by another.[28]

Applying the relational ontology of love to the subject at hand, we repeat: reception and contest are not contradictory states but polar qualities pertaining to the same relationship. In prayer, the human person *receives* the grace of understanding, but not passively, not in a submissive manner—rather, through dialogue and resolute questing.

There is no better illustration of what is meant here than the one that Jesus himself presents in one of his most neglected parables on the nature of prayer: that of the importunate widow and the unjust judge (Luke 18:1ff.). Like the widow, who returned again and again to the judge despite his refusal to hear her, and who finally achieved her desire for "vindication" because of her sheer tenacity, so prayer must persist with God in its quest for understanding. The point is not that God is comparable

---

28. Unfortunately, women in particular have suffered from this conception of the nature of love, the image of divine love confirming for them the passivity they ought to demonstrate in relation to their fathers, husbands, and lovers.

to a hard-hearted and unscrupulous figure like the judge, but that the human being who wills to be blessed—in the case of theology, blessed with understanding—can receive this blessing only through an enduring and determined endeavor to acquire and assimilate what is there as gift.

Prayer conceived as a rapt reflection inspired by a presence transcending the self, as thought which dares to struggle with the source of thought, as a meditation on being which refuses to concede that existence is precisely and only what it *seems* to be—such prayer is both presupposed and fostered by the discipline of theology. If we were attentive to the linguistic nuance of Anselm's famous definition of theology—*fides quaerens intellectum*—we should have heard something very similar to this. For the participle "seeking" (*quaerens*) comes very close to depicting the whole posture of theology as prayer. The attitude of theology is an inquiring one—and not in the sense of a polite or detached curiosity, but as a quest upon whose outcome everything depends.

It is not necessary—perhaps it is not even desirable—that theological inquiry thus understood should be explicitly liturgical or *ostensibly* prayerful. On occasion, great theology may take the actual form of prayer, in the sense of direct address to God. Augustine's *Confessions* demonstrates this very movingly. But the important thing is not that theology should *look like* prayer, but that it should *be* prayer, namely, prayer in this most rudimentary sense of an earnest, hard-headed, Jacobian struggle for the blessing of understanding.[29]

23. Theology and the Church

23.1. Theology as a Discipline of the Disciple Community. It would of course be misleading to consider the church "an element" in theology in the way that faith, Bible, tradition, experience, and prayer are elements. The truth is that theology is a component of the life of the church, not vice versa. Yet there would be something vital missing from our delineation of the various sources and perspectives which exercise their special influences upon the theological task were we to leave out of account the living community whose work this is. As we have insisted in the introduction, theology is a discipline of the disciple community.

This community, with its quite specific needs, problems, and possibilities, brings to the discipline of theology certain qualities, as well as

---

29. For a more extensive discussion of the themes developed in this subsection, see my *When You Pray: Thinking Your Way Into God's World* (Valley Forge: Judson, 1987).

certain demands, which it does not receive by association with the other elements we have treated. When theologians neglect this rootedness of their discipline in the life of the disciple community, they not only stand in danger of creating a purely theoretical account of the faith, but they deprive themselves of an *embodiment* of belief which could provide a foundation for their otherwise insubstantial thought. To use the language I have chosen for these volumes, *thinking the faith* is inseparably linked with *professing and confessing the faith*.

23.2. Theologians and "The Theological Community." Theology is a work of the whole people of God; it is not the preserve of a professional elite. There are reasons, as we reminded ourselves earlier, why theology became, in the course of the "Christian" centuries, the prerogative of a guild. Given a situation where people are Christians by birth and public convention rather than through experience and constantly renewed decision, theology is virtually superfluous to the majority—at best, an option for the curious, the gifted, or the doubting. Where Christianity is indistinguishable from the general social milieu, theology easily becomes a vocational option for a privileged minority, just as law and medicine are for other minorities. The elitist reputation of theology is bound up, not only with its minority status, but with the fact that this minority has been for the most part drawn from the more affluent and influential segments of society—though, in the modern period, with less consistency than in the case of other professional guilds. In the churches, though not in society at large, we are still living with the consequences of this image of the discipline.

At the same time, all the signs of our time point unmistakably towards a return to what must be regarded as the normal situation (though it has been the exception, historically), where theology is a discipline of the whole community of faith. This normalcy is increasingly asserting itself today, as those Christians who resist the winnowing processes of secularity and alternative faiths are compelled to find a rationale for their belief. In many North American denominations, it is now mandatory for all who devise programs and activities for the church, including its finances, to provide acceptable *theological* grounds for their plans and visions.[30] When

---

30. This is particularly conspicuous in the area of ecclesiastical finances. In the past, North American churches of the "mainstream denominations" have been able to count on regular and almost automatic giving from their membership. Within the past decade or so, the financial officers of these denominations have experienced the necessity of inculcating a *basic theology* of Christian stewardship. Exhortation and technique ("every person visitation" and similar hard-sell programs for fund-raising) no longer suffice; stewardship must be seen as a dimension of the most rudimentary meaning of belief, and not as a second step that can be taken only by the most dedicated.

one adds to this the fact that many of those who are required to specify such grounds, or approve them, are laypersons (often the majority in these situations are neither professionally trained nor ordained), it becomes clear that professionalism in theology is no longer the rule, at least so far as the daily workings of ecclesiastical bodies are concerned.

This development cannot but be lauded by a scholarship which is in touch with Christian beginnings. That does not mean, however, that the situation is without drawbacks and dangers.

The special temptation present in an ecclesiastical setting where theology is regarded as the responsibility and privilege of the church as a whole is that theology will become a matter of consensus. In many Protestant denominations in North America just now, the question of *representation* is more decisive at every level of ecclesiastical life than any other, including competence or even "calling." There are good reasons why this is the case, and these must be sustained. The dangers of mediocrity and simplism should not tempt us to call for a return to the *sort* of excellence that is based on professionalistic norms and practices. Yet neither should these dangers be disregarded. For it is not only banality that we are risking but a conspicuous loss of the prophetic-critical dimension which belongs to the theological traditions of biblical faith. When the primary concern of the Christian community is that all segments and shades of opinion should be given equal voice in the articulation and implementation of the priorities of the faith, the result is too often a mishmash of views, programs, and activities lacking any sort of confessional thrust and in fact simply reflecting the variety and confusion of the ecclesiastical body in question. It becomes a case of supply and demand: "theology" is tailored to the expressed "needs" of the religious community. The prophetic-critical dimension of our tradition requires of us a greater readiness to stand before "the judgment that begins at the household of God" than is likely in such circumstances. Theology exists to serve the church—by all means! But not necessarily to serve up precisely what the church asks for. There is a matter of obedience to sources other than church—we have been discussing a number of them heretofore; moreover, a cursory acquaintance with church history will inform us that, with considerable regularity, the most important theological moments in that history were moments when theology had to *confront* the church, not when it simply catered to ecclesial wants.

Evidently, then, there is some necessity inherent in the dynamics of the gospel for permitting and sustaining a certain *dis*continuity between theology and church as well as the continuity we have noted above. A theology too continuous with the Christian community is apt to devolve into a simple justification of the ecclesiastical status quo. A degree of distance is required if theology is to do justice to the other ingredients of which it is comprised and the sources to which it is accountable.

Practically speaking, this seems to mean that there is a need within the church to sponsor a minority whose special vocation it will always be to pursue theological disciplines more rigorously than they can be undertaken by the whole community. Without ceasing to be the task of the entire disciple community, theology also becomes the vocation of a few "theologians" within it. These exercise a rabbinic function vis-à-vis the larger body; they are (to employ the Reformed terminology) "teaching elders," who are responsible to the community, but accountable also to the other inherent demands of the discipline. There is, I suspect, no guarantee that such an arrangement will ever circumvent the danger of elitism and professionalism. The only way in which the most unfortunate consequences of such an eventuality can be offset is through a radical recovery, on the part of the *whole* church, of the fundamental biblical dialectic of the individual and the community.

It has been very difficult, it would seem, for the church throughout the centuries to appropriate this dialectic. The most rudimentary reasons for that difficulty lie, of course, in the mystery of human sin: the rebellious and ubiquitous "I" continues to assert itself long after it has experienced the grace of justification! *Simul justus et peccator* (at the same time justified and sinner—Luther). But the social status of the church can also affect this issue. When the structures of the church mirror the structures of a hierarchically arranged society, for example, as they have done throughout the greater share of the history of Christianity, they provide the external circumstances favorable to egoistic self-assertion in the Christian community, and thus militate against the realization of the new and grace-given possibilities to which, for example, Paul is alluding in his metaphor of the body of Christ (*sōma Christou/corpus Christi*). Is it not possible that, as the church enters the quite different sociological situation which pertains at "the end of the Constantinian era," it could more fully realize the meaning of reconciliation and human communion in its own life?

23.3. One Body, Many Members. Part of what such a recovery must mean is the restoration of the *dynamic* character of the relation in question. The typical sentimentalism of North American Protestantism, combined with our seeming preference for linear, nondialectical thought,[31] results in a very questionable sort of idealism when it comes to the doctrine of the church. We entertain similar ideals for marriage and family life, for friendship, for community as a whole; and in all of these relationships a great deal of the frustration and suffering that is actually experienced is a direct consequence of false expectations.

These expectations are false because they seek to eliminate, always, the negative dimension inherent in the relationship: trust is unaccompanied by any element of distrust; faith admits of no doubt, hope of no despair, joy of no sorrow, etc. Above all, love contains no hint of its antithesis; it is simply and solely "love," pure and spotless! The *desire* to "eliminate the negative" is entirely human, and even somehow (from a Christian standpoint) right. But the negating dimension is not eliminated by wishing it away; and, what is more important, the attempt at dismissal is entirely premature. The so-called negative can in fact play a highly positive role within every relationship. Indeed, it is what keeps relationships alive— relational. Without the dialectical presence of its antithesis, the positive element by itself would create a static and stagnant situation devoid of life. Trust without any hint of existential distrust regularly devolves into presumption, faith without doubt into credulity, hope without despair into doctrinaire optimism, joy without sorrow into smugness of spirit. As for love, it is not even possible apart from the dimension of resistance or hesitation which can *seem* its opposite; for love requires of the self that it retains its own center of identity and is not absorbed in the other—"It takes *two* to love."

When these same false expectations are applied to our preconception of the Christian community, the effect is in some ways even more dev- astating than it is in our personal and secular relationships; for now such ideals are crowned with an aura of sanctity. Thus our image of Christian community, characteristically, is one in which all the negating dimensions that color our life in the world have (supposedly) been set aside: there are no longer any distinctions between persons; strife and division of every sort have been overcome; tensions have been resolved, and a new "oneness" has replaced the old state of alienation, and so on. The con- sequence of such a picture of the "true church" is that *most people never*

---

31. On the nature of dialectical thought, see Jacques Ellul, "On Dialectic," trans. Geoffrey W. Bromily, in *Jacques Ellul: Interpretive Essays*, ed. Clifford G. Christians and Jay M. VanHook (Chicago: University of Illinois Press, 1981), pp. 291ff. (In introducing his subject, Ellul states: "If I have chosen this theme for final reflection . . . , it is because I have the impression it might help to explain some of my 'contradictions,' and also (if American readers will pardon me) because I have known many American students over the past twenty years and have found that dialectical thinking is strange to them: they do not like entering into it" [p. 292]).

find it in any existing congregation; or if they find it, it is because they foster, in their congregations, an atmosphere of unreal "friendliness" into which individuals are required to fit themselves regardless of their actual condition. The *social* consequence of this image of the church is that, in their insistence upon *having* such a community, Christian people since the Reformation have invented a whole spate of denominations and sects (at least some 1500 on this continent), each one vowing to be the promised "fellowship," each in turn succumbing to the fate of all utopias.

The biblical conception of the church does not warrant this kind of religious idealism. Paul's analogy of the body is too often interpreted as a metaphor of total harmony. On the contrary, it is an astonishingly realistic image. The harmony of which it speaks is a dynamic, eschatological harmony, that is, a harmony which is made lively by the interactions of elements which are not "naturally" compatible, a harmony which is always *in process*, not in a state of achievement. Thus in the passage where Paul employs the *corpus Christi* image most imaginatively (1 Cor. 12:4ff.), the whole background of the discussion is the apostle's desire, over against an obvious attempt on the part of the Corinthian disciple community to avoid it, to explicate and vindicate the necessary *tension*— the *creative* tension—between the two principles involved in the image, viz., individuation and incorporation.

That there would be tension here, he affirms, is to be expected; for, given the pride of self (of which he is so vividly conscious), it is hardly surprising that individuals could enter into communality only with great and continuing adversity. Each wants to be preeminent, each wants to do everything (vv. 29ff.), each resents it that the other is gifted in matters where he or she is not, etc. Yet the solution appropriate to this egoism is not to ignore it, or to leave the fellowship and search for another, "true" church; rather, it is to school the spirit of the community to recognize that in an organism *each component* has its unique function, that the whole depends upon the proper functioning of the parts, that none is superior to the other (which is the rationale of his apt allusion to the parts of the body that may *seem* inferior [they are in fact "indispensable"— vv. 22ff.])—in short, that it is precisely the *otherness* of each, with all the potential and actual tension that this undoubtedly makes for, which ensures the full life and giftedness of the whole "body."

23.4. Implications for Theology of the "Body of Christ" Metaphor. An ecclesiology which has appropriated the eschatological dynamism of Paul's historic metaphor is productive of several implications for theological work:

(a) Theology as gift: We have seen that there are excellent reasons

why, in the post-Constantinian situation, theology has to become the work of the whole disciple community. It is also paramount in such a context that the church should continually seek accord among its members on matters of faith and obedience. But these necessities do not add up to the conclusion that theology is a matter of consensus. With notable exceptions (among which I should place the Barmen Declaration as prime instance in the present century), most of the theology that is done "in counsel" is conspicuously mediocre and often banal. It may give the impression of harmony, but what it regularly betrays is chiefly compromise.[32] Such "theology" has usually died the death of a thousand qualifications before it has ever seen the light of day. It may function as a barometer of majority ecclesiastical opinion, but rarely does it function prophetically, to call church and world to a more authentic expression of Christian and human obedience.

This is not a matter about which Christians today and tomorrow can remain indifferent. With the (largely good and in any case inevitable) breakdown of older authority structures in all branches of Christendom, and the withdrawal of many theological professionals from active participation in the churches, there is a regrettable tendency towards consensus theology at the level of ecclesiastical life. It is true that such common-denominator religious thought is challenged, on occasion, by theologies emanating from minorities within or around the churches, and that these latter do often represent prophetic judgments on the status quo. All the same, such minorities cannot assume responsibility for the whole spectrum of church membership, for they speak from specific points of identity and concern. Thus, by default, the theological posture of the larger church is regularly determined by ecclesiastical courts and committees which have, as a rule, insufficient depth of exposure to the whole process of doing theology about which we have been reflecting in these pages.

This tendency is more conspicuous in more democratic branches of the universal church, which are understandably less resistent to the undesirable aspects of radical democratization. In the Roman Catholic and other churches which can still assume some expression of the *magisterium*, the danger of theology by consensus is less evident—with the consequence

---

32. A prime example, in my view at least, is the so-called *BEM* document of the Faith and Order Commission of the World Council of Churches. Such documents undoubtedly serve the purpose of overcoming the most notorious aspects of "our sad divisions," but they can hardly be regarded as imaginative or prophetic theology (*Baptism, Eucharist, and Ministry*, Faith and Order Paper No. 111 [Geneva: World Council of Churches, 1982]).

that authoritative sources within the church can on occasion make pronouncements that are remarkably prophetic.[33] At the same time, these churches are tempted by their hierarchical traditions to "solve" the problems created by the demise of Christendom through reactionary measures designed to stave off the diaspora situation.

The response appropriate to this situation, in my view, is neither the typical Protestant laissez-faire attitude towards theology nor the traditional Catholic attempt to regulate doctrine, but rather an endeavor to bring about new manifestations of mutuality between the church at large and the theological scholars. From the side of the church this would mean a more consistent and serious recognition of the fact that theology is a gift. It is not given to everyone, at least not in the same measure, to probe the depths of meaning in the Christian message, or to spend a lifetime searching the Scriptures and traditions of the church. The gift entails sacrifice and discipline.[34] It cannot be picked up and set down again at will. Skills are demanded for the perfecting of this gift, as they are for any other; most of these skills are only acquired over a long period of time. Therefore, while this in no way excuses *all* who call themselves Christians from working at the understanding of what they believe, it is necessary to recognize that *some*, who have been called to this office, will have particular responsibilities for theological scholarship; and their contributions to the life of the whole church will be actively sought and their work supported.

From the side of the theologians, mutuality will require a new sense of *accountability to the church.* Theology is gift, but it is given for the

---

33. Examples: (1) The United States Bishops on nuclear warfare (U.S. Conference of Catholic Bishops, *Origins,* May 3, 1983); see also *Catholics and Nuclear War*, ed. Philip Murnion (New York: Crossroads, 1983), Jim Castelli and *The Bishops and the Bomb* (New York: Doubleday, 1983).

(2) The Canadian Catholic Bishops' statement on the economy (See G. Baum and D. Cameron, *Ethics and Economics* [Toronto: Lorimer, 1984], and J. Sheridan, ed., *Do Justice!* [Toronto: Jesuit Centre for Social Faith and Justice, 1987]).

34. In a world facing crises that may well lead to civilizational "catastrophe" (von Weizsäcker), *thought* is always a painful process. For those who care in an ultimate way about "the fate of the earth," it is often literally excruciating—a burden which can be personally devastating. The drugstore bookshelf religionists create the false impression that Christian faith delivers its practitioners from the pain of thought. This is no doubt borne out by the slick thoughtlessness of what these acolytes of the official optimism actually present. But the great thinkers of the faith have always had to suffer for their thought—not just as a consequence of what they thought, but for the thought itself. Not only Paul Tillich, but both of the Niebuhr brothers, whose lives were far less psychically traumatic than Tillich's, suffered periods of depression that Martin Luther would certainly have called *Anfechtungen*. See in this connection Richard Fox, *Reinhold Niebuhr: A Biography* (New York: Pantheon, 1985), p. 222 (on H. Richard Niebuhr's hospitalization), and Robert McAfee Brown, ed., *The Essential Reinhold Niebuhr* (New Haven: Yale University Press, 1986), pp. 250ff. ("Epilogue: A View of Life from the Sidelines," by Reinhold Niebuhr).

life of the church, not for personal aggrandizement or for the creation of an academic elite. The Constantinian situation pertaining throughout so many centuries, combined with the lamentable fact of overspecialization in contemporary academic life, has conditioned theologians to regard themselves not so much as members of the disciple community as members of the intelligentsia—the "high culture"; and therefore they are often (quite understandably) resented and spurned by those whose educational background is less developed. It is imperative that as the church in North America moves from the imperial to the diaspora model of Christian community the scholars of the faith, at every level of scholarship, should discover their primary identity within the *koinōnia*, and that the latter should welcome and support its scholars as the bringers of gifts which—*especially* in the diaspora situation—the disciple community sorely needs.

(b) Theology as conflict: There are tensions which Christian faith can only consider false and sinful, such as those created by the juxtaposition of an elitist theological guild and an anti-intellectual clergy and laity. But there are also tensions which *belong* to the community of belief, and if we are to make the transition into the kind of mutuality to which I have just referred we shall have to overcome our (bourgeois?) antipathy to conflict. We have seen that the harmony of the *sōma Christou* is a dynamic harmony: it is always becoming. It does not exclude, rather it includes tension, because it is founded upon the love of truth, not on superficial peace, and because it is ready to acknowledge and to be grateful for the negative dimensions within relationships which in the end may contribute to that harmony.

This conception of community has particular application to the relation between church and theology, because theology cannot be engaged in seriously without conflict. We have said that theology is *struggle*—the drive of the Spirit-inspired intellect to comprehend what is believed. Even within the individual self, theology creates tensions; for part of each of us wills—and strongly so—to avoid all struggle, to escape knowledge of the paradoxes and contradictions that already exist in our spirits and minds, to avoid dialectic, to achieve "peace of mind." When the theological quest is extended to the community as a whole, it will uncover existing differences and hostilities, and it will create other differences. It will not be possible to pursue theological understanding within the *koinōnia* so long as its members intend above all to make of it a place of no conflict.

We must face the prospect that these places which are free from conflict, these friendly churches with their smiling, well-mannered people and their coffee hours, may be in these difficult times little more than exercises in bourgeois civility, the cost of whose existence is Christian realism and obedience. Civility of any kind is to be preferred above self-assertiveness, bickering, and rudeness; but civility does not make the church, only love and truth do. The church, as Christ's body, is a place where *life* is being given—"dry bones" are being knit together with new life; "no people" are being created a people, God's people; the "dead" are being raised and made to walk "in newness of life" (Romans 6). Life entails the meeting of antitheses—love and hate, hope and despair, faith and doubt, health and sickness, truth and lie, life and death. Theology is born of the need to be close to the source of all this. And if this is indeed what is happening in the church, then theology can be impoverished only if it is absent from the congregation. But it is equally true that real theology, if it is allowed to exist within the congregation, will *stir up* the embers of life, and therefore disturb, with some regularity, the civility that so many of our congregations seem to think is of the essence.

(c) Theology as discovery: Yet it would be entirely misleading to leave this discussion with the acknowledgment that theology is conflict. Everyone who has had the privilege of serious theological reflection, study, and dialogue, and who is therefore well acquainted with the conflictual dimension of the discipline, knows that there is an abiding satisfaction in theological work which is *not* the satisfaction of our bellicose human impulse to do battle with one another. The quest for truth may not produce the kind of happiness demanded by our repressive instincts; but it does have its own rather profound and lasting joy.

> Christianity is certainly not melancholy, it is, on the contrary, glad tidings—for the melancholy. To the frivolous it is certainly not glad tidings, for it wishes first of all to make them serious.[35]

The joy is the joy of discovery—the discovery of what is true, what is real. Some things that are true do not make for happiness, and such things are indeed included in this discipline: sin, the demonic, death, the "dark night of the soul." But to face these things! To become honest about them! This is no little boon to the spirit, which spends so much of its time hiding from precisely such realities. And then, to contemplate the conquest of these melancholy realities by a love that goes into the night—how could such a prospect not excite the mind and the soul!

---

35. Søren Kierkegaard, *The Living Thoughts of Kierkegaard*, presented by W. H. Auden (Bloomington: Indiana University Press, 1966), p. 30.

But there is more, for this discovery is never a lonely one, it is undertaken in company—in company with several millennia of other explorers, a few of them named, many who "have no memorial" (Sir. 44:9); in company with a living community of searchers, a collegium which today is ecumenical and catholic in a way not the case in previous ages. This community is full of great variety. As at Pentecost, many voices are heard, many languages spoken. There is no obvious, universal agreement. But what is more important than agreement (which may or may not accompany it) is the feeling of reality—that one is not *acting* but is oneself; that the other is who he is, who she is—not a mask; that one is taken seriously, that one's testimony is heard, that there are points of meeting between one's thoughts and the thoughts of others. . . .

This experience, which has been the experience of all who entered into the discipline of theology at depth, *belongs to the whole church*. And it is one of the most regrettable aspects of the segregation of theology from the church that, in consequence, the church (the *laos*) has been so consistently deprived of the fullness of this experience. The converse is also true, however. For a theological guild which finds its identity and engages in its discipline at some distance from the disciple community is bereft of the insight, wisdom, and joy which could come to it *from* that source, and perhaps from that source only. For as we have repeatedly asserted, professional theology, like every other specialized discipline, regularly gives way to its own language-world, its own self-generated problems, its own internal interests. As an "ingredient" in theology, the church can—and must—boldly invade this inner sanctum of the theologians, call upon it to focus upon the primary data of the Christian faith and life, and turn its often esoteric pursuits towards the more genuine theological meditation and witness that is the basic discipline of the disciple community.

24. Theology and "the World"

24.1. No Theology without the World.   For a contextual theology, the world is not merely a passive recipient, an empty vessel into which theological content is to be poured; it is rather, as we have maintained in the first section, a partner in theology. While it is not one of the traditional sources of theology, the world in biblical thought as in the most responsible contemporary theology is rightly perceived as making demands upon this discipline and, often enough, spurring it on to new insight. It is, after all, God's world! No matter how far it may have fallen away from God,

God has not left this world to its own devices but is "at work in the world to make and to keep human life human."[36] We may say, then, that God speaks to us through the world—through the neighbor (who, as Luther insisted, could well be Christ incognito); through the myriad creatures, the seasons, the hills and seas, the trees; through events in which faith is enabled to perceive the judgment and mercy of God.

But theology needs the world also in this sense, that it needs to hear what we called, earlier, the world's story of itself—the one that it is telling just now. It needs to know what time it is, that is, what manner of spirit (*Geist*) informs the age, what mood is being displayed in the acts and speech of people, what fears and expectations are being enacted in world events, etc. Without this knowledge, the theological community literally cannot practice its discipline—or rather, what it practices will not be, in the genuine sense, theology. For theology, as we have seen, means the *meeting* of stories, the encounter of the human with the divine, the engagement of "the word of man" by "the Word of God" (Barth).

There are literally no limits to the ways in which the world makes its contribution to the dialogue of theology, and it would be very artificial to propose any such limits. Everyone who engages in theological work knows that the world invades his or her thought at every moment, sometimes consciously, sometimes subconsciously or unconsciously; because the world *is* with us, whether we will it or not. The world is in fact so profoundly with and *within* us that where all of the other theological elements cease and our world consciousness begins, or vice versa, it is virtually impossible to detect.

For example, we read the Bible as persons whose presuppositions have been thoroughly conditioned by our world; and while through scholarly reflection we may learn how to distinguish these presuppositions from those of the biblical writers, our interpretations of Scripture are always colored by our own worldly perception. The same thing is true, mutatis mutandis, of all the other components we have cited.

It is not my intention here, therefore, to propose a schema which would in effect narrow the breadth of worldly influence upon the work of theology; I should like, rather, to offer categories which might help

---

36. Paul Lehmann, *Ethics in Christian Context* (New York and Evanston: Harper & Row, 1963), chap. 3, pp. 74ff. This is not to say that God's *humanizing* work is *all* that God is "busy with." James Gustafson's criticism of Lehmann may be pertinent to some degree in this respect (*Ethics from a Theocentric Perspective*, pp. 50-53). If, however, "humanization" is understood to include—as today it must—the human recognition of our common ties with all other creatures, then Lehmann's theological-ethical formula is a very precise statement of the intent of the biblical God.

the reader to *expand* his or her appreciation of the ways in which the reality of the world impacts, or ought to impact, theology.

The categories I shall elaborate briefly are two basics, with a number of subthemes in each. The basic categories are suggested by the fact that our communication with the world is both *immediate* and *mediated*.

24.2. Immediate Commerce with the World.

(a) The world in me: No one is a theologian by birth. No one is even a Christian by birth, and the time has come when we can recognize this with all of its theoretical and practical implications. The fact is that one comes to faith and theological reflection upon the things of faith out of a quite definite worldly past (which may or may not have anything to do with religion, Christian or otherwise), and one's life as a child of the world does not end with one's introduction to faith. One brings to Christian theology, at whatever level one engages in it, the specifics of that past and of that present intercourse with the world. "The world" has in some concrete fashion formed itself in one's physical, emotional, intellectual, and spiritual being; and this is obviously the most immediate way in which that world enters into theological discourse.

If, for example, I come to know, or feel that I know, profoundly, what Paul means when he insists that we are justified by grace, through faith, not by works lest anyone should boast (cf. Eph. 2:8), it will be in part because of certain personal encounters, certain novels I have read or pictures I have looked at, certain impressions created upon me by incidents in which I have been involved, certain feelings that shaped themselves silently in my internal history. Unless the questions contained, implicitly, in the world as it has manifested itself to and in me are *met* by what is proffered as the Christian message, I shall have no reason in the first place to delve into Christian theology. If, on the other hand, the world *in me*—the microcosm—feels itself taken seriously, grasped, and perhaps even shaken by this message; if Christian teaching as it is communicated to me begins to impress me as something existentially gripping—as gospel—then I shall be ready to think that the macrocosm might also be addressed by this Word. At this point—and, I suspect, only at this point—theology in the proper sense begins seriously to occur.

The disciple community is a body of persons, for each of whom this personal incorporation of the world and its engagement by the gospel is their existential point of departure; and therefore the discipline itself is never without a powerful worldly component, even when its practitioners protest (as they sometimes do) that they have eschewed all traffic with the world! It is the unfortunate fate of too much "academic" theology that it tries to camouflage this obvious fact—partly, of course, *because* it is academic, and therefore feels obligated to minimize subjectivity and any suggestion of bias. But of course the primary data of Christian theology is *intensely* subject-oriented: it concerns the subject God and the subject *anthrōpos* in existential encounter; and therefore when the subject engaging in this discipline feels constrained to eliminate self from the process, the results are somehow unconvincing and even, sometimes, ludicrous. It is just as absurd for Christian theology to evict the self from its investigations as it is for the physical scientist to make the self prominent. For what the theologian is required to investigate is the dialogue between "the Word of God and the word of man," and the most *immediate* locus of this dialogue is the investigating self. Thus (to return to our root theme of contextuality), when generations of American and Canadian teachers of theology go about their discipline without any conscious reflection upon their own autobiographies, i.e., upon "the world" as it has come to them in their distinctively North American histories; and when, instead, they attempt to present this subject matter to their students as something transpersonal, transspatial, transtemporal, what they invariably end by doing is providing themselves and their charges with theologies which have evolved primarily in the worldly dialogues of Germans, Scots, Italians, Swiss, and others.

It is gratifying, therefore, that here and there it has begun to be possible for theologians, without being maudlin, to introduce autobiographical material into their theological reflections, and even to discuss the possibility of "theology as biography." Feminist theology has perhaps led the way in this.

All the same, this process can be carried too far. The world is not to be *equated with* one's personal experience of the world. When theology proceeds as if such an equation could be made, it usually ends in personalism if not in religious solipsism. Such a danger is by no means confined to pietistic circles, which perhaps court it in obvious ways. It is indirectly present in much of the theology of the First World particularly. *My* world may be sufficiently like the worlds of others who belong to my race, class, gender, and generation that the individualism of such an approach is less obviously exclusivistic than it might otherwise seem. But what recent critical theologies have helped us to realize is that so much theology has been conducted by persons whose worlds *are* similar— because they are white, male, and middle-aged members of affluent First World societies—that there is a kind of *corporate* solipsism associated with the entire enterprise. A theology wholly devoid of an autobiographical dimension, whether explicit or implicit, must be considered too bloodless to be Christian theology. But a theology whose autobiographical dimension is not supplemented and challenged by forms of immediate encounter with the world which transcend the personal has also to be held in doubt.

(b) The world in "them": Every life that is not pathologically sealed off from contact with other lives is touched daily by human beings, some of whom are so different from itself as almost to warrant the term *"wholly* other." Yet all of these others are bearers of worlds, or world-consciousness, which cannot be ignored by the theological community.

In the previous section of the study, we drew attention to the pluralistic nature of the context in which we are doing theology today. How, in such a context, does "the world" appear to and in the life of an oriental immigrant who is neither Christian nor middle class nor English-speaking; who is a refugee from another, very different world which no longer has any place for her; who is uprooted and—at age 40, perhaps—has to establish a whole new life for herself? Or what "world" does the typical Anglophone Protestant encounter in the Francophone Catholic of Quebec, or the Midwestern American in the Spanish-speaking migrant worker, or the black Baptist in the white Baptist?

In my classrooms in a large university set in the center of a metropolitan city of this continent, I see before me persons who are not only young (where I am middle-aged), not only black (where I am white), not only disabled (where I am relatively "fit"), not only Jewish or Muslim (where I am Christian), not only Catholic (where I am Protestant), not only female (where I am male), not only very rich or very poor (where I belong to the economic bourgeoisie), not only credulous or, on the other hand, cynical (where I am a believer who seeks "help" for his disbelief), but in countless hidden as well as open ways very different from me. And these are all bearers of worlds. To each, the world has presented itself uniquely, and each in turn represents a unique face of worldly reality.

In my home, I am surrounded by four women—with one of whom I am married, and three who are my adult daughters. As a male, educated by a society which has accentuated male perceptions of reality even when it has communicated these perceptions through women, I am still tempted to assume that what women have of "the world" within them is basically the same as what I have imbibed of our common environment. Even of these four beloved women, not to mention the many women whom I encounter on a less intimate basis, I am prone to think that their images, expectations, and anxieties respecting this world are entirely continuous with my own. Yet at least intellectually I know that this is not the case. For both their words and their ways constantly remind me that their

303

perception of reality is discontinuous with my own at many points, and sometimes radically so.

And why should our recognition of "the others" stop with other *human* beings? It belongs to our immediate concourse with the world also to encounter countless other creatures, which, while it may not be appropriate to attribute world *consciousness* and *perception* to them, nevertheless convey to us intimations of the world which are not strictly our own. These intimations are gleaned from perspectives very different from ours, since *like* ours—only less deviously because instinctively, naturally—they are centered in self: Will the world offer them the "food that they seek from God" (cf. Ps. 104:21)? Will it allow them to survive, to thrive, to multiply? Will *our* pursuits destroy theirs—their foliage, their young, their habitats?

There is, of course, no way in which the gap between the self and "the other" can be wholly overcome. What is perfectly obvious in the case of nonhuman beings—namely, that I shall never be able to see the world through their eyes—is also true of the other human beings. The world as it is experienced, felt, and lived by and in these other children of Adam and Eve is inaccessible to me in any direct way. Yet we may recognize degrees of awareness and sensitivity with respect to the world as it meets us through other beings, human and extrahuman. As a white, Anglo-Saxon Protestant, I cannot become an immigrant from Vietnam and see the world as he sees it; but I *can* listen to him. As a man, I cannot cross over the perhaps invisible but nevertheless real and complex boundary between male and female; but I can be more open to the testimony of women concerning the world of their experience, or less open. I shall never know what a sea gull experiences when it finds that its eggs do not possess firm enough shells to endure the process of hatching its young; but I can, if I will, become knowledgable concerning the subtle forms of pollution which create this problem, and I can, if I will, consider the world from the perspective of one who on this account feels a greater responsibility for species other than my own.

In short, the world as it confronts me through all of these others—through "them"—is as immediately present to me as they are present, if I am enabled sufficiently to overcome my own psychic confinement to self, my own egocentrism. All that theology seeks to understand has precisely to do with that overcoming; and therefore if any human beings are capable of such altruistic perceptions, Christians should be among them.

(c) The world seen through its victims: Divine grace not only frees

us from self so that we may begin to see life through the eyes of others, but it would direct us to view our world in particular from the vantage point of those who are most vulnerable to its moods and its malaise: the poor, the politically and economically oppressed, the weak and disadvantaged—in short, the victims. The disciple community is required by the very liberation claims that it investigates to acquire—what most human beings prefer to avoid—a closer, more informed, imaginative, and committed acquaintance with the world as it makes itself present to those who are most susceptible to its pain.

We are speaking of theology's *immediate* commerce with the world, and therefore of priorities. Classical theology has preferred to concentrate on what we must here designate *mediated* sources of worldly concourse; that is, it has acquired its knowledge of the world through secondary sources, sources of information and worldly wisdom once-removed from the actual living of worldly life—notably, of course, philosophy. What liberation theology in particular has been able to communicate to many Christians in our time is that in this once-remove there is already a certain presupposition concerning the world's contribution to the theological task. It is presupposed, namely, that in our attempt to discern the signs of the times we are dealing with impersonal realities—with worldviews and epistemological theories and moral values and the like, in short with realities which we, as intellectuals, can manipulate, creating out of them our own versions of truth and systems of meaning.

But when the world with which theology must seek to correlate its gospel is the unmediated world of the poor and oppressed, neither anthropological analysis nor theological response is so conveniently managed. It is much easier to arrive at a satisfactory theory of human alienation by studying the ordered reflections of sociologists and political economists than to subject oneself to the daily round of those most visibly alienated; and religious "answers" to human alienation can also seem more convincing in one's study or classroom than in the urban ghetto or the state prison.

A contextual theology cannot be satisfied with theory, either as regards its analysis of the existential predicament or as regards its kerygma. It is contextual precisely in its dissatisfaction with theory. The test is always what is actually *there* in the context. ("The theology of the cross calls the thing what it really is"—Luther.) And this test drives theology to the vincible and the vulnerable within its context—not to the strong, who are always able to rise above the actual influences of their contexts because of their strength; for in these assailable ones, whether they are

305

human or nonhuman beings, the real character of time-and-place manifests itself most explicitly. If "the world" as it writes its own story in the lives of these victims is overlooked by theology, or too easily answered from the side of "the Word of God," then it has been overlooked everywhere. Jesus sought out the lowest and most humiliated members of his society, the rejected ones, because he knew, no doubt, that if his message and his being could not speak to *them* it could not speak to the others either; for they were unable to hide from themselves and others, by reason of wealth or power or physical fortitude, the essential need of the general creaturely condition.

24.3. Mediated World Awareness.   There is no adequate substitute for immediate concourse with the world. Through a reflective self-awareness, an openness to others, and involvement with society's victims, the Christian theologian gains a knowledge of the world without which he or she could not be a faithful representative of the tradition of Jerusalem.

At the same time, firsthand commerce with the world is seldom sufficient in itself for the theological task. For one thing, despite the extension of this commerce beyond the confines of the self, narrowly conceived, the impressions and conclusions which are drawn by the theologian on the basis of her or his exposure to other persons and to society's victims are still the impressions and conclusions of an individual. While the subjectivism implicit in this is undoubtedly offset in important respects by the communality of the theological task, it is nonetheless entirely possible that, even working corporately, Christians will find in the world only what they wish to find, what their religious presuppositions already anticipate; and it is equally possible that they will overlook whole dimensions of what is actually present in the world because it does not correlate satisfactorily with their preconceptions. This is one reason—a negative one—why, in addition to its immediate world involvement, the theological community must also seek help in its "reading" of the world from other sources which are engaged in cognate pursuits.

There are also positive reasons why such help ought to be sought after. One of these relates to the complex nature of the world. No one person, no one discipline can possibly achieve a comprehensive knowledge of the totality. While the Renaissance man was, and in some respects remains, an important ideal, it is also steeped in the kind of individualism which is today not even viable. Even to understand the physical, quantifiable data of the planet, whole teams of researchers are needed. Theology has no secret door to fullness of comprehension. It *does* have, to be sure, an inherent longing for an informed awareness of "the totality," and an innate sense of the interrelatedness of all that is; and this gives it the possibility of being, here and there, an important *integrating* discipline in an age of specialization and the tragic fragmentation of knowledge. But theology needs to learn from other sources that are equipped to probe various dimensions of the world about which, otherwise, it would have no knowledge whatsoever; and the more serious the contextual thrust within the theological community, the more earnestly and humbly will it seek for help from these other sources.

Another positive reason why theology requires the wisdom of other human attempts at understanding the world is that is it able to recognize, in many of those attempts, an existential concern for the creation which parallels its own. There was a time—and it is not long past; indeed, in large segments of the Christian church on this continent it is still very much present—when it was characteristic of much religion that it could only behold in the sciences and humanistic studies of our civilization rivals to its own endeavors. So far as the past is concerned, this perception was not all due to the paranoia of the theologians; it was in part the result of a conspicuous bravado among the humane and physical disciplines of the Western world which, their sails filled with the winds of Enlightenment hubris, believed themselves the successors to religion. Religion was a futureless "illusion" (Freud), soon to be replaced by Science! But as we have already had occasion to notice, this mood is hardly the dominant one among representatives of the sciences and humanities today. In comparison with the recent past, our present context is one of a quite astonishing openness—if not to explicit religious teachings, at least to the quest for wholeness that belongs to the theological discipline at its best. This openness is a direct result of the humiliation of all human learning in the 20th century. One suspects and hopes that we have passed far beyond the naive and pathetic belief that the world can be saved by knowledge alone.

There are innumerable ways in which awareness of the world is mediated to the disciple community; but for the sake of convenience, as well as for purposes of making certain distinctions which I believe important to this discussion, I shall treat the subject, briefly, under four headings: the media, the sciences, philosophy, and the arts and humanities.

(a) The media: Karl Barth, we noted earlier, described the preacher as one who needs to have the Bible in one hand and the newspaper in the other. He did not mean *only* the Bible, nor did he mean *only* the newspaper. He was speaking figuratively; for, despite what Barthianism

has sometimes become in the hands of its more wooden exponents, Karl Barth himself was a thoroughly contextual thinker. He knew perfectly well that theology had to *address* the situation at hand, and that to do so it had to have access not only to the primary sources of the gospel but also to the best available wisdom concerning the state of the world.

The human situation can never be encompassed by what appears daily in "the newspaper," i.e., in any of the popular media; and, as we shall have to contend in a moment, there are reasons to suspect that a too exclusive reliance upon the media can lead to very questionable conclusions about the world. Yet a contextual theology cannot do without the information that is conveyed to us through the media, for in no other way is it possible to find out what is actually occurring in the world, at least at the level of "events."

This is even more necessary in our time than in the past, because no "event," however seemingly remote, is without consequence for our own context. In the earlier discussions we considered the close relationship between contextual and global theology. There, we maintained that a contextual theology, far from being an *alternative* to global theology, is its necessary correlate. Through its rootedness in the particular context, the disciple community finds itself drawn inevitably to the totality of which its specific "place" is part and from which it is truly inseparable. In turn, the community gains from its global awareness a perspective on its particular context which is essential to a right understanding of the latter. The events which occur daily throughout the globe are thus of vital interest to the disciple community. For the knowledge of these events, the media are indispensable.

It would be irresponsible to broach this subject in the North American context, however, without at once recognizing the limits and dangers of a too uncritical reliance upon the popular media for our understanding of the world in which we are living. The media are *limited* because they represent events as they occur, without the benefit of hindsight, and also because, for the most part, they are geared to popular consumption and therefore are seldom capable of either breadth or depth of analysis. But the most popular media on this continent are also plainly dangerous!

The *danger* stems from two factors in particular: biased interpretation, and the subtle hazards of the most popular ("hot") media, especially television.

It is of course inevitable that the interpretation of events will be biased, and it will surprise no one who has given serious thought to the matter that this is so with respect to the media in our context. But the fact is that many people in this same context have *not* given serious thought to the matter, and are prone to accept what they see on television or read in (often very superficial) newspapers and magazines as if it were simple fact. More important, in a capitalist society such as ours, where even most of the news of the world is "sponsored" by firms which have their own interests in the way that the world is presented to the public, the interpretation of events is generally slanted in favor of the values of the dominant culture. We are very familiar with the argument (regularly advanced within capitalist societies) that in nations where the media are publicly owned and government regulated they are biased towards the official ideology; but we seem less than imaginative in applying this same logic to our own situation. The truth is that the last several decades have demonstrated rather convincingly that many people in societies where the media are quite rigidly controlled by government (especially nations of the Russian bloc) tend to be far more cautious (not to say skeptical) about what they learn from these official channels than are North Americans, who rather blithely assume that anything entitled "News Broadcast" is eminently trustworthy.[37] Christians, whose primary loyalty is not to states and economic systems but to God, ought to manifest an openness to all interpretations, including those of sources distrusted by the dominant cultures of their own societies, *and* a certain critical distance from all interpretations. They will be especially wary of interpretations whose bias is towards the maintenance of the status quo in affluent societies like our own. Conversely, they will pay particular heed to sources which speak from, or sympathetically in relation to, the poor and oppressed, who are so often voiceless, and who otherwise do not have the power to influence public opinion.[38]

The dangers of the media themselves, specifically of television, have

---

37. "During the past 30 years general television has gradually taken over many of the functions historically belonging to the church. Television, not the church, now communicates what is going on outside the parish, telling us how to behave, what to wear, who has power and who is powerless, what to believe about the world and what is of ultimate value. In this sense, general television, far more than religious TV, is the church's real competitor" (William F. Fore, "Religion and Television: Report on the Research," *The Christian Century*, July 18-25, 1984, p. 713). See also William F. Fore, *Television and Religion* (Minneapolis: Augsburg, 1987).

38. There is, in fact, an increasing need for Christians themselves to be involved in the reporting and interpretation of world events. The ecumenical nature of the Christian church provides a unique opportunity for global communication, and the critical distance faith in God makes possible with respect to ideologies and empires gives the Christian movement a basis from which to interpret world events in a less prejudicial manner than can normally occur within either communistic or capitalistic societies. Certain Christian journals, like *The Christian Century, The Christian Science Monitor, Sojourners, Christianity and Crisis,* and *The United Church Observer,* rather consistently demonstrate this possibility.

only begun to be understood, and only by a few. It has to be asked not only whether the actual programming of television in our society is acceptable to Christians and others who have concern for social mores and for the future; beyond that it is necessary to raise questions about the medium itself. What does it mean for the *imagination* when a person's visual as well as auditory images are formed in his or her behalf, when, in short, nothing is left to the imagination? What must be said about the impact of such a medium on society when, by the time a child is ready for primary school she or he shall already have watched 5000 to 6000 hours of television, and upon entrance to college or university 21,000 to 26,000 hours, and by the end of a lifetime 9 full years?[39] More subtly still, what is communicated to the population of a nation or continent like our own when everything from violence in the home to mass starvation and jungle warfare is presented, neatly framed, to persons sitting comfortably in their living rooms and sipping coffee or martinis? Persons, moreover, who with the slightest movement of their fingertips, can turn it all off and select a more soothing universe![40]

Clearly, the media are indispensable to a theology which purposes to engage its worldly context. But it is just as obvious that they do not by themselves provide an adequate perspective on that context—that they are indeed a significant aspect of the context itself, on which perspective and much critical thought is needed!

(b) The sciences: Part of that perspective can be provided by the sciences. Contemporary theology has inherited a rather long and inhibiting tradition of mutual suspicion between religion and science, but both have begun to outgrow such an adolescent stage and to realize that they have more in common than was formerly believed.[41] As we have already suggested, this new potentiality for dialogue has come about, in part, because both religion and science have been reduced to greater modesty by 20th-century trends and events. Religion, particularly the Christian religion, where it has allowed itself to be informed both by modern scientific and modern biblical and theological scholarship, has relinquished its former propensity to believe itself in possession of scientific truth; and the sciences, excepting in their more quixotic representatives, have realized their

---

39. According to statistics published by the Canadian Broadcasting Corporation, Fall 1985.

40. A subtle aspect of the way in which TV "soothes" is that it very seldom probes deeply enough into any subject to engender depth of reflection in its viewers. "No one talks long enough to express anything complex. Depth of feeling, if it exists at all, has to be expressed in a word or a glance" (Bellah et al., *Habits of the Heart*, p. 280).

41. See Gerhard Ebeling, *The Study of Theology*, trans. Duane A. Priebe (Philadelphia: Fortress, 1975), pp. 82-83.

inadequacy as a surrogate religion. "I have come to believe," wrote a prominent North American scientist, "that in the world there is nothing to explain the world."[42] This modesty, where it is honestly and imaginatively at work, is beneficial to both pursuits, and it may be one of the most hopeful aspects of our present situation as a civilization that some scientists and some theologians are able to converse with one another on account of their shared concern for the future of the earth.

Certainly Christian theology needs both the physical and the social sciences. That is, if and insofar as it is a theology whose *theocentrism* is inclusive of an *anthropocentrism* and a *geocentrism*. Theological systems which do not manifest an ultimate concern for the creation but occupy themselves with the supernatural are always willing to *use* science in order to demonstrate the truth of their religious claims (that there is "a God," that the world was created, etc.); but theology which through an incarnational commitment to the creation intends to serve God *in* the world requires the testimony of the scientist for very different reasons. Such a theology needs to comprehend so far as possible what the world *is*, as a vital part of the awe and mystery that it contemplates, and it also needs to understand as precisely as possible what *is wrong with the world*.

It is particularly important for theology today to understand what is wrong with the world, and it is no longer sufficient—if it ever was—for the theological community to cast its analysis of the world's malaise in the ancient doctrinal language of sin and fallenness and the demonic. I do not suggest that this language ought to be abandoned, as theological liberalism tried to do; for if it is sufficiently rethought and reinterpreted it is both a useful and a necessary language. Our world cannot be understood or described at all if we only have access to the bland categories of Christian modernity! All the same, the traditional language which theology has employed to describe what is wrong with the world is, much of it, either so conventional or so arcane as to have no impact or so distorted by association with private morality as to be lacking in any wider, social dimension.

The physical and social sciences, which in their best representations are today less dominated by the religion of progress than they were in the 19th and early 20th centuries, have developed skills for measuring and describing natural and social problems that are indispensable to a contextual theology. Most, indeed, of the problems with which theological *ethics* must concern itself today are problems which have either been laid

---

42. Loren Eiseley, quoted by Richard E. Wentz in "The American Spirituality of Loren Eiseley," *The Christian Century*, April 25, 1984, p. 430.

bare by the sciences or can be detailed only by them. From biology and the other life sciences we have learned most of what we know, in an exact way, about the environmental pollution and the threat posed to ecosystems by a rampant and directionless technology. From demography we have come to know something of the problematic of a rapidly expanding world population. From ethically responsible physicists and chemists we have become more conscious of the effects of chemicals upon our environment and ourselves, and (40 years after Hiroshima) of the likelihood of a nuclear winter following atomic warfare. From the agricultural and engineering sciences we have a better conception of the state of earth's natural resources and its capacity for food production, and thus also of the limits by which whole populations of the planet are already profoundly affected.

Meantime, medical scientists have confronted society with a whole spate of problems consequent upon the "advances" which newly discovered drugs and operational procedures have made possible: When should persons be allowed to die "with dignity"? Who should decide about that? Or about abortions? How far should the transplantation of human organs be carried? Who should have access to life-saving machines and costly surgical techniques? How far should medical science go in eliminating chance from the propagation of the species through programs of genetic engineering? When is a human being alive and when dead? All such questions have obvious and direct bearing upon religious beliefs of every species; they are of particular significance to the Judeo-Christian tradition, some of whose emphases have generated the inventiveness that has brought these very questions to the fore.

The social sciences, especially psychology and sociology, are now regarded by many theologians as being as indispensable to theology as philosophy was once thought to be.[43] While these disciplines are evidently more susceptible to bias and even to ideological manipulation than are the physical sciences, they provide insights and perspectives on the personal and social behavior of human beings which are vital for any theology which attempts to understand today's world. Even ideologically committed versions of these sciences (and it is doubtful if any are, or perhaps even should be, nonideological) can illuminate the world that theology attempts to comprehend. The impact of Freudian, Jungian, and other schools of psychology and psychiatry on Christian theology during the past several decades could hardly be exaggerated. Nor can the influence of Marxist and other socioeconomic theory. It is not claimed that this

---

43. See Ebeling, *The Study of Theology*, pp. 95-96, 98, 102.

influence is unambiguously beneficial. Nevertheless it has enlarged the Christian perception of the world enormously, and it has also introduced into Christian consciousness an awareness of the psychic and social functioning of religion, including the Christian religion, in such a way that we can never again simply assume that *religion* is unambigously beneficial.

The sciences, then, have become partners in dialogue with theology, and in a way that was not true even four or five decades ago. Not only Christian ethics, but theology as such—namely, the "systematic" attempt at comprehension of the meaning of the faith—both may and must have discourse with the scientific disciplines if it is to realize even minimally its aim to understand and engage its worldly context.

Nevertheless, while science can illuminate much of that world, and while individual scientists, reaching through but beyond the conditions of their disciplines as such, are often especially helpful partners in dialogue today, the sciences do not provide theology with the fullness of perspective that it needs. They present aspects of the world to which only they have access; but these remain aspects. In the case of the natural sciences, the aspects of reality are confined to physical dimensions of the world; with the social sciences, to be sure, more wholistic images of the world are offered, but, on account of their preliminary commitments to special theories and worldviews, they are often less than satisfactory from the standpoint of a faith and discipline which needs to know "the little point where the battle is raging."

What we are encountering just here is no doubt a particularly knotty problem of theological method, but it cannot be ignored. We have used a number of expressions and images and metaphors heretofore, all of which imply the presence of this problem. We have spoken of theology as the meeting of stories, God's and the world's; and of the theologian's need to "know what time it is," and (just now again) of Luther's "little point." What these and similar turns of speech are driving at, so far as it relates to "the world" as an element in the theological task, is that theology needs the world's assistance in discerning *the basic spiritual climate* of the sociopolitical context that must be engaged. The media have their peculiar contribution to make to this quest. The sciences also, and it is indispensable. But where will theology turn to hear the human spirit, the collective spirit of the age, articulate its most fundamental state—the state that is undoubtedly being *enacted* in most of the events to which the media draw attention; the state that is *visible* in much of the data explored by the various sciences; but the state which has to be gathered into a coherent whole, that has to become *audible*; the state as "statement"?

(c) Philosophy: There need be little hesitation when it comes to answering this question for the classical traditions of Christian theology. Throughout the greater share of its history, and in certain contexts still today, theology has found its spokesperson for the mental and moral disposition of the world in the philosopher.[44] Already in the Newer Testament, notably in the Pauline and Johannine literature, philosophy has become the dialogue partner of Christian theology. It was natural that this should have happened; for theology needed, then as now, to hear from the world itself how it understood its condition. As Paul sought out the philosophers on Mars Hill, so Augustine conducted his discourse with the Platonists, and Aquinas with the Aristotelians, and Kierkegaard with the Hegelians, and Tillich and Rahner with the existentialists. For philosophy, in most of the societies with which, until now, the church has sojourned, has been the point at which the characteristic ethos of society has been articulated, refined, codified, and (to a greater or lesser extent) justified. While being once removed from primary experience, philosophy has nevertheless been representative of the deeper intellectual trends, psychic-noetic states, and ethical mores of society. To dialogue with philosophy under such conditions meant and means to attempt, as Christian, to understand and expose oneself to the most profound and articulate version of the human story, the story that humankind is presently telling about itself.

This being the case, it is not surprising that *the great shifts* in Christian theology have occurred almost entirely as responses to shifts in the history of philosophy. For these philosophical transitions represent and reflect alterations in the larger culture's self-understanding. When such transitions occur, Christian theology must either seek out the new story or else carry on as if the old one were still current—and risk becoming obsolete to the "high culture" along with it.

Thus, when in the High Middle Ages Western European thought shifted subtly from a more or less Platonic to a more or less Aristotelian approach to reality, Christian thinkers (especially Thomas) tried to find a way of addressing the faith to this new apologetic situation. One could think of the Reformation in a similar manner, though many devotees of Reformation theology like to imagine that the reformers were entirely independent of philosophic influence. Still, the impact of nominalism on

---

44. See David Tracy, *Talking about God: Doing Theology in the Context of Modern Pluralism* (New York: Seabury, 1963), p. 8; Ebeling, *The Study of Theology*, pp. 51-58.

Luther and of humanism on Calvin, Zwingli, Oecolampadius, and others cannot be overlooked. In our own time, nearly all of the important Protestant and Catholic theologians of the immediate past were drawn into dialogue with existentialism—not because (as they have all been accused of doing) they wished to exchange Christian beliefs for existentialist beliefs, but because they wanted to be in dialogue with the world. And existentialism was the most challenging voice of their world.

The situation in Anglo-Saxon cultures generally and in North America in particular is, however, by no means so clear-cut. It is true, of course, that some branches of theology have found in pragmatism, empiricism, positivism, and linguistic analysis the philosophic traditions with which they could dialogue. It is also true (and perhaps more pertinent to our discussion) that one school of theology in North America, process theology, has carried on its discourse in relationship with Whiteheadian thought. But, partly because of the captivity of philosophy by pragmatism in the whole Anglo-Saxon tradition and partly due to the more activistic orientation of North American society, philosophy has never been for us the kind of *spiritual* undertaking that it was both in the ancient and medieval worlds and in modern continental Europe, particularly Germany and France.[45] In fact "philosophy," with us, has been a rarefied, academic pursuit, professionalistic in the most restrictive sense of the term. It has hardly been representative even of the intelligentsia, let alone a refined statement of the *Zeitgeist*. For the most part, it has not addressed itself to the questions which must be addressed by any discipline that speaks for the deepest aspirations of a civilization—the questions which have made philosophy the capable dialogue partner of classical theology: the question of being (ontology), of meaning (teleology), of the good (ethics), of the beautiful (aesthetics), and others. In its most dominant expressions on this continent, philosophy has in fact often renounced such questions as being poetic or religious or in any case incapable of sound investigation. Individual practitioners of philosophy have sometimes been more receptive to these questions than their guild permitted, and with these (e.g., William James, Ernest Hocking) theology could engage in profitable discourse. But for the most part theology on this continent has *lacked* a philosophical partner in dialogue, and there can be no doubt that this is partially the reason why we have not developed a taste for indigenous

---

45. See Ebeling, *The Study of Theology*, chap. 5, pp. 53ff. For the importance of a "Protestant philosophy" in the French experience, see Edward Farley, *Ecclesial Man*, pp. 257ff.

theological reflection.[46] For (until recently), instead of turning elsewhere for the kind of representation of the culture that was needed for their discipline, most North American teachers of Christian theology have been content to continue discoursing with Platonism, Aristotelianism, Enlightenment rationalism, or existentialism—in other words, borrowed philosophies to match our borrowed theologies!

Theology must continue to search for its philosophic partner in dialogue, even when that partner cannot be identified with those who bear the name. Perhaps theology on this continent should more actively *encourage* deeper philosophical thought, for philosophy, by whatever nomenclature, is the attempt of the human mind to achieve its best wisdom (*sophia*) about its own condition—about "reality." It may be that ours is a historical context in which such wisdom is impossible to come by, or at least when it cannot be gathered into a coherent whole; for *scientia* (knowledge), of which we possess more than we can rightly appropriate, is no guarantor of *sapientia* (wisdom). Yet the philosophic quest, if we may so name it, surely belongs to the spirit of the human being, and it will not be deterred even by the prospect of failure—or even (as existentialism has so dramatically demonstrated) by the prospect that the meaning that it desires to find in being is purely illusory.

What many—both Christians and non-Christians—believe is that in our culture this aboriginal philosophic quest, where it has been abandoned by academic philosophies, has been taken up by others, notably by the arts.

(d) The arts and humanities: While the North American landscape— at least by comparison with continental Europe and the classical traditions with which Christian theology has dialogued in the past—may be wanting in philosophy, it is astonishingly prolific in art. All of the arts have relevance to theology, which is itself in some ways an art form rather than a science, for art mirrors the world in a special sense.

In whatever form, the uniqueness of the artistic representation of the world can be regarded both from a negative perspective (what art helps theology to *avoid*) and from a positive one (what it achieves that is salutary to theology). Negatively, we may contrast artistic creations with other human attempts to depict reality: thus, unlike the physical scientist, the

---

46. It is true, as David Tracy insists, that professional philosophy is useful to theology even when it refuses to go beyond the formal investigation of truth-claims: "Philosophical discussion will inevitably sharpen this issue of truth" (*Talking about God*, p. 8). But theology needs far more in a dialogue partner than one who can monitor its language and moderate its propensity to exaggeration, useful as that may be.

artist attempts to present the internal, invisible dimension of what is—the essence, i.e., that which gives the thing its being. Even the so-called still life, painted with painstaking precision (as in the "realism" of Alex Colville), attempts to communicate to us this invisible "something," which the external properties of the thing cannot contain. Again, in distinction from the social scientist, the artist does not intend to present data about reality which will demonstrate, or can be summarized in, general behavioral laws or consistent theories. The ideological impulse may be found within some artists, but it does not belong to art itself, and when it is dominant—as in the case of "official" art in the soviet states or some recent American films and television dramas (*Amerika*)—everyone readily senses the violation of the artistic urge that this implies.

Again, unlike formal philosophy, art does not purposely seek to advance beyond the particular in order to describe the universal. If something universal is in fact revealed through the art form, as it frequently is felt to do, it is because of the faithfulness of the artist to the particular.

All of these negative factors are interesting to theology and indicate reasons why theologians who look to the sources of worldly dialogue treated earlier ought at least to supplement their awareness of the world through regular exposure to the art of their cultures.[47] A theology too exclusively turned towards the sciences is tempted to cast the dialogue with the world in physical terms (creation/evolution; the possibility of the miraculous; ethical issues centering in material problems, etc.) and to neglect the transcendental, the teleological, and even perhaps, in the deepest sense, the ontological issues with which Christian belief must concern itself. A theology which has made the social sciences its primary entrée into the heart of the world is apt to concentrate so undividedly on establishing a dialogical rapport with this or that socioeconomic, political, or psychological theory that it is tempted to confuse the theory with reality—and reality is *always* more complex than theory. A theology which finds itself engaged in discourse, chiefly, with some particular philosophic

---

47. That Christian theology should be conscious of art is not as novel an idea as many imagine. Luther, in his correspondence, wrote: "I am persuaded that without knowledge of literature pure theology cannot at all endure, just as heretofore, when letters have declined and lain prostrate; nay, I see that there has never been a great revelation of the Word of God unless He has first prepared the way by the rise and prosperity of languages and letters, as though they were John the Baptists. . . . Certainly it is my desire that there shall be as many poets and rhetoricians as possible, because I see that by these studies, as by no other means, people are wonderfully fitted for the grasping of sacred truth and for handling it skillfully and happily. . . . Therefore I beg of you that at my request (if that has any weight) you will urge your young people to be diligent in the study of poetry and rhetoric" (quoted by D. J. A. Clines, "Story and Poem: The Old Testament as Literature and as Scripture," *Interpretation* 34 [1980]: 115).

school may, if the philosophy in question is sufficiently sensitive, avoid the ideological pitfalls of those who converse too exclusively with sociologists or psychologists; but the temptation for all philosophically orientated theology, and particularly in the modern period when philosophy itself has become increasingly rationalistic, is that it will accentuate the intellectual dimension of Christian faith and neglect the noncognitive dimensions. Pietistic and spiritualistic rejection of *theology* as such are in reality often (understandable) reactions to just this captivation of theology by rationalism.

It is by no means my intention here to disdain or discourage dialogue with the various human disciplines under discussion. Far from it! But some caution must be registered in this connection, because so much theology appears to satisfy itself too soon with one partner of worldly discourse, and until very recently the preferred partners have been the more "scientific"—that is, the more theoretical—disciplines. This no doubt reflects theology's own self-image, especially its traditional propensity to cast belief in a theoretical mode.

Positively considered, the uniqueness of the artistic representation of the world is related to its greater *immediacy* in relation to what it depicts or describes. Of all the "mediated" sources of world-awareness treated in this subsection, art is the most immediate. It is this in two senses: first, as concerns the person of the artist. It is hazardous to generalize too grandly about such matters, but it is not accidental that words like "feeling" and "sensitivity" have been habitually associated with artists and what they do. If it is possible in principle, to distinguish art from other forms of intelligence and creativity, it would surely have to be on the basis of the way in which the artist relates to his or her subject. Thought, certainly, and not only "feeling," is involved in this relation; but it is thought which arises out of a distinctive kind of proximity to the subject that would be regarded as inhibiting in other forms of investigation. The artist "suffers," it is often said; and this can become an absurd romanticism if it is misunderstood. Many artists do not suffer conspicuously or inordinately! But if suffering is understood in terms of identification—let us say as a matter of empathy or pathos; as a consequence of allowing the subject a place within one's soul, or of failing to safeguard oneself against the subject; if it is understood, in short, as a kind of exposure of oneself to the raw stuff of existence—then perhaps this ancient connection between art and suffering can be sustained. The artist "suffers" the world to pass through him or her—and if that can be accomplished without pain, then theology, too, had better reconsider its primary

318

data. Unlike the scholar, the researcher, the investigator of the nature of things, the describer of this and that, the artist has no protective detachment from his or her subject—or, more realistically stated, the insulating psychic defenses with which all of us shield ourselves from our world is, characteristically, less effective in the case of human beings who become artists.

To illustrate: Recently a young Innuit artist explained to me why he had to give up his art finally. He found that as he drew and painted the images symbolizing the life and struggles of his ancient northern people, the images were, so to speak, transferred to his own person. In depicting a scene in which a hunter was wounded, for example, he would find distortions occurring in his own face—the hunter's pain had become his own. Or in painting some representation of the awe of his tribe before the natural world—the bear or the wolf—his arm would suddenly become numb. The unguardedness of the artist, which in more "developed" cultures has undoubtedly been modified by educational distancing from first-order experience and by the distractions of the technological society, is often very close to the surface of consciousness in the art of indigenous peoples.

It is not surprising, in view of this immediacy of identification with the subject, that the artist frequently detects what is occurring, covertly, within a society both more accurately and more expeditiously than most other human beings—even, it may well be, before the victims of these occurrences, of whom we spoke earlier. For while the victims are those most vulnerable to the deleterious effects of society's pursuits (that is what it means that they are victims), they are very often "dumb before their shearers": something happens *to* them, but they are frequently—perhaps typically—innocent as to its causes, or even its wider manifestations. The artist feels some of the same effects—either directly, as has often been the case, or through sympathetic identification with the victims (Goya); but the artist also sees relationships between things, senses something of the causes as well as the less conspicuous effects, observes subtle connections, and is able to give expression to all this. "I think of art, at its most significant," said Marshall McLuhan, "as a DEW line, a Distant Early Warning system that can always be relied on to tell the old culture what is beginning to happen to it."[48] It is precisely this capacity of art to plumb the depths, to discern the hidden roots and consequences of events,

---

48. In *Understanding Media* (quoted in *The Dynamics of Change*, ed. Don Fabun [Englewood Cliffs, N.J.: Prentice-Hall, 1968], p. 5).

and to portray them vividly, that has made art so vital in every major revolution and reformation, and made authority fear it above all else.[49]

The second way that art contributes to the theological work of the disciple community is by helping to provide precisely that integrated or holistic image of the cultural context which exposes the essential *spirit* of the age, the *Zeitgeist*. It is this deep and ineffable spiritual mood that Christian theology needs most to sense if it is to engage the heart of its host culture, and not only some of its peripheral or superficial concerns. It was this recognition that prompted Paul Tillich to write: "Art in all its forms can show three states of mind: hopelessness, foolish hope, and genuine hope." And he added: "If we look at our present artistic creations we find that artistic expressions of hopelessness by far prevail. . . . Artistic interpretations of genuine hope . . . are rare today."[50]

The third way in which art is the most immediate of the mediated awareness we may acquire of our world has of course to do with its unique capacity for communication. A novel, even a complicated novel (Dostoevsky's *The Brothers Karamazov* or Melville's *Moby Dick* or André Langevin's *Dust over the City*) is able to speak to us—even to the less sophisticated among us—far more forthrightly than are more discursive discussions of perhaps similar themes. A drama like Tennessee Williams's *Cat on a Hot Tin Roof* communicates more in the space of 90 minutes about the breakdown of family life, the uncertainty of human sexuality, the disillusionment of those who dreamed dreams in America than can be achieved through many painful hours of historical and social scientific research. F. Scott Fitzgerald's *The Great Gatsby* already tells the story of decline and fall in the "New World," not only long before the sociological best-sellers of the past two decades but to better effect. Similar claims could be made for the paintings of Wyeth or the Group of Seven or Morriseau, and for the music of Copland, Ives, or some contemporary folk artists. A film like *The Decline of the American Empire* communicates in subtle and immediate symbols complex analyses of the postmodern world that even clever and well-informed journalists or social commentators must envy. Not all art communicates to all persons. Each of us has his or her specific capacities and incapacities where art forms are concerned—though these are subject to modification through education. But

---

49. Consider, for example, the Nazi rejection of the great art of Käthe Kollwitz or Ernst Barlach. Because this art depicted the real condition of many persons, indeed of whole classes, and therefore gave the lie to the "official art" of the party, with its smiling blond children and pleasant pastoral scenes, it was declared to be *Entartete Kunst* (literally, nonart), and proscribed. Ironically, the same works of art are used propagandistically today in eastern Europe to demonstrate the evils of capitalist societies.

50. "The Right to Hope," *The University of Chicago Magazine*, November 1965, p. 19.

it is extremely rare when art of some form does not "get through" to an individual.

By the same token, art is not without its problematic dimensions where theology is concerned. One such dimension is its great variety. Since art does mirror a society, it will mirror the many facets of that society, and how will the theological community determine which art should be taken with greatest seriousness? Another problematic dimension has to do with authenticity. Every age produces inauthentic as well as authentic art. Our own age has been highly productive of what has been described as *kitsch*, and it is not incidental to our subject that *religious kitsch* abounds in our culture.[51] Kitsch is cheap art, false art: it falsifies existence, usually through simplification and sentimentalization. It exaggerates the positive and eliminates what negates, thus lending to reality a harmony that it does not in fact possess. A theology of the cross can hardly be satisifed with such art. But who will determine what is false art and what is true? It has been aptly said, "One man's kitsch is another man's kitchen!"

Another particularly knotty issue, closely related to art's capacity to falsify existence, is the *use* of art for entertainment. Just as the media have conditioned us to sit passively and unmoved while viewing scenes of war and human degradation photographed from "real life," so the entertainment industry in North America has numbed our minds to the poignancy and drama and catharsis that art traditionally produced in earlier societies. Every supermarket and elevator shaft accompanies our mundane activities with Vivaldi and Bach and Samuel Barber and the Beatles—in the form of Muzak. Paintings and prints are purchased for their color schemes. Drugstore bookshelves are filled with books designed by their publishers, if not also their authors, chiefly to titillate—in a word, to *assist* in our (very human) desire to escape the real world. Even serious and socially illuminating films like *One Flew over the Cuckoo's Nest* can be received by us in the spirit of sheer entertainment, because the entertainment mentality has been so thoroughly and successfully inculcated in us. Clearly, art is never *unambiguously* accessible or useful to the disciple community in its search for truth about the world.

This points to the need for contact, on the part of the theological community, with worldly disciplines which can help to provide an intelligent and discerning *perspective* on its host culture's artistic self-expression. This means in particularly those disciplines traditionally grouped

---

51. See Gillo Dorfles, ed., *Kitsch: The World of Bad Taste* (New York: Universe Books, 1969), especially "Religious Trappings," pp. 129ff.

under the nomenclature "humanities"—especially history, languages ancient and modern, and the various disciplines which enable us to appreciate and analyze art itself, including literature and literary criticism, musicology, aesthetics, and so on. In a context of overproduction, pluralism, consumerism, entertainment, and cheap art, theology is more than ever in need of assistance from those who have devoted themselves to these humane disciplines; and it is a rather sad commentary on theological education today that many students entering seminaries and theological colleges are *less* well educated in the humanities than was the case four or five decades ago. (Many of them, in fact, have so concentrated on *religion* already in their undergraduate study, following the general pattern of early "specialization" in our fragmented centers of learning, that they are virtually innocent of serious historical, linguistic, literary, and other types of knowledge which we have insisted is requisite for the doing of theology itself.)

It is by no means easy in the North American context, however, to gain access to the kind of humane sciences which can provide such necessary background for Christian theology. This is partly due to vast alterations in public educational philosophy, and partly to new attitudes within the fields of the humanities themselves. With respect to the former, one must note that it is impossible, for instance, in most institutions of public education to learn the classical languages (Greek, Hebrew, Latin) which were once considered the very *basis* of the humanities, and which, even if one finds that claim extravagant, certainly constitute the only entrée into the beginnings of a *profound* awareness of the foundational cultures of our Western civilization. Without such beginnings of awareness, how will it be possible to assess what our civilization *has come to*? If we have only the present and its "values" to go by, what criteria will we bring to bear upon the analysis of the present?

It will be answered, rightly, that *history* can help to provide such criteria of judgment.[52] But, again, anyone who has been exposed to primary, secondary, and even college and university curricula—not to mention their human "products"—will realize that real historical awareness is not likely to result from such minimal and superficial offerings. The presentation of historical *data* (and there is little even of that) does not make for informed historical *consciousness*.

The other limiting factor in theology's search for concourse with the humanities is that, in the meantime, the humanities have tended to

---

52. See chap. 1, §5.2.

associate themselves more keenly with the sciences than with the arts (despite their continuing association with the latter in name), partly in order to justify themselves to a pragmatically orientated society, and partly on account of the power of the scientific-technological mind-set that has been part of the mythology of our era. There are splendid exceptions to this rule, but it remains the norm, at least for the present. Scientists and technologists qualify for large government and private grants; historians and departments of romance literature do not. Graduates in English seldom find jobs. The consequence of this is that the humanities increasingly seek to *imitate* the natural and social sciences. Everyone speaks about "research." That a nomenclature quite different from the word "research" might belong to the *sciences humaines*—the *Geisteswissenschaften*—is seldom considered. That the object of humanistic studies might be to "get back to the sources," to be discerning, even to have wisdom (such were the original aims of the Renaissance thinkers who introduced these "humane sciences") is not in our time part of the working rhetoric of the disciplines concerned.

This may mean that the Christian community itself should engage more actively in the attempt to preserve the humanities—not, of course, for selfish reasons alone (dialogue), but neither to their exclusion. The Christian movement does not depend upon the retention of classical or Renaissance culture; but besides being a "betrayal of the West" (Ellul), the demise of what was best in classical, Renaissance, and Enlightenment civilization would constitute an incalculable loss to the Christian movement—the movement which, after all, gave birth to and nurtured the humanist enterprise.

Conclusion

Considering the many components that are brought together in the work of theology, one may well ask whether such a discipline is even possible. Or is it a "discipline" at all? Is it not perhaps too inclusive to be regarded as a discipline? Might it not be described, rather, as a broad forum of contemplation—the manner in which some human beings attempt to arrive at coherence—a way of integrating the diverse and disparate elements of existence?

Once, when I was making a long journey by air, I was asked by a fellow passenger to describe my work as a theologian. Since it was a lengthy flight, and since my companion seemed willing to listen, I took my time and attempted to answer his question in a responsible way. At the end of my discourse, he looked at me very earnestly and, without a trace of irony in his voice, said: "It must be wonderful to think about everything, all the time!" I took this rejoinder as a compliment—not to myself, but to the discipline; for it was followed by a sort of confession, in which my traveling companion confided to me that he, too, had once wished to think "about everything all the time"; he had even, he said, "prayed." But now, as an executive for a large multinational firm, his life had become so centered in his work that he no longer could afford to be drawn into such flights of contemplation. It was, he said, a great pity.

If one defines the discipline of theology by reference to its greatest practitioners over the centuries, there is perhaps no more accurate way of describing this pursuit than the words which came quite spontaneously and even innocently to the mind of my fellow traveler that day: thinking about everything, all the time. To a world which has so refined the mode of knowing anything that a single individual may be thought presumptuous even to call himself or herself a biologist or a geographer, let alone a historian (!), it can only seem the height of foolishness when a man or woman—or even a whole community—sets out to "do theology." Even theologians manifest embarrassment over the grandiose shadow cast by their venerable discipline, "the Queen of the Sciences," and are often quick to explain that their "field" is of course only this or that period or this or that doctrinal area. To claim more—unless one is a Barth or Tillich, with one's writings nearly all behind one—seems to press beyond mere arrogance and into the arena of the absurd.

Yet a person, a victim of the age of specialization, recognizes in such a quest something basic to his own humanity: "I too once wished to think about everything all the time." There is something fundamental to *humanity* in the theological quest; and if it is lost, set aside by life's duties, or ruled out as impossible from the start, there remains, happily, some evidence of deprivation. Certainly theology, with all of the above-named threads of interest and need, and many more besides, cannot be regarded as "a discipline" in the way that our world now uses this language. But it *is* the discipline of the disciples of Jesus Christ—and therefore, perhaps, a truly *human* discipline after all.

CHAPTER ▪ FIVE

Theological Method

Every methodological reflection is abstracted from the cognitive work in which one actually engages. Methodological awareness always follows the application of a method; it never precedes it.[1]

25. A Fundamental Tension

25.1. Method Flows from Content.   Method refers to the manner in which the practitioners of any discipline reflect upon their subject matter with a view to its comprehension and communication. This being so, we may say that the entire content of the present volume is concerned, in the broadest sense, with theological method. We are asking what is involved in thinking the faith.

It will also be evident from the direction that our previous discussion has taken, however, that method cannot be regarded, in our view, as an independent consideration. The manner in which those who profess a given discipline deliberate upon their subject matter will depend upon the character of that subject matter. It is one thing to advance a legitimate method for the study and communication of phenomena observable to the senses and susceptible to experimentation under more or less controlled conditions; it is something else to enucleate a method appropriate to the investigation and communication of historical, literary, cultural, and other types of less objectifiable or nonobjectifiable phenomena. A method appropriate to physics or geology cannot be transferred to the arts or social

---

1. Paul Tillich, *Systematic Theology*, vol. 1 (Chicago: University of Chicago Press, 1951), p. 34.

sciences, nor vice versa, even though some aspects of the methods of each may be useful to the other.

Theological method is a particularly complex instance of methodological reflection. The reason for this is not *simply* that Christian theology has to do with nonobjectifiable realities—"God and the things of God." That the theistic basis of the faith is an important part of this methodological complexity is testified to by the mass of literature that has been devoted to it. But it is misleading to think that Christian theological method is complicated exclusively or even primarily by eternal questions which it shares, after all, with every other explicit theistic religion: whether God exists, whether God is responsible for the universe, whether God is all-powerful and at the same time merciful—the list goes on. These are not, in fact, the kinds of questions that the earliest Christians found they had to face; and while much of modern and contemporary Christian scholarship in the Anglo-Saxon world especially has expended itself on such questions, one may doubt that they are the dominant questions of our own age either. Undoubtedly the existence of God, which is *pre*supposed by biblical religion, is a vital concern for many of our contemporaries; but a much more immediate concern is whether *our own* existence has any purpose in it!

The complexity of Christian theological method has more to do with the latter than with the former concern. For it is the particular interaction of the Christian message and the human quest for meaning that colors the methodological discussions of Christian theology from the primitive church onwards. This interaction is characterized by tension; and this tension, which lies at the heart of the Christian faith experience, gives to theological method its peculiar problematique.

Our purpose in the present chapter will be, first, to describe this fundamental tension in the content of Christian belief; second, to demonstrate its effect upon theological method; and, third, in the light of these distinctions, to consider the course of methodological discussion in recent theology. Throughout, we shall draw upon the previous considerations concerning contextuality in theology and our own specific context.

25.2. Gospel: Continuity and Discontinuity. We said that the methodological complexity of Christian theology stems primarily from the peculiar interaction of the Christian message and the human quest for meaning, and that this interaction is characterized by *tension*. There are numerous ways of describing this tension, but it will be convenient for our present purposes if we employ the polar concepts of continuity and discontinuity.

The tension in question may then be stated as follows: while the core of the Christian message (kerygma) is *discontinuous* with human experience, the message is nevertheless obviously intended for human beings and must therefore in some way be, or become, *continuous* with their experience.

To elaborate: From the outset, the Christian message has been known as "good news"—*euangelion*, "gospel."[2] That it is "news" suggests at once the dimension of discontinuity. The message could hardly be regarded as news were it simply a recounting, reinterpretation, or refinement of something already present to human experience and knowledge. It was and is news because it was and is the introduction of something *new* (*novum*).[3] The writings of the "new" Testament, as well as much of the liturgical, poetic, hymnological, and homiletical traditions of the Christian faith, are steeped in this sense of the new. Through them all runs the announcement, "The most wonderful thing has happened!"[4] As the medieval advent hymn *In Dulci Jubilo* exhorts—

> *Good Christians all rejoice*
> *with heart and soul and voice!*
> *Give ye heed to what we say;*
> *News! News!*
> *Jesus Christ is born today. . . .*

A sense of abiding surprise is present in the community which receives this message—and this despite the fact (or because of it?) that the original disciple community, comprised as it was of members of the family of Israel, was already a community of waiting and longing precisely for

---

2. The original Old English *god spel,* meaning "glad tidings," conveyed an ambiguity, when presented in written form, on account of the first word, "god," which was naturally confused with the name for the deity. This "ambiguity of its written form led to its being interpreted as a compound, god-spel, f. *God* + *spel* in the sense of 'discourse" or 'story' " (*Compact Edition of the Oxford English Dictionary: Complete Text Reproduced Micrographically,* vol. 1 [London: Oxford University Press, 1979], p. 1178).

3. The concept of "the new" is of particular importance in much contemporary theology, including liberation theologies and the theology of hope. "The Christian hope is directed towards a *novum ultimum,*" writes Jürgen Moltmann in *The Theology of Hope* (London: SCM, 1965), p. 33, "towards a new creation of all things by the God of the resurrection of Jesus Christ. It thereby opens a future outlook that embraces all things, including also death, and into this it can and must also take the limited hopes of a renewal of life, stimulating them, relativizing them, giving them direction."

4. I owe this formulation to George Buttrick, whose first principle as a homiletician was stated precisely in this phrase. All Christian preaching, Buttrick insisted, must in one way and another convey this announcement.

something new. A messianic community. *That* the Messiah had come, and the *manner* of his advent—both constitute the basis of this aboriginal Christian wonderment. The old cause-and-effect sequence of the historical process did not produce the new reality; it was introduced into the midst of the old, a veritable non sequitur—something "new under the sun" (Eccl. 1:9).

There are countless ways in which the tradition testifies to this newness, but perhaps none is more provocative than the symbol of the *virgin birth*. Despite its misappropriation by fundamentalist religion in the North American context, the virgin birth is a particularly useful doctrinal symbol because, when it is understood theologically rather than biologically, it encapsulates the whole motif that we are concerned to understand here through the juxtaposition of the continuity/discontinuity categories. The dismissal of the virgin birth "dogma" by liberalism, *and* its determined retention by Christian fundamentalism, should not rob theology of the symbolic significance of this biblical myth.

The virgin birth symbolizes the discontinuity principle, on the one hand. The possibility that is given here (so declared the believing community) is not a merely *natural* occurrence, it is a purely *gracious* one. It has come to be as God's possibility, not humanity's. It is a "new creation," not just a further unfolding of the old. Left to nature, the salvific reality that is required if the historical process is to be prevented from oblivion ("saved") simply could not occur. What has come to be in and through Jesus as the Christ is as "*un*natural," as discontinuous with nature, human potentiality, or merely *historical* providence as a child emerging from the womb of a pure virgin.[5]

While the dimension of "the new" and therefore of discontinuity with what has gone before is indispensable to Christian faith and theology, however, it is held in tension with the polar accent upon continuity: the new thing under the sun as it were, meets, embraces, corresponds with, "answers" the old. Although it is astonishing news, this same *euangelion* is intended exactly for human ears. To be sure, it has not been *produced by* history; nevertheless, it has been well and truly *introduced into* the

---

5. Under certain circumstances, the literal interpretation of the virgin birth *can*, I believe, express this essential wonder. One supposes that it must have done so in the premodern epoch, and that it may still do so in human communities which have been insulated by circumstances from "the scientific worldview." But in the modern period (and contemporary biblical literalism is both a reaction to modern fact orientation and a reflection of it), the concentration upon the "fact" of an alleged biological "miracle" *detracts from* precisely the symbolic significance of the "dogma." Instead of being contemplated as a focal point for faith's primeval wonder at divine grace, it becomes a test for doctrinal orthodoxy.

historical process, and is in the most explicit sense an *historical* event (the rationale for early Christian rejection of the docetic tendencies which so obviously tempted many believers). This *god spel* announces what is certainly a miracle—for faith the *fundamental* miracle. But the miracle occurs in "the fulness *of time*" (Gal. 4:4), and not merely as a marvel from above, a cancellation of the laws of nature and history, an extraordinary supranatural occurrence before which human beings would simply have to bow in abject and uncomprehending humility.

And just this is the other side of the virgin birth symbol: this "impossible" event, possible only to God, clothes itself in the most possible, even ordinary and everyday occurrence: a baby is born to a young mother.

> *How silently, how silently,*
> *The wondrous gift is given.*

Everything about this event is mundane: a too-recently wed young woman, no one special, gives birth under hard circumstances. Nothing could be more common—then or now. And just this commonness is what must not be undone by the human desire for magnificence, by characteristically "religious" clamoring after the spectacular and the unusual—heavenly signs and oriental potentates and angelic hosts! These Lukan/Matthean testimonies must be recognized for what they are—mythopoetic and liturgical-theological statements concerning the (unseen) *significance* of these very ordinary occurrences. If this is not understood (and Christian history is unfortunately littered with misunderstanding at this juncture), the very point of the *incarnation* is lost in a motley array of legend and superstition. The history of the world is full, after all, of tales about gods-become-human. This, insisted the primitive church, is not another such tale. Every attempt to turn it into such must be subjected to the test of Scripture, which identifies this lust for the spectacular with human vainglory and with *tentatio* (see Matt. 4:11, par.).

Few have understood this as well as Luther, whose feeling for the extraordinary-within-the-ordinary (*finitum capax infiniti*) is in evidence throughout his writings, but especially in his homely meditations on the birth of the Christ:

> The name of the maiden was Mary. . . . Among the downtrodden people she was one of the lowliest, not a maid of high station in the capital city, but a daughter of a plain man in a small town. We may infer that she was of no account because she herself said in her song, "he hath regarded the

low estate of his handmaiden." Who knows whether Joachim and Anna, her parents, were alive at the time? In all likelihood she was an orphan. . . .

The journey was certainly more than a day from Nazareth in Galilee to Bethlehem. . . . Joseph had thought, "When we get to Bethlehem, we shall be among relatives and can borrow everything." A fine idea that was!

Bad enough that a young bride married only a year could not have had her baby at Nazareth in her own house instead of making all that journey of three days when heavy with child! How much worse that when she arrived there was no room for her! . . .

Joseph had to do his best, and it may well be that he asked some maid to fetch water or something else, but we do not read that anyone came to help. They heard that a young wife was lying in a cow stall and no one gave heed. Shame on you, wretched Bethlehem! The inn ought to have been burned with brimstone, for even though Mary had been a beggar maid or unwed, anybody at such a time should have been glad to give her a hand.

There are many of you in this congregation who think to yourselves: "If only I had been there! How quick I would have been to help the Baby! I would have washed his linen. How happy I would have been to go with the shepherds to see the Lord lying in the manger!" Yes, you would! You say that because you know how great Christ is, but if you had been there at that time you would have done no better than the people of Bethlehem. . . . Why don't you do it now? You have Christ in your neighbor. You ought to serve him, for what you do to your neighbor in need you do to the Lord Christ himself. . . .

. . . Those who say that Mary was not a real mother lose all the joy. He was a true Baby, with flesh, blood, hands and legs. . . .

Let us, then, meditate upon the Nativity just as we see it happening in our own babies. I would not have you contemplate the deity of Christ, the majesty of Christ, but rather his flesh. Look upon the Baby Jesus. Divinity may terrify man. Inexpressible majesty will crush him. That is why Christ took on our humanity, save for sin, that he should not terrify but rather with love and favor he should console and confirm.[6]

As Luther's charge to his congregation makes poignantly clear ("Let us . . . meditate upon the Nativity *just as we see it happening in our own babies. I would not have you contemplate . . . deity . . . !*"), the *continuity* principle is, for him, at least as important as the discontinuity principle—probably more so. Because *unless God's act in Christ is a credible participation in our own very mundane lives, the redemptive*

---

6. *The Martin Luther Christmas Book*, trans. Roland Bainton (Philadelphia: Westminster, 1948), pp. 19ff.

import of it is lost to us. The appearance of a god in the midst of human surroundings may indeed be "news," but it will not be *good* news unless our human lives, with all their promise and their failure, are existentially touched by the event. We may marvel at the extraordinary, but adoration ("What Mary and Joseph did next, nobody knows," continues Luther. "The scholars say they adored")—*adoration* presupposes the experience of spiritual *incorporation*—becoming part of the event. To be sure, the discontinuity principle is still very much the presupposition of Luther's Christmas sermon (why, otherwise, make it the subject of proclamation?); but it is present as a descant, so to speak, upon the theme of continuity—"our own babies"!

The birth, and likewise the entire story at the center of the Christian faith, serves to express the fundamental tension in Christian theology which manifests itself in theological method: continuity and discontinuity, the old and the new, accord and discord, meeting and distance, immanence and transcendence, folly and wisdom. These two poles inform the Christian story from beginning to end; and as the story is, so must the means of our telling it be. Content determines method. No method can be adequate which does not do justice to this tension.

It is important to recognize that the tension is not a merely intellectual one. It is a lived tension, grounded in the faith experience itself. For on the one hand the human being who hears (hearingly!) this gospel *does* find it to correspond with that within him or her which has been, as it were, waiting for just such a kerygma: forgiveness answering guilt, mercy answering self- and societal condemnation, reconciliation answering alienation, love answering estrangement. . . . Were this not the case, who could consider such a message "news," let alone *good* news? But this continuity factor is from the outset in dialogue with its antithesis. Existential discontinuity consists not only in the realization that there is nothing automatic in the process (grace is not a foregone conclusion!) but also in the more subtle fact that, strangely, there is that within the human person which positively *resists* this news. For it contains a clarity, a seering truthfulness, a *krisis* (judgment) that is unnerving to the human psyche, a depth of comprehension in which the human being cannot unambiguously rejoice. The "good" news is also—under the conditions of historical existence—bad news.[7]

---

7. "The Gospel is bad news before it is good news. It is the news that man is a sinner, to use the old word, that he is evil in the imagination of his heart, that when he looks in the mirror all in a lather what he sees is at least eight parts chicken, phony, slob" (Frederick Buechner, *Telling the Truth: The Gospel as Tragedy, Comedy and Fairy Tale* [New York: Harper & Row, 1977], p. 7).

We are reaching now into the deeper recesses of that complexity we have attributed to Christian theological method. Already within the disciple community itself, this complexity discloses itself in the community's attempt to comprehend its subject matter. But we have said that method has to do not only with comprehension but also with communication. As we move to the latter category, we shall see how the complexity glimpsed in the community's own faith dialogue, with its subtle combination of acceptance and rejection, belief and unbelief, is magnified by its missionary experience.

25.3. The *Skandalon* and the Search for Common Ground.   Not only does the gospel engage that within the self which "hungers and thirsts" for just such good news, but it convinces its hearers that the whole of humanity is waiting for such a message. The "evangelical" drive is inherent within the message itself. It cannot be kept to oneself, "hidden under a bushel" (Matt. 5:15, par.). It demands to be "shouted from the housetops" (Matt. 10:27; Luke 12:3).

Yet when the disciple community attempts to proclaim its glad tidings it finds itself spurned. It is met by a hostility that is not explicable on the basis of lack of comprehension alone. The discontinuity principle here is more than a cognitive disjunction between the message and those for whom it is meant. It is a matter of offense! To use Paul's word, it is a *skandalon*. Why? We shall have to consider this more closely.

To begin with, there can be no question about the imperative to communicate. The "missionary" impulse is not appended to belief as a kind of second step; it is inherent in faith itself—just as the *hearing* of stupendous news of any kind creates an instantaneous desire to share it. The *mission* of the disciple community is not an option, then, but, like the drive to comprehend what is believed (*fides quaerens intellectum*), the compulsion to *communicate* what is believed is built into its reception by faith. "We *cannot*," pleaded the first disciples, ordered by the authorities to be silent, "we cannot but speak of what we have seen and heard" (Acts 4:20). It is not a matter of choice, it is a veritable *destiny* (*anangkē*)! "*Anangkē* ["necessity," RSV] is laid upon me," writes the apostle Paul to the church at Corinth. "Woe to me if I do not preach the gospel!" (1 Cor. 9:16).

The motif is not unfamiliar to anyone who is cognizant of the prophetic tradition of Israel. It is the Newer Testament's continuation of a familiar biblical theme:

> If I say, "I will not mention him,
> or speak any more in his name,'

332

there is in my heart as it were a burning fire
  shut up in my bones,
and I am weary with holding it in,
  and I cannot.

(Jer. 20:9)

What we call theology is a vital aspect of the Christian response to this *anangkē*. Faith cannot be satisfied with comprehension; it has to be communicated. It cannot even find fulfillment in doxology. Doxology is indeed a dimension of theology, but to say that theology *is* doxology[8] is to risk overlooking the compulsory dimension in faith, the "apostolic" sense of having-to.[9] The apostles were well-acquainted with Jeremiah's frank and even desperate wish to be silent and to forget. Irresistible grace—*gratia irresistibilis*!

Seldom has Christianity on this continent understood that side of discipleship. Mission and evangelism in our experience have been absorbed by the general optimism and sentimentality of our religious affections, so that neither the prophets' reluctance nor the apostles' sense of "having to do it" has found a sympathetic echo among us. One suspects that this is not unrelated to the subject matter of our earlier discussions— the typical failure of Christianity in North America to engage in an indigenous theological struggle. Would our much-publicized "evangelical" zeal be so enthusiastic were we to seek, in our preaching and our theology, truly to *engage* our own culture, rather than merely to affirm or confirm or comfort it, or to play the expected role of chastising it and bringing it "back to Jesus"?

The *anangkē* of communication expresses itself in a resolute search on the part of the evangelical community for a *basis* for communication with those to whom it is sent. In the same passage where Paul uses the strong term "necessity," to describe his vocation as preacher, he proceeds at once to demonstrate the search for a common ground vis-à-vis his hearers:

For though I am free from all men, I have made myself a slave to all, that I might win the more. To the Jews I became as a Jew, in order to win

---

8. See G. Wainwright, *Doxology: The Praise of God in Worship, Doctrine and Life: A Systematic Theology* (New York: Oxford University Press, 1980).

9. The term "apostle" is not usually associated with compulsion, but it should be. As the word itself indicates (*apo* + *stellein*), the apostle is, above all, one who is *sent*. It would be well to remember this when we confess, as one of the four primary "marks" of the church (*notae ecclesiae*), its *apostolicity*.

Jews; to those under the law I became as one under the law—though not being myself under the law—that I might win those under the law. To those outside the law I became as one outside the law—not being without law towards God but under the law of Christ—that I might win those outside the law. To the weak I became weak, that I might win the weak. I have become all things to all men, that I might by all means save some. I do it all for the sake of the gospel, that I might share in its blessings.

(1 Cor. 9:19-23).

The impulse to communicate, and to do so in as empathetic and humanly accessible a manner as possible, has surely never been given a more eloquent expression.

The other side of this polarity is, however, equally conspicuous in Scripture—not least of all in the writings of St. Paul. While the sense of being bearers of a message intended for all persons begets in the disciple community an urgent quest for common ground, it is the experience of this *koinōnia* from the outset that its *god spel* is for the most part unwanted and unwelcome. The antecedents of this, too, can be traced to the story of the wandering peoples of Israel, the despised and rejected "servant of God," and of course to that One towards whose cross Israel's history "hastens" (Barth).

It is in a real sense not at all surprising that this should be the case. For, as we have already had occasion to observe, the disciple community understands—from within—the human response of rejection. This existential refusal of love is the strange companion of faith's spontaneous and joyous acceptance of love given. As the Christ himself was rejected even by those closest to him; as he was betrayed from within the ranks of the "called" (see John 6), so the continued doubt and turning away of the community of belief, like the turning back of Israel towards Egypt's "fleshpots," reminds the disciple community of the primeval no at the center of the story it is sent to tell: humanity's ancient and repeated no to its Creator—which in the mystery of grace becomes the raw material of God's yes to humankind. *Creatio ex nihilo*! The word of the cross must be communicated, for it is meant for "all!"[10] But while this presupposes that there is that within universal human experience which awaits precisely such news as this, and *can receive it*, there is also an undeniable antithetical proclivity. "He came to his own, and his own received him not"

---

10. See Karl Barth's remarkable sermon by this title in *Deliverance to the Captives* (New York: Harper & Row, 1959), pp. 85ff.

(John 1:11). Wherever the church has been faithful to the evangelical necessity laid upon it, it has inherited some portion of the rejection of its Lord by the world that God "so loved."

These two polaric factors in the church's attempt to communicate with the world—the drive and promise of communion on the one hand, the human refusal on the other; the quest for mutuality on the one hand, the experience of repulsion on the other—affect its methodological decisions in a fundamental way. Unlike human disciplines which are not so dependent upon their reception by those outside the "professional" circle, Christian theology is obligated by its own subject matter to devise a method which faithfully reflects the universal missionary thrust of its essential content. Theological methods which impede or distort the dialectic inherent in the gospel itself must be questioned. Thus, when the disciple community relinquishes its search for a common ground ("To the Jews I became as a Jew . . . To those outside the law I became as one outside the law . . . ," 1 Cor. 9:20f.), it not only falls into a ghettoized existence, often acquiring the status of a cult or sect, but it violates the continuity factor in its own evangel. On the other side, if the community minimizes or rationalizes the disparity between what it has to proclaim and what the world apparently wants to hear, it not only courts the life of a culture religion, a sanctimonious variation on the dominant themes of its host culture, but it ignores the theme of rejection (the cross!) that is at the core of the kerygma and without which the positive side of the story devolves into fulsome superficiality.

The question that this raises for theological method is how to devise a mode of reflection and communication which does justice both to the continuity and the discontinuity dimensions within the gospel. The great temptation of Christian thinkers throughout history has been to seek to *resolve* this tension. But resolutions, as we have just now implied, invariably end in the forfeiture of something vital to the evangel itself. We have immediate experience of the danger of such forfeiture in our own ecclesiastical history on this continent. Liberal Protestantism so belabored the continuity theme that it ended in a pitiful equation of Christianity and "bourgeois transcendence" (Käsemann). On the other hand, "evangelicalism" has produced a Christian ideology which offers its consumers a "total package," analysis as well as cure, question as well as answer, complete with stylized forms of "conversion" from the worldly status to that of the "saved." These are of course extremes. But they mirror, nonetheless, the larger picture. The Christian church as a whole has not been very adept at sustaining both elements in this fundamental tension of faith. Even sophisticated theology again and again falls into these same patterns of premature "resolution."

25.4. Complications in Method at the End of the Constantinian Era. Christian theology has always been compelled to give an account of the "how" of its knowing, and the more so because the "what" of its knowing is neither self-evident nor immediately palatable. Even in periods basically hospitable to religious belief, the Christian message begs the epistemological question. In times of skepticism and cynicism, it evokes a very strong demand that it explain itself. The epistemological question addressed to Christians ever since the breakdown of the medieval synthesis of "faith" (read: "religious authority") and reason has been an increasingly aggressive form of the question.

That it has been so is of course, in part, a consequence of the secularization of modern Western society. The "God-hypothesis" is at best difficult for sensitive contemporary persons to sustain. Even within the circle of faith, the species of doubt with which faith must dialogue today is informed by an agnostic or atheistic view of the world. But we have insisted that the *skandalon* of the gospel must not be equated with simple, intellectual reservations concerning the supernatural. Its offense, at least in the *post*modern context, is not its *theo*logical assumptions so much as its anthropological ones. It is very hard for our contemporaries—and ourselves!—to believe that there is good news for the human race. Who, in an age of global violence where human beings daily anticipate the ultimate violence of nuclear warfare, can receive the angelic message of "peace on earth"? Thus, as Charles Davis rightly observes, "The basic option is not between theism and atheism, but between faith and nihilism. . . ."[11]

This post-Constantinian, postmodern situation, to which we have addressed ourselves in a previous chapter,[12] creates serious complications in the methodological discussions of Christian theology, aggravating the problem that we have just outlined, viz., the tendency to opt either for an approach which minimizes the discontinuity between gospel and world or one which boldly acknowledges the disparity and takes its stand on the givenness of "revelation."

(a) Kerygmatic theology: To consider the latter reaction first, we must acknowledge straightaway that there is and has been very much in

---

11. In his review of Gordon Kaufmann's *An Essay on Theological Method*, in *Religious Studies Review*, 5/4 (October 1979): 266.

12. Chapter 3, §11.

the course of modern Western history to warrant the stress upon discontinuity coming from the side of what has been styled kerygmatic theology. In the final section of this chapter we shall elaborate on that statement. For the moment, we simply recognize the basic legitimacy of Barthian and similar protests against the type of neo-Protestantism which carries the continuity factor to such extremes that it finally has no prophetic word to offer to what is an eminently critical world situation.

Yet it must be asked whether the kerygmatic suspicion of the continuity factor is not, in some measure at least, a reactionary stance in the face of the modern world's disbelief. Perhaps no theologian of the 20th century has been more conscious of modern atheism than was Karl Barth. Yet the response of the Barthian school to this phenomenon has been to refuse to "take it seriously"—in the name of a *highly* serious christocentric belief.

The issue is focused on the question of the place of apologetics in theology. Barth himself refused to make room for the apologetic search for common ground. Expressions of this refusal can be found not only in his earlier career[13] but in his final publications. In his Chicago and Princeton lectures, for instance, Barth writes:

> Ever since the fading of its illusory splendor as a leading academic power during the Middle Ages, theology has taken too many pains to justify its own existence. . . . Theology had first to renounce all apologetics or eternal guarantees of its position within the environment of other sciences, for it will always stand on the firmest ground when it simply *acts* according to the law of its own being.[14]

Among those influenced by Barth, it has often seemed more difficult to dispense with the apologetic quest so thoroughly, though the inclination to do so persists. An interesting example of this is found in Hendrikus Berkhof's very helpful study, *An Introduction to the Study of the Christian Faith*.[15] Confronting the question whether theology ought to engage in "prolegomena,"[16] Berkhof writes that there is "much in favor of the

---

13. The struggle with Emil Brunner over the question of a "point of contact" (*Anknüpfungspunkt*) no doubt marks the height of the rejection of an apologetic.

14. Karl Barth, *Evangelical Theology: An Introduction*, trans. Grover Foley (New York: Holt, Rinehart and Winston, 1963), p. 15.

15. Hendrikus Berkhof, *An Introduction to the Study of the Christian Faith*, trans. Sierd Woudstra (Grand Rapids, Mich.: Eerdmans, 1979).

16. Ibid., pp. 1-8. *Prolegomena* is a term originating with Protestant Orthodoxy in the 17th century. It refers to the "introductory section of a treatise or system of thought in which basic principles and premises are enunciated. . . . The *prolegomena* are . . . the place where the discipline of theology . . . itself is defined" (Richard A. Muller, *Dictionary of Latin and Greek Theological Terms* [Grand Rapids, Mich.: Baker, 1985], p. 248).

practice of the Reformation theologians, who did not bother with preliminaries but came straight to the point." He continues:

> This wise soberness can no longer be followed, we believe, because of the different times in which we live. Between us and the Reformation lies the period of the Enlightenment and everything that followed. As a result, man's self-awareness has become infinitely greater while God has become more of a question mark for him. For modern man, God's salvation and the reality he knows have become two separate things; the world has become increasingly more prominent and salvation increasingly more vague. The Christian believer, too, cannot get away from that climate. A contemporary book about the Christian faith can ignore this climate only at the cost of some or much of its effectiveness. At certain periods in the past, omitting the preliminaries was no doubt the proper thing to do, and the writer did his readers a favor with such a direct approach. Today, however, a similar directness might fall cold on the reader and give the impression that the writer does not really care for him. It could foster the idea that when we speak about the faith, we deal with a world which exists all by itself, alongside of the ordinary, real world.[17]

Professor Berkhof concludes this excellent statement of the contextual conditions under which contemporary theology carries out its task, however, with what can only seem, in the light of it, a non sequitur: "We therefore opt for Prolegomena." Does one "opt" for anything as mandatory as what is depicted in the paragraph just cited?

Beyond that, having so "opted," Berkhof immediately appears fearful of the decision. What "aspect of reality," he wonders, shall we "make the base from which to understand the revelation the Christian faith speaks about?" We could easily "get onto the wrong track." Too much contemporary theology wants to base itself on "philosophical thought, even though the results are ephemeral." "It would be different," he concedes in a small-print paragraph, "if a theologian of great intellectual ability and clear vision were able to offer a Prolegomena which would be an analysis of existence (*Daseinsanalyse*) in which many of his contemporaries could recognize themselves and which would at the same time give them a new outlook on the Christian faith. Pascal's *Pensées* are an excellent example of this. But Pascal was not a systematic theologian, and *in general the theologian lacks the gifts needed for such a convincing design.*"[18]

This seems a curious admission for a theologian to make, despite

---

17. Berkhof, *Introduction*, p. 4.
18. Ibid., pp. 4-6 (emphasis added).

its admirable humility. In the first place, it presents what seems to me an all-too-restrictive definition of systematic theology; in the second, it presupposes that theology is quite exclusively the work of individuals, almost of *isolated* individuals. It appears not to consider the prospect that a *community* of scholarship, among whose members some educated guesses about "existence" might be ventured, is the matrix of all faithful theological reflection. Most importantly, thirdly, it begs the question how, in the *absence* of such decision making concerning the cutting-edge of one's time and place, one would be able as theologian to get on with the business of confessing the faith.[19] Given all this, it is not surprising that Berkhof decides in the end that the only "prolegomena" the theologian is equipped to "opt" for is an analysis, not of existence, but of *religion*!

While this kind of caution with respect to the search for a common ground is understandable in the light of liberalism's overemphasis upon apologetic, it seems to me an excessive reaction to the latter. If we are right in believing that the quest for common ground is built into the hearing of the gospel itself, then this quest cannot be abandoned just because it is subject to certain dangers. There is, we repeat, no *non*dangerous theology! Moreover, as we shall argue more extensively in the final section of this chapter, it may be seriously questioned whether the cultural conditions which prompted Barth and his followers to renounce the quest for a common ground still obtain. It is one thing to caution against an apologetic in a historical context which manifests a Promethean resistance of every transcendental hypothesis; it is something else to do so in the midst of a society which has begun to discover the flaw in its own Prometheanism.

(b) Apologetic theology: The questionable side of the Christian apologetic is of course its tendency to accommodate the Christian message to the "felt needs" of the world. In their zeal for finding common ground, Christian apologists throughout the centuries have frequently minimized the abyss separating redeemed Lazarus from damned Dives! Did not St. Thomas propose a too-easy synthesis between reason and faith, as if reason were only a buttress to belief and not also faith's adversary? Did not Schleiermacher concentrate too exclusively on that in the human experience which longs for reunion with that upon which it is "absolutely dependent"? Did he forget that the spirit of humanity also flees from the pursuing "hound of heaven"? In short, is not the history of Christian thought filled with the stories of those who were so keen to make the

---

19. See the Luther quotation in chap. 1, §3.3.

grace of Christ the fulfillment of nature that they forgot that the world crucified its Christ? And does not the decision for continuity with such a world invariably lead to the minimization or even the elimination of that existential discontinuity enacted in and mirrored by the cross?

This perennial danger of the apologetic approach is aggravated in the contemporary situation in two senses. In the first place, the growing secularity of our society, including the cultural disestablishment of Christianity and the almost wholly *voluntary* nature of religious commitment tempts the churches to seek points of contact with human experience and need wherever they can find it. Thus many cultural phenomena are baptized as crypto- or proto-Christian, and the prophetic critique of these phenomena which would be forthcoming if the churches were more loyal to their own sources and better traditions is conspicuously absent.

The primary example of such accommodation in the North American context is the equation of Christianity with "our way of life" and, more particularly, with the tenets of the free enterprise system and its fight against "communism"—that is, against what it simplistically defines as such. The process of melding Christianity with Americanism has been in the making for more than a century.[20] As Sidney E. Mead wrote in his seminal study of Christianity in the United States, "During the second half of the nineteenth century there occurred an ideological amalgamation of [denominational] Protestantism with 'Americanism,' . . . and we are still living with some of the results."[21] One of the results of this equation is that whatever is non-American is regarded by large numbers of "true believing" Christians on this continent (including many Canadians, whose orientation is wholly indistinguishable from their United States counterparts in this respect) as being questionable so far as its Christianity is concerned—and this includes not only large numbers of Christians in western Europe who are very critical of United States foreign policy, but (for many) the World Council of Churches itself. At a more serious level still, the tendency to draw such parallels issues in the production of "enemy images" (*Feindbilder*) such that enemies of the official society of our "First World" are ipso facto enemies of Christ himself.[22] In short, the dynamics of accommodation lead—where they always have led—to the incapacity to distinguish Christian belief from the reigning ideology of the church's host society.

---

20. Once, in the far West of the United States, I was accused of being "un-American." When I remarked that this was a rather odd accusation for a Canadian to deal with, my critic explained that it meant, simply, "un-Christian."

21. Sidney E. Mead, *The Lively Experiment* (New York: Harper & Row, 1963), p. 134.

22. See Walter Wink, "My Enemy . . . My Destiny," in *Sojourners* 16/2 (February 1987): 30ff.

The second way in which Christianity in our context is unusually tempted to overstress the continuity dimension of the evangel relates to the increasingly *conscious* anxiety level of people in our time. Whatever may be said of Schleiermacher and the beginnings of theological liberalism, it must be admitted that its apologetic sought to reach the hearts of highly self-confident human beings, full of glowing expectations for the future and feeling little need for divine intervention. The recipients of the contemporary apologetic are a very different breed. Resistance to "solutions" is minimal among them. Everyone with a half-thought-out way of coping in a world which has become incendiary is able to find an audience. The reputed return to religion on this continent is a direct consequence of human insecurity, and under such sociological circumstances—circumstances *very* different from those Schleiermacher confronted—it is not especially taxing to devise an *apologia* which finds, in Christian belief of this or that variety, an answer to every question. "Jesus" becomes the solution to human loneliness, lovelessness, "future shock," marriage and family breakdown, drug and alcohol abuse, apathy, and every other evil demon that has flown out of the contemporary Pandora's box. The discontinuity factor is negligible or nonexistent; the *skandalon* is unheard of; the "leap of faith" is a very small step, and pleasurable.

It is hardly our aim here to mock human need, which in our time is very great; it is our aim, however, to attempt to be faithful to the tradition we have inherited—not for the sake of the tradition, but for the sake of the existential truth to which it testifies. When an apologetic form of Christianity neglects the scandal of belief in favor of meeting—or seeming to meet—human beings directly and without struggle, it not only violates the tradition with its cross at the center, but it offers its hearers what is finally a very superficial form of salvation. For it is ready to give them—for nothing!—a yes which does not come to terms with the aboriginal no that is there within them. The plastic yes of bourgeois Christianity may pacify, for a time, the existential no that resides in the soul of the human being—provided enough communal and pastoral support is provided along with it. But it will never do battle with that no. The refusal of love will persist, repressed or suppressed, and will work itself out in many strange ways—including the sham "sincerity" of ecclesial communities which deploy this kind of apologetic.

Between a kerygmatic approach which manifests an inordinate fear of being too accessible to the world and an apologetic theology which bypasses the real gulf that human sin has created between Creator and creature, sound Christian teaching must always search for ways to sustain the discontinuity and continuity factors of the gospel in tension with one another. I want now to suggest two ways in which that attempt can be facilitated: first, the responsibilty of the theological community to distinguish between true and false scandals, which I believe constitutes the *major* task of apologetic theology; second, the necessity within the disciple community for a contextual perspicacity which is able to distinguish between moments requiring a greater stress upon the discontinuity factor, and other moments which can bear the perhaps more subtle strain of the gospel's continuity with human history and experience.

26. Christian Apologetics

26.1. Authentic and Inauthentic Scandals. There is, then, a place in Christian theology for both the kerygmatic emphasis, representing the factor of discontinuity ("news") *and* the apologetic emphasis, representing the factor of continuity (*"good* news"). The question is: How can these two emphases be kept in dialectical tension with one another? The answer, I believe, lies first of all in the way in which we regard the function of Christian apologetics. The thesis I shall develop here is that it is the task of the apologist *to create a climate in which the real scandal of the kerygma can be encountered.* The elaboration of this hypothesis requires that we inquire more deeply into the meaning of the term *skandalon.*

The origins of *skandalon* as a theological concept must be traced to Paul's argument in the opening paragraphs of his first letter to the church at Corinth—the locus classicus, not incidentally, of the "theology of the cross."

> For Christ did not send me to baptize but to preach the gospel, and not with eloquent wisdom, lest the cross of Christ be emptied of its power.
>
> For the word of the cross is folly to those who are perishing, but to us who are being saved it is the power of God. For it is written [Isa. 29:14], "I will destroy the wisdom of the wise, and the cleverness of the clever I will thwart." Where is the wise man? Where is the scribe? Where is the debater of this age? Has not God made foolish the wisdom of the world? For since, in the wisdom of God, the world did not know God through wisdom, it pleased God through the folly of what we preach to save those who believe. For Jews [i.e., in Paul's view those enjoying the apex of *religious* insight] demand signs and Greeks [the apex of *philosophical*

achievement] seek wisdom, but we preach Christ crucified, a stumbling block [*skandalon*] to Jews and foolishness to Greeks, but to those who are called, both Jews and Greeks, Christ the power of God and the wisdom of God. For the foolishness of God is wiser than men, and the weakness of God is stronger than men.

(1 Cor. 1:17-25)

During the present century, and drawing upon antecedents in Luther, Pascal, Kierkegaard and others, theologians have used the concept of the *skandalon* to refer, not to the "Jewish" rejection of the gospel, as Paul does here, but to the offense of faith in the Christ to human wisdom and religion as a whole. In some ways, however, the association of the "scandal" with "wisdom" is misleading, especially given the modern, rather exclusively *cognitive* connotations of the word "wisdom." The scandal of the cross is not simply an offense to the intelligence, but rather the fact that it touches too closely upon the essential stuff of our lives. It at once confirms what we darkly suspect to be the truth of our condition— that we are "lost," that our being is "being-towards-death" (Heidegger)— and it offers us new life only through a lived encounter with this lostness and death. There is the greatest offense for the human spirit in this message, not because it seems to us superficial or absurd, but because it causes us to face realities that we would rather not face.

Perhaps the most graphic scriptural illustration of the Pauline idea of the scandal of the cross is the episode concerning the encounter between Jesus and the "rich young ruler," who "turned away sorrowful"—not because he found Jesus' formula for his redemption ridiculous, but because he knew it to be too true (Matt. 19:16f.). It was "costly grace" (Bonhoeffer). He preferred to live with the illusion his riches enabled him to keep up—in Ernest Becker's terms, an unworthy illusion. He was not ready to take into his consciousness the negating abyss on whose edge he had built his life, or to pursue his incipient quest for "eternal life" within the terms of that kind of *Wahrheitsorientierung* (orientation towards truth).

To employ other words: the *skandalon* of the gospel is an existential one. It is the "ontological shock" (Tillich) of recognizing the utter contingency of our being, the folly of our reliance upon the props of material or intellectual or religious acquisitions, the vanity of success. It is the look on the face of El Greco's "St. Jerome," condemned out of the text that he is engaged in reading. It is the sting of the *krisis* felt by Kafka's "K," in *The Trial*, a judgment for crimes whose precise nature one cannot even comprehend, though one knows it to be just.

Therefore the disciple community must be vigilant against the propensity of both religion and nonreligion to turn the scandal of the gospel into something less than this. Very often, what is identified as the great drawback to faith is in reality a false *skandalon*. A false *skandalon* is when some aspect of Christianity is identified as the core of the faith as such, or so elevated as to be inseparable from the core.[23] A common example in conservative forms of Christianity is the elevation of the virgin birth symbol to the status of dogma, or the substitution of a miraculous resuscitation of Jesus' dead body for the profound theology of resurrection. Frequently, the so-called scandal marking the discontinuity between belief and unbelief turns out to be some piece of doctrine left over from a previous age and held up as essential to contemporary belief. It may be that the doctrine in question was perfectly accessible to worldly wisdom in the context of the earlier period, but now it has become incongruous with "scientific" knowledge. It functions as a test of "faith": those who are able to accept it, all evidence to the contrary, are bona fide members of the community, and those who cannot are excluded.

An obvious instance for the present North American religious situation is the pre-Darwinian concept of creation in six days. When this is presented to late 20th-century people as being of the essence of Christian belief, it constitutes an inauthentic scandal. For, despite the fact that many intelligent persons contest a narrowly evolutionist explanation of worldly beginnings, only the most escapist elements in contemporary society cleave to the Priestly account of creation in Genesis 1 as if it were, in the modern sense, a "scientific" description of earth's origins. It is not even a cosmogony in the *ancient* sense, though it contains some cosmogonical elements. To hold this saga as essential Christian dogma is to present a false *skandalon* in that it not only requires a rejection of the best wisdom of the world in such matters but (a fact still more important for our present discussion), in the process, it attracts so much attention to *itself* that it obscures the real *skandalon* of the cross. This is in fact the chief characteristic of inauthentic scandals: they detract from the authentic *skandalon*.

The authentic scandal of the gospel is not to be found along the

---

23. "There are two kinds of 'stumbling blocks.' One is genuine. . . . There is always a genuine decision against the Gospel for those for whom it is a stumbling block. But this decision should not be dependent on the wrong stumbling block, namely, the wrong way of our communication of the Gospel—our inability to communicate. What we have to do is to overcome the wrong stumbling block in order to bring people face to face with the right stumbling block and enable them to make a genuine decision" (Paul Tillich, *Theology of Culture* [New York: Oxford University Press, 1959], p. 213).

edges of the story that Christians tell, but at its center. It is not an idea, a method, a soteriological principle, a dogma—not even the most central of these! It is first of all a person. Paul's formula is very precise. He does not say that we preach the doctrine of Jesus Christ and him crucified and that this doctrine is foolishness to the wise and scandalous to the religious. He says, "We preach Christ crucified" (v. 23). It is the person, Jesus Christ, not our always limited ideas about this person, with whom the wise and the religious have problems. This One, being met, constitutes for the wise and the religious—that is, for all of us in one degree or another—an offense. For this person is precisely "the crucified one" (Jüngel). He is not a successful human being who could serve as a model for our own attempts at self-betterment and personal triumph. He is a broken person, whose brokenness and weakness powerfully calls into question all our pretense and our vanity. If we allow this "*logos* of the cross" to penetrate the carefully tended walls of our spiritual, psychic, and intellectual defenses, we easily sense (as Judas did!) that the living Spirit of such a One would effect in us a "transvaluation of values" (Nietzsche), a turning-upside-down of everything, a *metanoia* so complete that we should have to have great dissatisfaction with our present state ever to desire it! This is why incidental, peripheral, secondary, or even apparently important *ideational* elements of the tradition must never become the heart of the *skandalon*. The core must remain some articulation of the "message of the cross," negating its *own* importance in the very manner and mode of our announcing it, and so making room for the potentiality in it—if it is taken up by the Spirit of God—of putting human beings into touch with the Thou who ultimately *is* the core.

A further observation about the nature of the authentic *skandalon* brings us still closer to the intention of the apologetic "formula" that I have proposed above. It is this: the fact that the Christian message is *skandalon* in this existential sense does not mean that it is simply irrational or totally incomprehensible to ordinary rationality. Those who have interpreted the matter in these terms have done an enormous disservice to the subtlety of Pauline thought in the passage quoted above. The whole energy of the apostle, both in Corinthians and in all of his writings, the epistle to the Romans especially, is precisely to set forth the *sense* that is made by this "word of the cross." Its offense does not lie in the notion that it is gibberish! Nonsense can be dismissed without further ado. False scandals may be written off without great struggle of soul. However annoying or frustrating may be those encounters with "true believers" who represent some ancient dogma as if it were the very kernel of the kerygma, the offense lies primarily in the extra-theological dimensions of such encounters. One does not feel oneself confronted by the "fool-ishness of the gospel" borne by "fools for Christ," but simply set upon by foolish persons who take themselves and their ideas much too seriously! As for the message of such self-important witnesses, it can usually be dismissed without a second thought, or treated with polite condescension; for it really does not strike at the roots of one's existence. It shakes no foundations of the soul to hear that the world was made in six 24-hour days! Even the *profound*, even the *true* ideas and doctrines of the tradition, *qua* ideas and doctrines, are soon forgotten after all the heated discussions and passionate sermons.

The authentic *skandalon*, on the other hand, is never readily dispensed with. What makes it genuinely offensive is that it grasps us at the center of our life—which is, after all, also in large measure suprarational. Like love—and more than merely *like* love!—the authentic scandal of the cross tackles our spirits at their most vulnerable psychic depths, making demands upon them that seem impossible. "Impossible" here does not mean irrational—any more than it meant that for the rich young ruler. It means that we know the thing to be altogether *too rational*, too right! What the rich young ruler needed *absolutely* was just what Jesus told him: to let go of the superficial security of his possessions, to face his adamic nakedness, to learn to trust, to discover the connection between love and justice, to follow and not to seem to lead. The sting of the gospel is not that it is senseless. (*Credo quia absurdum* was always the quip of a rebel, sickened by too easy interpretations of belief!) The sting of the good news is that the kind of sense it makes touches us too profoundly where we actually live. What does not get very close to that generative source of our existence is not yet "the word of the cross."

26.2. Implications for Method. In the light of this distinction between true and false scandals, we may return to the discussion of theological method. My argument here was that an adequate methodology, given the nature of the content with which the disciple community contends, would be one which kept the two poles (continuity/discontinuity; the search for common ground/the recognition of offense) in dialectical tension. I claimed that this would be possible if the primary function of the *apologetic* search were to distinguish the authentic *skandalon*. On the basis of the foregoing differentiation between authentic and inauthentic scandals, we may interpret the meaning of that claim more fully.

Part of the reason for the difficulty between representatives of the kerygmatic (discontinuity) and representatives of the apologetic (continuity) sides of this whole debate lies in the fact that the apologetic approach has too often been equated exclusively with the positive aspect of Christian apologetics. That is, it has emerged as an attempt to lessen the distance between the biblical God and humanity, grace and nature, faith and reason—sometimes to the point of seeking to overcome this distance altogether. Certainly it is part of the search for common ground to show that aspects of ordinary human experience are in some ways positively continuous with Christian belief, and vice versa. But when the apologetic task is left at that, it not only runs a course of inevitable conflict with the other side of Christian experience, viz., its offense, but it fails to achieve the real potential of Christian *apologia*. Instead, it identifies the substance of Christian faith with intellectual assent to theistic and other ideas rather than with an existential encounter with incarnate truth and love.

To grasp something of the more profound potentiality of Christian apologetics, we may benefit from a simple lesson provided by the earliest Christian apologists, those writers of the second century C.E. who took it upon themselves to interpret the faith to their pagan neighbors and rulers. They were, for the most part, unsophisticated thinkers (Justin Martyr excepted), but they did follow a principle which more sophisticated Christian apologists have frequently neglected in their zeal for the establishment of impressive positive points of contact: they saw it as their *chief* task to clear away *misunderstandings* of Christianity in order that their readers might have to deal with the real thing, and not with a product of hearsay or superstition. When they tried to describe the Christian message in positive terms, the early apologists were not terribly imaginative or erudite; but at least they were following a methodological principle which, by the criteria established above, has something to commend it. In their way, they were dispelling what stood in the path of the profound kerygmatic *skandalon*.

Apologetics is in large measure a *negative* work—"clearing away" (Bultmann)—which has, however, the *positive* goal of making present or visible what is there to be encountered. Much debris must be removed before the authentically scandalous core of the gospel even can be heard. This is how Rudolf Bultmann perceived his program of "demythologizing," and whatever may be thought of the articulation of the gospel that Bultmann and his school produced, the principle at the heart of it is surely essential to every responsible Christian theology:

> The purpose of demythologizing is not to make religion more acceptable to modern man by trimming the traditional Biblical texts, but to make

clearer to modern man what the Christian faith is. He must be confronted with the issue of decision, be provoked to decision by the fact that the stumbling-block to faith, the *skandalon*, is peculiarly disturbing to man in general, not only to modern man (modern man being only one species of man). Therefore my attempt to demythologize begins, true enough, by clearing away the false stumbling-blocks created for modern man by the fact that his world-view is determined by science.[24]

The end of the matter is not the negative one of debunking, casting off the husks of doctrine and convention, showing the world what Christianty is *not*. The end of the matter is the exposing of unbelief (including the unbelief that is partner to belief) to the essential focus of discipleship, which is constantly being obscured by inessential aspects of the tradition that we use, repressively, to shield ourselves from the "scandalous" Truth. Human nature being prone to evade wherever possible any truth that probes too deeply the secrets of the heart, without the work of identifying the false scandals, people easily succeed in locating the focus of discipleship in some aspect or accompaniment of faith, often indeed with very peripheral matters. Not only once, but always and again, theological method must cut through this programmed confusion of the human spirit and point to the mystery at the center, which cannot be easily dealt with, either by outright unbelief or by what passes for true belief.

The search for common ground, then, is not simply an attempt to establish links between ordinary experience and discipleship which could make the latter seem more reasonable. At its most arresting, Christian apologetics works for the support of the kerygma. It pares away what is inessential both in the church and in human experience, so that a real meeting of humanity and the God of the gospel may occur. Certainly it is never simply a technique for encounter. The I–Thou meeting, the encounter of spirit with Spirit, cannot be managed even by the most assiduous Christian apologetics, and it is to this *meeting* that the *skandalon* belongs. But what Christian apologetics can do in some measure is to eliminate what stands in the way of such a meeting. This means the elimination not only of false images of God and false interpretations of the faith but also of false conceptions of ourselves. If human beings can be brought to some degree of honesty about their own condition, they may be open to a Word which speaks to that condition. *Open* does not mean ready to receive, without question, without protest. *Open* here in-

---

24. Rudolf Bultmann, "The Case for Demythologizing: A Reply," in *Kerygma and Myth*, ed. H. W. Bartsch, vol. 2 (London: SPCK, 1962), pp. 182-183.

cludes the degree of defensiveness with which, as human beings, we regularly hear the divine summons. For the grace which heals cannot be given apart from a deeper exposure to our own wounds.

27. Apologetic and Kerygmatic Theology in Relation to the Concern for Contextualization

27.1. Locating Methodological Discussion in Recent Theological History. If distinguishing the role of apologetic theology in relation to the kerygma is one important way of maintaining the dialectical relationship of continuity and discontinuity in theological method, a second and integrally related consideration is the development in the disciple community of a certain sensitivity to context. By way of illustrating this, as well as setting the methodological discussion within its historical framework, we shall think briefly about the most dramatic aspect of the immediate theological past as it pertains to methodology.

Our century has seen the split of Protestant theology into two quite different, and at times bitterly opposed camps in this connection. The division centers in the basic questions we have been pursuing in this chapter: How far can Christian theology go, legitimately, in its search for points of contact (*Anknüpfungspunkten*, to use the historic term) with worldly experience and wisdom? Is the Kierkegaardian "leap of faith" a wholly irrational one? What is the character of the Christian revelation? Is it compatible with rationality? Is the *skandalon* inconceivable and inaccessible to the human mind, understandable only through the intervention of the Holy Spirit? Is the God of the gospel "wholly other" (*totaliter alliter*)? Is a *natural theology* possible?

Early in the century, a lively and critical movement gathered about the figure of the preacher-become-theologian, Karl Barth, made its program the dissociation of the Christian message from the aspirations, mores, wisdom and (especially!) religion of its culture. The signal for this movement was the publication of Barth's *Römerbrief*, a commentary on St. Paul's Epistle to the Romans, which not only attacked the identification of Christianity with European civilization, as Kierkegaard had already done, but called in question the kind of biblical scholarship which, it felt, in the name of scientific-historical method betrayed the radical message of the Scriptures. In this and subsequent writings, Barth insisted that the God who is revealed in Jesus Christ is radically "other" than the deity pursued in humankind's various religions, including also what calls

349

itself the Christian religion.[25] He disavowed "natural theology" (*theologia naturalis*) entirely—this centuries-old attempt of Christians to demonstrate that quite apart from any "special revelation" (*revelatio specialis*) the "natural man" or "man the sinner" (*homo peccator*) has or can acquire knowledge of God. Even when his erstwhile collaborator and friend, Emil Brunner, tried to hold out for the "addressibility" (*Wortmächtigkeit*) of human beings by their Creator, Barth resisted. In fact, in one of his most adamant writings, entitled simply *Nein!*[26] Barth disallows any capacity whatsoever on the part of humanity-apart-from-grace for the reception of the divine Word. The human creature simply does not have a "capacity for God" (*capax Dei*).

In the same mood, Barth relinquished even his own earlier interest in existentialism (that is, the existentialism of Kierkegaard and Dostoevsky, in particular), as providing any sort of basis for faith, even if only *via negativa*.[27] Although in his later period Barth softened his stringent criticism of the Christian appeal to human rationality and "experience," he never moved *very* far away from his classical line in the preface to the second edition of the *Römerbrief*: "If I have a system, it is limited to a recognition of what Kierkegaard called the 'infinite qualitative distinction' between time and eternity, and to my regarding this as possessing negative as well as positive significance: 'God is in heaven, and thou art on earth.' "[28]

Over against this intensively kerygmatic approach, as it came to be known in subsequent discussion, other theological schools of our century have offered renewed attempts at Christian apologetics. Some of those who have been most active in this pursuit were themselves, initially, more or less part of the kerygmatic revolution.[29] They shared the distaste of Barth and his immediate circle for the liberal interpretation of Christianity. Many of them had experienced what Barth also discovered—the inability of liberal Christianity to make any clear, prophetic critique of a civilization

---

25. The Dutch theologian Hendrik Kraemer developed this aspect of Barth's thought in his *Religion and the Christian Faith* (London: Lutterworth Press, 1956).

26. See Emil Brunner, *Natural Theology*, trans. Peter Fraenkel (London: Geoffrey Bles, The Centenary Press, 1946), pp. 65ff.

27. His rejection of existentialism meant the total rewriting of the first volume of his *Dogmatics*. "I have cut out in this second issue of the book everything that in the first issue might give the slightest appearance of giving to theology a basis, support, or even a mere justification in the way of existential philosophy" (*The Doctrine of the Word of God: Prolegomena to Church Dogmatics*, I/1[New York: Scribner's, 1936], p. ix).

28. *The Epistle to the Romans*, trans. Edwyn C. Hoskyns (London: Oxford University Press, 1933), p. 108.

29. Among these were Bultmann, Brunner, Georg Merz, Friedrich Gogarten, and others.

faced with its own nemesis.[30] As the generation of youth called upon to defend this allegedly "high" civilization in World War I, these younger scholars were deeply impressed by the incongruity between the liberal ideals and the grim facts of war, economic disparity, and radical evil. But gradually many of those who had at first aligned themselves with Barth's all-out renunciation of liberal Christianity began to believe that the house ought not to be swept too thoroughly! Particularly after World War II, when the immediate disorder and preoccupations of the war-torn civilization had given way to prospects of a more reflective approach, a number of theological and biblical scholars emerged who asked again the question of the "common ground."

The most prominent of these—certainly so far as our North American consciousness is concerned, and probably in Europe as well—was Paul Tillich.[31] There is, as we shall see presently, good reason why Tillich should not be labeled simplistically "a Christian apologist." He never lost sight of the kerygmatic dimension of the Christian message. Yet he did resist the Barthian tendency to deny any continuity (except from God's side!) between "the Word of God and the word of man."[32] Tillich did not intend his exposition of Christian belief to be a return to liberalism, though he was (and still is) frequently accused of being a second Schleiermacher, Barth's avowed "alternative" in theological method. Nevertheless, Tillich did intend to reopen the age-old question of the possibility of a Christian *apologia*. He regarded any theology which is in principle opposed to such dialogue with the world as a contradiction in terms:

The famous 'No' of Karl Barth against any kind of natural theology, even

---

30. "I . . . weep over the constantly increasing barbarism, tedium, and insignificance of modern Protestantism, which has gone and lost . . . an entire third dimension (. . . the dimension of mystery) . . . only to be punished with every possible worthless substitute, only that it might with all the less check relapse into High Church, German Church, Christian Community, religious socialism, and similar miserable cliques and sects, only that in the end so-and-so many of its preachers and faithful people might learn finally how to discover religious insight in the intoxication of their Nordic blood and in their political *Führer*" (Karl Barth, *The Doctrine of the Word of God,* p. xi).

31. In his long essay on Tillich, originally intended for the second volume of his biography of his friend and countryman, Wilhelm Pauck names the great systematician "Heir of the Nineteenth Century." Part of what this phrase intends is the belief, which seems to me accurate, that Tillich wished to perpetuate the program begun by Schleiermacher, viz., that of interpreting and commending Christian belief to religion's "cultured despisers." It is of course another matter altogether (and quite untenable) to assert as some have done that Tillich is just Schleiermacher reintroduced to the 20th century. (See Wilhelm Pauck, *From Luther to Tillich: The Reformers and Their Heirs,* ed. Marion Pauck [San Francisco: Harper & Row, 1984], pp. 10ff.)

32. The title of one of Barth's most influential publications, a collection of addresses and papers written by Barth in the first three decades of this century, but offered to the English-speaking world only in the late 1950s (*The Word of God and the Word of Man,* trans. Douglas Horton [New York: Harper & Brothers, 1957]).

of man's ability to ask the question of God, in the last analysis is a self-deception, as the use of human language in speaking of revelation shows.[33]

Tillich called his own theological method "the method of correlation," that is,

> the correlation between existential questions and theological answers. "Correlation," a word with several meanings in scientific language, is understood as "interdependence of two independent factors". . . .
>
> In this method, question and answer are independent of each other, since it is impossible to derive the answer from the question or the question from the answer. The existential question, namely, man himself in the conflicts of his existential situation, is not the source for the revelatory answer formulated by theology. One cannot derive the divine self-mani-festation from the analysis of the human predicament. God speaks to the human situation, against it, and for it. Theological supranaturalism, as represented for example, by contemporary neo-orthodox theology, is right in asserting the inability of man to reach God under his own power. Man is the question, not the answer. It is equally wrong to derive the question implied in human existence from the revelatory answer. This is impossible because the revelatory answer is meaningless if there is no question to which it is the answer. Man cannot receive an answer to a question he has not asked. . . . Any such answer would be foolishness for him, an un-derstandable combination of words—as so much preaching is—but not a revelatory experience. The question, asked by man, is man himself. He asks it, whether or not he is vocal about it. He cannot avoid asking it, because his very being is the question of his existence. In asking it, he is alone with himself. He asks "out of the depths," and this depth is he himself.[34]

Tillich's "System," accordingly, moves in the opposite direction from Barth's. In each of the five doctrinal areas[35] that it treats, the *Systematic Theology* begins first with the human condition ("the question"), and proceeds to the positive or constructive exposition of the meaning of the Christian message pertinent to that aspect of reality ("the answer") only after the author has been able to show that the human condition in this respect actually poses a "predicament" to which the theological tradition is able to address itself—with which it is "correlated."

---

33. Tillich, *Systematic Theology*, vol. 2, p. 14.
34. Ibid., p. 13. See also vol. 1, pp. 59-66.
35. The nomenclature of the five areas demonstrates the nature of the methodological movement: "Reason and Revelation," "Being and God," "Existence and the Christ," "Life and the Spirit," "History and the Kingdom."

To those committed to the Barthian position, this appears to minimize the radical gap (discontinuity) between gospel and world ("the infinite qualitative distinction between time and eternity"), to overlook completely the "fallen" condition of humanity which can receive the message of the cross only as foolishness and scandal, and to endanger, therefore, the uniqueness of the Christian confession by making it too easily compatible with human being and thinking. Challenged to answer how, in that case, they themselves can communicate their gospel to the world, the Barthians respond that that is in any event a matter of grace, not of their work, and that the Word of God does not need to have an advance foothold in the life of humanity in order to become effective. The Word creates its own "point of contact"; it "authenticates itself" (Barth). It does not require any preparation (*praeparatio evangelica*) or the apologetic honing of any preexistent "question." It comes, certainly, as a strange, new message onto the scene of our humanity. But it is God's Word, and contains, therefore, its own power to grasp, judge, and alter our situation.

These two approaches do not represent the only ones from which Christians may choose, certainly, but all *Protestant* discussions of methodology at least must be worked out in dialogue with these positions; for they represent our immediate past, and they are still strongly present on both sides of the Atlantic. It is particularly important for a theology which tries to be contextually involved with the North American experience and history to declare itself with respect to these positions. The earlier sections of this chapter have done so implicitly. I shall try now to be quite explicit.

To speak first of the Barthian methodology: The considerable appeal of the kerygmatic position should not be underestimated. It can obviously commend itself to those whose primary Christian source is the Bible, especially the prophetic and Pauline traditions. The Bible also knows about the God "whose ways are not our ways, nor his thoughts our thoughts" (cf. Isa. 55:8), the God whose "wisdom" seems like "foolishness" and whose "foolishness" is the only "wisdom" faith knows. This position can also draw upon very important Reformation roots. Indeed, it can seem a veritable resurgence of essential Reformation teaching, buried so long beneath the modernism and faddism of liberalism. It shares Luther's distrust of an uncritical reliance on "Reason," it insists with Calvin upon the sole authority of Scripture, and with the Radical Reformation it accentuates the work of the Holy Spirit. Above all, it is a clarion statement of the theology of grace alone—*sola gratia, sola fide, per Christum solum.*

353

The appeal of kerygmatic theology should also be considered, however, from a more historical-sociological perspective; for its allure has by no means confined itself to the theological level. It has provided many sensitive Christians living in an age at once skeptical of religion and indifferent to it with a sense of confidence and the courage to believe. For it not only has given them a very complex and thoroughgoing account of the meaning of the Christian kerygma (to speak of Barth alone, nothing since Thomas's *Summae* has equaled the *Church Dogmatics* in scope and depth); but in addition it has offered them a methodology which is somehow tailored to the age of anxiety. This method, with its realism about the world but its even more emphatic insistence upon the real triumph of the Word of God *over* worldly realities, offers an effective shelter from the pervasive doubts of such an age as ours. What Bonhoeffer in one of his letters from prison called the Barthian "positivism of revelation"[36] means in effect that it is possible to be quite honest about the "impossibility" of the world (including the world inside oneself) and, at the same time, to maintain a position of categorical hope. For whatever the world may produce by way of disbelief, doubt, evil, death, and damnation, it has already been overcome by transcendent grace, entering time in medias res. Perhaps one of Karl Barth's most telling sentences is his (almost sotto voce) comment in *Evangelical Theology* that "there is certainly a justification for the doubter. But there is no justification for doubt itself (and I wish someone would whisper that in Paul Tillich's ear)."[37] Doubt may certainly be admitted—it can be forgiven. But it should not be taken seriously, as if its presence or its cultivation could contribute anything to our theological sensitivity. It is in fact fundamentally *unreal*. So "the theologian should only be sincerely *ashamed* of it."[38] The theologian may entertain great doubt—"in the present period no one, not even the theologian, can escape it." But "this age has a boundary," and the kingdom, which *is* our reality, does not have to be correlated with our experience.

This is an enormously appealing point of view in a world which, even long before August 1, 1914, could be described by one of its most sensitive poets (Keats) as a place "where but to *think* is to be sad."[39]

But is such a point of view capable of providing the courage to be in a context far less black-and-white than the one in which it originally took shape?

---

36. *Letters and Papers from Prison* (London: SCM, 1953), p. 148.
37. Barth, *Evangelical Theology*, p. 131.
38. Ibid.
39. From John Keats, "Ode to a Nightingale."

The error in this consistently kerygmatic theology—perhaps the most consistent kerygmatic theology in the history of Christian thought—lies, I think, in the fact that it mistook a particular historical moment for the whole human condition, and devised its method accordingly. The appropriateness of the "theology of crisis" (as the Barthian emphasis was first named) for Europe between and during two world wars is, in my view, hard to deny. At a moment when significant forms of the Christian religion could seem to support, or at least not to condemn, the most imperialistic and oppressive systems that the world had ever known, it was imperative for someone in the name of the crucified Christ to announce that there is an "infinite qualitative distinction" between the glory of God and the glory coveted by the kingdoms of this world. Liberalism, having courted a too undialectical continuity between the the Christian faith and the achievements of Western civilization, was incapable of uttering such a word. The apex of the timeliness of this kerygmatic emphasis can be identified with the promulgation of the Confession of Barmen, which was largely Barth's own work.[40] In the face of the powerful "German Christian movement," which grandly endorsed the whole policy of Adolf Hitler, including his anti-Jewish program,[41] an obedient faith had to speak about the total otherness of God, the absolute distinction between *faith* and *religion*, and the abyss separating *Blut und Boden* cults from the ecumenical faith of Christ's church. Without Barmen and the whole background of kerygmatic theology which made possible the stand of the Confessing Church, the church in Germany and Europe generally would bear a much greater weight of guilt than it does in relation to this entire episode.

But the contextual basis of all this has been greatly underestimated by many, both among those who were prime movers in the movement and those who were subsequently influenced by its kerygmatic fervor. The particular behavior of certain individuals and nations during a given period of the late 19th and early 20th centuries has been taken as a revelation of the permanent condition of humanity, and the theological response to this behavior has been identified as the *vere theologia*. What we have here is an instructive example of the way in which a faithful and prophetic contextual theology devised by Christians in one situation

---

40. See Arthur C. Cochrane, *The Church's Confession under Hitler* (Philadelphia: Westminster, 1962). See also my essay, "Barmen: Lesson in Theology" in *Toronto Journal of Theology* 1/2 (Fall 1985): 180ff.

41. See Cochrane, *The Church's Confession*, appendix 2, "The Guiding Principles of the Faith Movement of the 'German Christians,' " June 6, 1932, pp. 222-223.

can be turned into a doctrinal pillar of salt when it is applied universally. The very brilliance of its timeliness blinded some of its creators and (especially) its latter-day supporters to its foundation in the *kind* of revelation which takes history very seriously. Instead of accepting it for what it was, a courageous and significant rendition of prophetic faith in the light of world-shattering occurrences, those caught up in this theological movement have made it a monument to eternal truth. One senses that Barth himself, who was no doubt one of the most gifted theologians in the history of the church, felt himself increasingly trapped in his own movement—as was Luther, as was Francis, as, indeed, most of the greatest exponents of faith may have been. Barth realized that new historical circumstances had come into being with the end of World War II, and his commentators note significant changes in his thought as a consequence: the "judgment of God" has given way to a new accentuation on divine mercy, the no! has given way to more than a tentative yes, and the otherness of God has found a fascinating new form of expression in the exposition of God's "humanity"![42] But how much farther might Barth have gone if he had not felt bound by consistency or by responsibility for the nurture of the people who now looked to him as the father of a school?[43]

---

42. Karl Barth, *The Humanity of God*, trans. Thomas Wieser and John Newton Thomas (Richmond: John Knox, 1960).

43. While Barth himself should not be made responsible for "the Barthians," it is nevertheless legitimate to ask to what extent he appropriated the historical and circumstantial distinctions obtaining at the end of World War II particularly, and in a non-European framework. He may have acted as a contextual Christian thinker in the 1930s, but was he perhaps constitutionally incapable of a consistently prophetic contextuality?

The 1951 meeting of the World Council of Churches in Geneva, where Barth and Niebuhr again met, is *very* instructive in this regard, and Reinhold Niebuhr's rather generous comments on the encounter leave no doubt about which of the two theologians was contextually nuanced in his approach to thinking the faith.

To begin with, Barth's all-too-typical European superiority complex is well to the fore: " 'Yes, we sat there and talked for ten whole days. . . . Americans (Niebuhr at their head!) with bright, healthy teeth, great determination and few problems.' To Barth, Robert Calhoun remembered, the Americans were country bumpkins with too much self-assurance and too little capacity for serious thought. He erupted with anger when Niebuhr's remarks on the conference theme ignored the Christian's 'final hope' of victory over evil in favor of a more worldly focus on incremental advances in social justice. Barth lamented that 'we have to tear our hair so much over Christian hope, of all things, instead of rejoicing at it.'

"For Niebuhr Barth was being his usual irresponsible, ahistorical self. The Christian message was *not the same in all contexts*. Americans had to be cautioned against the pretensions of the powerful. Europeans against the despair of the powerless. These were not 'different gospels. But different facets of the gospel are variously relevant.' Barth's view was itself historically conditioned, 'a natural expression of the Christian faith in those parts of the world where a Christian culture has broken down, where, as in France, the prevailing cultural mood is one of despair.' American Christians, by contrast, 'had no right to express their faith in such purely eschatological terms, that is, in terms which minimize the conquest of evil in particular instances and which place the whole

The historical period in question is of great importance for methodological reflection, for it points up again—and as a matter of our immediate historical heritage—what may, as we have seen, be a rudimentary problem of Christianity: the *thirst for finality*. This is of course not only a Christian problem, and there are dimensions within Christian faith which strongly warn against precisely such a quest. But are there also not things in our tradition which aggravate and encourage it?

Does the christological core itself, perhaps, with its insistence that the Christ reveals supremely and "finally" the very mind and heart ("The Word") of the Eternal, tempt us to give more permanence to our theological positions than they deserve? Karl Barth, it will be remembered, concentrated his whole energy as a theologian upon the christological core, to the point of being charged with Christomonism. The truth or falsehood of that accusation is, to me, less interesting than the question whether Barth gave sufficient weight to the thought that if the living God revealed the divine self supremely in a human *life*, then, as Luther put it, God's "revealing" must also be regarded as a "concealing." For no human life can be exhausted by descriptions of it (John 21:25). Certainly Barth knew this better than anyone in the earlier phases of his career. But did the thirst for finality, compounded by success and the inevitable temptations of age, overcome the modesty that such an insight necessarily brings? Was Reinhold Niebuhr right in suspecting, from the outset, Barth's "absolute Christ-idea"?[44]

Tillich's "method of correlation" is certainly more amenable to contextuality in theology than is Barth's "positivism of revelation." It is indeed possible that, so far at least as his methodology is concerned, Tillich has exercised more influence upon subsequent movements in theology for which the "context" has priority than has any other major figure of our recent past.

There are, however, three problems in Tillich's methodology which will concern most of us who attempt to articulate the Christian faith in a contextual mode. The first of these is suggested by the word "correlation" itself. The image conjured up by this term (and I think it is the image

---

emphasis upon God's final triumph over evil.' It was up to them to uphold the historical liberal Protestant quest for a 'responsible' society. *Niebuhr was urging a pluralistic, shifting Christian prophecy that tailored its judgment to circumstances. God was beyond history, but the Christian witness was profoundly shaped by it.* At the conference itself, Barth's forces carried the day, perhaps because of his threat to bolt the meeting altogether. In the end, Niebuhr glumly recalled the following year, 'we did nothing more than to capitulate more than was wise to Karl Barth' " (Richard Fox, *Reinhold Niebuhr: A Biography* [New York: Pantheon, 1985], pp. 243-244 [emphasis added]).

44. Fox, *Reinhold Niebuhr*, p. 117.

Tillich intended) is one of considerable harmony. To be sure, the two things to be "correlated" (question and answer; human situation and divine revelation; etc.) are "independent factors."[45] The question, as he puts it, cannot be derived from the answer, nor the answer from the question. This is the kerygmatic element in Tillich's method, and it prevents one from accusing him (as some of his less discerning critics have done) of offering the sort of synthesis of situation and gospel, reason and faith, and so on, which has more in common with Catholic natural theology than with classical Protestantism. Nevertheless, the two "independent factors" *do* correspond very harmoniously in Tillich's system, and without great difficulty. The question cannot produce the answer, but it recognizes the answer as its appropriate counterpart, and vice versa. There appears to be little awareness here of a gospel which, while it may indeed *be* the "right answer," is offensive precisely for that reason!

This feeling for the correlative relationship between situation and message, context and text, question and answer is, of course, more than a methodological technique. Tillich knew very well that method is derived from one's preliminary convictions concerning the *content* which is to be investigated.[46] His method of correlation presupposes his ontology or theory of reality. And his ontology is one in which the principle of *continuity* is strongly dominant: the being of the creatures is necessarily and essentially continuous with the Being who is the "ground of being," even though "existence" introduces separation and distance—in short, discontinuity. If there can be (must be!) for Tillich a *methodological* correlation, it is because there is a prior metaphysical one—to the point, as Barth would insist, of embracing an *analogia entis* (analogy of being).

From our present point of view, the difficulty in this approach is that it greatly reduces the methodological *tension* we have pointed to as the central factor in Christian theological method. The principle of continuity is so prominent, both in the method as such and in its ontic presupposition, that the dimension of discontinuity finally seems more poetic than real. Discontinuity *is* present in Tillich's discussion of the faith, of course. It is there in his concepts of creation and redemption (it is simply irresponsible to accuse him of pantheism, as some have done); it is certainly there, also, in his concepts of sin and alienation, of nonbeing, of the

---

45. Supra, p. 599.

46. In the *Systematic Theology*, therefore, he insists that while problems of communication make it necessary first to treat "reason and revelation," the epistemological question, what really comes first is what appears second in his ordering of the doctrinal areas, viz., "being and God." Ontology precedes epistemology.

demonic, and elsewhere. But it is not given a sufficiently solid status, so to speak, to counterbalance the power of its antithesis. It is more like a minus-quality than something asserting itself actively—a kind of shadow reality which, however existentially distorting, can never really threaten the essential continuity running through all that "is."

By contrast, in the *Hebraic* background of Christian faith, the discontinuous, negating, separating dimension is very much part of the "really real." It is true that biblical religion, with its "The Lord thy God is One Lord," could never embrace the sort of dualism present, for example, in Zoroastrianism. And yet, with its clear distinction between Creator and creation, its radical belief in the freedom of the creature, its sense of the reality of evil, biblical religion does assume something like a *provisional* dualism: the one God from whom everything flows and upon whom everything is dependent, nevertheless *permits* the possibility of a radical independence on the part of the creature, because only so can this God expect the creature freely to love. If the principle of continuity is overstressed, love becomes a matter of necessity and of nature rather than freedom and grace. The dangerous and even evil potentialities of the discontinuity factor must be risked by a God who will have our love as a product of our willing it, and not as a programmed response.

In the end, what distinguishes Tillich's method from that of the prophetic tradition is a different theory of reality. Tillich's ontology, in the long tradition whose roots lie in Athens rather than Jerusalem, is substantialistic; for the biblical tradition, reality is through and through *relational*.[47] The relational understanding of reality must be differentiated from Tillich's kind of ontology, in which the relatedness of Creator and creatures, creatures and creatures, is simply a given—built into the scheme of things. In biblical faith, on the contrary, the creaturely *capacity* for relationship is not necessarily actualized. Its realization presupposes an act of turning, of intention, of decision, on the parts both of Creator and creatures. That God is turned towards humanity is the primary declaration of biblical faith throughout. That God's orientation towards humanity has found its response, representatively, in the man Jesus' vicarious turning towards God is the declaration of the Newer Testament. But all of this assumes a theory of being which is quite different from the *analogia entis* of scholasticism and the ontology of Tillich. The biblical ontology is not about *being* as such but about *being-with*, and therefore it also presupposes

---

47. See my discussion of this in *Imaging God: Dominion as Stewardship* (Grand Rapids: Eerdmans, 1986).

the genuine prospect of *not* being-with, of being-against and being-alone—in short, of discontinuity.

In this way, we can see that the element of discontinuity, far from being a merely negative factor, is a necessary concomitant of the biblical understanding of the nature of being. Even the *skandalon* serves an important end: it prevents us from being simply overwhelmed by the divine "power of Being": it guarantees us sufficient distance from God and God's incredible, irresistible love and grace to enable us, now and then, to love God freely and not as a matter of coercion or necessity. The preservation of the dimension of radical discontinuity at the level of theological method is therefore important to the whole discussion of the content of belief which follows from this method.

The second critical comment to be offered in connection with Tillich's methodology is really a criticism of his generation—the generation of our great teachers. As such, it is not so much a criticism as it is an observation concerning the differences between their situation and our own. We may, I think, observe about them—and especially about the systematic theologians among them, Tillich himself included—that they were able, apparently, still to think categorically in a way that has been denied us. If Barth and his followers gave way to the temptation to regard what was a timely and strategic theology as "the true theology," Tillich and his disciples have been equally prone to think in terms of permanency. Because Tillich made "the situation" so central to the theological task, he introduced an element into methodology which would militate against the human and religious quest for finality. This is the vital side of the "method of correlation," which saves it from petrification and keeps it open to the moving edge of time. And yet the method is explained by Tillich in such a way that one wonders to what extent he would be willing to take it beyond the realm of methodological *theory*. What if the highly specific realities of his situation had been permitted to make their way, as it were, more graphically and explicitly into the pages of his three-volume system of theology? It is one thing to speak theoretically about the correlation of situation and message, question and answer; it is something else to bring into proximity to one another the traditions of the faith and the existing events, conflicts, and attitudes of one's world. Whoever knows the story of Tillich's personal life—his own conflicts of spirit, his deep involvement in the shattering events of the first part of the 20th century—will realize that he was himself existentially caught up in an attempt at "correlation" far exceeding the "method of correlation" calmly outlined in the measured sentences of his *Systematic Theology*! If he had permitted this existential attempt at correlating the Christian message and life to inform more immediately the discussions of his formal work might he, perhaps, have been more emphatic than he was concerning the dimension of discontinuity?

I put this question not out of biographical interest but in order to illustrate more concretely the transition I believe has occurred between the generation of our teachers and our own. Although they were subjected to external events which have shaped our present time, and in many cases subjected to these events more intensely than are many of us, they brought to their interpretation of their situation and their faith principles far more fixed than anything known to us—principles of order and authority and wholeness and consistency which came to them from the Protestant and Catholic past. To put it in a word, *theory* was possible for them in a way that it is not possible for us today. "Systematic theology" was possible for them—and in a real sense it could still be done by them along the lines already laid down by the Middle Ages and classical Protestantism. This was their strength—and their weakness.

It was a weakness, because the kind of order, authority, wholeness, and consistency that it enabled at the theoretical level was purchased at the expense of a once-remove from life. Not that they were *personally* aloof or remote from the affairs of their world—far from it. But when they addressed themselves to the theological task, particularly when they set out to be theologians in the strict sense, they had, apparently, access to reservoirs of theory and objectivity which lifted them above the immediacy of their own troubled times and lives. And while "transcendence" is a dimension that Christian theology cannot do without, a faith which takes historical existence as seriously as biblical faith does ought not to be tempted to let that dimension translate itself into an analytical once-remove.

To speak candidly: there is a tendency in the works of our precursors in this field to discuss the Christian faith without any intensive attention to the particularities under which the discussion is taking place. To those among our own generation who *have* become conscious of the inherent demands of contextual particularities, the great works of theology produced by our immediate predecessors seem singularly lacking in explicit references to their own situation. It is not fair, I think, to say of these works that they could have been written at any time, in any place; yet *by comparison with* some of the more imaginative theology today, especially as it emerges from the ranks of the oppressed, these older works betray very little about their actual situation, even when (as with Tillich) "the situation" is vital to the whole process. It is even typical of them that they (politely?) avoid sharing with their readers the specifics of their own existence: that they were for the most part males, for example, and white, and at least economically if not also personally "bourgeois"; that they were citizens of affluent nations; that they could still live and move among the intelligentsia and command a certain respect, and so on. They did not regard such information as being in good form; and yet this same convention, a very typical one of their class, enabled them to hide from themselves and us many of the realities by which their *thinking* was decisively shaped. The fact that they could discuss *the discipline* without asking frankly and critically about their own identity as *disciples* may have seemed to them an advantage. We must regard it as a disadvantage, a barrier in the way of theological *praxis*.[48]

The third way in which present-day advocates of contextuality in theology must question Tillich's method of correlation is closely related to the above observation—namely, *the absence of what we may call place-consciousness in this method*.

When Tillich juxtaposes human question and revelatory answer, situation and message, he is exemplifying the long tradition of apologetic theology from the second-century apologists to Augustine and Anselm, Aquinas, Schleiermacher, and others. Insofar as this tradition takes the ever-changing historical situation seriously and attempts to relate the Christian gospel to it, it is the precursor of theological contextuality.

Does this mean that contextuality in theology is merely an extension of this long apologetic tradition? In a way, it is. But something new *has* been added in contemporary contextual theology which does not belong conspicuously to the long apologetic tradition. The simplest way of designating that new element is to call it the *sense of place*. Let me elaborate.

What we have by way of a tradition as Christians, once the center of Christian discourse moved beyond the eastern end of the Mediterranean Sea, is, as we have said from the outset of this study, largely a European phenomenon. Moving through the history of Christian thought, the names that we encounter up to and including the present time are largely European names. All of these names betray, in their work, the evolving history of Europe and Europe's satellites—even when their work is less

---

48. It could be asked, in this connection, whether the continuing popularity of the rather tentative writings of Dietrich Bonhoeffer is not due as much to their thoroughly personal and confessional nature as to the fact that they are the works of a modern martyr. In a way that is unique in his generation, Bonhoeffer speaks out of a profound awareness of his own *discipleship*—and of its "cost."

apologetic and more kerygmatic. There are of course very important distinctions between the ideas of these different theologians, for they are responding to the dynamics of time, and over a very long period of time. There are also extremely significant similarities—significant enough to warrant writers of historical texts, for example, to speak of "the Christian tradition" in the singular. For however varied and even provincial it has been, the *place* in which this tradition evolved does have a certain unitary character. Even the Reformation break with the past is explicable chiefly in temporal rather than spatial terms—though its predominance in *northern* Europe may be somewhat provocative. Regional variations notwithstanding, the relative unity of place here means that many things immediately pertinent to the "modest science" of theology could be assumed by most of the evolving tradition: climactic conditions, producing far-reaching consequences for human survival and self-understanding; political structures, which from the ancient Roman to the British Empire created material and spiritual forms of social unity; the greater movements of history, with population shifts and wars and class structures spilling over local boundaries; evolving schools of thought—philosophy in the larger sense—which already by the early Middle Ages were exercising a ubiquitous influence upon all European theology through the developing court and cathedral schools; a common fund of legend, myth, saga, and song, which in albeit variegated form found its way into all the corners of the continent; and even (given, once more, room for regional nuance) certain fairly common social and moral assumptions, partly influenced by Christianity but in many cases antedating official Christian morality, such as the hierarchic structuring of authority, the dominance of the male, the right to property, and the whole range of concepts connected with the human domination of the nonhuman species.

So thoroughly does the phrase "the Christian tradition" simply assume this long European locus of the faith, that when it moves out into the non-European world, as it began to do in the 16th century, it must attempt to translate the conditions of its *place* to the other places into which it moves. And sometimes—as in North America—it is astonishingly successful in doing this, simply, in the process, ignoring and suppressing the indigenous peoples, *their* climate, *their* politics, *their* values, and, above all, their *religious* traditions.

Nor are we speaking only of the past when we note this tendency. The place assumption inherent in the Christian tradition as we have inherited it is manifested in our own readiness in North America today to accept as immediately applicable to our situation analyses of the human condition which are very obviously "Made in Europe." When at age 47 Paul Tillich moved to the United States he could assume without contradiction that existentialism constituted the articulate core of the *Zeitgeist* with which Christianity had to enter into dialogue—even though most of his students and hearers were completely baffled by that term. One could speak of the Marxist and other presuppositions of later European theologians in essentially the same vein, though modern communications have *somewhat* broadened North American awareness of such everyday European phenomena.

Contextuality means in a special sense, then, the discovery of the place-dimension of the human condition. It builds upon the apologetic tradition with its consciousness of changing time, but it adds to this the recognition that within any given time there are very different spatial realities that must be taken seriously by a faith that is genuinely incarnational. Jesus did not come only "in the fulness of *time*"; he came to a very specific place—not Rome or Alexandria, but obscure Bethlehem. The place already says a great deal about the embodiment of the evangel.

This discovery of the significance of place is, of course, bound up with the dramatic spread of Christianity into parts of the world which could never be Europeanized in the manner which befell North America. In Asia, Africa, and Latin America, 20th-century Christians have recognized in their own indigenous cultures presuppositions and expectations *very* different from even the rudimentary assumptions of European Christianity. Although their reinterpretations of the faith seem to "Western" Christians, often enough, almost betrayals of orthodox Christianity, the theologians of these new churches can argue convincingly that the apostolic tradition sets important precedents for taking earnestly precisely what is *there* in the host culture, and not importing cultural assumptions from the so-called Western world, no matter how hallowed they may be through long association with Christian belief.

To say that contextuality refers in a particular way to the discovery of place, however, is not to confine the context to geography. It also refers to a more metaphoric use of the term "place," as, for instance, it is used in expressions like "knowing one's place." That is, it refers to explicit conditions which set one apart from others. In any period of history, persons share a great many things in common (they are *con*temporaries) in spite of their particularities—as in our time, for example, we all exist under the shadow of the bomb. But there are spaces within the general time frame called the last fifth of the 20th century whose characteristics are such that they represent specific conditions with high theological significance. To be black in a predominantly white world; to be a woman in a male-dominated culture; to be French- or Spanish-speaking in a great sea of Anglophones; to be poor and without work in a still affluent, work-orientated consumer society; to be handicapped or unattractive physically in a society that has all but divinized the body—these constitute "contexts" which put to theology quite explicit questions, by which the theological answers must be *informed*.

Thus, while theological contextuality stands in a clear line of continuity with the whole apologetic tradition, it represents in some ways also a departure from this tradition. For it insists upon a *radical concretization* of the human condition and the Christian response to it. Theology inspired by the idea of context is no longer willing to indulge in *general* observations about the human situation, such as can be (and habitually have been) practiced by those who are conscious of the time factor, but are prevented by this consciousness from elaborating analyses which in fact overlook the explicit circumstances of the *polis*, and more especially of its countercultural elements and its victims.

In the last analysis, therefore, contextualization in theology must be seen as the methodological dimension of a much more momentous shift in Christian theology. I am referring to the movement of theology (not all of it, to be sure, but its most serious contemporary expressions) away from the suprahistorical, the eternal, the unconditioned, and towards *this* world. As soon as Christian faith begins to insist that it is indeed this world that representatives of the gospel of the cross have to take with utmost seriousness, it has registered its preference for theological contextuality. For there is no way of taking this world seriously without beginning with the concrete realities of the particular *place* where one is. Only God can have "the *whole* world in his hands"; human beings can grasp the whole only by taking hold of that part nearest them.

The Tillichian method of correlation contains important directives for a method of doing theology that is informed by context, then, but it cannot provide an entirely satisfactory background for such a method.

27.2. The Role of the Context in Theological Method. We may state the argument developed above in still another way. It is conceivable that between the generation of our teachers and ourselves what has occurred is the emergence of a religious and social climate in which the context both can and must play a more decisive role in our methodology than it has done heretofore. The reason why the context *can* play such a role is bound up with many of the factors we have treated earlier in this study: (1) The breakdown of Christendom is mirrored in the breakdown of theological systems in which the whole universe was present and accounted for. (2) The plurality of religions and quasi-religions in our present situation introduces alternatives not only at the level of belief but at the level of the paths to belief. (3) Auschwitz and the fundamental rethinking of faith that it has caused among us has brought us to a more serious consideration of the dynamic, nonsystematic theology of Judaism. (4) The critique of all ideologies by minorities which suffer on account of them has made us aware of the vested interests hidden beneath our theory. In short, many things have worked together to deny to our generation the production of great systems of thought, and to make us more conscious of the particularities that are almost always lost sight of by those who search for universals. We are frequently heard to lament the absence of "theological giants in the land," who like the great ones of our youth could produce vast tomes and establish "schools." But what from one standpoint is the humiliation of theology may from another be its rejuvenation. Denied access to the secrets of the universe, it can become, perhaps, more concretely orientated towards the earth, as a theology centered in incarnation and cross might well be expected to be.

What this means for method is clear enough. It means that whereas our forebears were able to evolve methods which could satisfy them and their circles of influence for a lifetime if not forever, we must learn to be more tentative and open. We cannot decide for or against *any* methodology a priori, be it kerygmatic, apologetic, or some admixture of the two. Given the origins and the history of our faith, we *can* assume, I think, that the meeting of gospel and world will always entail something like the dialectical tension to which I spoke earlier in this chapter: the tension between continuity and discontinuity, between the common ground and the *skandalon*. But what we cannot say in advance is which element in this tension will have to be accentuated. That will depend upon the specific character of our context, our time-*and-place*.

It is for example quite conceivable that there are situations in the world today where the disciple community must announce a *kerygma* just as critically detached from the culture as was Karl Barth's version of the gospel in Hitler's infamous Reich. Something like this would seem to be called for particularly in certain Third World and other contexts where the most oppressive regimes give themselves off officially to be "Christian." But only the insensitive today could assume that such an accent upon the *discontinuity* between God and the world would be appropriate in every place, or even in those places for all time. On the contrary, what seems increasingly the case in our own society is that the dimension of discontinuity hardly needs stressing at all. It is already conspicuously present—except for pockets of complacent "Christianity" where it can be imagined that God is very much "on our side."

What it comes to is this: that method in theology, too, must and can be subjected to contextual consideration. It is not as if a contextual approach could be taken to the *content* of the faith, while the method of theology remains fixed. *A confessional theology requires a methodology whose informing principle is strategic.* Everything must be geared to the concrete realities of time-and-place; everything must serve the *here and now* beloved by God. Neither a predilection for harmony nor an abiding sense of the disconnectedness of things should be held on to as if it were always and everywhere valid. The context calls sometimes for one and sometimes for the other emphasis. The combinations of this fundamental tension have not yet been exhausted, nor will they be until time itself runs out.

CHAPTER ▪ SIX

Knowing in Christian Faith and Theology

Richard: *You know I don't believe in God, Grandmama.*

Mother Henry: *You don't know what you talking about. Ain't no way possible for you not to believe in God. It ain't up to you.*

Richard: *Who's it up to then?*

Mother Henry: *It's up to the life in you—the life in you.* That *knows where it comes from,* that *believes in God. You doubt me, you just try holding your breath long enough to die.*[1]

28. Modes of Knowing

28.1. How Do You Know? Whenever Christians make statements about the biblical God, or even statements which, while they may not concern the divine person directly, assume belief in transcendent meaning, they can expect to elicit the question, How do you know? When Christian preachers announce the reality of God's love, God's willingness to forgive, the judgment of God against social evils, the meaningfulness of the historical process, and so on, they must assume today that there are people in every pew who are asking them, silently but insistently, How do you know? Even the well-dressed and polite congregations of our middle-class churches; even old ladies and gentlemen who are not usually cast in the role of skeptic—all may be asking, How is it possible to know this?

---

1. James Baldwin, *Blues for Mister Charlie* (New York: Dell, 1964), pp. 33-34.

Really to *know*? And the one who is in the pulpit is also asking this question, in all probability—perhaps without admitting it.

It is better for us to ask this question explicitly and consciously. In fact, we shall be well acquainted with our socioreligious context only insofar as we have made this question in some genuine sense our own. For this question, which is much more than an intellectual question only, is one form of *the* question to which as disciples of the Christ in our time and place we must endeavor to find the answer—to use Tillich's methodological metaphor.

It is of course not the only form of the question by which contemporary Homo sapiens is addressed; and it is misleading when theologians take up the epistemological question as if it were the exclusive interest of 20th-century persons in search of faith. In one sense, the questions presupposed by the main doctrinal areas of Christian theology are far more important: Is it permitted any longer to assume the possibility of transcendence (Theology)? Is the human creature in any appreciable way unique, special (anthropology)? Is salvation possible in a world that is no longer able to distinguish between "is" and "ought," existence and essence (Christology/soteriology)? Is the historical process—are our own personal histories—in any sense purposeful (eschatology)? Yet all such questions presuppose a preliminary consideration of the epistemological question. For, especially in a society which has severely limited the things that human beings may be credited with knowing, the claims of Christian faith can be entertained seriously only if they are accompanied by strong evidence that their advocates have opened themselves existentially to the rigors of the epistemological question. The discipline to which we are called is perhaps more demanding at this point, given our particular historical-geographic context, than at any other.

This is not to say that Christians are obligated to demonstrate to their world, on its own terms, the *legitimacy* of their mode of knowing. So far as many of our contemporaries are concerned, such a demonstration is in any case unthinkable. To take on the world as it presents itself in our technological society, and to seek to convince it that "God-talk" is quite permissible and meaningful, is to abandon oneself to an indefinite engagement with epistemological discourse of the sort which is never able to advance beyond the how of knowing to the what. Just that has been the fate of much Anglo-Saxon theology in our time. It lives in a methodological cul-de-sac.

What is required of us, then, is not that we prove to all concerned our "right" to pursue this "arcane science" (Bonhoeffer); on the contrary, it is that we give evidence of recognizing at depth that such a right, if it ever existed, does not exist today. It was taken away from the church by the modern world, which decided that Christians had badly abused precisely this right and that from now on they would have to *earn* whatever noetic rights they wished to have. Part of the earning of such rights has to do with our attitude towards the quest for truth. The world will listen to us only if it senses that we know that our knowing is in fact a risking, trusting, hoping, imagining, envisioning—in short, a reaching out into mystery, and not without difficulty, and not without doubt.

At the same time, it is not required of Christians today that we bow in abject humility before what the dominant systems and methods honored by our society recognize as legitimacy in the realm of knowledge. There is for us also at this point a discontinuity to be encountered, a *skandalon*. We cannot submit the subject matter of our knowing to the tribunal of the technological society—and we should not! The gap between that world's knowing and ours must be made quite plain. All the false scandals connected with the church's reputation for knowing must be cleared away so that the authentic scandal may become present in all of its boldness. The true offense of the faith so far as its epistemological aspect is concerned has nothing to with the quantity of data Christians have been traditionally credited with knowing. It has to do with the *quality* of their knowing, that is to say, with the nature of what is known, and the mode of knowing it. Suffice it here to say—in an anticipatory way—that this "what" is not properly designated "it" but only "Thou"; and this *first principle of our knowing* sets us at once in conflict with a society which has made it less and less possible for human beings even to say "thou" to one another, let alone to address an "Eternal Thou" (Buber).[2]

By the same token, the pursuit of this mode of knowing will not find Christians alone and friendless in such a world. For the very reductionism present in the dominant rational systems by which the technocratic society is regulated has produced in the last analysis its own internal protest. In a manner that was not true even for the great teachers of the faith to whom we have made reference in the preceding chapter, there is in our present context a recognition on the part of many sensitive persons in all disciplines that the reduction of knowing to quantitative and functional terms has robbed our culture of spirit and meaning, making of it

---

2. The first great disutopic novel of the century, Zamyatin's *We*, depicts the mass culture in just such terms. When the protagonist wishes to find a language appropriate to love ("I wanted to say 'thou' "), he cannot do so in a society that can only say "we" (Yevgeny Zamyatin, *We*, trans. Mirra Ginsburg [New York: Viking, 1972]).

a "one-dimensional" society.[3] Eschewing all wisdom but that which could, as it was thought, give Homo sapiens supremacy over nature and history, our species has arrived at a point where, as we have seen, its vaunted mastery could destroy what it set out to control. Many of the most thoughtful minds of our civilization have in consequence been driven to ask after an alternative form of thinking and being that seems to have been lost in the rush for facts and power. Is it not possible, then, that we shall find allies all along the way in our search to describe anew, for the postmodern era, the sort of knowing that is linked with trusting and with mystery? May we not also hope, in that case, to discover common ground and the prospect of a profitable exchange with those who are "not of this fold"?

28.2. Levels of Knowing. We may begin this search by making a distinction that is by no means peculiar to Christianity, but is nevertheless basic to Christian epistemology. It is common experience that there are different levels or dimensions or categories of knowing. I do not mean by this a merely quantitative distinction—knowing more and knowing less. What I refer to, rather, is a frequently experienced need to categorize human cognition according to types or qualities. There are distinct levels of knowing, that is to say, in the sense that one kind of knowledge is markedly different from another. To know a fact of mathematics (that 6 and 6 are 12) implies a kind of knowing quite dissimilar to what is intended when someone says to his mortal enemy, "I know *you*, sir!" or when the apostle Peter assures Jesus, "Lord, you *know* that I love you" (John 21:15f.) When a woman explains to her husband, "We've overspent the budget again this month," and he replies, "I know," a very different sort of knowledge is implied from what may be alluded to two minutes later in the same exchange, when the husband, shedding his customary nonchalance, gives expression to his frustration over money and work and perhaps life itself, and his wife, in sympathy, responds, "I know, I know." In the same sequence, using the same terminology, qualitatively distinct messages are conveyed. We understand one another when this happens. No one has to spell it out. It is quite unnecessary to explain that one "I know" means, "Yes, I understand this deplorable fact: the budget is overspent," while the other conveys the comforting reassurance of compassion, love, and conjugal trust. These nuances of meaning, so very important in everyday life, are communicated from one person to another almost automatically.

---

3. See Herbert Marcuse, *One-Dimensional Man: Studies in the Ideology of Advanced Industrial Society* (Boston: Beacon, 1964).

It should not surprise us, in that case, that similar distinctions also apply to the language of faith and theology. If it seems to be part of human experience in general that knowing occurs at varying levels, then one could expect this to be the case also where religious belief is concerned.

Is it possible to classify the different levels of knowing which apply to Christian faith and theology? Classification is difficult even in areas where quite precise distinctions can be noted and described. There is usually an arbitrary element in such distinctions. All the same, it may help to establish differentiations that can aid our perception of the reality which ultimately evades classification and description if we recognize three *types* of knowing which seem to apply to our subject matter. For convenience, and without committing ourselves in any rigid way to the nomenclature itself, we may designate these: knowledge, acknowledgment, and trust.

28.3. Knowledge. We begin by positing the kind of knowing which is the possession of information—data. Some conventions of our society would warrant our calling this level of knowing simply, "knowledge." A person is said to be knowledgeable when she has a good grasp of the data associated with a particular discipline or profession. Much of our time in childhood and youth is spent in the acquisition of this kind of knowledge—too much of our time, according to some critics of North American educational systems! Yet without the knowledge that fire burns and heavier things fall and energy can be transferred and things are valued according to their supply and demand, it would be impossible to live in the world. Moreover, the contemporary world seems to demand more and more of this type of knowledge for anyone who wants to avoid being victimized by forces in the society which will certainly govern our lives more effectively if we do *not* know such things.

There is a tendency among some Christians, particularly mainline Protestants in North America, to minimize or even to denigrate altogether this level of knowing. Such a criticism comes from the side of persons who believe, with some justification but little understanding of the subtlety of the relation between faith and knowledge, that the *essential* thing in Christian belief has very little to do with the intellect but much with the heart, or the hands: feeling and doing. There is a history of anti-intellectualism within the general history of the Christian movement, and it has in many ways found a fertile soil in the New World, where piety and activism have too often been more highly valued than *thinking* the faith.[4]

---

4. Martin E. Marty reminds us of Tocqueville's telling insight on this subject: " 'The majority

But in fact Christian belief also assumes the necessity of knowing in this preliminary sense. The same sort of knowing that is implied when someone recites the mathematical datum 6 plus 6 equals 12 is part of what Christian theology has to treat in its epistemology.

Indeed, this type of knowing in Christianity plays an important role in the whole process of the movement of anyone towards belief. There is simply a great deal to be known in the sense of the acquisition of information; and there is a way in which this kind of knowing must *come first*. In a way, everything else depends upon it.

It is for this reason that Christianity from the outset has been a *teaching* religion, as was and is its parental faith of Judaism. The disciple community is a teaching community; its discipline is inextricably linked with the fact that it both learns continuously and communicates what it tries to comprehend. More is always involved in learning and teaching, certainly, than the mere imbibing and imparting of information. But information—and therefore knowledge in the sense in which we are presently using the term—is all the same an important aspect of this discipline. This applies rather obviously to Christian education. It applies as well to Christian *preaching*, which is always *partly* the communication of information (though when it is nothing more than that it does not deserve to be called preaching). Christianity *must* be taught, and Christians *must* teach. This is built into belief. It is inherent in belief not only because of that "necessity" which, as we have seen previously, is "laid upon" those who hear, and whose hearing itself creates the need to share what is heard. It is inherent also on account of the sheer fact that Christianity is a *historical* faith. That is, it is based upon event—upon a whole series of historical events with one especially clarifying (*kairos*) event at the center.

Part of the reason why the Protestant reformers from Wycliffe and Hus onwards stressed Bible knowledge as requisite for every Christian believer lies exactly in this recognition that such a faith requires continuous nurture through the recollection of its own foundational events. When recitation of and reflection upon these events gives place to more immediate, personal, and experientially based "spirituality," as this has happened in circles of liberal Christianity during the present century, there

---

[in America] draws a formidable circle around thought. Within its limits, one is free: but woe to him who dares to break out of it.' Religion, [de Tocqueville] saw, was a major element in the formation of this circle. He believed there was no country in the world where the Christian religion retained a greater influence over the souls of men than in America" (*Righteous Empire: The Protestant Experience in America* [New York: Harper Torchbooks, 1970], p. 90).

is a very real danger that Christianity as such will be dissolved. And, as George Lindbeck insists, the dissolution of Christianity has implications for the whole civilization that has been formed, in large measure, by the Christian story.

> If the Bible has shaped the imagination of the West to anywhere near the degree that Northrop Frye, for example, has argued, then the West's continuing imaginative vitality and creativity may well depend on the existence of groups for whom the Hebrew and Christian Scriptures are not simply classics among others, but the canonical literature par excellence, and who are also in close contact with the wider culture.[5]

Historical occurrences are not known automatically. We are not born with historical knowledge, though we may in some way be born with a thirst for historical knowledge—for remembering. But the knowledge of events has to be acquired. The character of these foundational events—what happened, what the original participants and observers said about what happened, what was said *by* the central figures of these occurrences, especially by Jesus—all of this has to be transmitted from one person to another, one generation to another; for it is not something transhistorical, an eternal truth of which everyone may become aware quite naturally in the course of her or his life. It is historical, part of the past; it is not still occurring—not, at least, so far as the *foundational* events are concerned. "It is finished." And even if these events were still occurring—even if they were somehow recurrent events (as in a parabolic, mythic, and liturgical sense they are)—there would still be the need for transmitting information. For as the Newer Testament makes quite plain, the events as such do not communicate the thing that has to be communicated. The events have to be *interpreted*. They must be "borne witness to"—fulfilled, as it were, by words, by thought.

It is not that the events are inadequate; it is that *we* are inadequate. We do not see what is there to be seen, or hear what is there to be heard. So the God of the Scriptures does not simply "act." To name this God the acting God, and to discuss "God's mighty acts" is misleading—particularly in an activistic culture like our own. For the God of the Bible also *speaks*—is also *Deus loquens*. God's acting is inseparable from God's speaking. God's acting *is* God's speaking. God speaks through the mouth of the prophets, the law-givers, the evangelists, for

---

5. George Lindbeck, *The Nature of Doctrine* (Philadelphia: Westminster, 1984), p. 127.

THE DISCIPLINE

Surely the Lord God does nothing,
without revealing his secret
to his servants the prophets.

(Amos 3:7)

Thus Jesus, God's Word enacted, must not only *be* and *do*, but he must also interpret his being and his doing. He must disclose information. Indeed, he must be known *first* as "Teacher," "Rabbi."

This information is not by itself effective. It depends upon the being and the doing to which it points. And more: it depends upon a movement which no teacher, not even the rabbi Jesus, can cause to occur—what we may think of, poetically, as the movement from brain to heart. The object of the information that the disciple community receives and imparts is that it should make possible some such movement as this, but it cannot do this by itself. This movement is the subject of the next two phases of our discussion about the levels of knowing. All the same, so far as Christian belief is concerned, the kind of knowledge that is implied in this first distinction has a decisive chronological priority. What Lindbeck calls "experiential-expressive" religion may seem, for a time, more exciting and more personally fulfilling than what is offered by a disciple community that requires of its membership, older and younger, an ongoing and disciplined exposure to historical narrative and interpretation; but without this basic *knowledge*, there is in the long run nothing whatsoever to ensure the cohesion of the disciple community *or* the uniqueness of its service to the larger human community. Knowledge in this first sense is thus indispensable, and a vital aspect of the discipline to which the disciple community in our particular context is called today must involve the most serious pedagogical efforts to inculcate precisely such knowledge in those who remain within the churches of the "postliberal age."

Let us not, however, underestimate the difficulties of such a mandate! On the one hand, it leads to the temptation (which in North American Christianity today must be regarded as a very great *temptation*) to ignore all the warnings of the scientific mind and the experience of modernity as a whole, and to "return" to a defensive and positivistic biblicism. On the other hand, those who are able to resist *that* temptation are faced with another, namely, to be debilitated by the skepticism of both modern and postmodern secularity concerning all claims to knowledge of this sort. For already in the initial stages of our epistemological quest we encounter the skepticism and—not infrequently—the scorn of our world. Already the aggressive "How do you know?" of our fact-driven society accosts

376

us. For history, too, has been forced into the role of "objectivity." And what concrete evidence do we have for these historical data which describe the foundational events of our religious tradition and must be given chronological priority in our knowing? What can be proved about the history of the people of Israel? More, no doubt, than can be proved about Jesus "the Christ"! Can we even "get back to the historical Jesus"? Albert Schweitzer demonstrated the pitfalls of such a quest already in the early decades of this century.[6] We intend to base our faith on events, and yet we cannot show beyond the shadow of a doubt that these events ever actually occurred! We say that "Jesus Christ and him crucified" is the cornerstone of our belief; but before we even come to the *meaning* of such a statement we are confronted by the fact that we cannot be absolutely certain that such a thing took place.

This demonstrates, among other things, the inadequacy of factual knowledge as the foundation of belief. No one is saved by knowledge—a truth which won the battle (if it was indeed won!) against the Gnosticism of the early Christian centuries. The historical data which form the substantive basis of our faith can by no means be dispensed with, yet they do not of themselves give the possibility of faith. Even if they were not limited; even if the data *could* be demonstrated in a more objective manner—even then this would be unsatisfactory as a basis for belief. The disciples of Jesus who actually spoke and walked with him had, presumably, more knowledge of this sort than could be acquired today even by the most astute and patient scholars. Observing as they could in an immediate way—not only hearing his words but seeing his facial expressions as he uttered them; not only watching in a spectator manner but participating in the events of his life—they could surely gain more information about this central figure of our belief than if many books *had* been written (see John 21:25) and much evidence preserved. Yet with all their firsthand knowledge not one of them "believed"! The belief with which, *later*, they approached the recollection of these foundational events was certainly not independent of the immediate experience of their life with Jesus in the flesh—just as *our* belief, if we manifest such, is never independent of their *testimony* to that experience (*sola scriptura*). Yet between the fact-knowledge they had from their firsthand experience (and we from their testimony) and the post-Pentecostal state of belief or trust there is no comparison. The latter state, this *believing* knowledge, depends upon the former; but it is qualitatively different from fact-knowledge.

---

6. Albert Schweitzer, *The Quest of the Historical Jesus,* trans. W. Montgomery (London: A. & C. Black, 1910).

Something had to happen to "the facts" of their raw experience before they could become foundational for belief. Similarly, something has to happen in the life of the one who has acquired biblical and doctrinal knowledge (*gnōsis*) before it can become the conceptual ground of our trust in God.

28.4. Acknowledgment. In order to understand a little better the mystery of the movement from *gnōsis* to *pistis*, fact to faith, we may posit a second type of knowing which differs from both. This second type is suggested by the fact that *some* of the data people come to acquire becomes significant for them. Not all information that we pick up is immediately significant. Most of it, indeed, remains in the limbo of semi-consciousness or half-remembered things. At two or three years of age, a child may be taught that 5 plus 5 are 10, and the proud parents stand and beam while the toddler recites this ineluctible datum of human experience. But the information is not really significant to the child, beyond the obvious fact that it gains a certain amount of prestige and self-satisfaction from reciting it (something which can be observed about many persons well beyond the state of childhood).

A few months later, however, the child stands before a candy counter with a nickle in one pocket and 5 pennies in another; and in the case before it there is a particularly enticing red candy which may be acquired for 10 cents. Now the information that 5 plus 5 are 10 becomes highly significant information. Now the child *knows* this! Did it not also know this mathematical datum before? Yes, but the child's present state of knowing, as it stands in rapt attention before a desirable object, is very different from rote knowledge.

We have a whole vocabulary for describing the difference in question. We say, for example, that the child has "assimilated" the mathematical information, or that this information has been "absorbed into" its experience. What has occurred between the acquisition of the knowledge concerning the sum total of 5 and 5, and this new state of mind, is that the individual has acted upon the information he or she had received. Before, it was merely something there. The child did take it in, to be sure—did memorize it; so that it was never *totally* uninvolved with respect to this bit of knowledge. But now, in circumstances which have rendered this information existentially significant to the child, it does something to the information. It makes it its own, responds to it, *acknowledges* it.

In the foregoing, I referred to the mystery of the movement from fact to faith. It is possible to see something of this mystery already at this second stage, before we even reach the state of faith or trust. For

378

there *is* a kind of mystery between knowing and acknowledging some-thing. It could not be said with precision how the child got from the one state to the other. Or let us say that even if, in some instances of this kind, it were possible to describe at least the external circumstances which accompanied this movement, it would hardly be possible to describe these in such a way that they could then be taken up as a prescription, a method for turning data into *significant* data. To be sure, educators are always trying to do just that; because what all good educators desire is to move their charges from the state of knowledge to the state of acknowledgment. Thus they are forever attempting, methodologically, to analyze the mys-tery of this process and to turn it into a foolproof technique. But the fact remains that it is an area full of great unpredictability. Certain useful things can be learned which will no doubt aid the process, or remove obstacles to its occurring. But still it happens that what for one person comes to be highly significant information remains, for another, who may have been exposed to the very same occurrences and educational pro-cedures, mere data.

This distinction is also very important in Christian theology. Between the data-knowledge first described and the believing-knowledge to which we shall turn next, there is this intermediate state. It is a point in Christian experience which may cover a very long period of time or a very short one. Some of the scriptural and other data which one has received becomes *significant* information. Suddenly, or quite gradually, one realizes that some aspect of Christian teaching is meaningful to oneself. It may have become so inconspicuously—like Kierkegaard's "thoughts which wound from behind"—or on the other hand it may have occurred as a flash of insight. In any case, what was before mere information, eliciting no special interest, has become important, useful, or clarifying information. One is no longer neutral with respect to it. One has acted vis-à-vis this data—in some manner one has accepted it.

Two observations should be made at this point. First, remembering the dimension of mystery, we need to recognize the difficulty of explaining precisely why certain information, which was formerly *only* information, became significant. Obviously it always has something to do with personal experience. Something happened to one, some new constellation of events and attitudes, and in the process what was previously mere fact became relevant fact. It helped to explain something. It became a window through which one could catch a glimpse of meaning not grasped previously. A question was answered, or made more tantalizing. Yet it would be un-convincing to show an absolute correspondence between the experience and the new appreciation for this aspect of Christian teaching. Always in the face of such explanations one has to ask to what extent the Christian teaching itself, perhaps at an unconscious level, shaped the experience.

The second observation is that, applied to Christian experience, this second type of knowing seems never to occur in an all-embracing way. That is, it does not happen that the *whole body* of Christian doctrine becomes significant. What is acknowledged is rather this or that aspect of Christian teaching. It may be something central in theology, such as the doctrine of justification by grace through faith; or it may be rather peripheral or at least less basic—for example, some part of Jesus' Sermon on the Mount. Often the acknowledgment of a particular idea or dogma *opens one to the possibility* that there may be more to the rest of Christian teaching than one had anticipated.

Yet the *acknowledgment* of some particular dogma or precept of the faith does not necessarily lead to belief. Many of the people who have always been on the fringes of the Christian church have been persons who could certainly acknowledge some aspects of Christianity, but who did not and do not believe in the sense of faith-commitment as such. As for those for whom the acknowledgment of some aspects of the faith does become a stage on the way to belief, it is probably true that what they acknowledged was, or came to be, one of the more important, central teachings of the faith—the forgiveness of sin, the sufficiency of divine grace, faith "not works," the suffering love of God in the face of human suffering. There are, however, many possibilities here, and the programming or classifying of this cognitional movement should not overlook the enormous variety of the ways in which people are brought to discipleship.

This needs to be recognized, for there is a danger, well-documented in Christian history, that *patterns* are too easily established. Augustine's or Luther's or Wesley's faith pilgrimage becomes normative for whole segments of the church. It is assumed that one will always move, let us say, from the studied contemplation of Paul's argument in his epistle to the Romans to the acknowledgment of the "justification by grace through faith" concept to the experience of salvation. Especially in the Protestant traditions, authoritative patterns of this sort are established on account of conventions stemming from strong, foundational personalities; and these patterns become the basis of programs of Christian education, preaching, church membership, and so on.

The truth is, surely, that the Christian tradition is exceedingly rich in ideas and responses, and that there is really no predicting what aspect of this tradition will grasp an individual, or why some acknowledge this aspect while others fasten upon quite another dimension of the tradition. Catholicism has understood this much better than the Protestant denominations, and this is one reason why the Catholic church has been able, despite great internal variety, to remain more or less "one body." In North America especially, what "Protestantism" seems to mean to large numbers of Protestants has more to do with such typologies of religious experience than with the broader traditions of the faith, including those testified to in the Bible itself. In fact, it is difficult for persons in our context to experience more immediate and open exposure to Scripture and tradition in the broader sense, because their approach to these almost invariably is guided by certain communally predetermined assumptions about them. Those individuals, therefore, who are predisposed to affirm such assumptions—or are particularly in need, perhaps, of personal acceptance by their confessional community—move without great difficulty to the stage of "acknowledgment." But, as we have noticed heretofore, an increasingly large number of persons reared in Christian homes and parishes on this continent find it impossible to emulate or even to sympathize with the basic belief patterns and acknowledged "values" of their congregations, and consequently discover no entrée into the faith as such.

What this means for theology both at the theoretical and practical levels is that, beyond the need for a more disciplined and serious introduction to the basic data of the faith (at the "knowledge" level), there is in our context an equally important need to free rudimentary Christian teaching from denominational and sectarian strictures, so that the *breadth* preserved in Scripture and tradition may become accessible to more persons within and on the periphery of Christian communities. At present, this breadth is still restricted to those who are training for careers within the churches—and to minorities even within this classification. Yet without some acquaintance with the great variety of dogma, symbols, and perspectives that constitute the whole tradition of Jerusalem, the points at which what we are calling acknowledgment can occur are limited— and sometimes gravely limited. Human experience and human need are always nuanced; and this nuancing must be met, if its curiosity is to be aroused, by a tradition which is capable of many shades of meaning and interpretation.

28.5. Trust. In human experience there is also a kind of knowing which is different from either the acquisition of data or the assimilation and acknowledgment of this data. If we had only these two categories, we would not know what to do with a whole dimension of our experience of knowing.

This would be particularly true of the kind of knowing that we engage in vis-à-vis other human beings. When I say that I know my friend, I obviously mean something quite different from either the possession of knowledge *or* the acknowledgment of certain ideas or truths. I mean that there exists between myself and this other person a certain *relationship*. It is this relationship as such that I have in mind when I say that I know this other human being. It is not the details of her history or the characteristics of her physical or mental make-up that I intend. Nor is it just that some of these characteristics have become significant for me. Rather, when I say, "I know her," I am alluding to a knowledge which quite transcends both the information I possess about this other human being and those aspects of that information which have gained some special meaning for me. The relationship did not occur merely as a result of the information I possessed about her, or even as a consequence of the fact that some of that information became important or meaningful. There was a time when I could say that I knew a good deal *about* this person, but I could not say, "I know her"—not, at any rate, if I were being accurate in my use of language. There was also a time when I could say that aspects of this person's character interested me in certain ways, i.e., when some of the data I learned about her corresponded with traits or questions or needs within myself. But even then I could not say that I knew her. Between the state of acknowledgment and the more personal sort of knowing, knowing which implies depth of relationship, there is once again a gap. The overcoming of this gap does not occur automatically. It is not a matter of simple evolution—occasionally it is almost revolutionary! There are many persons whom I somehow "acknowledge" (i.e., the data I possess about them is significant to me), but who do not exist for me as persons of whom I can honestly say, "I know him"; "I know them." Something has to happen, some new dimension has to be introduced, if I am to pass from the state of acknowledging someone to the state of knowing him or her in this third, interior sense.

What has to happen? What does in fact happen? It is extremely hard to describe it. Art can describe it better than discursive thought. But perhaps we may notice some things about this transition, without being too superficial.

For one thing, this third kind of knowing seems to occur in one as a matter of *decision*. I decide—but it would be better to say that *I find myself deciding*—that this other one has some kind of claim on me and, correspondingly, that I have some kind of responsibility for this other. We may call this "decision," not so much in the sense that it is deliberately, consciously willed; and not in order to distinguish it sharply from a sense of compulsion or destiny (because in fact in very much of the knowing that occurs at this level there is a strong sense of "having to"; indeed it would be hard to imagine the deepest form of such knowing, love, as if it could ever be totally free from the sense of destiny or compulsion). But I use the word "decision," rather, to mean that whatever occurs when a person moves over into this kind of personal knowledge of someone else, it is something which involves not only *rational* activity but the activity of the whole self. This means in a specific sense the activity of what we call the *will*. The "Will you?" and "I will" of traditional marriage ceremonies is a formal acknowledgment of this very distinction. Willing, in this sense, is a summing-up of the whole person, inclusive of thinking and inclusive of feeling, but transcending both. The knowing that is implied here is not just the summation of all that I know about this other one, and it is not just the recognition that some of the things I know are matters which touch me. It is the knowing of an encounter between persons who indeed know that they will *never* know each other fully in the fact-knowledge sense, and will *never* acknowledge in one another fully everything that really *is* significant about the other, but who nevertheless determine to commit themselves to one another.

The discontinuity between the three types of knowing is most conspicuous at this point. I seriously doubt that this third kind of knowing can occur apart from the first and second types—reports of love at first sight and the like notwithstanding! But neither the data that I receive in the first kind of knowing, nor the *significant* data of the second type are sufficient to *produce* the third. There is an hiatus between the second and third types of knowing. The overcoming of this hiatus cannot be engineered. Often, people try to manipulate others into this third form of knowing, but it cannot be done. This is the stuff out of which human pathos and tragedy are made. But the bridging of the gap, which even at the strictly human and "natural" level can hardly be described apart from recourse to transcendental language, is finally what makes life worth living.

In a real sense, we have already entered the theological application of this third type of human knowing; but now we must do so explicitly. With Christian faith and theology, as in human experience generally, it must be seen that there is no easy transition from the state I have called acknowledgment to this third state, which now we may describe as the state of belief, trust, or commitment. There are countless persons for whom much of Christianity "makes sense." What Christians believe is not something neutral for such persons—is not mere data. They may even live by certain Christian precepts and ideals. Yet they would not call themselves Christian believers, for they sense, rightly, that between their acknowledgment of Christian truths and the "I believe in . . ." of the Christian confession there is a certain leap of faith. They realize that belief involves a fundamental *trust*—a commitment of the *self*, not merely of the mind. Like those who look at human love from outside the experience of it, they know that while belief *involves* rational reflection upon data and ideas, it *is* infinitely more than this.

It is the recognition of the suprarational element in belief that has caused one stream within the Christian tradition to conclude that in the last analysis belief is *ir*rational. Christian spiritualism, from Montanism to present-day charismatic movements, manifests a tendency to eliminate rationality from belief, or even to court the irrational. This is wrong, but it is based upon something right, namely, the insistence, over against all Christian intellectualism and the *kind* of orthodoxy which assumes that the holding of correct dogma is primary, that "believing" is and must be a form of knowing which transcends rationality and all the data accessible to reason. My point here, however, is that such a form of knowing is by no means exclusive to Christianity. It is true that in Christian faith this knowing is applied to an "object" that is different from other objects— that is, the Christian claims that this knowing applies not only to his wife, his friend, his neighbor, but . . . to God. But at least in terms of the *kind* of knowing, as distinguished from the object or content of the knowing, what Christian faith says is not in essence different from what is experienced universally by human beings. At the deepest level, what one means as a Christian when one affirms that one "knows" ("believes in") God is not different from what any human being means who says that she "knows" a friend, child, partner. . . . The *reasonableness* of belief in God is a question to which we must turn in the subsequent section of this chapter. But it will make that a more meaningful discussion if we can agree, at the end of the present section, that "knowing" in the experience and terminology of Christian theology is as such continuous with knowing in human experience and language generally—also in this third sense. Christian knowing, in short, is not of another order, as if in the Christian the ordinary faculties and potentialities of "the thinking animal" had been replaced by something else! What—or rather who—is known may be considered unusual, indeed unbelievable, in an age of religious unbelief; but the mode of knowing itself is *entirely human.*

28.6. Conclusions and Transition. Three observations follow from the foregoing discussion: (*a*) The first is related to Christian apologetics. We have noted that our present context is one which manifests a conspicuous plurality of religious and quasi-religious alternatives. It is very important in our dialogue with those who do not belong to the Christian disciple community that we always seek to distinguish the level on which the discussion is taking place. The vast majority of encounters between alleged belief and alleged unbelief or alternative belief involve persons speaking at cross-purposes, because they are assuming different types of knowing. It can almost be taken for granted that most of those who attack Christian belief are arguing on the basis of the second type: acknowledgment. They think—often with reason—that Christians are persons who acknowledge certain data as having significance, as being literally true. They themselves want to say that it is not significant, not true. Such discussions can be worthwhile *if* the Christian understands that the objections to the faith are being expressed at that level. Too often, however, Christians do not understand this, and immediately seek to defend themselves as if they were offering an *apologia* for belief as such, rather than attempting to explain some of the concepts with which Christian belief may, to a greater or lesser extent, be bound up.

(*b*) Second, the distinction between knowing, acknowledging, and trusting has important practical implications for life within the disciple community itself. One of these is that we should not assume, either about ourselves or others, that *belief* must always mean the *acknowledgment* of all the data that comes to us in the tradition. There are persons who may be described as authentic believers, who nevertheless *acknowledge* very little of the traditional data. Some of them do not even *know* this data (in the first, "knowledge" sense of knowing). Others know it but do not find it significant, though they may be open to learning its significance for themselves. In the cases of many Christians who have not been formally educated in theology, whole vast areas of doctrine are like foreign lands, unvisited and undreamed of. How many laypersons—how many clergy!—have given themselves studiously to the study of the evolution of trinitarian theology, to the concept of perichoresis, to comprehension of the *Filioque* clause, to serious consideration, even, of the nature of the authority of Scripture?

Again, there are persons of great learning who find much of what has been preserved in the tradition to be inessential. *Belief (fiducia)*, in both instances, can be entirely sincere and authentic. And the reverse is also true: there are persons who both know and acknowledge very much in the tradition, and are sometimes men and women of influence and authority in the churches, who nevertheless do not "know" in the third sense that we have described, i.e., they do not trust. The knowledge and acknowledgment of *much* does not guarantee belief, nor does the knowledge and acknowledgment of *little* signify disbelief.

(c) Third, however, the second observation poses a problem in practical Christianity: if belief cannot be easily correlated with knowledge and acknowledgment; if people often truly believe who do not know or acknowledge very much with respect to the traditions, doctrine, and dogmas of the faith, then why should Christians exert themselves to understand this tradition and communicate it to others? This, as we have seen, is a rather pertinent question in the North American context, where the effort of understanding what is believed is rarely undertaken with enthusiasm.

While this question is frequently a spurious one or the product of intellectual sloth, it can also be quite serious. It comes close to the heart of the basic paradox of knowing in Christianity. For it contains the recognition that in the last analysis it is not possible for human beings by their efforts either to know the "Thou" of biblical faith or to communicate God's presence and "Word" to others. It implies that God, if God is to be known in the third, interior sense of knowing, must engage in an act of self-communication—must *reveal* God's self.

Yet the statement of Paul remains true:

> How are men to call upon him in whom they have not believed? And how are they to believe in him of whom they have never heard? And how are they to hear without a preacher? And how can men preach unless they are sent? . . . So faith comes from what is heard, and what is heard comes by the preaching of Christ.
>
> (Rom. 10:14-17)

Trust in God, as I have maintained throughout this discussion, does not lie on a continuous line with knowledge and acknowledgment. There is a gap between knowing and acknowledging the data that belongs to the Christian faith. There is an even greater discontinuity between acknowledgment and trust. There is also, however, an element of continuity between these levels of knowing. At least it must be said that trust does not occur apart from the hearing of information. Something has to happen to this information before it can be anything more than what the writer of Job called "the hearing of the ears." What has to happen—to state this in the language of our doctrinal tradition—is that the Holy Spirit must translate what is heard externally into the kind of "language" requisite to its internal reception—*Testimonium spiritus sancti internum*. We have seen that there are analogies to this process in every human relationship. The point just here, however, is that this transformation by the Spirit, this miracle of communication, *presupposes* the attempt of the human being with his or her various faculties to comprehend and share the Christian message. Belief does not occur without this very human activity. It does not come straight out of the blue, the consequence of a direct encounter with deity. It is mediated.

Precisely here, the *method* to which Christian theology is bound reflects most transparently the character of the theological *content* of this tradition. Unlike the gods of power and miraculous feats of whom the long story of humankind is filled, the God of covenant love will not bypass the processes of history and nature. God will not circumvent the human, including human rationality, volition, and discourse, in God's self-communication. This is not because the biblical God is *bound* to what is temporal, historical, natural, rational, human. Clearly, the whole tradition of Jerusalem envisages a sovereign Lord *who would be able, were it the divine intention, to communicate directly to each and every human being without any human mediation.* But it is just as apparent from the tradition that this God does not will to do this. Even if such a form of communication sometimes occurs with respect to specific biblical figures, the Bible does not regard it as *normative.* The normative mode—so normative, in fact, as to render direct epiphany or miraculous appearance highly suspect, and never wholly distinguishable from the demonic!—is the indirect, the mediated revelation. God confines God's self to the structures of creation, to what is historical, natural, human, finite. God will not be known apart from the poor testimony of "the preacher"—the teacher, the curious and passionate individual seeker after truth, the neighbor who, according to Reformation doctrine, is priest to neighbor.

> When God wants to speak and deal with us, he does not avail himself of an angel but of parents, of the pastor, or of my neighbour. This puzzles and blinds me so that I fail to recognize God, who is conversing with me through the person of the pastor or father. This prompts the Lord Christ to say in the text [Jesus' encounter with the woman at the well—John 4]: "If you knew the gift of God, who it was that is saying to you, 'Give me a drink,' then I would not be obliged to run after you and beg for a drink."[7]

The point of this is not the exaltation of "the preacher," i.e., the

---

7. Martin Luther, quoted by John M. Todd, *Luther: A Life* (New York: Crossroads, 1982), p. 351.

witnessing community, the *medium* of divine communication, but the preservation of a kind of knowledge of God which permits the human knower to retain his or her integrity and dignity. The trouble with religious systems which rely upon direct supernatural epiphany is that in the process of the divine revelation, the human partner is effectively overcome— taken by storm. "Divinity can crush a man" (Luther). The God whose power subjects itself to, and is a function of, the divine love will not overwhelm our humanity. While, therefore, God can be known only through God's own grace, God's approach to us is in the humble form of the ordinary: ordinary events, ordinary creatures, ordinary people, ordinary thought and discourse.

29. Reason and Revelation

29.1. Introductory: Establishing Our Perspective on the Relationship of the Two Terms. Epistemology concerns "the 'knowledge' of knowing."[8] Having set the stage for this question by reminding ourselves of the different ways in which "knowing" applies both to life and to Christian belief, we turn now to the two specific categories employed by our long tradition in its attempt to articulate the reality of the knowledge of God appropriate to Christian discipleship.

Neither of the terms "reason" and "revelation" is readily comprehended. The history of their usage is surrounded not only by heated debate but by argumentation which is, much of it, the product of imprecise hearing, unclarified presuppositions, and the vested interests of many reputed verities, not all of them by any means theological or religious![9] The question posed by the juxtaposition of these terms is a more specific version of the same question we have been encountering throughout this second part of our study: How, according to the Christian tradition, does the knowledge of God in God's self-revelation relate to ordinary human rationality, and vice versa? In the foregoing discussion of theological method, as well as in the above introductory analysis of knowing, we have moved towards a broad response to this question. We are now obliged to make our response within the terms of reference carried by these two recognized categories of the discipline.

It will be possible to do so only if we first try to establish working

---

8. Paul Tillich, *Systematic Theology*, vol. 1 (Chicago: University of Chicago Press, 1951), p. 71.
9. The 18th-century debates, whose effects we will feel for some time still, were especially notorious in this respect. See H. Richard Niebuhr, *The Meaning of Revelation* (New York: Macmillan, 1955), pp. 1ff.

definitions of the two terms themselves. For their meaning is not only obscured by past debate, it is also conditioned by our present historical and geographic context. When we ask about the relation of reason and revelation, we are not asking an abstract question but a contextual one. The answer to this question will be greatly determined by the way in which, in a given age or society, these two terms are conceived.

In particular it will be conditioned by the contextual meaning of the term "reason," for this, being the more common and universal category of the two, sets the stage for the dialogue between them. If, in a given cultural context, reason is so defined as to exclude a priori any dimension of transcendence or mystery, it is probable that there will be little openness to the claims of revelation. On the other hand, there is no cause to presuppose that reason is *always and by definition* inhospitable to what is meant by "revelation," since in its history Christianity has experienced various attitudes on the parts of the representatives of reason towards its testimony to revelation. Our first task here, then, is to apply our earlier discussions of the character of our context to the analysis of reason.

There is no doubt that we are part of a historical environment in which reason has been generally defined so as to engender great suspicion of whatever cannot be submitted to objective testing. In such an age—and more particularly in our own North American setting which, as we have seen, is the cutting edge of the technological society—it is impossible to find any high degree of mutuality between the kind of knowing signified by the term "reason" and that intended by the term "revelation." In fact, the only way of securing a working arrangement between the two concepts in the modern period has been by reducing the meaning of revelation rather drastically—usually by associating it with noncognitive, attitudinal, or emotional states. A place is made for "the things of God" by pointing to the "gaps" in reason's competencies. Those who have not wanted to end with a truncated view of revelation have for the most part taken refuge in doctrinaire versions of revealed truth, such as those of Catholic or Protestant orthodoxy, neoorthodoxy, or fundamentalism. They have concluded that the church's ancient dialogue with reason, even if it had been legitimate in earlier epochs, could no longer profitably be engaged in; or that, in any case, reason's worldly representatives were now past the point of discourse with religious belief. Hence, since the 18th century we have witnessed a split of the Christian movement into one party willing to accommodate itself to the world's increasingly narrow view of reason, and another party so determined to preserve the fullness of revealed religion (and its power!) that it could willingly or reluctantly bow out of the ancient dialogue, or perhaps continue it—but with its premodern exponents.

In keeping with the earlier cultural analysis, it is the thesis of the following discussion that our present moment, which has been called postmodern, is characterized by significant changes in the meaning of "reason" especially; and that these changes, while they by no means remove the difficulties in the meeting of the two noetic categories and their representatives, at least have the effect of reopening the possibility of meaningful dialogue. The demonstration of this hypothesis will require, first, a discussion of reason with respect particularly to the changes in our society's perception of its meaning; second, an analysis of the meaning of revelation against the background of the discussion of reason; and third, an exposition of the character of the mutuality which could inform their relationship today.

29.2. Two Types of Reason.   The story of Christianity could be written from the standpoint of the church's obsession with worldly rationality. If this were done, it would be possible, of course, to observe moments of proximity and mutuality as well as moments of hostility and alienation throughout the nearly two millennia. Yet there would also be a rather conspicuous long-range movement in this history of discourse, and this would be a movement of *separation*: Reason gradually but steadily, and with revolutionary breaks here and there, disentangles itself from religion in general and Christianity in particular until it seems totally independent and in fact the regnant alternative to an anachronistic piety. The latter stage was symbolically enacted in the French Revolution, when ancient cathedrals and churches were made over into "Temples of Reason."

The beginnings of Christianity with respect to this dialogue are of course ambiguous, for reasons to be discussed presently. But from the point of its movement into the Hellenistic world, and prominently after its political establishment, early Christianity was able to express itself in a very positive way vis-à-vis worldly rationality. In particular, Augustine, especially in his early and middle stages of Christian belief, became the spokesperson for this mutuality. Reason in Augustine's world could be open to mystery—was itself, indeed, steeped in transcendence. Thus, for example, in his *Soliloquies*, the Christian Augustine's guide to the knowledge of God and the soul is *Ratio*.[10]

This same comprehensive conception of reason governed the Middle Ages and is conspicuous in Anselm, Bonaventura, and most of the early

---

10. *Augustine: Early Writings*, Library of Christian Classics 6 (Philadelphia: Westminster, 1953), p. 23.

schoolmen. But with the beginning of the High Middle Ages reason has already, so to speak, given notice of its independence. It has shifted its focus from the internal to a greater preoccupation with the external world, from intuitive meditation to empirical observation, from the soul to the senses as its point of departure: *Principium cognoscendi est a sensu!* (the beginning of understanding lies with the senses). Even so, Christian apologetics through the genius of Albertus Magnus and his even greater pupil, Thomas Aquinas, found a way of sustaining the discourse with reason. Under these auspices, the meeting of reason and revelation, "natural" and "revealed" truth, was no longer the mutual intertwining, the merger of human and divine which belonged to the Platonic-Augustinian worldview. This real marriage of faith and human thought had now been replaced by a less intimate form of cohabitation. Yet Thomas was able, brilliantly, to demonstrate to the satisfaction of his age that while reason operates differently and brings other kinds of truth, neither its operations nor its fruits contradict the beliefs of "revealed religion."

The first great break in the alliance appeared with the early humanist developments of the Renaissance. Now reason began to develop its own field of investigation and to rival the champions of revelation. It began, that is to say, to fashion an alternative view of the universe. In response, the theologians of the late Middle Ages—especially Duns Scotus and William of Ockham (perhaps significantly both Britishers!)—constructed a form of theology under the nomenclature of nominalism (or terminism) which was prepared to give rationality its scope and to build the Christian story upon the foundations of an independent revelational truth undergirded (especially in Ockham's case) by the authority of Scripture. The breakdown of the famous "medieval synthesis," which had reached both its high point and its turning point in Thomas, had occurred, and with it the dissolution of the Middle Ages themselves.

The Protestant Reformation, viewed from the perspective of this same discourse, is complex indeed. As we have already seen, attempts to interpret Luther as an antirationalist are absurd. On the one hand, Luther certainly distrusts the scholastic attempt to render reason compatible with faith (he is too much aware of the *skandalon* for that!); on the other hand, his thought *can* be interpreted as a search for the lost rationality of the Platonic-Augustinian variety (his own protestations notwithstanding), i.e., intuitive reason as over against the incipient empiricism of the Thomists. His sacramentalism and Christ mysticism would be impossible apart from this link with the earlier Augustinian and medieval world. The more "modern" men Calvin and Zwingli suggest another story entirely. In them (and it is not accidental that they were both trained in the humanist tradition), the reason with which faith has to dialogue is much more bound to evidence and logic. On the whole, it would be true to say that their own lives indicate an increasing difficulty in regard to the prospect of bringing revelation and reason into proximity with each other, thus confirming their protomodernity.

Subsequent developments in the career of worldly reason made this difficulty even more conspicuous, especially within Protestantism, which, unlike Catholicism prior to Vatican II, could not rely so unrestrictedly on entrenched sources of authority and consequently had always to justify itself in relation to the existing forms of intellectual respectability. With the Enlightenment, as we have noted in the first part of this study, reason announced not only its complete independence of religion but, on the whole, its hostility towards it—and particularly towards the more suprarationalistic expressions of Christianity. This was mitigated somewhat, particularly in the Germanic experience, by the romantic rebellion against empiricism and rationalism. But in the world of deed especially, rationalism paid very high dividends, being the spiritual force behind the industrialization of Western societies. Thus, while romantics and idealists protested in their art and their salons and gardens, rationality went its own way, with technique as its inseparable partner, and organized the world accordingly. "Technical reason," to use Tillich's nomenclature, is the last stage in the divorce of reason and religious belief.

But it may well be that with this last and most unbending separation of reason, as conceived by modernity, from any sustained discourse with faith and piety, a new turning point has been reached which in some definitive way could reverse or significantly modify this whole, uneasy history that we have been outlining. For with the restriction of rationality to technique, the independence of reason may have reached its limits. Reason is perceived by many today, indeed, as manifesting a destructive and potentially annihilating independence. Not only the religious, but many who make no profession of religious belief, perceiving the dilemma of a society whose rationalism has led it to a Babylonian captivity of the spirit and community of humankind far more threatening than anything achieved in the name of revealed religion, search in the past, present, or hoped-for future for some alternative view of reason with which to counteract the destructive movement of a rationality narrowly confined to empiricism and technicism.

This search expresses itself frequently in a distinction between two types of reason. We shall cite a number of recent scholars, representing both nonreligious and religious viewpoints, in which this distinction appears.

(*a*) Karl Jaspers, in *The Future of Mankind*, distinguishes between what he calls "intellectual thought" and "rational thought":

> Of all-encompassing importance is the distinction between two ways of thinking. *Intellectual thought* is the inventor and maker. Its precepts can be carried out and can multiply the making by infinite repetition. The result is a world in which a few minds devise the mechanics, creating, as it were, a second world in which the masses then assume the operative function. *Rational thought* on the other hand does not provide for the carrying-out of mass directives but requires each individual to do his own thinking, original thinking. Here, truth is not found by a machine reproducible at will, but by decision, resolve, and action whose self-willed performance, by each on his own, is what creates a common spirit.[11]

Jaspers thus not only criticizes the "functionalist" view of reason in itself, but he shows the social consequences of such a view. This is a frequent concern of those who ask about the meaning of rationality today. It is very much the concern of the Marxist writer Paul A. Baran.

(*b*) In a scathing critique of the contemporary intelligentsia,[12] Paul A. Baran, a British socialist, distinguishes between two human types resulting from the two conceptions of thinking under discussion—"intellect workers" and genuine "intellectuals":

> What marks the intellectual and distinguishes him from the intellect workers and indeed from all others is that his concern with the entire historical process is not a tangential interest but permeates his thought and significantly affects his work. To be sure, this does not imply that the intellectual in his daily activity is engaged in the study of all historical development. This would be a manifest impossibility. But what it does mean is that the intellectual is systematically seeking to relate whatever specific area he may be working in to other aspects of human existence. Indeed, it is precisely this effort to *interconnect* things which, to intellect workers operating within the framework of capitalist institutions (not also in Marxist societies?) . . . necessarily appear to lie in strictly separate compartments of society's labour—it is (I say) this effort to interconnect which constitutes one of the intellectual's outstanding characteristics. And it is likewise this

11. Karl Jaspers, *The Future of Mankind* (Chicago and London: University of Chicago Press, 1961), p. 7.
12. In *The Monthly Review: An Independent Socialist Magazine*, vol. 13, no. 1 (May 1961).

effort which identifies one of the intellectual's principle functions in society: to serve as a symbol and as a reminder of the fundamental fact that the seemingly autonomous, disparate and disjointed morsels of social existence. . .—literature, art, politics, the economic order, science, the cultural and psychic condition of people—can all be understood (and influenced) only if they are clearly visualized as parts of the comprehensive totality of the historical process.

By contrast, the "intellect worker" pursues his or her little corner of investigation without any thought for the interconnectedness of everything or the ends that are served by his or her work.

Interpreting their function as the application of the most efficient means to the attainment of some stipulated ends, the intellect workers take an agnostic view of the ends themselves. In their capacities as specialists, managers, and technicians, they have nothing to do with the formulation of goals; nor do they feel qualified to express a preference for one goal over another . . . . They admit that they may have some predilections as citizens, with their predilections counting for no more and no less than those of citizens. But as scientists, experts, scholars, they wish to refrain from endorsing one or another of these "value judgments."

The consequences of the victory of this restrictive view of rationality, applied socially, are devastating, says Baran:

It should be perfectly clear that such abdication amounts in practice to the endorsement of the status quo, to lending a helping hand to those who are seeking to obstruct any change of the existing order of things in favor of a better one. It is this "ethical neutrality" which has led many an economist, sociologist, and anthropologist to declare that *qua* scientist he cannot express any opinion on whether it would be better or worse for the people of underdeveloped countries to enter the road to economic growth; and it is in the name of this same "ethical neutrality" that eminent scientists have been devoting their energies and talents to the invention and perfection of means of bacteriological warfare, etc.

Thus the identification of reason as an empirical-technical pursuit of ever more efficient means to ever more destructive ends leads, according to this nonreligious thinker, to the tragedy of a society incapable of exercising control over its future. Limits to such "growth" depend upon the reintroduction of operative forms of thought which have been effectively ruled out by progress.

(*c*) Martin Heidegger: While Baran catalogues the consequences of the reduction of reason to technique for society as a whole, Heidegger sees it as the nemesis of Homo sapiens as such. In his famous "Memorial Address" of 1955,[13] marking the occasion of the 175th anniversary of the composer Conradin Kreuzer, the great German thinker takes the occasion to discourse on the nature of thought in our time. "Even a memorial address," he begins, "gives no assurance that we will *think* at a memorial celebration." He continues:

> Let us not fool ourselves. All of us, including those who think professionally, as it were, are often enough thought-poor; we are all far too easily thought-less. Thoughtlessness is an uncanny visitor who comes and goes everywhere in today's world. For nowadays we take in everything in the quickest and cheapest way, only to forget it just as quickly, instantly. Commemorative celebrations grow poorer in thought. Commemoration and thoughtlessness are found side by side.

Having set the tone in this auspicious way (a thing that I doubt the good burgers of the area had bargained for!), the philosopher asserts that "man today is *in flight from thinking.*"

> But part of this flight is that man will neither see nor admit it. Man today will even flatly deny this flight from thinking. He will assert the opposite. He will say—and quite rightly—that there were at no time such far-reaching plans, so many inquiries in so many areas, research carried on as passionately as today. Of course. And this display of ingenuity and deliberation has its own great usefulness. Such thought remains indispensable. But— it is thinking of a special kind.
>
> Its peculiarity consists in the fact that whenever we plan, research, and organize, we always reckon with conditions that are given. We take them into account with the calculated intention of their serving purposes. Thus we can count on definite results. This calculation is the mark of all thinking that plans and investigates. Such thinking remains calculation even if it is neither working with numbers nor using an adding machine or computer. Calculative thinking computes. It computes ever new, ever more promising and at the same time economical possibilities. Calculative thinking races from one prospect to the next. Calculative thinking never stops, never collects itself. Calculative thinking is not meditative thinking, not thinking which contemplates the *meaning* which reigns in everything that is.

"There are then," Heidegger continues, "two kinds of thinking, each

---

13. Martin Heidegger, *Discourse on Thinking* (New York: Harper, 1966).

justified in its own way: calculative thinking (*rechnendes Denken*) and meditative thinking (*besinnliches Denken*)."

Besinnliches Denken (thinking about *meaning* [=German: *Sinn*]) is for Heidegger *the* truly human activity: "You may protest that mere meditative thinking finds itself floating unaware above reality. It loses touch. It is worthless for dealing with current business. It profits nothing in carrying out practical affairs. . . ." But meditative thought pursues ideas without which all the "practical" thinking the world can offer is vain and without direction.

"And you may say, finally, that mere meditative thinking, persevering meditation, is 'above' the reach of ordinary understanding." To this charge of elitism, Heidegger replies that in the first place the only truth in it is that meditative thought *does* require "practice":"It is in need of even more delicate care than any other genuine craft." Second, it is by no means the preserve of professionals, however: "Anyone can follow the path of meditative thinking in his own manner and within his own limits. Why? Because *man is a thinking, that is, a meditating being*."

Aristotle's "man is a rational animal" does not refer primarily to the fact that humanity is capable of calculation; the beasts, and now very complex machines, are also capable of such "thinking." It refers to the human capacity for "thinking about meaning."

In all of this, Heidegger is not simply registering his protest against modern technology—adding his complaint, as it were, to the list of others who are "against the machine." He knows as well as Jacques Ellul and George Grant do that technology as such is only "symptomatic" of the disease.[14] "It is not that the world is becoming entirely technical which is really uncanny. Far more uncanny is our being unprepared for this transformation, our inability to confront *meditatively* what is really dawning in this age."[15]

Contemporary humanity, in Heidegger's view, is "in a perilous situation." What is the danger? That we may be destroyed by an atomic holocaust? That we may run out of vital resources? No. One suspects Heidegger might at this point agree with René Dubos, who claims that our real danger is our astonishing adaptability to such horrors![16] The real

---

14. Ellul's word. See Jacques Ellul, *The Technological Society* (New York: Alfred A. Knopf, 1964), p. 34, and George P. Grant, "A Platitude," in his *Technology and Empire: Perspectives on North America* (Toronto: Anansi, 1969), pp. 137ff.

15. "What demons obsess our technology to make that contemplation impossible to which we ought to turn from time to time if we want to find the right use of technology itself?" (C. F. von Weizsäcker, *The Relevance of Science: Creation and Cosmogony*, The Gifford Lectures of 1959–1960 [London: Collins, 1964], p. 9).

16. *Life,* July 24, 1970, p. 2.

danger, from Heidegger's viewpoint, could occur even if the other dangers are averted, and indeed (if B. F. Skinner had his way) *as a result of our averting them!* The real danger, in his opinion, is that we may virtually *lose our reason*: "The approaching tide of technological revolution in the atomic age could so captivate, bewitch, dazzle, and beguile man that calculative thinking may someday come to be accepted and practiced as *the only way of thinking.*"

And he concludes:

> What great danger then might move upon us? Then there might go hand in hand with the greatest ingenuity in calculative planning and inventing indifference towards meditative thinking, total thoughtlessness. And then? Then man would have denied and thrown away his own special nature— that he is a meditative being. Therefore the issue is keeping meditative thinking alive.

(*d*) George Grant: The question that must confront all who reflect carefully on the human condition today, however, is whether it is not already too late to ward off the victory of "calculative rationality." It is perhaps indicative of the advanced nature of that victory in the North American context that, of the four thinkers treated in connection with the present distinction, the one who seems most alarmed by the prospect of the takeover of "instrumentalist thought" is the Canadian political and social philsopher George P. Grant. There are of course those who would account for this on purely personal grounds, seeing Grant as a representative of classical philosophic and religious traditions, who cannot feel at home in the postindustrial society. Yet the possibility exists that, on the contrary, a society as steeped in technocracy as is ours calls forth in a few a prophetic critique of itself, and that anyone who retains or acquires sufficient memory of premodern alternatives to technological society will have some part in that critique.

To think Christian faith is to be brought into at least one sphere of influence where the premodern alternative cannot be wholly avoided: the "tradition of Jerusalem." More accurately, while superficial Christianity certainly can and does avoid existential encounter with premodern alternatives to modernity, and while most of what identifies itself as "Christian" on this continent does seem eminently superficial, reflective and serious Christian thought is constantly thrown up against contrasting views of life between the biblical and older traditions of the faith and contemporary pursuits and "values." It is not surprising, therefore, that George Grant, who is himself a Christian, is heard by a Christian minority on this continent, and that his thought about the world is perceived as having considerable theological significance.[17]

Where the subject of reason is concerned, Grant's analysis parallels in most ways the three previously discussed thinkers—though, as I have suggested, he seems more conscious than they of the ubiquity of "technical reason," and of the difficulty of challenging it or even of understanding, profoundly, what it *is*. Reason, he writes, "is thought of simply as an instrument."

> It is used for the control of nature and the adjustment of the masses to what is required of them by the commercial society. This instrumentalist view of reason is itself one of the chief influences in making our society what it is; but, equally, our society increasingly forces on its members this view of reason. It is impossible to say which comes first, this idea of reason or the mass society. They are interdependent. Thought which does not serve the interests of the economic apparatus or some established group in society is sneered at as "academic." The old idea that "the truth shall make you free," that is, the view of reason as the way in which we discover the meaning of our lives and make that meaning our own, has almost entirely disappeared. In place of it we have substituted the idea of reason as a subjective tool, helping us in production, in the guidance of the masses, and in the maintenance of our power against rival empires. People educate themselves to get dominance over nature and over other men. Thus, scientific reason is what we mean by reason. That is why in the human field, reason comes ever more to be thought of as social science, particularly psychology in its practical sense. We study practical psychology in order to learn how other people's minds work so that we can control them, and this study of psychology comes less and less to serve its proper end, which is individual therapy.[18]

In all of Grant's writings, there is a poignant consciousness of the fact that the "instrumentalist" conception of reason is particularly potent in the North American context—poignant, because Grant knows from within the beauty and goodness of what was envisaged for this "new world." His essay "In Defense of North America" is a moving testimony to his identification with the destiny of this society.[19] But he is also aware of the tenuousness of our hold upon any alternatives to the technological

---

17. See my essay, "The Significance of Grant's Cultural Analysis for Christian Theology in North America," in Larry Schmidt, ed., *George Grant in Process: Essays and Conversations* (Toronto: Anansi, 1978), pp. 120ff.

18. George Grant, *Philosophy in the Mass Age* (New York: Hill and Wang, 1960), pp. 9-10.

19. In George Grant, *Technology and Empire* (Toronto: Anansi, 1969), pp. 15ff.

society which could provide for us a vantage point from which to assess what has become of us. The instrumentalist view of reason, he believes, "has found its most popular formulation in North America, in the philosophy known as pragmatism. . . . This is not surprising, for it is in North America that control over nature and social adjustment has reached its most explicit development."[20] Among us, therefore, it is both rare and difficult to comprehend what reason is:

> Indeed, to think "reasonably" about the modern account of reason is of such difficulty because that account has structured our very thinking in the last centuries. For this reason scholars are impotent in the understanding of it because they are trying to understand that which is the very form of how they understand. The very idea that "reason" is that reason which allows us to conquer objective human and non-human nature controls our thinking about everything.[21]

Grant's analysis is important, especially for a contextual theology in the North American setting, because it both draws upon the distinction between the two types of reason and reminds us that, precisely in our context, we cannot *assume* this distinction. It has first to be understood, so far as possible, by ourselves, as Christians and theologians; and insofar as we are enabled to understand it, we must make it a *conscious* and *deliberate* part of our witness. In doing so, however, I think that we can count upon the support of significant minorities within our own cultural sphere—including *some* of the natural and social scientists who, in their own fields of investigation, have recently had cause to be skeptical at least of the managerial dimensions of modernity's account of reason.

29.3. The Importance of This Distinction for Christian Epistemology. Too much theology in the English-speaking world especially, where the philosophic tradition of empiricism-cum-pragmatism and the economic-industrial tradition of technologism have both been enormously successful, has been content to dialogue with a form of rationality which, from the perspective of these commentators, is severely limited. More than limited, it is reductionism of the worst kind, and its victim is the human "thinking animal." Theology in our sector has been far too much at pains to make itself agreeable to a view of reason which insists that

---

20. George Grant, *Philosophy in the Mass Age*, p. 10.
21. George Grant, "The Computer Does Not Impose on Us the Ways It Should Be Used," in *Beyond Industrial Growth*, ed. Abraham Rotstein (Toronto: University of Toronto Press, 1976), p. 124.

whatever one claims to "know" must be capable of empirical verification. Thus, much of the theological discussion at the level of epistemology in Britain and North America has been a kind of prolonged version of that "natural theology" developed in the Middle Ages which tried to demonstrate certain religious verities (especially the existence of God) by reference to the evidence of the senses and the application of logic.

But even where it seems to be successful, such a theology is satisfying only to the most arid type of religious intellectualism. Neither faith nor unfaith can be content with the kind of knowledge that reason of the calculating variety is able to derive. Such knowledge remains at the level of data, even when it attempts to climb to the second level—acknowledgment. The greatest exponent of empirical method in the service of faith, Thomas Aquinas, certainly never meant the fruits of this method to be received as *satisfying*! And since the time of Thomas, the feats that can be performed by empirical rationality, while they have been greatly expanded along technical lines, have been correspondingly curtailed philosophically. In Thomas's world, it was still permitted for a reason which began with the evidence of the senses to cross over the apparently invisible line between secondary and primary causation without being noticed! This is no longer permitted. But would it make any real difference if it were? As Paul Tillich has observed, "technical reason" does not even touch the primary sort of "knowing" that Christian belief confesses when it says *Credo in Deum*. . . . It can neither prove nor disprove the "knowing" which this confession assumes, which as we have seen in the foregoing section is not fact-knowledge but knowledge-in-relationship, fundamental trust.[22]

The inability of theology to engage reason as it is defined by the dominant conventions of our Anglo-Saxon civilization, however, does not mean that theology either should or needs to abandon the dialogue with reason. It simply means that it has to refuse to concede to these dominant conventions that they are the guardians of true reason! If it cannot dialogue with "official" representatives of rationality, then the disciple community can with good conscience shake the dust from its sandals and go out in to the marketplace to find forms of reason more amenable to dialogue.

The point of the foregoing sketches of the thought of four modern thinkers is to indicate that Christian theology with imagination does not have to go very far in *today's* world to discover representatives of reason who are ready to pose the kinds of questions in which theology has a

---

22. Paul Tillich, *Systematic Theology*, vol. 1, p. 74.

vested interest—questions of meaning, of the good, of the nature of being, etc. The thinkers whom I have cited are themselves not so important as are the concerns which they have verbalized. They are the amanuenses of a significant minority, a protesting element within the technological society that is literally sick unto death of the constricting, humiliating, and finally quite literally *annihilating* consequences to which Western humanity's reduction of thought to calculation has led.

This new potential openness to the transcendent on the part of worldly thought does not mean that dialogue between faith and reason has become easy, nor does it imply that Christians are now at liberty to ignore the rigors of objectivity and act as if "scientific method" were already a thing of the past. There are technical questions, questions of logic, questions requiring empirical evidence, coherence, with which all responsible thought must continue to live. But, despite the continuing power of "instrumentalist" rationality and its manifold threat to civilization, the world can never return *unanimously* to the bravado of post-Enlightenment rationality, which pushed God out onto the periphery (Bonhoeffer) and declared itself in charge. That deity has failed. *That*, surely, is the god that has died. With the death of that deistic god, who was only the premature, cloaked deification of proud, autonomous reason, the God who "humbled himself" (Phil. 2:5-11) may again achieve a hearing.

The latter possibility, however, depends in considerable measure upon the willingness of the biblical God's earthly witnesses to reflect the divine lowliness in their approach to the new, less autonomous rationality of thinking human beings. Here again we can see the indelible connections between the theological discipline and the character of the disciples. A disciple community which is unwilling to adjust its understanding of its unique category of knowing, revelation, for the purpose of facilitating the dialogue with reason will in no way make good the opportunity for such a dialogue that is there, potentially, in worldly reason's new modesty. We have spoken of the history of Christianity in terms of the gradual withdrawal of reason from the dialogue with faith. We could also speak of this history from the perspective of a revelation-conscious community which was interested, not only and perhaps not even primarily in defending the truth of revelation, but in defending the *power* that it had in the world as the guardian of ultimate truth. An imperialism of revelation may indeed be as much the source of the split between reason and faith as an imperialism of reason, and especially when revelation has been identified with theological and ethical absolutes susceptible to "possession" by the religious.

Reason has begun to be humbled by reflection, late in time, upon its own performance over the past two centuries, upon its failure to bring in the enlightened society that its several versions promised, and upon its still more dismal failure to anticipate the negating potential within its own schemes. While there is no justification for complacency in a technocratic culture which may yet destroy itself by the means introduced through its own human ingenuity, there now exists a critical and vigilant minority which has begun to understand how reasoning, divorced from discourse concerning ends, is captured by mindless processes that are almost invariably death-serving. This minority, whose minority status should not blind us to its historical and perhaps providential significance, often manifests a clear capacity for dialogue with religious faith.

But such a dialogue depends also upon the religious, and it is by no means obvious that the representatives of "revealed truth" are ready to take up the invitation to discourse implicit in our context. There are still Christians who would be glad to continue the well-established tradition of suppressing the quest and the labors of human reason by offering final, revelational truth. The situation of a reduced and perhaps contrite reason even encourages them in these efforts. The habit of triumphalism is deeply ingrained in the Christian character! The crumbling of rational mastery can seem like a veritable portent of the kingdom. The capitulation to skepticism on the part of many of the world's former champions of the goddess of the intellect can appear the seal of divine approval upon a return to authoritarian forms of religion in which the claims of science and the human mind are set aside with a flourish. This is one of the greatest temptations of the Christian community today. It is the *characteristic* temptation where the ancient discussion between reason and faith is concerned. It calls for great soberness. Nothing at all can be gained by an authoritarian, revelation-based religion which gloats over every humiliation of the human mind. The point of the cross is not that the faithful should win arguments, but that the world might know peace. Partly, this peace depends upon the exposition of a theology of revelation which does not humiliate but can fulfill and exalt the quest of the intellect—which joins with others of good will to "keep meditative thinking alive," or, where necessary, to give birth to it.

30. What Is Revelation?

30.1. Revelation as Christian Theology's Point of Departure.
We turn now to a term very central to Christian doctrine, and one which

leads us inevitably to the core of the gospel itself. I shall develop my answer to the question posed by the above heading in four steps, each one consisting of the elaboration of a thesis.

The first thesis is that *revelation is the basic epistemological presupposition of Christian belief and theology.* Christian faith does not base itself on general observations about the world, human being, nature, divinity, and so forth. It does not begin with a religious Weltanschauung, inward experience, or reasoned conclusions about the nature of existence. It begins with revelation. That is, its point of departure is a disclosure, an "unveiling" of something not otherwise accessible to human knowing. This is the literal meaning of the root terms (in Latin, *revelatio*; in Greek, *apokalypsis*) behind the concept. Something is given to the understanding which it could not by itself acquire. One is brought into a room whose door one could not open, whose door one probably did not even know about. A vista is opened up. Another dimension of reality is envisaged. This is the word-picture behind the concept.

Christian faith begins with revelation, not only historically but also existentially. Historically, the beginning of the Christian movement is traced by the writers of Scripture to the experience of Pentecost. Something existed before Pentecost, to be sure—a rather anomalous and puzzled group of people attracted by the rabbi Jesus. But the church could not come to be out of this almost random collection of persons until there had been an "unveiling" of the meaning of what had been taking place in their midst. This disclosure was primarily an internal event (the external realities described in Acts 2 are certainly more emblematic than literal). Internally, barriers to the perception of what had taken place among them had to be removed. Their eyes had to be opened, as we told of the two who had walked along the Emmaus road (Luke 24:13ff.). The historical, external event had happened, but in itself it could not constitute the revelatory beginning of the Christian movement. For revelation is not revelation until it is revelation *for* someone.[23] And that cannot occur until those for whom it is intended have been enabled to perceive it. Thus revelation is both an internal and an external event, both subjective and objective in character. It requires not only the redemptive work of "the Son" but also the enlightening, regenerating work of "the Spirit."

Our thesis is that Christian belief and theology presuppose this divine work of revelation as their basic epistemological assumption. There have been attempts to overcome the particularity of this assumption, as we

---

23. See ibid., p. 111.

have already noticed. But even liberal theology had to live with it, finally. The more radical forms of theological liberalism tried to avoid the seeming narrowness of this "door" (John 10:9) by claiming that the religion which came to its highest expression in Jesus is simply the supreme form of a consciousness present in some measure in everyone. But then the skeptical world, with its keen eye for hidden assumptions, asked: Why Jesus? And immediately this reminder of the scandal of particularity cast sensitive liberal thinkers back upon the revelational basis of their belief. They had to justify choosing, out of all the historical possibilities, this one person as the supreme manifestation of the highest human meaning and calling. They could not justify this on strictly rational grounds, and no one ever can. It is a matter of conviction and decision. It is the consequence of a disclosure which authenticates itself sufficiently to faith but which faith cannot authenticate for the unbelieving (including also the continuing unbelief of the believer himself or herself!). When therefore it is said that the fundamental epistemological presupposition of Christian theology is God's self-revelation in the Christ through the Spirit, it is said that theology treats of a mystery of knowing which cannot be immediately or fully shared beyond the community of belief.

30.2. The Disclosure of a Presence. But what is this mystery? *What* is revealed? This leads to the second thesis concerning revelation, namely, that *in the Christian understanding of it, revelation is at base the disclosure of a presence.*

Such a proposition sounds innocent enough, but in reality it is a highly polemical statement. The object of this polemic is not primarily the world, with its skepticism, but the Christian fellowship itself, with its perennial temptation to reduce revelation to manageable, manipulable dimensions—to objectify it. Indeed, perhaps the most common and entrenched definition of revelation within the various churches on this continent is one that is really the antithesis of the above proposition. For it equates revelation with ideas, dogmas, principles—"revealed truths." In Roman Catholicism, the term covering this view, first used in the Middle Ages, was *depositum fidei.*[24] The mystery that is unveiled in the Christian

---

24. "This comprises the body of teachings and commands given to the apostles and to their successors, the bishops, which are to be retained, taught, and offered to all mankind. The deposit is the sum of revelation and tradition and is entrusted to the Church that Christ founded and its *magisterium*, or teaching and defining role. It is attested to in Scripture (John 16:13) that through the illuminating action of the Holy Spirit the Church will grow and is recognized by the apostles (1 Tim. 6:20) as having been "committed" to them.

"Vatican Council I declares: 'Faith's doctrines which God has revealed are not put before us as some philosophical discovery to be developed by human ingenuity but as a divine trust (*depositum*)

revelation is the handing over (depositing) of revealed truths into the keeping of the church. At least in the writings of the greatest theologians there was, behind this concept, the awareness that the truths in question could never be adequately stated in human language.[25] Nevertheless, the reservations of refined minds do not easily transfer themselves to popular expression or the operating of a vast hierarchic organization; therefore, what prevails still in the average mentality of the church is a *propositional* conception of revelation. Some truths can be gained by ordinary if diligent inquiries of the mind (natural religion); others must be received in faith upon the authority of the church, the trustee of divine revelation (revealed religion).

The shape assumed by propositionalism in the Protestant tradition is different from this only in terms of the source of revelational authority. For traditional Catholicism it is the church. For traditional Protestant orthodoxy it is the Bible. No doubt this distinction introduces something more significant than the foregoing sentence suggests. But Protestants ought not to be too sure that the replacing of "the Bible" for "the Church" as the locus of "revealed truth" preserved or preserves them from the presumption of doctrinaire Catholicism. The Bible, too, can be a tyrant! Not in itself—but then, it is never "in itself," it is always in the hands of its interpreters; and there are few tyrannies more oppressive than those of the small-minded who consider their precepts invincible because they find them confirmed by The Book!

Original Protestantism did not make the equation, revelation equals Bible. For the Reformers personally—especially for Luther—the revelation which is faith's basis transcends the Scriptures. Luther's simple metaphor, that the Bible is "Christ's cradle," is sufficiently high in its estimate of the Bible to justify including his name among the endorsers of the *sola scriptura* principle of the Reformation. But as his actual treatment of the Bible makes clear, especially his rather cavalier way of consigning whole sections (like the Epistle of James) to the sidelines of truth, the Bible *as such* is for him only the *witness* to the Word. The Word itself—the ultimate truth that is revealed—cannot be put into words,

---

handed over to the Spouse of Christ for her faithful safeguarding and infallible exposition (Vat. Sess. iii, cap. 4, Dz. 1800). . . .

"Vatican II states: 'The Roman Pontiff and the bishops, in view of their office and the importance of the matter, strive painstakingly and by appropriate means to inquire properly into that revelation and to give apt expression to its contents. But they do not allow that there could be any new public revelation pertaining to the divine deposit of faith (LG 25). . .'" (*The Catholic Encyclopaedia* [Nashville and New York: Thomas Nelson, 1975], p. 158).

25. The language of Vatican II confirms this.

for "it" is the Christ in person. Scripture's words can only point to the Word incarnate, and they are authoritative for us only when they do so—only when they "drive to Christ" (*Christum treibet*).[26]

It is not quite so clear with the other chief reformers of the 16th century that they were ready to apply such critical theology to Scripture. Certainly neither Zwingli nor Calvin were prepared to *equate* the Bible with revelation. For them, too, revelation is a dynamic and personal encounter. All the same, their humanistically grounded respect for "the sources" led them to place much more faith in the Word written than the still-medieval man Martin Luther could ever have done. In the Holy Scriptures, said Calvin, "God opens his own holy mouth."[27] Everywhere? Always? Reformed doctrine is capable of a variety of interpretations here. But whether one judges that Calvin and his colleagues themselves opened the way for a propositional understanding of revelation based upon the Scriptures, it is certain that this temptation and reality has dogged the steps of the Reformed wing of Protestantism ever since; and in its more unbending forms, biblical propositionalism of revelation has been every bit as oppressive as the ecclesiastically managed *depositum fidei* of official Roman Catholicism. The Reformed influence being the strongest classical Protestant influence on this continent, biblicistic revelationalism has been our quite natural temptation.

Against this propositional or positivistic conception of revelation, the idea of revelation in more recent theological thought claims that what is revealed in Christian revelation is not, in the first place, a *what* but a *who*. A presence! The hidden mystery unveiled in external and internal event is God's own person. The knowledge of God intended by the term "revelation," says Karl Barth, is knowledge of God "as a *Person*. . . . He is one who knows and wills, who acts and speaks, who as an 'I' calls me 'Thou,' and whom I can call 'Thou' in return."[28] *Deus absconditus*

---

26. It is not incidental to Luther's understanding of the character and role of Scripture in the life of faith that he sometimes writes as if the Old Testament *alone* is properly called Scripture: "What a fine lot of tender and pious children we are! In order that we might not have to study in the Scriptures and learn Christ there, we simply regard the entire Old Testament as of no account, as done for and no longer valid. Yet it alone bears the name of Holy Scripture. And the gospel should really not be something written, but a spoken word which brought forth the Scriptures, as Christ and the apostles have done. This is why Christ himself did not write anything but only spoke. He called his teaching not Scripture but gospel, meaning good news or a proclamation that is spread not by pen but by word of mouth. So we go and make the gospel into a law book, a teaching of commandments, changing Christ into a Moses, the One who would help us into simply an instructor" ("A Brief Instruction on What to Look For and Expect in the Gospels," *Luther's Works*, vol. 35, trans. E. Theodore Bachmann [Philadelphia: Fortress, 1960], p. 123).

27. *The Institutes*, Book I, Chapter 6.

28. Karl Barth, *The Knowledge of God and the Service of God* (London: Hodder and Stoughton, 1960), pp. 33-34.

(the hidden God) becomes *Deus revelatus* (God revealed). God reveals Godself as "the Eternal Thou" and therefore also as One who can never be contained in propositions.[29] Revelation is not, then, the communication of *ideas* about God and the things of God, even though ideas are included in the experience of revelation, as they are included in the experience of meeting another *human* being. Revelation, however, is the "divine–human encounter" (Emil Brunner).[30] As Archbishop William Temple put it in his Gifford Lectures of 1932–1934,[31] what is disclosed in the revelatory event is "not truth concerning God but the living God Himself."

It is necessary to notice a very important consequence of this encounter view of revelation: If the subject of revelation is God's own presence, then the mystery which is revealed is at the same time concealed in the revelation. Mystery used in connection with revelation in Christian theological discourse, ought not (as Tillich writes) "be applied to something which ceases to be a mystery after it has been revealed."[32]

This may sound contradictory, initially. But it is by no means so. There are analogies to it in everyday experience. The possession of information about another human being is one thing: one can contemplate it, arrange and rearrange the various pieces of data, as a biographer does with his or her subject; one can communicate it, wax eloquent about it, control it, possess it! We are all able to be quite knowledgeable about persons we have never met or do not know very well! It is something else to encounter another human being personally, to learn to know this other one—perhaps intimately. What one knows about such a human being, *primarily*, in that case, is that with all one's (data-) knowledge, the other remains other—remains a mystery who cannot be manipulated, communicated, possessed, but only can be lived with. When we think that the human beings with whom our lives are most closely bound are fully comprehended by us ("Now I know what makes you tick!"), we have in that moment violated them, reduced them to objects, made of the mystery of their being a graven image. If we are wise, we know that these human beings—namely, the very ones who have *revealed* more of themselves to us than any other creatures of our acquaintance—are at the

29. "The Eternal *Thou* can by its nature not become *It*; for by its nature it cannot be established in measure and bounds . . .

"And yet in accordance with our nature we are continually making the eternal *Thou* into an *It*, into some *thing*—making God into a thing" (Martin Buber, *I and Thou*, trans. Ronald Gregor Smith [Edinburgh: T. & T. Clark, 1937], p. 112).

30. See Brunner's work by this title, *The Divine–Human Encounter*, trans. Amandus W. Loos (London: SCM, 1944).

31. *Nature, Man and God* (London: MacMillan and Co., 1951), p. 322.

32. Tillich, *Systematic Theology*, vol. 1, p. 109.

same time *concealed* from us. The very nature of their revelation of themselves prevents us from knowing them in the way that, with a very questionable part of ourselves, we should like to know them: that is, to "have," to keep, to manipulate and control them—to stop their ineffable otherness from disturbing our peace!

Precisely the danger of the propositional conception of revelation is that it permits itself to be "had," kept, and exploited. It lends itself very readily to the power instinct—as one can easily discern in the manipulative tactics of biblicistic evangelists who announce that they have "got it right here in the Bible." The God who reveals, not supranatural information, but self cannot be "had," any more than one's friend, husband, wife, parent, or child can be possessed. God eludes our grasp in the moment of encountering us. God invites our companionship, our being-with; and the invitation immediately curtails our dark impulse (perhaps the aboriginal "religious" impulse) to make God our servant, to enhance our own power infinitely by commanding God's infinite power. The Emmanuel who will be "*with* us" will *not* be possessed *by* us.

This view of revelation as encounter with the divine presence—and in particular the implication of it about which I have just now been reflecting—is at the heart of the theology of the cross. If "God hides himself in his revelation," if "the power of God is hidden beneath its opposite" (Luther), this is not because the biblical God wills to withhold self and truth from us, but because this God is well aware of our human propensity to use the divine for our own enhancement. In the reality and symbol of the cross, biblical faith expresses its permanent protest against the "religious" pursuit of the divine glory for personal gain. There *is* no glory here—"There was no beauty in him, that we should desire him" (Isa. 53:2, KJV). Moreover, as the resurrection, the ascension, and the advent of the Holy Spirit all confirm, each in its way, the Christ who *is* the revelation cannot be contained, retained, possessed, used. Christ can only be encountered and lived with—as Lord, as presence, as person, as thou.

The reopening of the dialogue with human reason today, which we affirmed at the conclusion of the preceding subsection, depends upon our Christian willingness to enucleate a humbler view of revelation; it depends, we might have said, upon the detriumphalization of Christian theology. The key to this door lies exactly here, in the tradition which knows that God's *revealing* of self, as the revelation of *self*, is therefore also simultaneously a *concealing*. Christians must learn how to say, with Israel, "Truly, thou art a God *who hidest thyself*, O God of Israel, the Savior" (Isa. 45:15).

No single lesson in theology is more needful among North American Christians today than this. For in both liberal and conservative camps, our particular brand of the *theologia gloriae* manifests itself most conspicuously in our readiness to identify our *doctrine* with revelation—or, which is the same thing, our failure to grasp the hiddenness of God *in* God's self-revelation.

30.3. Revelation and Historical Event. The third thesis has already been anticipated in the foregoing, but it adds an important dimension and qualification to the second. It is that *revelation in the Christian understanding of it is mediated through historical events, the decisive event being the one of which Jesus as the Christ is center.*

In some respects, this is the most difficult aspect of the Christian view of revelation, because here the presence is identified explicitly with a historical person. The particularism of this identification seems, among other things, to make dialogue with other faiths impossible, or at least difficult; and in the context described earlier in this study, with its plurality of religious beliefs, this is no incidental matter.

As was demonstrated during the period of theological liberalism, however, there is no escaping the fact that Christians are bound to a revelational religion which is christocentric. The scandal of particularity stands. But does this particularity *need* to manifest itself in religious exclusivism? That is the question. It is the conviction of this study that while historical particularity certainly is unavoidable, given the Christian view of revelation, religious exclusivism is *not* a necessary or even a logical consequence of this particularity, and in fact it can be our entrée to a more inclusive faith.

The condition requisite to the latter possibility is that Christians take more seriously than they have been wont to do that the revealed presence in our christocentric faith is associated with the living person, Jesus, and not simply with our Christologies! Dialogue with the others who are "not of this fold" cannot occur meaningfully if the christocentric revelation to which we hold is a theoretical *reduction* of the person Jesus. In particular, dialogue with Judaism has been bedeviled by the Christian habit of confronting the Jews, not with our devotion to the Jewish teacher Jesus and the transcendence revealed in and through his life, but with our own christological formulas, our dogmatic truths, our eternal theology. Given the finality which, as we have seen, such christological speculation has courted, especially under the conditions of establishment, this can be no basis for interfaith dialogue any more than it can be a basis for dialogue with unfaith.

An important aspect of what is meant by contextual thinking in Christian theology is that divine truth is encountered by us only under the conditions of time and place. As H. Richard Niebuhr has insightfully stated, "The cumulative evidence of history and sociology continues to impress upon us, against our desire, the conviction that our reason is not only in space-time but that time-space is in our reason." He continues:

> The patterns and models we employ to understand the historical world may have had a heavenly origin, but as we know and use them they are, like ourselves, creatures of history and time; though we direct our thought to eternal and transcendent beings, it is not eternal and transcendent; though we regard the universal, the image of the universal in our mind is not a universal image.[33]

Our christologies are products of space and time; Jesus, the Christ, transcends them all.

In other words, we Christians must learn—what Protestants are supposed to have imbibed as "the Protestant principle"—that if *Jesus* is Lord, then no theories *about* Jesus can legitimately function as sovereign truth. The liberals were at least right in this, that they tried to speak more about Jesus and less about Christology. The attempt should not be abandoned just because the liberal picture of Jesus suffered from projections of 19th-century idealism and sentimentalism. Before ever there was Christology there was Jesus; and Christology which becomes too prominent is bound to obscure the person to whose mystery it was intended to witness. Quite astonishingly, in the light of empirical Christianity's too consistent representation of him, not only Jews, but non-Christians of every hue, are still prepared to "see Jesus" (John 12:21). His "charisma" has somehow outlasted the reductionism of his followers. But these others do not meet Jesus in the testimonies and the persons of his followers with any great regularity. Frequently they only meet a parody of him in our doctrine—or worse, a mask for our own ideologies and prejudices. When Christians have learned how to speak about Jesus without in reality seeking to convey their own proud ideas under the guise of that revered name, a larger ecumenical dialogue will be quite possible despite the scandal of particularity, and perhaps even because of it!

---

33. H. Richard Niebuhr, *The Meaning of Revelation*, p. 10.

Revelation, we affirm, means the revelation of a presence. But it should not be adduced from this that Christian faith is founded on a purely spiritual, nonspecified, transhistorical experience of the divine presence. From the outset, the church *identified* this presence on the basis of quite specific historical events and persons, culminating in the one to whom a Jewish fisherman dared to say, "You are the Christ" (Matt. 16:16). The presence has found its form and its face in this one, for the community of the Newer Testament. In this historical person, but also in the history of the people in whose lineage this person stands—the people to whom (as Paul never tires of saying) this person has come "first": in this history, the divine revelation is rooted. These events are its points of reference. God reveals God's self through these events initially, and God's continuing self-revelation, according to faith, always involves the remembering of these events and is in this sense "dependent revelation" (Tillich).

The historical concreteness of this theology of revelation contrasts sharply with spiritualistic theories of revelation. Earlier in this work I spoke favorably of Montanism and various charismatic forms of Christianity throughout Christian history up to today. But the critical commentary on these movements cannot be avoided. Wherever the Holy Spirit has been conceived as the *successor* to the Christ, the concept of revelation in the disciple community suffers from a lack of concreteness and direction. The consequences for the community are usually devastating. For without any rootedness in history revelation becomes personalistic and arbitrary, and the church is victimized by a thousand tongues each claiming divine inspiration. By contrast, the role of the Spirit in revelation as it is depicted in Scripture is, as we have already seen, that of the "Enabler." While the *koinōnia* is brought into being by a revelation effected by the Spirit of God, that which is disclosed is truth made present in "the Son." Without the Spirit, the *koinōnia* could not exist. But what the Spirit bears witness to is not itself, and not even (in an immediate and simply *theistic* sense) "God," but . . . Jesus—which means, of course, also the people out of whom and to whom Jesus came.

Trinitarian theology at its best is intended to express precisely this conception of revelation. Revelation means that "the Spirit" bears witness to "the Son" as the one in and through whom "the Father" comes among us—becomes Emmanuel. The Spirit reveals the Son, who in his earthly life and ministry revealed the Father.

What is preserved in this trinitarian theology of revelation is very important. It means that the presence that is with us in the revelatory experience is not merely an undifferentiated, ineffable otherness, a *mysterium tremendum et fascinans*, but rather a Thou whose *self*-identification

411

precludes our making of this presence whomever or whatever we will. God has become accessible to humanity on humanity's own terms—terms we could somehow understand, if only we would! The presence has characterized, defined, exemplified, clarified, declared itself. It is not just the "Something behind it all." The God of the Scriptures will not be whatever we want God to be. We are not left simply to speculate or to stand in awe of mystery. The mystery is not hidden in *that* sense. The mystery has shown itself—and in very humble and ordinary occurrences, in lives and a life not at all unfamiliar to us. Yet, it is precisely the nature of what is exemplified in these events and these lives which elicits our awe, our sense of the holy. Not what is unknown but what is known, manifested, given, openly displayed to us in these events and lives: this is the source of our reverence. The difference between Christian mysticism and the genus of religious mysticism which has frequently invaded empirical Christianity lies just here: Christian mysticism is not the "abstract mysticism," for example of Pseudo-Dionysius but the "concrete mysticism"[34] of a Bernard of Clairvaux, a Francis, a Meister Eckhart, a Luther. The source of the mystery is that God should come so close, not that God is so far away! That God should be so available, so concretely and fully present! In short, that God should *love*: that is the mystery at the heart of Christian revelation.

Love is the essence of the character God manifests in the events that reveal God's presence. Revelation is first of all the movement of a loving presence towards world and self.[35] This cannot be said too often, and it should not be hedged about with qualifications. At the same time, the tendency to define the love of God by reference to our own preconceptions of love, without due attention to the historical events in which God clarifies the nature of the divine love, is a recurring temptation of the belief. Mawkish and one-sided expressions of love in North American religion have all but ruined the depths of the Christian understanding of the divine love by presenting it in word, art, and symbols devoid of the dark dimension with which the love of God in the biblical witness is inextricably associated. God does not love *easily*—neither, for that matter, does anyone else! God's love is evidently a matter of excruciating decision and

---

34. This distinction is Tillich's. See, e.g., *Systematic Theology*, vol. 2 (Chicago: University of Chicago Press, 1957), pp. 83-84.

35. "This faith-love is divine revelation in the primary sense of the presence of the divine reality in our minds and hearts. As responded to, it creates a fundamental stance in the subject which, like an originating idea, takes possession of the mind and heart and widens the horizon within which the person thinks, judges, decides, and acts" (Charles Davis, *What Is Living, What Is Dead in Christianity Today* [San Francisco: Harper & Row, 1986], p. 114).

struggle—and this applies to both of the biblical testaments. It is a matter of grace. The beloved is in so many ways not lovable! Anselm and the ancients knew this in a way that sentimental neo-Protestantism did and does not. The love of God is *suffering*-love, *agapē*. And there is judgment in it—as there is in all love which is not deserved (and when is love ever deserved?). A theology which takes seriously the revelational basis of faith will be wary, therefore, of baptizing cultural conceptions of love as if they automatically reflected the divine love. The *ḥesed* of God is disclosed in the events to which the Scriptures bear witness. It is not easily identifiable with any form of human faithfulness and self-giving, though it will always find analogies in human history and experience.

Love needs no other end besides itself. Yet as the love of God unveils itself in the revelatory *kairoi* of biblical testimony it is clear that what it wills for the creature is not just the creature's *knowledge* that he or she is loved, fully and ultimately; but this love wills the *fulfillment* of the creature, and of the whole creation. This is expressed in the symbols of liberation, redemption, salvation, and the kingdom. God wills not only to be present, lovingly, to God's creation, but to be present as one whose love delivers creation from the consequences of unlove. Thus God encounters Israel in events, the typical character of which is deliverance from oppression. The liberation of Israel, especially in the symbol and reality of the Exodus, prefigures not only the liberating work of the Christ but the whole movement of the divine grace towards an ultimate liberation. The new creation towards which scriptural eschatology yearns is not fully continuous with the old, for it is God's possibility and not history's inevitable movement. But neither is it (as we have said earlier) the setting aside of the old. Love seeks the fulfillment of the beloved, not its replacement.

In such ways as these must we discuss the presence who is the subject of revelation. For it is not merely a phantom deity, an "oblong blur," but an articulated presence. The notion that revelation should be mediated through historical event is of course not unique to Christianity. It is central especially in Judaism, and Judaic religion is presupposed by the Newer Testament as the model of its conception of revelation. In Judaic religion as in Christianity, the problem posed by the historical grounding of revelation is of course the relation of past and present. How can events which are past still incorporate for the present the revelatory basis of faith?

The answer lies in the nature of the faith under discussion. A vital dimension of biblical faith is remembrance, commemoration. The community of faith remembers. Israel remembers the Exodus. But the remembering is more than mere recollection. It is a recall in which—because

413

God the Spirit is its enabler—that which has occurred occurs again. Remembering the liberation from Egypt, Israel experiences again an existential liberation. "We were Pharaoh's slaves in Egypt, and the Lord brought us out with a mighty hand . . ." (Deut. 6:20-21). The liturgy, preaching, and sacraments of the Christian community are built around this same conception of the dialectical relation between remembrance and faith.

It is useful to refer to Tillich's distinction between "original revelation" and "dependent revelation" at this point. For Christians, the original revelation is that which is centered in the formative events of the life, death, and resurrection of the Christ. This is the original revelation in the sense that it is normative for all subsequent revelation in the Christian community. This is the *kairos*-event in which the revealing presence articulates and announces its identity and its intention. God is here revealed to be this kind of God—the God of suffering love and of the deliverance of sufferers. Without this original revelation, subsequent claims of revelation would be essentially arbitrary—rather, they would be given whatever content the recipients of the alleged revelatory experiences felt they should have. In the original revelation, as we may say, the good shepherd lets the sheep hear his voice, so that in the future his voice will not be mistaken for that of false shepherds, hirelings.

But the original revelation is not by itself sufficient. That is, the testimony of those who first experienced the presence of the revealing God in and through this event is by itself no substitute for revelation. This is why the Bible should never as such be considered the depository of revelation. If the original revelation could be contained in the witness to it, then it would not only be original but final—completed. Clearly, however, it is not the intention of the biblical God to reveal the divine self only to a generation—the generation of those who experienced the Exodus; the generation of those who were contemporaries of the Christ. The function of the original revelation, rather, is to establish the identity of the revealing God, so that in every subsequent generation the Spirit-enabled remembrance of this presence could become the historical basis and norm of authenticity and of sound teaching.

The connection between revelation and historical event is therefore neither arbitrary nor irrational. Revelation without historical grounding ends in a vague and airy spiritism or in abstract mysticism. Historical event without the revealing testimony of the Spirit ends in a rationalized religion of the letter. One could say, partly facetiously but also earnestly, that God, like everyone else, must be known by God's deeds. Otherwise,

God becomes (what again and again "God" has been for people) an empty transcendental form to which human beings attribute such content as complies with their own neuroses and ambitions.

30.4. The Reception of Revelation. Revelation refers not only to a disclosure on the part of God, its initiator, but also to the reception of this disclosure by an act of faith—trust. Our fourth thesis concerns the latter aspect of the subject. *Revelation is that disclosure of the divine presence which grasps the whole person, not only the spirit and not only the mind, and functions in the disciple community as its "ultimate concern."*

It will be recognized that there is again a polemic hidden in this very positive statement. The revealing presence grasps "the whole person, *not only the spirit and not only the mind. . . ."* It can hardly be overlooked that the two things which have been most characteristic of the Christian *reception* of revelation have been on the one hand an undue spiritualizing of the concept and on the other hand an intellectualization of it. North American religious experience, past and present, manifests an abundance of spiritualistic forms of Christianity in particular—partly because these forms were not accepted in the more static and doctrinally strict ecclesiastical bodies of the "Old World" and found refuge here, and partly because spiritualistic religion is more attractive to the individualism and anti-intellectualism of large segments of our population. In fundamentalism, however, as well as in Protestant orthodoxy of various types, we have had to do also with the opposite tendency within ecclesial communities, viz., the reduction of revelation to "revealed truths" to which assent is demanded.

The spiritualization of revelation means the tendency of certain branches of Christendom to turn revelation into ecstatic spiritual experience, vague as to its content though often quite explicit and stylized in its form. In the more radical instances of this practice, especially where the ecstatic impulse is not counteracted by something else (e.g., biblicism), revelation *becomes* the experience as such. In such religion, it is not so important what or who is revealed, *or what kind of ethical practices this leads to*; what is important is that one should have been grasped by supranatural power, that one should have had a "religious experience," should have "been saved," "born of the Spirit."

This is not to deny that ecstasy has a part in the disciple community. It would be hard to envisage that anyone could experience in some manner the presence we have been discussing here and remain unmoved at the emotional level. What needs to be questioned, however, is the tendency in spiritualistic religion so to accentuate the ecstatic dimension of revelation that in the end nothing is revealed except one's personal capacity for ecstasy—a thing which many North American Protestants, being rather fearful of ecstasy but at the same time fascinated by it, obviously find appealing.

On the other hand, the intellectualizing of revelation refers to the tendency within the church—and especially in more "established" denominations—to regard revelation as something to be received by the mind only: to be accepted intellectually, believed in the sense of rational assent (*assensus*), and worked with at a theoretical level of reflection. The reception of revelation characterized by this attitude has of course helped to produce the propositional understanding of revelation that we have discussed in the second observation. In fact, *only* a propositional conception of revelation could lend itself to the intellectualizing of revelational "content." When revelation means in the first place encounter with a presence, its reception could never be *purely* intellectual.

The criticism of the intellectualistic distortion of revelation does not imply a denial of the involvement of the intellect in the reception of revelation. Far from it! The faith which receives revelation is not a mindless faith, which spiritualistic forms of revelation sometimes make it appear. But if revelation can be submitted to the human intellect *in its entirety*, then it can no longer be regarded as an encounter with the "eternal Thou." The I–Thou encounter on the human level always contains intellectual elements, and the mind derives from it certain conclusions and directives which *can*, certainly, become the subject of intelligent reflection and discussion. But no encounter between persons is ever *solely* intellectual (though intellectuals are notorious for trying to make it so!). If encounter between human beings is never wholly intellectual, it can hardly be imagined that the encounter between a human person and the Thou who is our ultimate counterpart would be capable of pure ratiocination.

The reduction of revelation to spiritualistic or to intellectualistic versions of the revelatory experience is perhaps in the last analysis a defensive tactic of the human psyche. Sensing that the revealing presence wills to address and redirect the whole of our being, we consign the encounter to some part of our life and thus limit the ubiquity of its influence. But revelation can play no vital role in life unless it grasps us totally: not only at the level of spirit; not only at the level of mind; but at a level of being deeper than either of these, and inclusive of both. If it can be compartmentalized, it is not revelation in the Christian sense. For revelation means being shown a way so compelling, so absorbing, that one can no longer pursue the old path without being pursued by the vision of the new. The old path may indeed be followed still—*all* the "heroes" of Scripture could have understood St. Peter's flight from Rome along the Appian Way! But revelation means that another way has been envisaged and opened up. From that point onwards, one's life is a dialogue with that other way. It is the way the first Christians had in mind when they called themselves *communio viatorum*—the people of the way. It is the way of the cross. "The intelligence's enlightenment by love is a terrible teaching (in the literal sense of the word). Contemplate what happens to those who have been deeply illuminated by love."[36]

31. Revelation and Reason

31.1. The Quest for Mutuality.   Having defined our conceptions of the two key terms of this discussion, we are now in a position to inquire how they are related to one another in thinking the faith. I shall develop my response to this question, again, in four theses.

The first affirms the obligation that Christians have of keeping their accounts of what they believe in a form which at the same time respects the categories of reason, as these are understood within their historical context, and remains faithful to the revelational basis of the gospel. Expressed in thesis form: *Both reason and revelation are integral to the knowing that belongs to Christian faith and theology.*

It will be evident from the preceding discussion of revelation that in my view this must be given noetic priority. That will be the subject of the second thesis. This noetic or cognitive priority—that is, the recognition that revelation must remain the point of departure for Christian thought— however, does not lead to the conclusion that reason is to be eliminated from the Christian doctrine of knowing, or given a merely subservient or functionary role. The discounting or distrust of reason stems, in those thinkers from Tertullian to Barth where it is found, more from a high evaluation of revelation than from a low opinion of reason. It is often a clear by-product of the experience (which we discussed in the fourth thesis of the previous subsection) that revelation introduces one to dimensions of being and truth so new, so discontinuous with previous experience, that one feels ordinary thought would be quite incapable of discovering anything remotely akin to it, or perhaps even of comprehending it.

---

36. George Grant, *Technology and Justice* (Toronto: Anansi, 1986), p. 55.

Thus in Karl Barth's early essay "The Strange New World within the Bible,"[37] the Bible, as witness to the revelatory Word of God, depicts a realm of meaning and being undreamed of in our philosophies. It views everything from another vantage point. It turns the world upside down, creating something like Nietzsche's "transvaluation of values." It finds human wisdom foolishness, and human goodness "filthy rags." It looks for meaning in a manger and on a cross.

> The Bible tells us not how we should talk with God but what he says to us; not how we find the way to him, but how he has sought and found the way to us; not the right relation in which we must place ourselves to him, but the covenant which he has made with all who are Abraham's spiritual children and which he has sealed once and for all in Jesus Christ.[38]

Reason simply doesn't know what to do with all this. It can only receive it as something utterly unheard of. For faith, however, it is the message of salvation. . . .

This "fideist" position is understandable as a response of new-found belief to the wonder of God's self-manifestation and its meaning for human existence. It is also, as we observed in an earlier section, an appropriate emphasis within historical contexts where the church is in danger of a too facile adaptation of the faith to what passes in the world for truth. But as a permanent and consistent position it is artificial and self-defeating.

Its artificiality becomes obvious when it finds itself, on account of its a priori rejection of ordinary human thinking, having to distinguish and defend itself even from non-Christian reflection that is obviously very *close* to the conclusions of faith. A polemical revelationism is understandable, if not always wholly justifiable, in historical moments when the representatives of rationality are clearly hostile or indifferent to belief, or are leading the human project into paths which a prophetic faith cannot approve. Against the bravado of the rationalist who believes that the whole of life can be interpreted without reference to a givenness at the heart of things, it is always necessary to affirm, with Pascal, that "the heart has its reasons which reason does not know."

But the earlier discussions of reason have reminded us that "reason" does not refer to a fixed position; it is historically conditioned. Many of

---

37. Karl Barth, *The Word of God and the Word of Man*, trans. D. Horton (New York: Harper, 1957), pp. 28ff.

38. Ibid., p. 43.

the most honorable and sensitive representatives of human rationality in our own present context understand very well that "the heart" has its own reasons. Their conceptions of reason question functionalist definitions of reason precisely because "the heart" has been eliminated from the latter. Indeed, a significant trend in human thinking within our context today seems to be away from the earlier self-sufficiency of empiricist and pragmatist versions of thought towards a conception of thinking which contains within itself a dimension of depth that Christians ought to be able to recognize. This is even noticeable in the sciences, which in the first place have never been so steadfastly devoted to empiricism as many theologians imagine, and which today have begun to be sensitive to the many dilemmas which a too consistent emphasis upon objectivity and mastery has created. If revelation, in order to preserve its uniqueness, must refuse discourse even with a *friendly* reason, then is this not a travesty of incarnational belief?

The exclusion of reason by revelationist theology is also self-defeating. By this I mean that it leads to the kind of "closed shop" situation where only those who have been able to make the leap across the chasm separating faith from everything else can have any part in the disciple community. This not only conjures up a segregated image of the church, but it can scarcely avoid the noxious suggestion that salvation comes by right opinion. Historically speaking, fideism has almost always ended with a gnostic view of salvation. Persons are redeemed by knowledge (*gnōsis*)—secret knowledge, inaccessible to any but the initiates of revelatory experience. This in turn raises impossible forms of the problem of authority. Who defines the *vere theologia* (true theology)? Who can be trusted to articulate the meaning of revelation? Where ordinary reason is forbidden any vital role in the epistemology of faith, extraordinary forms of *authority and control* come to be exercised. No matter how important it is to maintain the noetic priority of revelation as the point of departure for belief and church, reason must at least be permitted to contribute questions and to establish checks and balances against the power temptations of the (often self-appointed) representatives of revelatory truth within the disciple community.

That, however, is surely only a *minimal* role for human rationality in the community of faith. Without dissolving the discontinuity between ordinary human thought and Christian belief, it is both possible and necessary to claim continuity as well. As we have expressed it earlier, the decision whether discontinuity or continuity should be stressed in any given historical situation depends upon the Christian perception of the situation as such. Today especially, wherever "meditative reason"—as it is exemplifed in many human disciplines—has freed itself from the Promethean pretentions which characterized our Enlightenment past, there is every incentive to look for positive links between human reflection generally and Christian belief, and the more so because our world needs all the support it can get from persons who, from *whatever* perspective, are sensitive to its fragile beauty and its created goodness.

In sum, there may be times and places where the obedient stance of Christian discipleship is to refuse dialogue with the recognized exponents of rationality. The *normal* situation, however, is one in which the disciple community is obliged by its own evangel and mission to seek out and engage reason's representatives. The gospel is intended for human beings, thinking creatures; and it is only when human thought assumes an inordinate self-sufficiency that revelatory belief can find no point of contact with it. In our present context, while the technocratic bid for control is very prominent at the managerial level, there are few really thoughtful men and women who consistently exemplify that kind of autonomy.

31.2. The Noetic Priority of Revelation.   The second thesis relates more specifically to the role of revelation in Christian thought, and the third to the role of reason. We affirm that, *in the relation between reason and revelation in Christian epistemology, revelation has noetic priority.*

This is the permanent truth of the kerygmatic position. What the Christian claims to know *qua* Christian is not, in the first place, something that is derived from the application of rationality to experience, but something offered from beyond the capacities of human thought and will. It is not produced by human reason, nor can it even be fully comprehended rationally. It is a given, a mystery, a being grasped.

We remember, however, that this which is noetically prior is in fact no *thing*. It is not, for instance, information—secret data—as in Gnosticism. Much that Christians believe in the line of data (doctrine, concepts, ideas) *can* be and *is* anticipated in human thought and experience. Far more than has been thought, in the past, can in fact be seen as the common property of human religious and secular thinking and is not exclusively Christian. Indeed, at almost every point of doctrine, parallels or reminiscences can be found in human philosophy, psychology, political ideologies, religion, and so on. As Christianity emerges out of its Constantinian cocoon, which has insulated both the church and its doctrine from lively contact with other religious and worldly traditions, we are often astonished and even embarrassed by the similarity between many of our primary concepts and those from other sources. One of the effects of the end of the Constantinian era is in fact a kind of defensive reaction to this discovery, born of the need to show that, after all, what Christians believe *is* very different! But why should it be? If revelation has something to do with the unveiling of truth, ought not one to expect that it could relate to truth *wherever* and by *whomsoever* truth is discovered?

As we have had numerous occasions to reiterate here, however, the truth for biblical faith cannot be equated with information, data, ideas. "I *am* the Truth," said Jesus. Revelation is the presence of the "I am" (Yahweh). *This* is what is noetically prior. *This* is the "first principle of our comprehension." The presence of the one who is Truth casts a whole new light on everything—including the truth that is already known. On account of this loving ("agapeistic"—Davis), liberating presence, the things of daily life and thought are given a different meaning and direction. The discontinuity between ordinary human thought and the thinking of the disciple community is to be found, not primarily in the different ideas and concepts deriving from one or the other source, but primarily in the new *perspective* upon the whole of reality which is given to belief in and through the presence of the revealing God.

This perspective is what theology tries—or should try—to bring to the analysis of the human condition. It would be foolish for theology to pretend that its view of the human condition is unbiased or objective in the way that these terms are used in contemporary scholarship. It is thoroughly biased! Christians understand humanity, history, nature, the future, in the way that they do because they assume from the outset that all of these are enfolded in a love that is eternal, that will not let them go. As we stated at the outset, the theology of the cross means God's *abiding commitment to this world.* Therefore Christians do not see *anthrōpos* merely as a biological or social being, but as a creature of the God whose presence they experience—a creature of this God, fallen from the divine intention for its creaturehood, alienated from its fellow creatures on account of this aboriginal alienation, missing the point of its creaturehood, seeking to rise above it but actually falling beneath it, yet not abandoned, but sought after, pursued, loved . . . . The point of departure in all of this is not divine information, vouchsafed to us through church or Bible, but the very presence (*Mitsein!*) of the one in relation to whom all of this becomes real.

Revelation is *noetically* prior: that is, it brings about a new situation in terms of our *awareness* of what is already the case. It clarifies and illuminates our darkness. It evokes the question that we did not know how to ask, or dared not ask. But the question was already there, because we *are* the question. And the "answer" to the question that we are cannot be given in propositions or theories or doctrines—answers! It can only be given—as it was given to Job—by the presence of the Answerer. Job did, of course, receive answers of a sort from the "voice out of the whirlwind" (Job 38ff.). But by themselves these answers cannot suffice. In the first place, the most impressive of the answers provided by "the voice" were in fact questions! In the second, the positive answers given by the revealing "voice" had for the most part already been rehearsed (ad nauseam) by Job's all-too-omniscient "friends," particularly Elihu.[39] But the point is that the answers cannot satisfy the questioner's needs. For Job's questions are not theoretical ones; they are existential, they are . . . his life and what has become of it! He has to know whether there is anything "out there" to meet his desperate cry for meaning, any reality worthy of his waiting, any Thou to correspond to his eternal restlessness, any Lord to receive the service he is ready to give, any lover of his life and all life to offset all this death. This immense creaturely destitution can only be responded to adequately by the Creator's presence as such. To know ourselves eternally befriended—this is revelation. And if this occurs, then it does not matter that the befriending presence proffers more questions than answers.

31.3. Potentiality for Dialogue. *While reason is not able to anticipate revelation, it is able to comprehend the human condition in terms that are frequently sympathetic to faith's analysis; therefore reason is always potentially capable of dialogue with revelation.*

Our third thesis returns to the theme of mutuality broached in the first. Given that revelation refers to encounter, presence, and to the acquisition of a new perspective on existence as a whole (the second thesis), we may now appreciate that the dialogue with human reason is on a different footing from what would be the case were revelation primarily the impartation of extraordinary information. In that case, revelatory information could only *compete* with rational information. For instance, revealed truth might insist that God exists while "unaided reason" insisted that God does not exist, or that God's existence cannot be demonstrated. There you have a conflictual situation which is determined to be so by the very preunderstanding of both sources of "information." Unfortunately, this has been the characteristic nature of the dialogue between the two categories, and, for the most part, it continues to be so in our context. But if revelation refers first and foremost to encounter with the divine

---

39. See Samuel Terrien, *Job: Poet of Existence* (Indianapolis and New York: Bobbs-Merrill, 1957).

presence and the new perspective upon the world which such an encounter provides, revelation is not predetermined to clash with the consequences of rational thought; its primary function in regard to reason is rather to bring to bear upon reason's conclusions about the world a dimension that reason cannot itself produce.[40]

This is what is meant when it is said, in our present thesis, that reason cannot anticipate revelation; for revelation is first the presence of the revealing God. This presence cannot be conjured up, argued towards, or called into being by the human intellect. Moreover, as we have already noticed, our tradition leads us to think that there is much in the mind and will of humanity, under the conditions of historical existence, that wants precisely to avoid just this presence!

But when this rudimentary acknowledgment of the fact that revelation is a matter of encounter and grace has been made, there is no need to hedge it about (as fideism does) with the insistence that reason can anticipate nothing at all of the consequences of such a view of revelation. We have already suggested that most of the *ideas* present in the teaching of the Christian tradition have been, in one way or another, anticipated and explored in non-Christian settings. It must be assumed from historical evidence therefore that human rationality is capable of reflecting on existence in ways that at least parallel or are tangentially related to Christian concepts. This is true not only of peripheral matters such as ethical precepts or miracle stories or myths which reflect thoughts similar to those of the tradition of Jerusalem. It is also true of the more central informing concepts of our faith—the idea of grace, of the necessity of forgiveness, of the internal tensions of judgment and love, of alienation between persons and with nature, and so on. Throughout human history, and still today, it is possible to discover many parallels with all of these key concepts.

But we may go beyond the recognition that such parallels exist at the ideational level and admit that human awareness is even able to envisage what it would mean for the spirit of Homo sapiens were it to feel

---

40. George Lindbeck notes that both Luther and, at the other end of the spectrum, Aquinas, "despite their material differences, can be viewed as holding that revelation dominates all aspects of the theological enterprise, but without excluding a subsidiary use of philosophical and experiential considerations in the explication and defense of the faith. Similarly," he concludes, "a postliberal approach need not exclude an ad hoc apologetics, but only one that is systematically prior and controlling in the fashion of post-Cartesian natural theology and of later liberalism. . . . In the conceptuality employed in this book, the logic of coming to believe, because it is like that of learning a language, has little room for argument, but once one has learned to speak the language of faith, argument becomes possible" (*The Nature of Doctrine*, pp. 131-132).

itself affirmed by a spiritual reality beyond its own dynamism—befriended! In the contemporary sense of the *absence* or *eclipse* of God, just this awareness is very real. In much imaginative literature and art within our context, for instance, it is possible to find a poignant realization of what it could mean to the human spirit and project were it to know itself befriended by something or someone transcending its own being. A new genre of science fiction, imaginatively presented in the films of Stephen Spielberg, for example, explores precisely this theme—and contemporary audiences, obviously sensing a profound need for such a message, are invariably moved. "Calculative reason" as such may not encourage such fantasies; but even the most technically orientated rationality, which is the very medium of science fiction, cannot prevent "meditative" thought from entertaining them. Human rationality cannot *produce* the presence by which the human spirit would be fulfilled; but it can ask for it and long for it. And it does!

This positive role of reason in Christian epistemology is supported not only by evidence from experience but also by theological assumptions which belong to the tradition of Jerusalem. The very fact that Christian theology will not consider the human condition apart from the perspective of the God whose presence is given in a self-revelation means that the human creature is, in the Christian view, eternally bound to its creator. It is the creature of this God, and therefore no matter how thoroughly humanity separates itself from its source, or is separated by impersonal or cosmic factors, it is conditioned by its origins in God's intentionality. We have been witnesses in our time to the phenomenon of a secular version of Homo sapiens which has seemed both incapable of and disinterested in asking the question of ultimate meaning and destiny. Many of our contemporaries still appear able to pass through life without ever putting to themselves, in any earnest manner, the question "Who am I?" and all the related questions. These attitudes, however, are greatly dependent upon external circumstance. It is not accidental that secularism is a 19th-century phenomenon, and that it achieved its greatest successes in the Western world among the middle classes. The question of ultimate meaning can be avoided when people are caught up in the excitement of the immediate. But as we saw in the first part of this study, the perpetuation of the secular, progressivist way is today possible only on the basis of an increasingly neurotic and repressive narcissism. The world—nature itself!—is teaching the human creature to ask questions and engage in searches that Western technological humanity had formerly consigned to "the dark ages." There is a search for meaning in our time that is increasingly open, being increasingly desperate. I suspect that we have not seen the end of the lengths to which "ordinary human rationality" will go to find an outlet for its finally irrepressible ontological and teleological questions.

While this means that the ancient dialogue with reason can be re-opened today in a way that may not have been possible even at the beginning of this century, it does not mean that the dialogue can ever be easy. It does not mean, either, that Christians can assume that *their* answers to the ontological and teleological questions humanity again insists upon asking will be the ones to which the majority even of Westerners turn. The hard questions raised by modern and postmodern skepticism, and written into the events of our era, cannot be answered easily by anyone. The test of our Christian authenticity is not whether we can answer these questions, but whether we can permit the world to ask them—and provide a forum for their asking!

To do this, we must let go of the conditioned urge, born of centuries of Christian "answering," to turn every question or questing situation into an occasion for the announcement of religious answers. In North America, this propensity is heightened by our notorious impatience—our need for the "quick fix"—and our incapacity for dialectical thought. Popular religion is answering religion, and under the apocalyptic conditions described earlier both the questions and the answers treated by the most vociferous forms of religion on this continent are increasingly trivial. Over against this simplism, serious representatives of God's revelation in Jesus as the Christ must learn how to identify themselves with the *questions* of a humiliated and fearful rationality, and to ask these questions with the same earnestness as the sensitive representatives of worldly concern ask them. When we have achieved that kind of solidarity with the human questions; when we can count ourselves among those who "hunger and thirst for righteousness" and for God, then we shall have the right to explore again, in new ways, the revelatory answer to the human question. Only as we participate in the suffering of the intellect and the humbling of the human enterprise shall we have any possibility of bringing comfort from the side of the suffering God. This is what it means to apply to this aspect of Christian theology—to the dialogue of reason and revelation—the perspective called *theologia crucis*.

31.4. Revelation, Reason, and Contextuality. The fourth thesis concerning the relation of revelation and reason has been anticipated in many ways throughout this study, but it will be useful to bring to bear upon the present discussion the importance of our special concern for contextualization. We state simply, then, that *this relation between reason and revelation will always be conditioned by contextual factors.*

We said earlier that reason is historically conditioned. It does not always and everywhere mean the same thing. "Our reason is not only in space-time, time-space is in our reason."[41] Significantly, reason as it has entered into the theological discourse of the 20th century presents itself most frequently in the guise of *the questioner.* This has not always been so. In the apologetic theology of St. Thomas, for instance, reason is very much *the contributor.* It brings to the dialogue with faith highly positive contributions, which in Thomas's time could seem to support and bolster the (different) contributions of revealed religion. Still, with Schleier-macher, reason (now understood in company with "feeling") comes to the dialogue with belief bearing many truths and insights gleaned from experience.

In our own period, however, reason does not appear on the scene of human reflection with answers so much as with questions. Even its answers (such as the answers of technology) are in reality grave questions, and are perceived as such by many reasonable persons. Thus when a sensitive modern theological apologist like Paul Tillich gives human rationality a highly important place in the theological "system," what reason brings to the discussion is not the wondrously supportive arguments for God that are brought forward by a Thomas, or even the psychically compelling rationale of a Schleiermacher, but (to use Tillich's own metaphor) "the question." And the question is not an academic one, but one which is full of angst and unfulfilled longing.[42] Tillich did not have to invent such a characterization of human rationality; it is there in every major work of art, in much that emanates from the natural and social sciences, in the formative events of the age, in the lines on the faces of "ordinary people" (Judith Guest).

In such sociohistorical circumstances, the relation between reason and revelation becomes highly provocative, so far as the Christian disciple is concerned. When reason held its head high and thought itself in charge of the human dance, even going so far as to consider itself the redeemer of the species, then it could only encounter revelational truth as its rival and ancient enemy. From its side, revelation could only shake its head

---

41. H. Richard Niebuhr, *The Meaning of Revelation*, p. 10.

42. "Man is the being who is able to ask questions. . . . It implies . . . that we do not have that for which we ask. . . . If man is that being who asks the question of being, he has and has not the being for which he asks. He is separated from it while belonging to it. . . . etc." (*Biblical Religion and the Search for Ultimate Reality* [Chicago: The University of Chicago Press, 1955], pp. 11f.).

and call reason false hope and human arrogance, and resent its intrusion upon the ground of revelational authority. But the rationality with which we are called to dialogue in our present context is a reason "eclipsed" (Horkheimer). It has been shorn of its pride on the bloody battlefields of early 20th-century Europe, and in the contemplation of its own destructive and annihilating potentiality. It no longer brings forth valiant schemes for human salvation—or, if some of its representatives are still given to such grandeur, many others are ready to call them to account. Reason in the main presents itself today as an articulation of human frustration and, not infrequently, despair; it has discovered the depths of questions to which no purely rational answers can be given.

We should therefore be very wary, as Christians, of permitting preconceived doctrinal patterns of the relation of these two epistemological categories from informing our theology, our preaching, our ethical activity. Protestants especially must be careful not to cling to what they have received as "Reformation" or "biblical" or other grounds for *suspecting* human reason. The temptations of a revelational ideology are very enticing to classical Protestantism, and liberalism did not help this situation with its too uncritical capitulation to modern conceptions of rationality. But it appears to me that we have come to a time in history when what is called for is not the kerygmatic protest of faith against reason's vain pretentions (surely that is a matter of whipping a dead horse), but the most earnest attempt of Christian apologetics to comprehend, and to help give birth to a human quest for meaning that may be more desperate than any that has ever been. At very least, what remains of the meditative traditions of reason today is not the sly enemy of faith that many Christians, trained in the conventions of evangelical and kerygmatic discontinuity, are prone to think it. Like Christianity itself, reason is more like a beggar than a prince today. If the representatives of revelational belief can themselves more openly admit their indigent condition, it may be that two beggars can discover their common ground, and make common cause.

32. Authority in Faith and Theology

32.1. The Crisis of Authority. The final aspect of the knowing that belongs to faith which we shall treat in this study is the question of authority. This question is inherent in the problem of knowledge. "How do you know?" always means, among other things, "What is your authority for this claim?" The world asks this of the disciple community, and within the community the members ask it of one another. What guidelines for authority can be offered within the tradition of Jerusalem?

Before we attempt an answer to this question, and as the necessary contextual background for our treatment of it, we need to take stock of the situation in which we are asking about authority.

We come to this question as persons whose society reflects a notorious crisis of authority. At least in the Western world, since the end of the 19th century every authority has been thrown into question. In a way, all that has happened in the 20th century—the most formative internal as well as external events—has served to confirm that questioning of authority. The authority of civic leaders, of governments, of the various conventions in the arts; the authority of the intellectuals, even of the natural scientists, whose authority seemed secure not very long ago—all these have suffered a crisis of confidence and of authority. In a certain sense, our whole civilizational crisis could be expressed as the crisis of authority. We cannot trust the authorities that have been, and yet we cannot live without authority of some kind. The more chaotic and dangerous our global society becomes, the more we sense the need for authority. Yet experience has made us skeptical of all possible authorities. Hence we tend to drift, and to allow irrational and even capricious—and possibly demonic—forces within our midst to take charge. As a society we seem not to be able to muster the will that is required to check the autonomous and random rule of technologism, the bureaucratization of public life, the illogic of war, the insanity of violence and terrorism. Our cities reflect the increasing power of vandalism and seem to cover—but just barely— a rampant, working nihilism.

This situation of drift is also conspicuous in the churches, which in this as in many other respects mirror the culture at large. It has always been the case that the so-called religious freedom of the North American continent has led to a proliferation of denominationalism in which the question of authority was flagrantly begged. But today we have progressed beyond this tolerated ecclesial chaos to a state of religious dishevelment verging on the absurd. The most bizarre forms of "Christianity" can command the attention of millions of television viewers. What can only be judged by historically aware persons as flaming heresies can now be put forward in all pomp as the very essence of the faith—and few indeed will know the difference! Religious visionaries of every conceivable ilk set up shop in our towns and cities, or parade the streets offering instant wisdom, or stealthily recruiting our lost or drifting youth—and the anxiety of the populace is such that they can *all* find a following. The older forms of Christianity, too, have lost touch with their own foundational traditions, and are so crippled materially and in spiritual confidence that they can do no better, often, than to emulate pathetically the "success" tactics of the sects and cults.[43]

There are those who think that they can remedy the random, authority-less situation by recalling the churches to the old authorities which were accepted before the crisis of authority. They challenge the churches to return to the Bible as their authority; and this "back to the Bible" means precisely (with exceptions) a return to the *kind* of biblical authority which preceded the crisis of authority, as if the crisis itself could be brushed aside by a firm resolution not to notice what had brought it about. Others attempt to recall the churches to the authority of confessional traditions. Particularly in the Roman Catholic church, but also among the successors of the various offspring of Protestant Orthodoxy, there are those who feel that the way out of this confusion and anarchy is a simple return to the authority of the doctrinal tradition which formerly incorporated the genius of that denomination—a return to Thomas, or the Council of Trent, or Calvin and the Westminster Confession. Such "returns" almost always do grave injustice to the past. In this connection, too, recent or contemporary theologians and theological schools suffer the unhappy fate of being cast in the role of authority figures. As we have previously noted, for instance, the use that is made of Karl Barth's theology within some circles in North America is an almost ludicrous (or perhaps tragic) case in point.

Again, it is possible to see people in the churches trying to return to the authority formerly held by the *church authorities*—by the episcopacy, the synod, the pope, the conference, etc. Often against the will and better judgment of the church leaders involved, they are asked (explicitly or implicitly) to *become* authorities in the old sense. Some of them are of course happy to oblige! But the more characteristic resolution of this socioreligious impulse is the bureaucratic one: since the appointed or elected leaders, being sensitive postmodern men and women, do not feel qualified to lead in the premodern sense of that term, decision making falls upon those officers, administrators, and functionaries who in reality are only the secretariat of the ecclesial organization, but frequently become collectively what is called (a term borrowed, significantly, from the business world) "the head office." In the absence of authority, in church as in world, a surrogate authority comes into being—the bureaucracy. It

---

43. See in this connection Reginald W. Bibby, *Fragmented Gods: The Poverty and Potential of Religion in Canada* (Toronto: Irwin, 1987).

is not a genuine authority, because it is driven by "laws" of its own internal development. It does not serve the ends for which the ecclesial organization exists, but it evolves according to inherent organizational constellations and needs. The same thing can be observed about every large corporation and about government. It is part of being the technological society.

But this breakdown of authority—what is it? Socially considered, it is many things. But one of the things that it is *for the churches* is an accompaniment—perhaps a necessary accompaniment—of the end of the Constantinian era. The old Christendom pattern has given way, and with it the hierarchies of authority that belonged to it. This hierarchical authority was no doubt most perfectly achieved in the Catholic and Orthodox traditions; but it very quickly found Protestant expression as well. The tendency of Christians, especially of those whose systems were most reflective of the Constantinian model of Christianity, is to be very threatened by this breakdown. They react either by being debilitated and immobilized, or by calling for the various kinds of "return" to which I have referred above.

But a quite different attitude towards this situation is possible. After all, a crisis (*krisis*) is not only a moment of great danger, but also a moment of possible change. One *could* regard the ecclesiastical crisis of authority as the necessary condition for change—indeed, as an unprecedented opportunity for genuine transformation. It may be that now, after centuries of Christian commitment to patterns and models of church and authority within the church that have had little to do with faith, to ask about authority in a fresh way, a way untrammeled by patterns of authority that we have borrowed from the succession of empires and cultures with which we have made our bed. For it is almost impossible, as a student of ecclesiastical and political history, to avoid the conclusion that authority within the Christian churches has simply mirrored the authority systems which dominated in the successive societies with which the churches have been identified. With a few brave exceptions, Christianity almost from the beginning has hardly managed anything *original* by way of a doctrine of authority. It has mimicked, it has borrowed, it has adapted its models of authority from the authorities it found to be recognized and respected in its host societies. This was in fact a built-in necessity of Christian establishmentarianism. The church could only expect to be authoritative itself in a society if it *did* mirror the canons of authority dominant in the society. (A corollary of this is that the churches most successful in reflecting society's authority patterns have usually been the most successful generally. For example, the "free churches" in North America have been more "successful" than those [like the Anglican or Catholic churches] which mirrored earlier, European patterns of cultural authority—and for the obvious reason that an imperial or feudal pattern could hardly be adapted to the more democratic systems at work on this continent.)

The crisis of authority *could*, I say, be perceived against such a background of temptation and the quest for power by proximity to power, as containing within itself a highly positive theological dimension—a cleansing *krisis* enabling the church to discover *its own rightful sort of authority pattern*. For there has always been that in biblical faith which resisted the identification of divine authority with *any* human structures of authority. Prophetic religion has always involved the calling in question of whatever claims authority for itself, or for something of which it is in possession. The prophets, from Jeremiah to John the Baptist and Jesus himself, always raised about themselves an open crisis of authority. "By what *authority* do you do these things?" (Matt. 21:23, par.) Jesus was asked by the indignant religious authorities of his milieu.

Given this prophetic tradition, faith should be neither surprised by nor anxious about the crisis of authority which has come upon the whole church today. In a way, the disciple community can even welcome this crisis. It should not welcome the darkness and disarray which ensues from the crisis, but it can welcome the interrogation of all authority and perhaps it is able to see the hand of God in this interrogation. Because prophetic and critical theology has always understood that the point at which human beings most pathetically manifest their bondage to sin is the moment when they set themselves up as authorities in relation to other human beings— or, conversely, when they allow other human beings to do this in relation to them. Authority, supreme authority, belongs to God alone: this is the presupposition of the prophetic tradition. Divine authority therefore reduces to relativity and transitoriness everything that announces itself as authoritative, even when it claims to represent the divine authority—and especially then. Prophetic faith has always evoked a vast suspicion of authority. It is like Solzhenitsyn's statement in his book *August, 1914*,[44] concerning a certain woman in prerevolutionary Moscow who ran a school for girls, and whose aim was to make of the girls "good citizens, that is to say . . . individuals in whom there was an inherent mistrust of authority."

Prophetic faith is skeptical of authority—in a real sense the whole

---

44. Alexander Solzhenitsyn, *August, 1914*, trans. Michael Glenny (London: The Bodley Head, 1971), p. 51.

431

function of the prophet, negatively expressed, is to keep watch in respect to false authority; for it recognizes the propensity of human beings, possessing the mantle of authority, to usurp the place of the one authority. Thus prophetic religion can be very stringent even with respect to apparently honorable authorities. Even the *good* king, David, must be chastized (2 Sam. 12:7). For all human authority tends to become immodest. This is the assumption of the prophets of Israel. Biblical faith permits human authority and societal authorities, and it even establishes them (as the kingship of Israel was—albeit reluctantly—established by the prophet Samuel; 1 Samuel 8). It knows that authority is needed for the life of humanity in community. But the same prophetic faith which calls authority into existence, blesses it, and supports it, is constantly alert in relation to it; because the primary calling of this faith is to be vigilant for humanity—for the sheep of the good shepherd. The one who affirms that *"The Lord* is my shepherd . . ." (Ps. 23:1) must develop a scrupulous vigilance for hirelings (John 10:12f.), more particularly those who claim to represent "the Lord."

In our time, the confusion of authority affords Christians an opportunity to explore concretely the meaning of authority as it flows, not from the external sociological circumstances of its life in this or that society, but from the heart of this prophetic tradition. It could well be that there are benefits here, not only for the church but also for the society experiencing a crisis of authority.

The prophetic tradition begins, we have said, with the critical ultimacy of the authority of God. We shall discuss this under the heading, "The Authority above the Authorities." Then we shall examine the authority of Bible, tradition, and ecclesiastical office under the general caption, "Provisional Authority."

32.2. The Authority above the Authorities. In an important respect that is often overlooked, the Reformation of the 16th century, which gave the world many messages, provided us with one message which comes straight from the prophetic tradition of Israel about which we have just been thinking. Perhaps Calvin more than any of the other reformers captured this spirit in his leading theological doctrine of "the sovereignty of God." *God* is sovereign, and therefore nothing else may legitimately claim for itself absoluteness of authority. *Soli Deo gloria* (glory belongs to God alone). God's sovereignty relativizes every mundane authority. There is but one absolute. And since this absolute is the ineffable, eternal

Godhead, it can neither be possessed nor commanded nor contained; it can only be heard and obeyed.[45]

Unfortunately, what has come down to the churches from this Calvinistic teaching concerning the divine sovereign authority (and perhaps it is partly Calvin's own fault) has been one side of the matter only. This is the side which insists (frequently with a certain religious hardness of heart) that God is Lord, and it is our business to obey God very strictly.

But the other, underside of the teaching about God's authority is that whenever it is taken seriously it puts a great question mark over all human pretensions to mastery and ultimacy. It reduces all the powers of the human kingdoms, including ecclesiastical powers, to authorities that are at best penultimate, and in any case always exist themselves *under* authority. The connection that has often been made between Protestant (especially Reformed) thought and political democracy or constitutional government is therefore not accidental, even though[46] the latter is not necessarily an intentional consequence of the former. As soon as you say, "God is sovereign," you are saying (in a silent polemic), "Ergo, Caesar is not, Nero is not, King John is not, Charles the First is not, Napoleon is not, Hitler is not," In fact, behind the earliest Christian confession—*Jesus Christos Kyrios* (Jesus Christ is Lord)—stands the Roman cry, *Kaisar Kyrios* (Caesar is Lord). The Christian confession is rendered harmless and sentimental unless this is understood. Democracy by no means guarantees that the human lust for power will be restrained or that the voice of the sovereign Lord will be expressed in the *vox populae*! But political democracy at least lessens the chances of those who are most driven by the lust for power to succeed in their quest.[47] "The people," said John Knox, "yes, or a part of the people, may execute God's judgments against their king, being an offender."[48]

This relativizing of all mundane authority in the name of the authority above the authorities was present in the Lutheran side of the Reformation as well. It is what gave courage to the obscure teaching monk of Wittenberg to take on the entire Roman establishment. But on the Lutheran side, this factor is complicated by other, practical and doctrinal issues, which have proved complex and dangerous in subsequent history, right up until the time of the Third Reich. In his struggle against the entrenched

---

45. See John Calvin, *Institutes*, Book I, chaps. 11–12.
46. As George Lindbeck suggests, in *The Nature of Doctrine*, p. 128.
47. See George Grant on tyranny, in *Technology and Justice*, pp. 56, 73-74.
48. Harry Emerson Fosdick, *Great Voices of the Reformation: An Anthology* (New York: Random House, 1952), p. 245.

authority of papal Rome, Luther applied this same "Protestant principle" (Tillich) as is present in Calvin's and Knox's teaching about God's sovereignty: the divine authority transcends, relativizes, and judges every earthly authority. But in the subsequent internal struggle with the more radical elements of the Reformation, Luther found it necessary to strengthen the hand of the civil authorities by accentuating their positive authoritization by divine authority. Citing the 13th chapter of Romans, Luther insisted that the governing authorities must be obeyed because "they have their power from God." He used the ill-fated metaphor which depicts government as "the left arm of God."[49] The Germanic peoples and the world at large have had to suffer terrible consequences on account of this overemphasis upon the divine sanctioning of civil authority. If St. Paul himself, or Luther his exegete, had been able to foresee these consequences, they would surely have been more cautious in their underwriting of existing authority. A people reared upon the teaching that existing authority must be obeyed because it is—simply because it exists!—is in no position to criticize the insane policies of a Hitler, even when they have become aware of their insanity. Even a man of the superior intelligence and sensitive morality of a Bonhoeffer must engage in an almost overwhelming crisis of conscience before he can participate in a plot whose informing ethical principles citizens of England had already settled for themselves in the age of King John. The conditioning to obey and respect authority, combined with "an inordinate fear of anarchy" (Reinhold Niebuhr),[50] has been a powerful spiritual influence in the Germanic experience.

This is, however, not only "a German problem." It can be seen in our own present-day society that many are ready to trust authority implicitly (not only the authority of government, but also, for example, the authority of the military, the legal system, science, business, etc.) simply because it is authority, and because they are afraid to face the breakdown of authority, which seems to court chaos. All that we as citizens of such a society may say about the Germanic experience is that in that particular history this common problem of Western civilization was highlighted, and its character thus illuminated.

Despite this qualification which is both theoretically and existentially important, a central insight of the Reformation was and remains the "Prot-

---

49. On the question of Luther's attitude towards the state, see Wilhelm Pauck, "Luther and Butzer," in *From Luther to Tillich: The Reformers and Their Heirs*, ed. Marion Pauck (San Francisco: Harper & Row, 1984), pp. 11f.

50. *The Nature and Destiny of Man*, vol. 2 (New York: Scribner's, 1953), p. 195.

estant principle": if *God* is absolute, there can be no other absolutes; if *God* is omnipotent, there can be no other who is all-powerful; if *God* is sovereign, every other claim to sovereignty exists under an implicit question mark. And when it is seen in its most consistent theological application (which is not always), this means, of course, that all *religious* authority is also relativized by the one Lord. God who *is* authority also transcends all of our efforts to give explicit expression to that divine authority.

32.3. Authority as a Problem in Christian Faith and Theology. This recognition of the fact that the absoluteness of divine authority radically qualifies even our efforts to articulate and codify the authority *of God* leads to a necessary consideration of authority *as a problem* for Christian faith and theology. If the divine sovereignty is finally incapable of being stated in specific ways, translated into codes of ethics, commandments, rules of behavior, expressed in theological truths that are permanently valid, then is this authority finally not so elusive as to be ineffectual? If over against the false absolutes of inauthentic human authorities it is not possible for prophetic faith to point to specific truths and commands, commands and truths which judge the misleading testimony of inauthentic authority, then is prophetic faith not rendered impotent?

In answer, those who emphasize the work of the *Holy Spirit* respond that the Spirit guides us and causes us to know the truth and the will of God. But how shall we recognize the Spirit? There are many spirits! Today in North America, a society perceived by some observers as having abandoned open secularity for reactionary religion,[51] spirits abound! On the other hand, those who emphasize *the Word* are prone to answer that the Scriptures contain the testimony by which the spirits must be tested. But how in that case can one prevent the Scriptures from becoming false authorities, that is, authorities which tend to *replace* or supplant the transcendent authority of the living God?

A way through this dilemma is suggested by one of the biblical writings which has seemed to many who understand it only superficially to court the latter danger. This is the book of Deuteronomy. For various historical reasons, it became the task of the Deuteronomist to state (actually, to put into words) the intention of God. Now the prophetic tradition,

---

51. Tom F. Driver, *Christ in a Changing World: Toward an Ethical Christology* (New York: Crossroad, 1981), p. 3f.

as represented, say, by Jeremiah, a contemporary of the Deuteronomist, insists that what obedience means is not obedience to precepts or to "the letter," but to "the voice." It is the living God, *Deus loquens*, who must be heard. Again and again, therefore, Jeremiah, like the other prophets, reminds Israel that the one basic command of God is: "Obey *my voice*" (e.g., Jer. 3:13; 7:23; 26:13; 38:20; 42:6).

The Deuteronomist knows this too. The same formula can be found in his writing; in fact, it is the central focus of his message (e.g., Deut. 4:30; 5:22-26; 13:4; 27:10; 30:20). But he knows, as well, that the voice can be very difficult to hear—indefinite, ambiguous, drowned out by a multitude of other voices, around and within us. Or perhaps altogether eclipsed—silent, like Shusaku Endo's Christ-figure.[52] So the Deuteronomist creates a kind of codification of the divine will: in this situation you should do this, and in that situation that. He is very well aware of the dangers implicit in what he is doing. Human beings need something quite concrete; they are afraid of the voice—*and* of the silence. They will gladly take hold of specific codifications of the *Torah* and turn them into absolutes. The "laws" supplant the voice. Religion in our present-day context everywhere gives evidence of this eventuality. How can it be guarded against?

The answer of the Deuteronomist is subtle. He puts his codification of the law into sections of text surrounded by what amounts to sermonic address. And the point of these sermons is to keep ever before the reader this message: it is the *voice* that you must listen for above all. These laws can only tell you the *sort* of thing that you can expect to hear from the divine voice. If you hear things that radically contradict these laws and the spirit of them, then be on your guard! The voice you are hearing, then, might well be some other—perhaps a demonic voice, the voice of other gods, or of your own "conscience," which is by no means to be equated with "the God within" (see 1 John 3:19f.). In other words, the writer of the laws tries simultaneously to make God's will explicit, without its becoming absolute and thus replacing the living one who "will be who I will be."

32.4. The Mystery of the Divine Authority. This reference to the tetragrammaton (YHWH) leads to the next stage in our reflection on divine authority as above all other authorities. It is the essence of the biblical God's authority that it eludes forever our attempts to grasp and hold it—

---

52. Shusaku Endo, *Silence*, trans. William Johnston (Rutland, Vermont, and Tokyo: Sophia University in cooperation with the Charles E. Tuttle Co., 1969).

or even fully to understand it. It is absolute authority if it is authority which we know ourselves to be *standing under*, and therefore do not fully (in the modern sense of the term) *understand*. At the heart of the divine authority is the mystery of God as God, as the one "who will be who I will be."

Yet this mystery is not the kind of mystery that is a mere unknown quantity. As we have seen, it is a mystery which is only felt and seen by us on account of its unveiling of itself: it is the *Deus revelatus* who is simultaneously *Deus absconditus*. God is awesome to us, not because God keeps God's self distant and hidden from view, but because God comes near. The biblical God is revealed in acts of astonishing graciousness towards the creation. This is the center of all Christian mysticism, as distinct from the "abstract mysticism" that bases itself on the divine unknownness and unknowability. The mystery is simply this: that God should love. That I, even I; that we, even we, should be accepted, "justified."

This reference to the divine *agapē* is not incidental in a discussion of God's authority. Without it, the whole interpretation of divine authority is inevitably distorted. As has often happened in Christian theology and practice, interest in authority becomes a thing-in-itself and is extricated from the context of the divine love. But the mystery that lies at the heart of the divine authority is nothing other than the love of God. The authority that God wills to exercise, according to the tradition of Jerusalem, is the authority of suffering love. In fact, God's authority is nothing more and nothing less than God's love expressing itself in concrete ways. With the God of Abraham, Isaac, and Jacob, the "Abba" of Jesus the Christ, authority is never for the sake of authority as such; it is always for the sake of love. It has no other purpose than to make effective and specific the divine *agapē*. Reducing this to a kind of theorum, we may say: *The authority of God is nothing other than the love of God expressing itself in the imperative mood.*

If this is grasped, and grasped as the most vital aspect of the mystery of the divine authority, a great many things fall into place. For one thing, it helps one to understand why no one expression of the divine authority, whether Bible, tradition, or ecclesial authorities, could ever legitimately become more than provisionally, penultimately authoritative. If the mystery behind the sovereign authority of God is God's "spontaneous and unmotivated love" (Nygren), then this conditions the kind of authority that such a God would employ.

An illustration will help to make the point. There are parents who from the beginning of their children's lives make it clear that certain practices are expected and others forbidden. This can be a very effective kind of authority if it is strictly instilled and consistently applied. It makes for an ordered household, and it saves the parents from the agony of situational decisions. But it is not necessarily motivated by love of the child. It is more often generated, rather, by the adult desire for order, convenience, peace and quiet, predictability—in short, chiefly for the sake of those who are *exercising* the authority. Authority born of love, while it certainly must provide guidance and direction for the children (we are not speaking about sheer permissiveness), nevertheless wants above all to avoid destroying the spontaneity and individual potentiality of the child by pouring it into a preconceived behavioral mold. So while it guides and advises, it also waits. It takes risks in doing so, because little human beings unused to the ways of the world can and do make mistakes! But the parent who loves knows that he or she cannot protect the child from all the mistakes that await it, and their often sad consequences. The parent counsels, waits, responds, and meets the problems as they come, rather than trying to anticipate them all in advance and thus circumscribing the channels through which the child may explore its unique, creative possibilities. To the strict disciplinarian this looks like gross inconsistency, and there are, indeed, usually elements of inconsistency in it. But this is a necessary corollary of love for the child; because the only authority that is appropriate in love is authority which serves the beloved. The beloved, then, in a real sense determines what authority will mean in the concrete situation of her or his life.

If the Parent whom we name God wishes in relation to his/her children to exercise the kind of authority that is the expression of a supreme *love,* then that Parent is under the same limitations and possibilities of authority that pertain to any earthly parent having a comparable intent. The biblical God cannot, being love, "work it all out in advance." God too has to wait, must be "the waiting Father" (Thielicke).[53] God can only discern the appropriate authority *in the moment.* To state the matter, again, in a formulary sort of way: *If love is the form of authority, then its content will depend upon the situation of the beloved.* This is why the God of the Scriptures, especially of the Hebraic Bible, can *also* appear inconsistent—as to the mind of the "disciplinarian" the parents described above appear. God in the Bible does not always say or do exactly the same thing. This is not what God's *faithfulness* means. Such "consistency"

---

53. Helmut Thielicke, *The Waiting Father: Sermons on the Parables of Jesus* (London: James Clarke, 1964).

really is "the hobgoblin of little minds" (Ralph Waldo Emerson). God's consistency is God's constant love (*ḥesed*), and *therefore* God cannot be consistent in the legalistic sense of the term. Love serves the beloved! Does the beloved "child," Israel, become callous or tyrannous in relation to others? Then one kind of authoritative response is appropriate: the harsh word of judgment is given. Does the child become the victim of tyranny, the oppressive rule of Egyptians, Babylonians, or others? Then another kind of authoritative word/deed is called for.

What this means, to put it in perhaps an irreverent but nonetheless instructive manner, is that not even God can articulate authority a priori. God can express a basic *intention* for creation, for the creature. This is how, for example, the Ten Commandments and Jesus' Sermon on the Mount should be understood: the divine Parent articulates his/her vision for the child. But God cannot spell out the divine intention in absolutes which, in effect, would only displace and replace God's own *presence* as authority—the authority of the voice. Unlike many earthly fathers who are absentee authorities in the home, God-Father *must* be present. No preconceived rules of truth and behavior can replace the ever-present God. And this "must" is not an external determination; it is simply the implicit *necessitas* of God's own free determination to love.

32.5. The Provisional Authorities.   The most significant authorities with which Christian faith and theology have to do on the horizontal plane, as it were, are the three already mentioned above: Bible, tradition, and ecclesial authority. In the light of the preceding discussion of *absolute* authority, we may refer to these as *provisional*.

The word "provisional" contains two nuances, and it is useful to employ both of them in the discussion of these three authoritative sources. One meaning (let us say its negative connotation) is suggestive of the fact that these authorities are finite, historically conditioned, transient, secondary, penultimate. They are temporary measures pending a more satisfactory arrangement! They are, in other words, authorities whose authority is always conditioned and circumscribed by the authority above the authorities.

There is a second nuance in the word "provisional," however. It has been implicit in the earlier discussion of ultimate authority, but now we must make it explicit. To say that the Bible, tradition, and church authorities are provisional is not only to affirm that they are temporary and limited by a great authority; it is also to say that they are *provided*. They are given as gifts, as comfort, by a provident God. They are not permanent, but they are good enough for the time being.

Both of these ideas should be heard in the application of the adjective "provisional" to the three penultimate authorities. One can hear both of them in the statements of the patriarchs of the church as they began very early to wrestle with the question of authority in the disciple community. Unfortunately (perhaps inevitably, since so many of these were precisely "patriarchs" and themselves authorities within the ecclesia) what came to dominate the thought of the church was the second, more positive meaning of "provisional." The critical dimension was, and too often still is, subdued by the need to accentuate and bolster the authority of the provisional authorities. This is unfortunate, because unless the dialectical tension is maintained between the two connotations of the word "provisional," too much weight is given to these authorities and the disciple community is tempted to lend them the kind of trust that belongs only to ultimate authority. When church authorities and advocates of biblical and traditional authority speak too one-sidedly about the providential nature of these preliminary authorities, then the prophetic insight is lost, namely, that these same God-given authorities are capable of usurping the place of the one ultimate authority, who "is love."

(*a*) *The Bible:* If we consider first the authority of the Bible, this is not accidental. For of all the provisional authorities, it has been regarded in Protestant theology of all varieties as the most significant for faith and theology. This primacy of Scripture (*sola scriptura*) can be perceived, moreover, within the Newer Testament itself, where we are again and again given evidence of the fact that the earliest disciple community itself turned to "the Scriptures" (that is, to the sacred writings of Israel) in order to comprehend the meaning of what had happened in their experience of the Christ. The primacy of the Bible can also be observed in the writings of subsequent early Christian writers, especially in Irenaeus and others who had to combat external and internal influences and dangerous alternatives to the apostolic tradition. And throughout the history of the church, wherever something else tended to usurp the primacy of *this* provisional authority, there has been a need to restore it. The Reformation of the 16th century was only one such occasion, though no doubt the most conspicuous of them all.

From the perspective of the positive nuance of the term "provisional," we may and must derive a very high doctrine of biblical authority. When we do so, however, we must be careful not to rely upon mere *reverence* for the Bible, which easily verges on magic. It is not necessary to resort to superstition to establish the nature of biblical authority. This assumes, of course, that we are not looking to the Bible for the sort of "truth" contained in the idea that revelation is propositional. Propositional revelation based on verbal inspiration of the Bible, i.e., on the identification of the Bible as if it *were* revelation, always courts the occult, even when it is put forward by sober and puritanical souls otherwise not given to superstition!

The authority of the Scriptures does not have to resort to extraordinary or unusually supranatural grounds. The need for biblical authority in faith and theology is indeed, as we intimated earlier, rather reasonable: if our ultimate authority is the biblical God; if that God has revealed God's self in events, the central event of which is "Jesus Christ and him crucified"; if these events and the original reflection of the disciple community upon these events are described in the Bible, then, by any logic whatsoever, the Bible is the primary testimony to the divine authority. It is "the testimony of the eye-witnesses" (Barth).[54] What these eyewitnesses witnessed transcends their own capacity to articulate it—because, as we have seen, "it" is finally not an *it*. Nevertheless, their testimony to what occurred is all that we have; and since we confess a faith grounded in historical event, we are bound to this testimony. Their proximity to the foundational events is very important—not because what was *really* happening in these events could be seen with the naked eye (it could not!), but because these events do provide the objective basis for what the eye of faith seeks to understand and to see. The church very soon rejected those accounts of the "original revelation" which could not claim such proximity to the Christ-event, or which because of their very nature turned these occurrences into tales which could not possibly be received as *historical* events (e.g., the apocryphal accounts of Jesus changing shape and size or passing through walls). The primacy of Scripture does not rest *solely* upon proximity to the events; it also rests, for instance, on the cumulative experience of generations—the church of the ages which confesses that precisely through this medium it has heard the divine voice. But as soon as one says that the revelation of God is bound up with historical events, then one commits oneself to this account of the events in question as guide and corrective to faith. It is *provided*.

But we have said that "provisional" also (and indeed normally) means that the thing in question is conditional, circumscribed, secondary. In the case of the Bible this means that even this primary objective authority for faith and theology is limited by the authority above the authorities.

---

54. Karl Barth, *The Doctrine of the Word of God*, Prolegomena to Church Dogmatics, being vol. 1, part I, trans. G. T. Thomson (New York: Scribner's, 1936), pp. 98ff.

But let us think concretely: Is it permitted to say without qualification that the Bible is the Word of God? It seems to have become permissible in many North American expressions of Christianity today; indeed, for majority forms of Protestantism on this continent it seems to have become mandatory. As Reinhold Niebuhr observed, "The authority of the Bible was used to break the proud authority of the church; whereupon the Bible became another instrument of human pride."[55] By classical Reformation standards this must be declared a crass and dangerous reduction of the authority of Scripture. The Bible itself may sometimes *seem* to use such language about itself, or similar language. But over against passages like Rev. 22:18-19, which are employed by literalists to justify their alleged adherence to "the letter," one has to recall the far more typical and weighty practice of the biblical writers of reserving ultimacy for the living God. (Ironically, the 22nd chapter of Revelation, to which the literalist so often appeals, contains its own severe warning against the temptation to give credence and glory to anything less than the living God. When the writer of the book falls down at the feet of the revealing angel, the angel rebukes him and says, "You must not do that! I am a fellow servant with you and your brethren the prophets, and with those who keep the words of this book. *Worship God*" Rev. 22:9.) Like the other Johannine material of the Newer Testament, the Apocalypse manifests an awesome respect for the prophetic word; but the prophecy remains open-ended (22:10), and it must do so because the decisive thing for the prophet is not the inspired word but the living, "coming" one who inspires it. However thoroughly the Fourth Gospel was influenced by non-Hebraic sources, it is essentially Hebraic in its identification of "The Word" with person— with the *Logos* who "became flesh." God's Word cannot become *simply* words. Since it is the very mind and heart of God, the Word can only represent itself to us in one who *lives*. Only therefore of "the Word made flesh" may Christians say in an unqualified way, "This *is* the Word of God."

What may be said of the Bible as such, then? It may be said, surely, that it is the unique *witness* to the divine Word. If Jesus is, for Christians, God's Word, then the Bible is the unique means through which we are permitted to hear this living Word of God.

We may even go beyond this, however, on account of the church's historical experience of this book. Again and again—indeed, always, wherever there has been a genuine faith—individuals and communities

---

55. Niebuhr, *The Nature and Destiny of Man*, vol. 2, p. 231.

of Christians have heard through the medium of the words of this book what comes to them as more than "words, words, words" (*Hamlet*). An ultimacy of judgment and love speaks through this testimony—not always, not predictably, not consistently; but with sufficient regularity that the disciple community cannot be satisfied with the classification of this book alongside all others. On the other hand, because it knows that only the *voice* of the living God is ultimate, neither can it treat the Bible as if it were in itself a holy object, comparable to holy objects of other religious traditions. Its holiness does not lie in itself, but in the use to which it is put by the Holy One of Israel. There is no special quality of the book as such which could guarantee its effectiveness as the unique medium of God's Word. As with all other earthly things (bread, wine, water!) the words of this book must be transformed if they are to be vehicles of the divine presence. The Spirit must make these words live, by preparing our deaf ears and our hard hearts to hear what may indeed be there already for us to hear.

The Bible, therefore, remains a provisional authority, both in the sense that it is provided in our weakness to aid our remembering of the events which are foundational for our belief, and in the sense that, however unique and irreplaceable it may be, it is never in itself and as such that to which our faith looks for ultimacy of truth and meaning. In a word, faith looks *through* the Scriptures, not *at* them.

(*b*) *Tradition:* The Reformation's *sola scriptura* never meant what subsequent forms of Protestantism sometimes caused it to mean, i.e., that Christians ought to heed *only* the Bible. *Sola scriptura* means, rather, that among the penultimate authorities of the faith, only the Bible bears this *normative* weight. The reason for this is not to be found in innate Protestant distrust of existing authorities so much as in the enthusiasm of the Reformation rediscovery of the biblical testimony to the original revelation.

This rediscovery by no means implied for the reformers themselves that there was no longer any place for either the authority of tradition or the authority of living ecclesial authorities. What it did imply was that the authority of these latter must be made conformable to the Scriptures. Therefore, in the name of scriptural authority the reformers called the dominant traditional and ecclesial authorities of their own day into question, because they believed that these authorities had contradicted or distorted the witness of the Scriptures.

That was, however, only the first step. Having sought, as they believed, to purify existing authority by bringing scriptural judgment to bear upon it, they then set about precisely to discover in the tradition of the Christian movement theological authorities which could correct or replace the authorities dominant in the medieval world. In a real sense, in fact, the Reformation *was* the search for a tradition. One looked in the past for traditions which could function as alternatives to the traditions which had governed the conventions of the late medieval church. It was a case of tradition against tradition. Far from being a willful jettisoning of all past theological work, then, the Reformation was a positive search for a tradition which could serve the church—a church which took the biblical testimony seriously.

In this spirit, Luther returned to Augustine (whom he quotes almost as often as he quotes St. Paul), and Calvin, Knox, and others returned to the Apostolic Fathers, and others. It was not only a polemic in which they were engaged—the rejection of Thomism, for example. It was a matter of necessity. There can be no future without a foundational past— or, as in so many ways the radical wing of the Reformation demonstrated, where people try to have a future without a foundation in the past, they frequently fall victim to worse ills than could be experienced by any sort of traditionalism.

The past, both in religion and in human society generally, is what gives the possibility of a certain stability, perspective, and sense of direction. Without remembrance, hope is a poor, homeless orphan! North Americans in the early stages of our civilization thought that they could have hope without history. They wanted to escape from the burden of the past—and understandably so.[56] But in these latter decades we have discovered how shallow hope can be when it has no anchor in memory. Therefore no search is more existential with us today than the search for a past—for roots. Not having cherished and nurtured the roots out of which we sprang, we became, as a people, the victims of a capricious present. The technological society has no greater need than the need for a past, from which it can derive guidance, the knowledge of limits, and correctives to values that are as fickle as fashions and image-makers. The full consequences of our New World abandonment of the past have only just begun to move us.

In the sense that tradition refers to this legacy of past to present and future generations, tradition in Christian theology is a provisional authority in a highly positive sense. Perhaps the fully positive character of tradition is not discovered until we human beings find ourselves in the

---

56. See Robert Bellah et al., *Habits of the Heart* (Berkeley, Calif.: University of California Press, 1985), pp. 227-244.

position of having to hand over to the next generation what we have gained—and know how little of our own we really have! There could come to be a new appreciation for tradition (paradoxical as this may sound) on the part of a North American church which finds that it must contextualize its theology. Freed from the self-imposed bonds of a past that is not fully ours, and faced with the need to speak to the present and the future, we may find ourselves more truly involved in reflection upon the Christian tradition than we have yet been.

While this positive side of tradition must be emphasized, the other dimension must never be overlooked: tradition is provisional in the sense of being secondary and limited. It ought never become a substitute for our own attempt to hear, in our own time and place, what "the voice" has to say to us. It can never become a legitimate substitute for the authority of the living God, the Spirit. Tradition*alism* is one of the great enemies of the church for this reason. For it feeds upon what was given to preceding generations instead of gathering the manna of the morning. It is, besides, always the temptation of those who "hand over" (*tradere*) what they have received to do so without the necessary modesty, without recognizing that the living God may have something quite different to say to the new generation from what was said to the one that is passing away. There is usually in this handing over a not very cleverly concealed wish to extend the authority of those whose authority is passing away. And, sometimes, those who receive what is handed over are glad enough to take it in the spirit of dependency. It is comfortable to live on the labors of others, and not to have to expose oneself anew to the cold winds of one's own age and place.

Between overdependence and independence; between gratitude for that which is given and watchfulness that it does not become an excuse for intellectual complacency and lassitude; between remembering and hoping, the disciple community is a community with a tradition.

(*c*) *Ecclesiastical authority:* Very early in the history of the Christian movement, Christians realized the need for authority within the structures of the church itself, i.e., for living persons who were authorized by the community to exercise authority in the midst of the others. This is not the place to enter into the knotty historical discussion of whether the earliest forms of ecclesiastical authority were congregational, presbyterial, or episcopal. If anything, it would seem to have been a variety of forms, with the specifics of their organization being dependent (once again we should recognize this) upon contextual factors, which were of course not universally the same. Here, however, we are concerned about a theological and not specifically a historical problem: What can one believe about the authorities within the Christian community? My answer will be, here also, an application of the twofold nuance of the adjective "provisional."

In the first place, let us honestly admit that ecclesiastical authorities are necessary. Against the *kind* of charismatic enthusiasm which thinks it possible to dispense with ecclesiastical offices, I should say that such offices are of the essence of the church—though I should not be willing to say that specific *forms* (whether episcopal, presbyterial, or other) are of the essence. In some way, the disciple community must order its corporate life. Not for its own sake alone! For the sake of its mission. Authority in the church must always reflect this proviso: for the better realization of its vocation; for the life of the world. For the church does not exist for itself, but to be a *witnessing* community, whose witness is meant for the enhancement of all creaturely existence.

This end prejudices me in the direction of a *functional* conception of ecclesiastical office and authority. That is, ecclesiastical authority ought, in my opinion, to be designed to assist the disciple community to live as a witnessing community in its world; and this, if the argument of this present work means anything at all, must mean that authority in the church will depend in large measure upon the character of that world within which the *koinōnia* finds itself. *Flexibility* of office is therefore important.

It would be difficult, however, to imagine such a community without some form of ordering, marshaling, planning, deciding, that will give it the *freedom* it needs to perform this witness. While it has been perennially tempting for North American Christians to question authority per se, it is a mistake to imagine that freedom means an authority-less situation. Any community, if it is to act with a certain recognizable singleness of purpose, must submit itself to some kind of discipline and authority. Moreover, as the church very early discovered, it will not do simply to assume that "the voice"/the Spirit will direct, or that the Bible is sufficient, or that the tradition will carry us. So long as we are speaking about a human community—and the church is such!—we must also speak about a provisional authority *within* this community. There must be some way of determining what is the meaning and direction of the divine authority in the moment. Otherwise, while each individual may be able to act on his or her own, or while small groups of like-minded persons may perform integrated services, it will not be possible for the community as such to act—and "act" here also includes thought. Ecclesiastical authority is part, then, of the provision that a provident God makes for the community of belief. It is never perfect, never problemless; but it *can be* providential.

It is, on the other hand, an unmistakable lesson of church history that ecclesiastical authority of *every* type tends to corruption. The Christian understanding of sin must always be kept in mind where authority in the church is at issue. Because here, as at no other juncture in the whole discussion of authority, there is always the temptation for penultimate authority pridefully to covet, or to be caused by the sloth of the community at large to assume, ultimacy. It is not accidental that this temptation is strongest in connection with the authorities within the church structures; because it is only here that we are dealing, not with an object (the Bible), and not with documentary testimony of deceased persons and groups (tradition), but with living persons who, being sinful human beings, are always tempted to use power for their own ends and not for the service of God and the community. Here as at no other point it has happened over and over in the church that authority contradicts most flagrantly the model of authority given in the divine paradigm, the paradigm of the Christ who is Lord. I mean that here, in the difficult business of ecclesiastical guidance and administration, it too easily happens that authority becomes an end in itself rather than a means of facilitating the freedom of divine love and worldly stewardship. Whatever authority we work out for ourselves in the disciple communities of the future, it must be one in which there is an implicit vigilance against this temptation. It may become possible to achieve this in the future in a way that it has not been achieved in the past. For with the disestablishment of the Christian movement there comes a concomitant dissociation of Christian models of authority from the authority patterns of imperial societies. Perhaps the most surprising changes in the disciple communities of the future shall be those having to do with authority in Christ's church.

What has plagued the church throughout the centuries at this juncture has been its too self-conscious dependency upon authority patterns in the host societies. In most cases, sometimes more obviously than others, these societal models of authority were far too authoritarian—meaning monolithic, patriarchical, hierarchical, exclusivist, and many other things about which contemporary theological movements have become rightly indignant. These models were, besides, impoverished in respect to self-criticism. This is rather obviously the case of the Christian imitation of structures of authority in the classical Roman world, and in the feudal societies of the Middle Ages. Not only do these structures of authority tend towards Augustan absolutism, as in the concept of the divine right of kings, but they habitually want to rule out legitimate protest and criticism. In ancient Israel, even with the institution of the monarchy, the spirit of protest *against* authority was built into the communal process. The prophet may not have been *appreciated* by the king, but the king was not at liberty simply to stamp out the spirit of prophetic criticism at its roots, for the latter was part of the life of the community of Israel—older, in fact, and substantially more indispensable than the kingship.

When Latin Christianity patterned itself on late Roman forms of authority (i.e., forms of Roman authority from which the spirit of tolerance in earlier Roman government had all but given way to the absolute rule of emperors, with a clear-cut hierarchy from the emperor down), it took on a model from which both modesty and self-criticism were conspicuously missing. Individual popes and bishops might indeed transcend the model, but the model did not lend itself to these qualities. (A pope like Innocent III possessed personal qualities, we are told, which could only be admired; but the office lent itself to the habits of power, and Innocent III developed that side of his character to perfection!) Subsequent forms of authority did not greatly alter this until the time of the Reformation, because, in spite of the struggle of protesting movements in the Middle Ages and in spite of the attempt to institute conciliar forms of government in the church, the dominant model from the Roman civilization was deeply entrenched in European Christianity.

Significant alternative models *were* introduced by the 16th century's protesting movements; but while some of these were *potentially* radical, they could not be taken up and made actual, except for various experiments here and there, most of them short-lived. The reason why the radical models of authority could not be adopted even within the reforming movement is clear enough: while it introduced rudimentary reinterpretations of gospel and theology, the mainstream of the Reformation did not on the whole criticize the idea of Christian establishment.[57] That is, it did not bring to bear anything like a prophetic critique of the Constantinian marriage of church and society. The left wing of the Reformation in its radical phases did so; but it was just this aspect of the Radical Reformation that was defeated.

So long as the concept of Christian establishment is maintained, whether in the de jure or the de facto (cultural religion) form prevalent in North America, the need of the church to model its life after the society in general will manifest itself especially in its patterns of authority. In the established situation, it would be very difficult, if not impossible, for the church to have forms of government and authority radically different from

---

57. Despite the fact that in the so-called pre-Reformers, Wycliffe particularly, there had been a strong predisposition towards disestablishment.

those of its civil partner and protector. Thus it is not surprising today to find the major denominations of North American churches having systems of authority which reflect, not ancient Rome or feudal Europe, but the business and professional milieu of our dominant middle classes, with their "head offices."

This, however, is changing. As the disciple community discovers a message and a work in the world which differs, sometimes markedly, from the pursuits of governmental, financial, military, industrial, and other corporate structures in First World contexts, it discovers simultaneously that its own authority structures will not serve its newly discovered evangelical and ethical ends. There is thus a suggestion in our present situation that the most visible changes in the diaspora church that is coming to be will be those relating to the nature of ecclesial authority.

INDEX OF SUBJECTS

INDEX OF NAMES

INDEX OF NAMES